Shakespeare's England

Oxford University Press

London   Edinburgh   Glasgow   New York
Toronto   Melbourne   Bombay
Humphrey Milford *M.A. Publisher to the University*

PRINTED IN ENGLAND
AT THE OXFORD UNIVERSITY PRESS

PYNCHON FUND

Shakespeare's England

An Account of the

Life & Manners

of his AGE

Volume

II

Clarendon Press Oxford

1917

A Marriage Fête at Horselydown, from the picture by J. Hoefnagel, in the collection of the Marquess of Salisbury, G.C.V.O.

George Vertue Sculp.

CONTENTS

VOLUME II

LIST OF ILLUSTRATIONS

VOLUME II

ABBREVIATIONS EMPLOYED IN QUOTATIONS FROM SHAKESPEARE'S WORKS

All's W. = All's Well that Ends Well

Ant. & Cleop. = Antony and Cleopatra

A. Y. L. = As You Like It

Com. of E. = Comedy of Errors

Cor. = Coriolanus

Cymb. = Cymbeline

Haml. = Hamlet

1 Hen. IV = The First Part of King Henry IV

2 Hen. IV = The Second Part of King Henry IV

Hen. V = King Henry V

1 Hen. VI = The First Part of King Henry VI

2 Hen. VI = The Second Part of King Henry VI

3 Hen. VI = The Third Part of King Henry VI

John = King John

Jul. Caes. = Julius Caesar

Lear = King Lear

Lover's Comp. = A Lover's Complaint

Love's L. L. = Love's Labour 's Lost

Lucr. = The Rape of Lucrece

Macb. = Macbeth

Meas. for M. = Measure for Measure

Merch. of V. = The Merchant of Venice

M. Wives = The Merry Wives of Windsor

Mid. N. D. = A Midsummer Night's Dream

Much Ado = Much Ado about Nothing

Oth. = Othello

Pass. Pilg. = The Passionate Pilgrim.

Pericles = Pericles

Rich. II = King Richard II

Rich. III = King Richard III

Rom. & Jul. = Romeo and Juliet

Sonnets = Sonnets

Tam. Sh. = The Taming of the Shrew

Temp. = The Tempest

Timon = Timon of Athens

Tit. Andr. = Titus Andronicus

Troilus = Troilus and Cressida

Tw. N. = Twelfth Night

Two Gent. = The Two Gentlemen of Verona

Ven. & Ad. = Venus and Adonis

Wint. Tale = The Winter's Tale

chor. = chorus

epil. = epilogue

ind. = induction

prol. = prologue

st. dir. = stage direction

The text used is that of the Oxford Shakespeare, except where for special reasons it has been necessary to set it aside.

XVII

THE FINE ARTS

§ 1. PAINTING, SCULPTURE, AND ENGRAVING

BY

Lionel Cust

THE arts of painting, sculpture, and engraving in England during the latter half of the sixteenth century do not afford a very fruitful field for their historian. The pictorial and graphic arts can hardly be said to have been a spontaneous growth in the nation's development. The history of these arts in England is a series of episodes rather than a continuous and harmonious progress to maturity. The art of the painter, as of the sculptor, was in early days but a servitor to that of the architect, until the episode of Hans Holbein, and the encouragement given by the Tudor monarchs to foreign artists from the Netherlands or France to make their homes and their fortunes in England. Then a freer scope opened for art. Painting still, however, remained a craftsman's business, and realism rather than imagination was aimed at and attained. With the rise of the merchant-prince and rich tradesman, and the advent of travelled adventurers to share the social and political power of the feudal and territorial aristocracy, a greater luxury began to pervade the homes and lives of the wealthier classes. More money was available for spending on the building of new houses, on their fittings, on tapestry, pictures, and works of art for the decoration of the home. Portraiture, an honour reserved in former days for ruling princes or persons of high official rank and importance, quickly became the vogue among a race of new men and women. The portrait-painter, or ' picture-maker ', found plenty of customers. The great expansion of painting as a popular art in the Netherlands led to the export of many small portable pictures to be sold at fairs or popular festivals, holy pictures for pilgrimages and other pious occasions, drolleries, tavern scenes, and other lively subjects for booths at the fairs or the pack of the travelling pedlar. All these subjects would naturally induce imitations by English artists, and in this way what may be called a native school of painters began to develop itself in divers parts of England. Their productions, being usually of ephemeral and little more than local importance, and at their best but imitations of the works of the more highly trained artists of the Netherlands, have survived in few and inconsiderable examples.

Shakespeare himself shows little enthusiasm for the pictorial arts, but the allusions, scanty as they are, which figure in his plays and poems, all suggest that the pictorial arts were a part of the ordinary daily life of the people, with which any one of his readers or spectators would be familiar, and show the dramatist in an observant, if hardly appreciative, attitude. Let us follow Shakespeare's experiences, and we shall find him alluding to the art of painting in many different ways.

The little houses in Henley Street, at Stratford-on-Avon, in one of which Shakespeare was born, offered little scope for adornment by the artist. His grandfather, Robert Arden, lived however in greater state in his house at Wilmcote, for he mentions in his will no less than eleven 'painted cloths'. How universal such house decorations were throughout England in Shakespeare's youth is well attested by Estienne Perlin, a French visitor to England in 1558, when he wrote from his own observation : 'Les Anglois se servent fort des tapisseries, des toilles pinctes, qui sont bien faictes, ausquelles y a force magnifiques roses couronnées, ou il y a des fleurs de Liz & Lions, car en peu de maisons vous pouves entrer que vous ne trouvies ces tapisseries.' These painted cloths seem to have been paintings in *tempera* on canvas, originally intended to replace tapestry, and were probably introduced by Italian artists early in the sixteenth century. They are usually carefully distinguished from ' pictures in tables or paintings on panels ', and are important in the history of art, since the painted or stained cloth was the forerunner of the painting on canvas, which, gradually displacing the painting on panel, was almost universally adopted. In the inventory of Henry VIII's pictures taken in 1542, several paintings are described as 'stayned cloths'.

Shakespeare frequently alludes to 'painted cloths'.   At the close of *Troilus and Cressida* (v. x. 46–7) Pandarus

Der Handmaler.

Die Kunst der perspectiff ich pur
Bericht bin/vnd Contrafactur/
Dem Menschen ich mit farb kan gebn
Sein gstalt/ als ob diß Bild thu lebn
Statt/Schlösser/Wasser/Berg vñ Wäld/
Ein Heer / sam lig ein Fürst zu Feld/
Kan ich so eigentlich anzeygn/
Als stehe es da Leibhafftig eign.

The Painter, by Jost Amman.

says, 'Good traders in the flesh, set this in your painted cloths'; in *1 Henry IV* (IV. ii. 27–8) Falstaff speaks of his soldiers as 'slaves as ragged as Lazarus in the painted cloth, where the glutton's dogs licked his sores'.   Harrison describes the walls of Elizabethan houses as 'hanged with tapestry arras works or painted cloths wherein divers histories, herbs, beasts, knots, and such like are stained'. The 'histories' included episodes from the Bible and ancient mythology.[1]

With hangings of tapestry or arras work which invariably covered the walls of the chief rooms in the large houses, Shakespeare was perfectly familiar. Falstaff hid himself behind the arras in the inn, when he fell asleep and suffered his pocket to be picked by Peto (*1 Hen. IV*, II. iv. 585 ff.). Polonius met his death when hiding behind the arras in Queen Gertrude's chamber (*Haml.* III. iv. 23). Tapestry, as distinguished from 'hangings', usually presented like 'painted cloths' pictorial subjects, sometimes woven with gold and silver thread, as in the Great Hall at Hampton Court Palace. The base Iachimo, in his accusation of Imogen, gave an air of truth to his slanders by describing her chamber, which was

> hang'd
> With tapestry of silk and silver ; the story
> Proud Cleopatra, when she met her Roman.
> (*Cymb.* II. iv. 68–70)

Elsewhere Shakespeare suggests that tapestry was in his day in process of supersession by the painted cloth. When the tavern hostess, Mistress Quickly, laments the threatened necessity of pawning 'the tapestry' of her 'dining chambers', Falstaff consoles her by declaring his preference for the more modern and less expensive painted cloth :

for thy walls, a pretty slight drollery, or the story of the Prodigal, or the German hunting in water-work [probably *a guazzo* or *à la gouache*], is worth a thousand of these bed-hangings and these fly-bitten tapestries. (*2 Hen. IV*, II. i. 139–41)

As a boy Shakespeare must have been familiar, in addition to 'painted cloths', with the curious scenes of mural paintings in the Chapel of the Guild of the Holy Cross, which adjoined the Grammar School at Stratford-on-Avon. The walls of this chapel were covered with allegorical and legendary paintings in fresco. Among these had been a 'Dance of Death', but this seems to have been destroyed with other religious subjects by the pious reformers in the time of King Edward VI. The paintings,

---

[1] A remarkable series of 'painted cloths', evidently inspired by the Mysteries or sacred dramas of the Middle Ages, was painted for the Hôtel-Dieu at Rheims, and was, until 1915, in the Museum of that city.

GRAMMAR SCHOOL STRATFORD-ON-AVON

however, of the 'Invention of the Cross', with the legend of the Empress, St. Helena, the 'Murder of St. Thomas à Becket', 'The Day of Judgement', and 'St. George and the Dragon', were visible during Shakespeare's schooldays. The churches and chapels of England were frequently decorated with paintings in this way. Few, however, escaped the destroying hand of the reformer, and those which survive have only been rescued from under obliterating coats of whitewash.

After settling in London in 1586 Shakespeare would be brought into contact with the arts in a still more definite way. Henry VII was the first king to encourage the fine arts at the same time as he promoted commerce, and the dearth of native artists led to the employment of artists from the Netherlands and Italy. Henry VIII followed this policy further, stimulated by a desire to outshine his contemporary, Francis I of France, and to divert the springs of art, or at all events some portion of them, from France to England. These fountain-springs were unfortunately not of the purest artistic quality; they were tainted with the adulterated and unrefined paganism of the Renaissance, and such artistic effort as reached England was by no means the choicest in general tone. England in Tudor days liked strong meat. A reaction set in under the Protestant King Edward VI, when many artistic treasures were destroyed by religious fanatics, and it continued under the devout Roman Catholic Queen Mary, but under Elizabeth the arts returned to their grosser fancies.

The reign of Elizabeth saw the rise of the picture collector. The saloons and galleries of Leicester's castle of Kenilworth, near Shakespeare's birthplace, were adorned by portraits at full length or on smaller scale in the rich costumes of the period which Holbein had made fashionable. If Shakespeare ever performed before the Queen at Nonesuch Palace at Cheam in Surrey, the splendid residence of John, Lord Lumley (d. 1609), he would have seen there part of the extraordinary collection of historical portraits formed by the owner either by his own acquisition or by inheritance from his father-in-law, Henry FitzAlan, twelfth Earl of Arundel. Lord Lumley was one of the first great collectors of pictures, books, manuscripts, and other objects, both at Nonesuch and at his northern home, Lumley Castle. Most of these were dispersed after his death, but such as remained in the family seem to have passed to the contemporary representative of the great house of Arundel. Thomas Howard, second Earl of Arundel of that line, the father of modern art-collecting, began to form his collections during Shakespeare's lifetime, an example quickly followed by the Duke of Buckingham, and carried further by Charles I. Lord Lumley's collection was rather historical and personal than artistic. His successors first drew the treasures of Continental art across the sea, and disseminated a knowledge of the truer and better canons of art in English society. Shakespeare's friend Ben Jonson lived long enough to write of English noblemen's appreciation of Romano, Tintoret, Titian, Raphael, and Michael Angelo (*Underwoods*, xcv). It is clear that Shakespeare had seen pictures in collectors' galleries.

Pictures there were often protected by a curtain, as is noted in the inventory of Henry VIII's collection in 1542. With such method of protection Shakespeare was well acquainted : 'Wherefore have these gifts a curtain before 'em ?' asks Sir Toby Belch of Sir Andrew Aguecheek ; 'are they like to take dust, like Mistress Mall's picture ?' (*Tw. N.* i.iii.136–8).[1]

Under the early Tudors Italian artists were chiefly summoned for works of decorative painting, sculpture, and engraving. Their style was that of the full-blown Renaissance. Their skill, which was well exemplified at one time by such an artist as Torrigiano, ran rather wild in England, as in France, betraying notably at Nonesuch a fatuous affectation and ostentation. The religious wars in the Netherlands and the Alvan persecution drove to England many working artists of the reformed religion, and this invasion did more to lay the foundation of a national art than the showy superficialities of the Franco-Italian school. These artists from the Netherlands were quiet-working craftsmen, ready to turn their hand to such employment as would enable them to earn a livelihood, careless of personal distinction. With them the arts were an industry ; the painter and sculptor ranked with the weaver, the goldsmith, or the fuller, and took their share in supplying the wants of the community.

[1] Cf. 'We will draw the curtain and show you the picture' (*Tw. N.* i. v. 252) ; ' Come, draw this curtain, and let's see your picture ' (*Troilus* iii. ii. 47).

In one branch of painting, that of portrait-painting, the advance in England was steady. Since the days of Holbein the demand for portraiture had greatly increased, and not to

Der Bildhauwer.

Bildſchnitzen ſo hab ich gelehrt/
Vor jaren war ich hoch geehrt/
Da ich der Heyden Götzen macht/
Die man anbett vnd Opffer bracht/
Die ich machet von Holtz vnd Stein/
Auch von Criſtallen ſauber rein/
Geliedmaſirt vnd wolgeſtalt/
Die mit Gelt wurden hoch bezalt.

The Sculptor, by Jost Amman.

have your portrait painted was not to be in the fashion. The impetus came from the Netherlands, chiefly through Antwerp, but also through the great painting schools of Bruges and Ghent in Flanders, and of Delft and the Hague in Holland. Portrait-painting—or picture-making, as it was usually styled in Shakespeare's time—was not yet a refined or luxurious art. The artist was content to work from a sketch in pencil or chalk, with notes of special details of costume and other accessories. From such a drawing a painting was made, the details of costume and jewellery being toilsomely elaborated. The intellectual side of portraiture was sacrificed to the demands for a rich and showy effect. This is the kind of portraiture usually associated in error with the name of Zuccaro. It was in this department that the artists of the Netherlands especially excelled, such as Marcus Gheeraerts of Bruges, Paul Van Somer of Antwerp, and Daniel Mytens of the Hague. A truer and tenderer note, and one more characteristic of England itself, was struck by Cornelius Johnson (or Janssen), who, though of Netherlandish origin, was born in London, and may be regarded as the first English-born painter of any note. All these painters found capable craftsmen to imitate them. Skilful amateurs were not unknown, even in Shakespeare's own circle. Richard Burbage, Shakespeare's principal dramatic colleague, was a capable 'limner' and 'picture-maker', at least one specimen of whose brush survives at Dulwich; while Shakespeare himself could be looked to for the suggestion of an *impresa* (or miniature picture employed as an heraldic device) which his friend Burbage was ready to sketch and execute in colours.[1]

The picture-shop must have been to Elizabethan and Jacobean London as familiar as the Fine Art shops in Bond Street or the fashionable photographer in the twentieth century. When Henry Holland published in 1620 his collection of historical portraits called *Herωologia Anglica*, he collected his materials not merely from various private collections such as the 'Cecilian Gallery', the 'Pembrokian', 'Essex House', 'Winchester House', the 'Earl of Hertford's Gallery', but also from 'a shop in the Strand', 'a shop in Fleet Street', 'a shop in Blackfriars', 'a shop by Paul's'. A famous picture-shop was kept at Snow Hill, Holborn, by Robert Peake, who supplied both painted and engraved portraits, and was already active in Shakespeare's time. The story is well known how at a little later date Anthony Van Dyck, when walking down Snow Hill, was attracted by a portrait in Peake's shop window, and, after entering

[1] See below, p. 88.

to inquire, found the artist at work in the back shop and
engaged the man as one of his principal assistants. It is
clear that Shakespeare was familiar with such portraits as
Peake sold, and such a shop as he kept.   In *Sonnet* xxiv he
writes :

> Mine eye hath play'd the painter and hath stell'd [1]
> Thy beauty's form in table [2] of my heart ;
> My body is the frame wherein 'tis held,
> And perspective it is best painter's art.
> For through the painter must you see his skill,
> To find where *your true image pictur'd lies,*
> *Which in my bosom's shop is hanging still,*
> *That hath his windows glazed with thine eyes.*
> Now see what good turns eyes for eyes have done :
> Mine eyes have drawn thy shape, and thine for me
> Are windows to my breast, where-through the sun
> Delights to peep, to gaze therein on thee ;
>   Yet eyes this cunning want to grace their art,
>   They draw but what they see, know not the heart.

Elsewhere in the *Sonnets* Shakespeare makes much familiar
allusion to portraits, to ' painted counterfeits ' (*Sonnets* xvi,
liii).   He describes ' the painted banquet ' of his ' love's
picture ' on which the poet feasts his eye (*ib.* xlvii).

Another class of paintings serves Shakespeare for examples
of luxury.   In the Induction to the *Taming of the Shrew*
(ii. 51–8) the tinker is thus addressed by the lord's servant :

> Dost thou love pictures ? we will fetch thee straight
> Adonis painted by a running brook,
> And Cytherea all in sedges hid ;

and the lord adds :

> We'll show thee Io as she was a maid,
> And how she was beguiled and surpris'd,
> As lively painted as the deed was done.

These allusions are evidently to mythological pictures of
the Italian school, and suggest famous pictures by Correggio,
Giulio Romano, and other painters.   In the poem of *Lucrece*,
a ' piece of skilful painting ' of the siege of Troy is described
in detail and at considerable length (ll. 1366–1456).   At
Mantua, the painter Giulio Romano (in addition to his
renowned paintings in the Palazzo del Tè) executed in the
castle, between 1532 and 1536, a famous series of paintings of

---

[1] ' Portrayed ' : a technical term.

[2] ' Table ' was the technical term as late as 1700 for the board or other flat
surface on which a picture was painted.

the Trojan War, the wonders of which may have been described to the young Shakespeare and may have impressed themselves on his imagination. The 'Tale of Troy' was, however, a favourite subject for tapestry, and may have been repeated on 'painted cloths'. Shakespeare cannot be safely credited with real acquaintance with Continental art. His solitary allusion to an Italian artist is to the aforesaid Giulio Romano—'that rare Italian master, Julio Romano' (*Wint. Tale* v. ii. 108). But Shakespeare speaks of him as a famous sculptor instead of a famous painter. There is no evidence of his skill in sculpture outside an epitaph quoted by Vasari.

In such general criticism of the art of painting as Shakespeare offers his readers, he usually expresses the pleased astonishment of the inexperienced observer at seeing art reproduce nature at all. In his early poem, *Venus and Adonis*, he credits 'a painter' with surpassing 'the life'

> In limning out a well-proportion'd steed.   (l. 290)

In *Timon of Athens* (I. i. 21 ff.) Shakespeare introduces a painter and a poet, who discuss together the portrait and the poem which they have just respectively completed. The poem is described as a moral allegory and the portrait as 'a pretty mocking of the life' which improves on nature. Merely fanciful effects in painting were welcome to Elizabethan taste. Among these ranked high certain paintings in perspective, a *tour de force* in which some painters were wont to practise their skill. Shakespeare frequently alludes to these 'perspectives'. In *King Richard II* (II. ii. 18–20) he writes of

> perspectives, which rightly gaz'd upon
> Show nothing but confusion ; ey'd awry
> Distinguish form.

In *Twelfth Night* (v. i. 227) mention is made of

> A natural perspective, that is, and is not.

Specimens of these distorted figures, which can only be seen aright by looking through a hole in a slanting direction, appear in the portrait of Edward VI at the National Portrait Gallery, and in the painting of·'The Ambassadors' by Holbein at the National Gallery, where there is a perspective presentation of a human skull.

Another distinctive branch of painting, which was

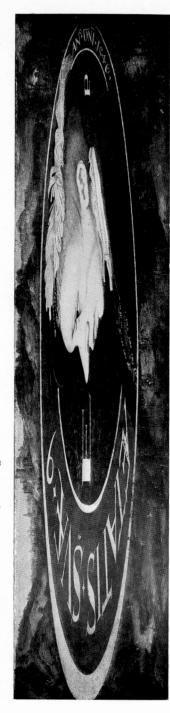

From the painting in the NATIONAL PORTRAIT GALLERY

A PERSPECTIVE PORTRAIT OF EDWARD VI

brought to high perfection in England during the reign of the Tudors, was the art of 'painting in little', 'limning' portraits in miniature. In that branch Nicholas Hilliard and Isaac Oliver had in Shakespeare's time already made themselves famous. Shakespeare bears witness to the popularity of portrait miniatures. Hamlet says to Rosencrantz and Guildenstern : ' My uncle is King of Denmark, and those that would make mows at him while my father lived, give twenty, forty, fifty, a hundred ducats a-piece for his picture in little ' (*Haml.* II. ii. 388–92). This passage has led to the supposition that in the more famous speech of Hamlet to his mother, beginning

> Look here, upon this picture, and on this ;
> The counterfeit presentment of two brothers.
> *(Haml.* III. iv. 53 ff.)

Hamlet was alluding to two miniature portraits, or 'paintings in little', pictorial accessories. The context, however, with its vivid descriptions of the paintings—' A station like the herald Mercury ', and ' like a mildew'd ear, Blasting his wholesome brother ' — demands the presence of two contiguous whole-length portraits on the walls of the queen's chamber, such portraits as were to be seen at Greenwich Palace, or at Nonesuch, or other noblemen's mansions.

Foreigners had a natural tendency to settle in places outside the jurisdiction of the Lord Mayor of London, where they could practise their trades with less restriction than within the city walls. Many artists were residents in the liberty of Blackfriars, with which Shakespeare's later years in London were closely associated. If in Blackfriars Shakespeare familiarized himself with painters' studios, the years which he spent in Southwark made him well acquainted there with the stonemasons' yards and wharves, in which the tombmakers and statuaries carried on their business. In Southwark there laboured Cornelius Cure (d. 1607) and his son William (d. 1632), who made the monuments of Queen Elizabeth and Mary Queen of Scots in Westminster Abbey. There also worked Bernard Jansen (1616–30), who provided sculptured ornaments for Northumberland House and Audley End, and was a partner of Nicholas Stone. The Southwark sculptors included, too, Gerard Janssen, or Johnson, from Amsterdam, who made Shakespeare's own monument for the church at Stratford-on-Avon. Shakespeare's allusions to sculpture are desultory. The commendations bestowed on the supposed statue in colours of Hermione in *The Winter's Tale* (v. ii. 105 ff. and iii. 15 ff.) suggest an exalted view of the capacities of the art. There are more pedestrian mentions of a carved chimney-piece in *Cymbeline* (ii. iv. 80–5), of a grandsire cut in alabaster in *The Merchant of Venice* (i. i. 84), and of a monument in a chapel in *Cymbeline* (ii. ii. 32). In *King Lear* (ii. ii. 62–4) Shakespeare makes Kent add to his contemptuous reflection on Oswald—'a tailor made thee'—the scornful comment : 'a stone-cutter or a painter could not have made him so ill, though they had been but two hours o' the trade.'[1] Had the dramatist any forebodings or actual knowledge of the fate which was in store for himself in the art of portraiture ?

A branch of the fine arts, which is inseparably connected with Shakespeare's name, although Shakespeare himself makes no allusion to it, was the newly-introduced art of copper-plate engraving. This art had been practised for pictorial purposes in Italy, Germany, and the Netherlands, but did not get a footing in England until the time of Elizabeth. As the invention of printing with movable types rapidly displaced the elaborate and expensive manuscript, so did the art of printing pictorial subjects, either from blocks in relief of wood or metal, or from copper plates engraved in intaglio, supplant and extinguish the art of the miniaturist or limner, which art became restricted to the execution of the ' portraits in little ' to which allusion has already been made. The earliest books published in England were illustrated with blocks, very roughly cut in imitation of miniature paintings, chiefly in outline, and seeming to demand colour. Copper-plate engraving offered a much more refined and artistic vehicle of book-illustration, especially in title-pages and portraits. Excellent map-engravers and seal-engravers were already in practice in England before certain working engravers from the Netherlands introduced their art into the English publishing trade. Archbishop Parker had a large share in encouraging such work, but the impetus came from abroad, where engraving as a means of book-illustration was in full vogue. Yet many Elizabethan practitioners were English born. The

---

[1] It should be noted that the word 'picture' was used equally for a painted figure in stone or plaster and for a figure painted on panel or canvas.

excellent map-engraver Augustine Ryther, who had the chief share in engraving Christopher Saxton's maps for Sir Thomas Seckford, Warden of the Court of Wards and Liveries, was a native of Leeds. Two of the earliest engravers of portraits and title-pages, William Rogers and Thomas Cockson, were Englishmen, though they may possibly have been trained in the engravers' schools at Antwerp, or in that of Crispin Van de Passe at Cologne. To Van de Passe's school the well-known engravers Renold Elstracke and Francis Delaram seem to have belonged.

The works of these engravers belong to bibliography, but they possess too much artistic merit to exclude them from the domain of art. There were engravers in London who were mere hack-craftsmen, working for the booksellers, though some of these show imagination and design. Among working engravers were the brothers John and Martin Droeshout, belonging to a refugee family from Brussels. Martin Droeshout has obtained undying, if unmerited, fame as the engraver of the portrait of Shakespeare, prefixed to the First Folio of 1623. There is no need to think that Martin Droeshout must have seen Shakespeare in person. This would not be necessary for his profession. A publisher wishing to find a portrait of a celebrity might betake himself to the shop of Messrs. Sudbury and Humble, at the sign of the White Horse, in Pope's Head Alley, Cornhill, where engraved portraits were on sale and engravers at work in the back shop. If an engraved portrait were not forthcoming there, he would pass on to Mr. Peake, the picture-maker, on Snow Hill, or to a shop in the Strand, at Blackfriars, or near St. Paul's, where he could obtain or have made to order a panel-portrait, such as the so-called 'Droeshout' portrait of Shakespeare in the Memorial Gallery at Stratford-on-Avon. Should such a portrait not be ready to hand, it was easy to concoct one, and if a new and seasoned panel were not forthcoming, there was always a plentiful supply of old panel-paintings, which could be adapted and utilized for the purpose. The portrait would be then handed to a working engraver, like the young Martin Droeshout, to be cut on a copper-plate, the impressions taken from such a plate varying in truth, strength, and durability according to the skill of the engraver.

Francis Meres, in his *Palladis Tamia, Wits Treasury,*

being the second part of Wits Commonwealth, published
in 1598, was one of the first critics to mention Shakespeare,
or to write with enthusiasm of his genius as poet and
dramatist. In the same book Meres discourses of Elizabethan
' Painting ', on which he pronounced this judgement : ' As
learned Greece had these excellent artists renowned for their
learning, so England has these, Hilliard, Isaac Oliver, and
John de Critz, very famous for their painting. So as
Greece had moreover their painters, so in England we
have also these, William and Francis Segar, brethren,
Thomas and John Bettes, Lockie, Lyne, Peake, Peter Cole,
Arnolde, Marcus, Jacques de Bruy, Cornelius, Peter Golchi,
Hieronimo, and Peter Vandevelde. As Lysippus, Praxiteles,
and Pyrgoteles were excellent engravers, so have we these
engravers Rogers, Christopher Switzer, and Cure.' Modern
research has done much to verify Meres's record of the
artists in England who were Shakespeare's contemporaries.

BIBLIOGRAPHY.—HORACE WALPOLE's *Anecdotes of Painting*, ed. Wornum,
contains much information. The best account of English engraving of the
period is SIDNEY COLVIN's *Early Engravings and Engravers in England*
(1545–1695), 1905. See also M. H. SPIELMANN's *British Portrait Painting to the
opening of the Nineteenth Century*, 2 vols., 1910; AYMER VALLANCE'S ' Art in England during the Elizabethan and Stuart Periods ', in *The Studio*, Special Spring
Number, 1908 ; also LIONEL CUST's Introduction to the *Catalogue of Early
English Portraiture*, Burlington Fine Arts Club, 1909, ' Notes on Foreign Artists
of the Reformed Religion working in England from about 1560 to 1660 ', *Transactions of the Huguenot Society*, vol. vii, pp. 45 ff., and various biographies of
Elizabethan and Jacobean artists in the *Dictionary of National Biography*.

§ 2. MUSIC

BY

W. BARCLAY SQUIRE

In order to understand the position which England occupied in the history of musical progress at the end of the sixteenth and the beginning of the seventeenth centuries, it is necessary very briefly to pass in review the development of the art during the hundred and fifty years which preceded the birth of Shakespeare. Roughly speaking, the period from about the middle of the fifteenth century until the end of the sixteenth is that in which the modern art of music had its origin. Based on foundations which reach back so far as to be lost in obscurity, the music developed by the school of which Dunstable (d. 1453) was, by common consent, considered the founder, the ' new art ', of which the ' foundation and origin ' took place in England, arose from a system of extreme intricacy, a system that had for its basis a scale consisting primarily of the ecclesiastical modes, not as regulated traditionally by St. Gregory, but as modified according to an arrangement said to have been invented, about 1024, by Guido of Arezzo. In this system the scale was divided into hexachords, i.e. groups of six sounds, so disposed as to place a diatonic semitone between the third and fourth notes of each series, the remaining intervals being represented by whole tones. The sounds of these hexachords were sung to the syllables *ut, re, mi, fa, sol, la,* while the notes of the entire octave were known as A, B, C, D, E, F, and G (or Gamma). This system remained in use until the latter part of the seventeenth century, and this ' gamut '—consisting of the whole series of two names of the notes—was taught to all beginners just as the scale is nowadays. Hortensio, disguised as a music-master, in *The Taming of the Shrew* (III. i. 67–70), thus begins ' the rudiments of art ' by teaching Bianca ' the gamut of Hortensio ' :

> More pleasant, pithy, and effectual,
> Than hath been taught by any of my trade.

It would be impossible within the limits of these pages to explain the intricacies of the musical system which reached its culminating-point at the end of the seventeenth century. Much about it was pedantic and unpractical, derived from mediaeval interpretations of Pythagoras as handed down by writers of whom Boethius was perhaps the most notable. But the main point to be borne in mind about it is that the first progress towards modern music arose from a system known as Descant, i.e. the art of combining two or more musical phrases or melodies. In the earliest times the groundwork of a vocal or instrumental composition was simply a more or less lengthy example of one of those ancient church tones, whose origin is so remote as to defy all attempts at discovery : these ' ground-melodies ', as they may conveniently be called, were known as the plain-song, or canto fermo, and the accompanying parts, sometimes written for a higher and sometimes for a lower voice or instrument, formed what is known as the ' counterpoint '. In this system of musical construction the main melody was in the plain-song, but, since the plain-song was generally assigned to one of the lower parts, its importance was necessarily obscured in performance by the superimposed counterpoint. The result was a form of music known as ' polyphony ', in which all the parts of the composition fitted in, so to speak, side by side, each component part of the whole being of equal melodic importance. It is hardly necessary to point out that in modern music (as usually written) the construction is entirely different, the highest part being devoted to the melody, and the subsidiary parts being merely added for the purpose of enriching or varying the harmony. In other words, whereas music down to about the end of the sixteenth century was entirely polyphonic, since then the old system has been replaced by homophony. The difference between the two may be further emphasized if it is remembered that in polyphony, musical composition was looked at horizontally, whereas in homophony it is purely vertical.

The art of polyphony is generally considered to have emerged from a purely theoretical stage under the influence of John Dunstable. Very little is known of him, and until recently most of his compositions were lost ; but of late years enough music by him and his immediate successors has been discovered to show that his influence must have been greater abroad than in his own country. Doubtless this was owing principally to political reasons. Music has always been an art depending almost for its existence upon its surroundings, and it was the ill-luck of the school of Dunstable that it arose at a time when England was in the throes of civil war, and when the court was too poor and too disorganized to play the part of foster-mother to a budding art. The Wars of the Roses seem to have driven English musicians abroad, and it was in the Netherlands, Burgundy, and Italy that the seed sown by Dunstable first bore fruit. With the advent of the strong government of the Tudors there was a prospect of better things. We find Henry VII sending to Italy to recall the learned John Hothby for service in his native land. Henry VIII also had distinguished native composers at his court, but such of their compositions as have survived show that their methods had made but little advance on those of a hundred years earlier, and it is not to be wondered at that foreign musicians should have been largely employed by the king. The Reformation dealt a severe blow to the progress of English music, for, after the Court, the Church was the chief support of musicians, and with the abolition of the Roman ritual the important branch of church music became of no practical use, and English musicians were reduced to cultivating their art for purely secular purposes. Meanwhile, on the Continent the art progressed by leaps and bounds. The Council of Trent curbed the extravagances of the theorists, who, by following too blindly the methods of an earlier age, had nearly succeeded in reducing church music to a most unedifying condition ; purified by wise reforms, the ecclesiastical compositions of men like Orlando di Lasso and Palestrina rose to a height of excellence that has never been surpassed, so that even now they are looked on as the true models of the loftiest and purest accompaniment of religious ritual. From about the third decade of the sixteenth century the printing-press was largely used in Italy (and to a less degree in Germany and France) for musical purposes. The astonishing number of secular vocal works, such as madrigals, canzonets, &c., which poured from the presses of Italy during this period shows how vigorously music must have flourished, and that the refined polyphony of the school of Palestrina and his contemporaries was by no means reserved for the service of the Church, but

was equally cultivated and appreciated in courts like
those of Ferrara, Mantua, or Naples, or in great commercial
centres like Venice. By the end of the century polyphony
had been carried to the highest degree of perfection, when
almost suddenly a new school arose, and the old system
gradually gave way to an entirely different method, in
which the single voice part was supreme—the method known
to musical historians as *homophony*. This new style of
music first sprang up in Florence shortly before the end
of the century : it arose from an attempt at finding something more suitable for dramatic expression than the polyphonic style, which had then reached its highest state of
development. Gradually the influence of the new style,
crude as it was in its beginnings, made itself felt in the
whole musical system : the old method of composition on
a canto fermo was abandoned, and the modern scales replaced the mediaeval hexachords.

It is necessary to bear in mind this summary of musical
history, in order to understand the condition of music in
England during the Shakespearian era. Originally, England was in the front rank of musical progress, but at the
time of the accession of Elizabeth it had fallen far behind
the Netherlands and Italy. The Wars of the Roses had
cut off the support afforded by the court and the households
of the great nobles ; the Reformation had dealt a further
blow by almost killing church music. The Council of Trent
saved church music abroad ; in England the reformers were
more drastic, and there was no Palestrina to show what
could be done in preserving what was good, while suppres-
sing the extravagances of pedantry. No doubt an attempt
was made to retain some kind of dignified church music. In
1564 we find Archbishop Parker writing to Burghley that
the French ambassador ' seemed to be glad . . . that we did
not expel musick out of our quires, telling them that our
musick drowned not the principal regard of our prayer ',
and in the previous year the archbishop, on a visit to
Sandwich, found ' their service sung in good distinct harmony and quiet devotion ; the singing men, being the
mayor and the jurats, with the head men of the town placed
in the quire fair and decent ', but the absence of any collections of church music printed in England (with the sole
exceptions of Merbecke's very scarce *Booke of Common*

JOHN BULL

Praier noted, of 1550, and the equally rare *Certaine Notes*, published by John Day in 1560 and 1565) shows that music of an ornate character was the exception in English churches. The cathedrals probably followed the Elizabethan injunctions in retaining anthems, but even here there were often restrictions as to any kind of ornate music, while such parish churches, as that of Sandwich, which had to rely on the musical services of the ' mayor and jurats and head men of the town ', were not likely to achieve anything very elaborate in the way of ecclesiastical music. Though we find that nearly all the English composers whose names are prominent during the latter part of the reign of Elizabeth and the early years of the seventeenth century wrote a certain number of anthems and Anglican services, some of which are indeed very fine, yet on the whole the church music of the period was distinctly inferior to the secular, and it is not until the appearance of Orlando Gibbons that there is anything to equal the splendid series of madrigals which make the period so important in the history of English music. It is noticeable that many of the chief musicians of the day clung to the old religion, and continued to write music for the Roman ritual for some time after it had been officially proscribed. Tye, Whyte, and Tallis, among the older men, Byrd, Bull, and Philips among those who lived on into the seventeenth century, all adhered, with different degrees of constancy, to the Roman communion, and (with the exception of Bull, who was chiefly an instrumental composer) some of their best work is to be found in masses and motets that can only have been performed privately. The revival in the present day of the masses of Byrd and Tallis, the motets of Philips, and the lamentations of Whyte, has shown that the Latin church music of the English school was not far behind that of Italy under Palestrina. In one branch of vernacular sacred music, indeed, there was plenty of activity. The English Reformation, which at first had shown a certain amount of Lutheran tendency, during the reign of Elizabeth, drew nearer to the school of Calvin, and with this change there arose a taste for psalm-singing, which is often alluded to by Shakespeare and other dramatists of the day. If not introduced by the Huguenot refugees who came to England from the Netherlands, there is no doubt that it was largely spread by the Flemish weavers who fled from the persecutions of Alva; and Falstaff's speech, 'I would I were a weaver, I could sing psalms or anything' (*1 Hen. IV*, II. iv. 148–50), alludes to a very definite fact in the history of English psalmody. The popularity of psalm-singing must have been enormous, for from 1560 to 1600 alone there appeared in England some ninety editions of metrical psalms with music.

But if the development of sacred music during this period was slow and fitful, secular music made astonishing progress. At the beginning of the reign of Elizabeth, England was, as we have seen, distinctly behind Italy and the Netherlands, but at the end of the sixteenth century it had more than made up for lost time, and produced a school of composers which fully equalled, and in some respects surpassed, any to be found on the Continent. At a first glance this sudden outburst of musical activity in England seems very surprising, but it may be accounted for by the fact that there existed in the country a large amount of musical talent, which only wanted a favourable opportunity to become prominent. There is plenty of evidence that in the fourteenth and fifteenth centuries the English were what is popularly known as 'a musical people', and during the troublesome times of the Wars of the Roses and the Reformation, music—in a rudimentary stage—continued to be cultivated by the people, even if it had not the opportunity of developing into a very highly organized art. During this period our national music was probably confined to simple instrumental works, played by artists of no great skill, and to ballad-tunes and songs. These formed the foundation of the English music of the late sixteenth and early seventeenth centuries. Many ballad-tunes are quoted by Shakespeare and his contemporaries in a way which shows that they must have been familiar to the audiences of the day, and many of them have survived as the themes of those elaborate sets of variations which are to be found in such manuscript collections of virginal music as the Fitzwilliam Virginal Book (preserved at Cambridge), Cosyn's Virginal Book (in the collection of His Majesty the King), or Lady Nevell's Book (in the library of the Marquis of Abergavenny). The taste for music among the people must have been very widely spread or there would not have existed so many itinerant musicians to satisfy the demand. The date of the Armada is that which is generally fixed for the birth of the great school of Elizabethan madrigalists, yet already in 1587 Gosson complains (in his *Schoole of Abuse*) that 'London is so full of unprofitable pipers and fiddlers, that a man can no sooner enter a tavern, than two or three cast of them hang at his heels, to give him a dance before he depart'; and in 1586 (if not earlier) one of the first of those companies of English actors and musicians who had so important an influence abroad made its appearance in Denmark. With the increase of luxury and the more settled political atmosphere that followed the defeat of the Armada, this native substratum of musical talent found greater scope for development. The experience gained slowly by the Netherlanders and Italians was quickly absorbed, and resulted in the appearance of an English school, which combined the freshness and vigour of the national melody with the technical ability of a highly-developed science. Music spread upwards from the masses to the classes; every great nobleman maintained among his household a certain number of musicians—'the music of the house', as Nerissa calls it (*Merch. of V*. v. i. 98) —whose duty was not only to perform but also to teach what was regarded as an essential part of a gentleman's education. If we exclude the members of the royal chapel and the organists of the great cathedrals, we find that most of the distinguished musicians of the day were in the service of great noblemen or country gentlemen. John Farmer dedicated his madrigals to his master, the Earl of Oxford, George Kirbye was in the service of Sir Robert Jermyn, Thomas Greaves was lutenist to Sir Henry Pierrepont, Henry Lichfild was in the service of Lady Cheyney, Thomas Vautor was a household musician to Sir George Villiers, Henry Youll was the teacher of the three sons of Edward Bacon, the third son of the Lord Keeper; John Bartlet dedicated his *Booke of Ayres* to 'his singular good Lord and Maister Sir Edward Seymore', John Ward was a highly trusted servant to Sir Henry Fanshawe, and Robert Johnson—the original composer of the songs in *The Tempest* —was apprenticed to Sir George Carey before becoming lutenist to James I. Of all these, with the exception of Johnson, printed collections of madrigals and songs exist; indeed, from the year 1588 until about 1630, the continuous

series of printed books of English vocal music is ample
evidence of the extraordinary musical activity of the age.
A well-known passage at the beginning of Morley's *Plaine
and Easie Introduction to Practicall Musicke,* first issued in
1597, describes how Philomathes was at a ' banket ' given
by Master Sophobulus, at which a discussion upon music
arose. Philomathes was invited to take part in it, but (he
says) ' refusing and pretending ignorance, the whole com-
panie condemned mee of discurtesie. . . . But supper being
ended, and Musicke bookes, according to the custome being
brought to the table ; the mistresse of the house presented
mee with a part, earnestly requesting mee to sing. But
when, after manie excuses, I protested unfainedly that
I could not, everie one began to wonder. Yea, some
whispered to others, demaunding how I was brought up.'
Thirty years later than Morley, Henry Peacham, writing of
music in his *Compleat Gentleman,* says : ' I desire not that
any Noble or Gentleman should (save at his private recreation at leasurable houres) prove a Master in the same, or
neglect his more weightie imployments. . . . I desire no more
in you than to sing your part sure, at the first sight, withall,
to play the same upon your Violl, or the exercise of the
Lute, privately to your selfe.' But even stronger than such
isolated quotations is the evidence to be derived from
Shakespeare that music played a very real and active part
in the social life of England. An industrious commentator
has calculated that there are about a hundred and seventy
passages in Shakespeare's plays and poems which introduce
the words ' music ', ' musical ', or ' musician ' ; that ' sing '
and its derivatives occur two hundred and forty-seven
times ; and that there are some thirty or forty passages dealing with musical instruments. In this respect Shakespeare
is far in advance of his contemporaries, though a very pretty
anthology of passages dealing with music might be made
from the lesser Elizabethan dramatists and poets. Moreover, the constant use of technical terms by Shakespeare
proves that he had more than a superficial knowledge both
of the art of composition and of the construction of musical
instruments. It is noticeable that his musical education,
wherever it was acquired, was strictly on the lines of the
polyphonic school, as sketched at the beginning of this
section. Such a passage as that in *Richard II,* beginning :

Music do I hear?
Ha, ha! keep time. How sour sweet music is
When time is broke and no proportion kept!

(v. v. 41 ff.)

cannot be understood without some knowledge of the elaborate system of proportions inherited by Elizabethan composers from the earlier English school, and the same knowledge of the technicalities of the polyphonic composers is displayed in Hortensio's gamut (*Tam. Sh.* III. i. 73 ff.) and in many other passages. The allusions to musical instruments, such as the lute, the virginals, recorders, are still more striking in the knowledge they show of the executive branch of the art, and more than one commentator has come to grief for want of the technical knowledge of which Shakespeare made such good use. At first sight it seems remarkable that the musical terms of the plays should be so consistently those of the old school of polyphony. We have seen that at the end of the sixteenth century there arose in Italy a new style of music, in which declamation by a single voice replaced the old intricate interweaving of several parts, no single one of which could be said to be more prominent as melody than the others. This homophonic style arose in the first instance from an attempt at imitating the Greek drama, and from it there sprang, in the early seventeenth century, the first musical dramas of Peri, Caccini, and Monteverde. In Italy the new school soon revolutionized secular music, and the older system of polyphony only survived for a time in purely liturgical music. This change dates from about the year 1597, yet in all the plays which Shakespeare produced from then until the performance of *The Tempest* in 1611, no allusion to the 'new music' can be discovered, and it is evident that, so far as England was concerned, it had little or no effect. When we consider the influence which Italy had on the English literature of the day, and also the fact that during the first quarter of the seventeenth century the masque reached its highest development in England, this seems rather surprising, especially as the masque was so closely allied to the opera. It may, however, be accounted for by the fact that the English masque was not, like the musical drama of the school of Peri and his successors, a deliberate attempt at

the production of a new art-form, but that in this country
it was made up of materials which were already at hand,
and more or less in everyday use in the existing theatres.
The accounts we possess of the English travelling companies which appeared so frequently in Denmark and
Germany from about the year 1585 onwards, show that
instrumentalists formed a large proportion in the composition of each troupe of performers (e. g. at Strasburg in 1605,
where there were seven instrumentalists in a company of
fifteen people), and the class of experienced theatrical
musicians from whom these wandering players were drawn
was quite able to supply music which fulfilled the modest
dramatic requirements of the masques.   Polyphony was no
more suited to the stage in England than it was in Italy,
but in England there was a large store of song-tunes and
ballads, the taste for which was a national inheritance, and
did not depend on musical science or culture.   It was this
store from which the theatre-musicians produced a school
of English melody totally distinct from the elaborate
dramatic attempts of the Italians.   The ' Ayres ' of such
men as John Dowland, Campion, Rossiter, short songs,
sometimes for a single voice, sometimes simply harmonized
for two, three, or four voices, but nearly always accompanied by a lute, are totally distinct from the intricate polyphonic madrigals of such composers as Wilbye, Gibbons,
and Weelkes, and yet they have no resemblance to the
Italian songs of Caccini and his contemporaries.   They are,
indeed, a native product, refined and polished imitations
or developments of national song-tunes, giving birth in
their turn to that peculiarly English musical form, the
glee or part-song.   It was these ' ayres ', as they were
generally called by their composers, which provided sufficient material for the dramatic music of the day.   Played
on viols they would serve for act-tunes or for such instrumental music as was needed ; as vocal solos, with lute
accompaniment, they were equally suited for the incidental
songs in plays.   This use of an essentially popular form
of composition in connexion with the stage had an effect
which has been strangely overlooked by English writers.
If grand opera had its origin in Italy at the end of
the sixteenth century, ballad-opera, and its equivalent,
the German ' Singspiel ', the ancestors of the modern

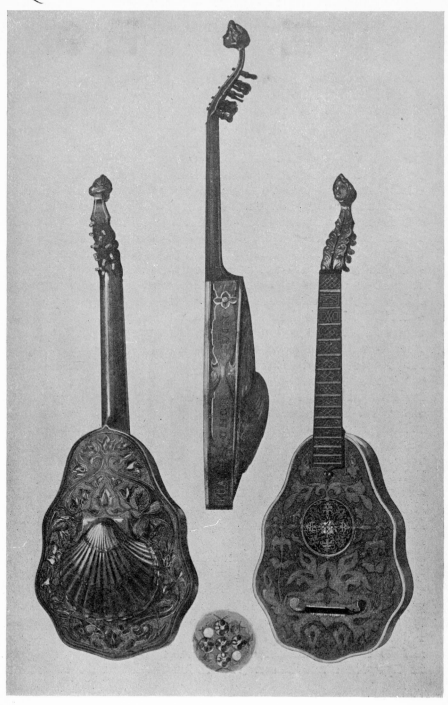

operetta, may with equal truth be said to have been introduced into Germany from England at the same date. This English 'Singspiel' first appeared on the Continent about 1596; it was spread over the country by various companies of English players and musicians—Robert Brown at Leyden, Frankfurt, and Nürnberg, Thomas Sackville at Brunswick and Nürnberg, and Richard Machin at Brandenburg, while all over the country there are found, between the years 1585 and 1635, English actors and English musicians, either in strolling companies, or settled down in the exercise of their art. From 1600 to 1605 Richard Machin was in the service of the Landgrave Maurice of Hesse, from 1617 to 1621 Thomas Simpson was a violist at the court of Ernest III of Holstein-Schaumburg, after 1614 Walter Rowe was a member of the band of the Elector of Brandenburg. Similarly we find Valentine Flood at Berlin in 1627, and later at Danzig; John Stanley at Berlin from 1628 to 1631, and John Price at Dresden in 1629, while William Brade, who had been successively in the service of the Duke of Holstein-Gottorp and of the town of Hamburg, in 1618 was living as court capellmeister at Halle, where his daughter married one Andreas Beger, a barber-surgeon, who was the teacher of Handel's father. But the most notable of the wandering English musicians of the age was John Dowland, who was celebrated by Richard Barnfield in his sonnet (sometimes attributed to Shakespeare) 'To his friend Maister R. L. in praise of Musique and Poetrie':

If Musique and sweet Poetrie agree,
As they must needes (the Sister and the Brother),
Then must the Love be great, twixt thee and mee,
Because thou lov'st the one, and I the other.
Dowland to thee is deare; whose heavenly tuch
Upon the Lute, doeth ravish humaine sense;
Spenser to mee; whose deepe Conceit is such,
As, passing all Conceit, needs no defence.
Thou lov'st to heare the sweete melodious sound,
That Phoebus Lute (the Queen of Musique) makes:
And I in deepe Delight am chiefly drownd,
When as himselfe to singing he betakes.
    One God is God of Both (as Poets faigne),
    One Knight loves Both, and Both in thee remaine.

Born in 1563, Dowland first appears in 1580 in the service of Sir Henry Cobham, English ambassador in Paris. Here he fell in with some English Catholic refugees, by whom he was persuaded to be reconciled to the old religion. In 1588 he was in England, but shortly afterwards he was invited to Germany by the Duke of Brunswick, from whose court he passed to that of the Landgrave of Hesse. He then travelled to Venice and Florence, returning by way of Bologna to Nürnberg. In 1597 he published his *First Booke of Songes*, which passed through five editions before 1613. In 1598 he entered the service of Christian IV of Denmark, with whom he remained, visiting England at intervals, until 1606, when he finally returned to his native country. He was appointed one of the king's musicians for the lutes in 1612, and must have died early in 1626. His music is to be found in many foreign collections, both manuscript and printed, as well as in his own four books of ' Songes or Ayres ', and in his very rare instrumental *Lachrymae, or Seven Teares, figured in seaven passionate Pavans*, which was published in 1605. Another interesting figure is that of John Bull, the most brilliant organist of the day, whose elaborate compositions for the organ and virginals show that he must have been an executant of extraordinary skill. Though he was Gresham Professor of Music and organist to James I, in 1613 he fled to the Netherlands, and in 1617 became organist of Antwerp Cathedral, thus forming a link between England and the Dutch organists, of whom Sweelinck was by far the greatest. Another such link we find in Peter Philips, an ecclesiastic, who first appears at Antwerp in 1591, and in 1598 was organist to the Archduke Albert. He was the most Italian in style of any of the English composers of the day, and in his later works shows some tendency towards the new style of homophony, though never entirely losing all his English individuality. With him may be associated Richard Dering, who in 1617 was organist to the English Benedictine nuns at Brussels, and, like Philips, wrote music in both the new and the old styles. But these men were only wandering stars of the great galaxy that shed such lustre over England at the beginning of the seventeenth century. Even to name them all, or to attempt to describe the varied excellence of their works, cannot be done here. Yet the subject of music in Shakespeare's England must not be left without some mention of a few of the greatest contemporary composers. First

among them comes the veteran William Byrd, ' a Father
of Musicke ', as he is described in an official register ; ' homo
memorabilis ', as an enthusiastic scribe has written against
his name in a manuscript in the royal collection. Associated
in his earlier days with Tallis, he lived on until nearly the
end of the reign of James I, producing, during his long
career, a very large amount of music of all kinds, much of
which is printed, while much still remains in manuscript.
His work is always interesting from its strong individuality,
strangely combining rugged grandeur and deep pathos, but
it is in his Latin church music that his greatness is displayed
to the fullest.   His *Cantiones Sacrae* and *Gradualia* are, as
Peacham truly says, ' meere Angelicall and Divine,' and
his three masses (to quote a recent writer) ' rank together
as, beyond all conceivable question, the finest settings of
the Mass that exist from an English hand ; they are not so
suave and broad as the work of Palestrina, but they are
somehow more human and personal '.   Less individual,
though often full of a distinct and rather quaint charm, is
his secular vocal music, while his instrumental pieces for the
virginals rival those of Bull in their instinct for effective
passages, at the same time remaining (unlike Bull's) invariably solid and sincere.   Taken all round, Byrd is one
of the very greatest musicians that England has produced ;
his greatness is only now beginning to be recognized, and
his true position among European composers will only be
realized when a complete edition of his works is available.
By the side of Byrd, and almost in the same rank, comes
his Anglican counterpart, Orlando Gibbons, the founder of
the best school of Anglican church music.   More modern in
style than Byrd, and showing in some of his anthems a
leaning to the tendencies of the new music, in the solidity
and massive spirit of his vocal writing he retains all that
is best of the old school.   He is splendid alike in his
madrigals and his church music, tempering austerity with
a note of human personality, though never soaring into the
heights of mystical fervour to which Byrd sometimes
attains.   His instrumental music is far less interesting
than his vocal ; some of the best of it is to be found in
Parthenia, a little collection of pieces for the virginals,
published about 1611, in which he was associated with Byrd
and Bull.

Following these two great masters comes a group which is only inferior owing to the more limited scope of the compositions it produced. John Wilbye, the greater part of whose life was spent at Hengrave Hall in the service of Sir Thomas Kytson and his widow, published only two collections of madrigals, sixty-five in all; but these are enough to place him in the very first rank of madrigal-writers, not excepting Luca Marenzio himself. Like Wilbye, John Bennet wrote very little; only one volume of his madrigals exists, but every madrigal is a gem, and throughout them all there runs a vein of exquisite pathos. More human and full of charm are the two sets of madrigals of Thomas Bateson, the Chester organist, beside whom may be placed Thomas Weelkes, organist successively of Winchester College and of Chichester Cathedral, a more voluminous writer, with a decided tendency towards quaint fancy and a picturesqueness that sometimes recall Orazio Vecchi. In some respects apart from his contemporaries stands Thomas Morley, whom one is tempted to describe as the type of the critic-composer, a master of technique, who knows all styles, and can write with equal facility and success grave church music of the Palestrina school, solid madrigals like Philips, dainty ballets like Gastoldi, and florid virginal music like Byrd. These men, Byrd, Gibbons, Wilbye, Bennet, Bateson, Weelkes, and Morley, are all in the first rank of the composers of Shakespeare's day, but close on their heels comes a crowd of organists, lutenists, and song-writers who are scarcely inferior to them: Farmer, Mundy, Este, Farnaby, Hilton, Lichfild, Pilkington, Tomkins, Ward, and many others—such an array of musical talent of the first order as England has produced at no other period of its musical history.

This brief sketch of the music of the day would not be complete without some mention of the instruments generally played on. The most intimate, because it was essentially the instrument used for accompanying solo songs, was the lute, with its pear-shaped body pierced by a sound-hole, attached to which was a neck covered by a finger-board divided by frets of catgut or brass into measured lengths. It was played by the fingers, unaided by a plectrum, and music for it was written in a special notation called tablature, in which the horizontal lines represent the

PARTHENIA

or

THE MAYDENHEAD

of the first musicke that

euer was printed for the VIRGINALLS.

COMPOSED

By three famous Masters: William Byrd, D: John Bull, & Orlando Gibbons,
Gentilmen of his Ma:ties most Illustrious Chappell.
Dedicated to all the Maisters and Louers of Musick

Ingrauen
by William Hole.

for

DORETHIE EUANS.

Cum

Priuilegio.

Printed at LONDON by G: Lowe and are to be soulde
at his howse in Loathberry.

strings of the instrument, the semitones above the open sound of each string being represented by small letters. A larger variety of the lute was the theorbo, or arch-lute, with deeper-toned strings and a larger neck. The lute was a very difficult instrument both to keep in good condition and to tune ; Thomas Mace, writing in 1676, recommends that it should be kept in a bed which is in constant use, and a later writer calculated that a lutenist eighty years old had spent sixty in tuning his instrument ! The violin, as we know it, had hardly come into general use in Shakespeare's time. It came into fashion under Louis XIV. At the beginning of the seventeenth century ' a French song, and a fiddle ' were looked upon as un-English. The place that it now occupies among instruments was taken by the viol, which differed from the violin in having deeper ribs and a flat back. Viols were made in four principal sizes—the treble or discant, the tenor, the bass (or viol da gamba), and the double bass (or violone). They generally had from five to seven strings, and their tone was more penetrating than powerful. They were often kept in sets, known as a ' chest of viols ', consisting of two trebles, two tenors, a viol da gamba, and a double bass. Of keyed instruments the organ in England, down to the end of the sixteenth century, had a single manual, but in 1605–6, Thomas Dallam built for King's College a two-manual instrument, the first English specimen of which we have any record ; pedals were a much later invention, and only appeared in England at the end of the eighteenth century, so that, in the absence of directions as to the use of stops, it is often difficult to decide whether music by early organists, such as Bull, is written for the organ or for the virginal or spinet. The virginal was a keyboard stringed instrument of oblong shape, often pentagonal (as is the beautiful instrument at the Victoria and Albert Museum, known as ' Queen Elizabeth's virginal '), but always with the keyboard placed on the long side. The strings, as in the later harpsichord, were plucked by quills attached to upright wooden ' jacks ', which were set in motion by the keys. Its tone is small, but extraordinarily clear and bright in quality, though quite differing from that of the modern pianoforte, and incapable of expressing any variety of light and shade. The chief wind-instruments were recorders, the ancestor of the modern flageolet, constructed with eight holes, and generally made in sets, the lower-toned instruments being fitted with keys ; their length varied from two to four feet, and their tone was peculiarly sweet and solemn. Mostly for open-air music we find hautboys, sackbuts (or trombones), cornets (wooden instruments covered with leather), trumpets, and drums. Combinations of various instruments such as we are accustomed to in the modern orchestra were only beginning to be tried experimentally ; ' consorts ' generally consisted of music played by the same class of instruments, and such a combination as that in Morley's *Consort-Lessons* (1599), which are written for treble lute cithern (a lute-shaped instrument with pairs of wire strings tuned in unison and played with a plectrum), pandora (an English variety of the cithern), flute, treble-viol, and baseviol, stands almost alone as the only printed instance that has come down to us of what Pandarus (in *Troilus*, III. i. 53) calls 'broken music'. Unfortunately, no complete set of the part-books of which the work consists is extant.

BIBLIOGRAPHY.—For the general musical history of the period the histories of Burney and Hawkins have not been superseded. The first two volumes of the *Oxford History of Music* deal at great length with the origins of mediaeval music, but pass over the end of the sixteenth century with much less detail ; the third volume deals almost entirely with the new style which arose in Italy in the seventeenth century. The best account of English music during Shakespeare's time is to be found in Chapters III and IV of ERNEST WALKER'S *History of Music in England*, 1907; W. NAGEL'S *Geschichte der Musik in England*, 1894-7, though diffuse, is also useful, and HENRY DAVEY'S *History of English Music*, 1895, is valuable for its accurate dates and summaries of original authorities. CHARLES VAN DER BORREN'S *Sources of Keyboard Music in England*, 1913, is important for its detailed account of the virginal and organ music of the period. Many little-known details as to the introduction of English musical plays abroad have been unearthed in J. BOLTE'S *Die Singspiele der englischen Komödianten und ihrer Nachfolger in Deutschland, Holland und Skandinavien*, 1893, and in W. CREIZENACH'S *Schauspiele der englischen Komödianten* [1895]. Three excellent special books on the musical allusions in Shakespeare's works are E. W. NAYLOR'S *Shakespeare and Music*, 1896, L. C. ELSON'S *Shakespeare in Music*, 1901, and G. H. COWLING'S *Music on the Shakespearian Stage*, 1913. For biographies of musicians the last edition of GROVE'S *Dictionary of Music and Musicians* is the best authority; for descriptions of instruments the Rev. F. W. GALPIN'S *Old English Instruments of Music*, 1910, is a treasure-house of valuable information.

The musical terminology of Shakespeare's age was familiar to all well-informed people and entered largely into literary and colloquial idiom ; in no author are musical allusions more frequent than in Shakespeare. Here follows

A SELECT GLOSSARY OF MUSICAL TERMS

WITH ILLUSTRATIVE PASSAGES FROM SHAKESPEARE'S WORKS

Compiled by C. T. ONIONS.

Accord. Harmony.
> ' Gamut ' I am, the ground of all accord. (*Tam. Sh.* III. i. 74)

Air. A melody or tune.
> A solemn air and the best comforter
> To an unsettled fancy, cure thy brains. (*Temp.* v. i. 58–9)
> If they but hear perchance a trumpet sound
> Or any air of music touch their ears,
> You shall perceive them make a mutual stand. (*Merch. of V.* v. i. 75–7)
> Your eyes are lode-stars ! and your tongue's sweet air
> More tuneable than lark to shepherd's ear. (*Mid. N. D.* I. i. 183–4)
> Moth. [*Singing.*]   Concolinel,—
> Armado.   Sweet air ! (*Love's L. L.* III. i. 3–4)
> A wonderful sweet air, with admirable rich words to it.
> (*Cymb.* II. iii. 19–20)

Anthem. A composition in unmeasured prose (usually from the Scriptures or Liturgy) set to music.
> Falstaff. . . . For my voice, I have lost it with hollaing, and singing of anthems. (*2 Hen. IV*, I. ii. 215–16)

Applied to a song of grief or mourning.
> breathe it in mine ear,
> As ending anthem of my endless dolour. (*Two Gent.* III. i. 240–1)
> Her heavy anthem still concludes in woe. (*Ven. & Ad.* 839)

A-re, B-mi, C-fa-ut, D-sol-re, E-la-mi. The names of A, B, C, D, E of the bass staff according to their position in the hexachords (*Tam. Sh.* III. i. 74–9 : see *Gamut*). In Guido d'Arezzo's arrangement of the musical scale, *A re* was A of the first hexachord (i. e. the note A on the lowest or first space of the modern bass staff), the lowest note but one of Guido's whole scale ; A of the octave, which was *la* of the second hexachord, and *mi* of the third, and *re* of the fourth, being distinguished as *A la-mi-re.*

Bagpipe. A musical instrument consisting of an airtight wind-bag and one or more reed-pipes into which the air is pressed by the performer. See *Drone.*
> when the bagpipe sings i' the nose. (*Merch. of V.* IV. i. 49)
> Falstaff.   'Sblood, I am as melancholy as a gib cat, or a lugged bear.
> Prince.   Or an old lion, or a lover's lute.
> Falstaff.   Yea, or the drone of a Lincolnshire bagpipe.
> (*1 Hen. IV*, I. ii. 82–6)

Bass, base. Epithet of strings of the lowest pitch.

> I have sounded the very bass string of humility. (*1 Hen. IV*, II. iv. 6)

The lowest part in harmonized musical composition ; the deepest
male voice, or lowest tones of a musical instrument ; one who
sings the bass part.

> The mean is drown'd with your unruly bass. (*Two Gent.* I. ii. 93)
>> Means and basses. (*Wint. Tale* IV. ii. 46–7)

In one passage *bass* is used as a verb for ' to provide a bass to '.

> . . . the thunder,
> That deep and dreadful organ-pipe, pronounc'd
> The name of Prosper : it did bass my trespass. (*Temp.* III. iii. 97–9)

Bass viol. A stringed instrument for playing the bass part in
concerted music ; a violoncello.

> He that went, like a bass-viol, in a case of leather. (*Com. of E.* IV. iii. 22)

Bear a part. To sing a part.

> *Ariel's Song.* Come unto these yellow sands . . .
> And, sweet sprites, the burden bear.
>> Hark, hark !
>>> [*Burden* : Bow, wow, *dispersedly.* (*Temp.* I. ii. 375–81)
> Come, Philomel, that sing'st of ravishment,
> Make thy sad grove in my dishevell'd hair :
> As the dank earth weeps at thy languishment,
> So I at each sad strain will strain a tear,
> And with deep groans the diapason bear ;
> For burthen-wise I'll hum on Tarquin still
> While thou on Tereus descant'st better skill.
>
> And whiles against a thorn thou bear'st thy part
> To keep thy sharp woes waking, wretched I
> To imitate thee well, against my heart
> Will fix a sharp knife to affright my eye. (*Lucr.* 1128–38)
>
> If the true concord of well-tuned sounds,
> By unions married, do offend thine ear,
> They do but sweetly chide thee, who confounds
> In singleness the parts that thou shouldst bear. (*Sonnet* viii)

Breast. Voice.

> *Sir Toby.* Welcome, ass. Now let 's have a catch.
> *Sir Andrew.* By my troth, the fool has an excellent breast.
>> (*Tw. N.* II. iii. 18–21)

Broken. Of a boy's voice : Cracked.

> My mouth no more were broken than these boys',
> And writ as little beard. (*All 's W.* II. iii. 65–7)

Compare :—

> I'll . . . speak between the change of man and boy
> With a reed voice. (*Merch. of V.* III. iv. 64–7)
>> . . . though our voices
> Have got the mannish crack. (*Cymb.* IV. ii. 235–6)

Broken music. Part music, concerted music ; especially music to
be performed by instruments of different classes (cf. p. 31 above).

> But is there any else longs to feel this broken music in his sides ?
>> (*A. Y. L.* I. ii. 150–1)
> Come, your answer in broken music ; for thy voice is music, and thy
> English broken. (*Hen. V*, v. ii. 261–3)

Pandarus. What music is this ?

Serv. I do but partly know, sir : it is music in parts . . .

Pandarus. . . . Fair prince, here is good broken music.

Paris. You have broke it, cousin ; and by my life, you shall make it whole again : you shall piece it out with a piece of your performance. Nell, he is full of harmony. (*Troilus* III. i. 19–21, 53–7)

Burden, burthen. The bass or undersong to a melody.

Julia. Best sing it to the tune of ' Light o' Love '.

Lucetta. It is too heavy for so light a tune.

Jul. Heavy ! Belike it hath some burden, then ?

(*Two Gent.* I. ii. 80–2)

Hero. Why, how now ! do you speak in the sick tune ?

Beatrice. I am out of all other tune, methinks.

Margaret. Clap 's into ' Light o' love ' ; that goes without a burden : do you sing it, and I'll dance it. (*Much Ado* III. iv. 41–5)

I would sing my song without a burden : thou bringest me out of tune.

(*A. Y. L.* III. ii. 263–4)

A refrain.

And, sweet sprites, the burden bear. (*Temp.* I. ii. 380)

with such delicate burdens of dildoes and fadings, ' jump her and thump her '. (*Wint. Tale,* IV. iii. 193–5)

Cadence. Used by Morley (1597), but not by Shakespeare, who has *Close.*

Carol. A religious hymn of joy.

No night is now with hymn or carol blest. (*Mid. N. D.* II. i. 102)

Catch. Originally, a short composition for three or more voices, which sing the same melody, the second singer beginning the first line as the first goes on to the second line, and so with each successive singer ; ' the catch was for each succeeding singer to take up or catch his part in time ' (Grove). Subsequently applied to rounds in which the words are so arranged as to produce ludicrous effects, one singer catching at the words of another.

Caliban. . . . Will you troll the catch

You taught me but while-ere ?

Stephano. . . . Come on, Trinculo, let us sing.

[*Sings.*

Flout 'em, and scout 'em ; and scout 'em, and flout 'em ;

Thought is free.

Cal. That's not the tune.

[*Ariel plays the tune on a Tabor and Pipe.*

Steph. What is this same ?

Trinculo. This is the tune of our catch, played by the picture of Nobody. (*Temp.* III. ii. 129–38)

Malvolio. Do ye make an alehouse of my lady's house, that ye squeak out your coziers' catches without any mitigation or remorse of voice ? . . .

Sir Toby. We did keep time, sir, in our catches. (*Tw. N.* II. iii. 98–102)

Chant. To sing.

O, fellow ! come, the song we had last night . . .

The spinsters and the knitters in the sun,

And the free maids that weave their thread with bones,

Do use to chant it. (*Tw. N.* II. iv. 42–6)

Cittern, cithern. An instrument of the guitar kind, but strung with wire, and played with a plectrum or quill. It was commonly kept in barbers' shops for the use of the customers. It had often a grotesquely-carved head.

> *Holofernes.* I will not be put out of countenance.
> *Berowne.* Because thou hast no face.
> *Holofernes.* What is this?
> *Boyet.* A cittern-head. (*Love's L. L.* v. ii. 608–11)

Clef, cliff. A character placed on a particular line of a stave, to indicate the name and pitch of the notes standing on that line.

> ' D sol re ', one clef, two notes have I. (*Tam. Sh.* III. i. 78)
>
> *Ulysses.* She will sing any man at first sight.
> *Thersites.* And any man may sing her, if he can take her clef; she 's noted. (*Troilus* v. ii. 9–11)

Close. The conclusion of a musical phrase or movement ; a cadence.

> For government, though high and low and lower,
> Put into parts, doth keep in one concent,
> Congreeing in a full and natural close,
> Like music. (*Hen. V,* 1 ii. 180–3)

Compass. The full range of tones which a voice or a musical instrument is capable of producing.

> You would sound me from my lowest note to the top of my compass.
> (*Haml.* III. ii. 390–1)

Concent, consent. Harmony. See *Close.*

Concert, consort. The accord or harmony of several instruments or voices playing or singing in tune ; a harmonious combination of voices or instruments ; harmonious music.

> Visit by night your lady's chamber-window
> With some sweet consort. (*Two Gent.* III. ii. 83–4)
> Their music frightful as the serpent's hiss,
> And boding screech-owls make the concert full !
> (*2 Hen. VI,* III. ii. 326–7)

The verb means 'to play or sing together', and is used with a pun in :

> *Tybalt.* Mercutio, thou consort'st with Romeo,—
> *Mercutio.* Consort ! What ! dost thou make us minstrels ? an thou make minstrels of us, look to hear nothing but discords : here 's my fiddle-stick ; here 's that shall make you dance. 'Zounds ! consort !
> (*Rom. & Jul.* III. i. 49–54)

Concord. A combination of notes which is in itself satisfactory to the ear, requiring no ' resolution ' or following chord : opposed to *discord.* By Shakespeare often used vaguely for harmony.

> you are too flat
> And mar the concord with too harsh a descant. (*Two Gent.* I. ii. 90–1)
> The man that hath no music in himself,
> Nor is not mov'd by concord of sweet sounds. (*Merch. of V.* v. i. 83–4)
> If the true concord of well-tuned sounds,
> By unions married, do offend thine ear. (*Sonnet* viii)

Cornet. A horn.

> Only in stage directions, e.g. *Hen. VIII,* II. iv, Trumpets, sennet, and cornets.

Crotchet. A symbol for a note of half the value of a minim, made in the form of a stem with a round (formerly lozenge-shaped) black head ; a note of this value.

> *Balthazar.* Note this before my notes ;
> There 's not a note of mine that 's worth the noting.
> *Don Pedro.* Why these are very crotchets that he speaks ;
> Notes, notes, forsooth, and nothing ! (*Much Ado* II. iii. 57–60)

> Then will I lay the serving-creature's dagger on your pate. I will carry no crotchets : I'll *re* you, I'll *fa* you. Do you note me ?
>
> (*Rom. & Jul.* IV. v. 119–21)

Cymbals. A pair of concave plates of brass or bronze, which are struck together to produce a sharp ringing sound.

> Till late in eighteenth century known only as the name of ancient and foreign instruments of the type described (especially as mentioned in the Bible). (*Cor.* v. iv. 54 : see *Sackbut.*)

Dead march. A funeral march.

> Enter Talbot, Bedford, Burgundy, and Forces with scaling-ladders; their drums beating a dead march. (*1 Hen. VI*, II. i. 8, stage direction)

Descant. A melodious accompaniment to a simple musical theme (the *plain-song*), sung or played, and often merely extemporized, above it, and thus forming an air to its bass : the earliest form of counterpoint. Hence, the soprano or highest part of the score in part-singing ; generically, a warbled song, a melodious strain ; figuratively, varied comment on a theme, amplification of a subject.

> you are too flat,
> And mar the concord with too harsh a descant :
> There wanteth but a mean to fill your song. (*Two Gent.* I. ii. 90–2)

> And look you get a prayer-book in your hand,
> And stand between two churchmen, good my lord :
> For on that ground I'll make a holy descant. (*Rich. III*, III. vii. 46–8)

The verb *descant* means 'to play or sing a descant ; hence, to warble'.

> Why, I, in this weak piping time of peace,
> Have no delight to pass away the time,
> Unless to see my shadow in the sun
> And descant on mine own deformity. (*Rich. III*, I. i. 24–7)

Diapason. The interval of an octave ; the consonance of the highest and lowest notes of the musical scale ; an air or bass sounding in exact concord, i. e. in octaves.

> So I at each sad strain will strain a tear,
> And with deep groans the diapason bear. (*Lucr.* 1131–2)

Discord. Want of harmony between two or more musical notes sounded together ; dissonance. A combination of two or more notes not in harmony with each other ; a chord which by itself is unpleasing or unsatisfactory to the ear, and requires to be 'resolved' or followed by some other chord.

> If he, compact of jars, grow musical,
> We shall have shortly discord in the spheres. (*A. Y. L.* II. vii. 5–6)

> It is the lark that sings so out of tune,
> Straining harsh discords and unpleasing sharps.
>
> (*Rom. & Jul.* III. v. 27–8)

Take but degree away, untune that string,
And, hark ! what discord follows. (*Troilus* I. iii. 109–10)

> . . . an should the empress know
> This discord's ground, the music would not please.
> (*Tit. Andr.* II. i. 69–70)

Division. The execution of a rapid melodic passage, originally conceived as the dividing of each of a succession of long notes into several short ones ; a florid phrase or piece of melody, a run ; a current phrase was *to run division*, i. e. to execute such a passage or variation, to sing or play a run.

> Thy tongue
> Makes Welsh as sweet as ditties highly penn'd,
> Sung by a fair queen in a summer's bower,
> With ravishing division to her lute. (*1 Hen. IV*, III. i. 207–10)

> Some say the lark makes sweet division ;
> This doth not so, for she divideth us. (*Rom. & Jul.* III. v. 29–30)

Drone. The bass pipe of a bagpipe, which emits only one continuous tone.

> *Falstaff.* 'Sblood, I am as melancholy as a gib cat, or a lugged bear.
> *Prince.* Or an old lion, or a lover's lute.
> *Falstaff.* Yea, or the drone of a Lincolnshire bagpipe.
> (*1 Hen. IV*, I. ii. 82–6)

Drum. A musical instrument of the percussive class.

> Beat thou the drum, that it speak mournfully. (*Cor.* v. v. 151)

D-sol-re. See *A-re.*

Dulcimer. A musical instrument in which strings of graded lengths are stretched over a trapezoidal sounding board or box and struck with hammers held in the hands.

> The most familiar use of the word is for the bagpipe of *Daniel* iii. 5, where 'sackbut, psaltery, and dulcimer' would be better rendered 'harp, dulcimer, bagpipe'. (Not in Shakespeare.)

Ear. The faculty of discriminating sounds, and especially of accurately recognizing musical intervals.

> *Julia.* He plays false, father.
> *Host.* How ? out of tune on the strings ?
> *Julia.* Not so ; but yet so false that he grieves my very heart-strings.
> *Host.* You have a quick ear. (*Two Gent.* IV. ii. 60–4)

> *Titania.* What, wilt thou hear some music, my sweet love ?
> *Bottom.* I have a reasonable good ear in music.
> (*Mid. N. D.* IV. i. 30–2)

E-la-mi. See *A-re.*

Fa. The name given by Guido d'Arezzo to the fourth note in his hexachords, and retained in solmization as the fourth note of the octave.

> I will carry no crotchets : I'll *re* you, I'll *fa* you. Do you note me ?
> (*Rom. & Jul.* IV. v. 120–1)

> O, these eclipses do portend these divisions ! Fa, sol, la, mi.
> (*Lear* I. ii. 152–4)

False. Out of tune.

> What, to make thee an instrument and play false strains upon thee not to be endured ! (*A. Y. L.* IV. iii. 69–70)

Lucius.   The strings, my lord, are false.
Brutus.   He thinks he still is at his instrument.
(Jul. Caes. IV. iii. 289–90)

Fancy. A composition in an impromptu style, ' when a musician taketh a point at his pleasure, and turneth and wresteth it as he list ' (Morley, 1597).

> A . . . sung those tunes to the over-scutched huswives that he heard the carmen whistle, and sware they were his fancies or his good-nights.
(2 Hen. IV, III. ii. 342–5)

Fiddle. A stringed instrument of music.

> *Lovell.*   . . . the sly whoresons
> Have got a speeding trick to lay down ladies ;
> A French song and a fiddle has no fellow.
> *Sands.*   The devil fiddle 'em ! I'm glad they're going.
(Hen. VIII, I. iii. 39–42)

Fiddler. Tam. Sh. II. i. 158 ; III. i. 1 ; *Troil.* III. iii. 308.

Fiddlestick. 1 Hen. IV, II. iv. 542 ; *Rom. & Jul.* III. i. 52.

Fife. A small shrill-toned instrument of the flute kind, used chiefly to accompany the drum in military music.

> When you hear the drum,
> And the vile squealing of the wry-neck'd fife.   (*Merch of V.* II. v. 29–30)
> The spirit-stirring drum, the ear-piercing fife.   (*Oth.* III. iii. 353)

Fingering. The action of using the fingers in playing upon an instrument.

> I did but tell her she mistook her frets,
> And bow'd her hand to teach her fingering.   (*Tam. Sh.* II. i. 150–1)

> I would this music would come. I am advised to give her music o' mornings ; they say it will penetrate. [*Enter Musicians.*] Come on ; tune. If you can penetrate her with your fingering, so ; we'll try with tongue too. (*Cymb.* II. iii. 12–16)

Fit. A strain of music, a stave.

> Doubtfully in *Troilus* III. i. 63.

Flat. Relatively low in pitch ; below the true pitch.

> *Two Gent.* I. ii. 90 : see *Descant.*

Flute. A wind instrument, consisting of a hollow cylinder or pipe, with holes along its length, stopped by the fingers, or by keys which are opened by the fingers ; blown through a mouthpiece at the end.

> the oars were silver,
> Which to the tune of flutes kept stroke. (*Ant. & Cleop.* II. ii. 202–3)

Fret. In musical instruments like the guitar, formerly a ring of gut, now a bar or ridge of wood, metal, &c., placed on the fingerboard, at the proper places for the fingers.

> I did but tell her she mistook her frets,
> And bow'd her hand to teach her fingering,
> When with a most impatient devilish spirit,
> ' Frets, call you these ? ' quoth she ; ' I'll fume with them ; '
> And, with that word, she struck me on the head,
> And through the instrument my pate made way. (*Tam. Sh.* II. i. 150–5)

> These means, as frets upon an instrument,
> Shall tune our heart-strings to true languishment. (*Lucr.* 1140–1)

The verb meaning ' to furnish with frets ' is used playfully :

> *Hamlet.* Call me what instrument you will, though you can fret me you cannot play upon me. (*Haml.* III. ii. 394–6)

Gamut. The lowest note in the mediaeval scale of music, answering to the modern G on the lowest line of the bass stave. Also, the ' Great Scale ' (of which the invention is ascribed to Guido d'Arezzo), comprising the seven hexachords or partial scales, and consisting of all the recognized notes used in mediaeval music.

> *Hortensio.* Madam, before you touch the instrument,
> To learn the order of my fingering,
> I must begin with rudiments of art ;
> To teach you gamut in a briefer sort,
> More pleasant, pithy, and effectual,
> Than hath been taught by any of my trade :
> And there it is in writing, fairly drawn.
>   *Bianca.* Why, I am past my gamut long ago.
>   *Hor.* Yet read the gamut of Hortensio.
>   *Bian.* ' Gamut ' I am, the ground of all accord,
>   ' A re ', to plead Hortensio's passion ;
>   ' B mi ', Bianca, take him for thy lord,
>   ' C fa ut ', that loves with all affection :
>   ' D sol re ', one clef, two notes have I :
>   ' E la mi ', show pity, or I die.
> Call you this gamut ? tut, I like it not :
> Old fashions please me best ; I am not so nice,
> To change true rules for odd inventions. (*Tam. Sh.* III. i. 65–82)

Good-night. ? Some kind of night-song. See *Fancy.*

Govern. To regulate an instrument by means of its stops.

> Nay, but his jesting spirit ; which is now crept into a lute-string, and new-governed by stops. (*Much Ado* III. ii. 60–2)

> *Hamlet.* . . . Will you play upon this pipe ?
> *Guildenstern.* My lord, I cannot . . .
> *Hamlet.* 'Tis as easy as lying ; govern these ventages with your finger and thumb, give it breath with your mouth, and it will discourse most eloquent music. Look you, these are the stops. (*Haml.* III. ii. 372–83)

Government is similarly used.

> Indeed he hath played on his prologue like a child on a recorder ; a sound, but not in government. (*Mid. N. D.* v. i. 123–5)

Ground. The plain-song or bass on which a descant is raised : see *Descant.*

Harmony. The combination of notes, either simultaneous or successive, so as to produce a pleasing effect ; tuneful sound.

> The technical sense of ' the combination of sounds so as to form chords ' is barely established in English in Shakespeare's time.

> *Alonso.* What harmony is this ? My good friends, hark !
> *Gonzalo.* Marvellous sweet music ! (*Temp.* III. iii. 18–19)

> Here will we sit, and let the sounds of music
> Creep in our ears : soft stillness and the night
> Become the touches of sweet harmony. (*Merch. of V.* v. i. 55–7)

>   like a cunning instrument . . . put into his hands
> That knows no touch to tune the harmony. (*Rich. II,* I. iii. 163–5)

> *Hamlet.* Will you play upon this pipe ? . . . Look you, these are the stops.
> *Guildenstern.* But these cannot I command to any utterance of harmony ; I have not the skill. (*Haml.* III. ii. 373–85)

377–378

Harp. A stringed musical instrument, which, in its usual form, consists of a framework of wood fitted with a series of strings of definite lengths which are played with the fingers (or, in some earlier types, with a plectrum).

> *Temp.* II. i. 91 ; *Mid. N. D.* v. i. 45 ; *Rich. II*, I. iii. 162 ; *I Hen. IV*, III. i. 123.

Hautboy. A wooden double-reed wind instrument of high pitch, having a compass of about 2½ octaves, forming a treble to the bassoon. (Now usually *Oboe.*)

> You might have thrust him and all his apparel into an eel-skin ; the case of a treble hautboy was a mansion for him, a court.
> (2 Hen. IV, III. ii. 353–6)

Holding. The burden.

> Make battery to our ears with the loud music ;
> The while I'll place you ; then the boy shall sing,
> The holding every man shall bear as loud
> As his strong sides can volley. (*Ant. & Cleop.* II. vii. 116–19)

Hornpipe. An obsolete wind instrument having the bell and mouthpiece made of horn ; a dance performed to the accompaniment of this ; music for this dance.

> One puritan . . . and he sings psalms to hornpipes.
> (Wint. Tale IV. ii. 47–8)

Hymn. A song of praise or prayer to God.

> To live a barren sister all your life,
> Chanting faint hymns to the cold fruitless moon. (*Mid. N. D.* I. i. 72–3)
> Our solemn hymns to sullen dirges change. (*Rom. & Jul.* IV. v. 88)
> I . . . like unletter'd clerk, still cry ' Amen '
> To every hymn that able spirit affords. (*Sonnet* lxxxv)

Instrument.

> Sometimes a thousand twangling instruments
> Will hum about mine ears. (*Temp.* III. ii. 149–50)
> Sound all the lofty instruments of war,
> And by that music let us all embrace. (*I Hen. IV*, v. ii. 97–8)
> They . . . would most resemble sweet instruments hung up in cases, that keep their sounds to themselves. (*Timon* I. ii. 101–5)
> *Clown.* Why, masters, have your instruments been in Naples, that they speak i' the nose thus ?
> *First Musician.* How, sir, how ?
> *Clown.* Are these, I pray you, wind-instruments ? (*Oth.* III. i. 3–6)

Jack. In the virginal, spinet, and harpsichord, an upright piece of wood fixed to the back of the key lever, and fitted with a quill which plucked the string as the jack rose on the key being pressed down. By Shakespeare applied to the key itself.

> How oft, when thou, my music, music play'st,
> Upon that blessed wood whose motion sounds
> With thy sweet fingers, when thou gently sway'st
> The wiry concord that mine ear confounds,
> Do I envy those jacks that nimble leap
> To kiss the tender inward of thy hand. (*Sonnet* cxxviii)

Jar. A discord.

> If he, compact of jars, grow musical,
> We shall have shortly discord in the spheres. (*A. Y. L.* II. vii. 5–6)

The verb is similarly used :

> *Host.* I perceive you delight not in music.
> *Julia.* Not a whit,—when it jars so. (*Two Gent.* IV. ii. 67–8)
> *Hortensio.* [*Returning.*] Madam, my instrument's in tune.
> *Bianca.* Let's hear.— [*Hortensio plays.*
> O fie ! the treble jars. (*Tam. Sh.* III. i. 38–40)

How irksome is this music to my heart !
When such strings jar, what hope of harmony ? (*2 Hen. VI*, II. i. 56–7)

Kettle(drum). A musical instrument of percussion consisting of a hollow hemisphere of brass or copper, over the edge of which parchment is stretched and tuned to a definite note.

> And let the kettle to the trumpet speak,
> The trumpet to the cannoneer without. (*Haml.* V. ii. 289–90)

> And, as he drains his draughts of Rhenish down,
> The kettle-drum and trumpet thus bray out
> The triumph of his pledge. (*Ibid.* I. iv. 10–12)

Key. The scheme or system of tones in which a piece of music is written.

> . . . having both the key
> Of officer and office, set all hearts i' the state
> To what tune pleas'd his ear. (*Temp.* I. ii. 83–5)

> In what key shall a man take you, to go in the song ?
> (*Much Ado* I. i. 194–5)

> Both warbling of one song, both in one key. (*Mid. N. D.* III. ii. 206)

> . . . with an accent tun'd in self-same key. (*Troilus* I. iii. 53)

Knock it. Strike up.

> Let the music knock it. (*Hen. VIII*, I. iv. 108)

La. The name given by Guido d'Arezzo to the sixth note in his hexachords, and retained in solmization as the sixth note of the octave. See *Ut.*

Lesson. A piece of music for practice ; an exercise.

> *Hortensio.* [*To Lucentio.*] You may go walk, and give me leave a while :
> My lessons make no music in three parts. (*Tam. Sh.* III. i. 60–1)

Lute. A stringed musical instrument, the strings of which were struck with the fingers of the right hand and stopped on the frets with those of the left.

> God defend the lute should be like the case ! (*Much Ado* II. i. 98–9)

> Bardolph stole a lute-case, bore it twelve leagues, and sold it for three
> half-pence. (*Hen. V*, III. ii. 46–8)

> O ! had the monster seen those lily hands
> Tremble, like aspen leaves, upon a lute,
> And make the silken strings delight to kiss them.
> (*Tit. Andr.* II. iv. 44–6)

> Dowland to thee is dear, whose heavenly touch
> Upon the lute doth ravish human sense. (*Pass. Pilg.* viii. 5–6)

> [Dowland wrote *A Short Treatise concerning Lute Playing ; with variety of Lute Lessons*, 1610.]

Madrigal. A kind of part-song for three or more voices (usually five or six) characterized by adherence to an ecclesiastical mode, elaborate contrapuntal imitation, and the absence of instrumental accompaniment ; also applied loosely to part-songs or glees not bound by these conditions.

To shallow rivers, to whose falls
Melodious birds sing madrigals. (*M. Wives* III. i. 17–18)

March. A composition of marked rhythm (of which the rhythmical drum-beats originally formed the essential part), designed to accompany the marching of troops. See *Dead march.*

[*A march afar off.*
Edward. I hear their drums ; let 's set our men in order.
(*3 Hen. VI*, I. ii. 69)

Mean. Alto or tenor. (*Two Gent.* I. ii. 92 : see *Descant.*)

He can sing
A mean most meanly. (*Love's L. L.* v. ii. 328–9)

Measure. The relation between the time-values of a note of one denomination and a note of the next, determining the kind of rhythm (duple, triple, &c.) ; the time of a piece of music.

The *triplex*, sir, is a good tripping measure. (*Tw. N.* v. i. 41)

Mi. The name given by Guido d'Arezzo to the third note in his hexachords, and retained in solmization as the third note of the octave. See *Ut.*

Minim. A note half the value of a semibreve and double the value of a crotchet.

In ancient music this note was of the shortest duration, hence its name, *nota minima.*

He fights as you sing prick-song, keeps time, distance, and proportion ; rests me his minim rest, one, two, and the third in your bosom.
(*Rom. & Jul.* II. iv. 22–4)

Mode, Mood. A kind or form of scale ; a particular scheme or system of sounds ; hence, the key in which a piece of music is written.

For all my reign hath been but as a scene
Acting that argument ; and now my death
Changes the mode. (*Quarto and 1st and 2nd Folios read* mood *or* moode.)
(*2 Hen. IV*, IV. v. 196–8)

Music. Formerly used both for a piece of music, and, more frequently, a band of musicians.

Come, we'll have you merry. I'll bring you where you shall hear music and see the gentleman that you asked for. (*Two Gent.* IV. ii. 31–3)

Play, music ! and you, brides and bridegrooms all,
With measure heap'd in joy, to the measures fall. (*A. Y. L.* v. iv. 185–6)

I have assail'd her with musics, but she vouchsafes no notice.
(*Cymb.* II. iii. 44–5)

Musician. A professional performer of music, especially of instrumental music.

I have neither the scholar's melancholy, which is emulation ; nor the musician's, which is fantastical ; nor the courtier's, which is proud.
(*A. Y. L.* IV. i. 11–13)

The nightingale, if she should sing by day,
When every goose is cackling, would be thought
No better a musician than the wren. (*Merch. of V.* v. i. 104–6)

An admirable musician ! O, she will sing the savageness out of a bear.
(*Oth.* IV. i. 197–9)

Noise. Musical sound, music.

> *Caliban.* Be not afeard : the isle is full of noises,
> Sounds and sweet airs, that give delight, and hurt not.
> *(Temp.* III. ii. 147–8)

> Why sinks that cauldron ? and what noise is this ? [*Hautboys.*
> *(Macb.* IV. i. 106)

A company or band of musicians.

> See if thou canst find out Sneak's noise ; Mistress Tearsheet would
> fain hear some music. *(2 Hen. IV,* II. iv. 12–14)

Note. A particular tone of definite pitch ; the character representing this.

> One clef, two notes have I. *(Tam. Sh.* III. i. 78)

> You would sound me from my lowest note to the top of my compass.
> *(Haml.* III. ii. 390–1)

Melody, music, strain of music. *(Two Gent.* I. ii. 78 : see *Set.*)

> Use like note and words. *(Cymb.* IV. ii. 237)

The verb is used for providing a text with musical notes.

> *Peter.* I'll *re* you, I'll *fa* you. Do you note me ?
> *First Mus.* An you *re* us, and *fa* us, you note us.
> *(Rom. & Jul.* IV. v. 121–3)

> *Thersites.* And any man may sing her, if he can take her cliff ; she 's
> noted. *(Troilus* V. ii. 10–11)

Organ-pipe.
> The thunder,
> That deep and dreadful organ-pipe, pronounc'd
> The name of Prosper. *(Temp.* III. iii. 97–9)

Part. The melody assigned to a particular voice or instrument in concerted music. *(Tam. Sh.* III. i. 60–1 : see *Lesson.*)

> We can both sing it : if thou'lt bear a part thou shalt hear ; 'tis in
> three parts. *(Wint. Tale* IV. iii. 296–7)

> *Pandarus.* What music is this ?
> *Servant.* I do but partly know, sir : it is music in parts.
> *(Troilus* III. i. 19–21)

Peg. In stringed musical instruments, a pin of wood or metal to which the strings are fastened at one end, and which is turned to adjust the tension in tuning ; a tuning-pin.

> O ! you are well tun'd now,
> But I'll set down the pegs that make this music,
> As honest as I am. *(Oth.* II. i. 202–4)

Pipe. A wind-instrument consisting of a single tube of reed or wood; especially used by shepherds and so associated with the *Tabor.*

> Playing on pipes of corn. *(Mid. N. D.* II. i. 67)

> Then put up your pipes in your bag, for I'll away. [*Exeunt Musicians.*
> *(Oth.* III. i. 20–1)

Plain-song. A simple melody or theme, upon which might be raised a running melody or descant.

> The plain-song cuckoo gray. *(Mid. N. D.* III. i. 138)

> *Nym.* The humour of it is too hot, that is the very plain-song of it.
> *Pist.* The plain-song is most just, for humours do abound.
> *(Hen. V,* III. ii. 5–8)

The devil fiddle 'em ! I am glad they're going :
For, sure, there's no converting of 'em : now
An honest country lord, as I am, beaten
A long time out of play, may bring his plain-song
And have an hour of hearing ; and, by'r lady,
Held current music too. (*Hen. VIII*, I. iii. 42–7)

Play. To perform on an instrument.

> *Host.* Hark ! What fine change is in the music !
> *Julia.* Ay, that change is the spite.
> *Host.* Would you have them always play but one thing ?
> *Jul.* I would always have one play but one thing.
> (*Two Gent.* IV. ii. 69–73)

> *Leonato.* We'll have dancing afterward.
> *Benedick.* First, of my word ; therefore play, music !
> (*Much Ado* v. iv. 123–5)

> *Page.* The music is come, sir.
> *Falstaff.* Let them play. Play, sirs. (*2 Hen. IV*, II. iv. 244–5)

The music plays ; vouchsafe some motion to it.
(*Love's L. L.* v. ii. 217)

'Sblood, do you think I am easier to be played on than a pipe ?
(*Haml.* III. ii. 393–4)

Point. A short strain or snatch of melody ; *point of war*, a short phrase sounded on an instrument as a signal.

Turning your books to greaves, your ink to blood,
Your pens to lances, and your tongue divine
To a loud trumpet and a point of war. (*2 Hen. IV*, IV. i. 50–2)

Prick-song. Music sung from notes written or ' pricked ', as distinguished from that sung from memory or by ear ; written vocal music.

A written descant or accompanying melody to a plain-song or simple theme ; descant or counterpoint accompanying a simple melody.

He fights as you sing prick-song, keeps time, distance, and proportion.
(*Rom. & Jul.* II. iv. 22–3)

Proportion. The relation of a note of one denomination to a note of another in respect of duration, determining the rhythm of a composition.

> Music do I hear ?   [*Music.*
> Ha, ha ! keep time. How sour sweet music is
> When time is broke and no proportion kept ! (*Rich. II*, v. v. 41–3)

Psaltery. An ancient and mediaeval stringed instrument, more or less resembling the dulcimer, but played by plucking the string with the fingers or a plectrum ; differing from the harp in having the sound-board behind and parallel with the strings. (*Cor.* v. iv. 53 : see *Sackbut.*)

Re. The second note of Guido's hexachords, and of the octave in modern solmization.

> *Peter.* I'll *re* you, I'll *fa* you. Do you note me ?
> *First Mus.* An you *re* us, and *fa* us, you note us.
> (*Rom. & Jul.* IV. v. 121–3)

Rebeck. An early form of the fiddle, having three strings and played with a bow.

Used as the name of a musician in *Romeo and Juliet* (IV. v. 136).

Record. To sing or warble.

Here can I sit alone, unseen of any,
And to the nightingale's complaining notes
Tune my distresses and record my woes. (*Two Gent.* v. iv. 4–6)
When to the lute
She sung, and made the night-bird mute,
That still records with moan. (*Pericles* IV. Gower 25–7)

Recorder. A wind instrument of the flute or flageolet kind.

He hath played on his prologue like a child on a recorder ; a sound, but not in government. (*Mid. N. D.* v. i. 123–5)
O ! the recorders : let me see one. . . . Will you play upon this pipe ? (*Haml.* III. ii. 367–73)

Reed-voice. A reedy or squeaking voice.

And speak between the change of man and boy
With a reed voice. (*Merch. of V.* III. iv. 66–7)

Relish. To sing or warble.

to relish a love-song, like a robin-redbreast. (*Two Gent.* II. i. 21–2)
' You mocking birds,' quoth she, ' your tunes entomb
Within your hollow-swelling feather'd breasts,
And in my hearing be you mute and dumb :
My restless discord loves no stops nor rests ;
A woeful hostess brooks not merry guests :
  Relish your nimble notes to pleasing ears ;
  Distress likes dumps when time is kept with tears.' (*Lucr.* 1121–7)

Rest. An interval of silence occurring in a melody or in any part of a concerted piece. (See *Minim* and *Relish.*)

Round. A song for three or more voices in which each succeeding singer takes up the melody at a certain interval behind his predecessor, and all the singers continue until they all come to the end of the melody at the same time. (Not in Shakespeare, who uses *Catch.*)

Sackbut. An obsolete musical instrument ; a bass trumpet with a slide like that of a trombone for altering the pitch. (Cf. *Dulcimer.*)

The trumpets, sackbuts, psalteries, and fifes,
Tabors, and cymbals, and the shouting Romans,
Make the sun dance. (*Cor.* v. iv. 53–5)

Scale. The series of tones and intervals taken as the basis of a composition ; especially those of the octave. (Not in Shakespeare, who uses *Gamut.*)

Sennet. A set of notes played on a trumpet as a signal for the approach or departure of a procession.

In several stage directions : *2 Hen. VI*, III. i, *Hen. VIII*, II. iv, *Lear* I. i.

Set. To put music to words.

Julia. Some love of yours hath writ to you in rime.
Lucetta. That I might sing it, madam, to a tune :
Give me a note : your ladyship can set. (*Two Gent.* I. ii. 76–8)

Sharp.　High, shrill ; a high or shrill note.

> *Lucetta.*　I do not like this tune.
> *Julia.*　You do not ?
> *Luc.*　　　　　No, madam ; it is too sharp.　(*Two Gent.* I. ii. 87–8)

> It is the lark that sings so out of tune,
> Straining harsh discords and unpleasing sharps.　(*Rom. & Jul.* III. v. 27–8)

Singing-man.　A man who sings in a church choir and is on the foundation of a cathedral or collegiate body.

> A singing-man of Windsor.　(*2 Hen. IV*, II. i. 101)

Sol.　The fifth note of Guido's hexachords, and of the octave in modern solmization.

> Ile re you, Ile fa you, Ile sol you.　(*Rom. & Jul.* IV. v. 121, First Quarto)
> O, these eclipses do portend these divisions !　*Fa, sol, la, mi.*
> 　　　　　　　　　　　　　　　　　　　　　　(*Lear* I. ii. 151–4)

Sol-fa.　The set of syllables ut (*now* do), re, mi, fa, sol, la, sung to the respective notes of the major scale ; the system of singing notes to these syllables ; a musical scale or exercise.

In Shakespeare only as a verb ' to sing to the syllables of the sol-fa ', hence, ' to sing from notes or a score '.

> I'll try how you can sol-fa, and sing it.　(*Tam. Sh.* I. ii. 17)

Soundpost.　A small peg of wood fixed beneath the bridge of a violin or similar instrument, serving as a support for the belly and as a connecting part between this and the back.

> Used as the name of a musician in *Romeo & Juliet* IV. v. 140.

Speak.　Of musical instruments, &c. : To emit a sound or note.

> There is much music, excellent voice, in this little organ, yet cannot you make it speak ?　(*Haml.* III. ii. 391–3)

Still music.　Soft or subdued music.

> *Enter Hymen, Rosalind, and Celia. Still Music.*　(*A. Y. L.* v. iv)

> In Gascoigne's *Jocasta*, v, occurs the following direction for ' the order of the laste dumbe shewe ' :—' First the Stillpipes sounded a very mournful melody '.

Stop.　A vent-hole of a wind instrument by which difference of pitch is produced ; also, a fret.

> You would play upon me ; you would seem to know my stops.
> 　　　　　　　　　　　　　　　　　　　　　　(*Haml.* III. ii. 387–8)

> Rumour is a pipe . . . of so easy and so plain a stop.　(*2 Hen IV*, Ind. 15–17)
> his jesting spirit, which is now crept into a lute-string, and new-governed by stops.　(*Much Ado* III. ii. 60–2)

Strain.　A musical phrase or piece of melody.

> What, to make thee an instrument and play false strains upon thee !
> 　　　　　　　　　　　　　　　　　　　　　　(*A. Y. L.* IV. iii. 68–70)

> That strain again ! it had a dying fall.　(*Tw. N.* I. i. 4)
> (*Jul. Caes.* II. iii. 256 : see the verb *Touch.*)

String.　A cord stretched over the soundboard of a musical instrument, made of catgut, wire, &c., and plucked by the hand or a plectrum, scraped with a bow, or struck with a hammer.

> *Julia.*　He plays false, father.
> *Host.*　How ? out of tune on the strings ?　(*Two Gent.* IV. ii. 60–1)

Take but degree away, untune that string,
And, hark ! what discord follows. (*Troilus* I. iii. 109–10)

You're a fair viol, and your sense the strings,
Who, finger'd to make men his lawful music,
Would draw heaven down and all the gods to hearken. (*Per.* I. i. 81–3)

Mark how one string, sweet husband to another,
Strikes each in each by mutual ordering. (*Sonnet* viii)

[Referred to as *calves' guts* and *catlings* in the following :
 If this penetrate, I will consider your music the better ; if it do not,
it is a vice in her ears, which horse-hairs and calves' guts, nor the voice
of unpaved eunuch to boot, can never amend. (*Cymb.* II. iii. 31–5)

Unless the fiddler Apollo get his sinews to make catlings on.
(*Troilus* III. iii. 308–9)

Catling as the name of a musician occurs in *Romeo and Juliet* (IV. v. 133).]

Strung. Fitted with strings.

Orpheus' lute was strung with poets' sinews. (*Two Gent.* III. ii. 78)

Bright Apollo's lute, strung with his hair. (*Love's L. L.* IV. iii. 343)

Tabor. A small drum, used chiefly as an accompaniment to the
pipe, for festive occasions ; used by clowns and jesters.

I have known, when there was no music with him but the drum and
the fife ; and now had he rather hear the tabor and the pipe.
(*Much Ado* II. iii. 13–15)

Viola. Save thee, friend, and thy music. Dost thou live by thy
tabor ?
Clown. No, sir, I live by the church. (*Tw. N.* III. i. 1–3)

O master ! if you did but hear the pedlar at the door, you would
never dance again after a tabor and pipe ; no, the bagpipe could not
move you. (*Wint. Tale* IV. iii. 181–4)

Tabourine. A kind of drum, less wide and longer than the tabor,
and struck with one drumstick only, to accompany the sound
of a flute which is played with the other hand.

Beat loud the tabourines, let the trumpets blow,
That this great soldier may his welcome know. (*Troilus* IV. v. 274–5)

Trumpeters,
With brazen din blast you the city's ear,
Make mingle with our rattling tabourines. (*Ant. & Cleop.* IV. viii. 35–7)

Three-man-song. A convivial part-song for three men ; a trio for
male voices.

She hath made me four-and-twenty nosegays for the shearers, three-
man-song men all, and very good ones ; but they are most of them
means and bases. (*Wint. Tale* IV. ii. 43–7)

Time. The duration of one note in relation to another, formerly
of the breve in relation to the semibreve ; hence, the rhythm
or measure of a piece of music, now marked by division of the
music into bars.

Malvolio. . . . Is there no respect of place, persons, nor time, in you ?
Sir Toby. We did keep time, sir, in our catches. (*Tw. N.* II. iii. 100–2)

Distress likes dumps when time is kept with tears. (*Lucr.* 1127)

[See also *Proportion*.]

Tongs. Used in burlesque or ' rough ' music.

> *Bottom.* I have a reasonable good ear in music : let us have the tongs and the bones.
> [Stage direction in the First Folio] *Musicke Tongs, Rurall Musicke.*
> *(Mid. N. D.* IV. i. 32–3)

Touch. The act or manner of touching or handling a musical instrument, so as to bring out its tones ; also, capacity, skill, or style of playing.

> For Orpheus' lute was strung with poets' sinews,
> Whose golden touch could soften steel and stones.
> *(Two Gent.* III. ii. 78–9)
>
> Come, ho ! and wake Diana with a hymn :
> With sweetest touches pierce your mistress' ear. *(Merch. of V.* v. i. 66–7)
>
> A cunning instrument . . . put into his hands
> That knows no touch to tune the harmony. *(Rich. II,* I. iii. 163–5)
>
> Dowland to thee is dear, whose heavenly touch
> Upon the lute doth ravish human sense. *(Pass. Pilg.* viii. 5–6)

Similarly the verb.

> Madam, before you touch the instrument,
> To learn the order of my fingering,
> I must begin with rudiments of art. *(Tam. Sh.* III. i. 65–7)
>
> Canst thou hold up thy heavy eyes awhile,
> And touch thy instrument a strain or two ? *(Jul. Caes.* IV. iii. 255–6)

Treble. The highest part in harmonized musical composition ; a treble voice ; the string or key of treble pitch in a musical instrument ; a musical instrument of treble pitch.

> His big manly voice,
> Turning again toward childish treble, pipes
> And whistles in his sound. *(A. Y. L.* II. vii. 161–3)
>
> *Hortensio.* [*Returning.*] Madam, my instrument 's in tune.
> *Bianca.* Let's hear.— [*Hortensio plays.*
> O fie ! the treble jars. *(Tam. Sh.* III. i. 38–40)
>
> A treble hautboy. *(2 Hen. IV,* III. ii. 355)

Triplex. Triple time.

> The *triplex*, sir, is a good tripping measure. *(Tw. N.* v. i. 41)

Troll. To sing in the manner of a round or catch.

> Let us be jocund : will you troll the catch
> You taught me but while-ere ? *(Temp.* III. ii. 129–30)

Trump. A trumpet of war.

> Whilst any trump did sound or drum struck up. *(1 Hen. VI,* I. iv. 80)
> Farewell the neighing steed, and the shrill trump. *(Oth.* III. iii. 352)

Trumpet. Occurs 51 times as a stage direction in 22 plays of Shakespeare ; examples in the text are numerous.

Tucket. A flourish on a trumpet ; a signal for marching used by cavalry troops.

> Then let the trumpets sound
> The tucket sonance and the note to mount. *(Hen. V,* IV. ii. 34–5)

Tune. A melody or air.

> *Caliban.* That 's not the tune.
> [*Ariel plays the tune on a Tabor and Pipe.*

Stephano. What is this same ?

Trinculo. This is the tune of our catch, played by the picture of Nobody. (*Temp.* III. ii. 135–8)

To jig off a tune at the tongue's end. (*Love's L. L.* III. i. 12–13)

My clown . . . grew so in love with the wenches' song that he would not stir his pettitoes till he had both tune and words.
(*Wint. Tale* IV. iii. 618–22)

Correct or proper pitch.

Keep tune there still, so you will sing it out. (*Two Gent.* I. ii. 86)

Hortensio. You'll leave his lecture when I am in tune ? [*Retires.*
Lucentio. That will be never : tune your instrument.
(*Tam. Sh.* III. i. 24–5)

I would sing my song without a burthen : thou bringest me out of tune.
(*A. Y. L.* III. ii. 263–4)

Like sweet bells jangled, out of tune and harsh. (*Haml.* III. i. 167)

Tune. To adjust the tones of (a musical instrument) to a standard of pitch ; to put in tune.

Take you your instrument, play you the whiles ;
His lecture will be done ere you have tun'd. (*Tam. Sh.* III. i. 22–3)

These means, as frets upon an instrument,
Shall tune our heart-strings to true languishment. (*Lucr.* 1140–1)

Ut. The lowest note of each hexachord in Guido's scale.

Ut, re, sol, la, mi, fa. (*Love's L. L.* IV. ii. 103–4)

Ventages. The stops of a wind instrument.
(*Haml.* III. ii. 380 : see *Govern.*)

Viol. An old instrument of the violin class, having from three to six strings.

And now my tongue's use is to me no more
Than an unstringed viol or a harp. (*Rich. II*, I. iii. 161–2)

Viol da gamba. A violoncello, bass-viol.

He plays o' the viol-de-gamboys. (*Tw. N.* I. iii. 27–8)

Virginals. A keyed instrument of the harpsichord class. (See p. 30.)

Virginalling. Playing (as if) on the virginals.

Still virginalling
Upon his palm ! (*Wint. Tale* I. ii. 126–7)

Wind. To blow.

But that I will have a recheat winded in my forehead, or hang my bugle in an invisible baldrick, all women shall pardon me.
(*Much Ado* I. i. 250–3)

Mid. N. D. IV. i. 108. Stage direction.

Wind up. To tune up the strings.

The untun'd and jarring senses, O ! wind up
Of this child-changed father ! (*Lear* IV. vii. 16–17)

Wrest. The key for tuning a harp.

But this Antenor
I know is such a wrest in their affairs
That their negociations all must slack,
Wanting his manage. (*Troilus* III. iii. 22–5)

§ 3. ARCHITECTURE

BY

J. ALFRED GOTCH

' THE cloud-capp'd towers, the gorgeous palaces, the solemn temples ' of Prospero's splendid utterance were no mere poetic images : they were the facts of the English country-side, and of great towns ; they came within the knowledge of any audience before whom *The Tempest* may have been played. The ' towers ' which exist at the present day—and there are many of them, remnants of feudal castles and houses—are not a tithe of those remaining in Shakespeare's time : and whereas now they are for the most part ruins ' where wasteful Time debateth with Decay ', then they were still the homes of great men, the centres of wide-felt influence. ' Gorgeous palaces ' were rising on every side, not only in London, but throughout the length and breadth of England : and it is these buildings which are now to be considered. ' Solemn temples ' there were in plenty : not the columned and pedimented temples which the imagination links with memories of Greece and Italy, but the cathedrals and abbey-churches, priories, and monasteries of English builders. The crowning glories of our native architecture which we know to-day are few in number compared with those which still existed in Shakespeare's time. He might have seen—very likely did see— vast churches, fellows of Westminster Abbey, of which now a few stones or perhaps even the memory alone exist. Some of them were still in use, some were being converted into dwellings, some were already dismantled, and may have prompted his comparison of leafless trees to ' bare ruin'd choirs where late the sweet birds sang ' (*Sonnet* lxxiii).

The contemporary architecture of Shakespeare's day was almost wholly domestic. There was hardly a new church built during his lifetime. The only vast public building which was erected in the period was the Royal Exchange in London, which was founded for commercial purposes by Sir Thomas Gresham, a private citizen of London. But the ' gorgeous palaces ' of the noble, the manor-houses of the squire, the simple homes of the yeoman were springing up in extraordinary profusion on every hand. In London the growth of smaller tenements in the suburbs increased so rapidly that from 1580 onwards it was restricted by proclamation and Act of Parliament. There is hardly a village in the country where a house was not built during the period covered by Shakespeare's life ; and these houses are more distinctively English than those of any other period. They have a character peculiarly their own, resulting from a combination of very interesting circumstances.

From the time of the Conquest down almost to Elizabeth's reign, safety from outside attack had been one of the controlling factors in the designing of houses. In very early times the accommodation provided had been extremely simple ; it consisted chiefly of a great hall, the room wherein the life of the household was passed ; but the hall was supplemented by a room for the lord at one end, and by a kitchen, or a kitchen department, at the other. Besides the lord's room there were practically no other private rooms ; the whole household lived, ate, and slept in the great hall. As time went on—and centuries elapsed in the process—the single room of the lord expanded into several chambers for the use of the family ; and the kitchen expanded into a series of apartments for the use of the servants. But the expansion was always hampered by the necessity for defence, and the same dominant motive controlled the size of the doors and windows, which were obviously the weak places in case of attack. It also tended to keep the windows from being placed in walls which faced the country, and confined them largely to walls which faced into a court ; and most houses were built round one or more courts which were entered through strongly defended gatehouses.

Such, very briefly, were the main conditions affecting the planning of houses previous to Shakespeare's time. In regard to their appearance, in other words to their architectural style, they followed down to the sixteenth century the building traditions of the country, traditions which applied equally to churches and houses, and with which all artisans —the masons, carpenters, plumbers, and the rest—were imbued. Style varied somewhat from time to time ; it went through a process of development having well-marked phases, each of which melted into the next, or, rather, each of which emerged from its predecessor, and grew out of what went before it. But early in the sixteenth century a new influence made itself felt, an influence which was not native to the soil, but had a foreign origin. It came from Italy—from Italy of the Renaissance. In architecture, the forms which the Italian Renaissance had invented or evolved began to invade our shores. They were brought, many of them, by Italian artificers, some by Frenchmen, and in later years by Flemings or Dutchmen. A number of Englishmen went abroad, both to France and Italy, to study foreign buildings. Some went of their own accord, others were sent by wealthy patrons. Italian ideas became fashionable. But it was not altogether easy to instil these ideas into the English workman. He had been brought up in the traditions of his fathers, and he now found himself expected to employ methods of design with which he had no intimate acquaintance. In the result he produced a curious mixture of the old and the new : a homely English dress with Italian trimmings ; a Gothic framework with Classic overlay ; or Classic features treated in a Gothic manner. It cannot be called a pure style, nor is it one on which students can best be trained in the elements of architectural design. It was curtly dismissed by writers of fifty years ago as a bastard style ; but like some of the bastards in Shakespeare's plays, it had a vigour and piquancy sadly lacking in the legitimate offspring. It was, indeed, a fit companion to the poetry with which it was contemporaneous. It had the naïvety, the curious mingling of the mediaeval and classic in an atmosphere of romance, which characterize *The Faerie Queene* : if it misses the profundity and noble rhythm of Shakespeare's maturity, it has the youthful *abandon* of *Love's Labour's Lost*, the pedantry of Holofernes and Armado, the homely humour of the rustics.

One very marked characteristic of mediaeval houses was their rather haphazard arrangement when once the hall and its immediate adjuncts were left. Other apartments grew out of this nucleus in a somewhat straggling way. No careful alignment was attempted, nor much balancing of one mass with another. But the Italian influence, before it had affected the ornamental detail very generally, seems to have wrought on the plan in the direction of making it

Fig 1 CHARLECOTE GATE HOUSE

symmetrical ; and accordingly all the notable houses of Elizabeth's time are laid out on symmetrical lines. The most obvious means of carrying out in a symmetrical way the ancient idea of the hall as the centre of the house with the family rooms at one end and the servants' at the other, was to adopt an outline shaped like the letter H or the letter E lying on its face, an arrangement in which the hall occupied the cross-stroke of the H or the back of the E, while the two adjoining departments were placed severally in the vertical strokes of the H or the top and bottom strokes of the E ; a projecting porch completed the resemblance to the latter by giving it a centre stroke. Practical considerations probably produced this particular form of house; but the Elizabethan designer would no doubt derive much pleasure from finding that in giving a convenient shape to his house, he adopted one which resembled the initial letter of Elizabeth's name.

It was not altogether an easy task to bring under the subjection of symmetry the series of rooms which hitherto had been freely put where they seemed at first sight most convenient. But it was a task which the surveyors of the time set themselves to master, and they brought great ingenuity to bear upon it. Chief among these designers was the well-known John Thorpe, whose collection of original plans is preserved in the Soane Museum in London.[1]

They were not all of the H or E type ; many of them were built round courtyards, thus carrying on the disposition which had been prevalent when defence was a primary consideration, but carrying it on now in many cases with a view to architectural effect. The court was entered through a gateway overlooked by the rooms occupied by the porter, who was thus able to keep an eye on all who entered, much in the same way as the porter watches the traffic through a college gate in the present day. Where the house itself did not form a quadrangle, there was very often a walled forecourt with a gatehouse where the porter lodged, together with some of the outdoor servants. An interesting example of such a gatehouse still exists at

[1] The authorship of some of these drawings is matter of controversy, but in any case they are contemporary evidence of how houses were designed between the years 1570 and 1620. Another equally interesting and valuable collection is in the possession of Col. Coke of Brookhill Hall, Alfreton ; it was made by another busy surveyor, named John Smithson.

Charlecote (Fig. 1), the home of the Lucys, with whose park tradition associates the deer-stealing episode of Shakespeare's young days. The difficulty which the porter experienced in controlling an eager crowd clamouring for admission is vividly depicted in the last act of *King Henry VIII*, and the reiterated knocking in *Macbeth*, caused through the dilatoriness of the drink-sodden porter, incidentally illustrates the importance of the gatehouse.

The smaller country mansions, though they could boast no gatehouse, often had an arch of entrance, lending dignity to the approach : many of these survive to the present day, and many others are figured in Kip's *Britannia Illustrata*, or *Gentlemen's Seats* (1708–9).

The aim was to make houses both comfortable and stately. A considerable increase of rooms effected the first object ; and a symmetrical disposition, combined with carefully arranged accessories, effected the second.

The increase of rooms led to the erection of many houses of palatial dimensions ; one of the first and largest was Hampton Court, built by Cardinal Wolsey. Henry VIII set the fashion in his gorgeous palace of Nonesuch, near Cheam in Surrey, which was only completed in 1557 after his death, and was one of Queen Elizabeth's favourite residences (see illustration, Chap. VII). Several spacious mansions, which private persons built in his predecessor's reign, were acquired by King James I for his own use, and became palaces in fact. Such were Holdenby House in Northamptonshire, built by Sir Christopher Hatton before 1580 (of which only a small part remains, converted into a modern residence), and Theobalds in Hertfordshire, built by Lord Burghley between 1564 and 1588 (destroyed in 1651). Holdenby was one of the largest private houses which England has seen. It was built round two noble courts, and in front of it lay a third or base-court, entered through a fine gatehouse. In the middle of the side walls of this outer court, which was the first to be traversed in approaching the house, were large archways, leading on one hand to the garden, and on the other to the village. The front of the house was full of windows, differing widely in this respect from the great houses of preceding ages, which generally presented large masses of expressionless wall-space to the approaching visitor. It was disposed in a truly symmetrical

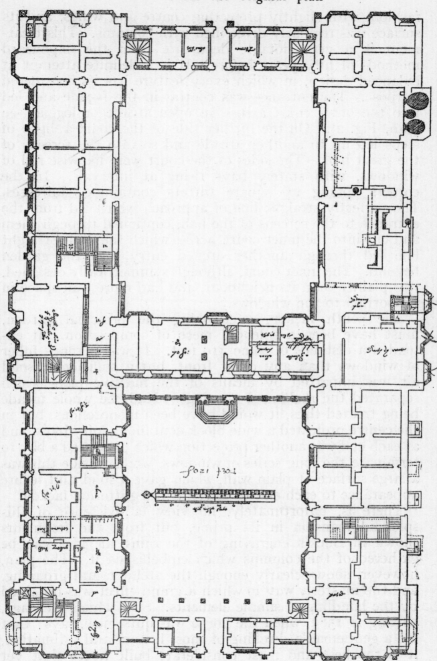

Fig 2 HOLDENBY HOUSE

fashion, with slightly projecting centre and wings, and its surface was regularly diversified with columns. This treatment is a very notable departure from the haphazard methods of fifty years before. It is a definite attempt at balanced design, in which every feature has its considered purpose. The entrance was central in the façade and led into the outer court across an open arcade or loggia (see plan, Fig. 2). On the further side of the court a flight of steps led up to another arcade and so into the screens of the great hall. The sides of the court were likewise full of windows, with stately bays rising at intervals. In the corners sprang up square turrets containing staircases. The perfectly straight line of approach which led from the entrance to the screens of the hall, continued through them and out into the inner court, across which the same straight line led through another arched entry into the garden beyond. The inner court, although symmetrically designed, was plainer than its neighbour, and had more wall-space in proportion to the windows.

The south façade, overlooking the principal garden, must have been a splendid piece of composition. It extended a distance of some 410 feet. It was perhaps fuller of windows than any other front, but a sufficiently solid air was imparted by means of the massive piers which separated the mullioned openings. Had the whole façade being treated thus, it would have been monotonous, but in the centre projected a wide block containing lofty bays, and at each end was another projection which presented a bay to terminate the long series of windows, while outside this was a large surface of plain wall, which gave a solid and secure appearance to each end of the long and glittering façade.

There is, unfortunately, no view in existence of this splendid mansion in its prime, but from the fragments shown in Buck's engraving of the ruins an idea can be gathered of the columns which embellished it. The plan, however, shows clearly enough the architectural grouping, and the masterly way in which a grand effect was obtained by the handling of simple elements. Sir Thomas Heneage, writing in 1583, when the house was quite new, says ' that for a gentleman's dwelling of most honour and estimation, it is the best and most considerate built house that yet mine eyes have ever seen '.

If Holdenby be compared with Hampton Court, which was built some fifty years earlier (about 1530), and was the only house which could vie with it in size, several points of difference may at once be noted. Holdenby is much more regular in disposition, and is indeed subjected to an almost rigid symmetry. Italian features are more freely introduced. At Hampton Court they only appear in small matters of detail : at Holdenby they play an important part in the design ; there are many columns, and there are at least two open arcades. Thirdly, the windows have increased in number and in size, thus adding greatly to the cheerfulness of the rooms. This, indeed, was one of the points which Lord Burghley noticed, when he visited Holdenby in 1579, when the house was approaching completion : ' I found ', he said, ' no one thing of greater grace than your stately ascent from your hall to your great chamber ; and your chambers answerable with largeness and lightsomeness, that truly a Momus could find no fault.' Momus, it will be remembered, was a carping deity who blamed Vulcan for not placing a window in the breast of a human figure which he had modelled in clay, so that all that was thought there could be brought to light.

Holdenby is typical of the gorgeous palaces of the time, and when its elaborate accommodation is compared with that of earlier houses, for instance with so fine a dwelling as Haddon Hall (begun in the twelfth century and altered from time to time), it at once becomes apparent that a remarkable development in comfortable housing had taken place. The great hall is still the centre of the establishment ; approached from its lower or entrance end is the kitchen department ; from the upper or daïs end access is obtained to the principal rooms ; and what a multiplicity of these there is ! Each one is well lighted, many have bay-windows, and almost all have fireplaces. In spite of the latter, the enormous amount of window-space gives point to Bacon's remonstrance, ' You shall have sometimes faire Houses, so full of Glasse, that one cannot tell, where to become, to be out of the Sunne, or Cold.' Some of these rooms are arranged in suites of two or three, forming convenient lodgings for a nobleman and his immediate retainers. This provision was especially necessary in houses where the Queen with her court was likely to stay on any of her progresses. Her principal officers were accommodated in separate rooms or in small groups, while ordinary gentlemen were placed, three or four together, in rooms of secondary importance. Such was the case when Elizabeth went to Theobalds in 1583, when the steward's room was occupied by ' Mr. Greville, Mr. Rawley (afterwards Sir Walter), Mr. Goodge, Mr. Cooke, &c.' It was the need for accommodating the queen on her progresses which led to the erection of some of these huge houses, as both Lord Burghley and Sir Christopher Hatton admitted.

Besides such vast places as Holdenby there were built many fine houses of moderate size, houses which, like Justice Shallow's, deserved Falstaff's hearty admiration, —''Fore God, you have here a goodly dwelling, and a rich ' (*2 Hen. IV*, v. iii. 5–6). It was these in which the H or E plan was occasionally adopted. Two examples are given from Thorpe's book (Figs. 3 and 4), where, it may be said in passing, the H type is the more frequent of the two. The two types are essentially the same, for the E only wants its wings extending at the back to become an H. The first of the two illustrated (Fig. 3) may be classed as an E. It was designed for Sir Henry Neville, but its location, if it ever was actually built, has not been discovered. The main wing is taken up by the great hall, the principal staircase, and the butler's rooms. The wing adjoining the upper end of the hall comprises the parlour and some smaller rooms, while the other contains the kitchen, larder, winter parlour, and (most probably) a ' lodging ' or bedroom. The upper floor of the parlour wing was taken up from end to end by the long gallery, and over the hall was the ' great chamber ', answering roughly to the drawing-room of to-day. Each wing has its own staircase—the wide distribution of rooms led to this necessity—and a staircase in the butler's room goes down to the cellar.

The other plan (Fig. 4) is of the H type ; the crossstroke accommodates the great hall, the buttery, and dry larder ; in the left wings are the parlour and principal staircase ; in the right are the kitchen and ' pastry '. To the front of the house is a large fore-court, ninety-four feet square, entered on the axial line, through a gatehouse.

The most striking characteristics of these plans are the simplicity of their disposition, their symmetry, and

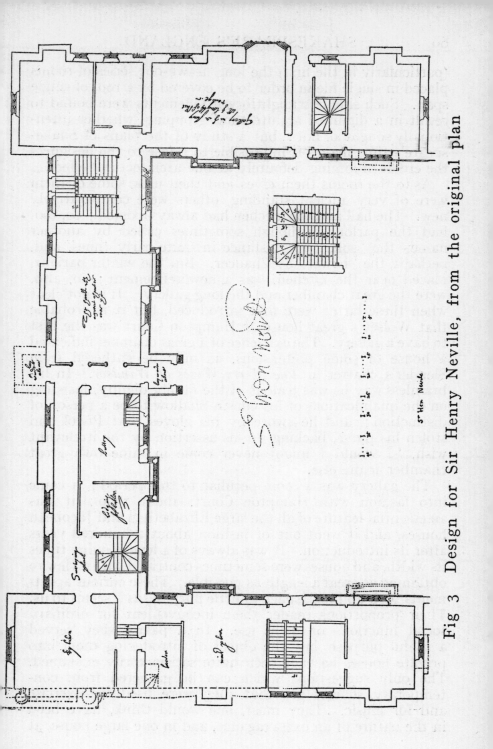

Fig 3   Design for Sir Henry Neville, from the original plan

(particularly in the first) the long-drawn-out series of rooms placed in single file in order to be covered by a roof of single span. Such simple straightforward elements were bound to result in a dignified architectural grouping, whether intentionally sought or not : but a study of the plans of Shakespeare's time makes it impossible to refuse to the designers the credit of aiming definitely at fine architectural effect.

As to the rooms themselves and their uses, some of them were of very ancient standing, others were comparatively new. The hall and the kitchen had always existed ; so, too, had the parlour, although sometimes called by another name—the 'solar' for instance in quite early times, and, perhaps, the 'bower' by Chaucer. But the winter parlour, placed near the kitchen, was a new refinement ; so, also, were the great chamber and the long gallery. It is not clear when these latter were first introduced, but it is probable that Wolsey's great house at Hampton Court was the first to have a gallery. The existence of a great chamber indicated a house of some pretensions, as may be gathered from Slender's chatter in *The Merry Wives of Windsor*. In his brainless way he was jealous of the family dignity, insisting on the qualifications of his cousin Shallow to be a person of distinction ; and he swore by his gloves that Pistol had stolen his purse, backing up his assertion by the irrelevant wish, 'I would I might never come in mine own great chamber again, else.'

The gallery was a room peculiar to this period ; it came into fashion with Hampton Court, about 1530 ; it was an essential feature of all the large Elizabethan and Jacobean houses, and it went out of fashion about a hundred years after its introduction. It was always of a length many times its width, and houses were sometimes contrived with a view to obtaining as great a length as possible. These curious apartments took up much space to little purpose, as it seems to us. Their proportions render them inconvenient for ordinary social functions or daily use. In a palace they served a useful purpose, but the object of introducing them into private houses has not been quite satisfactorily explained. The only suggestions which can be gathered from contemporary sources are that they were used for exercise and for music. They must, one would think, have been in the nature of an extravagance, and in one large house, at

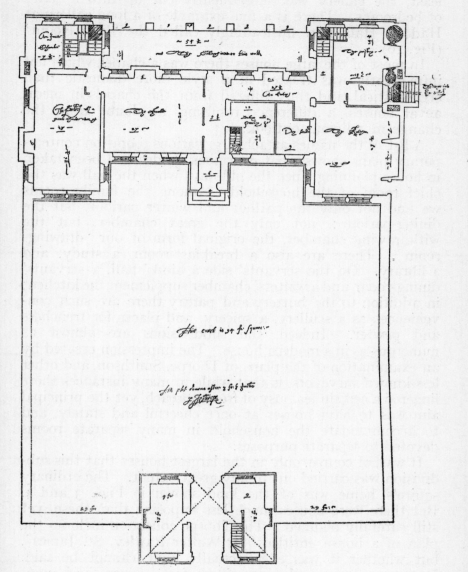

Fig 4 From an original plan

least, the gallery was subsequently cut up into a series of bedrooms. There is a fine example of a long gallery at Haddon Hall, now misleadingly called the 'Ball Room' (Fig. 10).

In most of the large houses there was a chapel, which not infrequently was treated in a style more domestic than ecclesiastical, and thus differed from the chapels in mediaeval houses, a difference resulting no doubt from the change in religious outlook.

A list of the names attached to various rooms on contemporary plans shows what enormous strides had been taken in house-planning since the old days when the hall was the chief room of the household. Among the family rooms we find not only the parlour and winter parlour, but the dining-parlour ; not only the great chamber, but the withdrawing chamber, the original form of our 'drawing-room'. There are also a breakfast-room, a study, and a library. On the servants' side a hinds' hall, a servants' dining-room, and a waiters' chamber supplement the kitchen; in addition to the buttery and pantry there are such conveniences as a scullery, a spicery, and places for trenchers and pewter. Indeed, the subdivisions are almost as numerous as in a modern house. The impression created by an examination of the plans of Thorpe, Smithson, and other less-known surveyors, is that while in many instances there lingered a certain jealousy of free approach, yet the principal aim was to have houses at once cheerful and stately, and to accommodate the household in many separate rooms devoted to separate purposes.

It was, of course, only in the largest houses that this subdivision was carried out to any great extent. The ordinary squire's home was of the kind shown in Figs. 3 and 4. But there were houses much less imposing than these, yet still carefully planned. The Thorpe collection includes the plan of a house entitled 'Sir Walter Rawley, St. James', but whether it was ever actually built cannot be said. It was to be a little over forty feet square, and comprised on the ground floor a hall, a parlour, a kitchen, pantry, and larder. It was almost truly symmetrical, with large bay-windows, which, together with the projecting porches and staircases, would have produced a striking architectural result. From the slight thickness of

Fig 6 MONTACUTE HOUSE SOMERSET

Fig 5
ARMADA HOUSE WESTON

Fig 7
BARLBOROUGH HALL

the outside walls, it would appear to have been intended to be built of timber and plaster ; but there is no record of its external appearance. It was, perhaps, a sixteenth-century ancestor of the modern bungalow. This diminutive example serves to show that expert designers not only concerned themselves with large mansions and manor-houses, but did not disdain the planning of houses which barely exceeded a cottage in importance.

Cottages, indeed, were built in plenty, and small farm-houses and houses for yeomen (Fig. 5) : but of their designers no record exists. They were almost certainly planned by masons, without conscious art, and they embodied the traditional treatment of the country-side. Houses in the small towns were of the type of several which are still extant at Stratford-on-Avon. They were usually two stories high, the upper one as a rule overhanging the lower, and being supported by carved brackets. On the ground floor there were, beside the hall, on which the front door immediately opened, a parlour partitioned off (which was apparently used at times as a bedroom by night), a chamber next the parlour, a buttery, and a kitchen-house which was built out on the yard or garden. Two or three bedchambers of varying size filled the upper story. Occasionally an attic chamber in the roof was lighted by a dormer window or a gabled window. From the front wall of the house there often projected on the level of the first floor a sloping tiled ledge, called a penthouse ; on the ground beneath there stood a stall, which served as shop-counter when the householder was engaged in retail trade. The façades were of timber and rough-cast, and the roofs were tiled. In the streets in the centre of the town the buildings were contiguous ; in the outskirts they were isolated, with enclosed passages or gardens separating them one from another.

William Harrison says of Elizabethan houses generally, that in old times they were generally built of wood posts and ' raddles ' covered with clay—what is now often called ' wattle and daub '. Where timber was plentiful, he says, houses were for the most part built of strong timber, ' howbeit such as be lately builded are commonly either of brick or hard stone '. Early in James I's reign the use of timber for outer walls, forefronts, and windows was forbidden under

heavy penalties, and the employment of brick or stone
was alone declared lawful.   Harrison was, therefore, quite
justified in emphasizing the employment of these more
permanent materials in his own day, as well as in making
the comment 'that if ever curious building did flourish in
England, it is in these our years, wherein our workmen excel
and are in manner comparable in skill with old Vitruvius,
Leo Baptista, and Serlo '.

Another matter to which Harrison calls attention is ' the
great multitude of chimneys lately erected'.   It must not
be supposed that there were few chimneys known before his
time.   There are many examples surviving of all periods
from the twelfth century onwards.   But the smaller class
of house was but sparsely furnished with them until the sixteenth century.   At Stratford-on-Avon they were hardly
known in the small tenements there at an earlier date, and
the Borough Committee's injunctions in 1582 to the inhabitants to make sufficient chimneys in all houses was far from
universally obeyed.   When in _1 Henry IV_ (II. i. 2–3) the
carriers were preparing to start from the inn at Rochester
on a dark morning, one of them observed that ' Charles's
Wain is over the new chimney ', which was evidently a noteworthy feature.   Again, one of Jack Cade's supporters
testified to the truth of his leader's assertion that he was the
son of a bricklayer by affirming that the elder Cade 'made
a chimney in my father's house' (_2 Hen. VI_, IV. ii. 160–1)
—a statement which would have special point at a time
when so many fireplaces were being added to old houses.

In connexion with the increase in the number and size
of windows, Harrison tells us that glass was now so easily to
be obtained that ' each one that may will have it for his
building', whereas in ancient times wooden lattices or sheets
of horn had been the customary materials for filling window-
lights.   Although glass in plenty had been used, especially
in churches, it is yet clear, from many existing examples,
that down to the end of the fifteenth century windows were
frequently left unglazed.   But in Elizabeth's time the stone-
work of the windows is always found to be grooved for
glass, and the grooving is not a matter of subsequent addition, for it occurs in buildings which we know were never
completed for occupation.

The few examples of planning which have been given have

not only served to show the kind of accommodation which was sought for in different circumstances, but have also indicated that the controlling factor in disposition was symmetry. This symmetry affected not alone the general outline, but the particular features, and it is quite usual to find window answering to window, door to door, chimney-stack to chimney-stack, and bay-window to bay-window (see Fig. 6). Sometimes the bay of the great hall, which was an admirable means of giving space and cheerfulness, was balanced by a similar bay at the other end of the front, which lighted nothing more than the buttery or pantry. Occasionally sham windows were introduced for the sake of uniformity, or lofty windows would have a floor carried across them, and thus the one large window of the outside would light two separate stories on the inside. These devices were occasionally adopted, but on the whole the imperious demands of symmetry were met in a reasonable manner.

In earlier days windows were used mainly for the purpose of giving light, and they were placed where they best served that end, without undue attention being bestowed upon their external effect. Indeed, in an irregular façade their exact position was not of great importance. They were also of comparatively small size, owing to the necessities of defence. But under the new influences, windows were used to produce external effect as well as to give light ; bay-windows,[1] in particular, were employed to give dignity and rhythm to a façade, while at the same time adding greatly to the charm of the rooms inside. Massive chimney-stacks were likewise introduced at regular intervals to increase the external effect. The result was at once stately and bright, and, as a rule, eminently reasonable from the point of view of daily life. If occasional extravagances were committed, people were too much pleased with the increased convenience and cheerfulness of their houses to be critical of every illogical device (see Fig. 7).

The general effect being obtained by a symmetrical treatment of the mass, by an ordered disposition of windows and chimneys, there still remained special features such as

[1] Shakespeare knew the illuminating effect of bay-windows. When Malvolio complains of the darkness of his prison house, the Clown derisively retorts : ‘It hath bay-windows transparent as barricadoes, and the clerestories toward the south-north are as lustrous as ebony ’ (*Tw. N.* IV. ii. 41–3).

doorways to be considered; the shape to be given to the windows and chimneys; and the treatment of the roof and of the projecting ' strings ' or courses of stone, which had always been used to bind a building together horizontally. It was in these details that the Italian influence made itself chiefly felt.

One striking characteristic of gothic architecture, the traditional architecture of England up to Shakespeare's time, is its strong vertical lines ; in classic, or Italian architecture, it is the strong horizontal lines which predominate.   Accordingly, in Elizabethan houses the latter characteristic is consciously adopted.   The narrow gothic string-course was replaced by the bold classic cornice ; the pointed heads of windows were abandoned in favour of straight heads ; much importance was given to long parapets at the base of the roof.   At the same time, the vertical idea was preserved in the steep gables, in the lofty chimney-stacks, in turrets, and (to a certain extent) in the shape of the windows.

The old traditional spirit was still strong, too strong to submit to the wholesale introduction of the Italian villa *en bloc*, even if there had been any one sufficiently familiar with Italian ways to do it.   It is true that several ingenious designers are known to have studied in Italy, but they were unable, even had they wished it, to persuade the ordinary Englishman to depart so far from his accustomed ways as to adopt an Italian plan.   Besides, the Italianizing of English architecture in Elizabeth's days was not done direct from Italy, but indirectly through France and the Low Countries. Gresham's Royal Exchange, which was designed and built by Flemings, imitated with its piazzas and its slender tower the Italianated Exchange of Antwerp.

A whole villa on the Italian model was apparently too much to attempt, but isolated features such as doorways could readily be designed in the new style, with round-headed archway, pilasters, and pediment.   Chimney-shafts could easily be made in the shape of classic columns, and string-courses in that of cornices.   Then again, if the classic spirit were strong upon him, the designer could divide his wall spaces with classic pilasters, or put sloping pediments over his principal windows.   Thus there is in Elizabethan houses a very great diversity of treatment, arising partly from the taste of the owner himself, but chiefly from the

Fig 8 MIDDLE TEMPLE HALL LONDON

knowledge and skill of the designer. In out-of-the-way places, and in many small houses, there is hardly any actual classic detail at all; merely a symmetrical plan, and square-headed windows. In others there is perhaps a quaint travesty of classic detail about the doorway. Where the mason was better instructed the doorway would be quite well designed in a quasi-classic manner, while in some of the grand houses there are pilasters and cornices, elaborate doorways and windows, fine pierced parapets and columnar chimneys. In such cases the actual detail—the profile of the cornices, the shape of the pilasters, the embellishments of the doorway—has been skilfully founded on, if not actually copied from, Italian examples. In other instances, no doubt, illustrated books were made use of, although no instance has yet been adduced of downright reproduction of an illustration, while in some small houses it would seem as though the mason had founded his design on a vague verbal description, so wide is the result from any known mark.

There can be little doubt, from the evidence of contracts which have been preserved here and there, that masons provided much of their own detail. They sometimes bound themselves to carry out the work according to a 'platt', or drawing, furnished by their employer; in other cases they were to take a certain existing building as a model, but the actual embellishment was generally left to their own skill and knowledge. Some notable builders, like Lord Burghley, not only collected the most recently published books on architecture, but obtained designs for particular features from various skilful surveyors or architects both native and foreign. Not a few of our native surveyors went abroad to study, among the best known of them being John Shute, John Thorpe, and Inigo Jones. Thorpe has left several plans which he made in France, and he evidently studied Androuet du Cerceau's book, *Les Plus Excellents Bastiments de France*, since he has copied one of its plans, with sundry slight alterations rendering it more suitable to English wants. Inigo Jones was led by his study of Italian buildings to a much more correct appreciation of their style than his predecessors had exhibited. It was he who 'purified' architectural taste in England, and drew it away from that phase of design which is characteristic of Shakespeare's

time.   Before he achieved fame as an architect, he had
acquired distinction as a designer of masques, a pursuit
in which his familiarity with Italian architecture was of
great assistance, and doubtless his skill in the handling
of architectural features in these ephemeral shows helped
him in the more serious work of his life, by bringing his
knowledge and capacity to the notice of wealthy patrons.
In many masques he collaborated with Ben Jonson, and
provided magnificent settings for the dramatist's concep-
tions ;   indeed, it is probable that the actual conception
was due as much to the architect as to the poet, if we may
judge from the title-pages of some of the masques.

An interesting reference to house-building occurs in
2 Henry IV (I. iii. 41 ff.), where the rebellious nobles take
counsel together as to their prospects of success.   Lord
Bardolph recommends caution, likening their enterprise to
the building of a house—

> When we mean to build,
> We first survey the plot, then draw the model ;
> And when we see the figure of the house,
> Then must we rate the cost of the erection ;
> Which if we find outweighs ability,
> What do we then but draw anew the model
> In fewer offices, or at least desist
> To build at all ?   Much more, in this great work,—
> Which is almost to pluck a kingdom down
> And set another up,—should we survey
> The plot of situation and the model,
> Consent upon a sure foundation,
> Question surveyors ; . . .
>
> or else,
> We fortify in paper, and in figures,
> Using the names of men instead of men :
> Like one that draws the model of a house
> Beyond his power to build it ;   who, half through,
> Gives o'er and leaves his part-created cost
> A naked subject to the weeping clouds,
> And waste for churlish winter's tyranny.

The 'models' referred to were drawn by surveyors like
Thorpe, among whose plans there are two sets for one
employer, one being smaller—'drawn anew in fewer offices'
—than the other.

Although it is not possible to lay the finger on any particular book or illustration and say 'Here is the original of

Fig 9   ROOM AT CARBROOK HALL SHEFFIELD

such and such a doorway, or gable, or cornice,' yet we can see in a general way whence the masons in the small buildings, and the trained surveyors in the large ones, obtained their details ; the comparison, however, goes to show that the English designer adapted rather than copied.

One of the characteristic features of Italian ornament, which must have set the unlearned English mason wondering, was the introduction of classic busts in niches in the walls. Wollaton Hall (built between 1580 and 1588) has a number of these—Plato, Aristotle, Virgil, Diana—and would have had more, according to the legend, had not the ship which was conveying them from Italy unfortunately been wrecked on the way. Legend is fond of deriving such Italian features direct from Italy. Thus the model of Audley End, which was built for Thomas Howard, Earl of Suffolk, between 1610 and 1616, was, by tradition, derived from the same source. But even if we read 'plan' for 'model'—as we certainly must in Lord Bardolph's speech—we can only conclude that legend embodied in a concrete form what was only a vague impression. For although Audley End was affected by the Italian influence, neither in its plan nor in its architectural treatment is it anything but English of the period. So, too, with the busts. At first they may have been imported ; Henry VIII undoubtedly obtained some from Italy for Hampton Court, and others may have been sent for Wollaton in 1588 ; but fifty years later Nicholas Stone was making them with the best, and sent one of Apollo down to Kirby Hall, in Northamptonshire, for which he charged £10.

Among other classic personages which adorned our English houses were the Nine Worthies. There is a row of them on Montacute House (see Fig. 6), in Somerset. But these heroes were quite well known to the ordinary Englishman, and they provided a diverting episode in *Love's Labour's Lost*, where a pageant of five arbitrarily chosen representatives of them was presented under the management of Holofernes, the schoolmaster.

Heraldry also played an important part in the decoration of houses both inside and out. Nothing is more usual than to find the owner's arms carved over his front door, and on his principal chimney-pieces ; while his family animal—be it bird, beast, fish, or fabulous monster—appears in all sorts

of places where ornament was required : on stone finials
outside, on newel-posts inside, in the panels of a screen, or
the frieze of a chimney-piece, or even—as was the *garb*
(or wheatsheaf) of the Hungerfords—fashioned into an
escutcheon round a keyhole.   Gresham's crest—a grass-
hopper—was carved on almost all prominent points about
the roof of the Royal Exchange.

In addition to the great chimney-stacks and the steep
gables, linked one to another by pierced parapets, the glittering windows and the wide doorways, flanked by pilasters
and surmounted with heraldry, there were, in the larger sort
of house, towers or turrets which rose above the roofs, and
were themselves covered with curved roofs of lead or copper,

all their tops bright glistering with gold,

as Spenser has it.   These turrets were usually disposed
symmetrically, and were often placed over staircases, which,
from the arrangement of the plan, had to be fairly numerous.
Sometimes they enclosed isolated rooms, especially in the
upper stories, rooms useful for the seclusion of unruly
heroines of the drama, such as Sylvia in *The Two Gentlemen
of Verona*, who was nightly lodged by her father in an upper
tower of his palace.

When houses thus fashioned on the outside to be attractive, there being no longer any need for the attractive to be
subordinated to the defensive, how were they treated on the
inside ?   It will be found that as much care was spent in this
direction as in the other.

The front door led into a broad passage, called the
'screens'; on one side were the buttery hatch and the doorway leading to the kitchens ; on the other side was the
screen separating the passage from the great hall.   Through
the screen led two doorways ; once beyond them, and you
were in the vast space of the hall (Fig. 8).   Behind was the
panelled woodwork of the screen, rich with intricate patterns
in low relief, with fantastic carving in high relief, and with
heraldry glowing with the few but vivid tinctures of its art.
High overhead were the curved roof-timbers crossing and
re-crossing each other in a kind of orderly confusion.   In
a side wall half-way up the hall was the massive chimney-
piece surrounding a vast recess wherein a tree-trunk might
be burnt.   On either side of its arched opening a column, or
a flat pilaster, or perhaps a grotesque human figure, helped

Fig 10 GALLERY AT HADDON HALL

to support the chimney-shelf at the height of a man's head. Above this again, framed in heavily carved mouldings, were the owner's arms—his own personal bearings in one panel, the family arms, with all the most notable quarterings, in the other. Perhaps in addition there would be a statue or two of some abstraction, of Justice and Virtue, of Arithmetica and Geometria; or maybe a carved panel of figures setting forth some incident of history, scriptural or mythological—Job displaying his sores to his comforters, or Apollo and the Muses performing a piece of music. On some convenient surface would be carved a short legend, either the owner's motto or some sententious saying in Latin, ' Ne sis Argus foris et domi talpa,' ' Amicus fidelis protexio fortis,' or what not. In the distance was the daïs, the low platform at the upper end of the hall, whereon the owner and his family sat at meals. At one end of the daïs was the recess of the great bay-window of which the lights were brought down low enough to give an outlook, while the rest of the windows were high above the floor, originally so placed, according to one old author, to shield the occupants from the arrow which flieth by day. The windows were bright with heraldry, setting forth in row upon row the great alliances of the owner's ancestors.

The walls themselves, according to Harrison, were ' either adorned with hangings of tapestry, arras work, or painted cloths,[1] or else they are ceiled (i. e. panelled) with oak of our own or wainscot brought hither out of the east countries, whereby the rooms are not a little commended, made warm, and much more close than otherwise they would be ' (Fig. 9). There is plenty of panelling left, of all degrees of richness, to confirm Harrison in this respect ; while of tapestry there is also a great wealth, albeit not now hanging in its old places. Besides the tapestry there was the chimney-piece, exquisitely carved with ' chaste Dian, bathing ' (*Cymb.* II. iv. 82) ; and the ceiling was fretted with golden cherubim—dainty little amorini in a fretwork of plaster.

The ceilings of Shakespeare's time were indeed the most characteristic product of the period. They had a character of their own unlike anything to be found in other countries. The whole surface was covered with a pattern formed by shallow plaster ribs (Fig. 10). Sometimes the ribs were

[1] See Chap. XVI.

narrow and the pattern was of simple geometrical form.   At
other times they were broad, ornamented with arabesques and
bent in intricate ways into panels of different shapes.   The
panels were enriched with figures of birds, beasts, fishes, and
flowers, or with shields of arms, so that yet again on his
ceilings the owner wrote his family history in a sort of heraldic
shorthand.   Occasionally pendants would hang down at set
intervals, producing an effect of great richness ; and from
such magnificence in the nobleman's house there are all
degrees of splendour down to the simple ceiling of a parlour
in the manor-house, or the city dwelling of the merchant.

Another characteristic feature of Elizabethan houses was
the staircase.   It was all the more remarkable because
before this time nothing of the kind was known in England.
Staircases had always been of the spiral or corkscrew type,
like those of church towers.   They may still be seen in many
a mediaeval building, in many a ' cloud-capped tower ', surviving from Norman times.   With the single exception of
a fine staircase at Burghley, dating from about 1556, and
evidently adapted from French examples, there is in existence
no intermediate step between the circular stone staircase and
the broad straight flights of the wood staircases of the
Elizabethan house.

But these wood staircases are almost as monumental as
those in stone.   They are wide and massive, ascending in
short flights of six or eight steps from landing to landing.
Not infrequently the steps are made from solid blocks of
oak, supported by deep, stout, sloping rails.   The handrail
is correspondingly massive, and the space between it and the
timber which carries the steps is filled with heavy balusters.
At every change in direction the main timbers are supported
by thick posts called newels.   In the plainest examples
some kind of ornamental work is bestowed upon the various
members.   In the richest, there is a wealth of almost
barbaric splendour.   The heaviness of the materials is
lightened by sunk patterns or carving, the balusters are
quaintly shaped, but above all the great newels are carried
up and either shaped into curious finials or crowned with
fantastic animals, not infrequently with vigorous representations of the beast which served as the owner's heraldic
cognizance.   They seem to ascend in a long and orderly
procession and form a fitting means of access from the

Fig 11 STAIRCASE AT HATFIELD HOUSE

splendour of the great hall below to that of the great chamber above (Fig. 11).

The staircase is perhaps as typical as any one feature of the change which came over house-building during Shakespeare's life. It exemplifies the desire for spaciousness, for comfort, for display, which actuated men in the making of their homes.

BIBLIOGRAPHY.—The chief Elizabethan treatise on Architecture was John Shute's *The first and chief groundes of architecture used in all the auncient and famous monyments with a farther and more ample discourse upon the same than hitherto hath been set out by any other*, London, 1563, with a dedication to Queen Elizabeth; *The First Booke of Architecture made by Sebastian Serly and treating of Geometrie*, London, 1611, in five books, was a translation from the Italian through the 'Dutch', dedicated to Prince Henry; Sir HENRY WOTTON's *Elements of Architecture* came out in 1624; BACON's *Essay on Building* first appeared in the edition of 1625. THORPE's drawings in the Soane Museum, KIP's *Britannia Illustrata*, London, 1708–9, 4 vols., supply important illustrations of the Elizabethan style.

Of modern works, reference should be made to REGINALD BLOMFIELD's *History of Renaissance Architecture* (1500–1800), 1897, JOSEPH NASH's *The Mansions of England in the Olden Time*, 2 vols., 1839– 49, 1869, and to the present writer's *Architecture of the Renaissance*, 2 vols., 1894, and his *Early Renaissance Architecture* (1500–1625), 1914.

XVIII

HERALDRY

BY

OSWALD BARRON

WHEN William Shakespeare was born in 1564, much of the pomp of heraldry had passed away. It was the proper business of those ages when Warenne shook out his chequers and Nevill displayed his red saltire over the knights that followed their renowned banners, when the knight rode in all the pride of armorials that embroidered his coat and horse-trappers, painted his shield, and crested his great helm. Heraldry was a flower of mediaeval war ; and Tudor fashions had no place for it in the line of battle. Tudor policy had its share in the change.

The army became the king's army ; it was no longer the old battle-array that was a gathering of the hosts of a score of barons. Those barons had been mowed down by civil strife ; their successors were the king's ministers at the council board, or his officers in the field. The royal leopards had devoured all lesser beasts in the armies of sovereigns who could not see without jealousy such a reminder of the old order as the molet of the Veres, or the silver crescent of Percy on a servingman's blue sleeve.

Heraldry still coloured the mimic warfare of tournaments, which remained a royal and noble sport until they fell into disfavour under the eye of a Stewart prince who did not love to look upon a naked weapon. But in Tudor tournaments armory was ousted by the conceits of the Renaissance.

Neglected by the soldier, armory found many foster-parents. By the sixteenth century the heralds had taught all men that the shield of arms was symbol and voucher of gentility, and that, without arms, wealth was ignoble. A man

> That has no pedigree, no house, no coat,
> No ensigns of a family

was, in Ben Jonson's definition, a 'mere upstart' (*Catiline* II. i). In every direction arms were displayed. They were worn upon the thumb that bore the seal-ring. They were engraved upon the silver dishes, bowls, and ewers which were found in plenty even in the houses of men of the middling sort. The sun shone through shields of arms into the squire's hall and the merchant's great chamber; painted scutcheons decked the wainscot. The broad chimney-piece showed the full achievement of arms—helm, crest, and 'word': the shield was below the barge-board of the gable and over the archway of the porch. The churches, already ablaze with ancient shields, received new bearings every year. No more saints and Trinities were demanded in the sixteenth century from the glass-painters' decaying craft, but there was still a call for shields for the chapel-window. Tombs and grave-stones must show the descent and alliances of the dead gentleman. Indeed, the undertaker remained the herald's good friend until our own days, when a black-framed hatchment has become a rare sight. To funerals, the heralds came in their tabards to see that the buckram scutcheons were in order, and to array the shield, pennon, and crested helm of such dead Elizabethans as wished, in Ben Jonson's phrase, to be 'buried with the trumpeters' and to have their 'style' pronounced at the graveside by the officers of arms after the fashion which is followed in our own days at state funerals. Shakespeare makes familiar reference to the herald's prominent place at funerals. The Volscian Lord describes the dead Coriolanus as

> The most noble corse that ever herald
> Did follow to his urn.   (*Cor*. v. v. 145–6)

Queen Katharine exclaims on her deathbed:

> After my death I wish no other herald . . .
> But such an honest chronicler as Griffith.
>   (*Hen. VIII*, iv. ii. 69–72)

The fees charged by heralds on these funeral occasions were high, and were a profitable source of their revenues. Garter King himself superintended 127 funerals of persons below the rank of nobility between 1597 and 1605. The family of one Sir George Rogers was charged £55 for the services of Clarenceux King of Arms and Rouge Dragon pursuivant at his funeral in 1582. In many a will of the period the testator's forethought makes harsh provision for warning off the heralds and their vain superfluities from the graveside.

In Shakespeare's day men no longer devised new arms for themselves, as their forefathers had done freely in the Middle Ages. For new coat armour they came obediently to the officers of arms, who bestowed those ensigns generously. The state of things was plainly put by William Harrison in his *Description of England* :

Whosoever studieth the lawes of the realme, who so abideth in the universitie giving his mind to his booke, or professeth physicke and the liberall sciences, or beside his service in the roome of a capteine in the warres, or good counsell given at home, whereby his commonwealth is benefited, can live without manuell labour, and thereto is able and will beare the port, charge, and countenance of a gentleman, he shall for monie have a cote and armes bestowed upon him by heralds (who in the charter of the same doo of custome pretend antiquitie and service, and manie gaie things) and thereunto being made so good cheape be called master, which is the title that men give to esquiers and gentlemen, and reputed for a gentleman ever after. Which is so much the lesse to be disalowed of, for that the prince dooth loose nothing by it, the gentleman being so much subiect to taxes and publike paiments as is the yeoman or husbandman, which he likewise dooth beare the gladlier for the saving of his reputation.

Charters reciting ' many gay things ' in their preambles, the new arms shining in gold and colours in the margin, the seals of the herald-kings dangling at the foot, remain in plenty among our private archives. The peculiar worthiness of the recipient, a man of singular virtue and discretion, well meriting to be taken into the fold of the gentry, is invariably proclaimed upon the parchment. In practice, those who came with fees in hand were kindly received without over-harsh inquiries into the nature of their claims or their ability ' to bear the port, charge, and countenance ' of their new rank.

There is a strange gap between the armory of Henry VIII's heralds and that of the age before them. The old armory is, as a rule, simply conceived and expressed in few and well-balanced charges. But the good tradition seems to have taken its death-wound during the hurly-burly of the civil war. The Tudor heralds set to building afresh upon a new foundation. Dazzled by the new ornament of the Renaissance they began to devise arms which gorged the shield with charges. Wolsey's bearings include an engrailed cross, a chief, four leopards' heads, two Cornish choughs, a lion passant and a rose; but although this be a characteristic example of the armorial taste of his age, other scutcheons are daubed with even greater numbers of charges. A reaction followed. The men who rose so suddenly under the Tudor policy began to compare their shields with those of the old houses, and to perceive that their new gentility was reflected in their bearings. Some, like the Petres, cast aside the elaborate devices, demanding something more after the fashion of the old coats. The heralds themselves, accumulating manuscripts of armories, were taken with the reaction, and many of their Elizabethan grants of arms show some desire to return to the old paths. Shakespeare himself, when he came to buy arms for his father, was well served, coming away with a simple shield that might, to a stranger's eye, have been inherited through a dozen generations of gentle Shakespeares.

A knowledge of heraldry was deemed in the sixteenth century a necessary part of a gentleman's education. A man who bore arms was expected to be able at need ' to blazon his own proper coat'. Peacham, in *The Compleat Gentleman*, devoted two chapters to the topic, and attached in his scheme of education an extravagant importance to the study, absurdly defining it as ' the most refined parte of natural philosophy '. A generous heraldic literature was at the disposal of students, and enjoyed a wide circulation. Gerard Legh's *Accedens of Armory*, published in 1562, ran through seven editions, the last being that of 1612. John Bossewell, gentleman, Legh's ape and plagiary, put forth the *Workes of Armorie* in 1572, a reprint being issued five-and-twenty years later. Other important treatises issued during Shakespeare's career were Sir John Ferne's *Blazon of Gentrie* (1586), Sir William Segar's *Booke of Honor and Armes* (1590), William Wyrley's *True Use of Armorie* (1592), John Guillim's *Display of Heraldrie* (1610), Thomas Milles's *Catalogue of Honor* (1610), and Edmund Bolton's *Elements of Armories* (1610).

Guillim's *Display*, augmented in successive editions, survived until the eighteenth century to be the favourite table-book of Sir Hildebrand Osbaldistone. Camden praised ' Edmond Bolton who learnedly and judiciously hath discovered the first elements of armory '. Segar described Bolton's book as ' absolutely the best of any in that kind.' But Legh's fanciful and pedantic *Accedens of Armory* was the prime authority in Shakespeare's era.

The wares of Legh, or of his disciple Bossewell, are such skimble-skamble stuff as would put the most reverent student from his faith. No student, indeed, will go to Legh for instruction, although some few of his fancies have filtered through the centuries to the latest heraldry books, for Bossewell was not the last of the plagiarists. Indeed it may be said for the credit of the Elizabethans that they also were plagiarists, and that the seed of their fantastic musings on armory is in such mediaeval treatises as those of John of Guildford and Nicholas Upton.

It is not easy to say what armory was to such men as Legh. Certainly it had nothing to do with exact archaeology. He has much to tell of Greeks and of Trojans, of Valerius and Pliny, but the practice of English mediaeval armory was either out of sight or of little value for him. As for the armory of his own day, his chief concern is to translate it into a tongue not to be understood of the vulgar, to overlay it with strange conceits, and to read from it mysterious symbolisms.

Purple, for example, which must be blazed as 'purpure', is, according to Isidore, the most noble of all colours; Plato is cited to prove that this majestic hue must not be used wantonly. Solomon's seal was this colour. Its planet is Mercury, whose stone is the 'Amatist', a very precious stone in Aaron's breastplate, and one that is enemy to drunkenness and giddy brains. When the colour purpure is combined with sable, it signifieth one who is lamentable as the lapwing; with sanguine it makes arms fit for that soldier who caused his man to brace him in a mail and lay him in a ditch. 'Such bearers of arms there are, sometimes, of whom I am weary to write.'

When we come to deal with beasts, all the ancient legends of the mediaeval bestiaries are set loose. The lion heals himself, when sick, with the blood of an ape; when old he is enemy to man, but never to children; he is always hot with the quartan fever, and the crowing of a cock is the hatefullest noise to him. In the old time they made shields for horsemen of his bones: Legh possessed one of these and held it 'a worthy antiquity'. The unicorn is the mortal enemy of the elephant; the ram 'is mild by kind and of authority is a duke'.

For the ordinary charges of shields, their description, by reason of the many ' diminutives ' discovered by these industrious writers, is reduced as it were to a table of weights and measures. You have the Bend, the Garter, which is half a Bend, the Cost, which is half a Garter, the Riband, which is half a Cost. Also there is the Bendlet whose width is left uncertain. What mediaeval armory knew as the Flaunche is measured up and found to differ from the Flasque and the Voyder. Any of these three may be given as a charge for the shield of the virtuous and learned person who has served his king as an ambassador.

'But', adds Legh, 'therein lieth a mystery.' There are many such mysteries in his book ; the keeping of them is with the heralds, whose high office Legh allows himself to compare with that of the angels. For as the angels have been messengers from God to man, even so the ' here-haughts ' go in their tabards from emperor to emperor, and from king to king. They and no others are keepers of those secrets which have accumulated since the early days of armory, since the siege of Troy and the wars of Semiramis, although ' the universal goodly order was not then as now '.

Such mysteries have a novel air to those who know the simplicity of mediaeval blazon. Legh, for example, lays down the precious rule which forbids the repetition of the words ' of ', ' on ', and ' with ', in blazonry. This may have mediaeval precedent, but the heralds of the Middle Ages would not allow themselves to be confused by the fancies of a Guildford or an Upton. For all these nice rulings, Legh and his imitator are ignorant even of the armory of contemporary heralds. They misname familiar charges. ' You bring in so many crosses and of so sundry fashion that you make me in a manner weary of them', complains one of the characters in the pedant's dialogue. Yet although Legh can bring in crosses entrailed and crosses urdee, and many other such pearls from the depths, he cannot so much as figure you rightly the famous crossleted shield of the mediaeval kings of Jerusalem.

It is plain enough that both Legh and his disciples write in high hopes of catching the patron's eye. They suggest glorious ancestries for the lawyers and statesmen who are in the front of affairs. When Legh gives you a shield of the form used of that valiant Captain Antonius, a *brown* man of colour and very hardy, who ' married with the famous Cleopatra, of Egypt, queen ', you are but mildly surprised to find that Marcus Antonius, the ' brown man ', bore the arms of Chief Justice Anthony Browne.

Burghley, however, the mighty minister who, fretful over his obscure origin, set to work the best imaginations of genealogists, is the patron whose eye these pedants yearn to catch. To him Legh's imitator Bossewell dedicates his volume. His own favourite among his many and various pedigrees is here treated as grave history. Both Legh and Bossewell tell the tale of how ' Sir John of Sitsilt ', a knightly shadow raised up as an ancestor for Burghley, disputed ages ago with Sir William of Facknaham for the possession of those very arms which glow in Burghley's hall-windows. Bossewell recites at length, and in a strange idiom purporting to be mediaeval French, the judgement that gave the Cecils their shield, offering, into the bargain, a picture of a mail-clad Cecil with that shield braced on his arm.

The heralds of Shakespeare's England were enjoying their great day. Incorporated for the first time under a charter of Richard III, in 1483, they received a second charter from King Philip and Queen Mary in 1555. In that year, too, the Crown granted the heralds, for their official residence, Derby House, on Paul's Wharf Hill, which led to the river from St. Paul's Churchyard. The building remained their home till its destruction in the Great Fire of 1666. The duties of heralds were elaborately defined by Sir John Doddridge, the solicitor-general, in 1600 : they were concerned with the granting of arms, the recording of pedigrees, and the supervision of funerals. At the head of the Heralds' College stood the Earl Marshal, and there ranged below him three kings (Garter, Clarenceux, and Norroy), six heralds (York, Richmond, Somerset, Lancaster, Chester, and Windsor), and four pursuivants (Rouge Dragon, Blue Mantle, Portcullis, and Rouge Croix). Clarenceux and Norroy were provincial kings, respectively governing the country north and south of the Trent. They made from time to time official visitations of their provinces, registering arms and pedigrees, and recording some few of the armorial insignia which adorned buildings or funeral monuments.

In 1590 there died the Earl of Shrewsbury, who had served in the office of Earl Marshal for the previous eighteen years.

During the greater part of Shakespeare's career, from 1590 to 1616 when he died, the headship of the college was in commission, save for the four years (1597–1601) when Robert, Earl of Essex, Queen Elizabeth's favourite, presided over Derby House. The commissioners of Shakespeare's day for the execution of the office of Earl Marshal included from time to time Lord Burghley, the Lord Treasurer, Lord Howard of Effingham, Lord High Admiral, the Earl of Dorset, another Lord Treasurer, and other high officers of state.

There were only two changes in the important office of Garter King during Shakespeare's London career. Garter King Sir William Dethick succeeded his father in 1586 after a short interregnum, and was finally deprived for irregularities in 1605. His successor, Sir William Segar, reigned for nearly thirty years (1603–33). Robert Cooke, Clarenceux King for a quarter of a century (1567–92), was one of the best known Elizabethan heralds, and his post was filled in 1597 by the scholar and antiquary William Camden, who retained his office till 1623—twenty-six years in all.

It was no loving household, this of the Elizabethan heralds. Sir William Dethick, Garter King of Arms, the grandson of a German armourer and son of another Garter who had grafted himself upon a Derbyshire stock of knights and squires, was violent and overbearing, and had blows and hard words for his fellows. He would brawl at funerals with the minister or the undertakers. The blood of some old German lanzknecht must have been hot in his veins ; his dagger was ever ready to slip from the sheath, as when he wounded his own brother within the royal precinct of Windsor. He drew it and fell upon two men in Westminster Abbey at the burial of the Countess of Sussex.

Clarenceux Cooke was the enemy of Dethick, who showered accusations upon him, including one of bartering grants of arms for entertainment in taverns by base persons. Queen Elizabeth is said to have encouraged Cooke's successor in office with the remark that, if he proved no better than Cooke, ' it made no matter if he were hanged '.

In many a manuscript of genealogies may be found the true pedigree of ' Sir William Dethick alias Derrick, now Garter ', engrossed lovingly with due regard for his mother's quality as the daughter ' of a Dutch Shoemaker in St. Martin's at the Red Cock', for his grandmother's style, 'daughter of a barber at Aken beyond the seas', for his father's 'false suggestion' of the Derbyshire origin of the family, and for the 'coats and crest usurped by the said Derrick'. Such entries must have been balm to the spirit of the writers, browbeaten officers under this terrible King of Arms.

Ralph Brooke, York Herald from 1593 to 1625, was another sour companion of that fellowship. His main grievance was the preferment of the great Camden, who was made Clarenceux King of Arms in 1597, an 'advancement *per saltum*, by the jump over other men's heads', moving Master Brooke to fierce attacks upon the genealogies in the 'much commended *Britannia*'. He had some lip-service for the 'rare knowledge' of that 'great learned Mr. Camden', but more contempt for the King of Arms elevated 'from the inferior province of boy-beating'. Camden took his revenge with a sharp reply in Latin, an idiom which York did not handle easily, 'putting him off with *quidam* and *iste* as an *individuum vagum*' and embittering the long quarrel.[1]

The abuses which were rife in the college during Shakespeare's time were often exposed. The bitterest censors were the ill-tempered officers of the college, who vented their spleen in pamphlets, many of which remain in manuscript. The corruption was assigned to an ordinance of the Duke of Norfolk, when Earl Marshal, in 1568. The Duke then formally authorized the three Kings of Arms not merely to grant coats of arms at their discretion, but to divide the fees amongst themselves. It was of advantage to the heralds to be busily employed. Robert Cooke is credited with having granted 500 coats. Sir William Dethick and his father are said to have far exceeded that number.

In 1599 William Smith, Rouge Dragon, wrote of the

---

[1] Brooke's quarrel with his colleagues has left a curious contemporary trace on a copy of the Shakespeare First Folio of 1623. In the year of Shakespeare's death Augustine Vincent joined the college as Rouge Rose Pursuivant. He acted as deputy for Camden in 1618, and became Windsor Herald in 1624. He defended Camden in print from Brooke's malicious attacks, and his discovery of Brooke's errors was printed by William Jaggard, the promoter and printer of the Shakespeare First Folio of 1623. A presentation copy of that volume from Jaggard to Vincent with a contemporary inscription is in the library of Mr. Coningsby Sibthorpe, of Sudbrooke House, Lincoln.

Favine's *Theater of Honour*, 1623, contains most of the head and tail pieces and initials used in the First Folio.

ELIZABETHAN TOMBS OF THE PEYTON FAMILY ISLEHAM
CHURCH CAMBRIDGESHIRE

growing scandal in 'A brief Discourse of the causes of Discord amongst the officers of arms and of the great abuses and absurdities com[m]itted by [heraldic] painters to the great prejudice and hindrance of the same office'. Smith points his scornful finger at two of Shakespeare's close associates and fellow actors, Augustine Phillipps and Thomas Pope, who had outraged truth and decency in endeavours to secure heraldic badges of gentility. On leaf 8a of his pamphlet Smith writes: 'Phillipps the player had graven in a gold ring the armes of Sir Wm. Phillipp, Lord Bardolph, with the said L. Bardolph's cote quartred, which I shewed to Mr. York [i. e. Ralph Brooke, champion of heraldic orthodoxy], at a small graver's shopp in Foster Lane.' Lower down on the same page appear these words,—'Pope the player would have no other armes but the armes of Sr Tho. Pope, Chancelor of the Augmentations.' Player Phillipps's fraudulently adopted ancestor, 'Sir William Phillipp', won renown at Agincourt in 1415, while Player Pope had taken the armorial honours of Sir Thomas Pope, the courtier and privy councillor, who died without issue in the first year of Elizabeth's reign after founding Trinity College, Oxford.

In another unpublished pamphlet of desultory notes in which Ralph Brooke, the severest of all censors of his colleagues, had a chief hand, heraldic offences in thirteen recent grants are described. On an outside page there is, however, a list of twenty-three names of persons who received coats of armour on false pretences. Among the names are 'Shakespeare' and 'Cowley' (probably Shakespeare's friend and fellow actor, Richard Cowley).

With detailed accusations, Brooke here avers that an embroiderer, calling himself Parr, who failed to give proof of his right to that surname, and was unquestionably the son of a pedlar, received permission to use the crest and coat of Sir William Parr, Marquess of Northampton, dead in 1571, as 'the last male of his house'. Three other men, who were accused of bribing the college into forging pedigrees, are named as a seller of stockings, a haberdasher, and a stationer or printer, while a fourth offender is stated to be an alien. In some instances Garter is charged with having pocketed the fee, thereafter prudently delaying the formal issue of the promised grant of arms until the applicant was dead.

The scandal increased under James I, until in 1616, the year of Shakespeare's death, Ralph Brooke tricked Segar, Garter King, into granting a coat to the common hangman of London, Gregory Brandon. That indiscretion led to the temporary imprisonment in the Marshalsea of both Garter and Brooke. A royal commission attempted reform early in 1619 with hopeful results. Henry Peacham, an earnest student of heraldry, wrote thus after the commission had reported : 'Coats sometimes are by stealth purchased, shuffled into records and monuments by painters, glasiers, carvers, and such ; but I trust so good an order hath been lately established by the right honourable the late commissioners for the office of the Earl Marshalship, and careful respect of the Heralds with us, that all hope of sinister dealing in that kind is quite cut off from such mercenary abusers of nobility.'

Ridicule of the thirst for heraldic honours and the discreditable machinery for slaking it often found its way on to the stage. Witless Sogliardo, the wealthy clown who would be a gentleman, in Ben Jonson's *Every Man out of his Humour*, stands for many an Elizabethan purchaser. He comes from the ' Harrots ' (i. e. Heralds), who speak to his ear the strangest language and give a man the hardest terms for his money that ever you knew. But he has his arms now upon a parchment. ' I thank God that I can write myself Gentleman now, here 's my patent,' says he ; ' it cost me thirty pound by this breath : ' ' it has as much variety of colours in it as ever you saw a coat have ', and the crest is ' your boar without a head, rampant.' The herald, says Puntarvolo, has well deciphered his man : ' a swine without a head, without brain, wit, anything indeed, ramping to gentility.' Jonson, a poor man's son, but with some vague story in his head of a grandfather who was a ' gentle Johnston ', had no patience with these new-made gentlemen by purchase, and when Puntarvolo suggests ' Not without mustard ' for Sogliardo's ' word ', one may possibly see in it a lick of the rough side of Jonson's tongue for the fellowpoet who had, in that same year, 1599, been wasting his hard-earned money upon such a parchment as the heralds would sell to any Sogliardo. For the ' word ' below the grant to old John Shakespeare was *Non sanz droict*.

Ben Jonson, the close friend of Camden, is mightily

cunning in the armorial lore of his age, delighting in its terminology, but he employs his heraldic learning chiefly in the way of satire. Not only in *Every Man out of his Humour* does the successful effort of the rich boor to obtain coat armour excite his scorn, but in *The Staple of News* he presents among his *dramatis personae* ' Piedmantle pursuivant at arms and heraldet ', a caricature of the Bluemantle pursuivant. Piedmantle, who had ' read the Elements [of Edmund Bolton] and Legh's Accidence and all the leading books ', illustrates in speech and act the ' manners ' and ' vices ' which Jonson imputes to the Heralds' College (*The Staple of News*, IV. i.) :

> here is Piedmantle ;
> 'Cause he 's an ass, do not I love a herald,
> Who is the pure preserver of descents,
> The keeper fair of all nobility,
> Without which all would run into confusion ?
> Were he a learned herald, I would tell him
> He can give arms and marks, he cannot honour ;
> No more than money can make noble : it may
> Give place, and rank, but it can give no virtue :
> And he would thank me for this truth.

In view of the free demand and supply of coat armour, there is nothing surprising in the well-known negotiations of Shakespeare and his father with the Heralds' College. Shakespeare's colleagues, Pope and Phillipps, were not the only actors to covet the badge of gentility. To John Heming, the actor-manager of Shakespeare's company, confirmation of arms seems to have been granted by Garter King, Sir William Segar, in 1628. The business of the grant of arms to Shakespeare was spread, it seems, over many years. All the documents that remain concerning it are rough drafts with their annotations remaining in the Heralds' College. One of these drafts, and the earliest of them, shows that in 1596 old John Shakespeare made his application to the heralds, his son's purse being without doubt opened to pay the fees. Arms inherited from a father were, according to the heraldry books, worthier than those a man might obtain for himself, and we may likewise credit the dramatist with some desire to restore the quality of his bankrupt father in his native town of Stratford-on-Avon, where he himself proposed to settle.

John Shakespeare had already shown a hankering after

these ' gay things '. The shield with the bend and justing spear had been devised for him, according to a memorandum on the first draft, by Robert Cooke, a King of Arms who had died in 1593 : ' This John showeth a pattern thereof under Clarenceux Cooke's hand in paper twenty years past.' Clarenceux Cooke, within whose province was Warwickshire, had his visitation commission in 1568, and it was in 1568 that John Shakespeare was bailiff of Stratford and justice of the peace. Therefore it is possible that ' twenty years past ' is to be taken as but a rough estimate of the date of the ' pattern '.

For some unknown reason, no grant was issued in 1596 ; the drafts never came to a fair copy on parchment. But in 1599 there was a new draft. William Dethick, Garter, and William Camden, Clarenceux, recite that John Shakespeare, now of Stratford-on-Avon, gentleman, comes of a great-grandfather, who, for faithful and approved service to King Henry VII, was advanced and rewarded with lands and tenements given to him in those parts of Warwickshire where the family has since continued in good reputation and credit.

No document has come to hand to support the first part of this boast. The first drafts halt between ' grand-father ' and ' ancestor ' in the description of the loyal for-bear ; ' great-grandfather ' is the second thought of the clerk in 1599. As for the good credit, John Shakespeare must have uneasily remembered the lean year which found him avoiding his parish church for fear of his creditors. But he had married the daughter and one of the heirs of Robert Arden of Wilmcote. Arden was a great name in Warwickshire, although the exact relationship of Robert with the knights and squires of the long Arden pedigree is as uncertain as John Shakespeare's own genealogy.

Moreover, it is recited that John Shakespeare had pro-duced his ancient coat of arms heretofore assigned to him whilst he was his Majesty's officer and bailiff of his town. This can mean no more than that the ' pattern ' of the arms which Robert Cooke had been ready to grant in 1568 was produced before Dethick and Camden ; and so it is that same ' shield and coat of arms ', namely, ' In a field of gold upon a bend sable a spear of the first, the point upward headed argent ', that Garter and Clarenceux in 1599 assign, grant, confirm, and exemplify to the said John, together with the crest of ' a falcon with his wings displayed, standing on a wreath of his colours, supporting a spear, armed, headed, and steeled silver '.

Although the grant itself, signed and sealed by Dethick and Camden, is not known to be extant, that it was issued is not to be doubted. The arms and the falcon crest are over Shakespeare's monument ; his daughter Susanna Hall shows the arms beside her husband's mastiff heads on seal and tombstone, and Elizabeth the poet's granddaughter quarters them with Hall. Quarrelsome Ralph Brooke, York Herald, attacked Dethick and Camden for sanctioning the use by a man in a base rank of a bearing which only the spear differenced from the shield of ancient magnates, the Lords Mauley. Dethick and Camden replied that the spear was ' a patible difference ', as indeed it was, adding that the man was a magistrate, a justice of the peace, who had married the daughter and heir of Arden, and was of good substance. In the matter of the Arden marriage, Brooke might have pressed them further. It is significant that the rough sketch of arms upon the draft shows the arms of the Warwickshire Ardens struck out. In their place are set the arms of the Cheshire Ardens, differenced, as Arden or Ardene of Hawnes in Bedfordshire was bearing them, with a martlet. Squire Arden of Parkhall was alive to question the claims of any persons thrust upon him as kinsfolk. There is, however, no evidence that either coat was allowed to John Shakespeare's wife, and no quartering for Arden appears on the poet's monument or in the arms of his daughter, ' good mistress Hall '.

In Elizabethan London, the faces of the heralds would be familiar to Shakespeare in ceremonial processions, at burials and funeral feasts. Camden was of his literary circle, and his visits to the college, while his father's shield was under discussion, doubtless extended his personal acquaintance among the officers. Falstaff likens the makeshift shirts of his ragged followers to ' a herald's coat without sleeves ', an allusion to the sleeveless tabard of the herald's official costume (1 *Hen. IV*, IV. ii. 49). Unlike Jonson's Piedmantle, the heralds of Shakespearian drama— Mountjoy and his English rivals—are stately figures of mediaeval temper, dignified messengers of their sovereigns on the battlefield, who do no dishonour to the royal lilies and leopards of their tabards.

In one fantastic branch of the heraldry of the Renaissance Shakespeare showed a practical interest. Noblemen of his day adopted the Italian fashion of adorning their shields at tournaments, and sometimes their household furniture and plate, with ' imprese ', artistic devices in miniature combining ingenious allegorical pictures with mottoes. Near the end of his career, in March 1613, the dramatist helped his friend Burbage, who was well known not only as an actor, but also as a painter, in devising an 'impresa' for the Earl of Rutland, a friend of the dramatist's patron, the Earl of Southampton, to bear on his shield and equipment at a forthcoming tournament at Whitehall.

Shakespeare fully shared the general heraldic knowledge of his time, if he lacked Ben Jonson's mastery of these matters. With the commoner usages and the heralds' language, he shows an easy familiarity. Justice Shallow writes himself ' Armigero ', as the Shallows had done ' any time these three hundred years ', during which period they had borne ' the dozen white luces in their coat '. The boast excites Parson Evans's taunt, ' The dozen white louses do become an old coat well ; it agrees well, passant.' The armorial jest is pursued by Shallow's cousin Slender, who asks if he ' may quarter ', and is told that he can do so ' by marrying ' (*M. Wives* I. i. 10 ff.).

One of the wildest fancies of the herald pedants of his age gives Shakespeare material for his lines in *Lucrece*, where Tarquin in his remorse exclaims :—

> The scandal will survive,
> And be an eye-sore in my golden coat ;
> Some loathsome dash the herald will contrive,
> To cipher me how fondly I did dote. (ll. 204–7)

There be nine ' rebatings ', says Gerard Legh, and goes on to explain what dishonourable additions must be made to the shields of ' boasters like Sir William Pounder ', of him that killeth his prisoner, lies to his sovereign, revokes his challenge, or is slothful in war. Arms, as Master Legh and his like eagerly assure us, are ensigns of honour. Yet this does not keep them from gravely devising the means

ACHIEVEMENT OF ARMS OF SIR
RICHARD PECKSALL (*ob.* 1571)

SHIELD OF MARGARET COUNTESS OF
LENNOX (*ob.* 1578)

whereby a man may make armorial advertisement, to all who look on his shield, of the fact that he is a drunkard or an adulterer.

Heraldic simile is common especially in early plays like *Henry VI*, for which Shakespeare was only in part responsible. The messenger from the fields of France comes with the word that :—

> Cropp'd are the flower-de-luces in your arms ;
> Of England's coat one half is cut away.
>   (*I Hen. VI*, I. i. 80–1)

And Iden, with Cade's gore upon his blade, says :—

> Ne'er shall this blood be wiped from thy point,
> But thou shalt wear it as a herald's coat,
> To emblaze the honour that thy master got.
>   (*2 Hen. VI*, IV. x. 73–5)

The language of armory colours much imagery in Shakespeare's *Lucrece*, where lines like this recur :—

> This heraldry in Lucrece' face was seen
> Argu'd by beauty's red and virtue's white.   (ll. 64–5)

A like predilection for heraldic metaphor is seen in Helena's words :—

> So, with two seeming bodies, but one heart ;
> Two of the first, like coats in heraldry,
> Due but to one, and crowned with one crest.
>   (*Mid. N. D.* III. ii. 212–4)

Like most Elizabethan writers the dramatist repeatedly plays on the word 'difference'—the distinction which marks the arms of the younger branches of a family. Beatrice says jestingly of Benedick (*Much Ado* I. i. 69–71) : 'If he have wit enough to keep himself warm, let him bear it for a difference between himself and his horse.' Ophelia bids Laertes 'wear your rue with a difference' (*Haml.* IV. v. 182). The heraldic term 'gules' (i. e. red) occurs in the plays. Timon bids Alcibiades 'with man's blood paint the ground, gules, gules' (*Timon* IV. iii. 59). The First Player says of the slaughtered Pyrrhus, 'Head to foot Now is he total gules' (*Haml.* II. ii. 487–8). 'Field', 'coat', 'shield', and 'crest' also fill a large place in Shakespeare's heraldic vocabulary.

But those who look in every line of Shakespeare for wisdom beyond his fellows' share will find nothing to warrant them here. He has not sought his armory far afield. An observant man, looking about him at the coloured windows and the tombs and idly turning the pages of the heraldry books, could supply all that Shakespeare has need of. It is the true heraldry of his own age. Talbot bidding his men

renew the fight,
Or tear the lions out of England's coat,

(*1 Hen. VI*, I. v. 27–8)

has Elizabethan words in his mouth, for the ' lion passant gardant ' of the Tudor heralds was a ' leopard ' for the mediaeval kings and their followers. From a dramatist who arms Falstaff on Shrewsbury Field with the pistol of one of those horsemen whom the writer had seen clattering through London streets, we look for no nice archaeology. Warwick, crying out that

Old Nevil's crest,
The rampant bear chain'd to the ragged staff,
This day I'll wear aloft my burgonet,

(*2 Hen. VI*, v. i. 202–4)

has forgotten the history of his house's armorial honours— for the rampant bear came to him as a badge brought by his Beauchamp wife ; ' old Nevil's crest ' was the bull's head.

BIBLIOGRAPHY.—The contemporary manuals on heraldry are mentioned in the text. The history of heraldry in Tudor times may be studied in JAMES DALLAWAY'S *Inquiries into the Origin and Progress of the Science of Heraldry in England*, 1793; and in MARK NOBLE'S *A History of the College of Arms, and the Lives of all Heralds from the reign of Richard III*, 1804. Shakespeare's treatment of the subject is fully expounded in ALFRED VON MAUNTZ'S *Heraldik im Dienste der Shakespeare-Forschung*, 1903. The story of John Shakespeare's coat armour is summarized in LEE'S *Life of Shakespeare*, new edition, 1915, the preface to which gives some recently discovered additional information about the abuses in the Heralds' College, and Shakespeare's share with Burbage in devising the Earl of Rutland's ' impresa '. A valuable summary of the state of heraldry in the reigns of Elizabeth and James I, with ample illustration from Ben Jonson's work, will be found in ARTHUR H. NASON'S *Heralds and Heraldry in Jonson's Plays*, 1907.

XIX

COSTUME

BY

PERCY MACQUOID

FOR the appearance of Elizabethan men and women in their habits as they lived we are almost entirely dependent upon portraits of the time, in which dresses are treated with a hard convention that gives little scope to the imagination. The wearers appear to be invariably painted in their best clothes, and, as the hard elaboration of detail is more in evidence than the true cut and style, it is only by comparison and inspection of actually surviving dresses that a satisfactory impression can be obtained. Such examples are exceedingly rare, but the Isham family dresses found at Lamport Hall, Northamptonshire, and now in the Victoria and Albert Museum, supply the needful information. This interesting collection of Elizabethan and Jacobean clothes reaches in date from about 1555, nine years before the birth of Shakespeare, to the reign of Charles II, the last example of the series being a wedding dress made for Sir Thomas Isham in 1681, but never worn, owing to his sudden death. The condition of the clothes is remarkably good, the few portions missing from some of the fabrics being small pieces cut out in the reign of Charles II for the purpose of dressing dolls, which were also discovered in the house.

The first impression given by these concrete links with the past is wealth and originality of colour combined with neat and minute detail ; the small size of the garments indicates that the stature of our ancestors must have been considerably below the modern standard.

The great wave of change that swept over England about the middle of the sixteenth century, developing what is known as the Elizabethan age, affected every form of design, completely altering the fashion of costume and obliterating the gothic features that remained in English dress of the first half of the century. In men's costume, the long tunic of the time of Henry VIII, cut open at the throat and filled in with pleated linen, the enormous puffed sleeves and shoes, gave way to a doublet fitting close to the figure, with tight sleeves, surmounted at the shoulders with small puffings and at the neck by a high close collar edged with a frill, whilst short and round upper hose or breeches headed the long stockings and small pointed shoes, a short shoulder cloak with a rapier and dagger completing the costume.

The clothes of the better classes were imitated and copied from the fashions set by royalty and the court, and the universal desire for fine clothes is continually alluded to by writers of the time. Harrison (1577–87) thus inveighs against the extravagant expenditure on dress :—

Oh how much cost is bestowed now adaies upon our bodies and how little upon our soules ! how manie sutes of apparell hath the one, and how little furniture hath the other ? . . . Neither was it ever merier with England, than when an Englishman was knowne abroad by his owne cloth, and contented himselfe at home with his fine carsie hosen, and a meane slop ; his coat, gowne, and cloake of browne blue or puke, with some pretie furniture of velvet or furre, and a doublet of sad tawnie, or blacke velvet, or other comelie silke, without such cuts and gawrish colours as are worne in these daies, and never brought in but by the consent of the French, who thinke themselves the gaiest men, when they have most diversities of jagges, and change of colours, about them. Certes of all estates our merchants doo least alter their attire,[1] and therefore are most to be commended : for albeit that which they weare be verie fine and costlie, yet in forme and colour it representeth a great peece of the ancient gravitie apperteining to citizens and burgesses, albeit the yoonger sort of their wives both in attire and costlie housekeeping can not tell when and how to make an end, as being women in deed in whome all kind of curiositie is to be found and seene, and in farre greater measure than in women of higher calling.

Women's dresses preserved their early Tudor character for a longer period than men's, since Elizabeth did not change her fashions until she had been for some time on the throne. The first alterations were the extreme prolongation of the corsage, the enlargement of the farthingale, and the growth of the ruff. Then the times became rich

[1] This is illustrated in the plate by Caspar Rutz reproduced here.

With silken coats and caps and golden rings,
With ruffs and cuffs and farthingales and things;
With scarfs and fans and double change of bravery.

(*Tam. Sh.* IV. iii. 55–7)

The ruff, introduced by Catherine de Médicis into France on her marriage with Henry II (1533), was then no more than a small and simple frill, encircling the neck as high as the ears, but it increased so quickly in size in this country that even before Shakespeare's birth an edict had been issued in 1562 against the wearing of great ruffs. This decree was evidently efficacious, as the ruff from that date till 1577 consisted merely of pleated frills of fine linen or cambric, sometimes edged with lace, of about three inches wide by two inches thick. But the rage for eccentricity of size must soon have recommenced. The proportions of the ruff began again to increase, and seem to have attained their greatest elaboration after 1580. In 1583 we find Philip Stubbes saying :

beyond all this they have a further fetch, nothing inferiour to the rest; as, namely, three or foure degrees of minor ruffes, placed *gradatim*, step by step, one beneath another, and all under the Maister devil ruffe ; the skyrts, then, of these great ruffes are long and side every way, pleted and crested ful curiously, God wot. Then last of all they are either clogged with golde, silver, or silk lace of stately price, wrought all over with needle woork, speckled and sparkled heer and there with the sonne, the moone, the starres, and many other antiquities straunge to beholde. Some are wrought with open woork down to the midst of the ruffe and further, some with close woork some with purled lace so cloyd, and other gewgawes so pestred, as the ruffe is the least parte of it self.

He adds that, when these fashionable ladies are caught in a shower of rain,

their great ruffes strike sayle and flutter like dishe-clouts about their neckes.

Stow states that ruffs, which were made of linen until the second year of Elizabeth's reign, were after this date constructed of cambric or lawn, and as no one could be found to starch or stiffen them well, the Queen imported Dutch women for this purpose. Amongst these was Mistress Dinghen Vanderplasse, who in 1564 met with great patronage from the rich classes, and was the first who publicly taught starching, charging four or five pounds per scholar, with twenty shillings extra for instruction in starch-making.

In 1597 we find Elizabeth herself giving command to the Lord Chancellor and privy council that after the 21st of February of that year no person shall use or wear such great and excessive ruffes, in or about the uppermost parts of their neckes, as had not been used before two years past ; but that all such persons shoulde in modest and semely sort leave off such fonde, disguised, and monstrous manner of attyring themselves.

Towards the end of Elizabeth's reign till the time of Shakespeare's death in 1616, changes took place in the shape of the ruff. The most fashionable ruffs consisted almost entirely of lace, often without pleats, and stood higher than ever at the back of the neck, no longer encircling it but open in front and ending in points at the V-shaped opening of the doublet.[1] Excessive exposure of the breast was peculiar to England at this time ; in a portrait of Lady Seymour of Trowbridge, existing at Petworth, no concealment of it is attempted ; portraits of other noble ladies show that the taste was general, and divines devoted many discourses to the obtrusive immodesty of women. The ruffs starched yellow with saffron and other dyes that came into fashion early in the seventeenth century seem to have deeply stirred the conscientious scruples of the Dean of Westminster. He forbade any gentleman or lady wearing a yellow ruff to attend service in the Abbey ; public opinion, however, forced him to forgo this prohibition, and his congregation continued to endanger their salvation for the sake of yellow starch. Shakespeare ridicules the fashion in old Lafeu's scornful speech about the ' snipt-taffeta fellow ', the ' red-tailed humble-bee ',

whose villanous saffron would have made all the unbaked and doughy youth of a nation in his colour. (*All's Well* IV. v. 2–4)

The farthingale, the other peculiar characteristic of female dress during Shakespeare's lifetime, developed in keeping with the ruff. Originally invented by a Spanish princess and called a *verdugado*,[2] this artificial adjunct was introduced under the name of *verdugadin* or *verdugale* at the French court in the first half of the sixteenth century, when the long gothic clinging skirts disappeared for ever. The farthingale was a round petticoat made of canvas distended with whalebone, cane hoops, or steel

[1] The portrait of Queen Elizabeth given in Chapter I illustrates the extreme of fashion from about 1595 to 1600.

[2] The literal meaning is ' fitted with rods or sticks ', from *verdugo*, a rod.

strips ; it was covered with taffeta or other material, the brocade, cloth, or velvet skirts being worn over this. During the latter part of the century it was enormously enlarged at the hips and called a cart-wheel farthingale, the circumference of the skirt being as wide at the hips as at the hem. At times a huge frill like a ruff headed the skirt, forming a flat circular surface projecting at right angles to the waist. Farthingales were also made in semicircular form, confined to the back of the skirt, leaving the front straight and so giving more freedom and a more graceful appearance. Falstaff, flattering Mistress Ford, says :

The firm fixture of thy foot would give an excellent motion to thy gait in a semi-circled farthingale.   (*M. Wives* III. iii. 67–9)

The upper part of the figure was squeezed into a long, stiff-pointed bodice, called the doublet both in men's and women's dress, stiffened with wood, steel, or whalebone, the lower point of the stomacher reaching below the level of the hips. Early in Elizabeth's reign sleeves were tight and straight, headed by rolls at the shoulders and cut and slashed, and criss-crossed with small puffings ; but by the year 1580 a large leg-of-mutton sleeve had become fashionable, padded and stiffened with embroidery, and often profusely sewn with jewels. The simple wrist-ruffs of the earlier period were then exchanged for cuffs of lace, six inches or more in depth and turned back on the sleeve. Petruchio abuses this new fashion in Katherine's sleeves in *The Taming of the Shrew* (IV. iii. 88–91). Towards the end of the century hanging sleeves were again introduced, the doublet or bodice being epauletted at the shoulders.

This abnormal costume remained in fashion with slight modifications through the greater part of Shakespeare's life ; it was most rigid and artificial in appearance, as it gave no expression to the lines and grace of woman's form. The wearers, indeed, resembled nothing so much as a trussed chicken set upon a bell. Stubbes condemns them bitterly in these words :—

When they have all these goodly robes upon them women seem to be the smallest part of themselves, not naturall women but artificial women ; not women of flesh and blood, but rather puppits or mawmets consisting of rags and clowtes compact together.

Ladies' hair from 1560 until the end of the century was

worn curled and taken back from the forehead, dressed over a pad, and often interwoven with pearls and jewelled ornaments. True golden hair was held in the highest estimation, but naturally all shades of auburn and red were favoured in a court whose Queen set the fashion by her own Tudor tresses, supplementing them as they faded with various wigs of these tints. Shakespeare alludes to the prevailing fashion in :

> Her hair is auburn, mine is perfect yellow :
> If that be all the difference in his love
> I'll get me such a colour'd periwig.
> *(Two Gent.* IV. iv. 196–8)

Women of fashion incurred much censure from the pulpit and scorn from the satirist for the general practice of dyeing their hair and wearing wigs. Face-painting was common among women and at court, and evidently was carried much farther than ever before. Harrison, Stubbes, Stow, Gosson, and other writers of the time see in it a token of a depraved mind, and imply that the use of face-paint is incompatible with moral behaviour. Nashe, in his *Pierce Penilesse his Supplication to the Divell* (1592), speaks of 'their cheeks sugar-candied and cherry blusht so sweetly', and Shakespeare has more than one reference to the habit :

> Your mistresses dare never come in rain,
> For fear their colours should be wash'd away.
> *(Love's L. L.* IV. iii. 270–1)

The heart-shaped hood associated with Mary Stuart was in favour till about 1575, but after that date the hair was dressed high and crowded with jewels, a little head-dress of material with ornaments and feathers being also worn. The jewels worn in the hair often took the form of little ships or other objects. Nichols records as a new year's gift to the Queen :

A Jewel being a ship of Mother-of-Pearl, garnished with rubyes ;

and in Montemayor's *Diana* (1598) occurs the following description :

The attyre of her head was in form of two little ships made of emeraldes, with all the shrouds and tackling of clear saphyres.

Falstaff has such ornaments in mind when he says :

Thou hast the right arched beauty of the brow that becomes the ship-tire, the tire-valiant, or any tire of Venetian admittance.
> *(M. Wives* III. iii. 59–61)

A popular form of female head-dress early in the reign was the coif, a tight-fitting cap following the shape of the head, banded in front with one or two rolls of coloured or gold tissue, finishing at the back in a fall that reached to the shoulders, and worn far back to show off the hair. Autolycus, crying his wares, sings :

> Golden quoifs and stomachers,
> For my lads to give their dears.
>
> *(Wint. Tale* IV. iii. 226–7)

In 1575 Van Meteren, writing on England, remarks that women habitually wore hats in the house :

The women are beautiful, fair, well dressed and modest, which is seen there more than elsewhere, as they go about the streets without any covering either of huke or mantle, hood, veil or the like. Married women only wear a hat both in the street and in the house ; those unmarried go without a hat, although ladies of distinction have lately learnt to cover their faces with silken masks or vizards, and feathers—for indeed they change very easily and that every year to the astonishment of many.

Stow states that :

Womens Maskes, Buskes, Mufs, Fanns, Perewigs and Bodkins were first devised and used in Italy by Curtezans, and from thence brought into France, and from thence they came into England about the time of the Massacre in Parris.

' Masks for faces and for noses ' *(Wint. Tale* IV. iii. 223) were of various colours, and were much worn by ladies of quality when riding. The eyeholes at times were filled with glass. They are frequently alluded to by Shakespeare. Julia, disguised, says of herself :

> But since she did neglect her looking-glass
> And threw her sun-expelling mask away,
> The air hath starv'd the roses in her cheeks.
>
> *(Two Gent.* IV. iv. 159–61)

The fan first made its appearance in England at Elizabeth's court, being introduced from Italy. It was worn hanging from the point of the stomacher ; it often contained a small mirror. At one time the Queen had no less than twenty-seven fans, chiefly the gifts of her admirers, their elaborate handles being of gold, silver, or agate, mounted with precious stones. One, presented by Sir Francis Drake, was of red and white feathers, with a gold handle inlaid with half-moons of mother-of-pearl and diamonds. Another, mentioned in an inventory of the time as belonging to the Countess of Bath, was made of swan's down and green velvet, sown with seed pearls. Fans were generally of circular form, and made of feathers or embroidered silk or velvet. Falstaff implies that the handles were worth stealing when he says to Pistol :

And when Mistress Bridget lost the handle of her fan, I took't upon my honour thou hadst it not.   (*M. Wives* II. ii. 12–14)

Women's shoes were slightly pointed, made of leather, cloth, or silk to match their dresses. For out-of-door use chopines or clogs were worn :

Your ladyship is nearer heaven than when I saw you last, by the altitude of a chopine.   (*Ham.* II. ii. 454–5)

Silk, worsted, and fine yarn stockings were in general use by the year 1580 ; the first pair of black silk stockings was worn by the Queen in 1560, a present from Mistress Montagu, her silk-woman. Such gifts to Her Majesty were usually made on New Year's Day and included all forms of clothing, as well as money, plate, and jewels. Thus in the year 1557–8 the bishops presented her with thirty, twenty, or ten pounds respectively, the list of these clergymen being headed by ' tharche busshop of Yorke ' £30. The temporal peers gave sums varying from £30 downwards, with jewels and occasionally dresses ; for instance :

Given by the Lord Cobham a petticote of yellow satten leyed al over with a pasmane of silver and tawnye sylke, fringed with silver and sylke lyned with tawnye sarcesnet.

The new year gifts of money for 1578 amounted to £993 13s. 4d., equivalent to about £8,000 of our currency. The peeresses invariably gave portions of dresses, either a ' doublet ', ' coate ', or ' kyrtill with a trayne ', but apparently never the entire costume ; some offered money, others ' feyer cushyns embrawdered with sylke ', or lengths of velvet and lawn, ruffs, fans, gloves and every conceivable conceit of the time. There is a charming bodice given

by the Lady Shandowes Dowager, a dublet of peche collered satten al over covered with white cut worke, and leyed with a lace of Venice gold, lyned with orenged colored sarcesnet and a swete bag of crymson taphata embrawdered with Venice gold and spangills ;

and the Lady Sheffield gave :

a dublet of sad tawny satten covered with white cut worke embrawdered with flowers of silver and spangills and lined with white sarcesnet.

FEMALE COSTUME — GENTRY

FEMALE COSTUME — PEASANTRY

Eighty different people made presents of dress to the Queen on New Year's Day 1578, and these presentations were over and above similar tributes showered upon her in her various progresses during the year. The accumulation of 3,000 dresses found at her death, generally considered so remarkable, would have represented the New Year's gifts of the previous decade in addition to her own considerable expenditure. Below is the inventory of her clothes taken in 1600:

Robes	99
French Gowns	102
Round Gowns	67
Loose Gowns	100
Kirtles	126
Foreparts	136
Petticoats	125
Cloaks	96
Cloaks and Safeguards	31
Safeguards	13
Safeguards and jupes	43
Doublets	85
Lapmantles	18
Pantofles	9
Fans	27
	1077

Robes were evidently dresses of ceremony or state; in this sense the word is repeatedly used by Shakespeare. Friar Laurence tells Juliet:

> Then—as the manner of our country is—
> In thy best robes uncover'd on the bier,
> Thou shalt be borne to that same ancient vault.
> *(Rom. & Jul.* IV. i. 109–11)

Gowns were over-dresses. Mistress Page, discussing Falstaff's disguise, reflects that

> There is no woman's gown big enough for him, otherwise he might put on a hat, a muffler, and a kerchief, and so escape.
> *(M. Wives* IV. ii. 73–6)

Falstaff complains that his skin is like an old lady's loose gown (*1 Hen. IV*, III. iii. 4), and Grumio insists in the face of the tailor that he did not order 'a loose-bodied gown' (*Tam. Sh.* IV. iii. 134). A kirtle (*2 Hen. IV*, II. iv. 297) was a jacket with skirt attached, a half-kirtle (ibid. v. iv. 24) the skirt alone. Cloaks reached to the ground; they were straight in front, but full at the back, with high-standing collars to support the ruff. There are several examples in the Isham Collection; one is of cream 'branched' damask (i.e. brocaded with isolated bunches of flowers in colours); there are no sleeves, but apertures edged with tabs of salmon-coloured silk for the arms. Lap-mantles were circular cloaks to envelop the entire figure.

In place of the tight-fitting whale-boned doublet with its padded sleeves, jumps or jackets were worn for morning dress by the less fashionable. There are two in the Isham Collection, of about 1600, one of loosely woven white silk with fine silver lines, still untarnished, the other a jacket, with tight sleeves, of salmon-coloured silk embroidered with a fine blue line.

Night-gowns are mentioned in wills and inventories, and were worn both by men and women at this period. They date from the beginning of the fifteenth century. They were generally made of silk or satin faced with fur, and fulfilled the purpose of a dressing-gown. Lady Macbeth's gentlewoman says:

I have seen her rise from her bed, throw her night-gown upon her.
(*Macb.* v. i. 5–6)

It is generally supposed that the night-gown proper or night-rail was not worn in England until the middle of the sixteenth century, and then only by royalty or the nobility. The rich may have slept in their 'smocks'. At any rate, Elizabeth wore 'night railes', for amongst the New Year gifts of 1588 we find Mrs. Wingfield giving her a 'night-raile of fyne camberick wrought all over with blak sylke', while her smocks are described as of 'fyne Hollan clothe' also wrought over with black silk. Shakespeare alludes to smocks as night-wear:

She'll be up twenty times a night, and there will she sit in her smock till she have writ a sheet of paper.   (*Much Ado* II. iii. 146–8)

O, ill-starr'd wench!
Pale as thy smock!   (*Oth.* v. ii. 271–2)

The following extract from a letter written in 1578 by Gilbert Talbot to his father, the Earl of Shrewsbury, shows that ladies walked about in their night attire rather freely, and that the Queen at the age of 45 did not refuse to display herself in this manner:

On May Day I saw Her Majesty and it pleased her to speak to me very graciously. In the morning about 8 o'clock I happened to walk in the tiltyard under the gallery where Her Majesty useth to stand to see the running at tilt, where by chance she was, and looking out of the window my eye was full towards her. She shewed to be greatly ashamed there of, for that she was unready, and in her night stuff, so when she saw me at after dinner as she went to walk, she gave me a great fillip on the forehead, and told my Lord Chamberlain, who was next to her, how I had seen her that morning and how ashamed she was.

Gloves were important and expensive items of a lady's dress. They were gauntleted and embroidered on the backs and cuffs with silk tassels and ' Venis gold ' and much perfumed. An entry in the household book of Lord North (1581) mentions presents of

Frogs and Flies for the Queens gloves 50 s., gloves for the Queen 15s. for myself 7 s.

Hero speaks of a present of gloves :

These gloves the count sent me ; they are an excellent perfume ;
(*Much Ado* III. iv. 61–2)

and Autolycus advertises

Gloves as sweet as damask roses.
(*Wint. Tale* IV. iii. 222)

They were also lined with fur :

You fur your gloves with reason.
(*Troilus* II. ii. 38)

Silks and velvets came from Italy or France. They were not manufactured in this country until about 1604, when they were made by

Master John Tyce dwelling near Shoreditch Church, the first Englishman that devised and attayned the perfection of making all manner of Tufted Taffeties, Cloth of Tissue, wrought velvets, branched Sattins and all other kind of curious silk stuffes.

These were all very costly : plain satin cost 12 to 14 shillings a yard, equivalent to about £5 of our money; figured Genoa velvets, and fabrics interwoven with metal and other colours, were extravagantly dear. The colours produced were very beautiful, and English selection ran for strong colour, as opposed to the quieter tones adopted by the French and Spanish courts. The names for the colours were sometimes descriptive, but often, on the other hand, entirely fanciful. Some of them are : Drakes colour satten, Ladie blush satten, Claie colour satten, Beasar colour, Heare colour, Gozelinge colour tapheta, Marigold, Isabel, Judas colour, Peas porridge tawny, Popingay blew, Lusty gallant. Devil in the hedge, Dead Spaniard. The patterns gradually became smaller as the century proceeded and were geometrical and conventional. These designs were enhanced by the addition of embroidery and of jewels attached to both the upper and lower portions of the dress. Plain silks or taffetas were sometimes shot or changeable (as the term then was):

The tailor make thy doublet of changeable taffeta, for thy mind is a very opal!   (*Tw. N.* II. iv. 75–6)

Shakespeare also alludes to the most expensive kind of velvet, cut in three heights:

Thou art good velvet ; thou art a three-piled piece, I warrant thee. I had as lief be a list of an English kersey as be piled, as thou art piled, for a French velvet.   (*Meas. for M.* I. ii. 33–7)

It is almost certain that neither rich nor poor wore anything under the skirt ; when it was cold, they put one petticoat over another. Nor is there any reason to suppose that rich men in cold weather wore anything but one linen shirt over another, besides their fur-lined coats and mantles. The fact that Charles I wore three shirts on the cold morning of his execution proves that by the middle of the seventeenth century nothing had been invented in the shape of warm underclothes ; the doublets, however, of both men and women were often thickly quilted and lined, and with the solidly constructed stays afforded much protection. Fur was comparatively common both for trimmings and linings, the sumptuary laws against its use by any one below a knight or dame being no longer rigidly enforced. At the same time, we have records that a waistcoat in cold weather was worn under the doublet, but over the shirt ; for in a contemporary pamphlet describing the execution of the Earl of Essex, which took place on a cold morning at eight o'clock in an open courtyard of the Tower on February 25, 1600, his dress is described as a

gowne of wrought velvet a blacke sattin sute a felt hatte blacke and a little ruffe about his necke. After his speech to the spectators he put off his gowne and on finishing his prayers opening and putting off his dublet he was in a scarlet wastecote, and then ready to lay downe.

This waistcoat was probably of silk, for we learn from Stow that :

In the yeere 1599 was devised, and perfected the Art of knitting or weaving silk stockings wastecoates, and divers other things, by engines or steele loomes by William Lee.

The dramatic change from black to scarlet was probably inspired by a similar arrangement of colour adopted by Mary Stuart at her execution in 1587. This is Froude's fine description of her last appearance, taken from ' Le Vray Rapport de l'execution faicte sur la personne de la Royne d'Ecosse '.

> She laid her crucifix on her chair. The chief executioner took it as a perquisite, but was ordered instantly to lay it down. The lawn veil was lifted carefully off not to disturb the hair, and was hung upon the rail. The black robe was next removed. Below it was a petticoat of crimson velvet. The black jacket followed, and under the jacket was a body of crimson satin, one of her ladies handed her a pair of crimson sleeves, with which she hastily covered her arms, and thus she stood on the black scaffold with black figures all around her, blood red from head to foot. Her reasons for adopting so extraordinary a costume must be left to conjecture. It is only certain that it must have been carefully studied, and that the pictorial effect must have been appalling.

At the accession of Elizabeth men's clothes were reasonable and restrained in their style—the ruff still small and close, and the double and upper hose tight-fitting—but the fashion and relative proportions of these soon began to alter, and rapidly, for, as Fynes Moryson wrote,

> No people in the world is so curious in new fangles as they of England bee.

This newfangledness was more marked in men than in women. An Englishman's dress in the period with which we are concerned was a byword in the rest of Europe, and the medley of taste and cut, borrowed from various countries, which he bore upon his person was proverbial. That this vanity was carried into all classes is shown by Stubbes, who says :

> it is impossible to know who is noble, who is worshipful, who is a gentleman, who is not, because all persons dress indiscriminately in silks, velvets, satens, damaskes, taffeties and such like notwithstanding that they be both base by birth, and servile by calling, and this I count a great confusion and a general disorder, God be merciful unto us.

After 1560 the doublet became longer and more pointed, with a shorter skirt ; the sleeves, braided and slashed, with puffings at the shoulders, were fairly tight. The upper hose or breeches, which in Mary's reign had been short and melon-shaped, now assumed, by reason of excessive padding, most absurd proportions, and were soon suppressed in favour of a shorter hose showing more of the leg. This was quickly followed by round hose gartered below the knee. Large leg-of-mutton sleeves resembling those worn by women, covered with embroidery and jewels, went along with them. Towards the end of the century puffed breeches, distended by wool and hair, were again brought into fashion, and these far exceeded in size their prototypes of 1566.

The chronology of these changes is as follows :

1550–60. Melon-shaped upper hose or breeches with long lower hose. Doublet reaching to waist with six-inch skirt. Puffed shoulders with tight sleeves.

1560–6. Similar upper hose, much enlarged. The doublet longer and more pointed, with a two-inch skirt. Sleeves rather looser.

1566–75. Small puffed upper hose again in fashion. The doublet still longer with no skirt. Sleeves slightly padded.

1575–90. Long round French hose reaching from the hips to below the knee, worn with stockings and garters. Padded leg-of-mutton sleeves. The doublet usually without a skirt ; excessively long and pointed, in many cases finishing far below the hips in the form of a pea-pod, hence called peascod-bellied doublets ; of Italian origin.

1590–1616. The upper hose was now enormous, reaching from the hips to just above the knee and fastened to the stockings by broad garters of silk or velvet trimmed with gold fringes. The doublet shorter, pointed, but hollow-bellied instead of convex. The sleeves were tight and simple with tabs or rolls at the shoulders.[1]

Stubbes in 1583 ridicules the ' dublets with great bellies . . . stuffed with four, five, or six pounds of Bombast at the least '. Shakespeare dresses Falstaff in a ' great-belly doublet ', which is no doubt a jocose allusion to his circumference rather than a precise description of his attire ; similarly he makes the page describe Armado thus :

with your arms crossed on your thin-belly doublet like a rabbit on a spit. (*Love's L. L.* III. i. 19–21)

[1] Some of these changes can be studied in the following illustrations to this book : the title-pages of Turbervile's *Booke of Faulconrie*, 1575, and of *The Noble Arte of Venerie*, 1576, in Chapter XXVII, the portraits of Prince Henry in Chapters III and XXII, and the portrait of the Earl of Southampton in Chapter XXII.

Shakespeare nowhere employs the term 'trunk hose', and it is not found earlier than 1637. His names for this garment are hose, round hose, breeches, and slops. Nashe, however, in 1592, speaks of trunk slops. 'Slops' was a generic term for wide loose breeches long before the Elizabethan period. Mercutio gives Romeo *bonjour*, and adds:

> There's a French salutation to your French slop.
> *(Rom. & Jul.* II. iv. 48–9)

Portia, describing her English admirer, says:

> I think he bought his doublet in Italy, his round hose in France, his bonnet in Germany.   *(Merch. of V.* I. ii. 78–80)

Other terms for wide hose were 'galligaskins' and 'gallyhose'. Shakespeare uses neither, but only the short form 'gaskins' *(Tw. N.* I. v. 27).

The long doublet and hose frequently ornamented with ribbings, spots, and stripes were suggestive of insects, and the wearer, with his winged triangular cloak and beeheaded bonnet, must have been in character with the court drones who hummed and buzzed round their queen in 1585. Shakespeare marks this feature when he makes Hamlet say of Osric:

> Dost know this water-fly?   *(Haml.* v. ii. 84)

What changed very little in fashion was the shape of the short cloak, which was invariably worn over the doublet and hose. Falstaff inquires of his page:

> What said Master Dombledon about the satin for my short cloak and my slops?   *(2 Hen. IV*, I. ii. 32–3)

Older men wore a long cloak or gown. Cloaks are continually mentioned in wills; one in 1573 gives the following details:

> I give to my brother Mr. William Sheney my best black gown, garded and faced with velvet and my velvet cap, also I will unto my brother Thomas Marcal my new shepe coloured gown garded with velvet and faced with cony also I give unto my son Tyble my shorte gowne faced with wolf and laid with Billements lace also I give unto my brother Cowper my other shorte gown, faced with foxe: also I give unto Thomas Walker my night gown faced with cony and my ruddy coloured hose.

Then follow other bequests of everyday canvas and cloth clothes to his servants, until we come to a frieze jerkin with silk buttons and another of the same material with stone buttons, and some hose lined with crane-coloured silk. The lining was under the strappings of the puffed upper hose.

Doublets and hose of frieze were worn as morning dress about the court, but probably as an affectation of simplicity. Sir John Harington writes :

the Queene loveth to see me in my laste frize jerkin, and saithe 'tis well enoughe cutt. I will have another made liken to it.

but adds that she simply spat on the fringed cloth suit of another gentleman, saying, ' the fooles wit was gone to ragges'.

We may presume that the ordinary gentleman in town wore cloth, or sometimes stout linen, stitched with coloured cording and embroidery. The accounts of William Darrell of Littlecote, during his last season in London, 1589, show him ordering a suit of plain fustian with silk buttons, and two doublets and cloaks of ' murry and black satten', both lined with a similar-coloured taffeta sarcenet. The satten cost him 12 shillings a yard and the sarcenet 7, 3 dozen silk points 3 shillings, 3 dozen silk buttons 1 shilling, 4 shirts 6 bands and 6 pairs of cuffs 4 pounds 6 shillings. The latter item seems large, but shirts were elaborately embroidered and cost anything from ten shillings up to 10 pounds ; even a cheap shirt cost a crown. The careful bequests of clothes in wills of this period can be well understood. For the making of these two suits William Darrell paid thirty shillings. His washing bill for this three months' visit to London is also instructive :

5 shirts, handkerchiefs, nightkerchiefs and socks . . .	18d.
6 shirts, 18 handkerchiefs and a waistcoat	24d.
6 shirts, handkerchiefs, nightkerchiefs, socks and collars .	20d.
5 shirts, 8 handkerchiefs, a nightkerchief, a collar and socks	20d.
4 shirts, 6 handkerchiefs, socks and nightkerchiefs . .	14d.
3 shirts, 4 handkerchiefs, and socks	10d.
3 shirts, 5 handkerchiefs	10d.
2 shirts, 4 handkerchiefs, 1 pair of socks and 5 sheets . .	13d.
6 shirts, 6 handkerchiefs and 1 pair of socks . . .	19d.
4 shirts, 5 handkerchiefs and 1 pair of socks . . .	13d.
1 tablecloth and 14 napkins	14d.

These are details from the daily expenditure of a country gentleman occupying a small house in Warwick Lane, a narrow thoroughfare which still connects Newgate Street with Ludgate Hill, where he lived in some luxury, having trout, game, fruit, and other delicacies of the country sent up from Littlecote to London by express messengers.

In the Isham Collection is a doublet of the same date and of similar cut to those mentioned in the Darrell accounts. It is of a deep turquoise malachite Genoa velvet, the pattern faded to a mossy green ; down the front is a row of silk buttons, placed so close that they touch. The short skirt is perforated with six eyelet-holes on each side, to take the silk points that tied the doublet to the upper hose.

The fronts of such doublets were stiffened inside six inches from the waist-line with a triangular piece of wood of the consistency of thick cardboard. Elaborate buttons were a prominent feature. Stow states :

The tenth yeere of Queen Elizabeth, many young Citizens and others began to weare Christall buttons upon their doublets, coats and jerkins. And within few yeeres after, began the generall wearing of buttons, of threed, silke, haire, and of gold and silver threed.

Crystal buttons were worn by vintners and other respectable tradespeople.

This leathern-jerkin, crystal-button, knot-pated, agate-ring, puke-stocking, caddis-garter, smooth-tongue, Spanish-pouch,—
(*1 Hen. IV*, ii. iv. 78–81)

is a string of epithets applied to the vintner by Prince Henry. Greene speaks of a pawnbroker dressed in a black taffeta doublet and a leather jerkin with crystal buttons.

The wide flat ruff worn with this phase of dress was introduced from the court of France, Henry III's ruff measuring over a foot from neck to edge and containing 18 yards of linen. Nine inches from neck to edge appears to have been the usual limit in this country, as in one of Elizabeth's sumptuary laws it was ordered to be clipped when reaching ' within a nayle of a yard in depth '. These wide dimensions continued till about Shakespeare's death, the huge puffed upper hose requiring a balance near the face. These must have made the legs look small, and so the wearing of very long boots reaching above the knee became fashionable. To such a point was this carried that Gondomar, the Spanish ambassador, is recorded to have said to James I :

I shall amaze my countrymen by letting them know at my return that all London is booted and apparently ready to walk out of town.

These boots were eccentric and costly, of russet cloth or leather, sometimes tight and smooth (*2 Hen. IV*, II. iv. 270), sometimes hanging loose about the leg and turned down and fringed, when they were called 'lugged boots'. Stubbes states they were also made of fine cloth with the tops elaborately embroidered, and Dekker prescribes :

Let it be thy prudence to have the tops of them as wide as the mouth of a wallet, and those with fringed boot-hose over them to hang down to thy ancles.

In Markham's *Cavelarice* (1607) there are full instructions for a horseman's boots and apparel, some of which are as follows :

A hat which must sit close and firme upon your heade. About your neck you shall wear a falling band, and no ruffe. Your doublet shal be made close and hansome to your bodie. Your hose would be large, rounde and full, your bootes must be cleane, blacke, long and close to your legge. Your bootehose must come some two inches higher than your bootes being hansomely tied up with points.

Women apparently at this time often hunted and hawked in men's riding costume with breeches and long boots. Leather or velvet shoes were the general footwear throughout Elizabeth's reign ; they were slightly pointed, slashed, or pinked,[1] and decorated with buckles, silver or copper gilt. Towards the end of the century large ornamental rosettes of silk were introduced which are stated to have cost as much as five pounds. 'Gabriel's pumps were all unpink'd i' the heel' (*Tam. Sh.* IV. i. 136) is one of Grumio's excuses for not meeting Petruchio according to appointment. Hamlet asks whether 'a forest of feathers' (which were much used on the stage) 'with two provincial roses' on his 'raced' (i.e. slashed) shoes are not sufficient qualification for his admittance to a theatrical company (*Haml.* III. ii. 291–4). The stockings of the well-to-do were of silk :

how many pair of silk stockings thou hast ; *viz.* these, and those that were thy peach-coloured ones !   (*2 Hen. IV*, II. ii. 17–19)

Hats, according to Stubbes, were of all shapes,

sometimes pearking upp like the spere or shaft of a steeple, standyng a quarter of a yard above the crowne of their heads, some more some lesse as pleased the fantasies of their inconstant minds, so

---

[1] Pinking was perforation, usually as a preparation for embroidery. hat of a haberdasher's wife—no doubt a confection of some elegance slightingly spoken of as a 'pinked porringer' (*Hen. VIII*, v. iv. 51).

Opulentus mercator Londinensis in Anglia.   Nobilis puella ornatus apud Londinenses.   Vulgarium fœminarum in Anglia.   Plebey adolescentis in Anglia habitus. Plebei adolescentis in Anglia habitus.

19

EXAMPLES OF COSTUME IN ELIZABETH'S REIGN

of velvet some of silk, some of wool and wiche is more curious some of a certain kind of fine haire. These they called bever hattes of xx, xxx, or xl shillinges price, fetched from beyond the seas from whence a great sort of other vanities doe come besides.

One form of the sugar-loaf hat was called 'copintank', 'coppid tank', 'coptank', and by Shakespeare 'copatain' (*Tam. Sh.* v. i. 69). The hat was a great asset in a well-dressed man's attire : he fought in it, and with it, using it as a parry ; he sat at church and at meals with it on, and only removed it with most profuse ceremony on meeting a lady, instantly replacing it : he remained uncovered only at court and in the presence of royalty. Ophelia remarks on Hamlet's hatless appearance :

> with his doublet all unbrac'd ;
> No hat upon his head. (*Haml.* II. i. 78–9)

There was a certain stiffness and formality in Elizabethan hats. The feathers with which they were decked were small, but as the size of hats increased in James's reign the feathers were worn larger. Small handkerchiefs of about four inches square, with a button or tassel at each corner or edged with gold lace, were folded and worn in hats as favours. Other objects, such as gloves and ribbons, were also stuck in the hat or cap, as passages in Shakespeare show (see *Hen. V*, IV. i. 232 ; *Haml.* IV. vii. 77 ; *Lear* III. iv. 85–6).

The last important change in man's costume that took place before the death of Shakespeare was the introduction of the falling collar in place of the ruff. Accepted portraits of the poet represent him with this. In the Windsor miniature of Essex, painted between 1590 and 1600, a small ruff surmounts this falling collar, showing a transitional and by no means successful style. These falling collars were no novelty ; instances of their use are continually found before 1600. In the well-known miniature at Windsor of Sir Philip Sidney, painted after his retirement, he wears a small square-cut lace collar and long close-fitting black boots topped with lace to match his collar and cuffs. The picture of Robert Dudley, Earl of Leicester, at Hatfield, probably painted about 1585, shows a combined collar and ruff ; we may safely assign to this date the beginning of the turn-down collar, which lasted with various alterations till the Restoration.

In all portraits of the latter part of the century the hair is worn longer at the sides than it was early in Elizabeth's reign. The trimming of beards was fantastic and various, nor does there appear to have been any generally accepted fashion. It was customary to dye them and to mould them in various forms according to the profession, age, or fancy of the wearer :

Quickly. Does he not wear a great round beard like a glover's paring-knife ?

Simple. No, forsooth : he hath but a little whey-face, with a little yellow beard—a cane-coloured beard.

(*M. Wives* I. iv. 20–4)

At the date of Shakespeare's birth women's dress amongst the middle and lower classes was sensible and economical, and his youthful eyes must have seen a style of dress very different from that with which he was familiar in his later manhood, for even gentlewomen in 1564 ordinarily wore simple cloth gowns. Coventry and Worcester were important centres of the manufacture of coloured cloth. The dress of a citizen's wife about 1570 was composed of a jacket-shaped bodice over a partelet or neckerchief of linen headed by a small ruff, together with a kirtled skirt, often looped up to show another coloured petticoat. An inventory of clothes taken at the early part of Elizabeth's reign in the cottage of a husbandman renting land to the value of twenty shillings a year, shows the value of dress of this class :

Hys wyves rayment Hur best gowne ten shillings, Her olde gowne five shillings A kyrtill of Russet nine shillings, Two Kyrtills of Fusten nine shillings, Hur best petticoat four shillings, Hur olde petticoat one shilling. A silver pynne one shilling and twopence. The best cappe two shillings and fourpence. A neckercher sixpence five kerchers five shillings. Her husbands clothes consisted of a gowne five shillings, a dublet and jacket six shillings and eight pence. Two payr hoses two shillings and eightpence. Two sherts one shilling and sixpence. A blak sleved cote three shillings and sixpence. A Fryse one shilling and eightpence. A canvass dublet tenpence, a cappe sixpence.

With the growth of luxury in the upper classes this simplicity of clothing gradually disappeared. Ruffs and farthingales began to make their appearance amongst the country people, and the poorer classes carried on their backs the greater part of what they earned. Aprons were worn by all classes, and, according to Stephen Gosson, were at times very elaborate :

> These aprones white of finest thrid
> So choicelie tide, so dearly bought
> So finely fringed, so nicelie spred
> So quaintlie cut, so richlie wrought ;
> Were they in worke to save their cotes
> They need not cast so many grotes.

Close-fitting linen caps, sometimes winged, with an over-cap of coloured cloth, were the customary head-dress for women and children. For out-of-door wear a hood was added, and frequently over this, particularly by married women, a high-crowned hat. One variety, called 'thrummed', was made from weavers' thrums, the small tufts of wool where the thread of the warp is tied. Mrs. Page mentions one :

> And there's her thrummed hat.
>
> (*M. Wives* IV. ii. 82)

Stubbes calls attention to the growing extravagance in the head-gear of this class :

to such excesse is it growen, as every artificers wyfe (almost) wil not stick to goe in her hat of Veluet every day, every marchants wyfe and meane Gentlewomen in her french hood and every poor Cottage Daughter in her taffatie hat, or els of woll at least, wel lined with silk, veluet or taffatie. But how they come by this, they care not ; who payeth for it, they regard not.

May Day and Morris dresses of this period were merely fancy costumes, and evidently of cheap material, as one is mentioned of gilt leather and silver paper, and another of spangled fustian with bells. Stubbes describes the colours used as ' greene, yellow, or some other light wanton colours '.

Townsmen wore fine cloth hats or bonnets, green blue and red being favourite colours with the younger men.

In 1571 an Act of Parliament was passed for the benefit of the cappers, enjoining the wearing of a woollen cap on Sundays and holy days by every person above the age of six years except women and certain specified officials. This cap is referred to under similar circumstances by Shakespeare and Marston :

Better wits have worn plain statute-caps. (*Love's L. L.* v. ii. 282)

Nay, though my husband be a citizen, and 's cap made of wool, yet I ha' wit.   (*Dutch Courtesan*, III. i)

Towards the close of the sixteenth century the round

cap with a low flat crown was commonly called a flat cap, and a flat cap came to indicate nothing more nor less than a Londoner, but especially a London 'prentice. In Jonson's *Every Man in his Humour* Kitely the merchant says :

> they . . . mocke me all over,
> From my flat cap, unto my shining shooes.

The rest of the dress was by preference of russet cloth, often a dark blue, seldom black, and made as a tight-fitting doublet rather longer in the skirt than that of gentlemen. Tight sleeves of a different colour, plain and loose upper hose, grey stockings and shoes, with a leather belt from which hung a pouch, completed the suit. Buttons were often of polished pewter, and the points and laces of some bright colour. Older men wore a half-circular cloak reaching below the knee. In an engraving of the end of the century a young man wears a leather doublet, a jerkin with long skirts buttoned to the waist, and a hat such as is usually still associated with Guy Fawkes. His rather long hose show just below the doublet, he carries a sword and a buckler with a point that exceeds in length that allowed by the edicts of the time, and his shoes are evidently of black velvet slashed to show the stocking hose, which in all probability were red or gay in colour.

A broadsword or dagger was the invariable equipment of every ordinary man qualified to wear weapons. At the beginning of Elizabeth's reign even agricultural labourers, when at work, put down in a corner of the field their sword, buckler, and bow. London apprentices, however, were forbidden to carry any weapon but a knife. Apprentices wore blue cloaks in summer and blue gowns in winter, with breeches and stockings of white broadcloth, and the flat caps already mentioned.

Servants in good families wore doublets of shorter waist and rather longer skirt than their masters, their upper hose or breeches were not padded, and the lower hose were gartered above the knee. Loose, hanging shoulder-sleeves were added towards the middle of the reign, and on these were embroidered the master's arms. A shade of blue was very popular for liveries. Grumio, giving directions about the underservants, says :

Let their heads be sleekly combed, their blue coats brushed, and their garters of an indifferent knit.   (*Tam. Sh.* IV. i. 93–4)

And the Duke of Gloucester, egging on his men to attack the Cardinal Beaufort, exclaims :

> Draw, men, for all this privileged place ;
> Blue-coats to tawny-coats. (*1 Hen. VI*, i. iii. 46–7)

Tawny was the shade adopted by dignitaries of the Church ; Wolsey's pillar-bearers were clothed in tawny velvet. By 'indifferent knit' is meant of quiet appearance. Such garters would have been of coarse wool ('caddis' or 'crewel'), occasionally bound over with a small scarf. They are mentioned in an account of 1571 thus—

> vi pece of gartoning crewle iijs.
> iij double peces of saye gartoning iijs. and ivd ;

and they are the subject of a joke by the Fool in *King Lear* (ii. iv. 7–8) :

> He wears cruel garters. Horses are tied by the head.

Gartering above and below the knee, called cross-gartering, was an eccentric fashion, to which there are many references in literature, as in *Twelfth Night* (ii. v. 169, iii. iv. 23–4) ; it was becoming obsolete towards the end of James I's reign, and was finally relegated to May and Morris dancers.

Yeomen, keepers, and those who managed hunting-dogs were usually dressed in Kendal green (*1 Hen. IV*, ii. iv. 250), with bugles, short hangers by their side, and a quarter-staff in their hands.

Plain canvas doublets were worn by inferior servants :

> Look you Francis, your white canvas doublet will sully.
> (*1 Hen. IV*, ii. iv. 84–5)

Ben Jonson in *A Tale of a Tub* (ii. ii) describes a rustic on his wedding day as wearing a leather doublet with long points, 'a paire of pin'd up breeches like pudding bags,' with yellow stockings, and hat turned up with a silver clasp.

Men of the poorest class wore skirted fustian tunics with loose breeches, coarse stockings, or canvas leggings buskined with leather or strips of cloth, and a hat differing little from that worn by the mediaeval peasant. There was no distinctive type of dress for the women of this class.

The Elizabethan period of costume is one of great distinction. The men's clothes conveyed a sense of elegance

446.1 I

and activity inseparable from the time. Women's dress
was more artificial, stilted, and overladen with ornament,
yet preserved a fine sense of dignity, and marked an
important epoch in the evolution of sartorial art.

JEWELLERY

Existing examples of Elizabethan jewellery and ornaments reveal the same ingenuity and industrious novelty
evident in other branches of contemporary art ; they
mostly bear decided traces of foreign influence, accounted
for by the fact that Hubert Moret, the celebrated English
goldsmith of the previous reign, worked with Holbein, and
that the school founded by them was further developed
and emphasized by the many Huguenot and Flemish
workers in precious metals who settled in this country
after 1572 and became members of the Goldsmiths Company. Taste and technique were also strongly affected
by jewellery of the Cellini school that drifted over here
from the Valois court. Cellini died in 1571, and
the individualities of his style were in vogue during the
greater part of Shakespeare's life. The earlier geometrical
arrangements of stones in heavy gothic settings gradually
gave way to the use of minute nude figures, realistically
modelled with exquisite taste and precision and set
amongst enamelled strapwork or arabesques, accentuated
at important points with precious stones ; this flat treatment was particularly suitable for the pendants so much
sought after and worn by both men and women. These
were of various shapes, oval, round, and heart-shaped, as
well as in the form of ships, lizards, dragons, birds, mer-
maids, and sea-monsters, the object being suggested by an
eccentric-shaped pearl or stone for the body, to which a
head and limbs were added in gold and small precious
stones.

The Darnley pendant, preserved at Windsor Castle,
which was made for the mother of Henry Darnley, the
Countess of Lennox, in memory of her husband who was
killed in 1571, is heart-shaped. Shakespeare alludes to
the form :

> I took a costly jewel from my neck,
> A heart it was, bound in with diamonds.
>
> (2 Hen. VI, III. ii. 106–7)

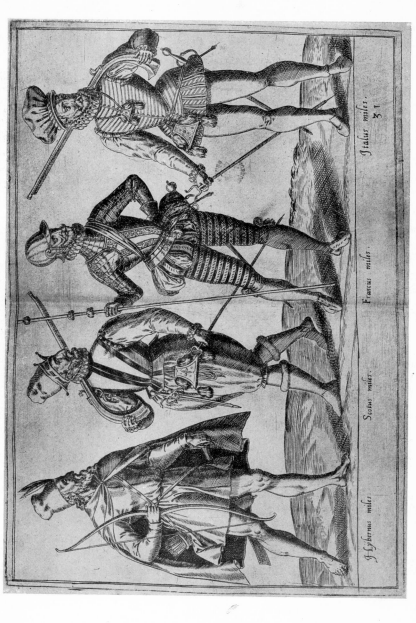

From CASPAR RUTZ *HABITUS VARIARUM ORBIS GENTIUM* 1581

Hybernus miles.   Scotus miles.   Francus miles.   Italus miles.
                                                        3 1

MILITARY COSTUMES—IRISH SCOTTISH FRENCH ITALIAN

A miniature was frequently inserted in the back of these pendants, and sometimes a portrait medallion in cameo set in jewelled ornament formed the obverse. These were made chiefly for gifts. In 1596, the Earl of Shrewsbury presented the admiral of the ship by which he went on his embassy to France with 'a Jewell of the Queen's Picture and a ring sent to his lady'. The lines,

> He that wears her like her medal, hanging
> About his neck,   (*Wint. Tale* I. ii. 307–8)

and

> Here; wear this jewel for me, 'tis my picture;
>   (*Tw. N.* III. iv. 231)

suggest portrait medallions or miniatures. They were suspended from chains or broad ribbons reaching just below the chest. Chains were worn by most citizens, and were provided by the wealthy for their retainers; every well-dressed gentleman wore a gold chain. In 1587, when Sir Christopher Hatton rode from Holborn to Westminster on the first day of his term as Lord Chancellor, he had in attendance, among others, forty of his gentlemen in blue liveries and chains of gold. These would have been plain; gentlemen's chains were often intricate in the link, frequently enamelled, black and white being a favourite combination. In 1596, the Earl of Shrewsbury, when in France, distributed, among other gifts from the Queen, four gold chains, varying in value from £100 to £52 apiece. The collars of SS, which are set down in the Order of the Coronation of Anne Boleyn (*Hen. VIII*, IV. i), were of Lancastrian origin, but of uncertain significance. These and other chains of office were flat and broad in the link, and at times very highly decorated.

Ladies wore long chains of stones or pearls. In 1588, a New Year's gift to Elizabeth is described as

a chayne, containing 22 aggetts slytely garnesshed with gold and 22 bawles of jheat slytely garnesshed over with seede pearles.

Stow quotes the price of a chain of pearls given by the Lord Mayor, aldermen, and citizens of London to Princess Elizabeth on her marriage in 1613 as 'a fayre chain of orientall pearle which cost about £2,000'.

Pomanders were very popular trinkets. Men wore them suspended from a long slender chain, and women from their girdles. They were either made in the form of a hollow perforated sphere to contain a ball of scent or constructed after the manner of an orange, the ' quarters ' being secured at the base by hinges opening outwards when the top was unscrewed, and containing various per-fumes and disinfectants, such as ambergris, musk, clove, and hartshorn. They were of gold or silver, engraved and ornamented inside and outside, and occasionally jewelled and enamelled. The love of perfumery was carried into other ornaments, such as carcanets and coronals. Anne of Denmark in 1607 possessed a dress, ' the fore part adorned with 48 tags 3 inches long of beaten and enamelled gold, hollow within and filled with ambergreece '. The pomanders alluded to by Autolycus (*Wint. Tale* IV. iii. 611) would have been the common wax perfume balls moulded into shapes and impregnated with scent.

Women's girdles remained in fashion till about 1600 ; they were of velvet covered with small plaquettes of embossed metal, or wholly of metal links, enamelled and jewelled ; from these were hung a variety of trinkets and sometimes a watch. Watches were introduced into England during Henry VIII's reign, but were worn only by the rich in Shakespeare's time. They were large, octagonal, oval, or round in shape, the outer cover being pierced with elaborate openwork to enable the strike to be heard. As they decreased in size towards 1580, they became personal ornaments of great value. Several are mentioned among New Year gifts to Elizabeth ; in 1581 we find a long gold chain set with diamonds and 'hanging thereat a rounde clocke fullie garnished with dyamondes.'

Malvolio pictures himself with a watch :

I frown the while ; and perchance wind up my watch.
(*Tw. N.* II. v. 66–7)

There is a reference to the strike movement in

Look, he's winding up the watch of his wit ; by and by it will strike.   (*Temp.* II. i. 12–13)

Carcanets were hanging collars of linked ornamental design set with important jewels surrounded by smaller stones, from which often hung little pendants. Their construction is accurately suggested in *Sonnet* lii :

Like stones of worth they thinly placed are,
Or captain jewels in the carcanet.

As they were of considerable value, their use was confined to

Royalty and ladies of the Court, the less wealthy being content with simple strings of pearls or other suitable stones. Queen Elizabeth was presented with three carcanets on New Year's Day 1588, one by Sir Christopher Hatton, another by the Lord Howard, and another by the Earl of Warwick, the contemporary description of which exactly explains its composition:

A sarceonet of gold, conteyninge 15 peeces, seven sett with foure rubyes, and one small diamond in the middest, the other seven sett with nyne pearles in a peece sett in gold, having a rowe of small pearles on thupside, and pendaunts of sparks of rubyes, oppalls, and ragged pearles.

Bracelets were composed of ornamental gold links, enamelled and jewelled, rows of pearls or beads of amber (*Tam. Sh.* IV. iii. 58), coral, agates, and bugles, which were long black tubular glass beads (*Wint. Tale* IV. iii. 224); they were also made of hair (*Mid. N. D.* I. i. 33). They were always worn outside the sleeve, which came down to the wrist. Shakespeare makes several allusions to them.

Rings were worn by all classes, the poorer kinds being of silver, brass, or pewter. An ordinary gentleman's signet ring was of plain gold, deeply engraved with his arms, or his crest and initials. The most valued stone for a ring was the pointed or table-cut diamond, but all stones were used. Shylock alludes to his turquoise ring, which Jessica had taken, and which he had of Leah when he was a bachelor (*Merch. of V.* III. i. 126–30). Many of the settings were exquisitely modelled and chased in delicate Renaissance designs; classical cameos and intaglios were also much used. The celebrated Essex ring, still in existence, is composed of a very small cameo of Elizabeth's head. Memorial rings were also popular; Shakespeare in his will leaves seven bequests of twenty-six shillings and eightpence each to buy rings. He alludes to *memento mori* rings in

> A death's face in a ring;   (*Love's L. L.* v. ii. 613)

and he makes rings important factors in the plots of several plays. They were also given with other jewels as prizes in contests of skill. The King says before the fencing match in *Hamlet*:

> And in the cup an union shall he throw,
> Richer than that which four successive kings
> In Denmark's crown have worn.   (v. ii. 286–8)

A union was a large fine pearl.

Brooches and ouches were worn by men in their hats, often to clasp the feather, and by women for the same purpose, as well as to ornament the front of the dress and stomacher. Falstaff uses the two terms in conjunction, ' Your brooches, pearls, and ouches ' (*2 Hen. IV*, II. iv. 52).

Ear-rings were not worn by women early in Elizabeth's reign because the ear at that time was concealed by the head-dress. Harrison, writing in 1587, says : ' Some lustie courtiers also and gentlemen of courage doo weare either rings of gold, stones, or pearle in their eares.' There is no mention of the word ' ear-ring ' by Shakespeare, but he alludes to them :

I would my daughter were dead at my foot, and the jewels in her ear ! (*Merch. of V*. III. i. 94–6)

Elizabeth, in her later portraits, and Anne of Denmark are generally represented as wearing long pear-shaped pearl ear-rings.

Jewelled sprigs of gold, hair-pins, and bodkins with most elaborate tops with falling jewels, were much used for decorating the hair, and a woman fashionably dressed for any important entertainment was besprinkled with stones, chains, and jewels, from the crown of her head to her girdle. Women of the middle class, who strove to emulate the manner of dressing of their richer sisters, had recourse to the counterfeit representations which were so abundant and so remarkable that they are said to have deceived even those accustomed to handle the finest specimens of goldsmith's work.

BIBLIOGRAPHY.—The important Isham Collection of clothes of this period is described at the beginning of this chapter. Much information is to be gathered as to details of fashion and changes in costume from the works of Stow, Harrison, and Stubbes, and from the dramatic, satirical, and other literature of the period (see the Bibliography to Chapter I). Wills, inventories, and household books are invaluable for records of expenditure on clothing ; see also NICHOLS's *The Progresses and Public Processions of Queen Elizabeth*, 3 vols., 1805 and 1823, and FEUILLERAT's *Documents relating to the Office of the Revels in the time of Queen Elizabeth*, 1908. Foreigners' accounts of English costume can be read in ESTIENNE PERLIN's *Description des Royaulmes d'Angleterre et d'Escosse*, 1558, and in W. B. RYE's *England as seen by Foreigners*, 1865. There are no books dealing in detail with the costume of our period, but the following may be consulted for a general view : JOSEPH STRUTT's *A Complete View of the Dress and Habits of the People of England*, 2 vols., 1796, 1799 ; new ed. by Planché, 1842 ; Planché's and Fairholt's works ; HUBERT HALL's *Society in the Elizabethan Age*, 3rd ed., 1888 ; and, for jewellery, H. CLIFFORD SMITH's *Jewellery*, 1908.

XX

THE HOME : FURNITURE : FOOD AND DRINK : CHRISTENINGS, WEDDINGS, FUNERALS

BY

PERCY MACQUOID

FURNITURE AND PLATE

HOWEVER scanty the supply of furniture was at the date of Shakespeare's birth, the universal growth of luxury during the next twenty years so promoted and improved its manufacture that many innovations, hitherto unknown, were speedily introduced amongst all classes.   How this luxury developed is best described by Harrison (1577–87) :

The furniture of our houses . . . is growne in maner even to passing delicacie : and herein I doo not speake of the nobilitie and gentrie onelie, but likewise of the lowest sort in most places of our south countrie, that haue anie thing at all to take to. Certes, in noble mens houses it is not rare to see abundance of Arras, rich hangings of tapestrie, silver vessell, and so much other plate, as may furnish sundrie cupbords, to the summe oftentimes of a thousand or two thousand pounds at the least. . . . Likewise in the houses of knights, gentlemen, merchantmen, and some other wealthie citizens, it is not geson to behold generallie their great provision of tapistrie, Turkie worke, pewter, brasse, fine linen, and thereto costlie cupbords of plate, worth five or six hundred or a thousand pounds, to be deemed by estimation. But as herein all these sorts doo far exceed their elders and predecessors, and in neatnesse and curiositie, the merchant all other ; so in time past, the costlie furniture staied there, whereas now it is descended yet lower, even unto the inferiour artificers and manie farmers, who by vertue of their old and not of their new leases have for the most part learned also to garnish their cupbords with plate, their ioined beds with tapistrie and silke hangings, and their tables with carpets & fine naperie.

He goes on to say that notwithstanding the great rise in prices, the community is able to buy and manufacture such furniture as up to that time ' hath beene unpossible '. He also states that three things connected with domestic

comfort are 'marvellouslie altred' in his time: one, the
increase of chimneys, which had been hitherto confined
to the religious and rich houses ; the second being the
great improvement in beds and bedding amongst country
folk, who had till then been content to lie on straw pallets
with a sack of chaff for a pillow. 'As for servants', he
goes on to say,

if they had anie sheet above them, it was well, for seldome had they
anie under their bodies, to keepe them from the pricking straws that
ran oft through the canvas of the pallet, and rased their hardened
hides.

The third is the change among the artisan and farming
classes of their 'treene [1] platters into pewter, and woodden
spoones into silver or tin'. We have a record only ten years
earlier than this of the poor quality and state of the furniture
even in the royal palace of Sheen in a letter written by
Lord Buckhurst in 1568 :

Two daies before the Cardinals arivall, I spake with Her M. officers
with whome I had conferens for the better accomodating of the
Cardinal. I brought them in to everie part of the hous that I possessed,
and shewed them all such stuf and furniture as I had. And where
they required plate of me, I told them that I had no plate at all.
Such glasse vessell as I had I offred them which they thought to
base. The table whereon I dine me self I offred them ; and for
that yt was but a square table they refused yt. One onelie tester
and bedsted not occupied I had, and thos I delivered for the Cardinall
himself ; and when we cold not by any menes in so shorte a time
procure another bedsted for the bishop, I assighned them the
bedsted on which my wiefes waiting women did lie, and laid them on
the ground. Mine own basin and ewer I lent to the Cardinall and
wanted me self.

Even the Queen, when she left one palace for another, moved
her surroundings with the court, and was accompanied by
some four to six hundred two-wheeled carts, each drawn
by six horses and laden with trunks.

The lower and middle classes were content with the
rough and scanty furniture inherited from their predecessors or with pieces of coarse gothic discarded by fashionable householders. A typical inventory of the year 1592
from the house of Henry Field, a tanner, friend and
neighbour of John Shakespeare, shows the furniture
possessed by a tradesman in a small country town [2] at

---

[1] Made of 'tree', i. e. wooden.
[2] See Sir Sidney Lee's *Stratford-on-Avon*.

the time when the changes mentioned by Harrison were
in progress.   In the hall of this house, which evidently
served as a kitchen and room for meals, there was one
table upon a joined frame, five small joint-stools, a small
chair, a wainscot bench, and painted cloths.   The table
would have been on a frame, morticed or joined on bulbous
legs uncarved.   The term 'joined' distinguished them from
the trestle form, which could be taken to pieces and was
used up to the middle of the century.   Capulet alludes to
this trestle shape when he cries 'turn the tables up'
(*Rom. & Jul.* I. v. 31), for, when the pegs holding the
stretchers to the trestles were withdrawn, the top could
be lifted from its slots and the whole piece stacked against
a wall to make more room.   The joined or joint-stools of
the last half of the sixteenth century resembled tables in
miniature and were used at meals both by rich and poor ;
in a large hall, they were packed when not in use, with
the legs turned inwards under the tables, resting on the
stretchers.

The joint-stool, being the piece of furniture most commonly encountered, inevitably lent itself to jocular reference.   There is a pleasant allusion in *The Taming of the
Shrew*.   Petruchio tells Katherine that he is moved to woo
her.   'Mov'd !' she exclaims,

> in good time : let him that mov'd you hither
Remove you hence. I knew you at the first,
You were a moveable.
>
> *Pet.*   Why, what's a moveable ?
> *Kath.*   A joint-stool.
> *Pet.*   Thou hast hit it ; come, sit on me.   (II. i. 196–9)

The Fool in *King Lear* makes use of the old proverb, ' Cry
you mercy, I took you for a joint-stool' (III. vi. 55).

Chairs were so scarce even in important houses that the
master and mistress of the house or the principal guests
were alone entitled to sit upon these rare commodities at
the high table.   The 'small chair' of the inventory must
have been a plain panel-backed oak armchair without
carving.   The 'wainscote bench' is interesting as iden-
tifying the settle with Elizabethan times ; an allusion is
made to it in 'and sleeping upon benches after noon'
(*1 Hen. IV*, I. ii. 4).   Such a seat was formed of a long chest,
with a panelled back about three feet high, finishing at

both ends with arms. They were placed facing the fire in winter and with their backs to the fire in summer. A couple of settles or benches usually stood near the great fire-place. The box of the settle often contained guards of wicker-work, which were used to protect the stockinged legs from being scorched. What comfort there was was supplied by loose cushions, since no stuffing was upholstered to the woodwork before the early part of the seventeenth century.

In the parlour of the same house was a small table upon a frame, two joint-stools, two chairs, a press, a joined bed and a small plank, also three painted cloths, one feather bed, one flock bed, two bolsters, one pillow, one bed covering of yellow and green, four old blankets, one old carpet, and two chests containing articles of linen. The chairs were probably of the kind known as ' turned chairs ' made of beech wood. The joined bed stood about four feet high at the back. It was generally carved and ended in short knopped posts of about three feet in height at the footrail, and was the ordinary type of bed for middle-class people. In another room, mention is made of a truckle bed,[1] a little round table, and two old chests. In two other rooms there were more beds, coffers, and a ' press of boards with shelves '; the last was a cupboard of plain wainscot for clothes, which were also kept in the coffers. The bedding appears to have provided the only item of comfort in this house. The possession of feather beds and bedding was by 1590 considered necessary by all decent folk. The old carpet mentioned was probably of cloth or felt, and used for the table, not for the floor.

The furniture of cottages must have been of the roughest description ; there does not seem to be any authentic record that it was distinctive ; a common labourer's wages in 1593 being about £7 a year, there was but little margin for its purchase. A plain unpanelled chest no doubt fulfilled many purposes, and Shakespeare alludes more than once to three-legged stools,[2] always in poor surroundings. It can be gathered from inventories that the labouring class used wooden trenchers and bowls for eating and drinking, and often possessed pewter candlesticks and

[1] See p. 126 below.
[2] *Mid. N. D.* ii. i. 52 ; *Cymb.* iii. iii. 89.

spoons, flock mattresses, and canvas sheets for their beds, and sometimes an old feather bed.

In an Elizabethan mansion, the hall, where the meals took place, was furnished with an upper table capable of extension, known as a draw-top table, at which the family sat, chairs being set for the master and mistress of the house and stools for the younger members of the household and ordinary guests; along the sides of the hall were ranged plain long tables and forms for the servants and poorer dependents. When guests could not find room at the high table, the upper ends of the side tables were used for their accommodation, a salt being placed where the distinction of class commenced. There is an allusion to this in *Coriolanus*:

As if he were son and heir to Mars; set at upper end o' the table.
(IV. v. 204-5)

Dekker in the *Honest Whore* (1604) also mentions this distinction of place as follows:

Plague him, set him beneath the salt; and let him not touch a bit, till every one has had his full cut.

In an inventory of the goods of one Peter Fratevile of Stavely, taken in 1581, there is the item:

In the Hall one longe table, ii long fourems x shillings.

At the ends of the room stood court-cupboards on which the silver plate was arranged, and these were also the receptacles for wine, fruit, cordials, spoons, and table linen. The only allusion to these by Shakespeare is in

Away with the joint-stools, remove the court-cupboard, look to the plate. (*Rom. & Jul.* I. v. 7-8)

Great numbers of these court-cupboards were made, some plain, some richly carved and inlaid, for they were used by all householders; the term 'court-cupboard' distinguished them from the smaller livery cupboards containing the livery allowances of the servants, which were generally made to hang on the wall, and had large perforations in the doors for ventilation.

The stone floor was strewn with rushes, which were allowed to accumulate until they became offensive. In the household accounts of Lord North at Kertlinge, 1578, 15s. a load is quoted for rushes, equivalent to about £6 of our money. These may perhaps have come from some distance so that carriage added to their cost, but the continual supply required must have been expensive.

The hall was lighted by candles in wooden or iron coronas suspended from the ceiling, which had superseded the earlier torch-lights fixed in iron brackets on the walls. Dipped candles, with rushes for wicks, were generally made in the homes by each family from fat accumulated in the kitchens; they were therefore dark in colour. Better candles of wax or white tallow with cotton wicks were purchased from candlemakers or made by journeymen who travelled from house to house working at the rate of 4½d. a day. In 1602, 12lb. of white candles cost 4s. in London. Candles were also used on the tables, but existing specimens of English domestic candlesticks before 1600 are extremely rare. They are short and baluster-shaped, with a double spreading round base. They were made of latten, pewter, or silver.

Buffets about 4 feet in height, consisting of two shelves with drawers separated by bulbous supports, were an innovation of about 1580 and probably stood in the wainscoted parlour, a room that was often used for meals when privacy was required. They were essentially a piece of furniture for a sitting-room, and are usually of inlaid walnut or oak of fine quality. The chairs in such a room would have been panel-backed and carved, with plain arms and baluster legs. A small draw-table, when not in use for meals, would have been covered with a Persian or needlework carpet, and the floor with mats. Mats were made of broad-leaved rushes coarsely plaited, and were known as Bedfordshire mats, costing in 1576 5d. a yard. The window curtains were probably of cloth, with embroidered borders and valances.

The best furniture in an important Elizabethan house was placed in the long gallery, used as a withdrawing-room and ball-room. Along the elaborate wainscot were ranged buffets and cabinets of English or foreign workmanship, and these were more often made of walnut, rosewood, or ebony mounted in silver, than of oak. Window seats, chests, stools, and cushions on the floor formed the principal seats, for even here there would have been no great supply of chairs.

Decorative buffets with doors formed a sort of cabinet against the wall for the display of such rare pieces of

AN ELIZABETHAN INLAID BUFFET

majolica, china, bronzes, and other curios as had found their way to this country ; they were sometimes elaborately inlaid with checker-work marquetry of light woods and ebony, and they represent the highest quality of English furniture about 1585.

Other smaller cabinets on stands, often of exquisite workmanship, full of secret drawers, evidently stood out in the rooms, as they are decorated on all sides ; they often have a slide inlaid with figures of writing implements, clearly denoting their purpose. There is a fine specimen in the Victoria and Albert Museum, the cabinet of foreign make resting on an English stand inlaid with Tudor emblems. The perfect execution of this piece makes one realize the good taste and brilliant colouring of the furniture and decorations of an Elizabethan mansion. It must be remembered that the panelling of these houses, being of new oak, was not dark as it is to-day, that the stiles and rails were frequently painted a rich red, and the panels decorated with designs in green or other colours ; that the tapestries, being fresh from the loom, were bright and full of gorgeous harmonious tones, and these with the costumes, stained glass, needlework, and silk hangings formed a fine combination of decorative colour ; cabinets and tables inlaid with ivory, silver, tortoise-shell, precious stones, and coloured woods helped to complete this vivid effect. Ornamental tables of this kind still remain *in situ* at Hardwicke, though the brilliancy of their inlay has faded like the tapestry.

Such luxuries as day-beds were probably introduced towards the end of the sixteenth century, for before this time our ancestors could not loll in their stiffly-constructed uncomfortable oak chairs and settles. The earliest known existing example of a day-bed is in the gallery at Hardwicke. It is of oak, with two panelled ends raking outwards ; it is painted chocolate red, with floral arabesques, and the arms of Talbot and Cavendish. It is 7 ft. 3 in. long, with a long, loose mattress covered in red damask embroidered in coloured silks and gold. Day-beds are twice alluded to by Shakespeare :

> He is not lolling on a lewd day-bed.
>
> > (*Rich. III*, III. vii. 71)

> Having come from a day-bed, where I have left Olivia sleeping.
>
> > (*Tw. N.* II. v. 55–6)

The furniture of the great chamber or bedroom was an elaborate affair, the hangings of the bed, walls, and windows often costing a very large sum. The oak or walnut bedsteads, finely carved and inlaid, consisted of a panelled head and corniced tester, supported on two posts at the foot. Occasionally the posts stood on plinths separate from the frame. The bedding, which was carried on a wide criss-cross of ropes, was a pallet of straw or wool underneath two or more feather beds ; over the sheets and blankets lay another thin feather bed as a coverlid, with an embroidered quilt; curtains of needlework, tester valances, lower valances called basses, consisting of fine silks interwoven with gold and trimmed with most elaborate fringes, completed a structure that often cost considerably over £1,000 of our money. Some Elizabethan fringes for repairing the hangings of these beds have been reproduced in modern times, and have cost over £5 a yard.

The so-called ' Great Bed of Ware ', measuring 11 feet square, now at the Rye House in Hertfordshire, is an interesting example of this period ; it is referred to by Sir Toby :

> Although the sheet were big enough for the bed of Ware in England.
>
> (*Tw. N.* III. ii. 52–4)

All important beds, small or large, were made more or less on these lines until the beginning of the seventeenth century, when in fashionable households the carved oak posts, tester, and back, were discarded, and the structure was hung with embroidered silk, linen, velvet, cloth, or other material. The bed at Knole, prepared for James I and hung entirely with embroidered cloth-of-gold, cost the Earl of Dorset £8,000 in money of that time. Small truckle-beds or trundle-beds were placed at the foot of these standing beds for the accommodation of the personal servant at night; they were very low frames on small wheels, so that they could be ' truckled '[1] or ' trundled ' under another bedstead in the day-time. They are mentioned in *The Merry Wives of Windsor* (IV. v. 7), *Romeo and Juliet* (II. i. 39), and by Joseph Hall in the following lines :

> First that he lie upon the Truckle-bed,
> Whiles his yong maister lieth on his hed.

[1] A truckle is a small roller, wheel, or castor.

The curtains round standing beds were carefully drawn and often pinned at night ; draughty leaded glass, and ill-fitting doors, doubtless made these stuffy precautions necessary. Bequests of beds are very numerous ; there is the well-known legacy to his wife in Shakespeare's will ' of his second best bed ', and evidently unimportant standing beds were considered valuable, as Francis Fitton, in Cheshire, 1608, leaves to his niece, Lady Anne Newdigate,

my bedd of downe etc. in my bed chamber at London with a canopy of yellow double taffaty and a yellow silke quilte.

The decorations of an important bedchamber in Shakespeare's time is best described in his own words :

It was hang'd
With tapestry of silk and silver ; the story
Proud Cleopatra, when she met her Roman,
. . . a piece of work
So bravely done, so rich, that it did strive
In workmanship and value ; . . . and the chimney-piece
Chaste Dian bathing ; never saw I figures
So likely to report themselves. . . .
. . . The roof o' the chamber
With golden cherubins is fretted ; her andirons . . .
. . . were two winking Cupids
Of silver.   (*Cymb*. II. iv. 68–90)

Rushes were evidently strewn even in such a bedroom, for Iachimo, speaking of the same chamber, says :

Our Tarquin thus
Did softly press the rushes ere he waken'd
The chastity he wounded.   (*Cymb*. II. ii. 12–14)

There were no chests-of-drawers, few washing-tables, and, except in large houses, no regular dressing-tables. The top of a chest, furnished with cushions, served as a couch, and often as an extra bed, and a taller chest held the silver or brass ewer, basin, and other articles of toilet. These were, however, sometimes placed on a shelf affixed to the wainscot.

Chests or coffers were composed of three or more panels, either plain or painted, and often beautifully carved and inlaid with coloured woods. Clothes of all kinds, as well as napery, were kept in these. Inside all of them was a little hanging covered box supposed to have been made originally to hold candles—the old remedy against moth—

but certainly used as well for money, trinkets, and the smaller details connected with dress. The linen stored in the coffers of the poorer classes was homespun, but better qualities were imported from the Netherlands. Important houses certainly possessed more chests than chairs. The other furniture of a fine bedroom comprised a hanging cupboard, carved or inlaid with marquetry, two or more carved chests, a small table for the little standing looking-glass, which by the end of the sixteenth century had begun to make its appearance, and silver boxes and jars for the many essences, cosmetics, and paints used by an Elizabethan lady of fashion. Wall mirrors were exceedingly scarce and small. In the royal palace they were evidently not encouraged by the Queen, for, in the account of her death, we read that :

In the me ancholy of her sicknes, she desired to see a true looking glass, which in twenty years she had not sene, but only such a one as was made of purpose to deceive her sight ; which glasse being brought her, she fell presently into exclayming against these which had so much commended her.

When not strewn with rushes, the floors were matted, for in the ' North household accounts ' there is an entry :

Twelve score yards of matts for the great chamber £3 10s.

Eastern carpets and carpets of cloth and Turkey work were also used, but usually for covering tables and chests. At Gorhambury there is a carpet of Turkey work in perfect preservation with Elizabeth's cognizances and initials, made for and used by the Queen when making her frequent visits to Sir Francis Bacon. This Turkey work was a needlework imitation of an Eastern carpet, and was chiefly used for window seats, bed valances, and chair cushions. It was a treble cross-stitch on canvas in coloured wools, cut open to a close pile. There are constant allusions to it. In *The Comedy of Errors* IV. i. 104–5, there is mention of a desk

That 's cover'd o'er with Turkish tapestry.

As there was no such fabric made in Turkey at that date, this undoubtedly refers to a small carpet of Turkey work forming a table-cloth to the flat Elizabethan oak box-desk on legs. There has been much confusion between needlework and loom tapestry, and inventories make little discrimination between them. Weaving of tapestry was carried on in England before the sixteenth century, and there was a manufactory established, about 1509, at Barchester, in Warwickshire, by William Sheldon, but it did not assume any industrial importance till the founding of the Mortlake works three years after the death of Shakespeare. Tapestry, both figures and verdure, was imported in great quantities from Flanders throughout the sixteenth century; and the accumulation of it in this country towards the close of Elizabeth's reign was very great. The royal collection alone was enormous, and selections from it were in constant requisition for various functions. On the occasion of the royal visit to Cambridge in 1564, King's College Chapel was entirely hung with the ' Queen's Arras ', and in 1613, on the occasion of the marriage of the Princess Elizabeth to the Palgrave at Whitehall, the temporary banqueting-hall for the extra accommodation of the guests was hung with tapestry representing the fight between the English and Spanish fleets. Estienne Perlin, writing in 1558, remarks that the English make great use of tapestry and painted cloths, and that there were few houses in which some would not be found.

Painted cloths, often inventoried as ' steyned cloths ', were a form of wall hangings used as a substitute for the more costly tapestry, and chiefly represented biblical or mythological subjects, carried out in water-staining and tempera on canvas, the method being practically the same as that employed at the present day for the imitation tapestry in theatrical use. Such hangings were popular for bedrooms. Falstaff describes his men as ' ragged as Lazarus in the painted cloth ' (*I Hen. IV*, IV. ii. 27–8). Dekker advises his young gallant to sleep his bellyful regardless of the ' coarse painted cloth rhymes ', referring to the stereotyped maxims painted on scrolls issuing from the mouths of the figures. In an inventory of Sir Henry Parker's goods taken about the time of Shakespeare's birth there is an entry :

In the chamber over the kitchen. A steynid cloth over chymney, with Marie and Gabryell iiijd.

No doubt at times these painted cloths were direct copies from tapestry, but they were more often of local design after the manner of the crude pictorial ornamentations in water-staining on plaster walls, many of which are extant. In the Savoy House, Denham, there are some rooms decorated in this manner ; one being a series of scenes from *Exodus,* in which Moses and his followers are represented in the costume of about 1600, with texts on scrolls spouting from their mouths. Such pictures are referred to in the following passage :

Quick. I must be fain to pawn both my plate and the tapestry of my dining-chambers.

Fal. Glasses, glasses, is the only drinking : and for thy walls, a pretty slight drollery, or the story of the Prodigal, or the German hunting in water-work, is worth a thousand of these bed-hangings and these fly-bitten tapestries. (*2 Hen. IV,* ii. i. 157–63)

Hentzner, writing in 1598, mentions that beds were covered with tapestry, even those of farmers ; but this must have been needlework, probably a large pattern of flowers and birds worked on linen in coloured crewels, or else an imitation of some tapestry work in cross-stitch.

Towards the close of Shakespeare's life, important changes in furniture took place. The X-chair of Henry VIII, which had never wholly disappeared, again became popular,[1] the woodwork being entirely covered with velvet or silk, the back heightened, and the seat upholstered to the frame. There are several of these chairs at Knole with their X-shaped stools to match. A still more important innovation was sets of chairs without arms, with stuffed seats and backs, called farthingale chairs, the absence of arms being designed for the better accommodation of the outrageous size of women's skirts. There is a complete set of these also at Knole with couches and stools to match. Sets of furniture were not made before the early years of the seventeenth century, but chairs from this date onwards became comparatively common, and were no longer confined to the use of important members of the household. The ordinary furniture of this class was covered in cowhide studded with nails. When furniture began to be upholstered the multitude of cushions grew less ; until then they had furnished the chief element of comfort, being much used on the floor as seats. It is stated that Queen Elizabeth passed the last three days of her life resting on cushions placed on the floor.

Never at any time in the history of our silver plate has such elegance and mastery of design been displayed as during the sixteenth century, and in the three technical

---

[1] It is seen in Rogers's portrait of Queen Elizabeth reproduced in Chapter I.

points of engraving, chasing, and hammering, England could at that period hold its own with the rest of Europe. So highly was the possession of plate esteemed, that by 1585 even farmers and town folk had acquired some small articles of silver, and it is usual to find in contemporary inventories of such households mention of silver spoons and a drinking-bowl. Seal-top and apostle spoons are too well known to need description ; the type was universal, and the quality was much the same for rich and poor alike, except that those of country make were generally inferior to London hall-marked spoons.

Colleges, city companies, and similar institutions had great possessions of plate, and most of their drinking-vessels were of sterling silver. Hentzner mentions that, when a person of distinction remarked on the number of the cups at Gray's Inn and Lincoln's Inn, he was given the answer :

They were ready to make him a present of all their plate, provided he would undertake to supply them with all the glass and earthenware, they should have a demand for ; since it was very likely he would find the expense, from constant breaking, exceed the value of the silver.

Prelates and noblemen such as Archbishop Parker and Lord Burghley were famous for their taste in plate. The former made many superb gifts to various colleges, which are still preserved, and Lord Burghley, who was by no means addicted to ostentatious luxury, but merely kept up the necessary state attaching to his great position, left plate at his death in 1598 to the value of about £15,000 in money of that time. Both Lord Burghley and his son appear to have had fine and original taste in selecting plate for their Queen, and evidently went out of their way to find some novelty that might attract her, such as

one porrynger of white porselyn, garnished with golde, the cover of golde, with a lyon on the toppe therof ; geven by the Lord Threasorour all 38 oz.

or again—

one cup of grene pursselyne, the foote shanke, and cover silver guilte, chased lyke droppes. Geven by Mr. Robert Cecill, 15 oz.

Pieces of china, agate, crystal, and other stones mounted in gold or silver were considered greater rarities than silver plate, as for example—

Oone poringer of blodstone, garnished with four fete and two handles of golde, made like snakes. Geven by therle of Leycestor. 7 oz.

K 2

—also given to the Queen. The royal store of plate must have been enormous, not only embracing Plantagenet relics and the pick of the monastic treasures taken by Cromwell for Henry VIII, but also the accumulation of presents made to Elizabeth during a period of forty-five years. Out of this stock came the gifts to the various ambassadors and foreign princes who visited England. One of these was the gold enamelled standing-cup originally made for Charles V of France; it became Henry VI's property in 1450, but was given from the royal collection in 1604 by James I to Don Juan Velasco, the Spanish ambassador. It was brought back to this country and is now in the British Museum. Large standing-cups were used only at banquets and for decorative purposes. In wealthy houses these were supplemented by small standing-cups and bowls for use at table; the rich also prided themselves on the possession of cups formed of carved coco-nuts, ostrich eggs, nautilus shells, agate, and rock crystal. Shakespeare constantly mentions ordinary drinking-cups and bowls. He refers to a standing-cup in *Pericles* (II. iii. 65):

Here say we drink this standing-bowl of wine to him;

and in *Richard II* (III. iii. 147–50) to figured goblets,

I'll give my jewels for a set of beads,
My gorgeous palace for a hermitage,
My gay apparel for an almsman's gown,
My figur'd goblets for a dish of wood.

The stage directions for the christening of Princess Elizabeth in *Henry VIII* (sc. v.) include 'two noblemen, bearing great standing-bowls for the christening gifts'.

Quite as important as this form of cup and equal to it in elaboration of workmanship were the great salts marking the distinction of rank at table. These, with their covers, often stood over a foot in height. In addition to these there were highly-finished small salts such as:

a smale saulte of blewe stone, called lapus lazarus, with pillars slitly garnished with golde. Geven by the Lady Sidney;

and

a sault of golde, in the form of a globe, enameled grene, with a cover, with two personages naked, enameled white, with a lion in the toppe of the cover. Geven by the Lady Burley. 7 oz. dim.

The ordinary salt for daily use was of trencher form. Poorer members of the community used small plain cylindrical

AN EARLY ELIZABETHAN PANEL-BACKED CHAIR

salts of pewter, and drank from wooden, pewter, or horn bowls and beakers. Another very favourite form of drinking-vessel was the stoneware jug. This pottery was mostly imported from Germany; it was mounted with neckband, foot, and cover of elaborately engraved and chased silver, and was highly esteemed. This fashion came in about 1540 and lasted hardly more than a decade. As the bowl died out as a drinking-vessel, the tankard came in; but the shape remained slight until 1600; nor was the form adopted in pewter by the poorer classes until after Shakespeare's death.

The ewer and basin for use at meals gave a great opportunity for decoration; the best examples were of very elaborate workmanship. The dish centred in a raised boss enamelled with the arms of the owner, on which the base of the ewer fitted. Like all highly decorated plate of this period, they were gilt, to obviate abrasion. Pewter and brass ewers and basins were used by those who could not afford the more valuable metal. They were more or less indispensable before and after eating, since the fingers assisted the knife and spoon, forks being used in the early seventeenth century only by the ultra-fashionable or eccentric. Forks were of Italian origin,[1] long, slight, and two-pronged, of steel, with beautiful handles, and were accompanied by a knife to match, often in a highly ornamented case. They were taken by their owners with them when they dined abroad. Roasted and cold meats were offered by the carver on a broad flat knife; some of these were as much as four inches wide.

MEALS: FOOD AND DRINK: COOKING

The arrangement of meals remained much the same as during the previous reign. Grace was regularly said before meals, and to this there are many allusions by Shakespeare. Evans, the Welsh parson, says:

Od's plessed will! I will not be absence at the grace.

(M. Wives I. i. 275–6)

[1] Politique Would-bee in Jonson's *Volpone* instructs Peregrine, the gentleman traveller, how ' here in this height of Venice ' he must comport himself, and particularly,

then, must you learne the use,
And handling of your silver forke, at meales.

Forks for special purposes had been known in England since the middle of the fifteenth century; a bequest of 1463 includes a ' silver forke for grene gyngour ', and one of 1554 mentions a ' spone with a forke in the end '.

Breakfast was at 6.30. According to Harrison, it was no longer so substantial a meal as in former times, though Queen Elizabeth, in some royal accounts signed by herself, included in that meal bread, butter, beer, and wine, a stew of mutton, beef, and veal, besides rabbits and chickens.

Dinner was served from 11 to 12. Dromio of Ephesus says :

> The capon burns, the pig falls from the spit,
> The clock hath strucken twelve upon the bell.
> *(Com. of E.* i. ii. 44–5)

This was the great meal of the day, and every kind of food that we are familiar with nowadays appears to have been served, including fresh and salt-water fish, oysters, game of all kinds, vegetables and fruits. Merchants and gentlemen kept much the same table at dinner, contenting themselves with one to three dishes when alone, and having four to six when entertaining guests. There was usually a separate diet for servants.

Supper was taken about 5.30. This meal, except in special circumstances, was a modified version of dinner. Elaborate cooking with eccentric flavourings was popular among the rich, and with the universal increase of prosperity, extravagance in food became general. This is shown by the high prices given for luxuries, and the enormous quantity of meat consumed in a household. One of Hentzner's first impressions of this country was that ' the English were more polite in eating, devouring less bread, but more meat, which they roast in perfection '. Shakespeare records the foreign opinion of the English liking for meat in the following dialogue :

Orl. These English are shrewdly out of beef.
Con. Then shall we find to-morrow they have only stomachs to eat and none to fight.   *(Hen. V*, III. vii. 169–72)

The diet of a well-to-do bachelor who lived in lodgings in Warwick Lane, London, for four months in 1589 shows a monotonous quantity of meat day after day, except on Fridays, when he sometimes indulged in elaborate fish dinners.

On May 11 he had for dinner :

A pece of bief	xviij*d*.
A loyne of veale	ij*s*.
2 chickens	xiiij*d*.
Orenges	ij*d*.
For dressings ye veale & chickens & sawce	xij*d*.

and for supper :

A shoulder of mutton	xvj*d*.
2 Rabbettes	x*d*.
For dressinge ye mutton, rabbettes & a pigges pettie toes	viij*d*.
Colde bief	viij*d*.
Cheese	ij*d*.

On June 20 he evidently had friends to dinner, as several delicacies are introduced :

Butter	iiij*d*.
A pece of bief	xiiij*d*.
A legg of mutton	xviij*d*.
A loyne of veale	xxij*d*.
2 pecks of Pescodes	viij*d*.
3 Rabbettes	ij*s*.
A quart of creame	vj*d*.
3 quarts of Strawberies	xvj*d*.
2 li. of cheries	xx*d*.
Di: li. of muske confectes	x*d*.
Di: li. of violett confectes	xj*d*.
Orenges	iij*d*.
2 Lemans	vj*d*.
Bred	viij*d*.
Beare	ix*d*.

One of the Friday dinners, on May 2, is interesting :

A side of hab[er]dyn & another of grene fishe	xiiij*d*.
Foure playses	xij*d*.
ij whitinges	viij*d*.
Conger	viij*d*.
Butter	iiij*d*.
Lettise for sallett	ij*d*.
A pynt of white wyne & another of clarett	vj*d*.
Suger	ij*d*.
A pound of butter	v*d*.
For dressinge the fishe	viij*d*.
Oyle & suger for sallett	ij*d*.
More for butter	ij*d*.
A pounde of candles	iiij*d*.

He appears to have been a moderate drinker, contenting himself with an occasional pint of claret, Rhenish, or beer for dinner.

On May 23 he has among other things ' a pynt of Straw-beries, xij*d*.'—a very early date, even in old style, for this fruit, if grown without protection. On May 29 he gets three pints of strawberries for the same price.

Beef, mutton, and veal were the staple meats. Moryson wrote that

England abounds in Cattell of all kinds, and particularly hath very great Oxen, the flesh whereof is so tender, as no meate is more desired. . . . The flesh of Hogges and Swine is more savoury then in any other parts, excepting the bacon of Westphalia.

He adds that the people eat fish, oysters, wild-fowl, conies, hens, geese, fallow deer in pasties, and a variety of white-meats ; that hares though eaten are thought to nourish melancholy ; and that

English Husbandmen eate Barley and Rye browne bread, and preferre it to white bread as abiding longer in the stomack, and not so soon disgested with their labour.

In 1589 beef cost three farthings a pound, a leg of mutton 1*s*. 6*d*., a neck of mutton 6*d*., sugar 20*s*. a pound, pepper 4*s*. a pound, salt [1] 3 bushells for 6*d*.

The givers of private feasts and banquets strove to outvie each other in lavish display. Unnecessarily large quantities of food of every description, often with eccentric flavourings to the sauces, such as musk, saffron, and ambergris (the last costing 6*s*. a pound), were a common feature. Beer and ale were drunk at these feasts, and wines in great variety, such as sack, alicant, claret, musca-dine, Rhenish, and charneco ; the last, a kind of port, is mentioned once by Shakespeare (*2 Hen. VI*, II. iii. 63). Sack was the generic name for Spanish and Canary wines, and was popular with all classes. Shakespeare gives its correct price in Falstaff's tavern bill :

> Item, Sack, two gallons 5*s*. 8*d*.
>
> (*1 Hen. IV*, II. iv. 595)

---

[1] Salt was used for many purposes. In the Churchwarden accounts of St. Margaret's, Westminster, 1610, there is this entry :

Paid to goodwyfe Wells, for salt to destroy the fleas in the Churchwardens pew 6*d*.

Bastard was another wine of common quality sold in taverns :

> Why then, your brown bastard is your only drink.
>
> *(1 Hen. IV*, II. iv. 83–4)

Cider or pommage was made and drunk in the west country. Sugar, spices, and even ambergris were added to sack and other wines.

All manner of sweets, cakes, and comfits—' sugar meats ', as they were generically called—were in great demand. Among the most popular cakes were gingerbread, Naples biscuits, sold at 2s. 6d. a pound by a London confectioner, and marchpane. The last was made of pounded almonds, pistachio nuts, sugar, and flour, with various essences, highly ornamented and sometimes gilt.

> Save me a piece of marchpane   *(Rom. & Jul.* I. v. 9)

is a request of a servant after a banquet. Sugarplate, a dainty kind of sweetmeat, was made by taking ' gum dragon ' and laying it in rose-water for two days, after which powder of sugar was added, with the juice of an orange, beaten into a paste and moulded. A favourite sugary dish was sugar sops, which consisted of steeped slices of bread, sweetened and spiced. Eringo, the candied root of sea-holly, was another sweetmeat ; it is coupled with kissing-comfits, which were perfumed for sweetening the breath (*M. Wives* v. v. 22).

On great occasions sweets were modelled in sugar to represent animals or mythological events ; and even fortifications in pastry were a fashionable device during the reigns of Elizabeth and James. Dekker says :

> Custards stood like the sinful suburbs of cookery, and had not a wall so much as a handful high, built round about them.

Fruit was highly appreciated and much cultivated. Fynes Moryson mentions that England yielded at that time apples, pears, cherries, and plums, and that apricots, musk-melons, and figs ripened well in some places. Grapes were grown in the south and west ; early in the century wine was made from these, though with little success, and was discarded in favour of French wines. Cherries were grown chiefly in Kent ; in 1589 they fetched 3d. a pound and pears 1s. a peck. Imported oranges in December 1591 were sold at seven for 2d. These were

also grown in this country about 1590, under removable
protection, by Sir Francis Carew and others. Beatrice
says, punning on the word ' Seville ' :

Civil as an orange, and something of that jealous complexion ;
                                        (*Much Ado* II. i. 306–8)

and the following speech shows that they were then, as
now, sold by women in the streets :

You wear out a good wholesome forenoon in hearing a cause
between an orange-wife and a fosset-seller.   (*Cor.* II. i. 78–80)

Plums, cherries, gooseberries, and other fruits are mentioned by Shakespeare. Titania commands a varied
fruit diet :

> Feed him with apricocks and dewberries,
> With purple grapes, green figs, and mulberries.

                                        (*Mid. N. D.* III. i. 173–4)

Of vegetables, cabbages and beans were plentiful,
carrots and radishes cost 2*d.* a bunch, and a cucumber 2*d.*,
onions 2*d.* a rope, olives 1*s.* a pint ; and Harrison says
that ' the English eat dangerous fruits, like mushrooms '.
Shakespeare mentions salads, green peas, and potatoes.
By the last must be understood the yam or sweet potato
introduced by Sir John Hawkins. Aphrodisiac properties
were attributed to them, and these are referred to in
Troilus and Cressida (V. ii. 54), and in the following :

Let the sky rain potatoes ; . . . hail kissing-comfits and snow
eringoes. (*M. Wives* V. v. 20–23)

Gerarde declares that

the roots being roasted in the embers do loose much of their windi-
ness especially being eaten sopped in wine.

The other potatoes[1] (called ' Virginian ' at the time) were
considered a great luxury and mentioned, among the
articles provided for Anne of Denmark's table, as costing
2*s.* the pound. Artichokes were a favourite vegetable.
Lord Burghley, writing to his son in 1598, says that he
cannot recover his appetite ' and supped yesternight on
4 or 5 leaves of an artichok ' ; and Lady Shuttleworth had
them sent to her as a present in her last illness in 1592.
Their cost was about 10*d.* for eight.

The cooking of food took place at an open fire ; it was
roasted on spits or seethed and stewed in large pots hanging
from the series of rods and chains forming part of the

[1] See Chapter XII, vol. i, pp. 353 and 374.

tall andirons. The tops of these were constructed like brazier baskets that could be filled with hot fuel to cook sauces and the like. All ovens were of brick, some of them of immense size, and in kitchens of importance a double fire-place was usual, to accommodate all the meats to be roasted. The spits were sometimes turned by dogs, but more generally by lads, or even by vagrants who travelled from house to house for this purpose. In the accounts of St. Bartholomew's Hospital, Sandwich, there is in the entry for entertaining the Mayor on St. Bartholomew's Day, 1569, an item ' for turnynge the spytte iiii*d*.' The turnspit was the lowest menial in the kitchen. And so Benedict says of Beatrice :

She would have made Hercules have turned spit, yea, and have cleft his club to make the fire too. (*Much Ado* II. i. 262–4)

The wages of a cook in a gentleman's house early in James I's reign were £3 6s. 8d. a year. Extra cooks were evidently hired for entertainments, as Capulet says :

So many guests invite as here are writ.
Sirrah, go hire me twenty cunning cooks.
(*Rom. & Jul.* IV. ii. 1–2)

There were numerous servants under the cooks, as boy scullions and kitchen wenches. A kitchen wench is vividly described and at great length in *The Comedy of Errors* (III. ii. 97–144), and more briefly in *Coriolanus* (II. i. 227–8) :

the kitchen malkin pins
Her richest lockram 'bout her reechy neck.

In most gentlemen's houses, in addition to those in the kitchen, there were three superior house servants, serving men who waited at table, and three or four females for upstairs work. The aggregate wages of four female servants (including a housekeeper) in Mr. Shuttleworth's bachelor establishment at Gawthorpe in 1605 amounted to only 17s. 6d. a quarter. These servants, however, no doubt had their clothes provided, as there are many entries in the accounts for material for wenches' dresses, shoes, and aprons.

A butler's chief duty was to attend to the wants of the high table at meals, and to fill the silver cups and bowls or glasses. The use of glasses rapidly became fashionable, the rich preferring them to cups, of which they possessed a superfluity. They were chiefly of the Venetian style. Stow states that their manufacture began at The Crutched Friars by an Italian, Jacob Venaline, in the first years of Elizabeth's reign. In the next century they became cheaper. In December 1608 two Venice glasses were bought for 2s. Glasses used in ordinary households do not appear to have been expensive :

> October 1600, six drinking glasses 9d.
> May 1602, four ditto 7d.
> April 1610, a glass for the cook's use 1d.

Harrison wrote :

The poorest also will have glasse if they may ; but sith the Venecian is somewhat too deere for them, they content themselves with such as are made at home of ferne and burned stone.

Shakespeare speaks of them as used in taverns (*2 Hen. IV*, II. i. 159), and in *The Taming of the Shrew* the hostess of an alehouse says :

You will not pay for the glasses you have burst ? (Ind. I. 7–8)

After dinner in summer the afternoon was devoted to various sports, the more elderly retiring to an arbour in the garden, to eat fruit or to smoke and watch the various games. Of Lord Burghley it was written that his greatest disport was riding in his garden

upon his little muile, he seldom or never plaied at anie game, for he cold plaie at none, he wold sometymes looke a while on shooters or bowlers as he rid.

Ladies wasted no time in playing outdoor games, though some of the more energetic hunted and hawked. Apart from ordinary domestic duties, in which they took part not only by personal superintendence, but in practical hard work, they devoted much time to embroidery and needlework, and this was of a quality generally acknowledged at the time to be as good as any in Europe, an opinion which the existing examples of curtains, carpets, quilts, and cushions, &c., amply substantiate. A certain amount of time must also have been spent by both sexes in writing. It is interesting to note that ink was often homemade ; a house recipe for making it in 1599 consisted of 2 oz. of gum, 2 oz. of copperas, and 4 oz. of galls, costing 8d. In 1585 half a ream of paper and half a pound of sealing wax cost 2s. Sir Toby says :

Let there be gall enough in thy ink.   (*Tw. N.* III. ii. 54–5)

Tobacco was introduced into England in 1565. Under the year 1573 Harrison writes in his *Chronologie* that

In these daies, the taking-in of the smoke of the Indian herbe called Tabaco by an instrument formed like a litle ladell, wherby it passeth from the mouth into the hed and stomach, is gretlie taken up and used in England, against Rewmes and some other diseases ingendered in the longes.

Hentzner in 1598 mentions that the English are everywhere constantly smoking. The practice assumed such proportions that in 1604 James issued his celebrated *Counterblaste*. His protest must have been shared by many, for we find as late as 1616 in the will of Peter Campbell of Darly, who left his household goods to his son Roger, that the legacy was to be revoked should one of his brothers or sisters find him ' taking of tobacco '. Snuff-taking was as much in fashion as smoking. In 1589 in London, tobacco cost 5s. an ounce and pipes 6d. each. Shakespeare does not mention either smoking or tobacco.

THE TOILET

Personal cleanliness received considerable attention. There were public baths; and Hentzner describes bathing-rooms attached to the royal apartments at Windsor, one wainscoted with looking-glass. But the bath for ordinary people was a large wooden tub placed before the fire as in earlier times.

There were many varieties of sweet-scented soap in Elizabeth's time, besides those for household use, and the numerous recipes prove that much of this must have been made in the homes, although there was a soap manufactory in London as early as 1524. In accounts of 1583, we find a pound of soap for the house costing 4d., and in January 1612 two pounds of sweet soap made into balls, 9d.

Clothes at this time were frequently washed in the rivers and wells, a practice which drew forth certain sanitary regulations. At Lyme in 1608 an order was issued

that none do wash their bucks in the street stream, under a penalty of 6s. 8d.

In *The Merry Wives of Windsor* (III. iii. 162–70) there is a conversation about this buck (laundry) washing while Falstaff is concealed in the buck-basket.

It is uncertain when tooth-brushes were first used, but

care of the teeth is shown by an entry in the Shuttleworth accounts of 'halfe a yarde of cloth to rubb my Mrs. teeth ix*d.*'; and of the Rev. Dr. Bois, who was born in 1550, lived 83 years, and was renowned for his attention to hygiene, it was said that

after meat, he was careful, almost to curiosity in picking and rubbing his teeth, esteeming that a special preservative of health.

The first known occurrence of the name 'teeth-brush' (as it then was) is of the date 1651; but 'tooth-blanch' (i. e. a dentifrice), 'tooth-powder', and 'tooth-soap' are names at least as old as the sixteenth century. Toothpicks, introduced from abroad, were much in request. These when treated as trinkets were often of gold highly ornamented; many such are mentioned among the Queen's gifts. In *King John* (i. i. 189–92) the Bastard says:

> Now your traveller,
> He and his toothpick at my worship's mess,
> And when my knightly stomach is suffic'd,
> Why then I suck my teeth;

and Benedict in *Much Ado* (ii. i. 276–7):

I will fetch you a toothpicker now from the furthest inch of Asia.

The ewers and basins for washing in ordinary bedrooms were of latten or pewter, in great houses often of silver. In the household books of Lord North, 1576, the following occurs:

For the use of the Quene a rownd bason and ewer with a pot of silver weighing 57 oz. paid for the weight 5*s.* per oz. and 6*d.* per oz. for the fashion £15 10*s.*

The towels, of fine damask, were generally hung from a roller placed above the washing utensils.

CHRISTENING, MARRIAGE, AND BURIAL CUSTOMS

Even in Shakespeare's lifetime much superstition surrounded the birth and christening ceremonies of a child. In 1567 midwives took an oath not to suffer any other body's child to be set, brought, or laid before any woman delivered of a child, and not to use any kind of sorcery or incantation. In Herrick's *Hesperides* there is this further injunction to a midwife:

> Let the superstitious wife
> Neer the child's heart lay a knife;

> Point be up and haft be down,
> (While she gossips in the towne :)
> This, 'mongst other mystick Charmes,
> Keeps the sleeping Child from harmes.

The christenings of royal and noble infants were very elaborate ceremonies, the most imposing during this period being that of the Princess Mary in 1605, very minutely described by Stow. The font in this instance was silver-gilt, worked in all kinds of imagery. In 1559, at the christening of Sir Thomas Chamberlayne's son at St. Benet's Church, Paul's Wharf, the church was hung with cloth of arras ; and after the ceremony were brought wafers, comfits, and divers banqueting-dishes, and hypocras and muscadine wine to entertain the guests. This feasting was sometimes preceded by a christening sermon or address to the godparents. The fees for baptism varied according to the position of the family, and it was enjoined in 1560 that

to avoid contention, let the Curate have the value of the Chrisome, not under the value of 4d. and above as they can agree, and as the state of the parents may require.

The chrisom was a white cloth put upon the child after the ceremony. If it died within the month, this was used as a shroud for its burial and it was then called a ' chrisome child '. The Hostess says in *Henry V* (II. iii. 11–12) :

A' made a finer end and went away an it had been any christom child.

At this period the gifts generally took the form of a caudle-cup, a silver-mounted coral with bells, supposed to avert witchcraft and the evil eye, and apostle spoons. Wealthy godparents are recorded to have presented an entire set of these spoons, including the master spoon. When given singly they represented the patron saint of the month in which the child was born. When Archbishop Cranmer hesitates to be godfather to Elizabeth, King Henry says,

Come, come, my lord, you'd spare your spoons.
(*Hen. VIII*, v. iii. 166–7)

Base metal apostle spoons were made for gifts among the lower classes. Oak cradles were also given and carved with appropriate legends, those of the rich being sometimes covered with velvet trimmed with gold galon and fringes.

The extravagance in the upholstery of a state bedroom at this time for the child's mother is almost incredible.

We read in a letter written by John Chamberlaine to Mrs. Alice Carton in 1612 that

about this day sevenight, the Countess of Salisbury was brought a bed of a daughter, and lyes in very richly, for the hangings of her chamber being white satin embroidered with silver and pearl, is valued at fourteen thousand pounds.

Over fifty thousand pounds of our money seems a great expenditure for the furniture and decoration of a lying-in chamber, but it must be remembered that such events were important functions in this extravagant age, and that presents, receptions, and card parties in the room were considered necessary for the lady's recovery. This custom of visiting and making presents, usually of money, to the mother extended to all classes.

The customs and superstitions connected with marriage during the second half of the sixteenth century had altered little from those of the previous hundred years, and many of them can be traced to classical times, the Reformation having only affected the actual marriage ritual and somewhat lessened the hitherto strict legal importance of betrothal. Shakespeare shows that a form of betrothal still existed in his time, when he makes Olivia say to Sebastian :

> Now go with me and with this holy man
> Into the chantry by ; there, before him,
> And underneath that consecrated roof,
> Plight me the full assurance of your faith.
>
> (*Tw. N.* iv. iii. 23–6)

The breaking of a gold or silver coin, with the interchange of rings and small gifts, was still adhered to ; Portia and Nerissa both gave their lovers rings as a sign of betrothal, and Shakespeare gives the whole formula in *The Two Gentlemen of Verona* (ii. ii. 5–7) :

> *Jul.* Keep this remembrance for thy Julia's sake.
>
> [*Gives him a ring.*
> *Pro.* Why, then, we'll make exchange : here, take you this.
>
> [*Gives her another.*
> *Jul.* And seal the bargain with a holy kiss.

The actual wedding ring was the most important emblem of marriage. A popular form was two hands clasping a heart made of a jewel, or an enamelled hoop with small stones and a motto engraved inside. Herrick mentions these :

> What, posies, for our wedding rings ?

And Gratiano, alluding to his betrothal ring:

> About a hoop of gold, a paltry ring
> That she did give me, whose poesy was
> For all the world like cutlers' poetry
> Upon a knife, ' Love me, and leave me not.'
>
> *(Merch. of V.* v. i. 147–50)

The plain gold hoop was not introduced till Puritan times.

So-called ' rush ring marriages ' were sometimes a mock ceremony, chiefly practised by designing men in cases of seduction or as a provisional emblem of a promised future marriage. In earlier times these rings were used in the religious ceremony when an illicit connexion was made legal:

> Tib's rush for Tom's forefinger. *(All's W.* ii. ii. 25)

is an allusion to one of these customs ; and a little later D'Avenant writes in *The Rivals* (1664):

> I'll crown thee with a garland of straw, then
> And I'll marry thee with a rush ring.

Another important form of betrothal and marriage was by the gimmal, or jointed ring, which was composed of two hoops, each with its own bezel set with a stone, working on a hinge that enabled the hoops to be separated on betrothal, so that each of the affianced parties could retain one, the hoops being reunited on marriage to form the wedding ring. Sometimes these rings were made of three hoops, and then a witness to the betrothal held the third. These were constructed with a hand affixed to the side of the upper and lower hoops, closing over a heart on the centre portion.

English ladies at this time are occasionally represented in portraits as wearing their wedding rings on the thumb. In Southerne's *Maid's last Prayer* (1692) we find

> Marry him I must, and wear my wedding-ring upon my thumb.

This fashion originated from the Catholic ritual of marriage, in which the husband placed the ring on the top of the thumb of the left hand, with the words ' In the name of the Father ', then moved it to the forefinger with ' and of the Son ', then to the middle finger, adding ' and of the Holy Ghost ', finally leaving it on the fourth finger with the closing word ' Amen '.

Brides at this period probably wore white or russet with coloured favours, which were a great feature. These were made of ribbons, tied in a true-lover's knot (a form of Runic origin), and were emblematical of love, friendship, and the ties of duty between the contracting parties. They were stitched as a trimming on to the sleeves, body, and skirt, and it was customary immediately after the ceremony for the young men present to rush forward and pluck these off the bride's dress, and also remove her ribbon garters, this sometimes occurring even before she had left the altar. They were then distributed among the guests, who wore them in their hats sometimes for weeks afterwards ; the points on the bridegroom's doublet were treated in a similar fashion. The bride wore her hair down,[1] and was crowned with a garland of wheat-ears or flowers. In *The Fifteen Comforts of Marriage*, the favourite colours for brides' favours are given as blue, red, peach colour, orange, tawny, flame-colour and milk-white. Gold colour was rejected as signifying avarice ; flesh colour, lasciviousness; and popinjay green, wantonness. For garters blue or a perfect yellow were chosen to signify honour and joy. In Herrick's *Hesperides* there are these lines—

> Quickly, quickly then prepare ;
> And let the Young-men, and the Bride-maids share
> Your Garters ; and their joynts
> Encircle with the Bride-grooms Points

The bride's gloves also formed an important item of her costume, and these with some other pairs were generally presented to guests and the two bachelors who led her to church. The bridegroom was often conducted by the bridesmaids along the path strewn with flowers and rushes. In his account of the wedding of John Winchcombe, the wealthy clothier of Newbury, Thomas Deloney says :

The bride being attired in a gown of sheeps russet, and a kirtle of fine worsted, her head attired with a billiment of gold, and her hair as yellow as gold hanging down behind her, which was curiously combed and pleated, according to the manner in those days : she was led to church between two sweet boys, with bride-laces and rosemary tied about their silken sleeves. . . . Then was there a fair bride-cup of silver and gilt carried before her, wherein was a goodly branch of rosemary, gilded very fair, hung about with silken ribands of all colours : next was there a noise of musicians, that played all the

---

[1] A custom alluded to by Shakespeare in ' a new untrimmed bride ' (*John* III. i. 209).

way before her : after her came all the chiefest maidens of the country, some bearing great bride-cakes, and some garlands of wheat, finely gilded, and so she passed to the Church.

This description, though written of a marriage of an earlier date, may be taken to represent what took place at a country marriage during the latter half of the sixteenth century. Rosemary was emblematical of manly qualities, and on the morning of the marriage the bridegroom was presented with a bunch tied up with ribbons, which he wore throughout the ceremony. The nurse infers its signifi-cance when she says :

> Doth not rosemary and Romeo begin both with a letter ?
>
> *(Rom. & Jul.* II. iv. 221–2)

At the conclusion of the service a cup of muscadel with cakes or sops in it was drunk by the bride, the bridegroom, and the company. Gremio, describing Petruchio's wild wedding, says that the bridegroom

> quaff'd off the muscadel,
> And threw the sops all in the sexton's face ; . . .
> This done, he took the bride about the neck,
> And kiss'd her lips with such a clamorous smack
> That at the parting all the church did echo.
>
> *(Tam. Sh.* III. ii. 175–82)

The cup used was often a mazer bowl kept for the purpose. Such cups still exist in some churches. An inventory of goods belonging to Wilsdon Church in the sixteenth century contains this entry :

Two masers to remayne in the church for to drynk at Brideales.

The entrance to the house was strewn and decorated with flowers for the return of the bridal party. Armin's comedy *The History of the Two Maids of More-clacke* (1609) opens in the following manner :

> *Enter a maide strewing flowers, and a serving man perfuming the doore.*
>
> *Maide.* Strow, strow.
> *Man.* The Muskadine stayes for the bride at Church,
> The Priest and himens cerimonies tend
> To make them man and wife.
> *Maid.* By my maiden-head, a Joyfull time, ile pave their way
> With flowers.
> *Man.* While I perfume.

The feasting and festivities that followed sometimes lasted for a fortnight. Stow's *Survey* has an account of the wedding of a daughter of Mr. Nicholls, the bridge-master, which took place in London in July 1562 :

At the celebration whereof were present, my Lord Mayor, and all the Aldermen with many Ladies etc. and Mr. Becon, an eminent Divine preached a Wedding sermon. Then all the Company went home to the Bridge House to dinner : where was as good cheer as ever was known, with all manner of Musick, and Dancing all the remainder of the day ; and at night a goodly Supper ; and then followed a Masque till midnight. The next day the wedding was kept at the Bridge House with great cheer ; and after Supper came in Masquers. One was in cloth of gold.

A great wedding, with most important results to England, which took place in the latter part of Shakespeare's life, was that of the Princess Elizabeth to Frederick, Count Palatine. The whole ceremony is described by Stow, who begins his account of the bride thus :

She was attired all in white, having her hair hanging down at length in faire and seemely tresses.

Marriages appear to have taken place by preference in April and November ; May was a month to be avoided. There is an entry in the Shuttleworth accounts which shows that a marriage licence in 1586 cost 11s. 3d. When a marriage of the lower classes took place, a basin was put in the church on a table to receive the presents of the invited guests, and ale was drunk at the conclusion of the cere-mony instead of muscadel. Harrison records the expendi-ture of food at poorer weddings in these words :

In feasting the husbandmen doo exceed after their manner : especiallie at bridales, purifications of women and such od meetings, where it is incredible to tell what meat is consumed and spent ech one bringing such a dish, or so manie, as his wife and he doo consult upon.

The term 'bridale' was derived from the circumstance of a bride of this class selling ale on her wedding day, for which she received whatever price the friends assembled chose to pay her for it.

Funerals during Elizabeth's reign were also conducted with many of the traditional ceremonies and rites of pre-Reformation times, the passing-bell being one of these. The custom is mentioned in *Venus and Adonis* (701-2) :

And now his grief may be compared well
To one sore sick that hears the passing-bell.

AN EARLY JACOBEAN DINING TABLE

Immediately after a death had taken place in a well-to-do house, the chief rooms and staircase were draped in black cloth and a black mourning bed was introduced for the surviving head of the family, who occupied it for a stated time and there received the visits of condolence. These beds were common property in a family and lent round as occasion required, with the black velvet window-curtains and carpets thereto belonging. Guilds and colleges and similar institutions possessed highly ornamental palls, which they lent for the funerals of their members. One of early sixteenth-century date, still existing at the Fish-mongers' Hall, was used in this manner till Georgian times. It is of dark purple velvet and cloth of gold. The hearse or canopy was carried over the coffin, or, when a horse litter was employed, was fixed to this. When the Lady Anne meets the funeral procession of Henry VI she says:

> set down your honourable load,
> If honour may be shrouded in a hearse. (*Rich. III*, i. ii. 1–2)

Here the word ' hearse ' is not used in its proper and original sense, but, as always in Shakespeare, for a coffin on a bier.

It was customary for the mourners to carry small branches of bay, rosemary, or other evergreens as emblems of the soul's immortality, which they threw into the grave. These mourners were frequently poor people and were paid for their services. In 1575 Sir Thomas Gresham directed in his will that black gowns, of cloth at 6s. 8d. the yard, were to be given to a hundred poor men and a hundred poor women to bring him to his grave; and at Sir Christopher Hatton's funeral in 1592 the bier was preceded by one hundred poor people whose gowns and caps were given them, and was followed by more than 300 gentlemen and yeomen in ' gownes, cloakes, and coates ', &c. Richard says in *3 Henry VI* (ii. i. 160–1):

> Shall we go throw away our coats of steel,
> And wrap our bodies in black mourning gowns ?

The funerals of noblemen were often very costly, Sir Thomas Gresham's costing £800. They were also some-times conducted at night and, on occasion, by river. The infant Princess Sophia, who was born in 1607 and only lived for a day, was, according to Stow, very solemnly conveyed from Greenwich by Barge, covered with blacke velvet, accompanied with three other Barges, covered with blacke cloath into the Chappell Royall in Westminster.

It was not uncommon for English people of importance who died abroad to leave directions for their hearts to be sent back to England for interment. In July 1586 in Denham Church

the harte of Sir Robert Peckham, Knight, was buried in the vault under the chappell.

He had died abroad in 1569. Edward Lord Windsor of Bradenham, who died at Spa in 1574, bequeathed his body to be buried in the

Cathedral Church of the noble city of Liege, with a convenient tomb to his memory, but his heart to be enclosed in lead, and sent into England, there to be buried in the Chapel at Bradenham under his father's tomb in token of a true Englishman.

When a man of good family was buried in a church it was usual to hang his casque, sword, and coat armour in its tinctures over his tomb, special funeral armour often being made for the purpose. Laertes speaks of

> his obscure burial,
> No trophy, sword, nor hatchment o'er his bones.
> *(Haml.* IV. v. 213–14)

Coffins, except for royalty, when sometimes they were purple, were covered in black with bunches of yew and rosemary tied to the sides. The Clown's song in *Twelfth Night* (II. iv. 55–60) gives several details :

> My shroud of white, stuck all with yew,
> O ! prepare it. . . .
> Not a flower, not a flower sweet,
> On my black coffin let there be strown.

And Friar Laurence says :

> Dry up your tears, and stick your rosemary
> On this fair corse.   *(Rom. & Jul.* IV. v. 79–80)

The manner in which music was employed at burials in 1598 is best shown by the following extract from a book of that date :

It is a custome still in use with Christians, to attend the funerall of their deceased friendes, with whole chantries of choyce quire-men singing solemnly before them.

Another author of the time alludes to the 'howling and hollowing of the mourners', and Anthony Stafford, in his *Meditations and Resolutions* (1612), says :

It is a wonder to see the childish whining we now-adayes use at the funeralls of our friends. If we could houl them back againe, our Lamentations were to some purpose ; but as they are, they are vaine and in vain.

Among the sums paid for Lady Shuttleworth's funeral in 1592 are the following items :

For making a coffyn ij s. to the tayllors for making a covering to the litter, and barbing the horses with blacke x s. 3 peces of blacke cotten. 40 yardes xxvij s. ij d. a pounde of blacke thride xviij d. for the coveringe of the litter and barbing of towe horses the pryst iij s. iiij d. ; the clerke ix d.

And at Mr. Shuttleworth's funeral the following year

Mourners were paid xlvij s. & viij d.
the funerall sermon v s.
and 10 score and 11 people were dyned at sixe-pence and five-pence the meall.

In the accounts of the same household in 1583 there is an entry of 7d. to bury Thomas Burton, a servant, with another of 8s. 9d. for the ale and bread consumed at the funeral.

Little was spent on the burial of the poor. In the churchwarden's accounts of St. Margaret's, Westminster, there is an entry in 1603 :

Item, paid for the graves of 451 poor Folks. 1. 17. 7.

This may have been at the commencement of the plague of that date. At this time it was not usual to inter the lower class people in coffins. There is no doubt that the poor, especially in the more remote counties of England, continued the old custom of the wake, or nightly feasting before and after a funeral. Shakespeare uses the word in connexion with a night revel in *Sonnet* lxi :

For thee watch I whilst thou dost wake elsewhere.

Garlands and flowers were placed on the graves of both rich and poor, and especially on those of young unmarried women. The priest speaking at Ophelia's burial says :

Yet here she is allow'd her virgin crants,[1]
Her maiden strewments.   (*Haml.* v. i. 254–5)

And Belarius :

The herbs that have on them cold dew o' the night
Are strewings fitt'st for graves.   (*Cymb.* iv. ii. 284–5)

Funerals invariably ended with an elaborate feast of cold

---

[1] An Elizabethan word for ' garland '. The First Folio reads ' Rites '.

food of all kinds, with wines and ale ; sometimes a sum for that purpose was set apart in the will, and in such bequests it was even customary to prescribe the particular food that was to be eaten. These feasts lasted for many days, with excessive drinking and dancing. Shakespeare alludes to them as follows :

> Thrift, thrift, Horatio ! the funeral bak'd meats
> Did coldly furnish forth the marriage tables.
>
> (*Haml.* I. ii. 180–1)

And again, where Capulet bewails Juliet's seeming death :

> All things that we ordained festival,
> Turn from their office to black funeral ;
> Our instruments to melancholy bells,
> Our wedding cheer to a sad burial feast.
>
> (*Rom. & Jul.* IV. v. 84–7)

The poor had their feasts in like manner, the guests contributing offerings of food as at their weddings.

BIBLIOGRAPHY.—The general sources of information are the same as for the subject of the preceding chapter. The Collections of Lancashire and Cheshire wills and inventories from which extracts are quoted above are those published for the Chetham Society : *The House and Farm Accounts of the Shuttleworths*, Chetham Society, 4 parts, 1856–8, has also been used. Authorities affording miscellaneous details as to manners and customs are : F. PECK's *Desiderata Curiosa*, 2 vols., 1732, 1735; J. STRUTT's *Worda Angel-cynnan : or a compleat View of the Manners, Customs, Arms, Habits, &c., of the Inhabitants of England*, 3 vols., 1775–6 ; NICHOLS's series of volumes of antiquities, 1782, &c. For the significance of rings, WILLIAM JONES's *Finger-ring Lore, historical, legendary, anecdotal*, 1877, is important.

XXI

LONDON AND THE LIFE OF THE TOWN

BY

HENRY B. WHEATLEY

THERE were two routes by which Shakespeare might make his journeys to and from Stratford—one through Oxford and the other through Banbury. The former led by Shipston-on-Stour, Long Compton, Chipping Norton, Woodstock, Oxford, High Wycombe, and Beaconsfield; the latter by Pillerton Hercy over Edgehill, and on by Banbury, Buckingham, Aylesbury, Wendover, Amersham, and the two Chalfonts. Ogilby describes this as *the* London Road. The Stratford–Oxford route was the straighter and the shorter, and there is reason to believe that it was the one Shakespeare preferred. The Stratford–Banbury route, however, was sometimes used by him, as at Grendon Underwood, eight miles south of Buckingham, he met, according to Aubrey, the constable whose egregious humours were exhibited in the person of Dogberry. These two roads met at Uxbridge, and went on through Hillingdon and Brentford. The traveller walked or rode along the Uxbridge Road by Shepherd's Bush, the gibbet at Tyburn, the Lord Mayor's banqueting house in Oxford Road, and turned south by the village of St. Giles-in-the-Fields into Holborn. After passing St. Andrew's Church and St. Sepulchre's he would enter the City at Newgate.

It is probable that Shakespeare in his first journey (supposed to have been made in the year 1586) was on foot, and took about four days, with an average of about twenty-five miles a day; when he had obtained an occupation and was better off, it is probable that he engaged a horse for his journeys. Having arrived within the City walls, he would naturally be drawn to the Thames, where a dazzling scene was spread before his eyes. For centuries London had grown by the side of her river, and there only was to be seen London in her greatness. It did not matter that the streets were narrow, for the heart of the town was on the river. Few cities, if any, had such a length of river front, and Elizabethan London impressed all visitors by its size. It may seem small to us in comparison with what it has grown to be, but it had a unity which has been lost since buildings have grown on all sides, particularly in the north and south.

John Norden's two maps of London and Westminster give us a trustworthy idea of Shakespeare's London.[1] They mark the high importance of the river, which was for centuries the great highway of London, extending from the Tower to Westminster Abbey. The Thames has been appropriately styled the silent highway, because the traffic is comparatively noiseless ; but it was really London's gayest thoroughfare, and the people who enjoyed journeying upon it, and the watermen who guided the craft, were, from all accounts, somewhat noisy.

The Queen, the Archbishop of Canterbury, the Mayor, and the City Companies, all had their state barges there for grand occasions and lighter boats for ordinary use. Most of the great houses on the river had their stairs and boats attached. Then there were innumerable wherries for hire at all the public stairs, with their watermen crying, 'Eastward Ho!' or 'Westward Ho!'—cries represented in our literature by two famous plays—*Eastward Hoe*, written by Chapman, Jonson, and Marston, and *Westward Hoe*, by Webster and Dekker. Strype (1720), on the authority of the Watermen's Company, states that there were 40,000 watermen on its rolls, and of these 8,000 were in service. John Taylor, the water-poet, affirmed that 2,000 small boats were to be found about London, and that ' the number of watermen, and those that lived and were maintained by them, and by the labour of the oar and scull, betwixt the bridge of Windsor and Gravesend, could not be fewer than 40,000 '. Of course these numbers are conjectural, but during Shakespeare's lifetime the numbers were certainly very considerable. Taylor, in later days, complained of bad times, caused by too many coaches,

[1] In *Cymbeline* he takes from Holinshed the spurious ' Lud's town ', which was invented by the mediaeval chroniclers to account for the name ' London '.

too many watermen, and the decay of the theatres on the bankside. The watermen, although they were licensed with fixed fares, were often very extortionate in their demands and were notorious for their strong vocabulary. Taylor himself, who was a sort of king among his fellows, had a coarse tongue. Many poets have celebrated the river, but few have written more to the point than this self-named 'Water-poet':

> But noble Thames, whilst I can hold a pen,
> I will divulge thy glory unto men ;
> Thou in the morning, when my coin is scant,
> Before the evening doth supply my want.

In 1613 he arranged the details of the water pageant on the marriage of the Princess Elizabeth to the Elector Palatine. The Princess did not forget him, and afterwards entertained him at Prague during her transitory reign of one winter as Queen Consort of Bohemia (which caused her husband to be styled the Winter King, and herself the Snow Queen). The river was the scene of many royal pageants, and civic ceremonies of all kinds were constantly occurring. On these gala occasions the water was covered with vessels of varied sizes and the concourse was very great. Sometimes state funerals proceeded with splendour along the Thames.

The silent highway united east and west and north and south, and made London and Westminster one town, as no road could have done so successfully ; and the watermen were foremost in promoting this union. Shakespeare, living as he did during most of his sojourn in London on the Bankside, must have daily crossed the river and been well known to the watermen. He used them as Chaucer and Hoccleve did before him, and as Pepys did in the next century. We know that still later Samuel Johnson loved to fight a wordy duel with the Thames watermen.

Norden's maps of London and Westminster contain the names of most of the places mentioned by or associated with Shakespeare. Unfortunately the fields outside Bishopsgate are only partially shown, and the Theater and the Curtain at Haliwell, Shoreditch, were outside the limits of the map of London. Norden was a good Londoner, and he describes the City as most sweetelie scituate upon the Thamis, served with all kind of necessaries most commodiouslie. The aire is healthfull, it is populous, rich and beautiful ; be it also loving and faithfull.

As the Thames was London's greatest and most used thoroughfare, with a large proportion of its most important buildings on the north bank, it will be well in the first place to describe these in order as they appear in Norden's maps. There are, however, three places on the river outside Norden's *London* which first need some notice—Deptford, Limehouse, and Wapping. It was at Deptford on April 4, 1581, that Queen Elizabeth went on board the *Golden Hind*, and on the deck of the first English ship that had voyaged round the world knighted Francis Drake, its captain. This ship was retained here as a famous relic, and it is mentioned in Peacham's verses prefixed to Coryate's *Crudities* (1611) as among the chief English sights. It became a holiday resort, and dinners and suppers were supplied to visitors until the vessel fell into complete decay ; and gradually the public reduced it to nothingness by stealing pieces as keepsakes. Young Knowell in *Every Man in his Humour* (I. iii), to clinch an argument, says, ' Drake's old ship at Deptford may sooner circle the world again '.

Limehouse is mentioned in *Henry VIII* (v. iv. 68), where the porter alludes to 'the Limbs of Limehouse',[1] a phrase which may mean no more than the reprobates of that place. Execution Dock, just below Wapping Old Stairs, is described by Stow as 'the usuall place of execution for hanging of Pirats and sea Rovers, at the low water marke, there to remaine, till three tides had overflowed them '. John Taylor in his *Description of Tyburn* writes :

> And there's a waterish Tree at Wapping,
> Whereas sea-thieves or pirates are catch'd napping.

This reference to three tides has been ingeniously connected with a passage in *The Tempest*, where Antonio, denouncing the boatswain, says :

> This wide-chapp'd rascal, would thou mightst lie drowning,
> The washing of ten tides ! (I. i. 62–3)

Antonio evidently considered three tides too small a

---

[1] The name is due to the Lyme oasts, or lime houses. There was a Lime-kiln Hill until the latter half of the nineteenth century.

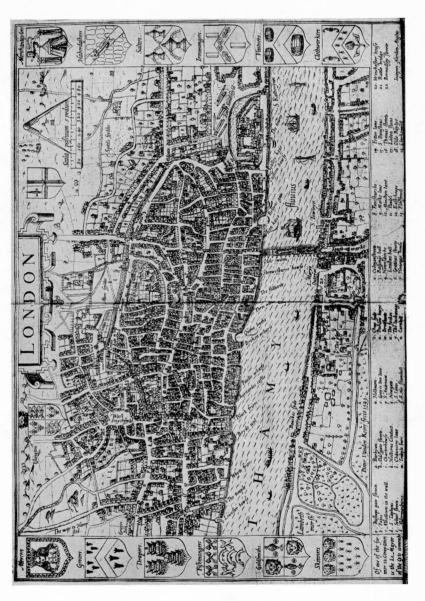

NORDEN'S MAP OF LONDON 1593

punishment for such a 'wide-chapped rascal' as the boatswain.[1]

The royal hospital, college, or free chapel of St. Katherine fills up the extreme eastern limit of Norden's map of London. It was founded in 1148 by Matilda, wife of King Stephen, augmented in 1273 by Eleanor, widow of Henry III, refounded by Eleanor, Queen of Edward I, and enlarged by Philippa, Queen of Edward III. It was placed under the especial patronage of the Queens Consort of England. Three years after the publication of Norden's map Queen Elizabeth appointed Sir Julius Caesar Master of the Hospital. In 1825 the hospital was removed to Regent's Park and the historical buildings were destroyed to make room for the St. Katherine Docks.

Next comes the Tower, the uses of which are thus summarized by Stow :

This tower is a Citadell, to defende or command the Citie : a royall place for assemblies, and treaties. A Prison of Estate, for the most daungerous offenders : the onely place of coynage for all England at this time : the armorie for warlike provision : the Treasurie of the ornaments and Jewels of the crowne, and generall conserver of the most Recordes of the Kings Courts of iustice at Westminster.

To the Tower Shakespeare has more references than to any other great building in London. The old but unfounded tradition that it owed its origin to Julius Caesar finds support in two of the plays : in *Richard II* (v. i. 1–2),

> This way the king will come ; this is the way
> To Julius Caesar's ill-erected tower.

and in *Richard III* (III. i. 68–9)—

> I do not like the Tower, of any place ;
> Did Julius Caesar build that place, my lord ?

In this play there is a scene on the Tower Walls where Gloucester orders : ' Look to the drawbridge there ' (III. v. 15). In another of the histories, there is a scene on Tower Hill at the entrance of the Tower. Humphrey, Duke of Gloucester, calls out at the closed gates:

> I am come to survey the Tower this day ;
> Since Henry's death I fear there is conveyance.

[1] J. W. Hales, *Notes and Essays on Shakespeare* (1884).

Where be these warders that they wait not here ?
Open the gates ! 'Tis Gloucester that calls.

(*1 Hen. VI*, 1. iii. 1–4)

A reference to the menagerie at the Tower will be found
in an unlikely place. Speed alludes to it when he says,
' You were wont . . . when you walked, to walk like one
of the lions ' (*Two Gent.* 11. i. 28–30).

The Tower was extra-parochial, and appears to have
been used for private marriages. Ben Jonson alludes to
this in *Every Man in his Humour* (iv. viii).

The Custom House was built in Elizabeth's reign, and
superseded an earlier building where Chaucer had worked.
Brainworm says to young Knowell in *Every Man in his
Humour*, ' Would we were e'en prest to make porters of,
and serve out the remnant of our days in Thames Street
or at Custom house key, in a civil war against the carmen.'
Three Custom houses have since been built on the same site.

Billingsgate was originally not confined to a fish market,
and at this time it was ' an open place for the landing
and bringing in of any fish, corn, salt stores, victuals, and
fruit (grocery wares excepted) '. Geoffrey of Monmouth
gives an account of a gate of wonderful design, with a pro-
digiously large tower and a haven of ships.

London Bridge was considered to be the glory of London,
and many important incidents in English history were
connected with it. Jack Cade ordered his rabble to burn
it ; much damage was done and many of the inhabitants
were killed (*2 Hen. VI*, iv. vi). The Bridge led to the great
highway to the south. The waterway was obstructed not
merely by the great breadth of the piers and starlings
and the narrowness of the arches, but by cornmills which
in the first half of the sixteenth century had been built
in some of the openings, and the great waterworks constructed at the southern end of the bridge in 1582. With
the flood tide it was impossible, and with ebb tide dangerous,
to shoot the arches of the bridge. The London watermen
were particularly proud of the skill with which they shipped
oars and shot the bridge, but amateurs were generally
unfortunate in their attempts. Prudent passengers insisted
upon being landed above bridge, generally at the Old Swan
stairs, and walked to some wharf, generally Billingsgate,
below it.

Shrewsbury House is better known as Cold Harbour, which was popularly regarded as a sanctuary. References to it in that capacity are common in the old plays. Morose in *The Silent Woman* speaks of taking sanctuary there. It was pulled down in 1600, when it was in the possession of Gilbert, seventh Earl of Shrewsbury.

The Stilliard, corrupted to Steel Yard, was the settlement of the powerful Hanse Merchants, or Hanseatic League, until they were expelled by Elizabeth before Shakespeare appeared in London. The Stilliard occupied four acres of ground; the site is marked by the present Cannon Street railway station.

' The Three Cranes in the Vintry ' was a very famous tavern; Scott makes the host of the Black Bear at Cumnor describe it as ' the most topping tavern in London '. It had been called ' The Crane in Vintry ' when there was only one crane at the wharf. Ben Jonson mentions it in *Bartholomew Fair* and *The Devil is an Ass.*

Queenhithe was of great antiquity and long the rival of Billingsgate for the wharfage of London, and in the first quarter of the seventeenth century it was the headquarters of the watermen, whose place of meeting was an alehouse called the Red Knight, as we learn from *Westward for Smelts.* Mistress Birdlime says in *Westward Hoe*: ' But I'll down to Queenhive, and the watermen which were wont to carry to Lambeth Marsh shall carry me thither.' It was from here that the Earl of Essex took boat for Essex House in February 1601, after he had fled down Friday Street on finding that his attempt to raise the City was hopeless and that he could not escape by Ludgate.

There were two Baynard Castles; the first was built by Ralph Baynard, or Bainardus, a Norman follower of William I, and afterwards came into the possession of Fitzwalter. The tower or castle, a bulwark of the City wall, was dismantled, and Fitzwalter gave the site and Montfitchet tower to Archbishop Kilwardby to be added to the property of the Black Friars, when they removed from Holborn in 1276. In 1428 Humphrey Duke of Gloucester built the second Baynard Castle on the banks of the river, with an entrance in Thames Street. This was the building inhabited by Richard Duke of Gloucester, when he had made the way smooth for him to receive the crown :

> *Glo.* If you thrive well, bring them to Baynard's Castle ;
> Where you shall find me well accompanied
> With reverend fathers and well-learned bishops.
>
> (*Rich. III*, iii. v. 97–9)

The house and precinct of Blackfriars was surrendered to Henry VIII on November 12, 1538, but nine years before the great hall had been appropriated for the trial of the King's divorce from Catherine of Arragon. The Court was opened on May 31, 1529, but it was not until Monday, June 21, that the King and Queen attended to hear the decision of the Court. This is the occasion of the great scene in *King Henry VIII*, ending with the King's command :

> Break up the court ;
> I say, set on. (ii. iv. 238–9)

Several of Queen Elizabeth's courtiers lived in Blackfriars, but its associations with Shakespeare is later than the publication of Norden's map.

Burbage's theatre, the site of which is marked by Playhouse Yard, was not opened until 1596, and Shakespeare did not buy the house near Puddle Dock until 1612.

Bridewell, named after the well of St. Bride, was in Shakespeare's day a house of correction, but it had previously been used as a palace ; in the words of Dekker :

> a Princes Court
> Is thus a prison now.

The first scene of the third act of *King Henry VIII* is laid in the Queen's apartment, then occupied during the trial, while the second scene is laid in the King's apartment, in the same palace at Bridewell.

Whitefriars was the friary of the Carmelites. The church was surrendered at the Dissolution, and, according to Stow, it was replaced by ' many fair houses, lodgings for noblemen and others '. Richard, Duke of Gloucester, sent the body of Henry VI to the old church:

> *Glo.* Sirs, take up the corse.
> *Gent.*   Toward Chertsey, noble lord ?
> *Glo.* No, to Whitefriars, there attend my coming.
>
> (*Rich. III*, i. ii. 226–8)

The place is better known in literature as Alsatia, a community of the lawless, whose privilege of sanctuary was abolished only in 1697.

Temple Gardens will always be associated with the story of the roses plucked by the adherents of the houses of York and Lancaster:

> *Plantagenet.* Hath not thy rose a canker, Somerset ?
> *Somerset.* Hath not thy rose a thorn, Plantagenet ?
> *Warwick.*   this brawl to-day,
> Grown to this faction in the Temple garden,
> Shall send between the red rose and the white
> A thousand souls to death and deadly night.
>
> (*1 Hen. VI*, II. iv. 68–9, 124–7)

Leicester House is better known as Essex House. It was originally the inn of the see of Exeter, held on lease from the Knights of St. John of Jerusalem. At the Reformation it came into the possession of William Lord Paget, when it was called Paget Place. Dudley, Earl of Leicester, obtained the house in Elizabeth's reign, and after his death in 1588 it passed into the hands of his stepson, the unfortunate Earl of Essex.

We now cross the city borders and pass into Westminster. Somerset House, named after the Protector Somerset, was during a portion of the reign of Mary appropriated to her sister. In 1596 Elizabeth granted the keeping of the house to her kinsman, Lord Hunsdon, for life. James I gave it to his Queen, Anne of Denmark, and commanded it to be called Denmark House.

The Savoy was built in 1245 by Peter of Savoy, Earl of Richmond, uncle to Eleanor, wife of Henry III. When it was in the possession of John of Gaunt, Duke of Lancaster, it was burnt down by Wat Tyler and his followers (1381). The second scene of the first act of *Richard II* is described as 'A room in the Duke of Lancaster's Palace'. In *The Second Part of Henry VI* (IV. iii. 1–3) Jack Cade cries out:

Now go some and pull down the Savoy ; others to the inns of court ; down with them all.

Cade's predecessor, Wat Tyler, had left very little to pull down.

Durham House is of interest as the residence of Sir Walter Ralegh for many years. The site is now occupied by the Adelphi.

446.1   M

Of Charing Cross there is but one mention in Shakespeare. A Rochester carrier tells his fellow:

> I have a gammon of bacon and two razes of ginger, to be delivered as far as Charing Cross. *(1 Hen. IV*, II. i. 26–8)

Whitehall is naturally often referred to in the historical plays, both by that name and by the older one of York Place:

> You must no more call it York-place, that's past;
> For, since the cardinal fell, that title's lost:
> 'Tis now the king's, and call'd Whitehall. *(Hen. VIII*, IV. i. 95–7)

A portion of the cellars of Wolsey's house still exists under the offices of the Board of Trade. The position of 'The Great Chamber' in which many of Shakespeare's plays were acted before Elizabeth and James I has been satisfactorily traced; a portion of this chamber was immediately over Wolsey's cellars. The stage stood rather to the south of the middle line of the Horse Guards Avenue, and exactly in the middle of the avenue, by the cabstand, is the site of the 'screens' at the back of the stage where the actors awaited their cues. Upwards of a hundred performances of Shakespeare's plays must have taken place during his lifetime at Whitehall Palace alone. The old Banqueting House, in which several of the plays were acted, was burnt down in 1619.

All around the grand old Hall of Westminster were the old buildings of the Exchequer, which were visited in state when the Lord High Treasurer took up office.

> *Gadshill.* Case ye, case ye, on with your vizards, there's money of the king's coming down the hill, 'tis going to the king's exchequer.
> *Falstaff.* You lie, you rogue; 'tis going to the king's tavern.
> *(1 Hen. IV*, II. ii. 58–62)

Near by was the notorious Star Chamber, which took cognizance, among other things, of riots. In 1590 a deer-stealer was bound over by Lord Derby to appear before Lord Shrewsbury to answer at this court for his misdemeanour. This may have suggested Shakespeare's reference to the court in *The Merry Wives of Windsor*:

> *Shallow.* Sir Hugh, persuade me not; I will make a star-chamber matter of it; if he were twenty Sir John Falstaffs he shall not abuse Robert Shallow Esquire. (I. i. 1–4)

Westminster Hall was rebuilt by Richard II, and the first use that the new building was put to was to try the

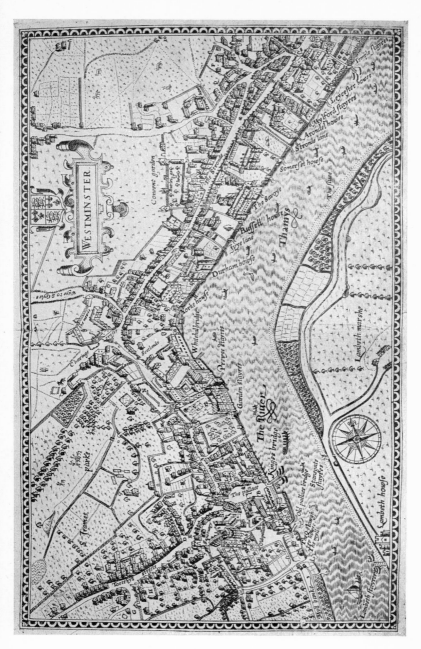

NORDEN'S MAP OF WESTMINSTER 1593

unfortunate king himself. The deposition forms the pathetic fourth act of *King Richard II*.

The Abbey, the coronation place of our kings, is not overlooked by Shakespeare. The Duchess of Gloucester dreamt that she

> sat in seat of majesty
> In the cathedral church of Westminster,
> And in that chair where kings and queens are crown'd.
>
> (*2 Hen. VI*, I. ii. 36–8)

Henry IV asks upon his deathbed :

> Doth any name particular belong
> Unto the lodging where I first did swound ?
> *Warwick.* 'Tis called Jerusalem, my noble lord.
> *K. Hen.* . . . It hath been prophesied to me many years
> I should not die but in Jerusalem,
> Which vainly I suppos'd the Holy Land.
> But bear me to that chamber ; there I'll lie ;
> In that Jerusalem shall Harry die.   (*2 Hen. IV*, IV. v. 231–9)

The Jerusalem Chamber has so many historical associations that it is almost a national shrine. It was originally the Abbot's private drawing-room, but, after the dissolution of the Abbey and the appropriation of the Chapter house to national purposes, it became the meeting place of the Dean and Chapter, as well as of important commissions.

We pass now to the south side of the Thames. Owing to the existence of London Bridge, Southwark has always formed a busy continuation of the city of London. Being on the high road to the sea coast, it was full of large galleried inns from which coaches were continually running. The Tabard, from which Chaucer's Canterbury pilgrims started, has the widest fame of all. It is at the White Hart in Southwark that Cade complained that the peasants had left him (*2 Hen. VI*, IV. viii. 26). S. Towleyes in Norden's map is St. Olave's, and is the origin of Tooley Street. St. Mary Overy, the present Cathedral of St. Saviour gives a fine architectural effect to the neighbourhood. Winchester House is just below the church. It was the town residence of the Bishops of Winchester, who possessed much property of ill repute in the neighbourhood. Bankside is of special interest as the home of the South London theatres, and because Shakespeare himself lived there for a considerable period. In 1593 there were a ' Beare howse ', which afterwards became the

Hope theatre, and the playhouse, a little to the south-east, known as the Rose theatre. The Globe and the Swan had not yet been built. The Globe is referred to by Shakespeare as ' this wooden O ', and there is one mention of Paris Garden (or as the First Folio has it—Parish Garden), where the bears were kept :

> *Porter.* You'll leave your noise anon, you rascals.
> Do you take the court for Paris Garden ?
>
> (*Hen. VIII*, v. iv. 2–2)

St. George's Fields, a wide open space through which the Canterbury Road was driven, is the occasion of one of Shallow's silly boasts :

> O, Sir John, do you remember since we lay all night in the Windmill in St. George's fields ?

This was a notorious place, and Falstaff had to call Shallow to order :

> No more of that, good Master Shallow, no more of that.
>
> (*2 Hen. IV*, III. ii. 211–12)

It will be seen that most of the great houses and the grand buildings from the Tower to Westminster Abbey were on the river front, but there are some others to consider in taking stock of the main topographical features of sixteenth-century London. The walls and gates were intact, and the main roads out of London were fairly well kept. The great southern road from London Bridge was well frequented, and the great eastern road from Aldgate, through Whitechapel, Mile End, on to Bow was a handsome thoroughfare with fields on either side. Shallow says:

> I remember at Mile-end Green, when I lay at Clements' Inn.
>
> (*2 Hen. IV*, III. ii. 301–2)

There were several gates on the north ; but it was from Bishopsgate that the great northern road started. Moorgate was merely a postern leading to Moorfields, which were not drained until 1606, and formed for long an impassable morass. When Prince Henry exclaims :

> What sayest thou to a hare,[1] or the melancholy of Moor-ditch ?

Falstaff answers :

> Thou hast the most unsavoury similes.　(*1 Hen. IV*, I. ii. 87–9)

Cripplegate was also only a postern, but in a convenient position, and a village grew up near it outside the walls.

---

[1] A melancholy animal.

Newgate opened upon the [great West road by which Shakespeare entered London.

Fleet Street was the show place of the town, and here was exhibited a constant succession of puppets, naked Indians, and strange fishes, to which the people eagerly flocked. Trinculo says :

A strange fish ! Were I in England now, as once I was, and had but this fish painted, not a holiday fool there but would give a piece of silver : there would this monster make a man ; any strange beast there makes a man. When they will not give a doit to relieve a lame beggar, they will lay out ten to see a dead Indian.

(Temp. II. ii. 28–35)

Among the sights were a 'motion' or puppet show, of London and Nineveh, and one of Eltham and the giant Dutchman. Shakespeare does not omit to mention London Stone, the greatest antiquity of the City. Camden considered it to have been the central milestone of the town, similar to that in the forum at Rome. It is now a small rounded stone in a stone case built into the outer or street wall of the church of St. Swithin, in Cannon Street.

Jack Cade, following a then old tradition, struck his staff on London Stone and exclaimed :

Now is Mortimer lord of this city. And here, sitting upon London-stone, I charge and command that, of the city's cost, the pissing-conduit [1] run nothing but claret wine this first year of our reign. And now, henceforward, it shall be treason for any that calls me other than Lord Mortimer. (2 Hen. VI, IV. vi. 1–7)

A marked feature of old London was the number of gardens and open spaces, of which a few are still to be seen. Walbrook was famous for its gardens from Roman times. Gerarde the herbalist superintended Lord Burghley's gardens in the Strand, and he himself possessed some in Holborn, nearly opposite Gray's Inn, as well as in the Strand. The strawberries of Ely Place (Rich. III, III. iv. 32) are as well known as the roses of Temple Gardens. Sir Christopher Hatton obtained in 1576 a lease of the gate-house and part of the buildings in the first courtyard of Ely Place and the garden and orchard of the Temple for the term of twenty-one years. The rent was a red rose, ten loads of hay, and ten pounds per annum ; Bishop Cox, on whom the hard bargain was forced by Queen Elizabeth, reserving

[1] The popular name of a conduit near the Royal Exchange, which ran with a small stream.

to himself and his successors the right of walking in the gardens and gathering twenty bushels of roses yearly.

To the great chamber at Whitehall may be added two other important buildings where Shakespeare's plays were acted before the Court : Gray's Inn, where *The Comedy of Errors* was performed on December 28, 1594, and the Middle Temple Hall, twice mentioned in the plays (*1 Hen. IV*, III. iii. 221, *1 Hen. VI*, II. iv. 3), where *Twelfth-Night* was presented on Candlemas, 1602.

To the frequenters of the noble Cathedral of St. Paul which dominated the large churchyard might well have been applied the words of condemnation passed by Christ upon the Jews of old : ' It is written, my house is the house of prayer, and ye have made it a den of thieves.' Ben Jonson opens the third act of *Every Man in his Humour* in the middle aisle of St. Paul's, called commonly ' Duke Humphrey's Walk' or ' Paul's Walk'. This was long the common news-room of London, the resort of the wits and gallants about town. Here lawyers stood at their pillars, like merchants on change, and received their clients. Here masterless men set up their bills for service. Here the rood loft, tombs, and font were used as counters for the payment of money, and here assignations were made. Here also ale and beer, baskets of bread, fish, flesh, and fruit were sold, and mules and horses were led, until the scandal became so great that in 1554 the Mayor and Common Council prohibited such ' unreverent ' practices. Dugdale says that Inigo Jones's portico to the west front was built as ' an ambulatory for such as usually walking in the body of the church, disturbed the solemn service in the choir '. Shakespeare and Ben Jonson have drawn the living picture of the frequenters of the place in Bardolph, bought by Falstaff ' in Pauls ' (*2 Hen. IV*, I. ii. 57), and in Bobadil, ' a Paul's man ' (*Every Man in his Humour*).

Whatever be the exact explanation of

Humphrey Hour, that call'd your Grace
To breakfast once forth of my company, (*Rich. III*, IV. iv. 176–7)

Shakespeare must certainly be alluding to Duke Humphrey's walk, where, it is presumed, needy loiterers who could not buy or beg a meal were constrained to spend the dinner hour—' to seeke his dinner in Poules with Duke Humphrey ', as Gabriel Harvey says.

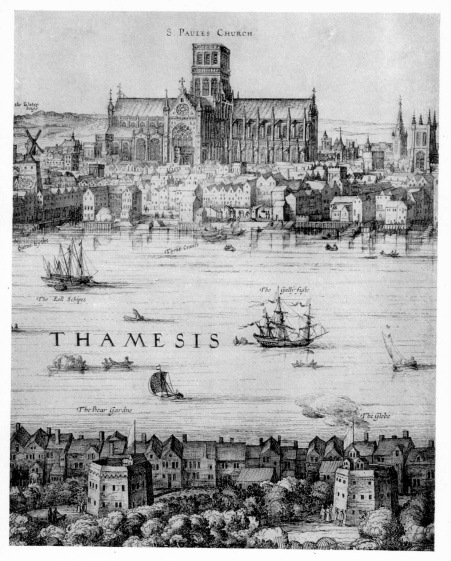

ST PAUL'S CATHEDRAL
The BEAR GARDEN and the GLOBE THEATRE

Great and solemn scenes were, however, enacted in the Cathedral, and two of these occurred shortly after the arrival of Shakespeare in the capital.   They were the funeral of Sir Philip Sidney on February 16, 1586–7, which proved how deep was the grief of the whole country for the loss of its most popular hero, and the rejoicings after the defeat of the Spanish Armada on November 24, 1588, when the national joy at the great deliverance was unrestrainedly expressed.   The funeral procession was accompanied by 700 mourners of all classes of the people, and each of the seven United Provinces sent a representative to the funeral. In the great thanksgiving for the defeat of the Armada the Queen drove from Somerset House to St. Paul's, her palfrey of honour being led by the Master of the Horse, the Earl of Sussex.

A large portion of old London was occupied by the great religious houses, or what remained of them.   By their suppression in the reign of Henry VIII a great change had been made in the appearance of the city.

Some were continued as charitable establishments ; thus the Greyfriars by Newgate and the Priories of St. Bartholomew and Bermondsey became Christ's Hospital for the education of young children, St. Bartholomew's Hospital, and St. Thomas's Hospital ; others were destroyed or given to courtiers ; others again became ruinous and were cleared away, new buildings being raised on the sites.

We have already seen that the Thames formed London's pre-eminent highway, and that as a consequence the narrow streets were much neglected.   With the increase of traffic caused by the carriers' carts and the increased number of coaches, they often became blocked.   The hubbub was great, caused by the cries of itinerant salesmen, the clamour of the bells, the singing of the ballad-monger, the beggar with his clapper, clap-dish, or ' clack-dish ' (*Meas. for M.* III. ii. 139), ' those tunes . . . that he heard the carmen whistle ' (*2 Hen. IV*, III. ii. 344–5), and the violent bad language of the crowd.   Before 1564 there were no coaches, but by 1601 it was thought necessary to introduce a Bill into the House of Lords ' to restrain the excessive and superfluous use of coaches within this realm '. This Bill was rejected and more coaches appeared, to the great injury of the watermen.   But the convenience of the coach to fashionable well-dressed gallants in saving them from the defilement of the streets must have discounted the claims of other forms of traffic. For at no time was the extravagance of dress greater than in Elizabeth's reign, and unquestionably men were more gorgeous in their attire than women. Costumes were continually changing, and greater eccentricity was consistently aimed at. Much of this was most effeminate, especially the treatment of men's hair. The use of extravagant lovelocks, the wearing of jewels and roses in the ear, is beyond our understanding to-day. Eccentricity in boots and shoes was so great that the law was called in to restrict it.

The cries in the streets were much the same as those recorded in the fifteenth-century poem *London Lickpenny*. 'Hot peas', 'Hot fine oatcake', 'Whiting, maids, whiting', were heard on all sides ; costermongers with their apples, shopmen with their constant repetition of their cry of 'What do you lack?' joined in the din. 'Rock samphires' formed one of the chief condiments of the time, used as a pickle or fresh in salads ; it grew on rocky cliffs near the sea, and was common in the south of England:

> Half way down
> Hangs one that gathers samphire ; dreadful trade !

says Edgar in *King Lear* (IV. vi. 15–16), standing over Dover cliffs, where the plant is recorded to have been gathered as late as the year 1886. The Elizabethan dramatists transferred the cries of London to the streets of Rome, and Heywood's song in *The Rape of Lucrece* includes samphire in the list:

> I ha' rock-samphire, rock samphire.

Other cries in London were 'small coals', 'have you any old boots', 'buy a mat', 'new brooms, green brooms'.

Then outside the prison doors were piteous cries for the poor women in the dark dungeons, and 'bread and meat, for the tender mercy of God, to the poor prisoners of Newgate', or for those who were 'for the Lord's sake' (*Meas. for M.* IV. iii. 21) in Ludgate gaol. Mingled with these were the moanings of the prisoners themselves,

> the cries of the damned in the Fleet. (B. Jonson, *Epigrams*)

But the most dangerous cry was 'Clubs', which

signified the arising of a fray. Its frequency in the streets
of London proves the inefficiency of the police. The
porter in *King Henry VIII* says :

I missed the meteor once, and hit that woman, who cried out
' Clubs ! ', when I might see from far some forty truncheoners
draw to her succour, which were the hope o' the Strand, where she
was quartered.   (v. iv. 53–7)

The authorities themselves sometimes used the cry on
serious occasions. The mayor, when the partisans of
Humphrey, Duke of Gloucester, and Beaufort, Bishop of
Winchester, quarrelled before the Tower, cried out :

I'll call for Clubs if you will not away.
                                            (*1 Hen. VI*, i. iii. 85)

The streets were cleared for an important procession by
an officer called a whiffler :

The deep-mouth'd sea,
Which, like a mighty whiffler 'fore the king,
Seems to prepare his way.   (*Hen. V*, chor. 11–13)

When James I and his Queen proceeded from the Tower
to Whitehall on March 15, 1604, a very great pageant was
produced. Seven fine arches of triumph at short intervals
were erected from the designs of Stephen Harrison, which
were, as far as we can judge from the engravings, the finest
ever used in a London pageant.

The prestige of the Government of London—Regum
Angliae Camera, the Chamber of the Kings of England[1]—
was not so high in the Elizabethan age as it had been,
and the feud between the courtier and the citizen had
just begun. The Lord Mayor was still a man of consequence, although he had somewhat fallen from the
high rank he held in the Middle Ages as a frequent
counsellor of the king. The importance of his office
is shown in several of the plays, as in *King Henry VIII*,
where he is introduced in the last scene as a witness to
the christening of the infant Elizabeth, and in *King
Richard III*, where Sir Edmond Shaa is introduced as
a prominent supporter of Gloucester in his struggle for
the throne.

Middleton, in *The Triumphs of Truth* (1613), writes :

Search all chronicles, histories, records, in what language or letter

---

[1] ' Welcome, sweet prince, to London, to your chamber,' says Buckingham
to the Prince of Wales (*Rich. III*. iii. i. 1).

soever let the inquisitive man waste the dear treasures of his time and eyesight, he shall conclude his life only in this certainty, that there is no subject upon earth received into the place of government with the like state and magnificence as is the Lord Mayor of the City of London.

Associated with the Lord Mayor in the government of the city were the twenty-six aldermen of the wards, and the sheriffs, each of whom had his own compter or prison, the one of these being in the Poultry and the other in Wood Street.

Crime was rampant in the streets of London, and the watchmen, constables, serjeants, and catchpoles were quite incompetent to deal with the criminals. The most ingenious mode of punishment which the governors could devise was to execute the criminal as near to the scene of his crime as was possible. The chief place of execution was Tyburn.

> Thou mak'st the triumviry, the corner-cap of society,
> The shape of love's Tyburn, that hangs up simplicity,
> (*Love's L. L.* iv. iii. 53–4)

says Biron, alluding to the triangular form of the gallows.

The administration of justice left much to be desired. Well-bred in *Every Man in his Humour* speaks in disparaging terms of a Guildhall verdict, and the general opinion of London juries was not high. A Bishop of London wrote to Cardinal Wolsey in behalf of his Chancellor, desiring the Attorney-General to stop a prosecution against him ' because London juries are so prejudiced that they would find Abel guilty of the murder of Cain '. Thomas Fuller corroborates this by quoting a proverb to the effect 'that London juries hang half and save half'.

Prisons were numerous ; there were five in Southwark alone, the Clink, the Compter, the Marshalsea, the King's Bench, and the White Lion ; besides these there were the Cage, the Cripplegate, the Fleet, Ludgate, and Newgate ; the Tower has been already named.

Besides the Tower and the Marshalsea (*Hen. VIII*, v. iv. 92), Shakespeare alludes to the Compter or Counter, which had become a common name for a debtor's prison, in the punning description of the common serjeant, put into the mouth of Dromio of Syracuse :

A back-friend, a shoulder-clapper, one that countermands
The passages of alleys, creeks, and narrow lands ;
A hound that runs counter and yet draws dryfoot well ;
(Com. of. E. IV. ii. 37–9)

and in Falstaff's address to the Lord Chief Justice's servant :

You hunt-counter : hence ! avaunt !
(2 Hen. IV, I. ii. 102–3)

More explicit is Falstaff's reference in *The Merry Wives of Windsor* :

Thou mightst as well say, I love to walk by the Counter-gate, which is as hateful to me as the reek of a lime-kiln.　(III. iii. 84–6)

In the Middle Ages the water supply was abundant on account of the large number of springs, but, as London grew, these were less trusted, and until Sir Hugh Middelton formed the New River (1609–13) the inhabitants depended entirely on the Thames. Water had to be fetched from the river itself or from the conduits by which it was conveyed thence. These conduits, often marked by an ornamental structure, and not infrequently bearing a human or other figure from which the water spouted, were familiar objects, and appear in Shakespeare in more than one allusive passage.

The old shepherd in *The Winter's Tale* is compared in appearance to

a weather-bitten conduit of many kings' reigns.
(Wint. T. v. ii. 61–2)

Lavinia's wounds, says Marcus, pour forth blood

As from a conduit with three issuing spouts.
(Tit. Andr. II. iv. 30)

Capulet, in his upbraiding of the weeping Juliet, uses the word ' conduit ' in very rough and homely simile :

How now ! a conduit, girl ? what ! still in tears ?
Evermore showering ?　　　(Rom. & Jul. III. v. 130–1)

The weeping Lucrece and her maid are set in a lovely picture in these two lines :

A pretty while these pretty creatures stand,
Like ivory conduits coral cisterns filling.　(Lucr. 1233–4)

The man who supplied the houses was the water-bearer, or carrier, who drew off the water into large wooden tankards, broad at the bottom but narrow at the top,

which held about three gallons. This vessel was borne
upon the shoulder, and to keep the carrier dry two towels
were fastened over him, one to fall in front and the other
to cover his back. The classical example of the water-
bearer in the literature of the time is the character who
follows this occupation in *Every Man in his Humour* ; he
is named Oliver Cob, and dwells ' at the sign of the Water
Tankard hard by the Green Lattice '.

The London amusements of the sixteenth century seem
to have been numerous and various enough to satisfy the
tastes of all classes of Londoners. Burton writes thus
approvingly in *The Anatomy of Melancholy* :

The country hath his recreations, the city his several gymnicks,
exercises, feasts, and merry meetings—What so pleasant as to see
some pageant as at Coronations, wedding, and such like solemnities, to
see an Embassadour or a Prince met, received, entertain'd with Masks,
Shews, Fireworks, &c.

A long list of town amusements appears in *The Pleasant
and Stately Morall of the Three Lordes and Three Ladies of
London* (1590) :

Lord Pomp, let nothing that's magnificall,
Or that may tend to Londons graceful state,
Be unperfourm'd, As showes and solemne feastes,
Watches in armour, triumphes, Cresset-lightes ;
Bonefiers, belles, and peales of ordinance
And Pleasure, see that plaies be published,
Mai-games and maskes, with mirth and minstrelsie,
Pageants and school-feastes, beares, and puppit plaies.

The theatre, bear-baiting and bull-baiting, card-playing
and gaming, dancing, and fencing are all dealt with in
another chapter of this book, and need only be mentioned
here as a part of London life.

London had been famous for its cookshops since the
twelfth century ; in the fourteenth century many of these
houses were turned into inns. In Shakespeare's time
tavern life had become very popular, and in his plays
there are 'many references to these places of entertainment.

The Boar's Head in Eastcheap was one of the chief London
inns in his day, but there is no authority for supposing
that Prince Henry, Falstaff, and the other roysterers really
met at that hostelry. The first reference to the Boar's
Head as a tavern is in a lease dated 1537. In *2 Henry IV*

(II. ii. 159–62) the Prince inquires after Falstaff, 'Where sups he?' to which Bardolph replies, 'At the old place, my lord, in Eastcheap'. The statue of William IV in King William Street nearly marks the site of the old inn.

The Dagger in Holborn, an ordinary and tavern, is mentioned by Ben Jonson in *The Alchemist* and *The Divell is an Asse*, but it appears to have been a low-class gambling-house frequented by disreputable characters. It was famous for its strong drink ; Dagger ale and Dagger furmety were highly appreciated, as well as Dagger pies, ornamented with a representation of a dagger and a magpie on the point. There was another Dagger tavern in Cheapside, mentioned in *The Penniles Parliament of Thred-Bare Poets* (1608) and in *The Pleasant Conceites of Old Hobson* (1607). It is a matter of dispute which of these two Daggers produced the celebrated pies.

The Mitre and the Mermaid were the rival taverns in Cheapside ; both of them were really in Bread Street. They lay back from the street and had entrances in both thoroughfares. The Mermaid [had also an entry from Friday Street.[1]

The Mitre is frequently mentioned by the dramatists. Middleton seems to have esteemed it more highly than the Mermaid:

Goldstone. Where sup we, gallants ?
Pursenet. Name the place, master Goldstone,—
Goldstone. Why the Mitre, in my mind, for neat attendance, diligent boys, and push excels it far.
All. Agreed. The Mitre then.   (*Your Five Gallants*, 1607)

Again in *A Mad World, My Masters*, Sir Bounteous exclaims :
Why this will be a true feast, a right Mitre supper.

There was another Mitre in Fleet Street, with which Shakespeare and Ben Jonson are reported to have been connected. This, however, must not be confused with Dr. Johnson's Mitre.

The Mitre and the Mermaid may have been equally esteemed in the sixteenth century, but the fame of the latter from its association with Shakespeare has become world-wide. Social clubs held at the best of these taverns

---

[1] Ben Jonson changed the names of the taverns mentioned by him in *Every Man in his Humour* ; the Mermaid of the 1601 quarto became the Windmill in the folio of 1616, and the Mitre of the quarto became the Star of the folio edition.

had become common and in great favour towards the end
of the century, but what club that ever existed could
compare with the one at whose meetings might be seen
and heard such men as Shakespeare, Ben Jonson, Francis
Beaumont, John Fletcher, Carew, Donne, Selden, and
Ralegh ? One of these members put into exquisite verse
his remembrance of the flow of wit, which makes us truly
grateful, though we grieve at not having more :

> What things have we seen
> Done at the Mermaid ! heard words that have been
> So nimble and so full of subtle flame,
> As if that every one from whence they came
> Had meant to put his whole wit in a jest,
> And had resolv'd to live a fool the rest
> Of his dull life ; then when there hath been thrown
> Wit able enough to justify the town
> For three days past ; wit that might warrant be
> For the whole city to talk foolishly
> Till that were cancell'd ; and when that was gone
> We left an air behind us, which alone
> Was able to make the two next companies
> (Right witty though but downright fools) more wise.
>
> (Francis Beaumont, *Epistle to Ben Jonson*)

The Devil at Temple Bar owed its designation to its
proximity to St. Dunstan's Church ; the original sign
represented St. Dunstan pulling the Devil by the nose.
Ben Jonson has given a lasting distinction to the tavern
and the landlord, Simon Wadloe, the original ' Old Simon
the King '. From the mention of the ' Mermaid ' in the
first draft of *Every Man in his Humour* it may be
inferred that Jonson was a frequenter of this tavern before
the Club was established by Ralegh in 1603. It was some
years after this that he established the Apollo Club at the
Devil. He drew up his *Leges Conviviales* about the year
1624, and placed over the entrance to the Apollo Club
some verses beginning :

> Welcome all who lead or follow
> To the Oracle of Apollo.

The Pegasus in Cheapside is mentioned in *The Returne from
Parnassus* (1602), and in Randolph's *Jealous Lovers* (1632),
Shakespeare transfers it to Italy :

> Near twenty years ago, in Genoa,
> Where we were lodgers at the Pegasus.
>
> (*Tam. Sh.* iv. iv. 4–5)

LONDON BRIDGE

Thomas Heywood made a humorous rhyming catalogue
of London taverns, beginning :

> The Gentry to the *King's Head*,
>   The Nobles to the *Crown*,
> The Knights unto the *Golden Fleece*,
>   And to the *Plough*, the Clown.
> The Churchman to the *Mitre*,
>   The Shepherd to the *Star*,
> The Gardener hies him to the *Rose*,
>   To the *Drum* the man of war.
> To the *Feathers* Ladies you ! The *Globe*
>   The Seaman doth not scorn !
> The Usurer to the *Devil* ; and
>   The Townsman to the *Horn*.
> The Huntsman to the *White Hart*,
>   To the *Ship* the Merchants go :
> But you that do the Muses love,
>   The *Swan*, called river Po.
> The Bankrupt to the *World's End*,
>   The Fool to the *Fortune* hie ;
> Unto the *Mouth*, the Oyster Wife ;
>   The Fiddler to the *Pie*.

The manners and customs of taverns are abundantly
illustrated in the drama. A painted lattice was the sign
of an alehouse, sometimes green, but more often red.
Falstaff at the Garter Inn at Windsor calls Pistol to account
for his ' red-lattice phrases and bold-beating oaths ' (*M.
Wives*, II. ii. 28–9), fit only for the pothouse. The vintner
was said to be known by his shining shoes, which were
considered to be fit only for shopkeepers, after boots had
come into fashion. In Massinger's *Guardian* the question
is given, ' How shall we know the vintners ? ', the answer
being, ' If they walk on foot, by their rat-coloured stockings
and shining shoes.' The favourite phrase of the innkeeper
was ' Said I well ? ' and of the drawers, ' Anon, anon, sir,'
of which the modern equivalent is ' Coming, sir '. No inn-
servant is credited with a good character. So Celia says :

The oath of a lover is no stronger than the word of a tapster ; they
are both the confirmers of false reckonings. (*A. Y. L.* III. iv. 31–3)

Scorn is thrown upon ' a tapster's arithmetic ' (*Troilus*
I. ii. 121). Waiters were tempted to cheat by the absurdity
of the frequenters of the taverns, who paid whatever was
asked because it was beneath the dignity of a gallant to
cast up his bill.

Passing to commerce and trade, we have first to notice the place

> where merchants most do congregate, (*Merch. of V.* 1. iii. 50)

the Royal Exchange, founded by Sir Thomas Gresham. The first stone was laid June 7, 1566, and in 1571 the Queen, after dining with Sir Thomas Gresham in Bishopsgate Street, visited the newly erected ' Burse ' and caused the herald to proclaim it the Royal Exchange, ' so to be called from thenceforth and no otherwise '. It soon became almost as favourite a lounge as St. Paul's. The merchants went on business and others to see and be seen. Kitely, in *Every Man in his Humour*, says, ' I will meet him on the Exchange anon ', and Bobadil boasts that he has been ' on the Exchange, at my lodging and at my ordinary '. In Gresham's time the bell for closure was rung at twelve noon and at six in the evening, but subsequently the Exchange was kept open to a later hour. Gresham's building was often called the Old Exchange or Old Change to distinguish it from the New Exchange or Britain's Burse in the Strand, built by the Earl of Salisbury in 1609. In both there were shops ; there are references in plays to buying and selling there.

Old London was practically divided into districts according to trades. Many changes had been made before Shakespeare's day, but the divisions still existed, and even now some localized trades subsist.

In a notice of the trade of Shakespeare's London it seems proper to begin with the book trade. In the thirteenth century Paternoster Row was inhabited by ' paternostrers ' or makers of prayer beads (rosaries), and by sellers of various objects used in the services of the Cathedral, such as books of devotion, candles, censers, and the like. The ' paternostrers ' were succeeded by mercers, and eventually by booksellers and publishers.

In Shakespeare's time and for long afterwards St. Paul's Churchyard was the head-quarters of the book trade, and vaults in old St. Paul's were used as storeplaces for the booksellers' stocks. It is well to remember that the yard was not a public thoroughfare, but more like the close of a country cathedral, with a high and strong wall around it, within which was included the deanery on the south and the bishop's palace on the north. The shops of the publishers in the Churchyard were of two kinds : the ordinary houses within the close having plenty of accommodation not only for a stock of books but also for the occupier and his household; and the little sheds or stalls of one storey fixed against the walls of the Cathedral, with accommodation for a small number of books, which were kept by such printers and publishers as had larger shops elsewhere. Some of the publishers were sellers of other than their own books and kept a show of foreign publications on their tables and shelves. From these shops Shakespeare would have been able to obtain the books he made use of for the plots of his plays. We have authority for saying that books were sometimes lent by these booksellers.

The prominent position of the Churchyard as the head-quarters of the bookselling business is seen from the fact that more than half of the plays of Shakespeare were issued from this place.

The riches of the goldsmiths' shops was a constant subject of wonder and admiration, and Cheapside or Gold-smith's Row was styled the 'Beauty of London'. As late as the fourteenth century the north side of the road was open ground reserved for jousts and other entertainments. The market was held in the middle of the street. The south side of West Cheap was therefore properly called Cheapside. Dick the butcher (with the inevitable pun on 'bill') asks Jack Cade:

My lord, when shall we go to Cheapside and take up commodities upon our bills ?   (*2 Hen. VI*, iv. vii. 133–4)

As to the localities of the various trades Stow gives us valuable information:

Men of trades and sellers of wares in this City have oftentimes chaunged their places, as they have found their best advantage. For where as Mercers, and Haberdashers used to keep their shoppes in West Cheape, of later time they helde them on London Bridge, where partly they yet remaine. The Goldsmithes of Gutherons lane, and old Exchange, are now for the most part removed into the Southside of west Cheape, the Peperers and Grocers of Sopers lane, are now in Bucklesberrie, and other places dispersed. The Drapers of Lombardstreete and of Cornehill, are seated in Candlewickstreete, and Watheling streete : the Skinners from Saint Marie Pellipers, or at the Axe, into Budge row, and Walbrooke : The Stockfishmongers in Thames streete : wet Fishmongers in Knightriders streete, and

Bridge streete ; The Ironmongers of Ironmongers lane, and old Jurie, into Thames streete ; the Vinteners from the Vinetree into divers places. But the Brewers for the more part remaine neare to the friendly water of Thames ; the Butchers in Eastcheape, Saint Nicholas Shambles, and the Stockes Market ; the Hosiers of olde time in Hosier lane, neare unto Smithfield, are since remooved into Cordwayner streete, the upper part thereof by Bow Church, and last of all into Birchoverislane by Cornehil : the Shoomakers and Curriors of Cordwayner streete, remooved the one to Saint Martins le Grand, the other to London wall neare unto Moregate, the Founders remaine by themselves in Lothberie : Cookes or Pastelars for the more part in Thames streete, the other dispersed into diverse partes. Poulters of late remooved out of the Poultrie betwixt the Stockes and the great Conduit in Cheape into Grasse streete, and St. Nicholas Shambles : Bowyers from Bowyers row by Ludgate into divers places, and almost worne out with the Fletchers : Pater noster makers of olde time, or Beade makers, or Text Writers, are gone out of Pater noster Rowe, and are called Stationers of Paules Church yarde : Pattenmakers of Saint Margaret Pattens lane, cleane worne out : Labourers everie worke day are to bee founde in Cheape, . . . horse coursers and sellers of Oxen . . . and such like, remaine in their olde Market of Smithfield.

This account by a contemporary is so full and important that it needs no addition. Something more may, however, be said of the pepperers (now the grocers), because Shakespeare took a special interest in their trade. John Sadler, a native of Stratford-on-Avon, came to London some years after Shakespeare. He was without friends and found much difficulty in obtaining any occupation, but at last a grocer in Bucklersbury agreed to take him on trial, and, being satisfied, bound him apprentice for eight years. When the apprenticeship came to an end Sadler entered into partnership with a fellow-townsman of Stratford, Richard Quiney, who married Sadler's sister on August 27, 1618. The father of Quiney was a friend of Shakespeare, and his brother married Judith, the poet's younger daughter. There can be little doubt that Shakespeare was a visitor to the business house of his two fellow-townsmen. He would be well acquainted with 'Bucklersbury in simple time' (*M. Wives* III. iii. 79).

The suburbs of a walled city have always had a bad name. This was so in London, and the scenes of *Measure for Measure*, which are placed in Vienna, suggest the vicious surroundings of the English capital. 'The skirts o' the town' were inhabited by disorderly persons who were not wanted within the walls, and who found the freedom outside more convenient to them. Chettle in *The Kind Hart's Dreame* (1592) wrote:

The suburbs of the cittie are in many places no other but dark dennes for adulterers, theeves, murderers, and every mischief worker.

The literature of the time is full of such allusions. Stubbes in his *Anatomie of Abuses* justly denounced suburb-gardens and garden-houses, and another writer observed ' how happy were cities if they had no suburbs '. Portia in *Julius Caesar* makes a striking allusion to the infamy attached to the word suburbs.

> Dwell I but in the suburbs
> Of your good pleasure ? If it be no more,
> Portia is Brutus' harlot, not his wife. (II. i. 285–7)

Two notorious localities are named by Shakespeare : Pickt-hatch [1] (*M. Wives* II. iii. 20), where the houses had hatches or half-doors guarded with spikes, and Turnmill Street (or as the First Folio has it, ' Turnball-street '), near Clerkenwell Green, the resort of bullies and rogues (*2 Hen. IV*, III. ii. 333).

The times, however, were changing, and the suburbs were beginning to reform themselves. Around the wide roads from some of the principal gates well-inhabited districts gradually grew up. Hoxton is now quite close to the centre of London, but in the reign of Elizabeth it was a country place cut off from the City by Moorfields. In *Every Man in his Humor* Knowell's house is described as in Hogsden, which was then according to Stow ' a large street with houses on both sides '. Master Stephen refers to his uncle's property as ' Middlesex land ', and he himself is called a country gull, in opposition to Master Matthew, the town gull. Islington was some way north of the City, and its gravelly soil made it a suitable site for a prosperous village, although it was not free from disturbing elements. The brick kilns at Islington had a population of rogues and vagabonds, and when Queen Elizabeth took a country drive there in 1581, these dangerous characters surrounded her carriage, and filled the air with their clamour. Hamp-

---

[1] Near the Charterhouse Wall in Goswell Road ; Pickax Yard once marked the spot.

stead and Highgate, Kentish Town and Tottenham Court, were distant country places. The nearness of field and open country to the walls of London gave the inhabitants the opportunity of rising early on May-Day to seek for May-dew, which was esteemed a sovereign salve for the complexion. Stow relates how

In the moneth of May, namely on May day in the morning, every man, except impediment, would walke into the sweet meadowes and greene woods, there to rejoyce their spirites with the beauty and savour of sweete flowers and with the harmony of birds, praysing God in their kind, and for example Edward Hall hath noted that K. Henry the eight, as in the 3 of his raigne and divers other yeares, so namely in the seaventh of his raigne, on May day in the morning with Queen Katheren his wife accompanied with many Lords and Ladies, rode a maying from Greenwitch to the high ground of Shooters hill.

These pleasant rural scenes have no charms for Philip Stubbes, who lays stress on the evils of the custom, affirming that

All the young men and maides, old men and wives, run gadding over night to the woods, groves, hils, and mountains, where they spend all the night in pleasant pastime, and in the morning they return bringing with them birch and branches of trees and deck their assemblies withall.

Stubbes's view is not corroborated by others, for later writers describe the practice much in Stow's terms, saying that the custom was to go out in the early morning in family parties.

BIBLIOGRAPHY.—STOW's *Survay of London*, 1598, 1603, is the most valuable contemporary authority on the subject, as the work of a contemporary of Shakespeare. It is founded on documents and personal knowledge. Successive editors continued it until it grew into two folio volumes edited by Strype, 1720, 1754–5. In consequence Stow has been frequently quoted for information respecting what had occurred long after his death. The original was reprinted by W. J. Thoms, 1842, 1876, and by Henry Morley, 1889, 1893. The 1603 edition was admirably edited by C. L. Kingsford in 1908 (Oxford, 2 vols.), with corrections from MS. sources, particular attention being given to Stow's faulty etymology of local names.

HARRISON's *Description of England*, attached to Holinshed's Chronicle, 1577, 1587, is of great value. Dr. F. J. Furnivall's reprint of Books II and III for the New Shakspere Society, 1877, contains much additional matter.

Maps of London were common in the sixteenth century, but being often pasted on the walls of houses they were generally destroyed. The earliest known to us is a view of London, drawn by A. VAN DEN WYNGAERDE, about 1550, in the Sutherland Collection (Bodleian Library). This was redrawn on a smaller scale and engraved by N. Whittock. It is a pretty view, but untrustworthy, as the original has been tampered with, and a representation of Bermondsey Abbey is added from another source at the south-east corner of the view. The drawing was accurately reproduced for the first time from the original by the London Topographical Society.

HOEFNAGEL'S plan of London, published in Braun and Hogenberg's *Civitates Orbis Terrarum*, 1572, with the heading *Londinum feracissimi Angliae Regni Metropolis*, is a very fine and well-engraved map, but the detail is so full that it is difficult to follow, in spite of the clearness of the lines. The map was reproduced with French descriptions in Belleforest's *Cosmography*.

The map attributed to RALPH AGGAS is on a much larger scale, but a very inferior engraving. The date of first publication is unknown ; it was probably to a certain extent indebted to Hoefnagel. Two copies only are known : one in the Pepysian Library, Magdalene College, Cambridge, and the other in the Guildhall Library, London, both published in the reign of James I.

NORDEN'S two maps of London and Westminster, 1593, are reproduced in this volume. Norden's map of Middlesex is valuable as showing clearly the suburbs of Elizabethan London. J. C. VISSCHER'S view of London, 1616, is specially interesting as a fine panoramic picture of Shakespeare's London. All these plans have been reproduced by the London Topographical Society.

A greater number of books and pamphlets on the evil manners of some of the people of England, and of London in particular, were published in Elizabeth's reign than in any other period. PHILIP STUBBES's *The Anatomy of Abuses*, 1583, holds a prominent position in this class. It was reprinted for the New Shakspere Society, 1877.

NATHAN DRAKE'S *Shakespeare and his Times*, 1817, 2 vols., 4to, is a trustworthy book, of which part ii is devoted to Shakespeare in London. G. W. THORNBURY'S *Shakespeare's England*, 1856, 2 vols., contains an excellent picture of the time, but is not always accurate in details, and few authorities are quoted. HUBERT HALL's *Society in the Elizabethan Age*, 1887, contains illustrations of characters in town and at court. *Shakespeare's England*, by E. Goadby, 1881, 1889, contains a chapter on London.

T. F. ORDISH'S *Shakespeare's London*, 1897, new ed. 1904, and H. T. STEPHENSON'S *Shakespeare's London*, 1905, are important contributions to the subject in recent times. Sir WALTER BESANT'S *London in the time of the Tudors*, 1904, *London in the time of the Stuarts*, 1903, and WILLIAM PAGE'S *History of London*, vol. i, 1909 (Victoria County History), contain useful information on customs, &c.

XXII

AUTHORS AND PATRONS

BY

D. NICHOL SMITH

THE relations of authors and patrons underwent a
gradual change during the sixteenth century. In older
days a poet had trusted to the bounty of a royal or noble
protector. He was in a sense a servant, however lightly
he may have treated the bond. His recognized privilege
of presenting a ' Compleynt to his Purse ' implied depen-
dence on his part and obligation on the patron's. The
relationship was a survival from the days of the minstrels ;
and it finally broke down when literature came to have a
value in the open market.

The change was due mainly to the great development
of printing, notably during the reign of Edward VI. Direct
encouragement was thus given to authorship, and there
arose before the end of the century a class of authors by
profession who, whether or not they were able to live by
their writings, made their writings their chief occupation,
and lived by them as well as they could. The rise of the
man of letters, the change in the methods of patronage,
and the increase of the importance of the printer are
different aspects of one large movement.

But the professional author received little from the
printer. The common offer for a pamphlet was apparently
forty shillings. ' I lost by your last booke ', says Danter
the printer to a Cambridge student in *The Returne from Parnassus*, ' and you knowe there is many a one that payes me
largely for the printing of their inventions, but for all this you
shall have 40 shillings and an odde pottle of wine.' [1] Wither
complained in *The Schollers Purgatory* that the printers could
' hyre for a matter of 40 shillings some needy Ignoramus '.[2]

[1] *The Returne from Parnassus*, part ii, ed. W. D. Macray, p. 88.
[2] *The Schollers Purgatory*, n. d. [1624], p. 130.

In both these passages the sum named is purposely small; and it is certain that an accomplished pamphleteer could command a higher price. ' Glad was that Printer ', said Nashe of Greene, ' that might bee so blest to pay him deare for the very dregs of his wit.' [1] Of himself he said, ' When I doo play my Prizes in Print, Ile be paid for my paines, that 's once.' [2] But what is known of the number of copies printed and the price at which they were sold indicates that even a pamphlet that was likely to prove popular cannot have brought its author a substantial sum.[3] A common method of payment was to give the author several copies which he could dispose of for his own profit. Richard Robinson's *Eupolemia* (1603)—the only Elizabethan document that gives a direct statement of literary earnings—shows that Robinson as a rule received twenty-five copies and considered himself fairly treated. Sometimes an author was paid both in books and money; John Stow, for instance, received '£3 and 40 copies for his pains in *The Survey of London*, and 20s. and 50 copies for his pains in the *Brief Chronicle* '.[4] It appears to have been not uncommon for an author to pay for the printing of his inventions, though this was a method that would not be employed by the impecunious authors of the popular literature. Nashe has his gibe at Gabriel Harvey because he ' gives money to be seene and have his wit lookt upon, never printing booke yet for whose impression he hath not either paid or run in debt '.[2] Other authors are known to have given their works to the printer. Gascoigne repudiated as a calumny the report that he had received great sums of money for the publication of his *Posies* : ' for answere heereof ', he proclaims, ' it is moste true (and I call Heaven and Earth too witnesse) that I never receyved of the Printer, or of anye other, one grote or pennie for the firste Copyes of these Posyes.' But in such cases the social position of the author has to be remembered. We know nothing of Spenser's dealings with his printers, but it may be presumed that he never thought of receiving

---

[1] *Foure Letters Confuted*, ed. R. B. McKerrow, i. 287.

[2] *Have with you to Saffron-Walden*, iii. 128.

[3] Mr. McKerrow suggests that more than £5 can hardly have been paid for a pamphlet sold at sixpence a copy.

[4] *Registers of the Company of Stationers*, ed. Arber, vol. v, p. lv[i]. In 1702 we find Sir Roger L'Estrange receiving £300 and 50 copies for his *Josephus* (*Hist. MSS. Com.* 11th Report, App. vii, p. 113).

money for the publication of his poems. He was more likely to have paid the printer than to have been paid by him, and he was probably content to have copies for distribution among his friends. There is ample material dealing with the printers' and booksellers' relations with the authorities and the public and with each other in the reign of Elizabeth. The little that is known about their relations with the authors is derived from casual allusions ; and it shows that they were able to look very carefully after their own interests.

The author who endeavoured to make a living by his writings was forced to find another source of income, and he found it in a patron. There are many references to the necessity of this form of assistance. Lodge made it the theme of his third eclogue in *A fig for Momus* (1595) :

> The Muses have some friends, who will esteeme
> A man of worth, and give desert his dewe ;

but if frugal patrons ' skantle learning with a servile pay ', it were better for the poet to ' hould the plough a while, and plie the cart '. Massinger spoke frankly of his own experience in his address to the patrons of *The Maid of Honour* (1632) : ' I heartily wish ', he wrote, ' that the world may take notice, and from my selfe, that I had not to this time subsisted, but that I was supported by your frequent courtesies, and favours.' A personal tie sometimes prompted or dictated the choice of a particular patron ; but needy authors are continually found seeking for a patron,[1] and presenting a work to him on the chance of his favour. A very large number of the Elizabethan dedications fail to reveal any reason why they should be made to one man rather than another.

The change from the conditions which prevailed during the first half of the century is not definitely marked, but on the whole it is clear. Sir Thomas Elyot thought of his *Governour* as a duty to his king and country, and could dedicate it only to Henry VIII. Ascham wrote his *Toxophilus* with the aim of effecting a social reformation, and won for it Henry's protection. It was at Henry's command that Berners translated Froissart. Latimer's sermons

---

[1] Cf. *The Pilgrimage to Parnassus*, ed. Macray, p. 20, ' looking still when I shoulde meete with some good Maecenas that liberallie would rewarde my deserts, I fed soe long upon hope, till I had almoste starved '.

before Edward VI, which were ' gathered, writ, and brought into lyght' by Thomas Some, were fitly dedicated by him to the Lady Katherine, Duchess of Suffolk. Thomas Wilson dedicated *The Rule of Reason, conteyning the Arte of Logike,* to Edward VI ; and having been encouraged by the Earl of Warwick, then Chancellor of the University of Cambridge, to write its sequel, *The Arte of Rhetorique,* he duly commended it to his Chancellor's patronage. Margaret Ascham, with like fitness, dedicated her husband's *Scholemaster* to a later Cambridge Chancellor, Sir William Cecil, afterwards Lord Burghley. There is an obvious reason in all these books for the choice of the patron. At the beginning of the reign of Elizabeth there were still no signs of the indiscriminate dedicating which became common in later years, when authors would ply the art of flattery, and when patrons might feel no obligation.

The conditions of patronage at the court of Elizabeth appear to have remained much as they were at the court of Henry VIII, but side by side with them there were growing up new conditions as a result of the great spread of literary activity. When authors were drawn from every rank of life, methods and motives of patronage were bound to vary with their social positions. A gentleman of the court, even when he was a great poet, could not regard literature as a profession. It might be his main occupation, he might know that by it alone he would be remembered, but he did not wish it to be thought the serious business of his life. The early poems of Spenser were moves in the difficult game of preferment. They helped him to win the private-secretaryship to Lord Grey of Wilton, which made Ireland his home for the rest of his life. When in 1589 he returned to London with the first three books of *The Faerie Queene* he hoped that they would carry him to high office ; and in 1596, when he issued the next three books, he still looked to the poem for his advancement. This unrivalled tribute to the glories of an English monarch was enriched with the noblest of dedications ; it was dedicated to Elizabeth ' to live with the eternitie of her fame '.[1] But Elizabeth did not give Spenser the reward that he sought. He had to rest content with a pension of £50 a year, a sum corresponding to at least £300 now. Counted merely as

---

[1] These great words were added to the dedication in 1596.

money it was a great gift, but it was a disappointment to the poet, who craved for a post that would remove him from his exile in Ireland. Sir John Harington, Elizabeth's godson, had his translation of the *Orlando* imposed upon him by her as a task. He had circulated among the ladies of the court his version of the story of Giocondo in the twenty-eighth book, and Elizabeth, as a punishment for the youthful frolic, forbade him the court till he had produced a translation of the whole poem.[1] When his *Orlando Furioso in English Heroical Verse* was published in 1591 it was therefore humbly recommended to her gracious protection. His only reward may have been the permission to return to court ; or he may have received, as on many other occasions, a personal gift. Edward Fairfax also inscribed to the Queen his *Godfrey of Bulloigne, or The Recoverie of Jerusalem* (1600). Elizabeth was thus the patron of the three great heroic poems of her reign—*The Faerie Queene* and the English Ariosto and Tasso. Another princely book which could have no meaner patron was North's translation of Plutarch's *Lives* (1579).

The search for office by the method of gaining the Queen's favour with poems or other literary gifts is well illustrated by George Gascoigne. He had been employed by Leicester to provide part of the entertainment on her famous visit to Kenilworth in 1575, and he was also present at the ensuing visit to Woodstock, where he saw that her learned judgement was greatly pleased with the prose tale of *Hemetes the Heremyte*. Next New Year's Day he presented her with a copy of the tale accompanied by versions of it in Latin, Italian, and French, hoping thereby to give proof of his sufficiency for her service. His request for employment was soon granted, and another work in manuscript,[2] *The Grief of Joye*, followed as a thank-offering and as a witness to the serious and dutiful use of his leisure. *Hemetes* has the special interest of containing a frontispiece which represents Gascoigne in the act of offering his gift. The author, who had fought in the Low Countries and was a member of Gray's Inn, supplied the explanation in a sonnet :

> Beholde (good Queene) A poett with a Speare
> (Straundge sightes well markt are understode the better)

---

[1] *Nugæ Antiquæ*, second ed. (1779), vol. i, p. [iii].
[2] Both are printed in J. W. Cunliffe's edition of Gascoigne, ii. 473–557.

GASCOIGNE PRESENTING HIS BOOK TO THE QUEEN

A Soldyer armde, with pensyle in his eare,
With penn to fight, and sworde to wryte a letter,
His gowne haulffe off, his blade not fully bownde,
In dowbtfull doompes, which waye were best to take ;

and he offered to serve

as maye become me beste
In Feilde, in Towne, in Cowrte, or any where.

As this frontispiece (which is here reproduced) was designed
in prospect of what it purports to represent, its historical
value does not lie so much in its details as in its illustration of the custom of making literary offerings in person.
Ascham presented his *Toxophilus* to Henry VIII in the
picture gallery at Greenwich,[1] and even Richard Robinson
was allowed to present his *Third Proceeding in the Harmony
of King Davids Harp* to Elizabeth at Richmond, when
she was ' goyng to the chappell in the morning '.

A servant of the Crown would be expected to present
to his sovereign a book dealing with his office. Richard
Jones, the printer, dedicated to Sir Christopher Hatton,
the Lord Chancellor, *The Booke of Honour and Armes* (1590),
but Sir William Segar, as Norroy King of Arms, could
dedicate only to Elizabeth his *Honor Military and Civill*
(1602). Books on all kinds of subjects boasted her name—
Foxe's *Actes and Monuments* (1563), Shute's *Groundes of
Architecture* (1563), Sanford's *Epictetus* (1567), Lyte's translation of the great *Herball* of Dodoens (1578), Mulcaster's
Positions (1581), the edition by Raph Rabbards of George
Ripley's *Compound of Alchymy* (1591), Savile's *Tacitus*
(1591) and *Scriptores post Bedam* (1596), Andrew Maunsell's
Catalogue of English printed Bookes (1595), John Davies's
Nosce teipsum (1599), Philemon Holland's *Livy* (1600).
But she knew when her royal acknowledgement was
an ample reward. When Robinson presented his *Harmony of King Davids Harp* she received it graciously ;
he was told that she was glad to have a subject who could
do so well and that he deserved commendation ; but he
also heard from the Master of Requests that Her Majesty
had enough to do in relieving her needy soldiers and
requiting their pains, and that, as she had not set him
on the work, he was not to be paid any wages. Nor did
a dedication to Elizabeth necessarily serve as any protection to a book. Giles Fletcher on his return from Russia,

---

[1] Works of Ascham, ed. Giles, vol. i, p. xxxiv.

where he had been employed in the Queen's service, duly inscribed to her his short treatise *Of the Russe Common Wealth* (1591). But the company of Muscovy merchants, fearing that some passages in it would prejudice the friendly relations between the two countries, and their trade, complained to Burghley and procured its suppression.[1]

Of the two English versions of the Bible produced during Elizabeth's reign—the Geneva and the Bishops'—only the former was dedicated to her. It was in origin a private enterprise, undertaken by Protestant exiles at Geneva during the reign of Mary, but a Protestant monarch was on the throne when it was completed, and a loyal address was duly prefixed. It was sanctioned in so far as it was allowed to be printed under episcopal supervision; but though it was the popular Bible of the reign, it continued, as it began, without royal authority. For the official Bible, which was produced mainly by the English bishops, no dedication was thought necessary. Similarly there was a dedication to Henry VIII in Coverdale's Bible and Matthew's Bible, but not in the Great Bible. And just as on the title-page of the Great Bible Henry VIII was represented on his throne, so on the title-page of the Bishops' Bible there is a portrait of Elizabeth; and the supremacy of the Crown is further symbolized within the volume in the portraits of her great favourite and her great minister—the Earl of Leicester,[2] who occupies most of the title-page to the second part beginning with the book of Joshua, and Lord Burghley, who ornaments the initial B at the beginning of the Psalms.[3] The first official Bible to contain a dedication was the authorized version of 1611.

Leicester and Burghley both rank with Elizabeth as patrons. Indeed, the number of authors whom Leicester befriended, and the continual testimony to his encouragement, give him the right to be considered the chief patron of the earlier part of the reign. Several works were dedicated to him before he was raised to his earldom. One of the earliest was Blundeville's *New booke containing the*

---

[1] *Letters of Eminent Literary Men* (Camden Society, 1843), pp. 76–9.
[2] Reproduced in vol. i, p. 4.
[3] Mr. A. W. Pollard speaks of this as an instance of ' punning capitals ' (*Records of the English Bible*, 1911, p. 33). This Bible was published in 1568, and Sir William Cecil did not become Lord Burghley till 1571. In the second folio edition (1572) the portrait was removed to the title-page of the third part beginning with the Psalms.

arte of ryding. It was dedicated to him because he was Master of the Horse, just as Turbervile's *Noble Arte of Venerie* was dedicated to Lord Clinton, the Master of the Hart Hounds. But as early as 1565 Arthur Golding, in the prose dedication of his *Fyrst Fower Bookes* of Ovid's *Metamorphoses*, spoke of Leicester as already well known for his support of learning and authorship; and he repeated these praises in the verse epistle prefixed to the complete translation in 1567. He wished his patron long life

> that all such students as
> Doo travell too enrich our toong with knowledge heretofore
> Not common too our vulgar speech, may dayly more and more
> Proceede through thy good furtherance and favor in the same,
> Too all mens profit and delyght, and thy eternall fame.

John Stow spoke to the same effect in the dedication of his *Summarie of Englyshe Chronicles* (1565).

> Because, bothe by the universall reporte of all men, I heare, and also by myne owne experience I perfectly know (right honourable and my very good lorde) how honorably and cherefully divers workes presented to your lordship have ben accepted : I (though of al others most simple) was thereby encouraged, to offer to your honour this my simple worke, in token of my bounden duty. . . . I was the bolder to dedicate to your honour, because I know your lordships good inclination to al sortes of good knowledges.

Ascham, whose son Dudley was Leicester's godson, said in a letter in 1566, ' I surely fixed my hope to have had more stay of your lordship's goodness than of any man else.' John Florio spoke of Leicester's ' continuall delight in setting foorth of good letters, and earnest zeale in maintaining of languages ' when he offered him his *First Fruites* (1578) ; and he added with emphasis that to his knowledge Leicester was ' the onely furtherer, maintayner, and supporter of all well disposed mindes toward any kinde of studie '. Greene, in dedicating his *Planetomachia* (1585), remarked on the numbers who dutifully presented the fruits of their labours to this Maecenas of learning. So, too, did Geffrey Whitney in *A Choice of Emblemes* (1586). In the lengthy dedication, which is notable for its attempt to describe the history of patronage from earliest times, Whitney alluded in particular to Leicester's fame for his services to Literature :

> For leavinge your native countrie, where so manie godlie and vertuous are countenanced : So manie learned advaunced, and so

manie studious incoraged by your honour. What other countrie
in Christendome, but knoweth that your lordship is a . . . lovinge
patron of learninge, and a bountifull Mecœnas to all the professors
of worthie artes, and sciences : whereof my selfe is a witnes, who
have often harde the same in other countries, to your everlastinge
memorie. . . . Divers who are nowe famous men, had bin, throughe
povertie, longe since discouraged from their studies : if they had
not founde your honour, so prone to bee their patron.[1]

These are more than conventional praises. Leicester's
authors seem to have approached him with a stronger
sense of his large-minded benevolence than they generally
felt towards their other patrons. He was ' a supporter
of any kind of study '. Spenser, who started his career
in Leicester's service and always looked to him for support,
dedicated to him his *Virgils Gnat*, and ventured to address
him with greater frankness than allegory could conceal
in *Mother Hubberds Tale*. At the other extreme of poetry
Edward Hake offered to Leicester's protection his *Newes
out of Powles Churchyarde* (1579). The ' good acceptation '
of the *Summarie of Englyshe Chronicles* caused Stow to
choose the same patron for his *Chronicles of England* (1580) ;
Stow's rival, Richard Grafton, also inscribed to Leicester the
Abridgement of the Chronicles of England (1563) ; and he
was likewise the patron of Holinshed's *Historie of Scotlande*
(1577). Thomas Cooper dedicated to him on his appointment as Chancellor of the University of Oxford the great
Latin-English dictionary, *Thesaurus Linguae Romanae &
Britannicae* (1565). A mainstay of the Puritans, Leicester
was the patron of Arthur Golding's translation of Calvin's
Sermons upon the Booke of Iob (1574) and of Calvin's *Two
godly and learned Sermons* (1584), translated by Robert
Horne, bishop of Winchester, and dedicated by Anthony
Munday ; and he gave Thomas Cartwright the mastership of his hospital at Warwick, with an annuity of £50.
At the same time he was a jealous supporter of the drama,
the ' Earl of Leicester's Players ' being for many years
the most prominent acting company. The range and
diversity of his interests finds even additional proof in the
dedications of James Rowbothum's *Pleasaunt and wittie
Playe of the Cheasts* (1562), Thomas Gale's *Certaine Workes
of Chirurgerie* (1563), North's *Morall Philosophie of Doni*

[1] Cf. Gabriel Harvey's *Gratulationum Valdinensium Libri Quatuor* (1578),
bk. ii.

(1570), and Mulcaster's *First Part of the Elementarie* (1582). Leicester was the universal patron. He may have been erratic in his rewards. Stow speaks of having received from him nothing but ' hearty thanks with commendations '.[1] But there can be no doubt of his interest in all kinds of literature, and his encouragement of them.

Unlike Leicester, Burghley was not accessible to all classes of authors. He did not encourage the poets. Spenser hints at this in the sonnet addressed to him at the conclusion of the first three books of *The Faerie Queene*. To one who bears the burden of the kingdom's government, the poem he fears may appear but 'ydle rimes, .. the labor of lost time, and wit unstayd '. In the opening stanza of the fourth book, published six years later, when hope of preferment was vanishing, he spoke with greater freedom :

> The rugged forhead that with grave foresight
> Welds kingdomes causes, and affaires of state,
> My looser rimes (I wote) doth sharply wite,
> For praising love, as I have done of late.
>
> .   .   .   .   .   .
>
> To such therefore I do not sing at all,
> But to that sacred Saint my soveraigne Queene.

The allusion to Burghley is unmistakable. It may betray Spenser's personal resentment towards the chief obstacle to his ambitions, but it confirms what is clearly indicated elsewhere. Burghley's indifference to the poets and dramatists is hinted at even in Richard Field's dedication of Puttenham's *Arte of English Poesie*. ' Perceyving ', says Field, ' the title to purport so slender a subiect, as nothing almost could be more discrepant from the gravitie of your yeeres and Honorable function, whose contemplations are every houre more seriously employed upon the publicke administration and services, I thought it no condigne gratification, nor scarce any good satisfaction for such a person as you ' ; and he is therefore careful to point out, by way of excuse, that many passages in the treatise show it to have been written for the recreation and service of the Queen. The kind of book which Burghley favoured had a direct bearing on the welfare of the State. In particular he helped the historians. Grafton dedicated to him his *Chronicle at large* (1569), Holinshed his *Chronicles*

---

[1] *Annals*, 1592, p. 815.

(1577), and Camden his *Britannia* (1586) ; and it was at his instance that Camden began in 1597 his *Annales regnante Elizabetha*.[1]   Though in his old age Camden could boast that he ' never made suit to any man, no, not to his Majesty ',[2] he was proud to allude to Burghley, even in the text of his *Britannia*, as his ' right honourable Patron, highly accomplish'd with all the ornaments of virtue, wisdom, and nobility '.   Arthur Golding translated *The historie of Leonard Aretine* (1563) while in the household of Burghley, and was encouraged by him to translate also Caesar's *Martiall exploytes in the Realme of Gallia* (1565) ; and twenty years later he dedicated to him also his translation of *The Rare and Singuler worke of Pomponius Mela of the situation of the world* (1585).   As Chancellor of the University of Cambridge, Burghley was the patron of Thomas Wilson's *Three Orations of Demosthenes in favour of the Olynthians* (1570), Ascham's *Scholemaster* (1570), and John Baret's *Alvearie or Triple Dictionary* (1573). And there could have been no more obvious patron for the *Catalogus arborum in horto Iohannis Gerardi* (1596) and for Gerarde's *Herball or Generall Historie of Plantes* (1597) than the great nobleman whose princely gardens were renowned throughout Europe.   They are all serious books with which Burghley's name is associated.   The one contemporary poem in which he appears to have taken real interest was his friend Sir Thomas Chaloner's *De Rep[ublica] Anglorum Instauranda Libri Decem* (1579).   He gave the manuscript to William Malim, master of St. Paul's School, to prepare for the press, and contributed to the introductory matter of the volume some Latin verses of his own.   In January 1595–6 George Peele, then in failing health, offered to Burghley by the hand of his eldest daughter, 'necessity's servant', what he called 'the history of Troy in 500 verses', perhaps a revised version of *The Tale of Troy* published in 1589.   Peele's letter (which is reproduced as an illustration to Chapter X) gives no indication that he had any reason to rely on Burghley's good-will.

Sir Philip Sidney has a place by himself among the Elizabethan patrons.   Though the nephew of Leicester,

---

[1] ' Life of Camden ' prefixed to *Britannia*, ed. Gibson, 1722, f 1.
[2] *V.CL. Gulielmi Camdeni Epistolae*, 1691, p. 247, letter to Usher, July 10, 618.

he did not owe his power to his high birth, nor could he owe it to his slender fortune. He was a comrade in letters who gave the great encouragement of example. ' The president of noblesse and of chevalree ' and ' the hope of all learned men ', as Spenser called him, was also by common consent the most accomplished writer of his day. Spenser delighted to proclaim his debt to his earliest and most influential patron,

> Who first my Muse did lift out of the flore,
> To sing his sweet delights in lowlie laies.

Whether or not Sidney had any direct influence on the composition of *The Shepheardes Calender*, the poem was the pledge of their active friendship. Next to it, the most important work dedicated to Sidney was Richard Hakluyt's first book, *Divers voyages touching the discoverie of America* (1582). Hakluyt knew Sidney well at Christ Church, and could speak of his continual readiness to help and of his ' accustomed favour towarde these godly and honourable discoveries '. While at Oxford, Sidney also assisted Camden.[1] His skill in arms and horsemanship pointed him out as the patron of Nicholas Lichefild's translation from the Spanish of L. G. de la Vega's *De Re Militari* (1582), and of Christopher Clifford's *Schoole of Horsemanship* (1585). His earnest Protestantism brought him the dedication by John Stell of *The Bee hiue of the Romishe Churche. . . . Translated out of Dutch into English by George Gilpin* (1580). At the same time his chivalrous and intellectual accomplishments won the admiration of Giordano Bruno, who addressed to him both *Spaccio de la Bestia Trionfante* (Paris, 1583) and *De gl'Heroici Furori* (Paris, 1585). He was the one English author of his time who had a European reputation ; Du Bartas, for instance, some years later, grouped ' le milor Cydné ' with Sir Thomas More and Sir Nicholas Bacon as the three pillars of the English speech. Of no significance in itself, but important in its unexpected results, was the dedication of Stephen Gosson's *Schoole of Abuse* (1579). Gosson, who was also a member of Christ Church, chose with thick-headed assurance the most distinguished member of his college as the patron of his ' invective against Poets and such like Caterpillers of a Commonwealth.' In Spenser's

---

[1] ' Life of Camden ', *Britannia*, 1722, d 2.

words, he 'was for hys labor scorned, if at leaste it be in
the goodnesse of that nature to scorne: suche follie is it,
not to regarde aforehande the inclination and qualitie
of him to whome wee dedicate oure Bookes'. Sidney at
first did not think of replying, but the spread of the controversy at length forced him to take up his pen in ' a
pittiful defence of poore poetry' and thus to give us in
his *Apologie* the first great critical treatise in English.
His scorn must have been too gentle for Gosson, who later
in the same year dedicated to him also *The Ephemerides
of Phialo*, and shamelessly remarked on the safety which,
notwithstanding the fury of the storm raised by the *Schoole
of Abuse*, he had enjoyed in Sidney's patronage. Thomas
Lodge, who had replied at once to Gosson in his ' Defence
of Poetry' (1579), dedicated to Sidney the work in which
incidentally he made his second contribution to the controversy, *An Alarum against Usurers* (1584).

No patron was held in greater affection than Sidney,
no fellow craftsman was more ready to offer his help.
Spenser acknowledged his debt and repaid it in noble verse ;
but even those who cannot have experienced the bounty
of Sidney's gentle nature came to think of him as the
perfect patron. Thomas Nashe was still an undergraduate
at Cambridge when Sidney left England for the Low
Countries and the fatal field of Zutphen, and could speak
only from hearsay when, six years later, he lamented the
loss that struggling authors had sustained in Sidney's
death :

Gentle Sir Phillip Sidney, thou knewst what belongd to a Scholler,
thou knewst what paines, what toyle, what travel, conduct to
perfection : wel couldst thou give every Vertue his encouragement,
every Art his due, every writer his desert : cause none more vertuous,
witty, or learned than thy selfe.

But thou art dead in thy grave, and hast left too few successors
to thy glory, too few to cherish the Sons of the Muses, or water
those budding hopes with their plenty, which thy bounty erst
planted.[1]

This passage is none the less valuable because Nashe did not
know Sidney ; it expressed the common opinion. ' Report
delivers of the Renowned Sidney ', said John Budge the
bookseller, in 1615, ' that the most unfiled worke, the poorest
hand could offer up, hee received with thanks, making the

---

[1] *Pierce Penilesse*, ed. MᶜKerrow, i. 159.

GEORGE CHAPMAN by WILLIAM HOLE (?)

love of the man to supply the worth.'[1] It soon became almost a fashion to write regretfully of the good old days of intelligent patronage. There were more reasons for it than Sidney's death; the attitude of the patrons was bound to be affected by the great increase in the profession of literature. But the complaints were coloured with the thought of Sidney's reputation. Fulke Greville dedicated 'all his monuments' to the memory of the friend of his youth.

The seventeen sonnets added to *The Faerie Queene* have the incidental interest of providing a list of the chief patrons about the year 1590. The most prominent at this time was Essex, who may be regarded as the true successor of Leicester. A poet himself in the intervals of more ambitious pursuits, he was a friend to the poets. In Daniel's words, he was 'the Mercury of peace, the Mars of war'.[2] Spenser looked forward to giving a place in *The Faerie Queene* to the celebration of his heroic achievements. In the calamitous circumstances of Spenser's death, Essex was at hand with the offer of help; and he defrayed the expenses of the poet's funeral. Shakespeare spoke of the welcome that awaited him when he returned from Ireland 'bringing rebellion broached on his sword' (*Hen. V*, v. chorus 32). Chapman chose him as the first patron of his *Iliad* because he was 'the most honored now living instance of the Achilleian vertues eternized by divine Homer'. Technical treatises on military matters were submitted to his martial censure, such as Sir Roger Williams's *Briefe discourse of Warre* (1590) and George Silver's *Paradoxes of Defence* (1599). Willingly or unwillingly, he had books of all kinds dedicated to him, so diverse in character as Thomas Newton's *Herbal for the Bible* (1587), Thomas Watson's *First sett of Italian Madrigalls Englished* (1590), Henry Holland's *Treatise against Witchcraft* (1590), John Mundy's *Songs and Psalmes for all such as either love or learne musicke* (1594), Ralph Brooke's *Discoverie of Certaine Errours in the much commended Britannia* (1596), Sylvester's translation of the *Second Weeke* of Du Bartas (1598), and William Gager's *Meleager* (1592). The last of these, a Latin play that had been performed at Christ Church

---

[1] Harington's *Epigrams*, 1615, dedication.
[2] *Civile Warres*, 1595, bk. ii, conclusion.

before Leicester and Sidney, was inscribed to Essex in memory of his brother, Walter Devereux. The dedications to Essex did not escape the scrutiny of the government, who rightly distrusted his headstrong ambitions and his popularity. The Queen is known to have taxed him with the patronage of *A Conference about the Next Succession to the Crowne of Ingland* (1594), printed abroad by Parsons under the name of ' R. Doleman '; the book had been dishonestly dedicated to Essex in order to compromise him politically.[1] John Hayward's *First Part of the Life and raigne of King Henrie the IIII* (1599) was suspected because of the account of the deposition of Richard II ; both author and printer were prosecuted, and the laudatory but innocuous Latin address to Essex was ordered to be cancelled.[2] Another kind of interest attaches to his association with the Elizabethan translations of Tacitus. Richard Grenewey dedicated to him his *Annales* and *Germania* (1598) ; but in Henry Savile's *Ende of Nero and Beginning of Galba* and *Agricola* (1591)—which was dedicated to Elizabeth—there is a prefatory note, entitled 'A. B. To the Reader', that he was believed to have written. Edmund Bolton said in his *Hypercritica* that ' Fame gives it him ', and Ben Jonson showed no doubt of the authorship in his conversations with Drummond. The initials were evidently meant to suggest the name of Anthony Bacon, who may have had some share in it. On the other hand his greater brother, Francis Bacon, is said to have given assistance in writings which appear under Essex's name.[3] It was on the career of Francis Bacon that Essex exerted the full force of his patronage. He did what he could for Bacon's advancement in the legal profession, and forced on him a gift of land to the value of £1,800. But this was not the patronage of literature.

Sir Francis Walsingham is described in Spenser's sonnet as

> the great Mecenas of this age,
> As wel to al that civil artes professe
> As those that are inspird with Martial rage.

---

[1] *Sydney Papers*, ed. Arthur Collins (1746), i, p. 357, letter from Rowland White to Sir Robert Sydney, November 5, 1595 ; *Lives of the Devereux, Earls of Essex*, by W. B. Devereux (1853), i, pp. 312, 313.

[2] *Letters written by John Chamberlain* (Camden Society, 1861), pp. 47–8 ; H. R. Plomer's article on the book in *The Library*, second series, vol. iii (1902), pp. 13–23 ; Bacon, *Apophthegms*, 58.

[3] See *The Advancement of Learning*, ed. W. Aldis Wright, p. xvi.

These high praises are hardly borne out by the mere number of dedications, though Thomas Watson also spoke of him as 'chiefe patron of vertue, learning, and chivalrie'. His active interest in colonial enterprise made him the great patron of books of discovery and adventure. Above all he was the patron of *The Principall Navigations, Voiages and Discoveries of the English nation* (1589). In dedicating it to Walsingham Hakluyt described it as 'the fruits of your owne incouragements'. Several books of Protestant theology also sought his vigorous protection. The poet most closely associated with him as a patron was Thomas Watson, who lamented his death in *Meliboeus* (1590). On the other hand it was the poets who had the first claim on the patronage of his younger cousin, Sir Thomas Walsingham. He was a friend to Marlowe, who, when under warrant for arrest, took refuge in his house; and to him Edward Blunt felt bound to dedicate the posthumous edition of *Hero and Leander* (1598). He writes :

I suppose my selfe executor to the unhappily deceased author of this Poem, upon whom knowing that in his life time you bestowed many kind favors, entertaining the parts of reckoning and woorth which you found in him, with good countenance and liberall affection : I cannot but see so far into the will of him dead, that whatsoever issue of his brain should chance to come abroad, that the first breath it should take might be the gentle aire of your liking.

Walsingham was also the 'constant friend' of Chapman, who dedicated to him *The Conspiracie and Tragedie of Charles Duke of Byron* (1608). Had Walsingham not 'stood little affected to these unprofitable rites of dedication', Chapman says he would have declared him to be the patron of other works.[1]

Other notable patrons of what may be called the older generation were Sir Christopher Hatton, the Earl of Oxford, Lord Charles Howard of Effingham, Lord Hunsdon, and Sir Walter Ralegh.

The Countess of Pembroke looked on the encouragement of the poets as a duty to the memory of her brother, Sir Philip Sidney. She owed much to him. To have the *Arcadia* written under her eyes and for her sole pleasure was the most liberal of educations. But there would have

---

[1] On the authenticity of the dedication printed in modern editions of *All Fooles* (1605), see T. M. Parrott's edition, 1907, pp. 139-42, and letter in *The Athenæum*, June 27, 1908, pp. 788-9.

been no *Arcadia* had Sidney not found continued inspiration
in the native gifts of this 'most dear, and most worthy
to be most dear lady'. Her own writings show how well
she was qualified to be regarded as his representative,
and to have books dedicated to her both 'for his and for
her own especial sake'. Thomas Howell, a retainer of
the Pembroke family, had dedicated his *Devises* to her
as early as 1581. Abraham Fraunce, the friend of Sidney
and Spenser, attached himself to her service and found
in her the patron of *The Lamentations of Amyntas . . translated out of Latine into English Hexameters* (1587), *The
Arcadian Rhetorike* (1588), *The Countesse of Pembrokes
Emanuell* (1591), and *The Countesse of Pembrokes Yvychurch*
(1591) ; and though the unsuitability of the subject kept
him from offering her *The Lawiers Logike* (1588), he addressed it to her husband, the second earl. Spenser, who
was moved by remembrance of the heroic spirit of Sidney
to include a sonnet to her in the first volume of *The Faerie
Queene*, and to dedicate to her *The Ruines of Time* (1591),
sang of her with grateful admiration in his *Colin Clout* (1595) :

> all I praise, but in the highest place,
> Urania, sister unto Astrofell,
>
> .   .   .   .   .   .
>
> She is the well of bountie and brave mynd,
> Excelling most in glorie and great light :
> She is the ornament of womankind,
> And Courts chief garlond with all vertues dight. (ll. 486–99)

Nicholas Breton dedicated to her *The Pilgrimage to Paradise*,
ioyned with the Countesse of Penbrookes love. (1592) and
Maries Exercise (1597), and called himself her 'unworthy
poet'. Nashe addressed her in his preface to Sidney's
Astrophel and Stella (1591) as 'eloquent secretary to the
Muses, most rare Countesse of Pembroke . . . whom Artes
doe adore as a second Minerva, and our Poets extoll as the
Patronesse of their invention'; and he added that his praises
of her virtues came short of the general report. Francis
Meres, the professional echo of current opinion, spoke of
her in *Palladis Tamia* (1598) as the representative English
patroness, worthy to be put in comparison with Octavia,
the sister of Augustus and the bountiful patroness of
Virgil. But no one spoke of her more eloquently than
the poet who knew her best. Samuel Daniel never forgot

the encouragement which he received from her in the household at Wilton. He called Wilton his best school.[1] In dedicating to her his *Delia* (1592) he said :

I desire onely to bee graced by the countenance of your protec-- tion : whome the fortune of our time hath made the happie and iudiciall Patronesse of the Muses (a glory hereditary to your house) to preserve them from those hidious Beastes, Oblivion and Barbarisme.[2]

He dedicated his *Cleopatra* (1594) to her as a companion piece to her own *Tragedie of Antonie,* a translation of Garnier's *Marc-Antoine.* And in 1609, in the dedication of his *Civile Warres,* he again spoke of her continued encouragement, adding that he would ever hold himself bound to her and her noble family. There were many other poets who felt her influence or enjoyed her bounty. Even Thomas Kyd was prompted by the example of her *Antonie* to make his translation of Garnier's *Cornelie,* though there is no evidence that he won her interest. She was the centre of the little Senecan school which held to the dramatic tenets of Sidney's early *Apologie,* and included Sidney's devoted friend, Fulke Greville. In her later life dedications to her became less frequent, but they still continued. What she had inherited from her brother passed in turn to her son. She was 'Sidney's sister, Pembroke's mother'. But for her own merits she was ' the subject of all verse ', as William Browne, one of her younger friends, called her in the epitaph which for long was attributed to Ben Jonson.

A representative list of the other patronesses during Shakespeare's lifetime may be formed from the dedications of Spenser's poems and the six dedications in Florio's translation of Montaigne. Among them Lucy Countess of Bedford has a clear pre-eminence. During the reign of James I she became more important than even the Countess of Pembroke, whose activities belong chiefly to the last years of Elizabeth. Drayton, Daniel, Jonson, Chapman, and Donne sang her praises.

It is to Shakespeare that Southampton owes his fame as a patron. There is abundant proof of his love of learning [3]

---

[1] *A Defence of Ryme,* ad. init.

[2] The prose address was replaced by a sonnet to his ' great patroness ' in the second edition (1594).

[3] He gave £100 in 1605 to the Bodleian Library (*Annals,* ed. W. D. Macray, 1890, p. 422), and collected books to the value of £360 for the library of his old college, St. John's, Cambridge.

and delight in poetry. But what is known of him apart from his connexion with Shakespeare would not of itself suggest that he was a patron of great importance. Florio boasted in his *Worlde of Wordes* (1598) that he had lived some years in Southampton's ' pay and patronage ', but Southampton shared the dedication of this dictionary with two others, the Earl of Rutland and the Countess of Bedford. Gervase Markham dedicated *The Most Honorable Tragedie of Sir Richard Grinvile* (1595) to Lord Mountjoy, and added three sonnets, the second of which is to Southampton, but there is no indication in it that Markham enjoyed any degree of intimacy ; while he acknowledges Mountjoy's favour, he only makes a bid for Southampton's. Robert Pricket's *Honors Fame in Triumph Riding. Or, The Life and Death of the late honorable Earle of Essex* (1604) was likewise dedicated to Southampton along with two other peers, and because of the part he had taken in Essex's rebellion. The works dedicated to him solely appear to be few in number. The best known of them is Nashe's *Unfortunate Traveller* (1594), but, for some unknown reason, and contrary to the usual custom, the dedication was withdrawn in the second edition. Others are William Burton's translation of Achilles Tatius (1597) ; [1] *The Historie of the Uniting of the Kingdom of Portugall to the Crowne of Castill* (1600)—an anonymous translation from Contestaggio, dedicated by Blunt the bookseller ; and Thomas Wright's *Passions of the minde in generall* (1604). There is also a manuscript version [2] by Thomas Wilson of the *Diana* of Montemayor (1596)—not the printed version by Bartholomew Yong (1598), which was dedicated to Penelope Rich. Altogether it is not a remarkable list. [3] The attempt to include other works by Nashe than his *Unfortunate Traveller* rests only on conjecture. The patron who is described at the conclusion of *Pierce Penilesse* (1592) may or may not be Southampton ; but the evidence for the identification of Southampton with ' the right Honorable the lord S.' to whom Nashe presented *The*

---

[1] See *The Times Literary Supplement*, February 10, 1905, p. 50, and H. R. Palmer's *List of English Translations* (Bibliographical Society, 1911), p. 1.

[2] British Museum Addit. MS. 18638.

[3] This list does not claim to be complete, but it has been made with a greater attempt at completeness than the lists of works dedicated to other patrons.

HENRY WRIOTHESLEY EARL OF SOUTHAMPTON

Choice of Valentines is nothing but the first letter of his name, and the evidence supplied by the matter of the introductory sonnet is strong on the other side. And as a whole the allusions in contemporary poetry to his patronage of literature are not remarkable. Sir John Beaumont laid stress on it in his elegy on Southampton's death :

> I keepe that glory last, which is the best,
> The love of learning, which he oft exprest
> In conversation, and respect to those
> Who had a name in artes, in verse or prose.

But Daniel, Chapman, and John Davies of Hereford, spoke rather of the part that he played in Elizabethan politics. There is nothing to associate Daniel with Southampton except the verse epistle addressed to him in 1603 on his misfortunes, and there are no signs in it of intimacy.

But it is enough for the fame of any man to have been the patron of Shakespeare, and it is Southampton's glory to be the only patron that Shakespeare is known to have had. The difference of tone in the dedications of *Venus and Adonis* and *The Rape of Lucrece* is remarkable. Aloof and formal terms give place, within a year, to expressions of affection whose like will not easily be found. ' The love I dedicate to your lordship ', says Shakespeare, ' is without end. . . . What I have done is yours ; what I have to do is yours ; being part in all I have, devoted yours.' There is no other dedication like this in Elizabethan literature. As *The Rape of Lucrece* was the last book that Shakespeare published, he did not again have occasion to speak of Southampton by name, and further proofs of their friendship must be sought in the *Sonnets*. A seventeenth-century tradition told of a gift. ' There is ', says Rowe, in his 'Life of Shakespeare', 'one instance so singular in the magnificence of this Patron of Shakespeare's, that if I had not been assur'd that the story was handed down by Sir William D'Avenant, I should not have ventur'd to have inserted, that my Lord Southampton at one time gave him a thousand pounds, to enable him to go through with a purchase which he heard he had a mind to.' If the tradition is true, the gift has no equal in the history of patronage. He was most active as a patron before he attained his twenty-eighth year, when he shared in

Essex's rebellion. He cannot be described as one of the great patrons of the reign of James I, though his interest in literature never abated.[1]

Southampton died in 1624, but the collected edition of Shakespeare's works, the First Folio of 1623, was not dedicated to him. Heminge and Condell selected as its patrons the Earl of Pembroke and his brother, the Earl of Montgomery. Their address provides the only scrap of evidence, as yet known, that can be advanced in proof of Pembroke's association with Shakespeare. But what they say does not necessarily imply personal relations :

But since your L. L. have beene pleas'd to thinke these trifles some-thing, heeretofore ; and have prosequuted both them, and their Authour living, with so much favour : we hope, that (they out-living him, and he not having the fate, common with some, to be exequutor to his owne writings) you will use the like indulgence toward them, you have done unto their parent. There is a great difference, whether any Booke choose his Patrones, or finde them : This hath done both. For, so much were your L. L. likings of the severall parts, when they were acted, as before they were published, the Volume ask'd to be yours.

There is nothing in this to show intimacy, or even greater interest than was generally taken in the performance of Shakespeare's plays. The identification of Pembroke with the ' Mr. W. H.' of the Sonnets is at best a wild conjecture. And the story that the Countess of Pembroke sent her son a letter in which she said ' we have the man Shakespeare with us '[2] must be discredited. This letter is not now to be found ; and if it ever existed, the chances are that it was a nineteenth-century forgery. It is to be expected that Pembroke knew Shakespeare, but there is nothing to suggest that his relations with Shakespeare corresponded in any way to his relations with Ben Jonson. Every New Year's Day he made Jonson the tactful gift of £20 to buy books ; and Jonson dedicated to him his favourite play, Catiline (1611), and what he called ' the ripest of my studies ', the Epigrams (1616). What appears to be the first book dedicated to Pembroke is Francis Davison's Poetical Rapsody (1602). About the same time Daniel addressed to him the Defence of Ryme. Thereafter

---

[1] For another account of Southampton as a patron, see Sir Sidney Lee's Life of Shakespeare (1915), pp. 664-71.
[2] See Extracts from the Letters and Journals of William Cory (1897), p. 168.

he gradually took over from his mother the duties of patronage that were traditional in the family since the days of Leicester. But he did not reach his full importance as a patron till about 1610. The distinctive title which Chapman gave him in the dedicatory sonnet in the *Iliad* (1611) is 'the learned and most noble patron of learning'. John Budge, the publisher of the first separate edition of the *Epigrams* of Harington, said, in inscribing it to Pembroke, that 'your Sidneian blood, and your famed favor to now despised Poesie, challenges the dedication of these Epigrams'. William Browne presented the second book of *Britannia's Pastorals* (1616) to

> that rare Lord, who judge and guerdon can
> The richer gifts which do advantage man ; [1]

in later life he was received into the household at Wilton. Pembroke was on terms of friendship with Donne, his kinsman George Herbert, and William Vaughan, who dedicated to him the sixth edition of his *Directions for Health* (1626). Other books—such as Nathanael Carpenter's *Geography delineated forth in two bookes*, bk. i (1625)—were dedicated to him as Chancellor of the University of Oxford, where Pembroke College bears his name. But his patronage during the later years of his life belongs to another age than Shakespeare's.

The one book in which James I showed an active interest was the authorized version of the Bible. He had, in the words of the translators, a 'vehement and perpetuated desire of the accomplishing and publishing of this worke', and it was presented to him in terms of flattery which now seem strangely out of place. Many other books were dedicated to him as King, such as Philemon Holland's translation of Plutarch's *Morals* (1603), Knolles's *History of the Turks* (1603), Bacon's *Advancement of Learning* (1605), Sylvester's translation of Du Bartas (1605), Camden's *Britannia* (sixth edition, 1607), Guillim's *Heraldry* (1610), and Minsheu's *Ductor in Linguas* (1617). But as a patron of literature he showed neither the taste nor the capacity of his son, Prince Henry. More remarkable than the number of books dedicated to the Prince is the deference which writers of experience paid to his judgement and his wishes. Ben Jonson furnished *The Masque of Queenes* (1609)

---

[1] Commendatory verses by John Morgan.

at his desire with its copious marginal notes, and dedicated it to him in these words :

Your favour to letters, and these gentler studies, that goe under the title of Humanitie, is not the least honor of your wreath. . . . Poetry, my Lord, is not borne with every man ; nor every day ; And in her generall right, it is now my minute to thanke your Highnesse, who not only do honor her with your eare, but are curious to examine her with your eye, and inquire into her beauties, and strengthes. Where though it hath prov'd a worke of some difficulty to me, to retrive the particular Authorities (according to your gracious command, and a desire borne out of iudgement) to those things, which I writ out of fulnesse, and memory of my former readings ; yet, now I have overcome it, the reward, that meetes me, is double to one act : which is, that therby your excellent understanding will not onely iustifie me to your owne knowledge, but decline the stiffenesse of others originall ignorance, already arm'd to censure.[1]

Chapman, who had dedicated to Essex the earlier portions of his *Iliad*, found in Henry the patron of the complete translation. In an undated petition to the Privy Council, written in poverty and age, and with the prospect of endless imprisonment, he described himself as

attending, fower yeares our late lost Prince ; in a service commanded by his highnes (being the translation of Homers Iliads out of the Greeke) And being promist, with his often Princely protestation of likinge, (both out of his owne rare towardnes, and confirmation of the best in the Homericall language) three hundred poundes ; And uppon his deathbed a good Pension during my life ; Commaunding me to go on with the Odysses [&c.].[2]

Even Sir Walter Ralegh, himself a patron, spoke with no less fervour. At the end of the preface to his *History of the World* (1614) he said that

it was for the service of that inestimable Prince Henry, the successive hope, and one of the greatest of the Christian World, that I undertooke this Worke. It pleased him to peruse some part thereof, and to pardon what was amisse. It is now left to the world without a Maister.

And within the book, in a passage of striking interest, he again lamented his own and his country's loss :

Of the Art of Warre by Sea, I had written a Treatise, for the Lord Henrie, Prince of Wales ; a subject, to my knowledge, never

---

[1] The dedication in the quarto (1609) was not reproduced in the folio edition of Jonson's works (1616) because of Henry's death in the interval.

[2] This important extract from a transcript of the now lost original has been supplied by Mr. Percy Simpson, who made it while the transcript was in the possession of the late Mr. Bertram Dobell. Cf. *The Athenæum*, April 6, 1901, p. 433.

William Hole sculp:

PRINCE HENRY by WILLIAM HOLE

handled by any man, ancient or moderne : but God hath spared me the labour of finishing it, by his losse ; by the losse of that brave Prince ; of which, like an Eclypse of the Sunne, wee shall finde the effects hereafter.[1]

There is much more in all these passages than the flattery of a prince. They speak the language of genuine admiration ; and they are the more remarkable as Henry died at the age of eighteen. His household accounts for the years 1610–12 show several payments to men of letters.[2] One of them is a 'gift' of £10 to Thomas Coryat, who presented Henry with the noble copy of the *Crudities* (1611) that is now in the British Museum. Another is an 'annuity' of £10 to Michael Drayton, who was then engaged on the *Poly-Olbion*. The poem was dedicated to Henry, and adorned with a full-length engraving by Hole representing him equipped for a tournament.[3]

It was not uncommon, as has been seen, for a book to be dedicated to several patrons. The most notable instance is Florio's Montaigne, which has the names of six noble ladies grouped together on the back of the title-page (reproduced Vol. I, p. 276), the dedications to two of them following at the beginning of each of the three books. Drayton had separate patrons for his ' heroical epistles ' ; and May followed this method with each book of his Lucan.

It was also the regular custom to dedicate a new edition to a new patron, if the original patron had died in the interval. Two cases will show that this is not to be regarded as the device of mere adventurers in the search for rewards. Hakluyt dedicated his *Diverse voyages* to Sidney ; after Sidney's death he dedicated his *Principall Navigations* to Sir Francis Walsingham ; after Walsingham's death he dedicated the second edition to Howard of Effingham. Camden dedicated the first four editions of his *Britannia* to Burghley, the fifth (1600) to Elizabeth, the sixth (1607) to James.

A disappointed author did not always wait for his original patron's death. James Sanford inscribed *The Garden of*

---

[1] First edition (1614), bk. iii, p. 351.
[2] See Peter Cunningham's *Extracts from the Accounts of the Revels at Court* (Shakespeare Society, 1842), pp. xvi–xviii.
[3] The engraving is in two states, without and with the words *Henricus Princeps* (cf. Vol. I, p. 110) ; cf. Sidney Colvin, *Early Engraving in England* (1905), pp. 95 and 152.

Pleasure (1573) to Leicester, and offered the second edition, under a somewhat different title (1576), to Christopher Hatton. The probable explanation is that Leicester had not given him what had been expected. A late instance of a sudden change of patron is found in the two issues of Massinger's *City-Madam*. The play was brought out post-humously by ' Andrew Pennycuicke, one of the Actors ', in 1658, when it was dedicated ' To the truly Noble John Wrath Esquire '. In 1659 it was dedicated ' To the truly Noble and virtuous Lady Ann, Countess of Oxford '. The type had been kept standing, and the terms of the dedication were not in any way altered ; the only change was in the heading.

Once a publisher had entered a book on the registers of the Stationers' Company it became his legal property, and an author had, it would appear, to supply new matter in order to gain anything from a new edition. Even Fairfax had no rights in so great a poem as his *Godfrey of Bulloigne*. The second edition (1624) was brought out by John Bill, the King's Printer, who added to Fairfax's verses to Queen Elizabeth a new dedication to Prince Charles. While Fairfax was still living Bill said that he, the publisher, ' could not leave this second birth of so excellent an author without a living patron '.

Men like Jonson, Chapman, and Daniel knew their patrons, and offered their works in recognition of friend-ship. They could all have said, in Jonson's words to the Earl of Dorset in his *Under-woods* :

> You cannot doubt, but I who freely know
> This Good from you, as freely will it owe ;
> And though my fortune humble me, to take
> The smallest courtesies with thankes, I make
> Yet choyce from whom I take them.

But the great majority of the Elizabethan dedications seem to have been unauthorized. The lesser men com-monly selected now one name and now another to put at the head of their works, and took their chance of a reward. If report said that a nobleman was generous, he became subject to a plague of dedications, which, with obvious purpose, lauded his accustomed favour to learning, his encouragement of the sons of the Muses, his thought of ' not the gift, but giver's poor good will '. He could not feel himself under any obligation. There was good excuse for him if, like Pope's Bufo,

> grown more frugal in his riper days,
> He paid some bards with port, and some with praise.

And the bards on their part were ready to find a grievance if he remained cold to what was often little better than a polite form of begging.

No better illustration of this need be desired than a passage in the 'Epistle Dedicatorie to Sir Walter Ralegh' with which Thomas Churchyard introduced his *Sparke of Frendship and Warme Goodwill* (1588) :

Yet waying how little Fortune hath done for mee, and howe fewe creditors I have, that have either lent me anie porcion of preferment (or procured me but a peece of anie certaine living) I thinke my self somwhat able with the little talent God hath given me, to repay all the debtes that ever I could bring to perfect remembrance, saving one a most honorable Personage, that I dedicated my booke of Choice [1] unto, who got me two great Seales (besides common courtesies manie) to shifte withall a season. And furthermore, your selfe 6. yeres past bestowed good speaches to the Q. Maiestie in my behalfe, by the which I got some comfortable recreation, to quicken my spirites and keepe me in breath. And yet loe a matter to be mused at, I have sixteene severall bookes printed presently to bee bought (albeit they are but trifles) dedicated in sundrie seasons to severall men off good and great credite, but to be plaine not one among them all, from the first day of my labour and studies, to this present yeere and hower, hath anie waye preferred my sutes, amended my state, or given mee anie countenaunce, I hope I am not much indebted to those, nor fallen so farre in their dangers, but may easely get out, though I yeelde them no more, but a customable good will. So finding my Muses franke and free from their servitude, I addresse this woorke of unfeyned friendshippe to your good consideration.

Churchyard clearly had flitted from patron to patron, with little or no claim on the consideration of any of them.

There were continual complaints of the niggardliness of patrons. Nashe in particular never ceased to speak of it. He counselled his friends not to cast away many months' labour on 'a clown that knowes not how to use a Scholer'.[2] 'Many write bookes', he said, 'to knights and men of great place, and have thankes with promise of a further

---

[1] *Churchyardes Choise* (1579) was dedicated to Sir Christopher Hatton, as well as *Churchyardes Chippes* (1578).
[2] *Pierce Penilesse*, ed. McKerrow, i. 241.

reward for their paines : others come of with a long Epistle
to some rufling Courtier, that sweares swoundes and bloud,
as soone as ever their backe is turnd, a man can not goe
in the streetes for these impudent beggers.'[1]   The case for
the patron could easily be stated.   It is equally clear that
the author had no certainty of an adequate reward.

The contemporary criticisms of the system of patronage
vary with the standpoint of the writer.   On the one hand
there are the complaints of men like Churchyard and
Nashe.   Richard Barnfield lamented the indifference and
selfishness of the rich in *The Complaint of Poetrie, for the
Death of Liberalitie* (1598) :

> I never then, did write one verse in vain ;
> Nor ever went my Poems unregarded :
> Then did each Noble breast, me intertaine,
> And for my Labours I was well rewarded :
> > But now *Good wordes* are stept in *Bounties* place,
> > Thinking thereby, her glorie to disgrace.

Even Daniel, who had no reason to be dissatisfied with
his own experiences, and thought only of the proper
encouragement of literature, felt that much was amiss :

> And it were well, if in this season, when
> > They leave erecting Churches, Colledges,
> And pious monuments, they would build men
> > Who of their glory may be witnesses. . . .
> For, would they but be ples'd to know, how small
> > A portion of that over-flowing waste
> Which runs from them, would turne the wheeles and all
> > The frame of wit, to make their glory last,
> I thinke they would doe something : but the stirre
> > Still about greatnesse, gives it not the space
> To looke out from it selfe, or to conferre
> > Grace but by chance, and as men are in place.[2]

On the other hand there are the critics who, with equal
reason, spoke of the abuse of patronage.   After dealing
in *The Advancement of Learning* with the old ' trencher
philosophers ' who were usually little better than solemn
parasites, Bacon turned to his own times to say that
' Neither is the modern dedication of books and writings,
as to patrons, to be commended : for that books (such
as are worthy the name of books) ought to have no patrons
but truth and reason '.   John Stephens wrote a character

---

[1] *An Almond for a Parrat*, ed. McKerrow, iii. 341.
[2] Commendatory verses in Florio's *New World of Words*, 1611.

of the 'mercenary poet',[1] describing him as 'the most faithfull obsequious servant of him that gives most'. John Davies of Hereford spoke out boldly in 'Papers Complaint':

> under Lords wings Metaphoricall
> All Authors creepe, a shame upon them all . . .
> Away with *Patronage*, a plague upon't,
> That hideous Word is worse then *Termagant*.
> Call for no aide where none is to be found ;
> *Protect my Booke* : such Bookes, O *fates*, confound.[2]

Shakespeare too glanced at the abuses in the dedication scene at the beginning of *Timon of Athens* :

> When we for recompense have prais'd the vile,
> It stains the glory in that happy verse
> Which aptly sings the good.   (I. i. 15–17)

Other dedication scenes occur in Dekker's *Honest Whore* (second part) [3] and in John Daye's *Parliament of Bees* (Character 5). In the former of these the patron will not consider the advances of the author till he makes sure that the book has not already been dedicated to some one else.

> Kings may be Schollers Patrons, but faith tell me,
> To how many Lands besides hath this bird flowne,
> How many partners share with me ?

It was evidently a common trick to furnish several copies of the same book with dedications to different patrons, who might each be deluded into thinking that it was dedicated to him alone. Dekker described the trick fully in his *Lanthorne and Candle-light*. The patron had cause to beware of the flattery of an unknown author. He knew too that the recommendation which his name carried with it was sometimes a bigger reward than he would willingly have given. Authors in their need were ready to try their luck even with one whose only qualifications for patronage were position and wealth. Such a patron is described in Thomas Thorpe's mocking dedication of Marlowe's *Lucan* (1600) to his friend Edward Blunt. Another mocking dedication fittingly begins *The Guls Horne-booke* (1609).

---

[1] *Satyrical Essayes Characters and Others* (1615), pp. 239–44 ; cf. his essay ' Of Poetry ', pp. 102–13.
[2] *The Scourge of Folly* (1611), ' Papers Complaint ', pp. 241–2.
[3] Act I, ed. 1630, A4v B1 ; Pearson's reprint (1873), ii. 101.

Sometimes a dedication was printed without a heading, which could be supplied in writing. There are, for instance, in the British Museum [1] two copies of Walter Bailey's *A Briefe Discourse of certain Bathes* (1587), in one of which the superscription has been inserted, while in the other it is wanting. It need not be assumed that there was any attempt at fraud. The recipient had no reason to regard himself as sole patron, and must have known that his name was written only in his own copy. Perhaps the author adopted this device as a convenient method of making several personal gifts. But the device lent itself to fraud, as the headings could easily be supplied in print, and Thomas Jordan used it fraudulently in 1664. [2] An instance in every way remarkable of a dedication specially printed for a gift-copy is in the first Quarto of *Cynthia's Revels*, entitled *The Fountaine of Selfe-Love* (1601), which Jonson presented to Camden. [3] In words which anticipate his great epigram on Camden, Jonson there spoke of himself as 'Alumnus olim, æternum Amicus'. *Cynthia's Revels* was publicly dedicated to 'The Court' in the Folio of 1616, but Camden was there paid the greater honour of being chosen as the patron of the first play, *Every Man in his Humour*.

Little is known of what the author received. Writers of social rank, as has been seen, hoped for office under the crown. Spenser was given a pension of £50 for his *Faerie Queene*. Shakespeare is said to have had £1,000 from Southampton. Chapman was promised £300 by Prince Henry; Drayton received from him an annuity of £10, and Sylvester one of £20. Jonson had £20 every year from Pembroke to buy books; he lived for long in the house of Lord Aubigny, whose 'timely succours' he acknowledged in the dedication of *Sejanus* and in the *Epigrams*; he was forced to accept the bounty of patrons because, up to 1618, 'of all his Playes he never gained two hundreth pounds'. [4] In the absence of further evidence about the reward for the dedication of minor works, what Peele was given by the Earl of Northumberland for *The*

---

[1] See *Catalogue of English Books to 1640*, vol. i, p. 87.
[2] See Collier, *Bibliographical Account*, vol. i, pp. 416, 419.
[3] This copy is in the Kemble collection, formerly at Chatsworth. The dedication leaf is inserted between signatures A and A2. The writer is indebted for these facts to Mr. Percy Simpson.
[4] 'Conversations with Drummond.'

Honour of the Garter may be taken as typical. Peele
celebrated in this poem the earl's installation as a knight
of the Garter in 1593, and he received for it £3.[1] Richard
Robinson once received £3, but his usual reward ranged
from two to ten shillings.

The habit of offering to a patron the published version
of a successful play appears to have been established by
Ben Jonson. Chapman speaks of the habit as recent in
the dedication of *The Revenge of Bussy D'Ambois* (1613).[2]
The reward which might be expected by a dramatist of
ordinary merit was evidently forty shillings. The authority
for this is the dedication of Nathaniel Field's *A Woman
is a Weather-cocke* (1612). ' I Did determine ', says Field,
' not to have Dedicated my Play to any Body, because
forty shillings I care not for, and above, few or none will
bestowe on these matters, especially falling from so fame-
lesse a pen as mine is yet.'

The system of patronage which began in the age of
Elizabeth continued till the eighteenth century. It arose
with the development of the printing trade, and it ended
when the growth of the reading public enabled authors
to obtain larger payments from their booksellers.

[1] Peele's works, ed. A. H. Bullen, ii. 316.
[2] Cf. the dedication to Sir Arthur Mannering, signed by Francis Burton,
the publisher, of *The Statelie Tragedie of Claudius Tiberius Nero* (1607).

BIBLIOGRAPHY.—The chief authorities are mentioned throughout the
chapter and in the footnotes ; and to them must be added R. B. McKERROW's
article on Robinson's *Eupolemia* in *The Gentleman's Magazine*, April 1906,
pp. 277–84. The subject is dealt with in PHOEBE SHEAVYN's *The Literary
Profession in the Age of Elizabeth*, 1909, and H. B. WHEATLEY's *The Dedication of Books*, 1887, and is touched on in H. G. Aldis's chapter on ' The Book
Trade ' in *The Cambridge History of English Literature*, vol. iv. See also
G. J. GRAY's *Index to Hazlitt's Handbook*, 1893.

XXIII

BOOKSELLERS, PRINTERS, AND THE STATIONERS' TRADE

BY

R. B. McKERROW

THERE were many things in the England of Shakespeare upon which we can look back with satisfaction and even with pride to-day, but among these the condition of printing, and of the book trade in general, is certainly not to be numbered. Not unpromising in its beginnings, the art of printing never developed in England as it did on the Continent: with very few exceptions the books produced here are not to be compared, whether in beauty, in correctness, or in perfection of workmanship, with the ordinary output of the chief foreign presses. More especially during the century 1551–1650 was there a steady decline not only in the mechanical art of the press, but in the enterprise, ability, and social position of the masters and men engaged in all the various branches of book production and distribution. In the earlier part of the period we indeed find a few printers, such as Richard Grafton, John Day, and Reynold Wolfe, who were men of education and even of learning, but how far are even these from ranking with the Etiennes at Paris and Geneva, Paolo and Aldo Manuzio at Venice, the Elzevirs at Leyden, or Christoffel Plantin at Antwerp! Later, the trade came more and more into the hands of an inferior class, until the great majority of those who dealt in books were tradesmen pure and simple, regarding their business solely from the point of view of immediate returns.

There were two chief reasons for this inferiority of the English book-trade. In the first place, the press was in the main a vernacular one, and lacked the consideration which would have been lent to it by the association of the

learned. The circulation of elaborate and expensive editions
of the Greek and Latin classics in England alone was
insufficient to make their production remunerative, even

Der Buchdrucker.

Ich bin geschicket mit der preß
So ich aufftrag den Firniß reß/
So bald mein dienr den bengel zuckt/
So ist ein bogn papyrs gedruckt.
Da durch kombt manche Kunst an tag/
Die man leichtlich bekommen mag.
Vor zeiten hat man die bücher gschribn/
Zu Meintz die Kunst ward erstlich triebn.

The Printer, by Jost Amman.

if England had been more favourably situated than it was
as regards manuscript sources, and the demand for such
works was easily and cheaply supplied by importation
from abroad. English printers and publishers not un-
naturally preferred to invest their money and labour in

wares more readily saleable, and so far as they printed the classics at all, devoted their attention mainly to cheap editions for school purposes. We meet with several complaints on the part of scholars of the difficulty of getting their works properly printed in this country, and of the want of enterprise shown by the trade in general.

The second and indeed chief cause of the general slackness was the censorship which was exercised by the Government over all kinds of book production. This, while far from efficient as regards the purpose for which it was instituted, produced its usual effect of diminishing the enterprise and lowering the character of all who came under its influence. It was indeed of such importance in its results upon the trade in general that it will be necessary to give some account of its beginnings and progress.

In the early years of printing in this country there appears to have been little, if any, attempt at control on the part of the authorities, and practically the sole official recognition which the trade received was the appointment from time to time of a King's Printer. Even when the State began to concern itself in the matter, its attention was at first entirely directed to the foreign printers resident in England, and to the importers of books from abroad, and its action was designed to protect the native workman. In 1484 an Act to regulate the conditions under which foreigners might trade in England had expressly excluded from its provisions scriveners, binders, and printers, who were allowed to carry on their business where and how they pleased. This complete free trade in books lasted until 1523, when an Act was passed forbidding aliens who practised any handicraft in England from taking other apprentices than English-born, and from keeping more than two foreign journeymen. The Act makes no special mention of printers, who are, however, of course included among handicraftsmen. In 1529 a more stringent Act was passed which had the effect of preventing any further establishment of foreign presses in England, but did not interfere with those already existing. The last of these ordinances which we need notice was in 1534, when the importation of *bound* books was prohibited, and the purchase from foreigners of any books printed abroad, except for the purpose of the wholesale trade, was forbidden. Aliens were, in fact, simply to act as importers, selling their wares to the English booksellers, not direct to the public. Mr. Duff notes that these enactments against aliens were so effective that ' whereas in the first forty years after the introduction of printing into England the majority of persons connected with the book trade were foreigners, the second forty years saw this state of things entirely changed, all the important men of business being Englishmen, and the foreigners decreasing in number and status '.

The year 1538 saw the commencement of a long series of enactments of a different kind; those, namely, which had for their object the suppression of treasonable or heretical literature. Before, however, we turn to these, it may be well to say something as to the purpose and justification of the Tudor censorship in general. Theoretically the control seems to have been theological, political, and moral; practically, however, it was exercised solely for political purposes, though the books censored were, for the most part, theological. It is generally hard for a later generation to understand the workings of the censorship in an earlier one, or to see why one book is deemed obnoxious, while another far more revolutionary in its teachings is allowed to pass, but it seems clear that the principal anxiety of those who directed the censorship was to prevent the circulation of anything which could bring into question the unity and authority of the Established Church, whatever at the time it might be. Heresy as heresy mattered little, what did matter was the danger of schism : there was nothing of religious bigotry, or even of the desire to save souls ; the intention was throughout political, to avoid the danger of civil dissension.

That the censorship was so exercised is its main defence, even, some may think, its justification ; for the unity of the English Church was, in the sixteenth century, vital to a degree which we can now scarcely realize. To the mass of the people outside London the Church was the chief visible symbol of the unity of the State : in days when communication was so slow and the dissemination of news so irregular, it must indeed have been practically the only one. Without it, a centralizing Government of the Elizabethan type would hardly have been possible.

The maintenance of that unity was, then, indispensable ; and if we grant this, we cannot greatly blame the Government for objecting, in so important a matter, to a freedom of discussion for which the times were clearly not ripe.

The various injunctions, proclamations, and decrees establishing or confirming the censorship are so closely interconnected and in some points so obscure that it is impossible to give an intelligible account of them in a few words, and those desirous of knowing more about them must be referred to Mr. Duff's introduction to his *Century of the English Book Trade* and to that by the present writer to *A Dictionary of Printers, 1557–1640*. The importance of the earlier decrees at any rate is overshadowed by the great change which was made in the conditions and status of the book-trade by the incorporation of the Stationers' Company on May 4, 1557.

Next to the establishment of Caxton's press at Westminster eighty years earlier, this was the most important event in the history of English printing. The Company was indeed not altogether a new thing. It had existed since 1404 in the form originally of a brotherhood of scriveners or copyists, and seems to have admitted printers to membership almost as soon as the art was introduced into England. Unfortunately, however, no records of its doings earlier than 1554 are now extant, and practically nothing is known of its early history. The incorporation in 1557 made probably little difference in the membership of the society, but it profoundly altered its position and power by constituting it the official authority over the whole of the book trade in the country, and holding it responsible for the doings of its members. For the future almost all decrees as to the printing and sale of books were issued in the form of instructions to the master and wardens of the Company, who were to see to their being carried out.

The charter of incorporation sets forth that the society shall consist in the first instance of a master, two wardens, and ninety-four freemen, all of whom are named, being ' freemen of the mystery or art of a stationer of our city of London and suburbs thereof '. They are authorized to hold meetings to elect their master and wardens from time to time, make such rules as are necessary for the well-being of the society, own a limited amount of property in London, and sue and be sued as a corporate body. They are given the sole rights of printing throughout England, saving that other persons may be permitted to print by royal warrant, and the wardens are empowered to search the premises of any 'stamper, printer, binder, or seller of any manner of books within our kingdom of England', and to seize any books printed 'contrary to the form of any statute, act, or proclamation made or to be made'. They may burn the books thus seized, and imprison the printer of them, or any one resisting them in their search, for three months, and fine him 100s., the fine going half to the Company and half to the Crown.

It is unnecessary to insist on the immense importance of this charter to the trade. Not only did it give the Company supreme power over printing, but the right of search permitted the wardens to exercise quite effective, if somewhat anomalous, control over all stationers, publishers, importers of books, or bookbinders not belonging to the Company, as well as over its own members. From the point of view of the Government it was an excellent piece of policy, for it is easy to see how much more effective a search for contraband literature or secret presses would be if made by the wardens of the Company, familiar as they were with every detail of the business, than if—as was formerly the case—it was entrusted to bishops and justices of the peace, who might fail to recognize printing materials even when they found them.

The charter of the stationers was confirmed by Queen Elizabeth in 1559, and in the same year began the strict censorship, which was maintained—at least in intention—throughout the reign. Twenty-one years before, it had been ordered that certain classes of books should not be printed without having been previously examined by the King or the Privy Council, but there is little evidence that this rule was strictly enforced. Now in 1559 we find new injunctions on much the same lines, but far more precise. According to these,

no manner of person shall print any manner of book or paper of what sort, nature, or in what language soever it be, except the same be first licensed by her Majesty by express words in writing, or by six of her Privy Council or be perused and licensed by the Archbishops of Canterbury and York, the Bishop of London, the

Chancellors of both Universities, the bishop being Ordinary, and the Archdeacon also of the place where any such shall be printed, or by two of them, whereof the Ordinary of the place to be always one.

The names of such as shall allow the book are to be added at the end—presumably at the end of the manuscript—' for a testimony of the allowance thereof'. Similarly, pamphlets, plays, and ballads, which appear not to come under the description of 'any manner of book or paper', are, before printing, to be approved by at least three members of the Court of Ecclesiastical Commission; and, lastly, all books dealing with religion, polity, or government, whether printed abroad or at home, are to be submitted to the same body, which may permit or prohibit them at its discretion. The only exception to these rules is in favour of books which have been or are generally used in universities and schools. The injunction is addressed especially to the Wardens and Company of the Stationers, who are evidently expected to see it carried out.

In 1559 and for some years after, a few printers made use, on their title-pages, of some such formula as 'Set forth and allowed according to the order appointed in the Queen's Majesty's Injunctions', to indicate that the terms of the injunctions had been complied with. Later we sometimes find 'Seen and allowed' (as on the title-page of the first edition of Bacon's *Essays*, 1597), less frequently 'Perused and allowed'; at the end of Stubbes's *Anatomie of Abuses* (1583) there is an example of a much fuller form:

Perused, authorised, and allowed, according to the order appointed in the Queen's Majesty's Injunctions.

We need not delay over a Star Chamber decree of 1566, much on the same lines, but further requiring that all engaged in the trade should enter into recognizances of reasonable sums of money to observe the law, and we may pass at once to the still more stringent enactment of 1586. By this it was provided that all printers should deliver a note of the number of their presses and of any which they should erect hereafter. There was to be no printing save at London, Cambridge, and Oxford. In view of the excessive number of printers already in business—some fifty-three in London, as we know from other sources—the erection of any new presses was forbidden until the

number should be diminished. On its being decided by
the Archbishop of Canterbury and the Bishop of London
that there was room for a new printer, they were to inform
the master and wardens of the Stationers' Company, and the
Company should then elect out of their number a fit person
to have the grant of a licence. Severe punishments were
decreed against the use or possession of any secret press
and against the printing of anything which had not been
perused and allowed by the Archbishop of Canterbury
and the Bishop of London or one of them. Lastly, the
number of apprentices that might be taken by any printer
is limited.

This was in several respects the most important enactment dealing with the press during the period. From
1586 until after Shakespeare's death there is nothing
which materially alters the position of affairs.

Such, then, were the chief regulations affecting the book
trade in the sixteenth century. They were severe enough,
and should have rendered quite impossible the sale and
circulation of literature obnoxious to the authorities. Like
many Elizabethan ordinances they seem, however, to have
been very irregularly observed—indeed, so much is indicated by their being several times renewed. Secret printing
seems to have gone on almost continuously until towards
the close of the century, and there must also have been
much smuggling of forbidden books from the Continent.
It is improbable that the demand for contraband literature was anything like what it was for Lutheran books in
Henry VIII's days, when, according to John Foxe the
martyrologist, 'some gave five marks, some more, some
less, for a book ; some gave a load of hay for a few chapters
of St. James, or of St. Paul in English ', but now there
were both the Catholics and the extreme Puritans to be
supplied, and one can imagine that the trade would be
fairly profitable. Even apart from that secret printing
which was in intentional defiance of the law, there seems
to have been much slackness in obeying the regulations
as to licensing. The authorities named in the injunctions
could not of course themselves peruse all the books which
were submitted for licence, and frequently delegated their
functions to others : it is not improbable that it was only
when books were by suspected authors or upon dangerous

subjects that any care was taken that the orders should be strictly followed. Unfortunately in the case of a very large number of works we have no evidence whether they were licensed or not.

Little or nothing in the shape of reports or discussions of the working of the censorship has come down to us. Our knowledge of it is, save for the injunctions and a few miscellaneous papers dealing with special cases, derived almost entirely from the records of the Stationers' Company. These records, which happily are almost complete from the date of the incorporation of the Company to the present time, deal of course with a variety of matters : among them are lists of apprentices taken by the various members, proceedings of official meetings, fines levied for offences, as well as the ordinary accounts of the Company, but their chief interest to us at the present day is that they include a series of entries of books published. This is of the highest bibliographical importance, for it enables us to ascertain the date of original publication of many works of which the early editions are undated or have disappeared, and incidentally tells us much about the licensing. The original purpose of these entries seems to have been as a register of copyright. Any member of the Company proposing to publish a book was apparently entitled and even required to have it entered to his name upon payment of a small fee, and, provided that no objection was raised to the entry on the ground of a prior claim, he then had the sole right of printing or publishing it for the future. Presumably the register was open to inspection by members of the Company in order that they might guard their interests in this respect. Transfers of copyright from one publisher to another were often, though by no means always, recorded in the same list.

The register of copyrights seems, however, to have served at the same time another purpose, namely, as a certification that the conditions imposed by the law had been duly complied with. Whenever a licence was required, the wardens of the Company apparently demanded the production of the licence before permitting the entry of the book in the register. Thus, although the Company in no way took any direct part in the censorship, an entry in the register—at any rate from about 1566

POLY-OLBION

JOHN MORRIS.

GREAT BRITAINE

By Michaell Drayton Esqr:

London printed for { M Lownes. I Browne. I Helme. I Busbie. } Engraud by W Hole

Engraved by WILLIAM HOLE

onwards—may be taken to imply, in the absence of any statement to the contrary, that the book had been duly submitted to the censors and passed by them. From 1569 onwards the name of the licenser—in early times generally the Bishop of London—is frequently given in the entry.

There is evidence that all books were supposed to be entered in the register of the Company, with the exception of certain classes of works which were the monopoly of particular firms, such as Bibles, almanacks, and a few school-books. Many books, however, were published without this having been done. The reason for the omission is not clear, for the fee demanded was too small to be worth serious consideration when set against the possibility of losing the copyright of a book by non-payment. In some cases it is probable that the printer was not anxious to call undue attention to his work, in others the cause of non-entry may have been simply carelessness, or the conviction that the book was not one which would run to a second edition, and that therefore it would be a waste of time and money to secure the copyright. Whatever the reason, this irregularity in the entries must make us suspect that there was similar irregularity in submitting works for licence.

The influence of the censorship upon the book trade was undoubtedly bad, in the main because it tended to stifle free competition among the printing houses. Success must have depended far less upon enterprise or good workmanship than on being in favour with the authorities. A printer who stood well with them would no doubt have a much better chance of getting books that had been submitted by him, or which he was known to be about to print, licensed quickly, than one who was regarded with dislike or suspicion. As we know from more than one complaint, the work of Puritan writers was especially liable to long delays, even when a licence was finally granted; and the whole system must inevitably have led to favouritism of the worst kind. On the other hand, it can hardly be maintained that literature suffered at all by it. There is, so far as the writer is aware, not a single instance of a work of literary importance having been lost to us through the refusal to license it; though of course we cannot say what might have been written had freer criticism of current affairs been permitted.　But even had there been no formal censorship, there would undoubtedly have been other checks on the publication of anything seriously obnoxious to Queen Elizabeth or her ministers.

The Puritan grievance is loudly voiced by Stubbes in *A Motive to good Workes* (1593) :

I cannot but lament the corruption of our time, for (alas) now-a-days it is grown to be a hard matter to get a good book licensed without staying, peradventure, a quarter of a year for it ; yea, sometimes two or three years before he can have it allowed, and in the end happly rejected too ; so that that which many a good man hath . . . travailed long in . . . shall . . . never see the light ; whilst . . . other bookes, full of all filthines, scurrility, baudry, dissolutenes, cosenage, conycatching and the like . . . are either quickly licensed, or at least easily tollerate.

By the censorship the whole body of the trade was affected alike, but there was another practice of the day which bore especially hardly on the smaller printing-houses.　This was the granting by the Queen of monopolies for the printing of certain classes of books.　Thus at one time Jugge had the sole right of printing Bibles and Testaments, Tottle of printing law-books, Roberts and Watkins of almanacks and prognostications, Marsh of certain school-books, John Day of the A B C. and the Catechism, and so on.　A decennial monopoly granted to Day for the printing of Ascham's *Scholemaster* is indicated at the foot of the title-page by the legend, ' Cum Gratia et Privilegio Regiae Maiestatis, per Decennium '.　Even persons who were not printers at all might be granted privileges of this kind ; thus, the musician, William Byrd, had a mono-poly of music-books and paper ruled for music, and one Francis Flower, a gentleman, had the sole right of printing Lily's Grammar, a right which he farmed out to a group of printers for £100 a year.　The existence of these patents was naturally a great grievance to the poorer members of the Company, for it deprived them of much of the most profitable work, and there was in 1582 a serious attempt at revolt, which at one time threatened to cause a split in the society.　Several of the younger members declared their intention of printing whatever seemed to them good, without regard to the patents, and their action resulted in the Star Chamber case of John Day against Roger Ward

and William Holmes for illegally printing the A B C. and
Catechism in contravention of his privilege. The matter
was eventually settled by the patentees agreeing to give
up a number of their most valuable monopolies for the
benefit of needy members of the Company.

The history of the formula, 'Cum privilegio ad imprimendum solum'—used by Shakespeare in *The Taming
of the Shrew*, IV. iv. 93, with allusion to marriage rites—is
somewhat curious. It has recently been pointed out by
Mr. A. W. Pollard that the original intention of the phrase
was to make clear that no other privilege had been granted
than that of a mere licence to print. Hence, in 1538,
printers were expressly forbidden to use the words 'cum
privilegio regali' without adding 'ad imprimendum solum'.
Later, however, it was taken to mean that the printer had
a monopoly of printing the book, and it is evidently in
this sense that Shakespeare understood it.

Up to this point we have treated the book trade as
though it were a homogeneous body all engaged in the
same business. It seems certainly to have been so regarded
by the Government, but, in reality, the distinctions between
the several branches of printer, publisher, bookseller, and
bookbinder, were clearly recognized, although there was
a good deal more overlapping than there is at present.
As regards the two first we shall not be far wrong if we
say that, at any rate towards the close of the sixteenth
century, all printers were also publishers, but many
publishers were not printers; this being indeed what we
might expect from the strict limitation in the number of
printers and from the fact that publishers did not necessarily belong to the Stationers' Company, whereas printers
did. There seems to be no evidence of any master printer
who was merely a printer, that is to say, who did not
himself deal to some extent in copyrights and issue books
on his own account. On the other hand, even as early
as 1582, we learn that the smaller printers were becoming
financially dependent upon the publishers. In that year
Christopher Barker, the Queen's Printer, reporting on the
condition of the trade, said that the provision of type, &c.,
was so costly that most of the printers were driven to
compound beforehand with the booksellers (i. e. publishers) at such low rates for their work that they made

little, if any, profit. The booksellers now, he says, keep no printing-house, but merely pay for the workmanship. In this report we have a clear indication that the two branches of the trade were tending to become altogether distinct, though it was some time before they actually became so.

Printing and publishing were then recognized as separate trades : can we say the same thing of publishing and bookselling ? On the whole it seems not ; but the evidence is too scanty to enable us to speak with certainty on the point. It seems clear that the publishers, as well as many printers, had open stalls either in St. Paul's Churchyard or before their own houses, at which they sold books ; what we do not know is whether the books which they sold were their own publications alone or whether they dealt in all books, new and second-hand. The most probable view seems to be that the larger publishers dealt chiefly in their own works, but also did a certain amount of business in foreign books as well as in English books of the better class, while the smaller firms, who published little themselves, carried on a general trade in the cheaper literature. Such general book-shops are referred to in the prologue to Rowlands's *Tis Merrie when Gossips meete*, and in Dekker's *Guls Horne-booke*.

A good deal of bookselling was, as we should expect, done at Oxford and Cambridge, and there were ' stationers ' at several of the larger provincial towns, but the amount of their trade in books cannot be ascertained with certainty. The lighter literature probably found a ready sale at the numerous fairs throughout the country, and ballads were sold by itinerant hawkers. London, however, was during the whole period the main book-mart for the country, and this not only because there was, save at the Universities, no printing outside it, but at least as much on account of the great influx from the provinces which took place into London at each of the four law-terms.

Few personal details have been preserved of the Elizabethan printers and publishers; not one of them seems to have been of remarkable attainments. Save for one or two of the University printers and a London compositor who was also a pamphleteer and dramatist—Henry Chettle —we find among them no scholars, no authors, and hardly even a compiler of importance. They were merchants pure and simple. One or two of them such as Waldegrave the Puritan have some small place in religious history, but the most noteworthy are known for their commercial achievements alone. For the most part they entered the trade at an early age as apprentices and could have had no opportunity for an extended education : only one or two were university men, who took up printing or publishing comparatively late in life, having been originally intended for some profession. They came from various classes of society : many were the sons of earlier stationers or printers ; others the sons of well-to-do tradesmen or of smaller professional men. Christopher Barker, the Queen's Printer from 1577 to 1588, owner of what was probably the largest business of the time, is said to have been related to a Garter King of Arms of the same name, and at the time of his death was a person of considerable wealth. The brothers John and William Jaggard, the latter of whom printed the First Folio of Shakespeare, were the sons of a barber surgeon of London. Robert Dexter, publisher of a large number of popular books, was the son of a sailor of Ipswich. Richard Field, the printer of Shakespeare's earliest works, *Venus and Adonis* (1593) and *Lucrece* (1594) was the son of a tanner of Stratford-on-Avon, and it has been plausibly conjectured that it was owing to his being a fellow townsman that these works came into his hands to print. He became one of the most important of contemporary printers, was Master of the Stationers' Company in 1616 and 1622, and died in 1624. Nothing is known of his connexion with Shakespeare, and after the two early poems he printed no more of his work. As Field's output consisted mainly of large and serious volumes, and as he hardly touched popular literature at all, this fact has no significance.

Turning now from questions of the trade in general, let us consider the actual process of the publication of a book in Elizabethan times. It is first to be remarked that there seems to have been a considerable circulation of works in manuscript. Not only was much verse circulated in this form, without ever getting into print at all, but occasionally larger works were thus handed about among the friends of the author. A well-known example is that of Sidney's *Arcadia*, which, written in the years 1580–3, was already famous by 1587, though it was not printed until three years later. There is evidence of a certain amount of trade in manuscript copies of books, carried on by scriveners, but this can hardly have been very large. Comparatively few of the manuscript copies of Elizabethan works which have come down to the present time have the appearance of having been written by professional scribes, though one would expect that from their greater neatness and legibility these would have been more valued and more likely to be preserved than private copies. They would of course in comparison with printed books have been very expensive, certainly no cheaper than a transcript of a modern work of equal size made at the present day ; indeed, considering that writing was by no means a universal accomplishment, it is reasonable to suppose that they would have been dearer. On the other hand printed books were, as we shall see, little more expensive than they are to-day.

Apparently transcripts of a manuscript were made without restriction,[1] for although such copying was as illegal as it is at present, detection was probably difficult and prosecution certainly not worth while. The same was probably true also of the printing of such transcripts : we find frequent complaints that a work has been published without the knowledge or consent of the author or his representatives, but instances in which action was taken in consequence are very few. We do, however, hear of one work the publication of which was stopped for this reason. This was Sidney's *Arcadia*, and the fact is known to us from a letter written in November 1586, a month after the author's death, by Sir Fulke Greville to Sir Francis Walsingham. The writer states that he has learnt from one Ponsonby, a bookbinder, that some one intends to print the work. Ponsonby, who is presumably identical with the bookseller of the name by whom the *Arcadia* was eventually issued, had inquired whether this was being done by the consent of Sidney's friends, and had advised that, if this was not so, notice

---

[1] Thomas Nashe, the satirist, complains in the dedication of his *Terrors of the Night*, that that work had—before being printed—' progressed from one scrivener's shop to another, and at length grew so common that it was ready to be hung out for one of their signs, like a pair of indentures.'

should be given to the Archbishop of Canterbury or to Dr. Cosin, who had copies for perusal with a view to licensing. Probably representations were made and the licence refused, for the book did not appear until 1590, but the course proposed for stopping publication strongly suggests that there was no regular or direct way of doing it, and that one who could not bring influence to bear with the licensers might have found difficulty in protecting his rights in similar circumstances.

Having obtained the manuscript, the publisher, before sending it to press, would have to see that the work was properly licensed and, if he thought fit, would enter it at Stationers' Hall. He would then, if not a printer himself, contract with one for the printing of the work. The printer might, if he had a large establishment, employ journeymen or apprentices to set it up in type on the premises, or he might, according to a curious and, one would imagine, most inconvenient system, give out the work to compositors to be set up in their own homes, only doing the actual printing himself. While the work was being printed the author would often visit the printing-house for the purpose of reading the proofs, and sometimes had the type corrected during the actual progress of the impression, with the result that differences frequently occur in copies of the same edition of a book, in some cases extending to the insertion or omission of whole lines. There is much of interest in the study of the actual processes of Elizabethan printing, a knowledge of which will often be found to throw light on points of textual criticism and even of literary history, but any attempt to discuss such matters here would lead us into technicalities alien to the design of the present work.

We may, however, notice in passing the employment from quite an early date of literary men as publishers' advisers, editors, or correctors of the press. In the economy of the Elizabethan printing-house such persons had never anything approaching the importance or status that they had on the Continent, but it seems clear that some of the chief printers had a connexion with one or more scholars or writers who assisted them when required. Thus John Foxe, after being a reader of the press with Johann Herbst, or Oporinus, at Basle during Mary's reign, lived on his

return to England for some time with the printer of the
English edition of his *Actes and Monuments*, John Day,
and took a prominent part in his business. We hear later of
Gabriel Harvey, Barnabe Barnes, Thomas Nashe, and other
literary men of the day as lodging in printers' houses,
and we may suppose that the arrangement was a profitable
one for both parties. Precise details on this point, as on
so many others affecting the means of livelihood of Elizabethan men of letters, are, however, wanting.

The number of copies of a book which in Shakespeare's
time formed an ' edition ' is another matter about which
little is known. In or about 1586 the Stationers' Company
had ordered that no more than 1,250 copies of an ordinary
book should be printed ; if more were needed the type
must be distributed and set up afresh, the object of this
regulation being that work should be more evenly distributed between compositors and press-men. An exception was made in the case of a few school-books and
others for which the demand was very great : of these
double the number, or even more, might be printed.
We may presume that in fixing the number 1,250 as a
maximum, regard would have been had to the number
of copies likely to be required of the most popular books,
such as Robert Greene's pamphlets and the like, and a few
favourite plays : more serious and more extensive works
could hardly have had a sale approaching this. It has
been estimated that the number printed of the First Folio
of Shakespeare's plays was from 500 to 600, but we have
no direct evidence on the point.

To turn now to the question of price. None of the very
few booksellers' catalogues that have come down to us
from early times makes any mention of price, and it is
consequently very difficult to arrive at a clear idea of the
average cost of new, and especially of the larger publications. We do not even know whether books, apart from
certain service-books for which a maximum charge was
fixed by the authorities, had any definite price at all, or
whether the bookseller got what he could for them. The
absence of any established style of ' publishers' binding '—
unless we regard the common limp vellum covers as one—
must have prevented the better class of books from having
a price absolutely fixed, but it seems likely that the price

THE
NEWE
Testament of
our Lord and Sauiour
IESVS CHRIST.

¶ Newly Translated out of
the Originall Greeke: and with
the former Translations diligently
compared and reuised, by his
Maiesties speciall Com-
mandement.

¶ IMPRINTED
at London by Robert
Barker, Printer to the
Kings most Excellent
Maiestie.
ANNO DOM. 1611.

Cum Priuilegio.

of pamphlet literature was fixed. Occasionally, but very rarely, the price of a book is mentioned in the book itself. Thus we learn that *The Forrest of Fancy*, a pamphlet by H. C. published in 1579, was sold at a shilling, and that the quarto of *Troilus and Cressida*, published in 1609, cost a testern, i. e. sixpence. The first of these works is a quarto of 80 leaves, that is to say of about twice the length of such a play as *The Merchant of Venice*. The quarto of *Troilus and Cressida* is slightly thicker than the average play : it contains 48 leaves. A work of either Nashe or Harvey, probably the former's *Have with you to Saffron-walden* (84 leaves), cost five groats (1s. 8d.) and, according to John Davies of Hereford, was very dear at the price. There are numerous references to twopenny and threepenny pamphlets, but it is doubtful whether these expressions are to be taken literally or have merely a depreciatory sense. Even more caution must be used in accepting the entries in diaries and accounts of prices paid for books, for on the one hand it is seldom certain that the book was a new copy, and on the other it may have been in an elaborate binding, which would of course add greatly to its value. On the whole we shall probably be not far wrong if we suppose the ordinary quarto play to have been sold, sewn or 'stabbed' at 4d. or 6d., or in a vellum wrapper at 8d. or 9d. The greater part of the pamphlet literature—Greene's, Dekker's, Rowlands's, &c.—would probably cost about the same. Of course if properly bound in leather such books would be considerably more expensive, but thin pamphlets would seldom, if ever, be bound in this way, unless several were bound together.

Of larger works it is quite impossible to say anything definite. They were probably sold bound, and much depended on the style of the binding. It has generally been said that the First Folio of Shakespeare cost £1 when new, but the statement should be received with caution, for it appears to rest on no more than a manuscript note cited by George Steevens [1] as occurring in a copy then in the possession of Messrs. White, booksellers in Fleet Street. The copy does not seem to be now known,

---

[1] The note seems to be first given in the Variorum Shakespeare of 1803, ii. 150, which appeared after Steevens's death. It is not in his own edition of 1793.

and until it is found we must not attach too much importance to Steevens's statement. It is not clear that the note of price is contemporary with the original publication, nor do we know how the volume was bound.

Assuming then that a play such as *The Merchant of Venice* cost 6*d*. in Elizabethan money, we have to consider what the equivalent value of this sum would be at the present day. We shall probaby not be far wrong if we say about 2*s*. 6*d*. or 3*s*.—in fact not very much more than the price of a new play at the present time, and modern plays are as a rule much shorter than Elizabethan. There seems, on the whole, little reason to think that, so far as new books were concerned, prices were appreciably higher than at the present day. Whatever cheapening there has been is in the reprints of standard works, for which nothing is paid to the author.

The only other point which remains for discussion is the question of the means taken by the publisher to bring new works to the notice of the public. Caxton, as is well known, soon after the establishment of his press in England, printed an advertisement to inform the public where certain service-books were to be procured, but after his time we hear hardly anything of publishers' advertisements for a century and a half. About 1650 it became quite usual to add at the end of a volume a list of other works to be sold by the same stationer, and the practice has continued. A few service-books contain a statement of the price not only of the book itself but of others, but with this exception there seems in this country to have been nothing of the nature of a bookseller's catalogue until the appearance of the well-known *Catalogue of English printed Bookes*, by the stationer, Andrew Maunsell, of which the first and second parts were issued in 1595. These two parts contain the divisions of theology and science : unfortunately the others, which would have included poetry and imaginative literature, never appeared. But even this work is not to be regarded exactly as a bookseller's catalogue, for, although Maunsell probably intended it to serve the purposes of his business, it is not merely a list of the books which he himself had for sale, but one as complete as he could make it of all that had appeared in England. It is in fact an attempt to do for this country what had been done for the learned literature of the Continent in the *Bibliotheca Universalis* of Conrad Gesner, or the condensed *Elenchus Scriptorum* of Wolffhart, and the public utility of the work was recognized by the Stationers' Company, who made to Maunsell a grant of money and books for his ' pains and charges ' in compiling it. Although no other catalogues from this time have come down to us, it is not impossible that something of the kind existed, for otherwise it is not easy to explain Thomas Nashe's suggestion in his *Strange Newes* (1592) that his enemy Richard Harvey had stolen the names of certain authors whom he professed to have read 'out of some Bookseller's Catalogue '. It may be that booksellers kept manuscript catalogues in their shops for the use of customers, or Nashe may be referring to some foreign compilation. Had the date been a few years later, one might have supposed him to refer to the famous half-yearly catalogue issued in connexion with the great book-fair at Frankfort, but this catalogue seems not to have begun before 1598. It probably had some circulation in this country, for in 1617 John Bill began to reprint it, and from 1622 to 1626 added to it a supplement of books printed in England. From about this date also we begin to find other evidence of the sale of books by such means. There are, for example, at the British Museum two booksellers' catalogues, dating from 1628 and 1637, of works purchased in Italy for sale in London.

It is then abundantly clear that, at the period with which we are here concerned, the issue of catalogues was by no means a usual or necessary part of a London publisher's or bookseller's business. He must have used other methods than this to make his publications known. Seeing that the area to which the trade was confined was so limited, a great part of the sale would probably be to customers who looked round the stalls and whose attention would undoubtedly be directed by the apprentices to anything new. ' What lack you, gentleman ? See a new book come forth, sir ! Buy a new book, sir ! ' cries the apprentice in Rowlands's tract, *Tis Merrie when Gossips meete*.

Various allusions point to a system of advertising by printing copies of the title-page alone and fixing these up at the recognized ' posts ' throughout the town—a practice

which would account for the frequency with which the
address at which a book is to be purchased is set forth
on the title-page, and for the fact that a title-page was
sometimes kept standing in type until a new edition of
the book was required. On the whole, however, we must
suppose that the trade was carried on with a very small
expenditure on advertisement ; that, in fact, books became
known chiefly by being talked of. After all, the literary
public was so small that it must have almost formed one
society, and the number of new books was so limited that
every one could be discussed.

Few words must suffice for the various arts or trades
subsidiary to printing, namely book-illustration, binding,
type-casting, and paper-making.

The history of book-illustration during the first century
of printing is of much interest, but in the period with which
we are concerned there is far less to say about it. Indeed,
one of the most remarkable facts connected with Elizabethan printing is the decline and almost complete extinc-
tion of the art of wood-cutting for the decoration of books.
In the early part of the sixteenth century woodcuts were
an important feature in a very large proportion of the
books issued, and, rough as they were, they seem to
have proved very attractive. These cuts, often copied
from Continental cuts, are especially numerous in the
work of Wynkyn de Worde and of Pynson, but they
occur in practically all the more popular literature of the
time. Printers seem, however, soon to have found them
too costly an item in the production of a book, and almost
from the beginning we find the same illustrations used
over and over again, sometimes in the same work, to
represent different subjects. Indeed, probably the less
distinctly a cut represented a particular person or scene,
the more useful it would be to its owner. Occasionally
a printer would have a block newly cut from an impression of the old one—thus usually reversing the design—
but often the actual blocks passed from printer to printer,
until in the last stage of wear and decay they are found
in chap-books or ballads of generations and even of
centuries later. A notable instance of these ' factotum '
woodcuts is a set of figures which seem to have originally
appeared in the *Terence en François* printed at Paris by

Antoine Vérard about 1500. These cuts were used again in the elaborately illustrated edition of the first English translation of a famous compendium of astronomy, moral precepts, and rules for health, printed anonymously in Paris in 1503 as *The Kalendayr of the Shyppars* (i. e. Shepherds). This version was, however, in such curious English that when imported into England the volumes proved to be unintelligible, and a new one was therefore made and printed in London by Richard Pynson three years later. For this he copied the series of figures referred to above, and, once naturalized in England, they became very popular. Their great virtue seems to have lain in the fact that each figure had a scroll over its head in which could be inserted in type the name of the character whom it was intended to represent, and several printers had sets cut for their own use, and employed them constantly. They appear at the head of several early editions of interludes, such as *Everyman, Youth, Hyckescorner,* and *Jacke Jugeler,* to represent the various characters of the play, and in other works of a popular kind. It need hardly be pointed out that the attempt which has sometimes been made to derive from them information about the dress worn by the players in these interludes, is absurd.

It may have been in some measure this economy of material on the part of the printers and the consequent lowering of the standard of illustration that brought wood-cutting out of favour, but other causes probably contributed. One may have been the Reformation, for many of the early illustrated books were religious, and the cuts represented incidents in the lives of saints. All such pictures were by Edward VI and Elizabeth rigidly suppressed, and thereby a large part of the field for illustration was at once cut off. Another cause was perhaps that the printers found that books might be decorated almost equally well by the use of ornamental initial letters and borders as by illustrations of the subject-matter, and these could be freely used over and over again without incongruity. A third cause may have been the introduction of copper-plate engraving, which, though much more costly, could be used sparingly in the more expensive work, and was regarded as infinitely superior to the current woodcuts. However this may be, pictorial illustrations, as distinct from diagrams, &c., became, early in Elizabeth's reign, scarce in works of the better class. Such woodcuts as we find are generally very rough, and occur chiefly in books of a popular character, such as plays and a few pamphlets, and even in these the illustration is generally limited to a cut on the title-page. There are indeed exceptions. Foxe's *Actes and Monuments* (1563) has numerous woodcuts, the first edition of Holinshed's *Chronicles* (1577) has a few, repeated over and over again, and Spenser's *Shepheardes Calender* (1579) has a series of twelve, one for each of the months : but this is one of the last books of any pretensions to be so decorated, and the idea of inserting them may have been suggested by *The Kalendar of the Shepherds* from which Spenser borrowed the title of his work.

It must not be supposed that the going out of fashion of woodcut illustration meant the disappearance of the wood-cutter. His art was still in demand for many subsidiary purposes. Ornamental initial letters were still cut, though most of them are much inferior to the earlier letters, of which they are often imperfect copies : woodcut title-pages are fairly frequent, and a few, such as that of the second edition of the *Arcadia* (reproduced opposite), are good, but the majority, though elaborate, have little artistic merit. Besides such things as these, he cut also coats of arms, which are frequently to be found in works dedicated to members of the nobility, printers' devices and the like ; while last, but by no means least, there was the constantly growing number of scientific works, herbals, books on natural history, medicine and physics, nearly all of which contain numerous woodcuts—intended, however, less to beautify the text than to render it intelligible.

The art of engraving on copper seems to have been practised on the Continent from about 1450, but it does not appear in England until about 1540, in which year was published Thomas Raynalde's *Byrth of Mankynde*, containing four plates of surgical diagrams. From that date the art grew steadily, though slowly, into popularity, but until towards the end of the century it was used chiefly for maps and diagrams. From about 1580, however, engraved portraits became numerous, and several engravers are known to have been working in London. The most

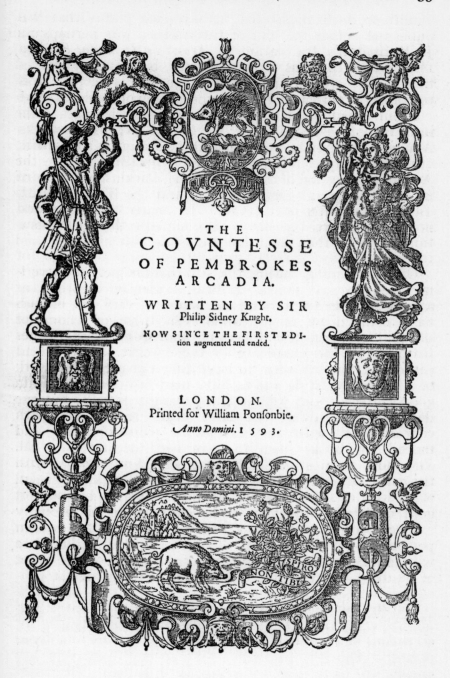

THE
COVNTESSE
OF PEMBROKES
ARCADIA.

WRITTEN BY SIR
Philip Sidney Knight.

NOW SINCE THE FIRST EDI-
tion augmented and ended.

LONDON.
Printed for William Ponsonbie.
Anno Domini. 1 5 9 3.

SPIRO
NON TIBI

ambitious book illustrated with copper plates that was published before the end of the century was perhaps Sir J. Harington's translation of Ariosto's *Orlando Furioso*, 1591, which contains forty-six plates, besides an engraved title. They are not of English design, but are copied from the plates of Girolamo Porro in the edition of Venice, 1584.[1]

From about 1600 elaborate engraved title-pages came into favour, especially for large and expensive works. Among them may be mentioned those of Coryat's *Crudities*, 1611 (see Chapter VII), Drayton's *Poly-Olbion* (1613), the Authorized Version of the Bible (1611), Parkinson's *Paradisi in sole Paradisus terrestris* (1629), and the *Works* of John Taylor, the water-poet (1630). In nearly all such work, however, the artist seems to have aimed rather at elaboration of detail than at producing a harmonious whole, and the general effect is rarely pleasing.

Of bookbinding during the Elizabethan period there is no need to say much. It was evidently regarded as a trade, not as an art, and the names of very few binders have come down to us, while even those of whom we do find mention are generally known for some other reason than the excellence of their work. Some of the earlier bookbinders seem to have aimed at producing work of a distinctive style and to have made an effort to obtain good materials and well-designed stamps or rolls, but the decorations used in the later years of the sixteenth century are, with few exceptions, commonplace, and indeed few books seem to have been decorated at all. The most usual styles of binding were limp vellum with ties for small or thin books, and plain brown calf or sheep, often with clasps, for larger works. Elaborate bindings of gold or silver, velvet or embroidery, were occasionally executed for presentation to the Queen or other exalted personages—it was no doubt of such a one that Shakespeare was thinking when in *Romeo and Juliet* (I. iii. 92) he wrote of the book ' that in gold clasps locks in the golden story '.

---

[1] The fact that the engravings are only copies was pointed out by J. J. Jusserand: see his *English Novel*, Eng. trans., 1899, pp. 12–13. He refers them to a Venice edition of 1588 which I have not seen. If the plates in this are identical with those of 1584, he seems, however, to go too far in saying that the English engraver, Thomas Cockson, only drew the portrait of Harington in the frontispiece, for several of the plates show considerable variation from the originals ; see, for example, plates 5 and 34.

There is testimony of a kind to the general existence of a sentiment that books of value deserved to be bound well, in the expression of scorn which Perdita bestows on a noble work 'vilely bound up' (*Wint. Tale* IV. iii. 22).

Der Buchbinder.

Ich bind allerley Bücher ein/
Geistlich vnd Weltlich/groß vnd klein/
In Perment oder Bretter nur
Vnd beschlags mit guter Clausur
Vnd Spangen/vnd stempff sie zur zier/
Ich sie auch im anfang planier/
Etlich vergüld ich auff dem schnitt/
Da verdien ich viel geldes mit.

The Bookbinder, by Jost Amman.

But as a general rule there seems to have been little demand for decorative work.

The chief bookbinders may have had establishments of their own, but the great majority were probably journeymen in the employ of stationers. A few owners of large libraries, such as Archbishop Parker, kept private book-binders in their employ, but there is no evidence that the practice was at all common.

In the early days of printing each printer seems to have cast his own type. There must from the beginning have been a separate trade of cutting the punches used in making the matrices from which the type were cast, for this was highly skilled work and could not possibly have been attempted by the ordinary journeyman ; but of the men who did this nothing whatever is known. So far as the present writer is aware, the earliest person who carried on an independent business in England as a type-founder was a certain Hubert Danvillier, a Frenchman, who came to this country in 1553. Whether from the beginning he worked independently or hired himself out to printers is uncertain, but he evidently had an establish-ment of his own in 1594, when Richard Watkins, a printer, placed one of his apprentices with him to learn the art of type-founding. One Antonius D'Anvillier, also a type-founder, who is first heard of in 1562, was perhaps a relation. In 1597, a certain Benjamin Sympson was working inde-pendently as a type-founder ; he seems to have been the first Englishman recorded to have been employed in the trade.

None of the type used in England during the sixteenth century was of a very high standard of excellence. The best was that used by John Day, who in this matter was by far the most enterprising printer of his time. To Day also belongs the credit of cutting the first fount of Anglo-Saxon type, which was used in an edition of a Homily of Ælfric edited by Archbishop Parker in 1567. A fount of Irish type was cut in 1571, and was used in Dublin in that year. Greek had been used in single words or phrases since 1521, but does not appear in any quantity until more than twenty years later. Hebrew is found in 1592.

The paper used by English printers during the reign of Elizabeth was for the most part imported from the Con-tinent, but this was not for want of attempts to make it here. Lord Say's fifteenth-century paper-mill (2 *Hen. VI,* IV. vii. 41) appears indeed to have been imaginary, but there is some reason to believe that a certain Tate made paper at Hertford early in the following century. He and others who engaged later in a like attempt, seem, however, to have met with little success, and in 1581 we learn that it had been found impossible to compete in price with the paper brought in from abroad, and that all manufacture here had ceased. In spite of this, John Spilman, of Lindau in Würtemberg, jeweller to the Queen, erected a mill at Dartford in or before 1588, and in 1597 he obtained an exclusive patent to buy rags and make white paper for fourteen years. He seems to have led the Privy Council to believe that he had been the first to establish a mill in this country, but, on the occasion of a dispute with the city authorities about the persons whom he employed to collect rags, the Lord Mayor stated that his claim was false and that previous to his time there had been mills at Osterley, near Brentford, and at several other places. Spilman's mill was flourishing in 1605, when it was visited by King James and the owner was knighted.

BIBLIOGRAPHY.—The best general account of the printing and publishing trade during the Shakespearian period will be found in H. G. ALDIS's chapter on 'The Book Trade, 1557–1625', in *The Cambridge History of English Literature*, vol. iv. Short biographies of all persons known to have been connected with the trade are given in E. GORDON DUFF's *Century of the English Book Trade, 1457–1557* (Bibliographical Soc., 1905), and *A Dictionary of Printers and Booksellers, 1557–1640*, ed. R. B. McKERROW (Bibliographical Soc., 1910). Much information on the subject of various printers and of the trade in general will be found in *The Transactions of the Bibliographical Society*, 13 vols., 1893–1916. The three volumes of wills of printers and publishers issued by the same society throw some light on their business relations and circumstances : H. R. PLOMER's *Abstracts from the Wills of English Printers and Stationers*, 1903 ; STRICKLAND GIBSON's *Abstracts from the Wills of Binders, Printers, &c. of Oxford*, 1907 ; and G. J. GRAY and W. M. PALMER's *Abstracts from the Wills of Printers, Binders, &c. of Cambridge*, 1915. For most matters connected with the Stationers' Company the authority is *A Transcript of the Registers of the Company of Stationers of London, 1554–1640*, by E. ARBER, 5 vols., 1875–94. Concerning the publication of Shakespeare's works see A. W. POLLARD's *Shakespeare Folios and Quartos*, 1909, and Sir SIDNEY LEE's *Life of William Shakespeare*. On questions of copyright in early times see an article by W. F. WYNDHAM BROWN on 'The Origin and Growth of Copyright' in *The Law Magazine* for November 1908. For wood-cutting see A. W. POLLARD's *Old Picture Books*, 1902, and for type-founding T. B. REED's *History of the Old English Letter Foundries*, 1887.

XXIV

ACTORS AND ACTING

BY

PERCY SIMPSON

THE ACTOR

THE age of Elizabeth showed a curious inconsistency in the attitude it adopted towards the drama. It patronized the theatre liberally, but placed a social stigma on the actor. The profession was not only regulated by law; it was officially discredited. This is an extract from a statute of 1572 :

And for the full expressing what persone and persones shalbe intended within this Braunche to be Roges Vacaboundes and Sturdye Beggers, to have and receave the punyshement aforesaid for the said lewde maner of Lyef ; It ys nowe publyshed . . . and set foorth . . . That . . . all Fencers Bearewardes Comon Players in Enterludes & Minstrels, not belonging to any Baron of this Realme or towardes any other honorable Personage of greater Degree . . . whiche . . . shall wander abroade and have not Lycense of two Justices of the Peace at the leaste, whereof one to be of the Quorum, wher and in what Shier they shall happen to wander . . . shalbee taken adjudged and deemed Roges Vacaboundes and Sturdy Beggers, intended of by this present Act.

(*Act* 16 *Elizabeth*, c. 5, § 5)

To be professionally liable to arrest was not encouraging, and the opponents of plays made the most of it. ' They forget they are i' the statute, the rascals,' says a truculent critic in Jonson, 'they are blazoned there, there they are tricked, they and their pedigrees ; they need no other heralds, iwiss ' (*Poetaster* I. ii). The Puritans of course pleaded that ' rogue and vagabond ' was a true indictment and pressed it home in a series of tracts. John Northbrook led the way with his *Treatise wherein Dicing, Dauncing, Vaine plaies or Enterludes . . . are reprooved* in 1579. Stephen Gosson, a convert from playwriting, followed with *The*

Schoole of Abuse, Conteining a plesaunt invective against Poets, Pipers, Plaiers, Jesters and such like Caterpillers of a Commonwelth in 1579. He wrote moderately about the 'quality': 'it is well knowen, that some of them are sober, discreete, properly learned honest housholders and Citizens well thought on amonge their neighbours at home'; he even added, 'as some of the Players are farre from abuse : so some of their Playes are without rebuke'. But when Thomas Lodge replied to him and he returned to the attack in *Playes confuted in five Actions*, he changed his tone and summed up without qualification from the Puritan standpoint :

Playes are the inventions of the devil, the offrings of Idolatrie, the pompe of worldlinges, the blossomes of vanitie, the roote of Apostacy, the foode of iniquitie, ryot, and adulterie, detest them. Players are masters of vice, teachers of wantonnesse, spurres to impuritie, the Sonnes of idlenesse, so longe as they live in this order, loathe them.

Invectives pleasant and unpleasant continued to appear till Prynne made a supreme effort in 1633 by publishing *Histrio-mastix*, a solid quarto of 1080 pages with masses of marginal quotations in which every conceivable authority, ancient or modern, sacred or profane, was pressed with a fine incongruity into the service of Puritanism.

Of course, there were actors and playwrights whose disreputable lives and broken fortunes lent plausibility to the Puritan attack. When John Stephens described 'A common Player'[1] in his *Essayes and Characters*, 1615, he commented, 'therefore did I prefix an Epithite of *common*, to distinguish the base and artlesse appendants of our citty companies, which often times start away into rusticall wanderers and then like Proteus start backe again into the Citty number'. Money difficulties or an 'inhibition' or the spread of plague sent better companies, such as 'the tragedians of the city', on their travels (*Haml.* II. ii. 351); but the strolling player was often one who was not good enough to get regular employment in London. Country audiences were less exacting and at a pinch were more easily imposed upon.

Middleton in *The Mayor of Quinborough*, v. i, has an

---

[1] For the term, cf. *Hamlet* II. ii. 372–4, 'if they should grow themselves to common players,—as it is most like, if their means are no better'. Stephens added his comment in the second edition of the *Essayes*.

amusing skit on a company travelling in Kent. Simon, the Mayor of the town, is told by his clerk, Aminadab:

Please your worship, here are a certain company of players—
   Simon. Ha, players !
   Amin. Country comedians, interluders, sir, desire your worship's favour and leave to enact in the town-hall.
   Simon. In the town-hall ? 'tis ten to one I never grant them that. Call them before my worship. If my house will not serve their turn, I would fain see the proudest he lend them a barn.

When the players are brought in, Simon inquires :

What think you of me, my masters ? Hum; have you audacity enough to play before so high a person as myself ? Will not my countenance daunt you ? for if you play before me, I shall often look on you ; I give you that warning beforehand. . . .
   First Player. Sir, we have play'd before a lord ere now, Though we be country actors.
   Simon.   A lord ? ha, ha ! Thou'lt find it a harder thing to please a mayor.

They begin a crude play, but Simon intervenes and insists on playing the Clown's part in it; as he is performing, they rob him of his purse and silver spoons and get clear away. Then the clerk discovers that they are a gang of professional thieves who

only take the name of country comedians to abuse simple people with a printed play or two, which they bought at Canterbury for sixpence [1] ; and what is worse, they speak but what they list of it, and fribble out the rest.

Even in a London company an actor's position, though free from legal difficulty, was precarious, and the playwrights were often badly paid. The struggles of those who worked for the manager Philip Henslowe are recorded in his famous *Diary*, preserved at Dulwich College. A significant feature is the entry of loans to actors and authors when in prison for debt ; any advance to the latter was usually made on the security of an unwritten play. The prosperous members of a company were those who held shares in the theatre which it occupied. Shakespeare himself was a shareholder in the Globe and the Blackfriars, and leading actors were admitted to this form of partnership. In Middleton's *A Mad World, my Masters*, v. i, a knight praises a member of a company which comes to act before him : ' I perceive

---

[1] The regular price for a play in quarto: so the preface found in some copies of the 1609 quarto of *Troilus and Cressida*. Cf. p. 229.

HISTRIO-MASTIX.
THE
PLAYERS SCOVRGE,
OR,
ACTORS TRAGÆDIE,

Divided into Two Parts.

Wherein it is largely evidenced, by divers *Arguments*, by the concurring Authorities and Reſolutions of *ſundry texts of Scripture*; of the *whole Primitive Church*, both under the *Law and Goſpell*; of 55 *Synodes and Councels*; of 71 *Fathers and Chriſtian Writers*, before the yeare of our Lord 1200; of above 150 *foraigne and domeſtique Proteſtant and Popiſh Authors*, ſince; of 40 *Heathen Philoſophers*, *Hiſtorians, Poets;* of many *Heathen,* many *Chriſtian Nations, Republiques, Emperors, Princes, Magiſtrates;* of ſundry *Apoſtolicall, Canonicall, Imperiall Conſtitutions;* and of our owne *Engliſh* Statutes, Magiſtrates, Vniverſities, Writers, Preachers.

That popular Stage-playes (the very Pompes of the Divell which we renounce in Baptiſme, if we beleeve the Fathers) are ſinfull, heatheniſh, lewde, ungodly Spectacles, and moſt pernicious Corruptions; condemned in all ages, as intolerable Miſchiefes to Churches, to Republickes, to the manners, mindes, and ſoules of men. And that the Profeſſion of Play-poets, of Stage-players; together with the penning, acting, and frequenting of Stage-playes, are unlawfull, infamous and misbeſeeming Chriſtians. All pretences to the contrary are here likewiſe fully anſwered; and the unlawfulnes of acting, of beholding Academicall Enterludes, briefly diſcuſſed; beſides ſundry other particulars concerning *Dancing, Dicing, Health-drinking, &c.* of which the *Table* will informe you.

By WILLIAM PRYNNE, *an Vtter-Barreſter of* Lincolnes Inne.

Cyprian, De Spectaculis lib. p. 244.
Fugienda ſunt iſta Chriſtianis fidelibus, ut iam frequenter diximus, tàm vana, tàm perniciosa, tàm ſacrilega Spectacula: quæ, etſi non haberent crimen, habent in ſe et maximam, et parum congruentè fidelibus vanitatē.
Lactantius de Verò Cultu cap. 20.
Vitanda ergo Spectacula omnia, non ſolum ne quid vitiorum pectoribus inſideat, &c. ſed ne cuius nos voluptatis conſuetudo delineat, atque à Deo et à bonis operibus avertat.
Chryſoſt. Hom. 38. in Matth. Tom. 2. Col. 299. B. & Hom. 8. De Pœnitentia, Tom. 5. Col. 750.
Immo vero, his Theatralibus ludis everſis, non leges, ſed iniquitatem evertetis, ac omnen cruitatis peſtem extinguetis.: Etenim Theatrum, communis luxuriæ officina, publicum incontinentiæ gymnaſium; cathedra peſtilentiæ; peſſimus locus; plurimorumque morborum plena Babylonica fornax, &c.
Auguſtinus De Civit. Dei, l. 4. c. 1.
Si tantummodo boni et honeſti homines in civitate eſſent, nec in rebus humanis Ludi ſcenici eſſe debuiſſent.

LONDON,
Printed by *E.A.* and *W.I.* for *Michael Sparke*, and are to be ſold at the Blue Bible, in Greene Arbour, in little Old Bayly. 1633.

he's your best actor.' He is told, ' He has greatest share,
sir, and may live of himself, sir.' Hamlet, on the success
of his play stratagem, claims a similar reward for authorship : ' Would not this . . . get me a fellowship in a cry of
players, sir ? ' ' Half a share,' Horatio replies, but Hamlet
claims a whole one (*Haml.* III. ii. 291–5). He insists on
the market scale of wages : thus, Robert Dawes was engaged
by Henslowe on April 7, 1614, to serve for three years ' for
and at the rate of one whole Share accordinge to the custome
of players ' (*Henslowe Papers*, ed. Greg, p. 124). Dekker,
in *Lanthorne and Candle-light*, ch. iv, assigns half a share
to ' an undeserving player '.

Shakespeare, who was both playwright and actor, had
thus a double claim. He worked throughout his career for
one company, the earliest that was formed in accordance
with the statute ; it was licensed as Lord Leicester's in
1572, became Lord Strange's on the death of its first patron,
then the Lord Chamberlain's, and on the accession of James,
the King's men. Other important companies were the
Queen's, founded under royal warrant in 1583; the Admiral's,
under Lord Howard of Effingham, first mentioned in 1586,
and renamed as Prince Henry's in the reign of James I ;
Lord Worcester's, which became Queen Anne's; and Lord
Pembroke's, first mentioned in 1593. It should be noted
that, when James succeeded to the throne, all recognized
companies passed under royal patronage.

In addition to these adult players there were two companies of ' Children ' or boy-actors, the Children of Paul's
and the Children of Queen Elizabeth's Chapel, the latter
of whom enjoy the unique distinction of a notice from the
pen of Shakespeare. Their competition damaged the
Chamberlain's company, and for once he was stung to make
a personal allusion.

But there is, sir, an aery of children, little eyases, that cry out
on the top of question, and are most tyrannically clapped for't :
these are now the fashion, and so berattle the common stages,—
so they call them,—that many wearing rapiers are afraid of goose-
quills, and dare scarce come thither.   (*Haml.* II. ii. 362–8)

In the induction to *Cynthia's Revels*, acted in 1600 by
these children, Jonson gives an amusing sketch of them.
One boy personates a gallant who has paid his money at
the door ' with much ado ' and sits down to smoke and

criticize :—' At the breaches ', i.e. the breaks in the text,
' he takes his tobacco ' is the stage-direction :

By this light, I wonder that any man is so mad to come to see
these rascally tits play here—They do act like so many wrens or
pismires—not the fifth part of a good face amongst them all—
And then their music is abominable—able to stretch a man's ears
worse than ten—pillories, and their ditties—most lamentable things,
like the pitiful fellows that make them—Poets.

A second boy acts the part of 'a more sober or better-
gather'd gallant', who embarks on serious criticism
and incidentally uses the slighting phrase about the
ordinary theatre to which Shakespeare refers : he professes to express the wish of the audience that the playwrights

would not so penuriously glean wit from every laundress or hackney-
man, or derive their best grace with servile imitation from common
stages.

These boys could be impressed by virtue of a warrant
for supplying the Royal Chapel with choristers ; and an
interesting document of the Star Chamber Proceedings
under Elizabeth (Bundle C 46, no. 39)—Clifton *versus*
Robinson and others—records the complaint of a Norfolk gentleman whose son had been ' impounded ' by
Nathaniel Gyles, James Robinson, and others, nominally
for the service of the King's Chapel, but actually for the
Blackfriars Theatre. Apprentices and schoolboys, it is
stated, are kidnapped ; cases are cited by name, among
them ' Nathan ffield, a scholler of a gramer schole in
London, kepte by one M^r. Monkaster,' i. e. Merchant
Taylors' under Mulcaster, and ' Salmon Pavey, apprentice
to one Peerce '—' being childeren noe way able or fitt for
singing, nor by anie the sayd confederates endevoured to
be taught to singe, but by them the sayd confederates
abusively employed, as aforesayd, only in playes & enterludes'. Field, the son of a Puritan preacher, was the
future dramatist [1] ; ' Salmon ', or more correctly Salathiel,
Pavey—the Christian name is evidence of Puritan up-
bringing—became famous for his skill in acting old men's
parts, and when he died in his thirteenth year Ben Jonson
wrote his epitaph (*Epigram* cxx).

[1] His portrait is reproduced here. The embroidered shirt which he is
represented as wearing is probably a stage costume.

Years he numb'red scarce thirteen
  When Fates turn'd cruel,
Yet three fill'd zodiacs had he been
  The stage's jewel,
And did act—what now we moan—
  Old men so duly
As sooth the Parcae thought him one,
  He play'd so truly.

The formation of these companies was obviously a development of the stage convention by which in Shakespeare's day the parts of women were played by boys; it is clear that they played them well, or managers would not have risked money on the experiment. 'Sirrah, go you to Barthol'mew my page,' says the lord in *The Taming of the Shrew*—

And see him dress'd in all suits like a lady. . . .
I know the boy will well usurp the grace,
Voice, gait, and action of a gentlewoman.
(Ind. i. 105–6, 131–2)

And there is positive evidence of their skill in such parts. Coryate in his *Crudities*, 1611, p. 247, relates as a surprising experience in Venice: 'I saw women act, a thing that I never saw before . . . and they performed it with as good a grace, action, gesture, and whatsoever convenient for a player, as ever I saw any masculine actor.' And Ben Jonson tells an anecdote of the actor, Dick Robinson, appearing at a gossips' feast, 'dress'd like a lawyer's wife', and specially notes his good taste in dress (*The Divell is an Asse*, II. viii).

A further proof is that a manager paid well for boys. 'Afore heaven 'tis a sweete fac't child', says a character in Chapman's *May Day*, 1611, Act III; 'methinks he should show well in womans attire. . . . Ile helpe thee to three crownes a weeke for him, and she can act well.'

Special attention was paid to training these boys' voices. 'They cry out on the top of question', says Shakespeare; and he probably means, they speak in a high key. In Marston's *What You Will*, II. ii, a schoolmaster says regretfully of one of his boys: 'I was solicited to grant him leave to play the lady in comedies presented by children; but I knew his voice was too small and his stature too low.' Compare Hamlet's greeting to the actor who had played women's parts:

What! my young lady and mistress! By'r lady, your ladyship is nearer heaven than when I saw you last, by the altitude of a chopine. Pray God, your voice, like a piece of uncurrent gold, be not cracked within the ring. (*Haml.* II. ii. 453-7)

Or Quince's remedy for the actor who was outgrowing such parts :

Flute. Nay, faith, let me not play a woman; I have a beard coming.
Quince. That's all one : you shall play it in a mask, and you may speak as small as you will. (*Mid. N. D.* I. ii. 50-3)

Or Cleopatra's fear that the quick comedians will improvise a burlesque upon her overthrow :

I shall see
Some squeaking Cleopatra boy my greatness
I' th' posture of a whore. (*Ant. & Cleop.* v. ii. 218-20)

All these passages lay stress upon the voice.

Finally, the jest in the epilogue to *As You Like It*— ' If I were a woman, I would kiss as many of you as had beards that pleased me '—owes its point to the fact that it was delivered by a boy; on the lips of an actress at the present day it has no meaning.

SHAKESPEARE AS DRAMATIC CRITIC

Of Shakespeare's own acting we have only a meagre record, and there is nothing that suggests—as contemporary references to Edward Alleyn [1] and Richard Burbage [2] do— that he was in the front rank of actors. There is a ring of sincerity in the solitary tribute paid to him on this point in his lifetime—Chettle's allusion in *Kind-Harts Dreame*, 1592, that he was ' exelent in the qualitie he professes '. But the only indication that he played an important part is given in the Folio text of Jonson's *Every Man in his Humor*, 1616, where his name heads the actor-list; and the only parts which have been definitely assigned

[1] See Nashe, *Pierce Penilesse* (*Works*, ed. McKerrow, i, p. 215): ' Not *Roscius* nor *Æsope*, those admyred tragedians that have lived ever since before Christ was borne, could ever performe more in action than famous *Ned Allen*.' Ben Jonson echoes this praise literally in *Epigram* lxxxix. Alleyn's portrait, reproduced here, hangs in the Council room of Dulwich College.

[2] He was the leading actor in Shakespeare's company, builder of the Globe Theatre, proprietor of the Blackfriars, and played the title parts in the original performances of *Richard III*, *Hamlet*, *Lear*, and *Othello*. His portrait, reproduced here, is believed to have been painted by himself.

to him—Adam in *As You Like It* and the Ghost in *Hamlet* —are rather disappointing. The cramped and clumsy epigram of Davies of Hereford in *The Scourge of Folly* which states that Shakespeare had ' plaid some Kingly parts ' carries us no further than to suggest the possibility of a sly under-current of allusion in Hamlet's promise to entertain the players—' He that plays the king shall be welcome ; his majesty shall have tribute of me ' (*Haml.* II. ii. 341–2).

But of his profound knowledge of the actor's art there can be no question. No other dramatist of that age has written such keen and subtle criticism of it, or alluded to it in his plays more frequently. It is often a source of vivid illustration.

> As in a theatre, the eyes of men,
> After a well-grac'd actor leaves the stage,
> Are idly bent on him that enters next,
> Thinking his prattle to be tedious.
> (*Rich. II*, v. ii. 23–6)

> [They] stand securely on their battlements
> As in a theatre, whence they gape and point
> At your industrious scenes and acts of death.
> (*John* II. i. 374–6)

> And, like a strutting player, whose conceit
> Lies in his hamstring, and doth think it rich
> To hear the wooden dialogue and sound
> 'Twixt his stretch'd footing and the scaffolage,—
> Such to-be-pitied and o'er-wrested seeming
> He acts thy greatness in :—and when he speaks,
> 'Tis like a chime a-mending. (*Troilus* I. iii. 153–9)

> Life 's but a walking shadow, a poor player
> That struts and frets his hour upon the stage,
> And then is heard no more. (*Macb.* v. v. 24–6)

> Like a dull actor now,
> I have forgot my part, and I am out,
> Even to a full disgrace. (*Cor.* v. iii. 40–2)

> As an unperfect actor on the stage,
> Who with his fear is put besides his part.
> (*Sonnet* xxiii)

These records of the actor-poet's experience are given with a strictly impersonal colouring, but some memorable passages in the *Sonnets* go further and lift the veil. He describes himself as ' in disgrace with fortune and men's

WILLIAM SHAKESPEARE ACTOR AND PLAYWRIGHT

eyes ', ' beweeping his outcast state ',[1] and in that sense of undeserved degradation ' desiring this man's art, and that man's scope ' (*Sonnet* xxix). The obloquy which assailed the actor is directly noticed :

> Alas, 'tis true I have gone here and there,
> And made myself a motley to the view,
> Gored mine own thoughts, sold cheap what is most dear.
>
> (*Sonnet* cx)

More famous still is the reference in the next Sonnet, where the poet reproaches Fortune,

> That did not better for my life provide
> Than public means which public manners breeds.
> Thence comes it that my name receives a brand,
> And almost thence my nature is subdued
> To what it works in, like the dyer's hand :
> Pity me, then, and wish I were renew'd.

Nearly all Shakespeare's references to acting harp upon its limitations ; the artist is characteristically struggling against the grossness of his environment. ' The best in this kind are but shadows ' (*Mid. N. D.* v. i. 215)—this comment, corroborated as it is by the other passages, remains his apologia for the drama. Sometimes he pleads inability, with the imperfect materials at his command, to express the greatness of his theme. The play of *King Henry the Fifth* vibrates with the spirit of the men who broke the Armada ; but on the stage of the Globe the wings of aspiration flagged :

> O! for a Muse of fire, that would ascend
> The brightest heaven of invention ;
> A kingdom for a stage, princes to act
> And monarchs to behold the swelling scene.
> . . . . . But pardon, gentles all,
> The flat unraised spirits that hath dar'd
> On this unworthy scaffold to bring forth
> So great an object. Can this cockpit hold
> The vasty fields of France ? or may we cram

---

[1] It may be noted that the famous passage ' All the world's a stage ' (*A. Y. L.* II. vii. 139–66) is introduced with a note of sadness:

> This wide and universal theatre
> Presents more woful pageants than the scene
> Wherein we play in—

which is exactly paralleled by Antonio's melancholy (*Merch. of V.* I. i. 77–9):

> I hold the world but as the world, Gratiano ;
> A stage where every man must play a part,
> And mine a sad one.

> Within this wooden O the very casques
> That did affright the air at Agincourt ?
>
> <div align="right">(<i>Hen. V</i>, chor. 1–4, 8–14)</div>

So he invited the audience to follow in the track of his
own soaring mind, to piece out defects and tone down
crudity with the shaping spirit of imagination :

> Into a thousand parts divide one man,
> And make imaginary puissance.　　　(Chor. 24–5)

More than once he echoes that appeal, but especially at
the crisis of the play :

> And so our scene must to the battle fly,
> Where—O for pity—we shall much disgrace,
> With four or five most vile and ragged foils
> Right ill dispos'd in brawl ridiculous,
> The name of Agincourt.　　　(IV. chor. 48–52)

It is extraordinary that, in contrast to this long array
of quotations which dwell on the defects of acting, only
three can be produced which speak of it in terms of appreciation.　There is Hamlet's praise of the player in the
' Hecuba ' passage, who

> Could force his soul so to his own conceit
> That from her working all his visage wann'd,
> Tears in his eyes, distraction in 's aspect,
> A broken voice, and his whole function suiting
> With forms to his conceit ! and all for nothing !
> For Hecuba !　　　(<i>Haml.</i> II. ii. 587–92)

In <i>Julius Cæsar</i> (II. i. 226–7) there is a tribute of another kind:

> But bear it as our Roman actors do,
> With untired spirits and formal constancy.

But the final reference to the art is essentially rhetorical ; it
is Cassius' exultant cry over his victim :

> How many ages hence
> Shall this our lofty scene be acted o'er
> In states unborn and accents yet unknown !
>
> (III. i. 111–13)

It is not the only passage in which Shakespeare has given
a touch of pose, of theatricality, to the character of Cassius.

But Shakespeare has not confined himself to incidental
or isolated allusions ; in a great passage of <i>Hamlet</i> he has
grappled with the problem directly and written a criticism
which is of supreme value, first, because it states definitely
the points which he considered essential to sound acting,
and secondly, because it makes quite clear the main principle

RICHARD BURBAGE

on which he based his conception of the art. He makes everything turn on two qualities—naturalness and self-restraint. 'Be rapid and easy in elocution; be quiet and appropriate in action'—that is the gist of his practical advice,

with this special observance, that you o'erstep not the modesty of nature; for anything so overdone is from the purpose of playing, whose end, both at the first and now, was and is, to hold, as 'twere, the mirror up to nature; to show virtue her own feature, scorn her own image, and the very age and body of the time his form and pressure. Now this overdone, or come tardy off, though it make the unskilful laugh, cannot but make the judicious grieve, the censure of which one must in your allowance o'erweigh a whole theatre of others. (*Haml.* III. ii. 21–32)

The dignity of the actor's art has never been more finely vindicated; theory and practice go so happily hand in hand.

Hamlet's directions about elocution bear with special force on the acting of Shakespearian drama:

Speak the speech, I pray you, as I pronounced it to you, trippingly on the tongue; but if you mouth it, as many of your players do, I had as lief the town-crier spoke my lines. (*Haml.* III. ii. 1–4)

Now we know from two explicit references in Shakespeare [1] that the time usually taken to perform one of his plays, in a theatre where no 'waits' were required for a change of scene, was two hours. But only such a delivery as Hamlet suggested would make it possible to get through a play in that time.

Hamlet's next point is the importance of artistic gesture:

Nor do not saw the air too much with your hand, thus; but use all gently: for in the very torrent, tempest, and—as I may say—whirlwind of passion, you must acquire and beget a temperance that may give it smoothness. Oh it offends me to the soul to hear a robustious periwig-pated fellow tear a passion to tatters, to very rags, to split the ears of the groundlings, who for the most part are capable of nothing but inexplicable dumb-shows, and noise: I would have such a fellow whipped for o'er-doing Termagant; it out-herods Herod. (*Haml.* III. ii. 4–16)

The Rape of Lucrece furnishes an interesting parallel in the description of the painting of the Greek forces before Troy: Nestor, the type of wise counsellor and persuasive orator, encouraging his countrymen to fight, is depicted

Making such sober action with his hand
That it beguiled attention, charm'd the sight.
(*Lucr.* 1403–4)

---

[1] See *Hen. VIII*, prol. 13, and *Rom. & Jul.* prol. 12.

Poet and stage-manager here meet on common ground.
In fact the painter's art, limited to portraying life under
its momentary aspects, could hardly express so much ;
Shakespeare transferred to canvas an artistic effect which
had appealed to him in his experience of acting.

A curious touch in *Titus Andronicus* (v. ii. 17–18) is perhaps
worth citing here for its indirect bearing on the question.
The maimed Titus asks, rather quaintly,

> How can I grace my talk,
> Wanting a hand to give it action ?

Some actor of this part must have used effective by-play,
for one of the spectators, T. M., refers vividly to it in
Father Hubburd's Tales, 1604, ' For all my lamentable action
of one arm, like old Titus Andronicus.'

The further references to ' tearing a passion to tatters ',
' strutting and bellowing ', ' imitating humanity so abomin-
ably ', must have had a pungent flavour at a time when
they recalled the mannerisms of particular actors. Shakespeare's contempt for the sham-tragic was boundless, and
it is noticeable in the Play scene how quickly and how
ruthlessly Hamlet stamps out any trace of it.

> Begin, murderer ; pox, leave thy damnable faces, and begin. Come ;
> the croaking raven doth bellow for revenge.
>
> (*Haml.* iii. ii. 267–9)

The quasi-tragic line lends itself rather well to mouthing ;
and the same grim irony in which an undertone of burlesque
blends subtly with the tragic note, is conveyed in the
sardonic dialogue of Richard and Buckingham :

> *Rich.* Come, cousin, canst thou quake, and change thy colour,
> Murder thy breath in middle of a word,
> And then again begin, and stop again,
> As if thou were distraught and mad with terror ?
> *Buck.* Tut, I can counterfeit the deep Tragedian,
> Speak and look back, and pry on every side,
> Tremble and start at wagging of a straw,
> Intending deep suspicion : ghastly looks
> Are at my service, like enforced smiles.   (*Rich. III*, iii. v. 1–9)

Hamlet tells us that dumb-shows pleased the groundlings ;
they were a form of art which put no strain on the intelligence. They were a picture-show in which the events of
a succeeding scene or act were exhibited beforehand.
A ' presenter ' introduced them and gave a brief explana-

tion. Gower presents dumb-shows in the verse preludes—
not written by Shakespeare—to Acts II and III, and in
Act IV, Scene iv, of *Pericles*. The origin of the dumb-show
is interesting : we find it first in plays of the Senecan type,
such as *Gorboduc* and *The Misfortunes of Arthur*, in which
declamation takes the place of action; so that the show
was designed to infuse the lifeless rhetoric with a faint tinge
of drama. With the advance of playwriting it naturally
disappeared, or it survived only in the modified form of
by-play serving to introduce a new scene, as in the beginning of the second act of Marston's *Tragedy of Sophonisba*.
Ophelia in the Play scene of *Hamlet* is puzzled by its
revival; she asks Hamlet the meaning of it, and then
comments, ' Belike this show imports the argument of
the play ' (III. ii. 150–1) ; and when Hamlet refers her to
the Prologue, who has just entered, she persists with the
question ' Will a' tell us what this show meant ? ' Shakespeare uses the dumb-show only in this scene, but very
significantly. Hamlet's object in ' The Murder of Gonzago '
is to probe the King's conscience ; so he imposes a double
test, first this quick rehearsal of the bare events without
the explanatory comment of the presenter—a noticeable
omission—then the prolonged strain of the fully acted
scene. No wonder the King broke under it. By a sheer
paradox of situation the stupid device of the dumb-show is
lifted to the plane of drama.

Of ' noise ' there were several varieties, but there is
a special reference to stage-fighting, with its alarums and
excursions and cannon going off. Scene xii of *The Contention of the two famous Houses of York and Lancaster*
opens very vigorously in this way :

Alarms within, and the chambers be discharged, like as it were
a fight at sea. And then enter the Captain of the ship and the
Master, and the Master's Mate, and the Duke of Suffolk disguised,
and others with him, and Water Whickmore.
Capt. Bring forward these prisoners that scorn'd to yield,
Unlade their goods with speed and sink their ship.

The clatter and scuffle of a land-fight also had attractions.
The prologue to *Henry VIII* says it is no play for those
' that come to hear ... A noise of targets ' (ll. 14–15) ; and
Shirley's prologue to *The Doubtful Heir*, modelled on this,
puts the point even more strongly.

No shows, no dance, and—what you most delight in—
Grave understanders,[1] here's no target-fighting
Upon the stage, all work for cutlers barr'd ; . . . .
No clown, no squibs, no devil in 't. Oh now,
You squirrels that want nuts, what will you do ?
Pray do not crack the benches.

The prologue to Jonson's *Every Man in his Humor* expresses a like contempt for the appliances used to produce the effects of thunder, lightning, and storm :

Nor nimble squib is seen, to make afeard
The gentlewomen, nor roll'd bullet heard
To say, it thunders ; nor tempestuous drum
Rumbles, to tell you when the storm doth come.

The realism with which Marlowe's *Faustus* was performed in 1620 is described by John Melton in *The Astrologaster, or the Figure-Caster*, p. 31 :

Another will fore-tell of Lightning and Thunder that shall happen such a day, when there are no such Inflamations seene, except men goe to the Fortune in Golding-Lane, to see the Tragedie of Doctor Faustus. There indeede a man may behold shagge-hayr'd Devills runne roaring over the Stage with Squibs in their mouthes, while Drummers make Thunder in the Tyring-house, and the twelve-penny Hirelings make artificiall Lightning in their Heavens.

Hamlet's final advice—to avoid rant—is pointed with a historic reference to the Herod of the miracle plays. ' Here Erode ragis in the pagond, and in the strete also ' is a stage-direction in a Coventry play of 1534 which shows him in the traditional part of tyrant, braggart, and child-killer. The actor who could ' out-herod Herod ' was ' far gone ' and ' suffered much extremity ' in histrionics. Shakespeare's stray allusions to this primitive type of drama must be for the most part memories of boyhood, and they introduce us to a delightful phase of his art—to Shakespeare the parodist. There is a lost play on the twelve labours of Hercules, referred to by Greene and Sidney, to which Bottom turned for tragic inspiration ; it was evidently in the Herod vein :

My chief humour is for a tyrant. I could play Ercles rarely, or a part to tear a cat in, to make all split.

The raging rocks
And shivering shocks
Shall break the locks
Of prison gates :

---

[1] An ironical term for the groundlings who stood under the stage : cf. *Barthol'mew Fair*, ind.; ' the understanding gentlemen of the ground '.

> And Phibbus' car
> Shall shine from far,
> And make and mar
> The foolish Fates.

This was lofty! . . . . This is Ercles' vein, a tyrant's vein.

> *(Mid. N. D.* i. ii. 30–43)

Or there is 'King Cambyses' vein'—the mock-pathetic—
which Falstaff adopts when he 'must speak in passion'
and personate the tearfully heavy father; Mistress Quickly,
no mean judge of art on that level, exclaims, ' He doth
it as like one of these harlotry players as ever I see!'
(*1 Hen. IV*, II. iv. 441–2). Preston's *Life of Cambises
king of Percia*, 'a lamentable Tragedie, mixed full of
plesant Mirth'—had its lachrymose moments, as in the
stage-direction, 'At this tale tolde let the Queene weep'.

Those picturesque figures of the old interludes, the
Devil and the Vice, also receive their share of allusion.
Shakespeare identified the Vice with Iniquity: Falstaff
is 'that reverend vice, that grey iniquity' (*1 Hen. IV*,
II. iv. 505–6), and Richard practises the equivocation of
' the formal Vice, Iniquity' (*Rich. III*, III. i. 82).
Iniquity plays this part in *The Nice Wanton*, 1560, and in
King Darius, 1565; but other types of vicious character
supply it elsewhere—Avarice, Hypocrisy, Haphazard, a
fashionable gallant. By the time of Shakespeare the term
' vice ' was synonymous with ' buffoon '; he carried a
wooden dagger, and to the joy of the groundlings thumped
the Devil with it. ' I'd not give a rush for a Vice that has
not a wooden dagger to snap at everybody he meets ',
says one of the gossips in *The Staple of News* (2nd inter-
mean). In Fulwell's old play, *Like Will to Like, quoth the
Devil to the Collier*, 1568, Nichol Newfangle the Vice tries
to bully the clowns Tosspot and Roister, ' Lest I stick you
bothe with this woodknife', but they take it from him: 'Body
of me they have tane away my dagger.' The Clown in
Twelfth Night celebrates another use of this weapon:

> Like to the old Vice, . . .
> Who with dagger of lath,
> In his rage and his wrath,
> Cries ' Ah, ah!' to the Devil—
> Like a mad lad—
> ' Pare thy nails, dad '.   (IV. ii. 138–44)

So Pistol is described as 'this roaring Devil i' the old
play, that every one may pare his nails with a wooden
dagger' (*Hen. V*, IV. iv. 75–7). And Falstaff sums up
Shallow : 'Now is this Vice's dagger become a squire'
(*2 Hen. IV*, III. ii. 347)—a gibe which Chapman may have
remembered in the last scene of *The Widow's Tears*—
'O desert ! where wert thou, when this wooddden dagger
was guilded over with the Title of Governour ? ' The
dagger of the Vice was sometimes gilded.

Hence, when Hamlet reproaches his mother with the
hideous contrast between her husbands, he concentrates
his contempt for his uncle in the mordant phrase 'a vice
of kings ', and adds, in allusion to the motley which the
Vice sometimes wore, 'a king of shreds and patches '
(*Haml.* III. iv. 98, 102). Applied to Falstaff, the term still
conveys through the underlying quibble some notion of the
comic ; but in its application to the king there is nothing
to relieve its merciless epitome of scorn.

THE CLOWN

In Shakespeare, however, the Vice is no more than
a historic survival ; it was the Clown who developed
with the growth of the drama, and even secured a firm
foothold in tragedy. Broadly speaking, there are two
types of Clown in the plays of Shakespeare—the rustic
and the domestic fool. The former is the original, and there
is some evidence to show that he even affected the later
conception. Samuel Rowlands in *The Letting of Humours
Blood in the Head-vaine*, 1600, Satire iv, makes a curious
comment on the pronunciation of contemporary actors :

What meanes Singer then ?
And Pope the Clowne, to speake so Boorish, when
They counterfaite the Clownes upon the Stage ?

Costard in *Love's Labour's Lost* and the Clown who brings the
asp in *Antony and Cleopatra* illustrate the average rustic ;
and Dogberry, the ' hempen homespun ' Bottom, or the
gravediggers in *Hamlet* are Shakespeare's finished sketches.
Of the domestic fools it is enough to mention Feste, Touchstone, and the Court Fool in *King Lear*. But a hard and
fast line cannot be drawn between the comic characters.
Speed and Launce in the *Two Gentlemen of Verona* are

described in the First Folio as 'clownish servants' to
Valentine and Proteus, which suggests a blend of the
two types. Then there is a set of characters not belonging
to either but having distinct points of contact with them,
such as the followers of Falstaff, whom the First Folio in
the actor-list prefixed to *Henry V* neatly labels 'Irregular
Humorists'; even the sardonic Thersites finds a place on
the edge of this dubious group.

Shakespeare took over certain traditional features of the
Clown—the word-play of the 'skipping dialogue' (*Tw. N.*
I. v. 215) with its repertory of quips and puns and wilful misunderstandings. 'Well, your old vice still; mistake the word,'
says Speed to Launce (*Two Gent.* III. i. 285–6); 'How every
fool can play upon the word!' says Lorenzo of Launcelot
Gobbo (*Merch. of V.* III. v. 48). And Feste gives evidence
against himself : he describes himself as being not Olivia's
fool, 'but her corrupter of words,' in the thrust and parry
of a word-fence with Viola which embodies Shakespeare's
criticism of the type and ends with a judicial summing-up :

> This fellow 's wise enough to play the fool,
> And to do that well craves a kind of wit :
> He must observe their mood on whom he jests,
> The quality of persons, and the time,
> Not, like the haggard, check at every feather
> That comes before his eye. This is a practice
> As full of labour as a wise man's art. (*Tw. N.* III. i. 68–74)

An important privilege of the domestic and court fool
was the freedom of speech which he could exercise upon
his superiors ; if he had the necessary tact—as Viola is
careful to note—he could 'play upon them' without
'fretting' them. Feste in *Twelfth Night* (I. v. 62–77)
openly proves his mistress a fool, and is commended for it.
'There is no slander in an allowed fool,' is her view of
the position, 'though he do nothing but rail' (ib. 100–1).
Even Goneril can only complain of 'this your all-licensed
fool' (*Lear* I. iv. 223), but though the ominous look on her
face checks him, she 'says nothing' to him personally
(ib. 218). When Jaques asks leave to wear the fool's
motley, he adds why he wants it :

> I must have liberty . . .
> To blow on whom I please ; for so fools have :
> And they that are most galled with my folly,
> They most must laugh. (*A. Y. L.* II. vii. 47–51)

If the fool went too far, it meant a whipping in the porter's lodge. 'Take heed, sirrah; the whip,' says Lear, and the Fool replies 'Truth's a dog must to kennel' (*Lear* I. iv. 123–4).

Shakespeare's supreme achievement with the Fool—to make him move freely in the tragic setting of *King Lear*—turns largely on this licence of criticism. It yielded an artistic solution of a literary problem. Critics might talk of 'indecorum', but the audience did not mind—in fact they were delighted—if the clown came in cheek by jowl with the king. Joseph Hall's protest against this contamination of a tragic theme eloquently shows it :

> Now, least such frightfull showes of Fortunes fall,
> And bloudy Tyrants rage, should chance appall
> The dead stroke audience, mids the silent rout,
> Comes leaping in a selfe-misformed lout,
> And laughes, and grins, and frames his Mimik face,
> And justles straight into the princes place.
> Then doth the Theatre Eccho all a loud,
> With gladsome noyse of that applauding croud.
> A goodly hoch-poch; when vile Russettings,
> Are match't with monarchs, & with mighty kings.
> A goodly grace to sober Tragick Muse,
> When each base clown, his clumbsie fist doth bruise,[1]
> And show his teeth in double rotten row
> For laughter at his selfe-resembled show.
>
>   (*Virgidemiarum*, 1597, Satires I. iii)

The lungs of such an audience were 'tickle o' the sere'. If the play were a comedy, well and good; if not, they expected a clown to relieve it with dancing and singing and extemporized doggerel, or there was trouble for the manager and a prospect of damage to the playhouse. Here again the songs of Feste and the rhymes of Lear's Fool show the consummate art with which Shakespeare transformed a coarse convention.

Two comedians of the time were very famous for their skill in improvising—Richard Tarlton and William Kempe; the latter was the original performer of the parts of Peter in *Romeo and Juliet* and of Dogberry. Peacham has recorded that

> Tarlton when his head was onely seene,
> The Tire-house doore and Tapistrie betweene,
> Set all the mulltitude in such a laughter,
> They could not hold for scarse an houre after.
>
>   (*Thalia's Banquet*, 1620, Epigram 94)

---

[1] He thumps the benches in order to applaud.

PORTRAIT OF TARLTON

The specimens of his wit which contemporaries thought worth preserving are instructive. The most interesting is in *Tarlton's Jests*, an insipid collection issued with his portrait [1] in 1611 :

An excellent Jest of Tarlton suddenly spoken.

At the Bull of Bishops-gate was a Play of Henry the fift, wherein the Judge was to take a box on the eare, and because he was absent that should take the blow, Tarlton himselfe (ever forward to please) tooke upon him to play the same Judge, besides his owne part of the Clowne : and Knel·then playing Henry the fift, hit Tarlton a sound boxe indeed, which made the people laugh the more because it was he : but anon the Judge goes in, and immediately Tarlton (in his Clownes cloathes) comes out, and askes the Actors what newes ; O (saith one) hadst thou been here, thou shouldest have seene Prince Henry hit the Judge a terrible box on the eare. What man, said Tarlton, strike a Judge ? It is true yfaith, said the other. No other like, said Tarlton, and it could not be but terrible to the Judge, when the report so terrifies me, that me thinkes the blow remaines still on my cheeke, that it burnes againe. The people laught at this mightily : and to this day I have heard it commended for rare.

From another of the jests we learn that it was the custom for the audience at the end of a play to ' throw up themes ' in rhyme, which Tarlton answered on the spot.

Kempe [2] was equally famous for ' extemporal wit ', and he also specialized in face-play. In the last scene of *The Pilgrimage to Parnassus*, acted at St. John's College, Cambridge, in 1598, a clown is 'drawn in with a rope' and told

Clowns have been thrust into plays by head and shoulders ever since Kempe could make a scurvy face. . . . Why, if thou canst but draw thy mouth awry, lay thy leg over thy staff, saw a piece of cheese asunder with thy dagger, lap up drink on the earth, I warrant thee they'll laugh mightily.

Now the gift of improvising jokes had its dangers when the comedian was cast for a part in a carefully constructed play ; the tendency to ' gag ' was irresistible. It is at any rate a plausible conjecture of Collier that Shakespeare's famous protest against interpolating clownery into his text was levelled at Kempe.

---

[1] It resembles the portrait reproduced here from Harleian MS. 3885, fol. 19, of the British Museum : in the MS. Tarlton is drawn standing within the loop of an ornamental T.

[2] He is depicted on the title-page of *Kemps nine daies wonder* (reproduced in Chapter XXVII, § 8) dancing the morris on the way to Norwich, ' attended on by Thomas Slye my Taberer '.

And let those that play your Clowns speak no more than is set down for them. For there be of them that will themselves laugh, to set on some quantity of barren spectators to laugh too, though in the mean time some necessary question of the play be then to be considered; that's villanous, and shows a most pitiful ambition in the fool that uses it. (*Haml.* III. ii. 43–51)

The First Quarto reinforces this criticism by quoting some topical jokes not found in the later texts, no doubt because the allusions became obsolete.

And then you have some again that keeps one suit of jests, as a man is known by one suit of apparel : and gentlemen quotes his jests down in their tables before they come to the play, as thus : ' Cannot you stay till I eat my porridge ? ' and ' You owe me a quarter's wages ', and ' My coat wants a cullison ', and ' Your beer is sour ' ; and blabbering with his lips and thus keeping in his cinquepace of jests, when, God knows, the warm Clown cannot make a jest unless by chance as the blind man catcheth a hare. Masters, tell him of it.

Other dramatists were more pliant, and kindly indicated to the Clown the points in the text where he was at liberty to air his wit. Some amusing stage-directions show how this was done : in *The History of the tryall of Cheualry*, 1605 (sig. E 4), we read ' Enter Forrester, missing the other taken away, speake any thing, and Exit ' ; and in *The Second Part of King Edward the Fourth*, 1600, by Thomas Heywood, ' Jockie is led to whipping over the stage, speaking some words, but of no importance. Then is young Aire brought forth to execution by the Sheriff and Officers.'

A later protest in *The Antipodes* of Richard Brome (II. ii), where a lord reads an actor a professional lecture with hints borrowed from *Hamlet*, is interesting as showing how the ' gag ' was worked in ; the Clown ignored his fellow actors, leaving them to mark time while he came forward and chatted with the audience :

> *Letoy.* But you, Sir, are incorrigible, and
> Take licence to yourself to add unto
> Your parts your own free fancy ; and sometimes
> To alter or diminish what the writer
> With care and skill composed ; and when you are
> To speak to your coactors in the scene
> You hold interlocutions with the audients.
> *Byplay.* That is a way, my lord, has been allow'd
> On elder stages to move mirth and laughter.
> *Letoy.* Yes, in the days of Tarlton and Kempe

Before the stage was purged from barbarism
And brought to the perfection it now shines with.
Then fools and jesters spent their wits because
The poets were wise enough to save their own
For profitabler uses.

Another inartistic practice of the theatre was the ' jig '—
an after-piece performed by the clown. 'Rehearsed . . .
as ordinarily as a jig after a play' is a phrase of Ben Jonson
(*Every Man out of his Humor*, II. ii), and *Jack Drum's
Entertainment*, 1601, speaks of it as being ' called for ' at
that point. It was extremely popular with the groundlings :
hence Hamlet's gibe at Polonius—' He's for a jig or a tale
of bawdry, or he sleeps' (*Haml.* II. ii. 530–1).
   The jig was a lyrical farce written in rhyme and sung
and danced to ballad measure. The title-page of a slight
book about Tarlton refers to its brevity—*Tarlton's Newes
out of Purgatorie. Onely such a jest as his Jigge, fit for Gentlemen to laugh at an houre*. It lasted at least twenty minutes.
Sometimes the clown performed it alone, but usually there
were two players. Kempe's 'newe Jygge betwixt a souldiour
and a Miser and Sym the clown', entered in the Stationers'
Register in 1595, requires three ; and there are four in the
excellent specimen which has been preserved among the
Shirburn Ballads (ed. Clark, pp. 244–54)—*Mr. Attowel's
Jigge betweene ffrancis a Gentleman, Richard a farmer, and
their wives*. It has four scenes sung to different tunes.
The first, ' To the tune of Walsingham ', represents the
' jolly Palmer ' Francis making love to Richard's wife, Bess :
she pretends compliance and makes an appointment.
In the second ' Enter Richard, Bess'es husband. To the
tune of The Jewishe dance'. They plot to substitute
Francis's wife for Bess : so in Scene iii 'Enter Mistris
Francis with Richard. To the tune of Buggle-boe', and
at the climax ' Enter Master Francis, with his owne wife
(having a maske before her face) supposing her to be Bessee,'
appropriately ' To the tune of Goe from my windo '. It is
a lively little piece, rough in workmanship, and evidently
depending for success on its rapid movement and the
variety of its tunes. The actor whose name heads the
jig may perhaps be identified with Hugh Atwell, one of
the Children of the Revels in 1609, when he played in
the original performance of Jonson's *Silent Woman*, and

afterwards an actor under Alleyn. But he was not the author : the piece was entered on the Stationers' Register in 1595 as ' A pretie new Jigge '.

The Clown's dress varied. Tarlton in his habit as he lived is described by Chettle in *Kind-Harts Dreame*: he wore a suit of russet and a buttoned cap, carried a tabor, and had a trick of standing on the toe. The russet suit probably appears in his portrait here reproduced. But he is not wearing there his ' great clownish slop ' or wide-puffed breeches which have received the honour of literary commemoration.[1] Marston also mentions the 'huge slop ' and the ' lugged boot ' as part of the clown's dress (*Sat.* xi. 174).

The traditional dress was the ' motley ' or ' patched ' suit with alternations of red and yellow.

> Oh that I were a fool !
> I am ambitious for a motley coat. (*A.Y.L.* ii. vii. 42–3)

' Pied ninny ', ' scurvy patch' (*Temp.* iii. ii. 73), and ' patch'd fool ' (*Mid. N. D.* ii. vi. 216) are humorous efforts of description. The hood was a copy of the monk's cowl, with asses' ears and a cock's crest—the ' coxcomb ' of *King Lear* i. iv. 105. ' What is your crest ? a coxcomb ? ' Katharina asks Petruchio (*Tam. Sh.* ii. i. 224). The bauble (*All's W.* iv. v. 32) or mock-sceptre, a stick ending in a fool's head, completed his equipment.

Another dress for the Fool was the long coat, borrowed from the dress of the natural idiot.[2] The title-page of Armin's *History of the two Maids of More-clacke*—which is probably a portrait of the author—shows this petticoat costume. It is described in the prologue to *Henry VIII* as a ' long motley coat guarded ', i.e. faced, ' with yellow '.

The long purse or wallet also appears at Armin's girdle ; it was the fashion to tip the Fool, and sixpence seems to have been the minimum (*Tw. N.* ii. iii. 27–37, iii. i. 50). The Clown in *Love's Labour's Lost* (iii. i. 143) was justly indignant at three farthings.

[1] In Rowland's *Letting of Humours Blood*, 1600, Ep. 30 ; and T. Wright's *Passions of the Mind*, 1604, p. 332.
[2] See Nashe, *Have with you to Saffron-Walden*, 1596, Ep. ded.

THE
Hiſtory of the two Maids of More-clacke,

VVith the life and ſimple maner of IOHN
in the Hoſpitall.

Played by the Children of the Kings
Maieſties Reuels.

VVritten by ROBERT ARMIN, ſeruant to the Kings
moſt excellent Maieſtie.

LONDON,
Printed by *N.O.* for *Thomas Archer,* and is to be ſold at his
ſhop in Popes-head Pallace, 1 6 0 9.

REHEARSALS, PROPERTIES, AND STAGE-ARRANGEMENTS

An interesting document, formerly in the possession of Malone,[1] states the terms of agreement between Robert Dawes, an actor, and Henslowe and Jacob Meade, to whom he engaged himself for a term of three years in April 1614. He binds himself to ' attend all suche rehearsall which shall the night before the rehearsall be given publickly out '; if he is unpunctual, to forfeit a shilling; ' if he come not before the saide rehearsall is ended ', to forfeit two shillings ; three shillings if he is not ' ready apparrelled . . . to begyn the play at the hower of three of the clock in the afternoone '; ten shillings ' if that he the saide Robert Dawes Happen to be overcome with drinck at the tyme when he ought to play '; and twenty shillings if he absents himself without permission or ' just excuse of sicknes '. Henslowe was a shrewd hand at a bargain, but Dawes, being a sharer in the theatre, must have been a competent actor : so the agreement probably runs on strict business lines. The graduated scale of fines is very instructive.

But Henslowe's rigid commercialism only takes us as far as the door of the ' tiring-house '; Shakespeare's picture even of amateurs so raw as the yokels of *A Midsummer-Night's Dream* shows us the life and bustle within. Peter Quince as stage-manager is methodical and businesslike ; he gets the whip hand of his awkward team and even reins in the plunging forehorse Bottom. He assembles the ' company ' and assigns the parts. ' Have you the lion's part written ? ' asks Snug nervously, ' pray you, if it be, give it me, for I am slow of study ' (*Mid. N. D.* I. ii. 69–70). Elizabethan plays were not in print before the performance : actors got their parts in manuscript— a full text of their own speeches with the ' cues '—the last word or words of any speech preceding their own. One playhouse manuscript of this kind has survived—the title part of Greene's *Orlando Furioso* preserved at Dulwich College ; it has been revised for performance by Edward Alleyn, who probably played it. It is written on slips originally pasted together so as to form a roll which the actor could work through his fingers as he learnt the part.

[1] Printed in the Boswell-Malone *Shakespeare*, 1821, vol. xxi, pp. 413–16.

This prevented the loss of loose leaves and saved the expense of binding.

Shakespeare has several allusions to the cues. Literally in *A Midsummer-Night's Dream*, III. i. 103–7, where Flute goes wrong at the rehearsal :

Why, you must not speak that yet ; . . . you speak all your part at once, cues and all. Pyramus, enter : your cue is past ; it is ' never tire '.

And figuratively in Edgar's plot against his brother :

Pat he comes, like the catastrophe of the old comedy : my cue is villanous melancholy. (*Lear* I. ii. 150–1)

To ensure that each actor did come pat, and to jog his memory if he were ' out ', was the duty of an underling— usually a boy—called the ' book-holder ' or the ' prompter ', who watched the cues, got the properties ready, and arranged for the music, alarums, and stage-thunder. Othello, when Brabantio orders his arrest and threatens him in the event of resistance, answers with the high-toned rebuke:

> Were it my cue to fight, I should have known it
> Without a prompter. (*Oth.* I. ii. 83–4)

The second part of *The Returne from Parnassus* opens with an amusing passage between a Boy, who was to have spoken the prologue, and the Stage-keeper. The Boy breaks down at the end of the first line.

Boy. Spectators, we will act a Comedy (*non plus*).

Stage. A pox on't, this book hath it not in it : you would be whipped, you rascal ; you must be sitting up all night at cards when you should be conning your part.

Boy. It 's all 'long of you, I could not get my part a night or two before that I might sleep on it.

Stagekeeper carrieth the boy away under his arm.

The ' Stage-keeper ' was one of the ' hired men ' who did menial work, sweeping the stage and supplying it with fresh rushes ; here, perhaps from motives of economy, he also acts as the ' book-holder '.

The prompter himself could refer to a skeleton outline of the play technically called the ' plot ', ' platt ', or ' platform ', seven specimens of which are known to us. They are written in two columns on paper mounted on pasteboard, and have a hole cut near the top to enable them to be hung on a peg in the playhouse,[1] so that actors

---

[1] See Greg, *Henslowe Papers*, p. 129 : the specimen here quoted is on p. 139. Bracketed letters mark the points where the paper has worn away on the pasteboard.

could also consult them. They mark off the separate
scenes and give the cast, often with the actors' names ;
and four of these plots have in the left-hand margin directions about music and properties. The most interesting
is *The Plott of the Battell of Alcazar*, Peele's play, of which
we have the text. This is the summary of Act I, Scene ii,
and the dumb show preceding Act II.

sound sennett Alarū	Enter in a Charriott Muly [M]ahamett & Calipolis : on each side pages moores attendant Pisano m^r Hunt & w· Cartwright and young Mahamet Antony Jeffes : exit m^r Sam manet the rest : to them m^r Sam a gaine exeunt
    brand and Chopping knife :	Enter the Presenter : to him 2 domb shew Enter aboue Nemesis, Tho : Dr[om] to them 3· ghosts. w· kendall Dab : to them [l]ying behind the Curtaines 3· Furies : Parsons : George & Ro :T[ai]lor one wth a whipp : a nother wth a [b]lody tor[c]h : & the 3^d wth a Chopp[ing] knif[e] : exeunt

The author naturally attended rehearsals and the first
performance ; he was not always so tactful and tolerant
as Quince. In the induction to *Cynthia's Revels* a gallant
walks on the stage and inquires for him. One of the
Children answers :

We are not so officiously befriended by him as to have his presence
in the tiring-house to prompt us aloud, stamp at the bookholder,
swear for our properties, curse the poor tireman, rail the music
out of tune, and sweat for every venial trespass we commit, as some
author would if he had such fine ingles as we.

Quince undertakes to draw up a ' bill of properties,
such as our play wants ' (*Mid. N. D.* I. ii. 109). Our
chief information about properties—a term which covers
all the requirements of the theatre, its costumes, furniture,
and miscellaneous articles—is derived from the *Declared
Accounts* of the Master of the Revels, who supervised court
performances, and from the *Henslowe Papers* at Dulwich,
especially the famous *Diary*. The latter collection is our
only authority for the public theatre. The most interesting
items in it are those made for particular plays. Henslowe's
stock included properties for three of Marlowe's plays.[1]

[1] See *Henslowe Papers*, ed. Greg, pp. 54, 116–20.

Thus in the inventory of the dresses of the Admiral's men for March 1598 there are 'Tamberlynes cotte, with coper lace' and 'Tamberlanes breches of crymson vellvet'; and among the properties 'Tamberlyne brydell', with which he guided the 'pamper'd jades of Asia', and 'j cage' for Bajazet. The caldron into which Barabas was precipitated at the end of *The Jew of Malta* appears in Henslowe's extraordinary spelling as 'j cauderm for the Jewe'. Similarly for the play of *Dr. Faustus* there are entries of 'faustus Jerkin his clok', 'j dragon in fostes'—the dragon-car in Scene vii,—'j poopes miter' for the papal banquet in the same scene, and—most interesting of all—a property called 'the sittie of Rome', apparently a painted cloth to illustrate the description given of Rome at that point of the play (ll. 831–45, ed. Tucker Brooke). A similar property, which cannot be identified—'the clothe of the Sone and Mone'—further shows that an occasional attempt was made to provide some rudimentary scenery.

Some of Henslowe's inventories record the prices of costumes. Hamlet's 'forest of feathers', which he mentions as necessary for the full equipment of a player, could be got for ten shillings [1] (*Diary*, ed. Greg, p. 79). A suit of motley cost thirty shillings (ib., p. 165); it is an interesting coincidence that Henslowe lent Lord Worcester's players the same sum 'to bye a sewte for w^m kempe' on September 3, 1602 (ib., p. 180). 'A man's gown of branched velvet and a doublet' cost six pounds (ib.). Sometimes the material is bought to make up—e. g. eight yards of cloth of gold for four pounds (ib., p. 69). Women's dresses, thanks to the boy-actors, are quite economical : 'taffeta and other stuff to make two women's gowns' cost nine pounds (p. 179), and, with extra stuff thrown in, was made up for thirty-four shillings (p. 180). The extravagant articles are the cloaks, on which sums varying from eighty to one hundred pounds in modern money are spent. Henslowe lent the company £19 to buy a 'rich cloak' (*Diary*, p. 96), and Alleyn and his brother paid £20 10s. for 'one blacke velvet cloake, with sleves ymbrodered all with silver and golde, lyned with blacke satten stryped with golde' (*Alleyn Papers*, p. 12).

[1] Multiply by at least five to get the equivalent value in modern money.

A very interesting entry is ' Bowght a robe for to go
invisibell ', which, together with a lady's gown, cost £3 10s
(*Henslowe Papers*, p. 123). This seems very cheap. On
would like to know more of a costume perhaps worn by Ariel
It may have resembled one of the methods of representing a
ghost. There are references which seem to show that a ghost
instead of wearing white, was sometimes clad in leather :

> A filthie whining ghost,
> Lapt in some fowle sheete or a leather pelch,
> Comes skreaming in like a pigge halfe stickt.
> > (*A Warning for Fair Women*, 1599, ind.)

Enter Brachiano's ghost, in his leather cassock and breeches, boots
a cowl.   (Webster, *The White Devil*, 1612, v. iv)

If this view is sound, the idea must have been to use a
dull-coloured material like buff as a contrast to the gorgeou
dresses and cloaks. But, as far as we have any clue to
Shakespeare's practice in this point, he seems to have
dressed his ghosts in the costume which they would naturally
have worn in real life. On the platform before the castle o
Elsinore the ghost of the King wears full armour (*Haml.* I. i
60 ; ii. 200, 225–6) ; indoors, in the bedroom scene, he wears
a dressing-gown. So at least the First Quarto informs us in
the stage-direction, ' Enter the ghost in his night gowne '.

The players turned an occasional penny by lending from
their wardrobe. When Drugger in *The Alchemist* has to
masquerade as a Spanish count, Face tells him

> > > > Thou must borrow
> A Spanish suit : hast thou no credit with the players ? . . .
> Hieronimo's old cloak, ruff, and hat [1] will serve ;
> I'll tell thee more when thou bring'st them.   (*Alch.* IV. vii)

Or they eked out their stock by hiring. Sir Henry Herbert
the Master of the Revels, records in his Office Book :

> I committed Cromes, a broker in Longe Lane, the 16 of Febru
> 1634 [O.S.], to the Marshalsey, for lending a church-robe with the
> name of JESUS upon it, to the players in Salisbury Court, to presen
> a Flamen, a priest of the heathens. Upon his petition of submission
> and acknowledgment of his faulte, I releasd him, the 17 Febr. 1634.

Quince's worries about properties are pure comedy
He brushes aside Bottom's inquiry about the colour of his
beard (*Mid. N. D.* I. ii. 93–9)—a nice point at a time when
the colour changed with the fashion [2]—and concentrates

---

[1] A gibe at the playwrights' eternal butt, *The Spanish Tragedy*.
[2] See Chapter XIX, p. 110.

n really grave problems. How is he to bring moonlight
nto a chamber (III. i. 63–6) ? His solution was actually
dopted at Whitehall in 1601, when the devices included,
ccording to Manningham, ' the man in the moone with
hornes on his backe looking downeward'. Quince's
ouching faith in the emblematic virtues of plaster, loam,
nd rough-cast, may be illustrated from the burlesque in
he *Twelfe Night Merriment* on the subject of Narcissus,
cted at St. John's College, Oxford, in 1602 ; this is how
he well into which Narcissus looks is made :

> Enter one with a buckett and boughes and grasse.

well there was withouten mudd
f silver hue with waters cleare
Vhome neither sheepe that chawe the cudd
hepheards nor goates came ever neare
Vhome truth to say nor beast nor bird
or windfalls yet from trees had stirrde.
    Hee strawes the grasse about the buckett
nd round about it there was grasse
s learned lines of Poets showe
Vhich by next water nourisht was,   Sprinkle water
eere to it too a wood did growe   Setts downe the bowes
o keepe the place as well I wott
Vith too much sunne from being hott
nd thus least you should have mistooke it
he truth of all I to you tell
uppose you the well had a buckett
nd so the buckett stands for the well
nd tis, least you should counte mee for a soto
very pretty figure cald pars pro toto.

> Exit.

uch properties as a well-head—minor pieces of furniture
vhich could be fixed on the stage—were in the stock of
very company. The Player King in *Hamlet* ' lays him
own upon a bank of flowers ' (III. ii. 146 st. dir.) ; and
here are similar references elsewhere.

> Come, sit thee down upon this flowery bed.
>   (*Mid. N. D.* IV. i. 1)
> How sweet the moonlight sleeps upon this bank !
> Here will we sit.   (*Merch. of V.* v. i. 54–5)

nd in Dekker's *Shoemaker's Holiday*, I. ii (1610, sig. C):

> *Enter Rose alone making a Garland.*
> Here sit thou downe upon this flowry banke,
> And make a garland for thy Lacies head.

This points to something more than the players sitting
upon the rushes of the stage, and we actually find that
Henslowe had 'two mossy banks' among his properties
(*Henslowe Papers*, p. 117). If it was inconvenient to
keep them on the stage throughout the play, they could
be pushed out at the moment when it was necessary
to indicate that the scene had changed to a wood or
a garden.

This abrupt method of changing the scene was often
employed to indicate a bedroom. It is noted twice in the
stage-directions of the First Folio—'Enter Imogen, in her
Bed' (*Cymb.* II. ii.), and 'Bed put forth' with the dead
body of Gloucester (*2 Hen. VI*, III. ii. 148). Both can be
happily illustrated from *The Spanish Curate*, by Fletcher and
Massinger, which has been printed from a playhouse copy
containing the manager's notes in the margins. In the
margin of Act IV, Scene i, is a note 'Bed ready'; it is
not wanted till Scene v. Early in that scene is a note
'Diego ready in bed, wine, cup'; then, at the required
point, where the text says 'Bring him out', there is a
stage-direction beginning 'Enter Diego (in a Bed)', with
the additional comment in the margin, 'Bed thrust out'.
Two notes on this subject in plays of Heywood are quaintly
worded: in *A Maidenhead Well Lost*, 1634, v. iii, a mother
is asked about her daughter.

> *Prince.* Pray may wee see her?
> *Wife.* My Lord you may.
> *Shee's drawne out upon a Bed.*

And in *The Golden Age*, 1611, Act IV:

> Enter the foure old Beldams, drawing out Dana's bed; she
> in it. They place foure tapers at the foure corners.

The absence of set scenery, shifted at frequent intervals,
forced these direct and plain methods upon the actors.
If we could recover a series of playhouse texts which the
manager had annotated for the use of the company, we
should realize vividly the simple conditions under which
plays were performed. Failing this source of help, we
can at any rate examine carefully the old stage-directions
which the modernizing editor often takes pains to obliterate.
A lost stage-direction for the death of Thisbe in the *Midsummer-Night's Dream* may be supplied from Edward
Sharpham's play, *The Fleire*, 1607, sig. E verso—'Faith

NATHANIEL FIELD

like Thisbe in the play, a has almost kil'd himselfe with the scabberd'. This must have been the direction—probably Shakespeare's own—for the original performance. We can certainly trace him in the stage-direction of Act I, Sc. ii, of *Hamlet*, as printed in the Second Quarto :

> *Florish. Enter Claudius, King of Denmarke, Gertradt the Queene, Counsaile : as Polonius, and his Sonne Laertes, Hamlet, Cum Alijs.*

This detaches Hamlet from the royal party, and heightens the dramatic point of the King's appeal to him, after the preliminary speech about the marriage and the directions to the ambassador :

> But now, my cousin Hamlet, and my son.

Editors adapt the commonplace direction of the First Folio and arrange a sort of Lord Chamberlain's procession : ' Enter the King, Queen, Hamlet, Polonius, Laertes, Voltimand, Cornelius, Lords, and Attendants.'

A fine effect intended by Shakespeare is similarly marred in the setting of Ophelia's funeral (*Haml.* v. i. 239). The First Quarto has the significant direction: ' Enter King and Queene, Leartes, and other lordes, with a Priest after the coffin.' Where in the modern rearrangement of editors and actors are the ' maimed rites ' of which Hamlet expressly speaks ?—' Enter Priests, &c., in procession : the Corpse of Ophelia, Laertes, and Mourners following ; King, Queen, their Trains, &c.' The stern and solitary figure of Shakespeare's text, cutting short the last rites with ' the bringing home of bell and burial ', deepens the pathos of Ophelia's fate. The ' Priests, &c.'—' &c.' means a crucifix, incense, and a choir of mutes—are clumsy intruders whom mere ignorance has foisted into the text.

This is not the only difficulty which has been wantonly created in this scene. How does the well-known figure in the ' inky cloak ' elude observation till the moment when he leaps into the grave ? By keeping in the background ? By dodging behind Horatio ? Or simply because the actors, complying with a stage convention, look elsewhere ? To complete the absurdity, Hamlet is supposed to have worn his court costume in the North Sea, fought the pirates in it, and brought it back undamaged. Mr. Poel makes the admirable suggestion that he should return in the dress of a common sailor. Then at the critical moment he can rush into the grave, telling Laertes and the startled court

This is I,

Hamlet the Dane, (ibid. 279–80)

without doing anything foolish.

That Shakespeare had an eye for these effects of costume is easily proved. In *The Tempest* he subtly suggests the magic atmosphere of the enchanted island by twice telling us (I. ii. 218–19 ; II. i. 65–8) that the dresses of the shipwrecked crew are even ' fresher than before ', ' rather new-dyed than stain'd with salt-water ' ; in Prospero's masque (IV. i. 138) ' certain Reapers, properly habited, join with the Nymphs in a graceful dance ', and with their ' rye-straw hats ' and working dress set off picturesquely the ' sedg'd crowns ' and fancy costume of the Naiads ; and in *Henry V* there is an artistic contrast, ignored by modern stage-managers, between the tattered, mudstained, rain-soaked English and the French nobles in shining armour and rich suits. ' We are but warriors for the working-day ', says King Henry :

> Our gayness and our gilt are all besmirch'd
> With rainy marching in the painful field ;
> There 's not a piece of feather in our host, . . .
> And time hath worn us into slovenry. (IV. iii. 109–14)

A very simple principle determines the location of the scene : it is left vague unless the action requires it to be fixed ; then the playwright frankly says so through the mouth of an actor. In this way there may even be a rapid change of locality in the course of a single scene. In the anonymous play of *George a Greene*, 1599, E 3 verso, there is a stage-direction :

Enter a Shoomaker sitting vpon the stage at worke, Jenkin to him.
Jenkin challenges him to go to the town's end for a bout at quarterstaff.

Jenkin. But darest thou walke to the townes end with me ?
Shoomaker. I that I dare do : but stay till I lay in my Tooles, and I will goe with thee to the townes end Presently.
Jenkin. I would I knew how to be rid of this fellow.
Shoomaker. Come sir, wil you go to the townes end now sir ?
Jenkin. I sir, come.
Now we are at the townes end, what say you now ?
Shoomaker. Marry come, let vs euen haue a bout.

At the words ' Ay, sir, come ', the pair walk up to the front of the stage till they reach their new destination. On a platform projecting out into the auditorium this would not be a difficult feat ; the depth of the stage lent itself to effects no longer possible behind the frame of the proscenium. ' Enter Hamlet and Horatio a farre off ' is the stage-direction in the Folio for *Hamlet* v. i. 60 ; over sixty lines are spoken before Hamlet directly addresses the Gravedigger. An interesting criticism of amateur actors put in the mouth of Will Kempe in *The Returne from Parnassus* shows how a skilled actor made such situations effective ; he is commenting on the university players :

. . . it is a good sport in a part to see them never speak in their walk but at the end of the stage, just as though in walking with a fellow we should never speak but at a stile, a gate, or a ditch, where a man can go no further. (Part II, IV. iii)

The opening of the third Act of *Julius Cæsar* gives an admirable illustration. Caesar's procession enters, and as it advances up the stage Artemidorus offers him a petition and is thrust aside by the conspirators :

What, urge you your petitions in the street ?
Come to the Capitol. (III. i. 11–12)

They are in the Capitol in the next line—a situation so bewildering to editors that some of them mark a new scene. The second scene of Act IV in *Othello* also causes ' great difficulties ', says Malone. It is Othello's terrible cross-examination of Desdemona—a scene which certainly requires the privacy of 'A Room in the Castle '. But immediately after Desdemona's exit, with Iago saying to her ' Go in, and weep not', Roderigo, wishing to see Iago, enters this private room of his enemy's house : so that pedantry would require us to add to the imperfect location, 'and afterwards, without a word of warning, the Court before the Castle '.

Sometimes the announcement of the scene is made by the ' Chorus ', who speaks the prologue or similar speeches of an introductory character at later points in the play, explaining the action. Rumour introduces *The Second Part of King Henry the Fourth*, and relates the result of the battle of Shrewsbury. Thence she has passed to

this worm-eaten hold of ragged stone,
Where Hotspur's father, old Northumberland,
Lies crafty-sick. (Ind. 35–7)

The Chorus in *Romeo and Juliet* describes at once the

> Two households, both alike in dignity,
> In fair Verona, where we lay our scene.   (Prol. 1–2)

And the Choruses in *Henry V* are a running comment on the play. This explanatory function of the Chorus is the point of Hamlet's reply, when Ophelia tells him he is a ' good Chorus ',

> I could interpret between you and your love, if I could see the puppets dallying.   (*Haml.* III. ii. 260–1)

In short, the Elizabethan playwright was explicit on points of stage-arrangement whenever the situation required him to be ; but he excelled in suggesting it by the life and movement of the action. The final defeat of Edward II in Marlowe's play is announced thus :

> *Enter the King, Baldock, and Spencer the sonne,*
> *flying about the stage.*
> *Spen.*   Fly, fly, my Lord, the Queene is over strong, . . .
> Shape we our course to Ireland there to breath.
> > (*Edw. II*, ll. 1778–80, ed. Tucker Brooke)

Talbot's recovery of Orleans in *The First Part of King Henry the Sixth*, Act II, Scene i, is still more vigorous, especially in the stage-directions of the First Folio. ' Enter a Sergeant of a Band, with two Sentinels ', whom he posts, and orders to report any noise. When he retires, one of the sentinels comments,

> Thus are poor servitors—
> When others sleep upon their quiet beds—
> Constrain'd to watch in darkness, rain, and cold.

Immediately ' Enter Talbot, Bedford, and Burgundy, with scaling Ladders : Their Drummes beating a Dead March '. They agree to make their attempts at different points. ' Ile to yond corner,' says Bedford. ' And I to this,' says Burgundy. ' And here will Talbot mount, or make his grave.' The sentry gives the alarm, and the stage-directions are, ' Cry, S. George, A Talbot ' : ' The French leape ore the walles in their shirts. Enter seuerall wayes, Bastard, Alanson, Reignier, halfe ready, and halfe vnready.' Later they rally, and then ' Alarum. Enter a Souldier, crying, a Talbot, a Talbot : they flye, leaving their Clothes behind.'

THE PERFORMANCE

When the manager had completed his arrangements, he advertised the coming performance by putting up ' bills ' on a ' post ', commonly used at this date for public notices. The anonymous play of *Histriomastix*, 1610, depicts a strolling player caught by the press-gang just as he is advertising a play :

> *Enter Belsh setting uppe billes. Enter to him a Captaine.*
> *Capt.* Sirra, what set you up there ?
> *Belsh.* Text billes for Playes.

He takes the money which the Captain offers him, innocently asking 'How many meane you shall come in for this ?' and is told that it is press-money and that ' Text billes must now be turn'd to Iron billes'. The earliest mention of these advertisements appears to be in the Stationers' Register for October 30, 1587, when John Charlwood secured a monopoly for printing 'all manner of Billes for players'; he paid half-a-crown, five times the usual fee, evidently for-the five companies. The only example is late and incomplete, in Sir Samuel Tuke's *The Adventures of Five Hours*, 1663 :

> *The Prologue Enters with a Play-Bill in his hand, and Reads,*
> This Day being the 15th of *December*, shall be Acted a New Play, never Plai'd before, call'd *The Adventures of Five Hours*.

Besides the business details, such as time, place, company, and title, the bill probably gave a sufficient notion of the piece to whet the appetite of the playgoer. The title-pages of a number of the Shakespearian Quartos are unblushing attempts at advertisement : in fact they were the only part of the book over which the publisher could claim to exercise complete control. Play-bill and printed title may well have been identical in *The Tragedy of King Richard the third. Containing, His treacherous Plots against his brother Clarence : the pittiefull murther of his innocent nephewes : his tyrannicall usurpation : with the whole course of his detested life, and most deserved death,* as the Quarto of 1597 words it, or in *The most excellent Historie of the Merchant of Venice. With the extreame crueltie of Shylocke the Jewe towards the sayd Merchant, in cutting a just pound of his flesh : and the obtayning of Portia by the choyse of three chests,* as in the Quarto of 1600.

These bills also circulated privately. Fitzdottrel in *The*

Divell is an Asse, I. iv, inquires if there is a play; Ingine answers,

> Oh here 's the bill, sir ;
> I had forgot to gi't you.   *He gives him the Play-bill.*

For performances at a nobleman's house or at court it was usual to submit the ' argument ' or plot of the piece. Hamlet had ' heard the argument ' of the play he patronized (*Haml.* III. ii. 245), and in Ford's *Lover's Melancholy*, III. iii, the author of the masque, who is described as entering ' with a Paper-plot ', hands the Prince a paper, saying :

> Pray my Lord
> Hold and observe the plot, tis there exprest
> In kind, what shall be now exprest in action.

In Jonson's masque of *Neptune's Triumph* there is even a distribution of programmes ; the author is described as ' entering on the stage to disperse the argument '.

The performance began at three.[1] Those of the audience who wished for good seats came early and whiled away the interval of waiting in various ways. Henry Fitzgeoffery in his *Notes from Black-Fryers*, 1617, describes the scene. He strolls into the playhouse, is disgusted with the piece announced for performance, but decides to ' sit it out '.

> Come, let 's bethink ourselves what may be found
> To deceive time with till the second sound—

i.e. till the trumpets announce the play. He describes various characters in the audience—Captain Martio, who in the order of merit would rank between Pistol and Bobadil ; Sir Island Hunt, a lying traveller ; a Cheapside dame, of doubtful morals ; a fashionable gallant dressed like Portia's English lover in an international costume (*Merch. of V*. I. ii. 78–81) ; another exquisite, ' Tissue-slop ', who enters from the tiring-house ; a singer and with him the author, supercilious and irritable :

> See how he draws his mouth awry of late,
> How he scrubs, wrings his wrists, scratches his pate.

A variety of articles were on sale before or during the performance. There was bottled ale : Beaumont in *The Woman-Hater*, II. i, describes a nervous poet ' towards the latter end of his new play' 'peeping betwixt the curtains so fearfully that a bottle of ale cannot be opened but he thinks somebody hisses '. Tobacco could be bought—

---

[1] See the contract quoted on p. 264.

Prynne records that women were offered pipes there [1]—and nuts and apples. The City apprentices, who were particularly noisy visitors on a holiday afternoon, are described as 'the youths that thunder at a playhouse and fight for bitten apples' (*Hen. VIII*, v. iv. 65–6); and an actor anticipates a practical use for these in the prologue to Tailor's play, *The Hog hath lost his Pearl*, 1614:

> We may be pelted off for ought we know,
> With apples, egges, or stones, from thence belowe.

The literary-minded purchased books and appear to have tried to read them!

> I suppose this Pamphlet will hap into your hands, before a play begin, with the importunate clamour, of *Buy a new Booke*, by some needy companion, that will be glad to furnish you with worke for a turn'd Teaster.
>
> (W. Fennor, *Descriptions*, 'To the Reader', 1616)

Dekker's suggestion—'Before the play begins, fall to cards'—seems more practical. This is offered in his amusing burlesque of books of etiquette, *The Guls Horne-booke*, published in 1609, where a chapter is devoted to explaining 'How a Gallant should behave himself in a Playhouse'. He should take his seat 'on the very rushes where the comedy is to dance'; but it is better not to come too early:

> Present not yourself on the stage—especially at a new play— untill the quaking Prologue hath by rubbing got colour into his cheeks, and is ready to give the trumpets their cue that he's upon point to enter: for then it is time, as though you were one of the properties, or that you dropped out of the hangings, to creep from behind the arras with your tripos or three-footed stool in one hand and a teston mounted between a forefinger and a thumb in the other.

He is also advised to 'laugh aloud in the middest of the most serious and saddest scene of the terriblest tragedy' and 'let that clapper (your tongue) be tost so high that all the house may ring of it'; and finally to rise in the middle of the play with 'a screwed and discontented face', 'no matter whether the scenes be good or no; the better they are, the worse do you distaste them'; and, if possible, to leave accompanied by a number of friends: 'the Mimics are beholden to you for allowing them elbow room.' Dekker gets some fun out of this variety of ass; Jonson

[1] *Histriomastix*, p. 363 (marginal note).

took him more seriously, and there is a tinge of bitterness in his description :

> But the sport is at a new play to observe the sway and variety of opinion that passeth it. A man shall have such a confused mixture of judgement poured out in the throng there, as ridiculous as laughter itself : one says he likes not the writing, another likes not the plot, another not the playing. And sometimes a fellow that comes not there past once in five year at a Parliament time or so, will be as deep-mired in censuring as the best, and swear by God's foot he would never stir his foot to see a hundred such as that is.   (*The Case is Altered*, II. iv)

' The people, generally,' the speaker goes on to say, ' are very acceptive,' but there are two kinds of hostile critic who infect an audience. ' One is the rude barbarous crew,' that ' will hiss anything that mounts above their grounded capacities'. The other are ' a few capricious gallants ', who

> have taken such a habit of dislike in all things that they will approve nothing, be it never so conceited or elaborate ; but sit dispersed, making faces and spitting, wagging their upright ears, and cry ' Filthy ! filthy ! ' . . . using their wryed countenances instead of a vice to turn the good aspects of all that shall sit near them from what they behold.

Shakespeare's kindlier temper made him incapable of such an outburst, but even he suggests that there is an element of truth in the accusation. The courtiers' banter of the Nine Worthies in *Love's Labour's Lost* and of Quince's company in *A Midsummer-Night's Dream* has no spite in it, but it is equally disturbing to the players. The induction to *The Taming of a Shrew*, the old play which preceded Shakespeare's, makes the transformed Sly, when he has ordered a piece to be performed before him, say to his supposed servant, ' Come, Sim, where be the players ? Sim, stand by me, and we'll flout the players out of their coats.' The ' tag-rag people ', clapping and hissing the actors in the theatre (*Jul. Cæs.* I. ii. 259–63), copied rather more noisily the conduct of their betters.

An exciting diversion was provided by the occasional capture of a pickpocket.

> Somebody once pickt a pocket in this Play-house yard,
> Was hoysted on the stage, and shamd about it.
>   (*Nobody and Somebody*, sig. I)

Kemps nine daies wonder explains that the offender was ' tied to a post ' on the stage ' for all to wonder at ' and doubtless to pelt with bitten apples. If 'some necessary question of the play' were in progress at the time, the Tragicomedy of the Cutpurse would imperatively call a halt.

The announcement that the actors were ready to play was made by trumpet. This was their usual means of introduction, both on the stage and on the march. In the induction to *The Taming of the Shrew* the Folio has a stage-direction 'Sound trumpets', and the lord says,

> Sirrah, go see what trumpet 'tis that sounds . . .
> *Ser.* An 't please your honour,
> Players that offer service to your lordship.
>
> (Ind. i. 74, 77–8)

So in *Hamlet* II. ii. 394 there is a 'Flourish for the Players' when they arrive at Elsinore, and in *A Midsummer-Night's Dream*, v. i. 107, for the approach of the Prologue. In the theatre there were 'three soundings'; after the last the Prologue entered in the black velvet cloak still worn traditionally in the Play scene of *Hamlet*. Heywood's play *The Four Prentices of London*, 1615, opens thus :

> *Enter three in blacke clokes, at three doores.*

1. What meane you, my maisters, to appeare thus before your times ? Doe you not know that I am the Prologue ? Do you not see this long blacke velvet cloke upon my backe ? Have you not sounded thrice ? Do I not looke pale, as fearing to bee out in my speech ? Nay, have I not all the signes of a Prologue about me ?

Music was of course required incidentally in most plays and for the concluding jig ; but the private theatres, at any rate, must have employed a regular band. Brathwaite, in the *Whimzies*, 1631, pp. 51–2, notes that 'at the end of every Act . . . the encurtain'd Musique sounds, to give Enter-breath to the Actors, and more grace to their Action '. Music between the acts is sometimes marked in the stage-directions. In *Gorboduc*, acted by the gentlemen of the Inner Temple in 1561, and *Jocasta*, acted at Gray's Inn in 1566, it introduces the dumb-shows. In *The Two Italian Gentlemen*, 1584, there are the following notes :

The first Act being ended, the Consorte of Musique soundeth a pleasant Galliard.

The second Act being ended, the Consorte soundeth again.

The third Act being doone, the Consort sounds a sollemne Dump.

The fourth Act being ended, the Consort soundeth a pleasant Allemaigne.

In Marston's *Wonder of Women, or The Tragedie of Sopho-*

nisba, 1606, which was 'sundry times Acted at the Blacke Friers' there is the same arrangement with more variety. The first Act ends with 'the Cornets and Organs playing loud full Music'; at the beginning of the third there is 'Organ mixt with Recorders for this Act'; before the fourth, 'Organs Violls and Voices play for this Act'; and lastly 'A Base Lute and a Treble Violl play for the Act'. This interval was called 'the act-time'.[1]

The Children at the Blackfriars, who acted this play, and the Children of Paul's, being royal and cathedral choristers, naturally perfected their stage-music. A remarkable tribute to the skill of the former is paid by the secretary of the Duke of Stettin, who attended a performance in September 1602. He records that for a full hour before the play there was 'a delightful musical entertainment'; it seems to have been mainly instrumental, but a choir-boy sang so beautifully to the accompaniment of a bass-viol that the visitors had not heard his equal except possibly among the nuns at Milan.[2]

If the performance were a tragedy, it was the custom to drape the stage in black:

> The stage is hung with blacke, and I perceive
> The Auditors preparde for Tragedie.
> (A Warning for Faire Women, 1599, sig. A 3)

Dekker further speaks of the theatre being darkened for night effects : he refers of course to roofed buildings :

> All the Citty lookt like a private Play-house, when the windowes are clapt downe, as if some Nocturnal or dismall Tragedy were presently to be acted before all the Trades-men.
> (The Seven deadlie Sinns of London, 1606, p. 19)

Hence Shakespeare's choice of metaphor in the lines which refer to the betrayal of Lucrece and the funeral of King Henry V :

> O comfort-killing Night, image of hell ! . . .
> Black stage for tragedies and murders fell ! (*Lucr.* 764, 766)
> Hung be the heavens [3] with black, yield day to night !
> (I Hen. VI, I. i. I)

So, after a prolonged wait and various minor catastrophes in the tiring-room, where one actor has not got

---

[1] See Middleton, *The Changeling*, opening stage-direction of Act III.

[2] See Wallace, *The Children of the Chapel*, pp. 106–7.

[3] The plural form suggests the theatrical use—'The coverings of the stage, which wee call the heavens' (Heywood, *Apology for Actors*, 1612, sig. D2 verso). Cf. the quotation from Melton, p. 254.

EDWARD ALLEYN

'good strings to his beard' (*Mid. N. D.* iv. ii. 37), another has 'a stitch new-fallen in his black silk stocking—'twill be drawn up ere you can tell twenty' (*Barthol'mew Fair*, i. i.), and a third, feeling 'a little o'erparted' (*Love's L. L.* v. ii. 585), looks white and nervous, the play proceeds to its final test. An art so subtle and elusive as that of the actor is hard to gauge, but the available evidence suggests that a high standard was maintained on the Elizabethan stage. Making due allowance for patriotic bias, we may accept the independent verdict of Fynes Moryson, a traveller who had had a wide experience of the Continent : ' as there be, in my opinion, more Playes in London then in all the partes of the worlde I have seene, so doe these players or Comedians excell all other in the worlde' (*Unpublished Chapters* of the *Itinerary*, p. 476). Shakespeare's triumph as a playwright was shared by his fellow actors, and the appreciation which Leonard Digges prefixed to Shakespeare's *Poems* in 1640 has a unique value because it records the experience of a playgoer :

> So have I seen, when Caesar would appear,
> And on the stage at half-sword parley were
> Brutus and Cassius : oh how the audience
> Were ravish'd, with what wonder they went hence,
> When some new day they would not brook a line
> Of tedious, though well-labour'd, Catiline ;
> Sejanus too was irksome, they prized more
> Honest Iago or the jealous Moor ;
> And though the Fox and subtle Alchemist,
> Long intermitted, could not quite be miss'd,
> Though these have shamed all the ancients and might raise
> Their author's merit with a crown of bays,
> Yet these sometimes, even at a friend's desire
> Acted, have scarce defray'd the seacoal fire
> And doorkeepers : when let but Falstaff come,
> Hal, Poins, the rest, you scarce shall have a room,
> All is so pester'd ; let but Beatrice
> And Benedick be seen, lo in a trice
> The cockpit, galleries, boxes, all are full,
> To hear Malvolio, that cross-garter'd gull.

There is a fine sincerity in this tribute, and as we read it we go back in imagination to a time when Shakespeare was alive to receive men's homage and to move them to mirth or tears on the stage of the Curtain, the Blackfriars, and the Globe.

BIBLIOGRAPHY.—The one original document of an authoritative character is *Henslowe's Diary*, ed. W. W. GREG, Part I, Text, 1904; Part II, Commentary, 1908: it is completed by the *Henslowe Papers*, ed. W. W. GREG, 1907. A few documents not included in the preceding are to be found in *The Alleyn Papers*, edited by J. P. COLLIER for the Shakespeare Society, 1843. W. C. HAZLITT edited for the Roxburghe Club, 1869, *The English Drama and Stage under the Tudor and Stuart Princes, 1543–1664*—a useful collection of legal documents, treatises, and poems. Important documents on stage history are included in the *Collections* of the Malone Society, Vol. I, 4 parts, 1907–11, Vol. II, part i, 1913. W. W. GREG's *A List of English Plays Written before 1643 and Printed before 1700* (Bibliographical Society, 1900) is a full bibliography of plays.

The first scholarly survey was MALONE's *An Historical Account of the English Stage*, in Vol. I, part ii of his edition of Shakespeare, 1790; revised in Boswell's Variorum edition of 1821, vol. iii: all statements are attested by quotations from Elizabethan literature or contemporary records. J. P. COLLIER's *The History of English Dramatic Poetry to the Time of Shakespeare*, 3 vols., 1831, is a storehouse of illustrative material, but facts and references are untrustworthy; it was reprinted with some additions in 1879. KARL MANTZIUS's *A History of Theatrical Art in Ancient and Modern Times*, translated by L. von Cossel, treats 'The Shakespearean Period in England' in vol. iii, 1904. W. POEL's *Shakespeare in the Theatre*, 1913, is a suggestive study written from the standpoint of the actor. Sir SIDNEY LEE's *A Life of William Shakespeare* in the new and enlarged edition of 1915 is a compact work of reference for Shakespeare's dramatic history.

The history of the various companies is treated in F. G. FLEAY's *A Chronicle History of the London Stage, 1559–1642*, 1890; J. T. MURRAY's *English Dramatic Companies*, 2 vols., 1910; A. FEUILLERAT's 'The Origin of Shakespeare's Blackfriars Theatre' in the *Shakespeare Jahrbuch*, 1912, pp. 81–102; and C. W. WALLACE's *The Children of the Chapel at Blackfriars, 1597–1603* [1908].

The Fool is discussed in F. DOUCE's 'Clowns and Fools of Shakespeare' in his *Illustrations of Shakespeare*, 1839, and, from the literary point of view, in LIONEL JOHNSON's essay in *Noctes Shakespearianae* (Papers of the Winchester College Shakspere Society), 1887, pp. 171–89.

XXV

THE PLAYHOUSE

BY

WILLIAM ARCHER AND W. J. LAWRENCE

THE EARLY ENGLISH THEATRES

IN 1576, when Shakespeare was a boy of twelve, and about ten years before he came to London, James Burbage, a joiner, erected within the precincts of the old dissolved Holywell Priory, in the parish of Shoreditch, the first permanent building designed for theatrical purposes in England, and one of the first in modern Europe.[1] A royal warrant dated May 7, 1574, had given Burbage and four other servants of the Earl of Leicester the right to perform 'Comedies, Tragedies, Enterludes and Stage playes' both in the City of London and elsewhere, subject only to the censorship of the Master of the Revels, and to the restriction that performances must not be given 'in time of common prayer' or of 'great and common plague'. The performances contemplated in this warrant no doubt took place in the yards of the larger inns, such as the Cross Keys in Gracechurch Street, the Bull in Bishopsgate Street, and the Belle-Savage on Ludgate Hill. But the City fathers were not inclined to acknowledge the royal jurisdiction within their boundaries. A few months before the date of Burbage's warrant, they had declined a request by the Lord Chamberlain that they would delegate to a nominee of his Lordship their right of licensing places of performance ; and on December 6, 1574, seven months after the date of the warrant, they issued an order asserting their own rights of licensing and of censorship, and imposing severe penalties on all who should ignore their authority. The preamble

---

[1] There were several earlier Continental playhouses, but none had quite the historical importance of the Theater. The Hôtel de Bourgogne dated from 1548, and there were playhouses of a simple, unorganized kind in Italy.

to this order gives a curious, if one-sided, picture of the old inn-yard play-places. Great disorders and inconveniences, it declares, had been found to ensue from

the inordynate hauntynge of greate multitudes of people, speciallye youthe, to playes, enterludes, and shewes ; namelye occasyon of frayes and quarrelles, eavell practizes of incontenencye in greate Innes, havinge chambers and secrete places adjoyninge to their open stagies and gallyries, inveyglynge and allewrynge of maides, speciallye orphanes, and good cityzens children under age, to previe and unmete contractes.

Furthermore, the lieges have been withdrawn from divine service and have been subjected to robberies ' by pickynge and cuttinge of purses ' ; ' besydes that allso soundrye slaughters and mayhemminges of the Quenes Subjectes have happened by ruines of Skaffoldes, Frames and Stagies, and by engynes, weapons and powder used in plaies.' From this and other evidence it is apparent that plays were popular, and that the feeling of sober-minded citizens was strongly against them. Consequently it is not surprising that a far-sighted manager should have taken measures to secure a convenient place for the exercise of his craft, outside the jurisdiction of the Common Council.

It has frequently been stated that the building of the ' Theater '—so Burbage called his playhouse—followed upon a formal expulsion of all players from within the city limits. The evidence on this point, however, is inconclusive ; but it is clear that, whether expelled or not, the players could not have felt secure under the sway of a hostile municipality. Moreover, though the conveniences of the inn-yards were doubtless great, their inconveniences must have been not small. Chief among them would probably be the fact that performances could be given only at such times as suited the innkeeper, and that he would be in a position to exact a lion's share of the takings.[1] It would not be unnatural, then, that, even apart from any menace from authority, James Burbage should desire to have a play-place entirely at his own disposal, and that, going outside the city where sites would be comparatively

---

[1] At the Theater the players received ' the profits arising from the dores ', and Burbage, as proprietor, the money gathered in the galleries. From this we may perhaps conjecture that the innkeepers allowed the players to charge for admission to the inn-yard, reserving to themselves the tax upon those spectators who entered the actual building.

inexpensive, he should erect, under the protection of his patent, what was practically an inn-yard without the inn.

He departed, however, from the shape of the inn-yard in making his structure circular instead of rectangular. Circular bull-baiting and bear-baiting rings already existed on the south bank of the Thames; and as Burbage's house was destined not only for plays, but for many performances which require an arena rather than a stage,[1] it is natural that he should have followed this model.

Burbage's playhouse was, then, an amphitheatre, with the difference that it could be, and habitually was, changed into a theatre by the erection of a movable stage.[2] One segment of the circle was convertible from auditorium into tiring-house, just as one end of an oblong inn-yard, by the aid of a few screens or curtains, was made to serve as tiring-house to the stage built out from it on trestles or barrels. Even when the amphitheatre was converted into a theatre, spectators continued (on some occasions at any rate) to occupy upper boxes at the back of the stage; and the same practice established itself even at the theatres in which the stage was a permanent structure.

It does not appear that the construction of a special building for theatrical performances was due to any desire to improve the arrangements and accommodations of the stage, or was accompanied by any considerable improvement. The play-house confessed its descent from the tavern in the term 'yard' applied to the pit (as we should now call it) where, as in the inn-yard, the spectators stood under the open sky; in the use of the word 'rooms' for the boxes, occupied by the wealthier portion of the audience; in the signboard by which the building was distinguished; and in the system of a first payment for admission to the 'yard', followed by a 'gathering' from those who passed from the yard into the galleries.

We have no direct and detailed evidence as to the

---

[1] In 1583 the Lord Mayor wrote to Walsingham complaining of the 'very great and dangerous inconvenience' of 'the assemblie of people to playes beare bayting fencers and prophane spectacles at the Theatre and Curtaine and other like places' (Malone Society *Collections*, I. i. 63).

[2] The technical name for the platform on which dramatic performances were given, from Chaucer's time till the end of the sixteenth century, was 'scaffold'. The term is used by Shakespeare in the opening Chorus of *Henry V*; in *Troilus and Cressida* I. iii. 156, he calls it the 'scaffolage'—a coinage of his own.

structure and arrangements of Burbage's 'Theater', or of the 'Curtain', which, a little later in 1576, was built in its immediate neighbourhood. The name 'Curtain' has no reference to the curtain which forms so distinctive a part of the mechanism of our modern theatre. The land on which the playhouse was built had been known as 'The Curtene' at least as early as 1538. Though its material was wood, the Theater, at any rate, was a building of some pretensions. Burbage and his sleeping partner, John Braines, spent fully £700 upon it—a large sum for those days. In August 1578, John Stockwood, preaching at Paul's Cross, refers to playhouses 'built with great charges . . . without the liberties', and denounces the Theater in particular as 'the gorgeous playing place erected in the fields'. Gosson (*Playes Confuted*) speaks of 'the beautie of the houses and the Stages'; and 'the painted stage' and 'painted theatres' are the phrases applied to the Shoreditch houses by Gabriel Harvey in his letters and by Spenser in *The Teares of the Muses*. We need not, therefore, be surprised when we find Johannes de Witt (a few years later) enlarging on the elaborate decorations of the Swan Theatre.

Many of the plays of Marlowe, Greene, Peele, Lodge, and Kyd were performed at the Theater. Here was acted the pre-Shakespearian version of *Hamlet*, if we rightly interpret Lodge's allusion to 'the ghost which cried so miserally at the Theator, like an oister wife, *Hamlet revenge*'. At the Curtain Jonson's *Every Man in his Humor* first saw the light, as also Shakespeare's *Romeo and Juliet* and doubtless many of his early plays. If there is anything in the tradition that Shakespeare, on his first arrival in London, acted as a horse-boy outside the theatres, it must have been at these Shoreditch houses. The Theater, after falling into disuse for some seasons, was pulled down in 1598 by the heirs of James Burbage, its materials being used in the construction of the Globe. The Curtain had a longer life. It was in existence in 1627, but was probably pulled down two or three years later. Its site was afterwards known successively as Curtain Court, Gloucester Row, and Gloucester Street, and is now roughly indicated by St. James's Church.

Within twelve months from the establishment of the

ROXANA
TRAGÆDIA

A plagiary
vnguibus
vindicata,
aucta, et
agnita ab
authore
Gulielmo
Alabastro.

TITLE-PAGE OF WILLIAM ALABASTER'S
ROXANA 1630 SHOWING A STAGE IN
THE MIDDLE PANEL AT THE FOOT

public theatre we hear of the first 'private' playhouse. There has been much uncertainty as to the meaning of the word 'private'; but it now seems highly probable that the term was first employed by a manager who was desirous of establishing a playhouse within the liberties of the city without traversing the regulations of the 'Act of Common Council' passed on December 6, 1574. The final clause of this Act excepted from its penalties

anie plaies Enterludes Comodies, Tragidies or Shewes to be played or shewed in the pryvate hous, dwellinge, or lodginge of anie noble-man, citizen, or gentleman, wch shall or will then have the same thear so played or shewed in his presence, for the festyvitie of anie marriage, assemblye of ffrendes, or otherlyke cawse, wth owte publique or comen collection of money of the auditorie, or behoulders theareof.'

The creator of the first private theatre was Richard Farrant, master of the Children of the Chapel at Windsor, a musician and playwright of some note. In December 1576 Farrant took a lease of the old frater of Blackfriars priory, a building which had recently been used as a private dwelling by Lord Cobham and others, and after arranging to house his family in the lower portion of the premises, fitted up a small theatre on the second floor. Here perform-ances were given by choir-boys under Farrant's care, and to assure his immunity from municipal interference, he gave it out that the theatre was merely a practising place for the boys 'for the better trayning them to do her Majestie service'. Caution was necessitated by the fact that the Common Council still claimed jurisdiction within the Liberty of the Blackfriars. So, in keeping with the terms of the Act of 1574, Farrant forbore to give his play-house any distinctive title, and it was known simply as 'the private house in the Blackfriars'. The term 'private theatre' did not come into vogue until the seventeenth century. Farrant died in 1580, and the little theatre, after passing through various hands, declined in vogue and came to an end in 1584. This first Blackfriars is not to be confounded with the second and much more important playhouse of thirteen years later.

Shortly after the Blackfriars was opened, a second private playhouse was established by Sebastian Westcott, master of the Paul's boys, in the Choir Singing School near the

Cathedral.[1] Although suppressed for several years from 1590, this house enjoyed happier fortunes and a longer lease of life than its predecessor, lasting up to 1608.

There were many fundamental distinctions between the private theatre in the initial stage of its development (i. e. up to the building of the second Blackfriars) and the public theatre ; but all were due, directly or indirectly, to the necessity imposed upon Farrant and his successors to keep within the Common Council regulations of 1574. A theatre that could plausibly pretend to 'privacy' in this sense was necessarily small. The bulk of the audience had to be accommodated on the floor level, though a small balcony, analogous to the music gallery in a Tudor hall, was no doubt admissible. As the audience must have been limited to some three or four hundred, high prices would naturally be charged, and the rougher element of the ordinary theatrical public would thus be excluded. It may seem strange that, even at high prices, it could pay to present plays to so small a public ; but it must be remembered that the actors were children, recruited and maintained for another purpose, and therefore not dependent, like adult actors, on a share in the takings. It is noteworthy that no boy companies ever acted in a public theatre. They were distinctively associated with the private houses. The boys being all good singers, and many of them also capable musicians, their staple form of entertainment was naturally a sort of musical comedy. There can be little doubt that the primary appeal of the early private theatre play lay rather in the wealth of its musical embellishment, the charms of its song and dance, than in its emotional content. The boy-player had his limitations. He was thoroughly at home in the conceits and fantasies of Lyly ; but for the stark melodrama he loved, the Elizabethan playgoer had to go to the public theatre.

The fifth London playhouse was probably erected at Newington Butts (near what was afterwards the site of Spurgeon's Tabernacle) in the middle of the fifteen-eighties. So little is known about it that its very existence has been doubted ; but this scepticism is unjustified. We know from Henslowe's *Diary* that plays were given in Newington

---

[1] Paul's is first mentioned in Gosson's *Playes confuted in five Actions*, 1580, but no doubt it had then been some time established.

in 1594; and when we find an inhibition 'of the use of playes at the theater and thother places about Newington' mentioned in the Acts of the Privy Council in May 1586, there is no reason to doubt that they took place in a permanent theatre. Mr. Fairman Ordish has pointed out that as the Shoreditch playhouses were near the recreation grounds of Finsbury Fields, so Newington Butts was itself a holiday resort, and was, furthermore, close to St. George's Fields. Among plays noted by Henslowe as having been acted here in June 1594 are 'the Jewe of malta', 'andronicous', 'hamlet', and 'the tamynge of A shrowe'. There can be little doubt that the playhouse was an unroofed or 'public' theatre. It was probably pulled down about 1600.[1]

We come next to Philip Henslowe's playhouse, the Rose, situated in the Bankside—that is to say on the Surrey shore of the Thames, a little westward from London Bridge. The name of Rose Alley still marks the site. This house, like the Curtain, took its name from the plot of ground on which it stood, called by Henslowe 'the Littell Roose', from an old tenement on the site. There exists a contract for the erection of this theatre by Henslowe, in partnership with one John Cholmley, dated January 1586-7. The cost of the building was estimated at £816, which would indicate a desire to outdo Burbage's Theater. It remained in use, with frequent intermissions owing to the plague and other causes, until 1603; but after that it disappears from theatrical records. *The First Part of King Henry the Sixth* was acted at the Rose.[2]

The next playhouse in order of time has a peculiar interest for us, as it is the only 'public' theatre of which an interior view exists. The manor of Paris Garden, somewhat further west than the Rose Theatre, was acquired in 1589 by Francis Langley; and in 1594, in spite of some opposition from the municipal authorities, he built there a playhouse, to which he gave the name of the Swan. It seems to have been a twelve-sided structure.[3] The Dutch

---

[1] Mr. W. W. Greg (*Henslowe Papers*, p. 52) has shown that some Surreyside playhouse was demolished when the Fortune was built. This may have been the Newington Butts theatre.

[2] For exterior views of the Rose, see Norden's map (1593) and Ryther's (1604). The latter shows the enclosure surrounding the plot of ground in which the theatre stood (cf. W. W. Greg, *Henslowe Papers*, p. 49).

[3] The twelve sides are indicated in the exterior view in Visscher's map (1616) and in the ground-plan in the Manor map (1627), reproduced in

traveller, De Witt, who visited it and described its glories in or about 1596, declares that it was built of a 'concrete of flint stones'. This has been doubted, on the ground that all the other sixteenth-century ' public ' theatres are known to have been built of wood ; but it is hard to see how De Witt could be in error on such a point as this. He declared, indeed, that the wooden pillars of the interior were painted in very skilful imitation of marble ; but it seems unlikely that the exterior would be painted to imitate flint rubble-work. However, he was certainly mistaken in his estimate that the theatre could seat ('in sedilibus admittat') 3,000 persons. In spite of its architectural pretensions and the fact that acting took place there intermittently until 1621, the Swan played no great part in theatrical history. One extant play, Middleton's *A Chast Mayd in Cheape-side*, is known to have been produced there ; and in 1602 it was the scene of a riot because a promised performance of a new pageant-play, entitled *England's Joy*, did not take place.

We have now to speak of one of the two playhouses with which the name of Shakespeare is most intimately associated. In February 1596, James Burbage, who twenty years before had built the Theater in Shoreditch, bought for £600 certain ' rooms ' in the old frater in the Blackfriars, in which Farrant's top-floor theatre had formerly been situated, and proceeded to convert them into a public theatre. But in January 1597, before the work could be completed, Burbage died ; and, on a petition of the inhabitants of the Precinct, who specifically objected to a ' public ' theatre being raised in their midst, the Privy Council, through the civic authorities, forbade the house to be opened. But beyond some modification of the original architectural scheme, this suppression only occasioned a temporary setback. To get out of the difficulty, Richard Burbage, James's son, the great tragedian of his time, decided to convert the theatre into ' a private house '. It was doubtless owing to these complications that the second Blackfriars was the first private theatre to have most of the characteristics of a public-theatre auditorium. We know for certain that it had three galleries ; the lowest,

Harrison's *Description of England* (ed. F. J. Furnivall, 1878, Part II, p. 66). As to De Witt's interior view, see *post*, pp. 298–300.

however, was but slightly raised above the level of the pit. Established in a hall whose dimensions were 46 by 66 feet, its seating capacity must have been small, not more than six or seven hundred.

On the completion of the theatre it was let by Richard Burbage to Henry Evans, one of Farrant's successors in the management of the earlier Blackfriars, who went into partnership with Nathaniel Gyles, Master of the Children of the Chapel Royal, and made the house for eleven years (1597–1608) the home of the company of 'little eyases' referred to in *Hamlet*.

Shortly after the suppression of the Blackfriars boys in 1608, Burbage leased the theatre to six of his fellow actors, of whom Shakespeare was one; Burbage himself making a seventh in the partnership. The new sharers, like Evans before them, paid a rent of £40. At the time of his death, Shakespeare still owned his seventh share in the Blackfriars; and the theatre continued in the occupation of the successors of his company until the Civil War. Even apart from Shakespeare's connexion with it, the Blackfriars was, in a literary sense, the most important theatre in London. Its name appears on the title-pages of over fifty quarto plays, whereas less than half that number are assigned by the publishers to the Globe.

In the lease of the land on which James Burbage erected the Theater, it was stipulated, under certain conditions, that Burbage should have the right to take down and carry away any buildings he might have erected. After his death in 1597, his sons, Richard and Cuthbert, decided to exercise this right of removal, though the agreement under which they claimed it had, strictly speaking, lapsed. Taking advantage of the landlord's absence in the country, and availing themselves of the services of one Peter Street, a builder, they carried out their plan on December 28, 1598. As the landlord's complaint put it, the Burbage party, to the number of twelve, did

ryoutouslye assemble themselves together, and then and there armed themselves with dyvers and many unlawfull and offensive weapons, as namelye, swordes, daggers, billes, axes, and such like, and soe armed, did then and there repayre to the sayd Theater and . . . attempted to pull downe the sayd Theater ; . . . and having so done, did then alsoe in most forcible and ryotous manner take and carrye away from thence all the wood and timber thereof unto the Bancksyde in the parishe of St. Marye Overyes, and there erected a newe play-house with the sayd timber and wood.

This new playhouse was the famous Globe, so called from its sign, which represented Hercules carrying the world on his shoulders, with the motto ' Totus mundus agit histrionem '. We have direct evidence that *Richard II*, *Romeo and Juliet*, *King Lear*, *Othello*, *Macbeth*, *Love's Labour's Lost*, *The Winter's Tale*, *The Taming of the Shrew*, and *Pericles* were acted here; and here, no doubt, the whole Shakespearian repertory was performed, including *King Henry V*, with its famous reference in the prologue to the theatre as ' this wooden O '. It was during a production of *King Henry VIII*, on June 29, 1613, that the discharge of two ' chambers ', or small cannon, set fire to the thatch of the roof over the galleries, and reduced the theatre to ashes in less than two hours. It was rebuilt in 1614 ' in far finer manner than before '; and it is this second theatre, as figured in Visscher's map of 1616, that has come to be regarded as the typical Elizabethan ' public ' playhouse. Shakespeare's share in the original structure seems to have been one-tenth, in the rebuilt theatre one-fourteenth. There has been much controversy about the precise site of the Globe; but the memorial tablet placed in 1909 in the wall of Barclay & Perkins's brewery is sufficiently near for all practical purposes.

The second Globe was externally an octagon, while its interior was no doubt circular, or nearly so. This was the prevailing shape of the ' public ' theatres, though there was some variation in the number of the sides; but there was one clearly established exception. On January 8, 1599–1600, Philip Henslowe and Edward Alleyn entered into a contract with Peter Street, the builder, for the erection of a playhouse in Golden Lane, Cripplegate; and this contract is fortunately preserved to us. From it we learn that the Fortune (as the theatre was named) was a three-story square structure measuring 80 feet outside and 55 feet inside; that the stories were respectively 12, 11, and 9 feet in height; that the galleries were 12 feet 6 inches deep, with, in each of the upper stories, an additional ' jutty ' forwards of 10 inches; and that the stage was 43 feet broad and 27 feet deep. Moreover, there was a ' shadow or cover ' over the stage, which, as well as the roof of the ' frame ' or main structure, was tiled instead of thatched. This contract is the most important document we possess with regard to the theatrical architecture of the time ; but unfortunately it gives us no details as to the structure and arrangement of the stage, merely providing that it is to be ' Contryved and fashioned like unto the Stadge of the Plaie howse Called the Globe', which the same builder had recently erected. The price to be paid was £440, but it appears from a note-book of Alleyn's that the building actually cost £520. Among the plays originally produced at the Fortune were Yarrington's *Two Lamentable Tragedies*, and Dekker and Middleton's *The Roaring Girle*. Like the house on which it was, to some extent, modelled, the first Cripplegate Theatre was burnt down. The fire occurred on December 9, 1621. Two years later the Fortune was ' built againe with bricke worke on the outside ', but this time in circular form. Dismantled in 1649, it fell into decay and was wholly pulled down in 1661.

At an undetermined date, but early in the seventeenth century, a public playhouse was built at the upper end of St. John Street, Clerkenwell. It was called the Red Bull and was remarkable, in an unruly period, for the turbulency of its audiences. Its actors, too, were rated by Gayton as ' terrible tear-throats ' ; so that it probably ranked as what was called in the nineteenth century a ' transpontine ' house. Here were produced Dekker's *If It Be Not Good, the Divel is in it*, and several of Thomas Heywood's plays, including *The Golden Age*. Enlarged in 1632, the Red Bull had a longer record than any other Elizabethan theatre. It was reopened as a playhouse at the Restoration, and as late as May 1664 was being used for fencing matches.

The Whitefriars, fourth of the private playhouses, was constructed about 1606 in the old monastic hall of the Whitefriars, near Dorset Garden, Fleet Street. Here the Children of the King's Revels performed, among other plays, Barry's *Ram-alley* and Mason's tragedy of *The Turke*. Afterwards, from 1610, the theatre was occupied by the newly constituted Second Children of the Queen's Revels, for whom Beaumont and Fletcher wrote some of their most important plays. Records of the Whitefriars cannot be traced later than 1621.

In 1613, immediately after the destruction of the Globe, Henslowe made such alterations in the old Bear Garden on the Bankside that it could be used indifferently as playhouse or arena. The Hope, as it was now called, was modelled on the Swan,[1] but it was specially stipulated that the half-roof or ' shadow ' over the stage was to be supported by the main structure, and not by pillars resting on the stage. Here Ben Jonson's *Bartholomew Fayre* was first produced. At the outset drama was so greatly in demand that bear-baiting took place only once a fortnight ; but before long the sport so encroached upon the art that the new name of the building tends to disappear, and it is commonly called the Bear Garden once more. There is no record of its employment for theatrical performances after 1616.

Fifth in order of the private theatres, the Phoenix (better known as the Cockpit, from the use to which the building had formerly been applied), dated from about the year 1617. It was situated in Drury Lane, and its rank among private theatres was nearly equivalent to that of the Red Bull among public theatres. Among the plays performed at the Phoenix were Middleton's *The Spanish Gipsie* and Shirley's *Hide Parke*. Shirley's fortunes as a playwright were largely associated with those of this house. Temporarily dismantled in 1649, the Phoenix was last used for theatrical purposes in 1664.

The last of the Elizabethan houses was Salisbury Court, a private theatre built in 1629 by Richard Gunnell and William Blagrove on the site of the old granary of Dorset House, near Fleet Street. Because of its position, Salisbury Court has been thought to have been a mere reconstitution of the Whitefriars theatre ; but this is an error. The site measured 140 by 42 feet. A residence for the players was also erected upon it. Here was performed that quaint comedy *The Antipodes* of Brome. Dismantled in 1649, Salisbury Court was last used as a theatre in 1662. Four years later it fell a victim to the Great Fire.

[1] For exterior views of the Hope, see Visscher's view of London (1616), Merian's map (1638), and ' Cittie of London ' map (1646).

THE STRUCTURE OF THE THEATRE

Some of the structural problems of the early London theatres remain rather obscure. The past ten years, however, have witnessed very substantial additions to our knowledge.

The general distinction between the Elizabethan stage and that of our own time is perfectly clear. In the modern theatre, we present a series of pictures within a frame called the proscenium, which we fill with a curtain while the pictures are being shifted. The Elizabethan theatre had neither proscenium nor curtain. Its stage was an unframed rostrum thrust boldly forth into the auditorium, and surrounded on three sides, if not on four, by spectators. It was, in short, not a picture-stage, but a platform-stage. In its whole history we can trace but three forms of approximation to what we now call scenery :

1. At the beginning of our period the ' multiple ' scenes, often employed at Court performances, seem also to have been adopted at the ' private ' playhouses which served as rehearsal stages for the Court. Under the ' multiple ' system, all the clearly defined localities in a play were simultaneously indicated by means of ' practicable' constructions, known as *maisons*, ' mansions ' or ' houses ', planted at the back and sides of the stage before the performance began—changes of locality being indicated by the movement of the actors from one ' mansion ' to another. In a system which placed a cave, a bed-chamber, and a blacksmith's forge simultaneously on the stage, there can obviously have been nothing pictorial. The ' mansions ' were properties rather than scenes.

2. At the very end of our period, between 1635 and 1641, one or two masques seem to have been given at ' private ' theatres, in which shifting tableaux of a scenic nature were presented within prosceniums designed for the occasion.[1] There is also some indication of an architectural treatment of the ordinary stage background, whereby its three entrances and upper stage assumed the appearance of a scene, not unlike what was called on the contemporary French stage a *chambre à quatre portes*.

[1] For the masque, with proscenium, see Nabbes's *Microcosmus* (1637). The point is fully discussed in Lawrence's *The Elizabethan Playhouse*, Second Series, pp. 121–47.

3. There are vague and doubtful indications here and there of the occasional employment of painted hangings on the small inner stage or recess (to be hereafter described) which was framed, as it were, by the panels of wall on either side of it.

On the whole, there is some reason to think that, if the Civil War had not intervened, the transition from the platform-stage to the picture-stage, which followed the Restoration, might have taken place some years earlier. But whatever experiments in the pictorial direction may have preceded the Civil War, they were forgotten at the Restoration, when even theatrical experts like Downes and Wright believed movable scenes to be an absolute novelty.[1]

On the other hand, the use of properties, sometimes of an elaborate nature, was inherited by the Elizabethan from the mediaeval stage ; though indeed it is rather superfluous to assign any definite ancestry to such a simple and obvious practice. Properties would often show quite clearly the nature of the locality to which the action was assigned. Thus an altar would indicate a church ; an arbour, a garden ; benches, tables, and flagons, an alehouse. Apart from references in the text, no other method of defining locality was commonly adopted. The popular belief that changes of scene were notified by the exhibition of placards has little to support it. Not infrequently, indeed, the play-wright had in his mind no definite locality ; and the modern editors' practice of assigning each scene to a particular spot is often quite unwarranted by the text, if not at variance with it. The name of the play, however, was generally hung out on a placard ; and on rare occasions

---

[1] Even when the proscenium and scenery had definitely established themselves, the tradition of the platform-stage profoundly modified the picture-stage of Italian origin. The projecting apron of the Restoration theatre, its proscenium doors and balconies, and its music-loft above the proscenium arch, were all adapted from the Elizabethan theatre.

In the print reproduced opposite there are represented : Falstaff and Mistress Quickly ; Clause, king of the beggars in Fletcher and Massinger's play, *The Beggars' Bush* ; the title character in *Greene's Tu Quoque*, 1614, a play by John Cooke, in which the actor Thomas Greene originally performed ; and the character in the underplot of Middleton's *The Changeling*, which is thus noted in T. Goffe's *The Careles Shepherdess*, 1656, ind. :

I heard a fellow
Once on this Stage cry, *Doodle, Doodle, Dooe,*
Beyond compare ; I'de give the other shilling
To see him act the Changling once again:

Frontispiece of F. Kirkman, *The Wits* (Kirkman's Drolls), 1672–3.
(Commonly misdescribed as the Red Bull print: see p. 307).

when the action was constantly shifting from country to country, as for instance in *Pericles*, *Antony and Cleopatra*, and *The Fair Maid of the West*, it would seem that some topographical indications, such as 'Palermo', or 'Vienna', or 'Bohemia', were displayed.

It is generally agreed that an upper gallery or balcony was an indispensable part of the normal Elizabethan stage. Its origin in the inn-yard is readily comprehensible ; and it can be deduced from countless directions, of the type of 'Enter so-and-so, above'.[1]   This upper stage, as it is generally named, represented now the upper story of a house, now the battlements of a town, now a gallery within a hall, and so forth.   Its relation to the lords' room, which, at an early period, was situated within stage regions, and to the 'music room', which was invariably placed in the same locality, cannot be accurately determined.   It is possible that all this upper region may have been used for dramatic purposes when the action of the play required it, and at other times for the accommodation of spectators and musicians.

From this point onwards, we are almost constantly in the regions of controversy.   Some students try (quite hopelessly in our judgement) to treat the Swan drawing as a complete and accurate presentment of a typical stage ; while others, feeling compelled to question its authority, cannot agree as to the modifications to which it must be subjected.

Of its genuineness there is no doubt ; but it has not the authority of a sketch taken actually on the spot.   It is

---

[1] Thus, in the First Folio, characters appear on 'the walls' of town or castle in *John* II. i. 200, IV. iii ; *Rich. II*, III. iii. 61 ; *1 Hen. VI*, I. vi, III. ii. 25 ('on the top'), 41, IV. ii. 2 ('aloft'), v. iii. 129 ; *2 Hen. VI*, IV. v ('Enter Lord Scales upon the Tower walking.   Then enters two or three Citizens below') ; *3 Hen. VI*, IV. vii. 16 (followed by 'He descends', l. 29) ; v. i. ; *Cor.* I. iv. 12 ; *Timon* v. iv. 2.   A street is indicated in *Merch. of V.* II. vi. 26, 'Jessica above' ; *Rom. & Jul.* III. v, 'Enter Romeo and Juliet aloft' ; *Tam. Sh.* ind. ii, 'Enter aloft the drunkard with attendants'; *Hen. VIII*, v. ii. 18, 'Enter the King, and Buts, at a Windowe above'; a gallery in *Rich. III*, III. vii. 94, 'Enter Richard aloft, betweene two Bishops' ; a room in Cleopatra's monument, *Ant. & Cleop.* IV. xiii, 'Enter Cleopatra and her Maides aloft', with the direction at l. 37, 'They heave Anthony aloft to Cleopatra'.   The 'upper stage' is so-called by Middleton (*The Famelie of Love* I. iii) in describing 'a play, where we saw most excellent Sampson excel the whole world in gate-carrying. . . . Believe it, we saw Sampson bear the town-gates on his neck from the lower to the upper stage with that life and admirable accord that it shall never be equalled unless the whole new livery of porters set to their shoulders.'

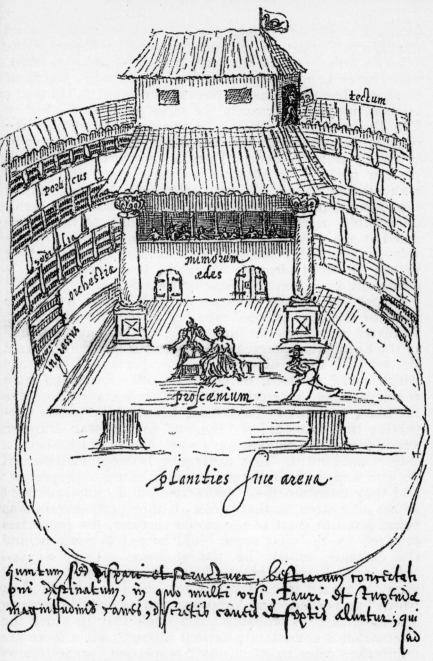

From De Witt's drawing of the SWAN THEATRE, about 1600.

found in a sort of commonplace-book kept by one Arend van Buchell (1565–1641), and purports to illustrate the 'observations' of Van Buchell's friend Johannes de Witt, who visited London soon after the Swan theatre was built in 1595. The sketch as we possess it cannot be De Witt's original, for it is on exactly the same paper as the rest of Van Buchell's book. We do not even know whether the original from which it was copied was drawn on the spot, or merely from memory. There is therefore no reason to pin our faith to its absolute accuracy where it conflicts with other evidence. It may, of course, be accurate for the Swan but not for other theatres; but this seems improbable, as the one play that we know to have been acted at the Swan—Middleton's *A Chast Mayd in Cheapeside*—unmistakably demands what is most notably lacking in the De Witt drawing; namely the recess which is commonly known as the Inner or Rear Stage.

Before stating the evidence for this recess, let us see how the theorists proceed who try to operate without it. Although there was not, and could not be, any 'curtain' to the Elizabethan stage, analogous to our modern act-drop, yet we have many allusions to some portion of the stage which could, at need, be curtained off. Reasoning from these passages, a certain school of students suppose the necessary curtains to have hung between the pillars supporting the 'heavens' or 'shadow' in the Swan drawing, and found on this supposition a whole theory of Elizabethan stage-management. They distinguish between scenes which do, and scenes which do not, demand the use of properties; and they maintain that 'propertied' and 'unpropertied' scenes alternated, so that, while an unpropertied scene was being acted in front of the closed curtains, the properties required for the next scene could be put in place behind the curtains, unseen by the audience. This so-called 'alternation' theory breaks down from whatever point of view we regard it. Though a few cases can be cited in which 'propertied' and 'unpropertied' scenes do seem to alternate, there is probably not a single play in which the alternation is consistently carried through, while there are numberless cases in which one 'propertied' scene follows immediately on the heels of another. Again, we have only to look at the Swan drawing to see that curtains hung between the pillars would leave what went on behind them visible to a considerable part of the audience, and would, on the other hand, prevent a certain portion of the audience from seeing what went on in front of them. The latter difficulty is absolutely insuperable; but upholders of the alternation theory try to get over the former difficulty by hanging lateral curtains between the pillars and the tiring-house. It would take too long to expound all the difficulties involved in these side curtains. Suffice it to say that Dr. Brodmeier, the leading German champion of this theory, gets over them by the simple plan of absolutely ignoring the Swan drawing and all other authorities, and, by pure conjecture, running walls back to the tiring-house from the outer edge of each pillar. By this means the pillars are practically converted into a proscenium, and the stage becomes almost like a modern stage with a large 'apron'. On such a stage, there could not be the slightest reason why, at the end of an act or scene, the curtains should not have closed upon a group or 'tableau', just as they do in the modern theatre. As a matter of fact, this never occurred. We never find any stage-direction equivalent to the modern 'Curtain', but always the direction 'Exeunt' or 'Exeunt omnes'.[1] It is absolutely certain, if stage-directions have any meaning, that no considerable number of people were ever 'discovered' by the opening, or concealed by the closing, of curtains. And it is no less certain that there was no rigid rule as to the method of placing properties on the stage. Sometimes, no doubt, they were 'discovered' *in situ* by the withdrawal of the 'traverses' which, as we shall see, screened the inner stage; but in the generality of cases they were brought on in full sight of the audience, often in the middle of the action and occasionally (as in *A Woman Kilde with Kindnesse*) by one of the characters. The conclusive proof that no large portion of the stage could be concealed by curtains lies in the fact that not only did living characters always walk off, but dead characters were always carried off, careful provision being made to that end either in the text or in stage-directions.

---

[1] There is an extremely small number of instances (notably Chapman's *Tragedie of Byron* and *Alphonsus Emperour of Germany*) in which no provision is made for clearing the stage. These instances, occurring only, we think, in private-theatre plays, offer a curious problem, but are too rare to invalidate the almost universal rule.

Had it been possible to shut off with curtains so large a space as that behind the pillars in the Swan drawing, there would have been no reason why (say) the corpses in *Hamlet* should not have been left in peace at the end, as they generally are on the modern stage. That they were not, we learn not only from the stage-direction, but from Fortinbras's command, ' Take up the bodies.'

On the other hand, if we look at the end of *Romeo and Juliet,* we find that no provision is made for the removal of bodies, except that Romeo himself has carefully to carry the dead Paris into the tomb of the Capulets (v. iii. 83–7). We note, too, that at a given point, Romeo must have opened the tomb—however it may have been represented —and disclosed Juliet lying on her bier. We have seen reason for rejecting the idea that half the stage could be curtained off, so as to conceal the building of a tomb ; and it is inconceivable that a ready-made ' property ' tomb actually containing Juliet, and large enough to contain Paris and Romeo as well, can have been carried on in sight of the audience. The doors, which alone give access to the stage in the Swan drawing, are not large enough to permit of the passage of such a structure. We find it flatly impossible, then, to conceive how this scene could have been presented on the stage figured by Johannes de Witt. But suppose that between the doors there was some sort of curtained recess, and the difficulty vanishes. Either the recess itself might figure ' Capel's monument ', and the opening of the curtains might represent to imagination the opening of the doors ; or a ' property ' tomb might be constructed at leisure behind the curtain, with a practicable door for Romeo to burst open. In either case, it is quite clear why there is no direction as to the removal of the bodies—because they all three lay in a curtainable space, supposed to be a tomb, from which it would be the height of absurdity to remove them. The same curtainable space was required in at least one other scene in the play—the so-called Potion Scene (IV. iii). At the end of Juliet's soliloquy, the First Quarto explicitly says, 'She fals upon her bed within the Curtaines '.[1] Supposing, then, that this curtainable space was where we

---

[1] Sometimes taken to mean the bed-curtains, but the final words in reality indicate the position of the bed, which had not been, in the words of the old stage-directions, ' thrust out '. See p. 270.

suggest—at the back of the stage between the doors—we see at once the difference, from the stage-manager's point of view, between the last act of *Romeo and Juliet* and the last act of *Hamlet*. In *Hamlet* it would have been absurd for all the ' morituri ' to crowd together in a narrow and remote point of the stage before their deaths ; wherefore it was necessary to arrange for the removal of the corpses. But it was not absurd—it was natural and necessary—for Romeo, Juliet, and Paris to lie together in the tomb of the Capulets ; wherefore the bodies were left lying, and the curtains were simply closed on them.

The existence of such a recess, or Rear Stage, is established by abundant evidence. An early and very clear allusion to it occurs in Greene's *Alphonsus, King of Arragon*, Act IV, scene i, where we read ' Let there be a brazen Head set in the middle of *the place behind the Stage*, out of which cast flames of fire'. Another very early instance of the use of the Rear Stage occurs in Marlowe's *Tamburlaine*, Part II, Act ii. Here we have the stage-direction :—

Scaena ultima. The Arras is drawn, and Zenocrate lies in her bed of state, Tamburlaine sitting by her: three Phisitians about her bed, tempering potions. Theridamas, Techelles, Usumcasane, and the three sonnes.

It has been argued that the utmost space we can allot to the Rear Stage would be insufficient to accommodate, without ridiculous crowding, so large a group around Zenocrate's bed. But the only persons stated to be about the bed are Tamburlaine and the three Physicians. It is quite possible—indeed the wording of the stage-direction rather favours the view—that the other six characters entered in the ordinary way by the doors when the curtains opened. But even supposing them all to have been revealed in a group or tableau, there could be nothing to prevent Theridamas, Techelles, and the rest from immediately coming forward and thus relieving the congestion on the Rear Stage. It is always easier for actors to advance and spread over the stage, than to retire and concentrate themselves on one confined and distant spot : a principle which explains the fact that we far more often find characters revealed by the opening of the curtains than concealed by their closing.

That the Rear Stage must have been immediately

beneath the Upper Stage is clear from the passage in Marlowe's *Jew of Malta*, where Barabas, having made a trap-door in his 'dainty gallery' through which he intends Calymath to fall, is himself precipitated through it into a cauldron beneath, 'discovered' by the opening of curtains. The Rear Stage was commonly used to represent the 'study' of a philosopher, poet, or magician. 'Enter So-and-so in his study' is a typical stage-direction. It is also found figuring as a cell, cave, shop, counting-house, tent, prison, and bedchamber. As properties, no less than people, were often revealed on the Rear Stage, there must have been ample access to it from behind; so that in all probability we may conceive it not as an alcove or bay, but rather as a sort of corridor at the back of the main stage.

It may be asked why, if we so far override the authority of the Swan drawing as to place a Rear Stage where De Witt shows a solid wall, we should without hesitation accept the two doors by which that wall is pierced. The answer is that countless stage-directions show that two doors supplied the principal means of access to the Elizabethan stage, at all theatres, whether public or private. We constantly come across directions in this form: 'Enter at one door So-and-so, at the other door Such-an-one.' The frequent recurrence of this expression, taken in conjunction with the Swan drawing, has led some people to imagine that two doors, and two only, gave access to the stage. On closer examination, however, we find that another form of expression is still more common: not 'at the other door', but 'at *an* other door'—a phrase clearly implying that there were more than two.[1] Again, there are a few stage-directions in which 'three doors', and a 'middle door' are explicitly mentioned; and the 'middle door', if we are right in the location of the Rear Stage, can have been nowhere else than in the back wall of that recess. The interpretation of these phrases is not far to seek: namely that, though there were in fact three doors opening upon

---

[1] In the First Folio we find 'at one door . . . at *the* other' in *Tit. Andr.* I. i (twice); *Rich. III*, II. iii; and *Hen. VIII*, I. i. But the commoner form, 'at one door . . . at *an* other', occurs in *Mid. N. D.* II. i (twice); *Hen. V*, V. ii; *3 Hen. VI*, II. v. 54; *Hen. VIII*, I. iv; *Troilus* IV. i; *Cor.* I. ix; *Tit. Andr.* IV. ii; *Ant. & Cleop.* II. vi. and III. ii; *Cymb.* III. i and v. ii. The expression 'at several doors' occurs in *Meas. for M.* V. i; *Tw. N.* II. ii; *John* II. i. 333; *Rich. III*, III. vii; *Hen. VIII*, II. i; *Cor.* I. viii; and *Timon* I. i.

the stage, two of them were so much more prominent and more frequently used, that playwrights often expressed themselves as though they alone existed. They would, indeed, be the only doors visible when the curtains of the Rear Stage were closed.[1] It need scarcely be pointed out that if we are right in supposing the Rear Stage to have been no mere alcove, but a corridor, it would provide two other entrances at its several ends. Exits and entrances could also be made through the curtains—a method which seems to have been specially appropriated to eavesdroppers.

The stage thus reconstructed is figured in Mr. W. H. Godfrey's drawing of the Fortune theatre, made (so far as possible) in accordance with the builder's specifications above mentioned. These specifications, indeed, fail us in regard to details of stage arrangement ; but the existence of a Rear Stage is so amply proved by stage-directions that it can scarcely be called conjectural ; while for the Upper Stage we have the evidence, not only of stage-directions, but of the Swan drawing. On the other hand, the oblique position of the panels of wall in which the two doors are placed must be admitted to be wholly conjectural. Although not supported by the Swan drawing, this arrangement is deducible from certain passages in which characters placed on the Upper Stage are represented as seeing things occurring on the Rear Stage, which would clearly be impossible in the absence of some such projection of the Upper Stage as is here figured. One of the most notable of these passages is in Peele's *The Love of King David and fair Bethsabe*, where the stage-direction runs :—

He [the Prologus] drawes a curtaine, and discovers Bethsabe with her maid bathing over a spring: she sings, and David sits above vewing her.

Moreover, since the interior of the first ' public ' theatres was circular and the tiring-house was the depth of the surrounding galleries, it is conceivable that the tiring-house front should partake of the general architectural scheme and carry on the curve of the galleries. And there is surely some significance in the fact that in many early plays we find entrances indicated at the sides or ends of the stage.

---

[1] It is evident from many stage-directions that the two main doors were always visible, even when the curtains were closed ; and this is one among the many reasons for rejecting the theory that the curtains were hung between the pillars. Thus the opening scene of *Eastward Hoe* has ' Enter Master Touchstone and Quicksilver at several doors. . . . At the middle dore, enter Golding, discovering a Goldsmith's shop, and walking short turns before it.'

Thus in *John a Kent and John a Cumber* (*c.* 1595), we have in Act III the directions :—

> From one end of the Stage enters an antique, queintly disguysed, and coming dauncing before them, singes . . .
> From the other end of the Stage enter another antique as the first.

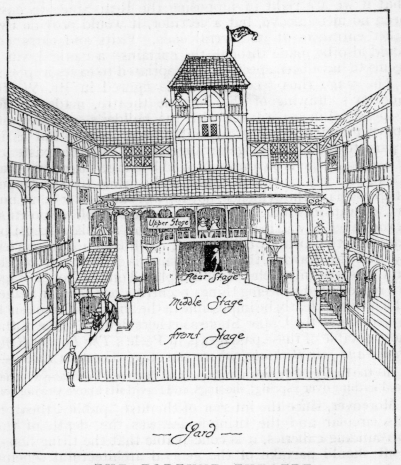

THE FORTUNE THEATRE

Mr. W. H. Godfrey's reconstruction from the builder's contract.

In Marlowe we rarely, if ever, find entrances indicated by doors, the usual formula being ' Enter (or exeunt) on one side So-and-so ; on the other Such-an-one '. These directions occur with considerable frequency in private-theatre plays of the later period. Indeed, so abundant is the evidence pointing to the use of side entrances that the testimony of the Swan drawing becomes doubly suspect. If it is correct, the Swan was far from a typical theatre.

It is probable that, from the building of Burbage's Blackfriars onwards, the stage of the private theatres was constructed as nearly on the model of the public stages as the narrower limits of the buildings would allow. Whatever the earlier differences, when once the ordinary adult players began to act in the private theatres a certain standardization would necessarily follow. We know that many plays were acted indifferently at the Globe and at the Blackfriars. Professor Wallace, who has discovered the dimensions of the Blackfriars hall (66 by 46 feet), argues that the stage cannot have projected into the pit, as did the stages of the public theatres, because in that case it could not have been more than from 13 to 19 feet wide, a space which certainly seems very contracted as compared with the 43 feet of the Fortune stage. In the one drawing we possess of the interior of a private theatre (see p. 297) the stage is represented as projecting into the pit and is extremely narrow. This cannot be said, however, to negative Professor Wallace's conjecture that at the Blackfriars the stage extended right across the hall, with the audience facing it, as in a modern theatre. On a stage 46 feet wide some 10 feet could be spared on each side for the stools of the gallants, who loved to exhibit themselves in this position, and in an ordinary theatre would seriously block the view of other members of the audience. T. M. in *The Blacke Booke* (1604) has a reference to one Barnaby Burning-glass as ' arch tobacco taker of England . . . upon stages both common and private ' ; and there is this very explicit passage from Dekker's *Guls Horne-booke* :—

Whether, therefore, the gatherers of the publique or private Playhouse stand to receive the afternoones rent, let our Gallant (having paid it) presently advance himselfe up to the Throne of the Stage . . . on the very Rushes where the Comedy is to daunce . . . beating downe the mewes and hisses of the opposed rascality.

The prices of admission differed at different theatres and at different times ; but, broadly speaking, the prices at public theatres ranged, in five degrees, from a penny to a shilling, and at the private theatres from sixpence to

half-a-crown.   The Prologue to *Henry VIII* specifies a
shilling, doubtless as an average price :

> Those that come to see
> Only a show or two, and so agree
> The play may pass, if they be still and willing,
> I'll undertake may see away their shilling
> Richly in two short hours.   (ll. 9–13)

As the purchasing power of money was then at least five
times greater than at the beginning of the present century,
it appears that the cost of playgoing was not, on the whole,
much lower than in our own time.   Prices, too, were
frequently doubled at the first performance of a new play.
The higher scale of prices at the private theatres was no
doubt determined by three facts : that the lighting was
artificial and expensive ; that the capacity of the houses
was small ; that the audience were all seated.   In the last
fact lay the radical distinction between the two types of
theatre ; for the history of the European stage has clearly
shown that a standing pit always makes for turbulence.
It is probable, however, that we are apt to exaggerate
the unruliness of the average Elizabethan audience.   The
fact that some theatres were noted for the roughness of
their frequenters proves that it was not universal.   Indeed,
we have direct testimony to the sobriety and attentiveness
of certain audiences.   It was probably only at holiday
periods—especially at Shrovetide—when a flood of apprentices, shoemakers, butchers, &c., was let loose upon the
town, that pandemonium reigned in the Bankside houses.
It is inconceivable that such a body of literature as the
Elizabethan drama should have been produced under
conditions that precluded all delicacy of delivery and
intimacy of comprehension.

One of the distinguishing characteristics of the Elizabethan audience, as contrasted with continental audiences
of the first half of the seventeenth century, was the free
mingling of the sexes.   This led to certain parts of the house
becoming a notorious resort for loose women—an abuse
which survived almost to our own day.   Reputable women,
however, did not hold aloof from the playhouse, which was
then, as now, a favourite place for the display of the latest
and most striking fashions.   It was at one time the custom
for ladies to wear vizard-masks, which served very much the

purpose of the modern parasol, and may, moreover, have spared their wearers some embarrassment when the playwright's coarseness went beyond what was permitted by the conventions of the age. Others at such moments took refuge behind their fans, in the ' nice conduct ' of which Elizabethan dames had nothing to learn.

Performances began about two or three in the afternoon, after the midday dinner of the period. The play of the day had usually been notified from the stage on the previous day, and was further announced on posters. An hour or two before the time of the performance the ensign of the house, bearing its symbol, was hoisted on the turret of public theatres ; and the immediate signal that the play was about to begin was given by three trumpet-blasts, blown at short intervals, from the same point. To make sure of places, the audiences assembled early ; and at the second Blackfriars, when occupied by the boy-players, the hour before the play was whiled away by a concert of excellent music. This probably established the principle of the overture at the private houses. It is furthermore certain that at those houses inter-act music (sometimes accompanied by song and dance) was regularly given. But it is not so certain that music extraneous to the play was customary at the public theatres. We know that a few public-theatre plays like *Sejanus*, based on the classic model, had an accompanied chorus between the acts ; but inter-act music does not seem to have been a normal feature. But the idea that the act-division was not recognized in the Elizabethan theatre, and that scene followed scene from beginning to end without the slightest break, will not bear examination. In the public no less than in the private theatres, musicians were regularly attached to the staff. In most plays music entered more or less into the business of the scene, and, even if this did not always apply to the public theatre, musicians were always required there for the concluding ' jig '.[1]

Though the Elizabethan drama was not subjected to the attentions of a critical press, criticism of a kind had already come into being. People who do not pay for their seats are notoriously ill to please, and it is significant that the first known ' deadheads '—the dramatists of the age—

[1] See Chapter XXIV, p. 261.

were among the first dramatic critics. Possibly they acted
on the principle of 'set a thief to catch a thief'. Hall in
his *Virgidemiarum*, 1597, girds at the 'synod' of poets,
who sat on the stage, and, as magistrates of wit, arraigned
every new production. But the office did not remain long
a specialized one. It was entrenched upon by a set of
gallants whom Dekker in his *Guls Horne-booke* denominates
the 'Colledge of Criticks', and who, sitting indifferently
on the stage or in the twelvepenny room, waited, tablebook
in hand, to catch the unlucky author tripping. This critical
conclave was no more beloved by the authors of that day
than are its successors by the playwrights of the present.
'There are a sort of these narrow-eyed decypherers', writes
Ben Jonson, in *Every Man Out of his Humor*, 'that will
extort strange and abstruse meanings out of any subject,
be it never so conspicuous and innocently delivered. But to
such, where'er they sit concealed, let them know, the author
defies them and their writing-tables, and hopes no sound or
safe judgement will infect itself with their contagious comment, who, indeed, come here only to pervert and poison the
sense of what they hear, and for naught else.' Here were
the elements of dramatic criticism in solution. But the
precipitation was delayed for something over a century.

BIBLIOGRAPHY.—For the general authorities on the subject of the Playhouse the bibliography of Chapter XXIV should be consulted under GREG,
MALONE, COLLIER, HAZLITT, FLEAY, and MURRAY. In addition there are
the following special contributions :—CECIL BRODMEIER's *Die Shakespeare-
Bühne nach den alten Bühnenanweisungen*, 1904, which sets forth the alternation theory ; PAUL MÖNKEMEYER's *Prolegomena zu einer Darstellung der
englischen Volksbühne*, 1905 ; RICHARD WEGENER's useful *Die Bühnenein-
richtung des Shakespeareschen Theaters*, 1907 ; G. F. REYNOLDS's *Some Prin-
ciples of Elizabethan Staging*, 1905, and *What we know of the Elizabethan
Stage*, paper in *Modern Philology*, vol. ix, No. 1, July 1911 ; WILLIAM ARCHER's
The Elizabethan Stage, article in *The Quarterly Review*, April 1908 ; V. E.
ALBRIGHT's *The Shakespearian Stage*, 1909 ; B. NEUENDORFF's *Die englische
Volksbühne im Zeitalter Shakespeares*, 1910 ; W. J. LAWRENCE's *The Eliza-
bethan Playhouse and other Studies*, First and Second Series, 1912–13 ; C. W.
WALLACE's *The Evolution of the English Drama up to Shakespeare*, 1912 ;
T. S. GRAVES's *The Court and the London Theatres during the Reign of Eliza-
beth*, 1913.
   Special studies of particular theatres are : T. F. ORDISH's *Early London
Theatres* (in the Fields), 1894 ; C. W. WALLACE's *The First London Theatre*,
1913, and *The Swan Theatre*, paper in *Englische Studien*, vol. xliii, pp. 340 ff. ;
WILLIAM MARTIN's *The Site of the Globe Playhouse of Shakespeare*, 1910 ;
A. W. CLAPHAM and W. H. GODFREY's *Some Famous Buildings and their
Story*, 1913 ; WILLIAM ARCHER's *The Fortune Theatre, 1600*, in the *Shake-
speare-Jahrbuch*, 1908, pp. 159–66 ; and W. W. BRAINES's *Holywell Priory
and the Site of the Theatre, Shoreditch* (London County Council Pamphlets:
Indication of Houses of Historical Interest in London, Part xliii, 1915).

XXVI

THE MASQUE

BY

PERCY SIMPSON

THE LITERARY DEVELOPMENT

THE masque is, historically, an expansion of the mediaeval
'mumming' and 'disguising'. It retained to the end
its undramatic character, even when set scenery and the
semblance of a plot had elaborated the early form. Dancing
was always the essential feature of the entertainment :
thus the disguising was originally a dance in masquerade,
for which the performers paid a visit to a noble's house,
usually at a time of festival. Sometimes they rode thither
in procession, danced in his honour, and rode away, so
that the function had something in common with the
'riding in Chepe' which fascinated Chaucer's idle apprentice [1] and the city 'pageant' which survives in the Lord
Mayor's Show. In 1377 the citizens of London rode out
from Newgate to Kennington to pay their court to
Richard II just after his accession. They consisted of
'130 men disguizedly aparailed & well mounted on horse-
backe to goe on mumming . . . with great noyse of min-
stralsye, trumpets, cornets & shawmes & great plenty of
waxe torches lighted'. First rode forty-eight, 'two & two
togither clothed in cotes & clokes of red say or sendall and
their faces covered with vizards well & handsomly made';
then forty-eight knights; and finally an emperor. At an
interval of one hundred yards a pope and twenty-four
cardinals followed; then forty-eight knights; and finally by
a piquant contrast 'came 8 or 10 arayed & with black
vizerdes like devils'. Entering the hall, they saluted
the royal party, 'shewing a peyr of dice upon a table to
play with the prince': the dice were loaded, so that he

---

[1] See *The Canterbury Tales*, A. 4377.

won their gold and jewels. He offered them wine, 'and they dronck with great joye. . . . And the prince and the lords danced on the one syde and the mummers on the other a great while and then they drank, & tooke their leave & so departed toward London.' [1]

This is the earliest record which describes a mumming fully. The main features are the *motif* of a congratulatory visit from the Pope and the Emperor, the dice-play, and the dance. The distinguished foreigner is a stock character in a show of this kind. The gaming in which the visitors lose to the host is also a convention. It does not involve any speeches; it is merely a form of dumb-show in which the mummers intimate by signs their desire to play. In the dance they do not mingle with the royal guests. All this was modified with the development of the masque, but in other characteristic points there is no change. The torches were needed to light a procession which took place just before Candlemas; but the large supply here used was evidently for scenic effect. They were always an accompaniment of the masque:

> Night, like a masque, was ent'red heaven's great hall,
> With thousand torches ushering the way,

is the beautiful image of a later poet.[2] The torch-bearers were supernumeraries. When Benvolio is arranging the masquing party which is to dance at Lord Capulet's, Romeo refuses to take any active part:

> A torch for me! . . .
> I'll be a candle-holder, and look on.
>
> (*Rom. & Jul.* I. iv. 35–8)

So Jessica in her page's suit, when she celebrates her freedom from home-ties by going to a masque with Lorenzo:

> *Lor.* Descend, for you must be my torch-bearer.
> *Jes.* What! must I hold a candle to my shames?
>
> (*Merch. of V.* II. vi. 40–1)

Effective contrasts of colour and costume were studied from the first. The torch-bearers had a sharply distinctive dress. Thus a masque of Moors mentioned in an inventory of the Revels Office for 1560 had white friars for torch-bearers, and they wore 'crimson headpieces'—probably to set off the white turbans which we may suppose the

---

[1] In British Museum, Harleian MS. 247, fol. 172 verso.
[2] William Barksted, *Mirrha*, 1607, sig. B 3.

PENTHESILEA in *The Masque of Queenes*
by Inigo Jones

Moors to have worn. The devils in the mumming at Kennington are a good foil to the pope and cardinals ; in this early use of the grotesque we can see the germ of the antimasque.

The masques introduced into Shakespeare's plays are usually in this primitive form of the masquerade dance at a nobleman's house. After the 'great supper' at Leonato's (*Much Ado* II. i) Don Pedro and the nobles enter as 'Maskers with a drum'[1] (l. 89) and mix with the ladies in conversation till the 'Musicke for the dance' (l. 162). The approach of a masquing party is always heralded by drum or trumpet. Shylock, hearing that masquers will pass his house, tells Jessica not to look out of the window,

> when you hear the drum,
> And the vile squealing of the wry-neck'd fife, . . .
> To gaze on Christian fools with varnish'd faces.
>
> (*Merch. of V*. II. v. 29–33)

At Timon's banquet there is a stage-direction, 'Sound Tucket. Enter the Maskers of Amazons, with Lutes in their hands, dauncing and playing.' Timon, hearing the trumpet, sends to inquire what it means, and his servant reports :

> Please you, my lord, there are certain ladies most desirous of admittance. . . . There comes with them a forerunner, my lord, which bears that office, to signify their pleasures.
>
> (*Timon* I. ii. 123–8)

Then ' Enter Cupid with the Maske of Ladies ' and

> *The Lords rise from Table, with much adoring of Timon, and to shew their loves, each single out an Amazon, and all Dance, men with women, a loftie straine or two to the Hoboyes, and cease.*
>
> (ib. 152 st. dir.)

Here Cupid is the presenter, and it became a common practice to bring in the masque with a formal speech of introduction. Verses by Lydgate to usher in mummings or disguisings to the king or the lord mayor have been preserved. A historic instance is dramatized in the play of *King Henry VIII* (I. iv), where Henry, attended by nobles, visits Wolsey at Hampton Court during a state banquet. ' Drum and Trumpet, Chambers dischargd ' is

---

[1] All the Shakespearian stage-directions which follow are quoted from the First Folio.

the intimation of their coming. A servant reports, after the usual inquiry, that they are

<blockquote>

A noble troop of strangers;

For so they seem : th'have left their barge and landed,

And hither make, as great ambassadors

From foreign princes. (ll. 53–6)
</blockquote>

To receive them, 'All rise, and Tables remov'd'. The royal party enters.

Hoboyes. Enter King and others as Maskers, habited like Shepheards, usher'd by the Lord Chamberlaine. They passe directly before the Cardinall, and gracefully salute him.

The Lord Chamberlain, as their spokesman, tells Wolsey that, hearing of that noble assembly,

<blockquote>

they could do no less,

Out of the great respect they bear to beauty,

But leave their flocks; and, under your fair conduct,

Crave leave to view these ladies, and entreat

An hour of revels with 'em. (ll. 68–72)
</blockquote>

At a later point (l. 74) the stage-direction is ' Choose Ladies, King and An Bullen', and then ' Musicke, Dance'. A banquet follows.

Wolsey's gentleman-usher, George Cavendish, was an eyewitness of this entertainment, and he has described it fully in his *Life* of the Cardinal, pp. 112–18. 'The banquets were set forth', he says, whenever Henry visited Wolsey,

with masks and mummeries in so gorgeous a sort, and costly manner, that it was a heaven to behold. . . . I have seen the king suddenly come in thither in a mask, with a dozen of other maskers, all in garments like shepherds, made of fine cloth of gold and fine crimson satin paned, and caps of the same, with visors of good proportion of visnomy ; their hairs, and beards, either of fine gold wire, or else of silver, and some being of black silk ; having sixteen torch bearers, besides their drums, and other persons attending upon them, with visors, and clothed all in satin, of the same colours.

The king came by water, and on his landing at Hampton Court

many chambers . . . were all shot off, which made such a rumble in the air, that it was like thunder. . . . Then immediately after this great shot of guns, the Cardinal desired the Lord Chamberlain, and Controller, to look what this sudden shot should mean, as though he knew nothing of the matter. They thereupon looking out of the window into Thames, returned again, and showed him, that it seemed to them there should be some noblemen and strangers arrived at his bridge, as ambassadors from some foreign prince.

The fiction is maintained, as the play records; when the masquers entered the presence chamber, 'they went directly before the cardinal where he sat, saluting him very reverently,' and asked his permission to hold the revels.

To whom the Cardinal answered, that he was very well contented they should do so. Then the maskers went first and saluted all the dames as they sat, and then returned to the most worthiest, and there opened a cup full of gold, with crowns, and other pieces of coin, to whom they set divers pieces to cast at . . . to some they lost, and of some they won. And thus done, they returned unto the Cardinal, with great reverence pouring down all the crowns in the cup, which was about two hundred crowns. At all! quoth the Cardinal, and so cast the dice, and wan them all at a cast, whereat was great joy made.

Wolsey then attempted to single out the king from his fellow masquers, but made a wrong choice; in the play he is represented as succeeding. The king changed his dress; a banquet followed, and the night was spent in 'banqueting, dancing, and other triumphant devices'.

The convention of the wandering foreigner also appears in *Love's Labour's Lost*, v. ii. 120-1, where the king and his companions visit the ladies 'apparell'd . . . like Muscovites or Russians', and

> Their purpose is to parle, to court and dance. (l. 122)

When the trumpet sounds, the ladies mask to receive them; then 'Enter Black moores with musicke, the Boy with a speech, and the rest of the Lords disguised'. If this disguising had taken place at night, the Blackamoors would have been the torch-bearers.

A boy was frequently chosen for the presenter. The Revels Accounts for 1582-3 contain the entry:

> geven in Reward to the boye that pronounced ⎱ x^s.
> the speeche before the maske of the Ladies. ⎰

For a single speech the pay is distinctly good. In Benvolio's masque his services are not highly rated.

Enter Romeo, Mercutio, Benvolio, with five or six other Maskers, Torch-bearers.

 Rom. What! shall this speech be spoke for our excuse,
Or shall we on without apology?
 Ben. The date is out of such prolixity:
We'll have no Cupid hood-wink'd with a scarf,
Bearing a Tartar's painted bow of lath,
Scaring the ladies like a crow-keeper;

Nor no without-book prologue, faintly spoke
After the prompter, for our entrance:
But, let them measure us by what they will,
We'll measure them a measure, and be gone.

(Rom. & Jul. I. iv. 1–10)

So Benvolio gives the plain directions:

Come, knock and enter; and no sooner in,
But every man betake him to his legs.   (33–4)

In the Folio the scene is transferred to Capulet's house. Benvolio gives the order, ' Strike, drum,' and instead of the ' Exeunt ' of modern editions, we have, ' They march about the Stage, and Servingmen come forth with their napkins ', clear the room for the dance, ' exeunt ', and then ' Enter all the Guests and Gentlewomen to the Maskers ', who are welcomed by Capulet. ' Musicke plaies : and the dance.' Finally, the host gives the usual invitation to a ' trifling foolish banquet '.

The masque became more complicated with the introduction of scenery, but at first this was very crude. A ' pageant ' or ' scaffold ' on wheels, like the movable stage used in the miracle plays, was constructed in the form of a castle, a mount, or a ship, and moved into the hall. A mimic warfare followed, which gave occasion for simple speeches such as a parley or a defiance, or even for a debate and some approach to dramatic dialogue. In 1501 ' banquets and disguisings ' in honour of Katharine of Aragon took place in Westminster Hall, and Stow has preserved an account of ' this most goodly and pleasant disguising convayed and shewed in pageantes proper and subtile '.[1] The first pageant was ' a Castle right cunningly devised, sett uppon certaine wheeles and drawne into the said great hall of fower great beastes with Chaines of gold '— a gold and a silver lion, a hart with gilt horns, and ' an Ibeke ', with two men inside each of these, ' one in the forepart and another in the hinder part secretly hid and apparelled, nothing seene but their legges '. Within the castle were ' viij goodly and fresh ladyes looking out of the windowes ', four in English, and four in Spanish costume; in the four corners were turrets with children ' singing most sweetly '. The castle moved up the hall and was stationed before the king and queen. The second

---

[1] In Harleian MS. 69, foll. 29 verso–30 verso.

ATALANTA a Design for *The Masque of Queenes*
by Inigo Jones

pageant was 'a shippe in like wise sett uppon wheeles
without any leaders in sight, in right goodly apparell,
having her mastes toppes sayles, her tackling and all
other apperteynances necessary unto a seemely vessell,
as though it had bene sayling in the sea'. The 'maskers'
worked the ship 'after the manner and guise of Mariners'
and anchored beside the castle. On board was a fair
lady dressed, out of compliment to Katharine, as a princess
of Spain ; 'two well beseene and goodly persons calling
themselves hope and desire' descended the ship's ladder
and advanced to the castle as ambassadors from the
Knights of the Mount of Love, on whose behalf they sued
for the ladies' favour. When rejected, they showed great
displeasure and retired with threats. 'Incontinent came
in the third Pageant in likenes of a great hill or moun-
taine', with the eight knights, who received the report of
their failure. Displaying their banners, they assaulted
the castle ; the ladies yielded and came down to dance
with them. When the maskers retired, the royal party
danced by themselves. 'This disguising royall thus
ended, beganne the Voydee to enter in this manner of
a bankett.'

This is a noteworthy advance on the masked dance
of mummers, and clearly points the way to the later
phase in which the 'inventor' worked the accessories
into an elaborate literary pattern. The masque attained
its full development at the court of James I, where a rare
combination of artistic gifts was employed to heighten
the presentment. The music was composed by Ferrabosco
or Lanier ; exquisite scenery and dresses were designed
by Inigo Jones ; and a certain solidity was given to the
frail and airy structure by the massive scholarship of
Jonson. The dance was still the nucleus of the entertainment. Its successive stages were the 'Entry', the 'Main',
and the 'Going out', with the 'Revels', a series of
lighter dances, often inserted after the Main. Effects of
contrast and surprise were carefully studied ; sometimes
there is almost an attempt to import dramatic method.
The masques are elaborately introduced. It is interesting
to compare the pilgrim figures in *The Queenes Masque of
Blacknesse*, 1605, Jonson's first experiment in this form,
with such crude predecessors as the City mummers and

the wandering Knights of the Mount of Love. Jonson's scene—or rather Inigo Jones's—was a vast sea stretching to the horizon with moving and breaking waves, and over all ' an obscure and cloudy night-piece '.

The Masquers were placed in a great concave shell, like mother of pearl, curiously made to move on those waters and rise with the billow ; the top thereof was stuck with a chevron of lights, which, indented to the proportion of the shell, strook a glorious beam upon them, as they were seated one above another.

Sea-monsters swam at the sides carrying the torch-bearers, twelve ocean-nymphs, who ' had their lights burning out of whelks or murex shells '. The twelve masquers were Aethiopian princesses, daughters of Niger, blackened with tropical heat, and seeking a more temperate clime, a land where the sun, no longer scorching,

> leaves that climate of the sky
> To comfort of a greater Light,
> Who forms all beauty with his sight.

They reach an island of snowy cliffs.

At this, the Moon was discovered in the upper part of the house, triumphant in a silver throne made in figure of a pyramis ; her garments white and silver, the dressing of her head antique and crowned with a luminary or sphere of light, which, striking on the clouds and heightened with silver, reflected, as natural clouds do by the splendour of the moon. The heaven about her was vaulted with blue silk and set with stars of silver, which had in them their several lights burning.

This pure and radiant figure is Aethiopia, or the moon-goddess as worshipped by the Aethiopians. She tells the wanderers they have reached their goal, the ' blest isle ' of Britannia, lit by the mild rays of a sun of majesty,

> Whose beams shine day and night, and are of force
> To blanch an Aethiop and revive a corse ;
> His light sciential is.

The Tritons sounded, and they danced on shore. Then, when they were ' about to make choice of their men, one from the sea was heard to call 'hem with this charm, sung by a tenor voice ' :

> Come away, come away,
> We grow jealous of your stay :
> If you do not stop your ear,
> We shall have more cause to fear
> Sirens of the land than they
> To doubt the Sirens of the sea.

CAMILLA in *The Masque of Queenes*
by Inigo Jones

They danced the revels, and 'were again accited to sea with a song of two trebles, whose cadences were iterated by a double echo from several parts of the land':

> Daughters of the subtle flood,
> Do not let earth longer entertain you.
> *First Echo.* Let earth longer entertain you.
> *Second Echo.* Longer entertain you.

Aethiopia warned the pilgrims at each full moon in the coming year to bathe

> in that purer brine
> And wholesome dew called ros-marine;
> Then with that soft and gentler foam,
> Of which the Ocean yet yields some,
> Whereof bright Venus, Beauty's Queen,
> Is said to have begotten been;

and the perfecting touch is to be given when they return, 'dry their faces'

> in the beams of yond bright Sun,

and find their blackness converted into beauty. They returned dancing to the sea, 'where they took their shell', and went out with a 'full song'.

So with varying effects of light set off against the dark background, and with verse that echoes the music and reflects the colour of the sea, Jonson made his first attempt to bring the masque within the domain of poetry. Even the choice of King James I for presiding luminary did not wreck the venture. The choice could hardly have been avoided, for the masque was the Queen's; and Jonson's elaborate invention was based upon a hint from her that she wished the performers to be 'Black-moors'. Similarly, when the return was made, not, as was expected, a year after, but in 1608, she commanded Jonson 'to think on some fit presentment which should answer the former, still keeping them the same persons, the daughters of Niger, but their beauties varied according to promise, and their time of absence excused'. The real reason for the delay was the struggle for precedence at these entertainments among the foreign ambassadors; the court, unable to arrange for the representatives of France and Spain to appear together, did not venture to invite either singly. So Jonson put forward the fiction that Night, resenting the princesses' change as a slight upon her own complexion, had kept them wandering in the ocean on their floating island. Their escape was the theme of *The Second Masque, Which was of Beautie*.

Such was Jonson's pioneer venture; his later masques exhibit a marked improvement in technique. He achieved a closer structural unity, and he strengthened them with an element of dramatic surprise. In fact he made a conscientious effort to dramatize his intractable material. Two of his devices were an obvious gain. He kept the masquers back at the beginning, preparing for their entry with a suggestive introduction and revealing them in a sudden transformation scene. In the marriage masque of *Hymenaei*, 1606, first Hymen entered with pages and musicians to the altar of union; then a 'microcosm or globe figuring man', with Reason seated above it 'as in the brain or highest part of man', was seen suspended; turning softly it discovered the men masquers, seated 'within a mine of several metals', so lit up that at first they were not seen. They entered 'with a kind of contentious music', and proved to be the four Humours and the four Affections, bent on disturbing the ceremony, till the appeal of Reason quieted them. 'Here the upper part of the scene, which was all of clouds and made artificially to swell and ride like the rack, began to open,' and revealed the region of the air, with Juno, queen of marriage, throned above, beneath her the rainbow, and on the sides eight lady masquers, named after her attributes. 'Their descent was made in two great clouds, that put forth themselves severally and, with one measure of time, were seen to stoop and fall gently down upon the earth.' Order, the servant of Reason, marshalled their opening dance.

Still more significant was the effect of contrast in the antimasque. Jonson in his finest effort in this genre, *The Masque of Queenes, Celebrated from the house of Fame by the Queene of great Britaine with her Ladies,* 1609, explains that Queen Anne, 'best knowing that a principal part of life in these spectacles lay in their variety, had commanded me to think on some dance or show that might precede hers and have the place of a foil or false masque.' The year before, in the masque at Viscount Haddington's wedding, he had used an antimasque of boys attending on Cupid; they had represented 'the sports and pretty lightnesses that accompany love', and had performed 'a subtle capricious dance to as odd a music, . . . nodding with their antique faces, with other variety of ridiculous gesture, which gave much occasion of mirth and delight to the spectators.' But this had been only an incidental device in the hue and cry after Cupid which formed the prelude; it was quite unconnected with the theme of the marriage and the climax of the masque. In his second attempt therefore Jonson carefully aimed at an underlying unity. The masque was designed to celebrate twelve famous queens, and especially Bel-anna, Queen of the Ocean: so he 'devised that twelve women in the habit of hags or witches, sustaining the persons of Ignorance, Suspicion, Credulity, &c., the opposites of Good Fame,' should be the foil, 'not as a masque but a spectacle of strangeness, producing multiplicity of gesture, and not unaptly sorting with the current and whole fall of the device'. At first the scene was 'an ugly hell, which, flaming beneath, smoked unto the top of the roof'. Eleven witches entered from it, differently attired, with rats on head or shoulders or ointment-pots at their girdles, and 'with spindles, timbrels, rattles or other venefical instruments'—a device of Inigo Jones, to which Jonson added a few classical properties. They danced and used a charm to fetch their dame, who came 'naked-armed, bare-footed, her frock tucked, her hair knotted, and folded with vipers; in her hand a torch, made of a dead man's arm, lighted; girded with a snake'. They plan to eclipse the glory of 'these bright nights of honour'. They ply all their charms, without avail, and end with 'a magical dance, full of preposterous change and gesticulation, . . . dancing back to back and hip to hip, their hands joined and making their circles backward, to the left hand, with strange fantastic motions of their heads and bodies.' Suddenly with a crash of musical instruments they and their hell vanished, and there appeared the House of Fame, with the queens at the top of it, 'sitting upon a throne triumphal, erected in form of a pyramid and circled with all store of light'. Heroic Virtue in the equipment of Perseus acted as their presenter; Fame, dressed in white, came to do them honour.

Descending, they made their entry in three triumphal chariots, with the witches bound captive to the wheels. After the dances they returned to their proper sphere, the House of Fame.

Elsewhere Jonson shows the same skill in presenting contrasted types while keeping the unity of conception. In *Oberon, the Faery Prince*, a masque of Prince Henry, where the main scene discovers a palace with ' the nation of Fays ', ' the first face of the scene ' is a dim landscape with a dark rock and trees, and the first characters to appear are Silenus and the Satyrs. In *Mercurie Vindicated from the Alchemists at Court*, the opening scene is a laboratory, the first antimasque is composed of Vulcan and a troop of threadbare alchemists, and the second of ' imperfect creatures, with limbecks on their heads '—the botched and bungling outcome of the alchemists' experiments to manufacture men ; but the main scene is ' a glorious bower, wherein Nature was placed, with Prometheus at her feet ' —Prometheus, who in the old classical legend wrought men out of earth and water ; with them are the masquers, the perfect children of Nature. One later masque, *Lovers Made Men*, 1617, attains complete unity : it opens with ' certain imagined ghosts ', ' the gentle forms of Lovers ' ' drowned by Love ', who drink of Lethe and are renewed ; so that masque and antimasque are fused by the transformation.

A further scheme of Jonson's to vary the pattern of the masque was the introduction of realism. *The Irish Masque at Court*, 1613, opens with a homely Irish dialogue of Dennis, Donnel, Dermock, and Patrick, and the antimasque was danced ' to the bagpipe and other rude music ' ; the masquers following 'with a dance in their Irish mantles to a solemn music of harps ' ; a bard sings a charm to them, and they ' let fall their mantles, and discover their masquing apparell '. In *Newes from the New World discovered in the Moone*, 1621, the dialogue is extended so far as to be indistinguishable from Jonson's ordinary methods in comedy ; and it merely leads up to four slight songs which introduce the dances of the masque itself in the Region of the Moon, from which the masquers ' descend and shake off their icicles '. This lack of balance no doubt indicates the taste of the Court, for which the dances alone

ARTEMISIA in *The Masque of Queenes*
by Inigo Jones

were important and a comic induction was tolerable. The increase in the number of antimasques or 'entries' of grotesque characters is also suggestive : Jonson in *Chloridia*, his last Court masque presented in 1631, has eight of these. The scene changes to a storm, with a dance of the nymph Tempest and the four Winds.

Fifth Entry.

Lightnings, three in number, their habits glistering, expressing that effect in their motion.

Sixth Entry.

Thunder, alone, dancing the tunes to a noise mixed and imitating thunder.

Seventh Entry.

Rain, presented by five persons all swoln and clouded over, their hair flagging as if they were wet, and in their hands balls of sweet water, which as they dance sprinkle all the room.

Eighth and last Entry.

Seven with rugged white heads and beards to express *Snow*, with flakes on their garments mixed with hail.

The presentment here is at least artistic ; it soon ceased to be so when these preliminary dances multiplied. Davenant in *Salmacida Spolia*, 1640, produced twenty of them, the ninth being 'Four Grotesques or Drolleries, in the most fantastical shapes that could be devised'. In such hands the antimasque had neither point nor relevance ; it was merely a variety entertainment.

The masque as a literary form can hardly have interested Shakespeare ; he wrote one slight example of it—'some vanity of his art'—in *The Tempest* (IV. i. 60-138). But a masque written for inclusion in a play was necessarily a fragment ; Shakespeare contented himself with sketching it in outline, and touched it here and there with poetry.

THE OFFICE OF THE REVELS

The duty of organizing the performance of masques and plays at Court was assigned to a 'Master of the Revels'. The term appears to have been given at first to the particular courtier who superintended the function of the moment, but in March 1544 it is found as the definite title of a Court official with an annual fee of ten pounds.

'The cheife busynes of the office' is defined in an important memorandum [1] of 1573, as resting

speciallye in three poyntes, In makinge of garmentes, In makinge of hedpeces, and in payntinge. The connynge of the office resteth in skill of devise, in understandinge of historyes, in judgement of comedies, tragedyes and shewes, in sight of perspective and architecture some smacke of geometrye and other thinges.

A staff of workmen—chiefly tailors, embroiderers, and painters—was employed ; they worked ten hours a day, and, if on night duty, six hours. The painters were to be specially watched :

Some one speciall officer to have commaundement over theym and Commission to rate their wages, and to punyshe theym for their absence or negligence, otherwise the Prince is like most commonlye to be ill served of those kinde of men bothe for absence wages wast and loyteringe whiche breadeth the Prince many tymes muche more charge then neadeth.

The Office, however, was badly organized ; in 'A note of sarten thinges which are very nedefull to be Redressed ', in the same manuscript is the statement that

there is no convenyent Romes for the Artifycers to worcke in but that Taylours Paynters Proparatiue makers and Carpenders are all fayne to worcke in one rome which is A very greate hinderannce one to Another which thinge nedes not for theye are slacke anove of them selves.

The Master of the Revels also ran into debt. In 1574 'The poore Creaditours and Artyffycers which serve thoffyce' petitioned the Queen for prompt payment of £1,550 5s. 8d., ' unpaide ij yeares and more ' : a solitary creditor has the courage to sign it—' poore Bryan Dodmer a creditour to save the labour of a great Number whose exclamacion is lamentable '.

The Revels Accounts give full information about the dresses and properties. The tailors and the officials who supervised them in the reign of Elizabeth showed little ' understandinge of historyes ' in their costumes ; they aimed only at colour and magnificence. In January 1579 a double masque was shown in honour of the French ambassador—a *Masque of Amazons*, who danced with the lords, followed by a *Masque of Knights*, who danced with

[1] In British Museum, Lansdowne MS. 83, foll. 160 verso, 161, 149, dated by Mr. E. K. Chambers in *The Tudor Revels*, pp. 49-50.

THOMYRIS in *The Masque of Queenes*
by Inigo Jones

the ladies, and fought the Amazons at Barriers : [1] the first was

A Masque of Amazons in all armour complete, parcel-gilt gilded within this office, with counterfeit morions silvered over and parcel-gilt (besides their head-pieces belonging to their armour), and a crest on the top of every six of them, having long hair hanging down behind them ; their kirtles were of crimson cloth of gold, being indented at the skirt and laid with silver lace and fringed with pendants of gold tassels, gold knobs, and set on with broaches of gold plaited upon the skirt with plaits of silver lawn, with tassels of gold laid under below instead of petticoats, with white silver, rich tinsel fringed with gold fringe ; buskins of orange-colour velvet ; antique fauchions and shields with a device painted thereon, and javelins in their hands. One with a speech to the Queen's majesty delivering a table with writings unto her highness coming in with musicians playing on cornets apparelled in long white taffeta sarcenet garments ; torch-bearers with the truchman wearing long gowns of white taffeta with sleeves of the same, and upon them had long crimson taffeta gowns without sleeves, indented at the skirt and fringed, laced, and tasselled with silver and gold, tucked up with the girding almost to the knee ; bows in their hands and quivers of arrows at their girdles ; head-pieces of gold lawn, and women's hair wreathed very fair.

The designer might fairly plead that for semi-mythical creatures like the Amazons he had to draw upon his invention ; but that excuse would not serve for the dresses of humbler characters. In the accounts of 1560 there is an inventory of dresses for eight clowns :—

viii coats of crimson satin guarded with yellow gold lawn, with half-sleeves of the same and under-sleeves of green damask turned up with yellow gold lawn.
viii pair of plain hosen of green damask.
viii aprons of white gold sarsenet edged with Venice gold fringe.
viii broad hats, crimson satin lined with green gold sarsenet.
viii pair of shoes of black velvet laced above the ancle.
viii flails and viii spades of tree foiled over.[2]

In real life nothing could have been simpler than the rough dress of the wild Irish kerns (*Rich. II*, ii. i. 157, *Macb.* i. ii. 30) ; but the court tailor dressed them in this fancy attire :

vi upper garments with bases of crimson cloth of gold fringed with green silk.
vi shirts of yellow sarsenet fringed with white and green caddis fringe.

[1] Bacon comments in his *Essay* on Masques and Triumphs : ' Double masques, one of men, another of ladies, addeth state and variety.'
[2] i. e. wood covered with gold-leaf, suggested by the gilded dagger of the Vice.

In the inventory of 1560 an interesting note appended to these garments states that they were 'translated into Almains for torchbearers to the Rutters' and were 'too much known' to be used again. The Office adopted the thrifty plan of re-using the old stock of dresses. Thomas Giles, haberdasher, complaining that the Yeoman of the Revels is too free in letting the wardrobe out to hire, states that dresses were always altered, 'for theye never com before her heyghnes twysse In on forme.' Thus various lengths of crimson satin originally made into 'large garments for two cardinals and two bishops' were 'translated into viii clowns' garments and hats'.

The record of the properties is equally entertaining. In *The Masque of Janus*, which appears in the inventory for 1572–3, snowballs were presented to the queen : they were made of 'ffyne white Lam . . . 8 skinnes at v^d the peece', and perfumed. For this masque the royal apothecary was paid 27s. 4d. Here is his bill :—

Robert Moorer for suger plate—xij^s. viij^d Musk kumfettes j lb—ij^s iiij^d / Corianders prepared j lb—xx^d. Clove Cumfettes j lb—ij^s iiij^d Synamon kumfettes—iij^s Rose water j quarte & j pynte of spike water—iij iiij^d / Gynger Cumfettes j lb—ij^s All whiche served for fflakes of yse & hayle stones in the maske of Ianvs the Roze water sweetened the balls made for snowballes presented to her Maiestie by Ianvs.

In *The Pedlars' Masque* of 1574 the 'haberdasher of small ware' is paid as follows for the contents of the pedlars' packs :

ffrenche pynnes & greate pynnes	. .	ix^s
Sylk poyntes Brayded 18 dozen	. .	xxj^s
White & sweete Inglish balls j dozen	.	vj^s
Gloves perfvmed ij dozen price	. .	xxviij^s
sylk Twyst to tye the papers	. . .	xij^d
Laces of sylke iiij doozen price	. .	xijs.
Venis Balls sweete j doozen	. .	xvj^s
Staves bowght of Carow j dozen	.	ij^s vj^d
ffayer wryting of pozies for the Mask	.	vj^s viij^d

Autolycus' stock in *The Winter's Tale* should be carefully compared ; the pedlars no doubt plied among the Court ladies, each of whom would receive a posy with her present.

Other items throw some light on the manufacture of the properties : 'for wooll to stuf the fishes' for *The Fishers' Masque*, 'xij^d'; 'for twoe lambes—v^s' to the

CANDACE in *The Masque of Queenes*
by Inigo Jones

basketmaker, who made them out of twigs ; ' dishes for
devells eyes, heaven, hell, and the devell and all, the
devell I should saie but not all.'   So the Clerk of the
Revels, aiming at humour but on second thoughts fearing
the auditor, rounds off a miscellaneous list of properties.[1]
In 1571 John Izarde received 22s. for ' his device in coun-
terfeting Thunder and Lightning in the playe of Narcisses '—evidently an improvement on the vulgar squib.
Another significant attempt at realism in this play is the
payment of 21s. 8d. to John Tryce

for mony to him due for Leashes, & Doghookes, with staves, &
other necessaries : by him provyded for the hunters that made
the crye after the fox (let loose in the Coorte) with theier howndes,
hornes, and hallowing, in the playe of narcisses. which crye was
made, of purpose even as the woordes then in utteraunce, & the
parte then played, did Requier.

Ten shillings was paid in 1578–9

ffor A hoope and blewe Lynnen cloth to mend the clowde that was
Borrowed and cut to serve the rock in the plaie of the burnyng
knight and for the hire thereof and setting upp the same where it
was borrowed.

Clouds were worked up and down, and ' steered ' by
pulleys ; and double girths were used ' to hange the soon
in the Clowde '. Canvas was used ' for howses for the
players and for other properties as Monsters, greate hollow
trees ' ; a very elaborate property of this kind, purchased
in April 1581, was ' The Mounte, Dragon with yᵉ fyer
woorkes, Castell with yᵉ falling sydes Tree with shyldes,
hermytage & hermytt, Savages, Enchaunter, Charryott,
& incydentes to theis ', which cost £133 6s. 8d.

THE ART OF INIGO JONES

A performance at the Court of Elizabeth was thus a
splendid and lavish spectacle : under her successor it was
something more ; the genius of Inigo Jones gave it the
crowning touch of art. Beginning with *The Masque of
Blacknesse* in 1605 and ending with Davenant's *Salmacida
Spolia* in 1640, he staged twenty-seven masques. The
main period of his activity lies outside the scope of the
present book, and he influenced the Restoration stage,
not the stage of Shakespeare. So only a brief notice is

[1] From the Accounts of 1574–5, ed. Feuillerat, p. 241.

attempted, based on the designs for dresses and scenery in the Duke of Devonshire's collection at Chatsworth ; eight of these sketches for the legendary and historic figures of *The Masque of Queenes* furnish illustrations for the present chapter. These are the designs for Penthesilea the Amazon, Atalanta, and Camilla, all from classical poetry ; and for the historical characters : Artemisia, queen of Caria ; Thomyris, queen of Scythia ; Candace, queen of Aethiopia ; Berenice, queen of Egypt ; and Zenobia, queen of Palmyra. 'These habits', says Ben Jonson in his acknowledgement to Inigo, 'had in them the excellency of all device and riches, and were worthily varied by his invention to the nations whereof they were queens.' Three colours are employed for each dress ; when used uniformly, they are for the bodice, the ' bases ' or outer skirt, and the petticoat. The bases are overlaid with ' labels ' or hanging strips of cloth, sometimes fringed or in the form of a leaf—a favourite device in Inigo's schemes of costume. He has varied it with broad labels below the bases in the dress of Camilla with its exquisitely blent colours of willow, carnation, and white, where the willow tint and the leaf ornament convey a romantic suggestion of her ' forest maidenhood '. Where the colours blend and cross in intricate details of design, he gives the dress-maker minute directions, as in the sketch of Candace. The variety of costume which Jonson praises is seen in the classical and helmeted figure of Penthesilea, in the different Oriental patterns for the dresses of Berenice, Candace, and Zenobia, and in the marked suggestion of barbaric richness for that of the Scythian Thomyris. The sketch of Atalanta was not used ; another heroine of romance was substituted in the final scheme. The sketch for Queen Anne herself, ' of whose dignity and person, the whole scope of the invention doth speak throughout ', has not survived : it would be interesting to see the design which was intended to be a consummation of such a group. Contrasted with the witches of the antimasque, and suddenly revealed in a shining palace under a reflection of jewelled lights, these exquisite figures show the artistic spirit which transformed the masque.

Other designs depict the allegorical figures or personifications so common in the masque. A frequent source

BERENICE in *The Masque of Queenes*
by Inigo Jones

of these is the *Iconologia* of Cesare Ripa, first published at Rome in 1593, and reissued with illustrations in 1603 and 1611. Each character is briefly described with suitable attributes or emblems. In *The Description, Speeches, and Songs, of The Lords Mask*, by Campion, Entheus, a type of poetic inspiration or ' poetic fury ',

was attired in a close cuirass of the antique fashion, bases with labels, a robe fastened to his shoulders and hanging down behind ; on his head a wreath of laurel, out of which grew a pair of wings ; in the one hand he held a book, and in the other a pen.

So he appears in Inigo's sketch. This is taken, with some modification, from Ripa's description of ' Furor poeticus ' ; Ripa's figure is nude and girt with ivy. This writer is constantly drawn upon for similar representations in the masques of Campion and Jonson.

Sometimes there are dramatic personifications of a type, such as the antimasque of twelve ' depraved Lovers ' in *Love's Triumph through Callipolis*, ' expressing their confused affections in the scenical persons and habits of the four prime European nations'. The sketches for ten of these have been preserved ; the ' angry quarrelling Lover ' is a Spanish captain, and the ' fantastic umbrageous Lover ' a scaramouch. This set drew its inspiration from Jacques Callot, and especially from some of the figures in his *Balli di Sfessania*. The ' glorious boasting Lover ' is an exact copy of Callot's ' Cap. Cerimonia ' ; others are adaptations, or only partial borrowings. The Callot group are familiar figures of Italian comedy, and Inigo followed up this suggestion. In Jonson's masque the Lovers leap forth ' with antic gesticulation and action after the manner of the old Pantomimi ', and have ' a Mistress leading them '.

The designs for scenery are exceptionally interesting. A few of them bear traces of having passed through the hands of the scene-painter ; they are splashed with spots of paint. The main characteristic of these sketches is their strongly marked Italian influence. Inigo evidently studied with great care the entertainments of the Florentine and other ducal courts and the working methods of the Italian theatre. A succinct notice of the latter is given in the *Libro Secondo d'Architettura* of Sebastiano Serlio, first published at Venice in 1566 and reissued later in various forms : one version, ' Translated out of Italian into Dutch, and out of Dutch into English', was printed in London in 1611 'at the charge of Robert Peake'. Three scenes—tragic, comic, and satyric—are described and illustrated in the chapter 'Of Perspective'. 'A street in perspective of fair buildings discovered' opens Jonson's *Vision of Delight*; Serlio's tragic scene with 'none but stately houses' leading up to a triumphal arch in the distance indicates the type. He explains the construction—use laths covered with linen, but wood when it is 'necessary to make some things rising or bossing out', painted cloths in the background, and 'All that you make above the Roofe sticking out, as Chimneyes, Towers, Piramides, Obilisces, . . . you must make them all of thin bords, cut out round, and well colloured'. Inigo's mechanism was rather to employ 'shutters', or wings, as we should now call them, running in grooves above and below and pushed out in a projecting series.

Serlio's satyric scene is a pattern often used for the masque—a woodland with cottages set among trees and a slightly winding path running up the centre of the stage. He writes with a naïve rapture of the scenes made by Jeronimo Genga for the Duke of Urbino :

> Oh good Lord, what magnificence was there to be seene, for the great number of Trees and Fruits, with sundry Herbes and Flowres, all made of fine Silke of divers collors. The water courses being adorned with Frogs, Snailes, Tortuses, Toads, Adders, Snakes, and other beasts : Rootes of Corrale, mother of Pearle, and other shels layd and thrust through betweene the stones, with so many severall and faire things, that if I should declare them all, I should not have time inough.

Inigo Jones had not only Italian precedents to guide him ; he had a personal knowledge of the country, which he twice visited. His careful studies of its architecture and his predilection for the art of Palladio are faithfully reflected in his theatrical designs, especially in palaces, forums, and temples—such as the gorgeous Palace of Oberon for Jonson's masque. The House of Fame in *The Masque of Queenes* unfortunately survives only in Jonson's description, but one feature of the design has a special interest : 'for the lower columns', says Jonson, 'he chose the statues of the most excellent poets, as Homer, Virgil, Lucan, &c. . . . For the upper, Achilles, Aeneas,

ZENOBIA in *The Masque of Queenes*
by Inigo Jones

Caesar, and those great heroes which these poets had celebrated.' He actually used this device in 1619 in his great design for rebuilding Whitehall, where as a variation on the rectangular courts he planned a circular corridor two stories high with Caryatides in the upper range and Persians in the lower instead of pillars or pilasters ; the Persian figures had Tuscan capitals above their heads, the Caryatides Corinthian capitals. Some masque or play, not now to be identified, laid the scene in the Forum at Rome. Inigo's sketch of the Forum is preserved at Chatsworth, as well as his adaptation of it for stage purposes, regrouping the architectural details so as to allow a middle space and exits and entrances for the actors.

Some of the pastoral landscapes are very beautiful : for instance, the opening scene of *Chloridia*,

consisting of pleasant hills, planted with young trees, and all the lower banks adorned with flowers ; and from some hollow parts of those hills fountains come gliding down, which in the far off land-shape seemed all to be converted to a river. Over all a serene sky with transparent clouds giving a great lustre to the whole work, which did imitate the pleasant spring.

Or pure fancy is employed, as in some of the scenes for Davenant's *Luminalia*—the cloudy night-piece with the moon, which opens the masque ; the ' new and strange prospect of Chimeras ', and ' the City of Sleep ', which form parts of the second scene. Or there is the effective contrast of a homely scene as in Davenant's *Britannia Triumphans*, where the ' Giant's Castle ' is followed by a set of English houses with a distant view of London and the Thames.

There are a few examples of what Inigo calls a ' Border of the Scene '—the picture-frame which originated the modern proscenium and entirely changed the setting of plays. Thus there is the border for Townshend's *Albion's Triumph*, as the masque describes it :

The first thing that presented itself to the eye was the Ornament that went about the Scene : in the midst of which was placed a great armes of the King's, with angels holding an imperial crown, from which hung a drapery of crimson velvet fringed with gold, tackt in several knots, that on each side with many folds was wound about a pilaster ; in the freeze were festoons of several fruits in their natural colours, on which in gracious postures lay children sleeping ; at each end was a double shield with a Gorgon's

head, and at the foot of the pilasters on each side stood two women,
the one young, in a watchet robe, looking upwards, and on her
head a paire of compasses of gold, the points standing towards
heaven ; the other more ancient, and of a venerable aspect, apparelled in tawny, looking downwards ; in the one hand a long
ruler, and in the other a great pair of iron compasses, one point
whereof stood on the ground, and the other touched part of the
ruler. Above their heads were fixed compartments of a new composition, and in that over the first was written *Theorica*, and over
the second *Practica*, shewing that by these two all works of architecture and engining have their perfection.

That is not only Inigo's design, but beyond a doubt Inigo's
wording inserted by Townshend in the text. One can
imagine the language of Jonson, who had been displaced
at Court by Townshend through Inigo's influence, if he
had seen that proscenium ; he would have regarded it
as a shameless effort at self-advertisement on the part of
the master-mechanic. For these distinguished collabo-
rators quarrelled hopelessly over the relative importance
of their rival contributions. In the literary manifesto on
the masque which he wrote as a kind of preface to *Hymenaei*,
Jonson drew a sharp distinction between the ' body ' and
the ' soul ' of the device, between the lasting impression of
' things subjected to understanding ' and the transitory
nature of ' those which are objected to sense ', and urged
that his royal patrons were not only rightly ' studious
of riches and magnificence in the outward celebrations ',
but ' curious after the most high and hearty inventions, . . .
grounded upon antiquity and solid learnings '. Inigo,
doubtless with the Court to back him, had a low opinion
of these ' removed mysteries '. He found in Davenant and
Townshend associates at once more pliant and less literary.
Probably he gave ample provocation, but he was justified
in resenting any slur upon the beauty and the sincerity of
his art. Jonson's scathing line,

Painting and carpentry are the soul of masque,

admitted of a simpler interpretation than he realized.

BIBLIOGRAPHY.—The Masques are best studied in the actual texts, which
usually add elaborate descriptions of the scenery and costume : in CAMPION's
Description of a Masque . . . in honour of the Lord Hayes and his Bride
1607, there is a copper-plate engraving of a masquer as a Knight of Apollo.
For editions up to the Civil War see W. W. GREG's *A List of Masques
Pageants, &c.*, published by the Bibliographical Society, 1902 ; a series of
texts in the order of performance is included in NICHOLS's *Progresses of Queen*

Elizabeth, 3 vols., 1823, and *Progresses of King James I*, 4 vols., 1828 ; H. A. EVANS in his *English Masques*, 1897, reprints a selection of sixteen masques with an introductory essay.

Documents relating to the Court drama are reprinted in J. |S. BREWER's and J. GAIRDNER's *Letters and Papers of the Reign of Henry VIII* ; A. FEUILLERAT's *Documents relating to the Revels at Court in the time of King Edward VI and Queen Mary* (*The Loseley Manuscripts*), and *Documents relating to the Office of the Revels in the time of Queen Elizabeth*, vols. xliv and xxi in Bang's *Materialien zur Kunde des älteren englischen Dramas*, 1914 and 1908 ; P. CUNNINGHAM's *Extracts from the Accounts of the Revels at Court in the Reigns of Queen Elizabeth and King James I*, Shakespeare Society, 1842.

The special works on the history and character of the Masque are O. A. SOERGEL's *Die englischen Maskenspiele*, 1882 ; R. BROTANEK's *Die englischen Maskenspiele*, 1902 ; and PAUL REYHER's *Les Masques anglais*, 1909. The last is very full and interesting. *Court Masques of James I*, by MARY SULLIVAN, 1913, is also a good study of this period. See also E. K. CHAMBERS's *The Mediæval Stage*, vol. i, ch. xvii, ' Masks and Misrule ' ; and the article on ' Masque and Pastoral ' by RONALD BAYNE in *The Cambridge History of English Literature*, vol. vi, ch. xiii.

E. K. CHAMBERS's *Notes on the History of the Reve s Office under the Tudors*, and A. FEUILLERAT's *Le Bureau des Menus-Plaisirs* (*Office of the Revels*) *et la mise en scène à la cour d'Elisabeth*, 1910, elucidate the history of the office.

For Inigo Jones consult P. CUNNINGHAM's *Life*, Shakespeare Society, 1848 : it contains 14 plates in facsimile, |not very happily chosen, of the sketches at Chatsworth ; the first plate of the ' Pilgrim ', absurdly described as Romeo, is Genorio, ' a voted Pilgrim ', in Walter Montagu's *The Shepherds' Paradise*. R. T. BLOMFIELD in *The Portfolio*, nos. 233–5, May to July 1889, criticized the Chatsworth sketches, with two illustrations ; W. J. LAWRENCE in *The Elizabethan Playhouse*, 1912, pp. 99–108, ' The Mounting of the Carolan Masques ', deals with Inigo's scenery and reproduces five designs now in the Royal Institute of British Architects. W. G. KEITH in *The Burlington Magazine*, vol. xxv, pp. 29–33, 85–98, ' The Designs for the first movable Scenery on the English Public Stage ' connects John Webb's staging of Davenant's *The Siege of Rhodes*, with Inigo Jones. Webb was Inigo's pupil.

XXVII

SPORTS AND PASTIMES

§ 1. HUNTING

BY

THE HON. J. W. FORTESCUE

IT is somewhat singular that the English, who pride themselves above all things upon their keenness in the chase, should know little of the manner in which it was pursued by their ancestors. Writers upon the subject fall back invariably, for want of better material, upon *The Boke of St. Albans,* the two pieces entitled *The Craft of Hontyng* and *The Maystre of Game,*[1] and the *Noble Arte of Venerie or Hunting* of George Turbervile, published in 1575. All of these, except the last, may be traced back to a single work by Gaston Phœbus, Count of Foix ; and the last is little more than a translation of *La Vénerie de Jacques du Fouilloux,* published in 1561, which, though superior to anything that had appeared before it, acknowledges many debts to the great Gaston aforesaid. We hardly recognize that all the refinements of venery, so far as we know them, are borrowed from France. The sounds of the horn, such as the mort and the recheat, are French. The noises of the voice are corruptions from the French, ' tally-ho ' from *theau le hau* or *thia hillaud,* ' illo ' or eleu from *illeoques,* and ' soho '[2] (according to the old treatises) from *sahow.* Even the word 'quarry' is but the French *curée* metamorphosed into English. Yet the English had their own methods, and for that matter even a few technical terms of their own, and it is needless to say that they preferred them to any other. In 1521, Francis the First of France gave the English Ambassador, Fitzwilliam, special

---

[1] Manuscripts of this work exist in the Cotton collection in the British Museum, and in the Digby collection in the Bodleian.

[2] ' Soho ' signifies a view of the game in *Two Gent.* III. i. 189; *Rom. and Jul.* II. iv. 139.

VENATIO.

Ioan. Stradi Academi. Florentin. figurauit.   Raphael. Sadeler scalp. et excud.

At Rex, ne innenum incipiant frigescere vires,   Venatu muggilet, pubemq; exercuat aruis.   Ille autem arcte alios pernix uolet equore, nec sit
Vix. olea. ittexlit dum redimita comas,   Per uga sit ludus cursu agitare feras.   Tramare incolitus flumina magna labor.

THE CHASE by JOANNES STRADANUS

facilities for learning the French manner of 'harbouring and hunting the hart'; and Fitzwilliam liked the English manner better, especially in the matter of harbouring. 'Nevertheless,' he added, ' I assure Your Grace they knew their deer right well, as well by his view, feeding and fewmishing, as also by such other tokens as a woodman should have.' [1]

Wherein then did the English practice differ from the French ? There is a series of passages in Ben Jonson's *Sad Shepherd* which should help us to answer the question, and are worth quotation, if only as a text of this essay :—

> Here 's Little John hath harboured you a deer,
> I see by his tackling.   *John.* And a hart of ten
> I trow he be, Madam, or blame your men.
> For by his slot, his entries and his port,
> His frayings, fewmets, he doth promise sport
> And standing 'fore the dogs. He bears a head
> Large and well-beamed, with all rights summed and spread.
> *Marian.* Let 's rouse him quickly and lay on the hounds. (i. ii)
> *Robin.* Had you good sport i' your chase to-day ? *Jo.* Oh, prime.
> *Mar.* A lusty stag. *Rob.* And hunted ye at force ?
> *Mar.* In a full cry. *Jo.* And never hunted change.
> *Rob.* You had staunch hounds then ? *Mar.* Old and sure, I love
> Not young rash dogs, no more than changing friends.
> *Rob.* What relays set you ? *Jo.* None at all ; we laid not
> In one fresh dog. *Rob.* He stood not long then ? *Scarlett.* Yes.
> Five hours and more ; a great large deer. *Rob.* What head?
> *Jo.* Forked ; a hart of ten. . . .
> *Mar.* . . . He that undoes him [the deer]
> Doth cleave the brisket bone, upon the spoon
> Of which a little gristle grows.   (i. vi)

The reader must be patient while this passage is subjected to analysis. In the first place it must be explained that the harbouring of a deer is the process of woodcraft whereby the lair of the largest stag discoverable in a wood is ascertained, so that he and no other may be hunted ; for the largest stag will be in all probability the fattest stag, and the fatter the stag the more easily will he be tired to death— a serious consideration in the days when hounds were always slow and never in good condition. The French method of harbouring was, and apparently is, to use a very keen-scented but mute hound in a leash, called 'limier ', which word was represented in English by 'lyam' or 'lyme

---

[1] *Cal. State Papers : Foreign and Domestic*, vol. iii, pt. i, no. 1160.

hound'. The English method, which is still in full practice in North Devon and West Somerset, is to work solely by the slot or footprint of the animal, tracking a stag carefully into a covert, and casting round about on paths or tracks habitually followed by deer, to be sure that he has not left it. This must be done with extreme wariness, lest the stag catch the wind of the harbourer and shift his position. It is true that the existence of the word 'lyam', or 'lym' (*Lear* III. vi. 72), points to the employment of a hound for harbouring in England also; and the phrase 'draw dryfoot' in the passage 'a hound that runs counter and yet ¦draws dryfoot well' (*Com. of E.* IV. ii. 39) hints at the work of a lym, which has often to carry forward a very stale scent from footprint to footprint. But the word 'lym' is of rare occurrence, and its omission from the passage under review is significant.

The slot, the entries, the port and the frayings and the fewmets are all tokens of woodcraft by which the size and weight of a deer may be judged. The footprint itself gives indications through its width and other signs. The entries are the marks, such as bent grass or broken twigs, made by a deer as he brushes through covert, and enabling the woodcraftsman to estimate how high he stands on the leg and how high he is in the side, for a great stag is a broad deer and a tall deer. The port is the sign that is given by the width of his head, that is to say of his horns. If branches or twigs far apart are scarred by his head, then his head is well-spread and likely to belong to an old stag. The frayings are the marks made by an old stag when he frays the velvet off the newly grown horn against a tree. If he be a tall deer with a great head, 'large and well beamed', that is to say wide and heavy of bone, the marks will be high up, and will score so deeply into the bark as even to kill the tree. Therefore fraying marks on a young sapling are never those of an old deer, who chooses something stouter to stand the wear and tear. The fewmets or fewmishings are the droppings of the deer, from which the old French woodcraftsmen professed themselves able to draw many conclusions.

Not one of these words—harbour, slot, entries, port, fraying, fewmishings—is to be found, in the sporting sense, anywhere in Shakespeare. Are we then to infer that rare

THE NOBLE ARTE OF
VENERIE OR HVNTING.

VVherein is handled and set out the Vertues, Nature, and Properties of fiuetene sundrie Chaces togither, with the order and maner
how to Hunte and kill euery one of them.

Translated and collected for the pleasure of all Noblemen and Gentlemen, out of the best approued Authors, which haue written any thing
concerning the same : And reduced into such order and proper termes
as are vsed here, in this noble Realme of England.

The Contentes vvhereof shall more playnely appeare in
the Page next followyng.

Ben Jonson knew more of hunting than did Shakespeare ?
Just the contrary.   Jonson knew nothing of woodcraft,
and must have copied the whole of the words out of a book
of sport, probably *The Noble Arte of Venerie*.   No man who
knew anything of harbouring would have adduced all the
possible signs of woodcraft in reference to a single deer,
for it is most unusual to encounter all of them on one day.
The frayings indeed occur but once a year.   Moreover, there
was no occasion for all these tokens, for Jonson's harbourer
had seen the stag with his eyes ;   otherwise he could not
have told that he ' had all rights summed and spread ' ;
and if the head were such as he described, that would be
sufficient to show him a good stag.   The rest of the passage
is equally the result of book-learning.   The stag was
' a lusty one, a great large deer '.   In that case he should
not have stood up for very long, even when hunted ' at
force ', that is to say not driven into a net or an enclosure
from which he could not escape, but fairly run to a stand-
still.   But on the contrary he stood up for five hours and
a half.[1]   The obvious inference is that he must have turned
up other deer—a very common trick with old stags.   But
we are met with the assertion that the hounds never
' hunted change ', that is to say that they never forsook
the line of their hunted deer for a fresh one.   This was
highly creditable to them, for it is not every hound that will
carry the scent of a hunted deer through that of the herd
and single him out from his fellows ;[2] so we may infer that
they were all old hounds, old and sure, such as our ancestors
delighted in.   It is true that relays were not employed, that
is to say that no fresh hounds were loosed upon the line after
the deer had been running for some time, in which case,
they, having spent none of their strength, whereas he would
have spent at any rate some measure of it, would have
pressed him more sharply.   Yet Jonson makes Will Scarlett
opine that the absence of relays would rather shorten than

---

[1] This is none the less no extravagant time for a deer to be on foot, if scent,
for any reason, be bad.   I have myself seen a deer chased for seven hours ;
and Francis I of France once chased one for nine hours.   *Cal. State Papers,*
iv. 1 ; no. 2136.

[2]   Single you thither then this dainty doe,

(*Tit. Andr.* II. i. 117)

says Aaron of Lavinia, and

Now, Clifford, I have singled thee alone,

says Richard exultingly at Towton field (3 *Hen. VI.* II, iv. 1).

lengthen the chase ; and assuredly Will knew better than that.

Finally this great large stag, when brought to bay, carried only ten points, ' forked, a hart of ten ' ; that is to say no more than sufficed to proclaim him a ' warrantable deer ' and to raise him above the herd of ' rascal '.[1] It is, however, significant that these very words, ' forked,' ' a hart of ten ' are precisely those, translated from the French, which are to be found in *The Boke of St. Albans* and in *The Noble Arte*. Jonson, however, had previously spoken of all his ' rights summed and spread '. Now a deer's rights (the three lower antlers, brow, bay, and trey) are

[1] The rascal, according to *The Maystre of Game*, includes all small deer with fewer than ten points. Shakespeare's use of the word is peculiar :

> Horns ? Even so. Poor men alone ? No, no ; the noblest deer hath
> them as huge as the rascal. (*A. Y. L.* III. iii. 58–60)

> Thou rascal, that art worst in blood to run,
> Lead'st first to win some vantage. (*Cor.* I. i. 165–6)

Reading these quotations together with the speech of John Talbot quoted a little lower down, it is plain that Shakespeare conceived of ' rascal ' as a deer with a great head and a small body, who would neither fight nor run. Such deer, though not unknown (Judge Madden quotes a remarkable instance, p. 228, n.) are very uncommon, though it is by no means unusual for a deer past his prime to carry an inferior head on a very large body. Shakespeare's rascal would be at a great disadvantage, for deer fight by shoving before they come to goring ; and here the light weight of his body would place him at the mercy of a stag of heavier frame. Moreover, the enormous mass of bone upon his head (there is a pair of horns, pictured to scale, in the Dresden Gallery, which are seven feet long) with no sufficient strength of body to carry it, would make such deer weak and helpless. Hence the legitimate conclusion that he could neither run far nor fight well ; for he would be overweighted and overbalanced by his head. He might very likely be in the foremost place in a herd, for, when a herd is moved, the hinds and young male deer always move in front, and the big stags bring up the rear ; but he could never bully anything bigger than a four-year-old. Judge Madden comments (pp. 228–9) on the intimate knowledge of woodcraft betrayed by Touchstone's speech ' Horns ? Even so, &c.', and adds ' it needs a wary and a practised eye to detect the rascality of the big-horned, self-assertive brute who to win some vantage thrusts himself in front of the herd ; and herein consists the woodman's art '. Undoubtedly Touchstone betrays knowledge of woodcraft in being aware that such peculiar deer existed ; but an abnormally large head upon a small body is an object which would strike even a comparatively unpractised eye. If Touchstone could have detected a rascal of this kind by his slot, the case would be different ; but Shakespeare seems to have known nothing of this all-important branch of woodcraft. It may be questioned if Shakespeare was correct in using the word ' rascal ' only in this restricted sense ; and if the term be extended to its legitimate limits, so as to cover all young male deer, then Shakespeare's similes are false ; for a young stag (as the sportsmen of the day well knew) can and will run better than any other, and can fight savagely enough if he husbands some strength for the bay ; which, however, as a rule he does not. The reasons are stated below for thinking that Shakespeare was more familiar with fallow than with red deer. But in any case it is dangerous to press his similes too far.

not and cannot be spread; they are almost invariably single tines and very rarely bifurcated; while the word ' summed ' was used properly only of the heads that bore four or more points on the top, that is to say of harts of at least fourteen. In fact the poet, like a modern journalist, had hastily prepared his subject from a book, and, eager to show the extent of his knowledge, had crammed in every detail which he could gather, with the result only of exposing his entire ignorance of the whole matter.

Two things, however, are noteworthy. Jonson must have been told that the lymar was not generally used in England, or he would certainly have stolen some technical terms concerning that hound's work. He must also have learned from some source the expression ' rights ', which is purely English, and not to be found in any text-book of French origin.

So much must be said of the insufficiency of Jonson to give us an idea of the chase in the time of Elizabeth; and in truth it is not clear how his shortcomings are to be made good. None the less beyond all doubt our ancestors did pursue the chase heartily, though according to no fixed rules. They used every kind of method and every kind of dog; they exchanged presents of hounds when they felt friendly; and they sometimes poached upon each other's manors when they felt otherwise. Thus Leicester gave a hound to Burghley, which Burghley commended mightily. ' She maketh my huntyng very certain,' he wrote; ' she hath never failed me; and this last weke she brought me to a stagg wh. myself had strycken with my bow, being forced to the soyle [that is to say the water, always the refuge of a deer hard-pressed], wher w^t help of a gretar water spannyell yt forced hym out of the water; your good brache [1] helped to pluck hym down.' Leicester himself was equally keen as a sportsman, and describes himself and his company at Theobalds as 'altogether hunters, doing nothing but ride about from bush to bush with a cross-bow about their necks '. Lastly (if the intrusion of family affairs may be forgiven) Mr. John Fortescue [2] found Lord Grey poaching upon his manor of Salden, and, after his keepers

---

[1] ' Brach ' by this time had grown to be synonymous with ' bitch '.

[2] Queen Elizabeth's cousin, and tutor; later Sir John and Chancellor of the Exchequer.

and Lord Grey's had exchanged broken heads, carried complaint of the matter to the King.[1]

But the thing for which our ancestors cared most was that their venison should be good fat meat. It was to this

From Turbervile, *The Noble Arte of Venerie*, 1575.

A Huntsman, presenting the Fewmets of a Hart, makes his Report

end that woodcraft busied itself over the tokens of a fat stag ; and that, when once he had been harboured, no means were despised for doing him to death. The prettiest work of hunting hounds in the world is that of a pack when a deer has 'beat the water ', that is to say, followed a stream up or down, thereby drowning all scent. Our ances-

[1] *Calendar State Papers : Domestic*, ann. 1547, 1580, pp. 448, 467–8, 472.

tors seem to have known nothing of all this. Burghley, when he was in difficulties with a deer in the water, sent for a water spaniel.

Our forefathers, when pursuing the chase, for the sake of sport preferred the most cunning of all hunted animals, the hare. This view is amply supported by Shakespeare. His knowledge of deer was considerable, but his experience of the chase of the deer, with hounds only, seems not to have been great. It is true that he compares Achilles sulking in his tent to a stag that refuses to leave covert:

> The hart Achilles
> Keeps thicket;   (*Troilus* II. iii. 272–3)

but of harbouring and the true refinements of the art of venery, which might have supplied him with many images, he says nothing. On the other hand, he knew all about driving deer into nets or enclosures from which they could not escape; and had undoubtedly seen game fall to his own cross-bow as well as to those of other men.

> Why do you go about to recover the wind of me, as if you would drive me into a toil?

says Hamlet (III. ii. 368–9); and John Talbot, surrounded by the enemy before Bordeaux, breaks out likewise into the language of sport:

> How are we park'd and bounded in a pale,
> A little herd of England's timorous deer,
> Maz'd with a yelping kennel of French curs!
> If we be English deer, be then, in blood;
> Not rascal-like to fall down with a pinch,
> But rather moody-mad and desperate stags,
> Turn on the bloody hounds with heads of steel,
> And make the cowards stand aloof at bay.
> (*1 Hen. VI*, IV. ii. 45–52)

Shakespeare must have seen many a deer, red or fallow, at bay, and heard the maddening clamour of horns and hounds; but always, no doubt, like a true sportsman, with sympathy for the victim. So Antony apostrophizes the corpse of Caesar:

> Here wast thou bay'd, brave hart,
> Here didst thou fall; and here thy hunters stand,
> Sign'd in thy spoil, and crimson'd in thy lethe.
> (*Jul. Cæs.* III. i. 204–6)

Here speaks the man who has seen a large field, stained, as was the custom, with the blood of the hunted stag, not the man of books, Jonson, who gives perfectly correct details about making the first cut into a deer's brisket.

But Shakespeare knew not many sounds of the horn. He speaks once of a recheat—the sound for calling hounds together—but only allusively (*Much Ado* I. i. 251), and once of the mort, which is used as a simile for a sigh (*Wint. Tale* I. ii. 119), perhaps because the mort consisted of a series of two notes, the first short and the second long. He was more at home with bow and cross-bow, shooting at driven deer, than chasing them to bay (*3 Hen. VI*, v. i. 65, *Rich. II*, II. iii. 128).

> *First Keeper.* Under this thick-grown brake we'll shroud ourselves ;
> For through this laund anon the deer will come ;[1]
> And in this covert will we make our stand,
> Culling the principal of all the deer.
> *Sec. K.* I'll stay above the hill, so both may shoot.
> *First K.* That cannot be ; the noise of thy cross-bow
> Will scare the herd ; and so my shoot is lost.
> Here stand we both, and aim we at the best.
> (3 Hen. VI, III. i. 1–8)

And Shakespeare was so good a sportsman that he hated to wound an animal. Thus the Prince in *Love's Labour's Lost* says :—

> But come, the bow : now mercy goes to kill,
> And shooting well is then accounted ill.
> Thus will I save my credit in the shoot :
> Not wounding, pity would not let me do't.   (IV. i. 24–7)

Moreover, he knew the fate of the wounded deer, or for that matter of the deer distressed in the chase ; for both alike are driven out of the herd. Thus Lavinia is described as

> straying in the park,
> Seeking to hide herself, as doth the deer,
> That hath receiv'd some unrecuring wound.
> (Tit. Andr. III. i. 89–

And there is the famous picture of the stricken deer that had, as is invariably the case, sought the water :—

> Under an oak whose antique root peeps out
> Upon the brook that brawls along this wood ;

[1] The constancy with which deer will follow the same paths or tracks through century after century is very remarkable. The writer has been witness to the fact on Exmoor ; and has been told that the spot where William Rufus was killed in the New Forest is still an excellent point of vantage for seeing, and, if necessary, shooting deer.

> To the which place a poor sequestered stag,
> That from the hunter's aim had ta'en a hurt,
> Did come to languish.   (*A. Y. L.* II. i. 31–5) [1]

Upon the whole, looking to his entire omission of many well-known terms of woodcraft, the writer inclines to the opinion that Shakespeare was more familiar with fallow than with red deer. He uses the word 'pricket',[2] which is common to both kinds, but never 'brocket' nor 'hearst' for the adolescent stag and hind ; he speaks of does far more frequently than of hinds ; and he never mentions a hind and calf, though there is a touch which shows his knowledge of the ways of mother deer.

> Then but forbear your food a little while,
> Whiles, like a doe, I go to find my fawn
> And give it food.   (*A. Y. L.* II. vii. 127–9)

And this greater knowledge of fallow deer is just what we should have expected from a man who had stolen them in Charlecote Park, possibly with the connivance of Sir Thomas Lucy's keepers.

> 'Tis gold
> Which buys admittance ; oft it doth ; yea, and makes
> Diana's rangers false themselves, yield up
> Their deer to the stand o' the stealer.   (*Cymb.* II. iii. 72–5)

The bow and arrow must have been a convenient weapon for poachers, being noiseless; and greyhounds, running mute, were equally well adapted to the purpose. But, on the other hand,

> When night dogs run all sorts of deer are chas'd,
>   (*M. Wives* v. v. 264)

so that the poacher could not always be certain of carrying off good venison. There was, however, the delight of out-witting the custodian of the park after a successful foray in the early winter,

> What ! hast thou not full often struck a doe,
> And borne her cleanly by the keeper's nose ?
>   (*Tit. Andr.* II. i. 93–4)

---

[1] Judge Madden, upon the line that comes a little later,
          Left and abandoned of his velvet friends,
comments that the covering of the newly-grown antlers is called velvet. But surely the reference is rather to the sleek coats of the 'fat and greasy citizens' of the rest of the herd, as contrasted with the dull broken coat of the wounded stag. It adds nothing to the force of the passage that the male deer's horns were not clean ; but it adds much that their coats were sleek, signifying good health and condition.

[2] *Love's L. L.* IV. ii. 58–63, where the terms for a buck in its second, third, and fourth year (' pricket ', ' sorel ', and ' sore ') are all mentioned.

And there was always the chance of poaching, without risk, a deer that had broken out of the park—a deer that 'breaks the pale And feeds from home' (*Com. of E.* II. i. 100–1). Lastly there was the satisfaction of cutting up a

From Turbervile, *The Noble Arte of Venerie*, 1575.

An Assembly, made in the presence of Queen Elizabeth.

'bribed' or stolen buck quickly, so as to get it out of the way before the keepers could come up (*M. Wives* V. v. 27).

But enough of the deer : it is time now to turn to the chase of the hare, which shared with the hart, the boar, and the wolf the distinction of being a beast of venery. 'The Hare is the Kynge of all venerie,' says *The Maystre of*

Game, 'for al blowyng and the fair termys of huntynge commen of the seekyng and fyndyng of the hare, for certayn it is the most merveilost beest that is.' The fox was held in no such honour, being mere vermin to be hunted to earth and dug out without mercy.

It was Mr. Bagehot who was the first to remark that whatever else Shakespeare might or might not have done, he had certainly hunted the hare, and quoted in support of his contention the following stanzas from *Venus and Adonis* :

> But if thou needs wilt hunt, be rul'd by me ;
> Uncouple at the timorous flying hare,
> Or at the fox which lives by subtilty,
> Or at the roe which no encounter dare :
> Pursue these fearful creatures o'er the downs,
> And on thy well-breath'd horse keep with thy hounds.
>
> And when thou hast on foot the purblind hare,
> Mark the poor wretch, to overshoot his troubles
> How he outruns the winds, and with what care
> He cranks and crosses with a thousand doubles ;
> The many musets through the which he goes
> Are like a labyrinth to amaze his foes.
>
> Sometime he runs among a flock of sheep,
> To make the cunning hounds mistake their smell,
> And sometime where earth-delving conies keep,
> To stop the loud pursuers in their yell,
> And sometime sorteth with a herd of deer ;
> Danger deviseth shifts ; wit waits on fear :
>
> For there his smell with others being mingled,
> The hot scent-snuffing hounds are driven to doubt,
> Ceasing their clamorous cry till they have singled
> With much ado the cold fault cleanly out ;
> Then do they spend their mouths : Echo replies,
> As if another chase were in the skies.
>
> By this, poor Wat, far off upon a hill,
> Stands on his hinder legs with listening ear,
> To hearken if his foes pursue him still :
> Anon their loud alarums he doth hear ;
> And now his grief may be compared well
> To one sore sick that hears the passing-bell.
>
> Then shalt thou see the dew-bedabbled wretch
> Turn and return, indenting with the way ;
> Each envious briar his weary legs doth scratch,
> Each shadow makes him stop, each murmur stay :
> For misery is trodden on by many,
> And being low never reliev'd by any. (673–708)

There is little more to say about hare-hunting than is contained in these stanzas ; but it is worth while to dwell on the passionate love of the ancient sportsmen, from Xenophon and Gaston de Foix downward, for the cry of hounds. Indeed it seems to have been the fashion, to judge from the passage in *Titus Andronicus* (II. ii. 5), to begin the day with a 'hunter's peal'—that is to say with horn-blowing, which set the hounds' tongues into activity, and produced a pleasing din. Of all cries, it is a question whether that of beagles or bassets is the more striking. Shakespeare apparently preferred the deeper and more robust music of the bassets.

> *Hippolyta.* I was with Hercules and Cadmus once,
> When in a wood of Crete they bay'd the bear
> With hounds of Sparta ; never did I hear
> Such gallant chiding ; for, besides the groves,
> The skies, the fountains, every region near
> Seem'd all one mutual cry. I never heard
> So musical a discord, such sweet thunder.
> *Theseus.* My hounds are bred out of the Spartan kind,
> So flew'd, so sanded ; and their heads are hung
> With ears that sweep away the morning dew ;
> Crook-knee'd, and dew-lapp'd like Thessalian bulls ;
> Slow in pursuit, but match'd in mouth like bells,
> Each under each. A cry more tuneable
> Was never holla'd to, nor cheer'd with horn.
>
> (*Mid. N. D.* iv. i. 118–31)

The reference to the Spartan kind suggests that Shakespeare had read a Latin translation of Xenophon's *Cynegetica* ; but the ideal of 'mouths match'd like bells, Each under each', was originally put forward by Gaston de Foix, from whom it was copied by all subsequent writers ; being finally pushed to absurd lengths by that inveterate maker of books, Gervase Markham. Whether, beyond the employment of both sexes of hound, any great effort was made to make a pack into a choir (for Gaston considered the music of his pack to be at least as sweet as that which was to be heard in the King's Chapel) may well be doubted ; but that the cry was full and merry there can be no question. 'Crook-knee'd and dew-lapp'd,' the hounds may well have been 'slow in pursuit'. Probably they spent half their time sitting on their tails and howling. Yet they seem always to have been wild, for they were invariably taken to the hunt in couples.

> My love shall hear the music of my hounds.
> Uncouple in the western valley ; let them go :
>
> (*Mid. N. D.* IV. i. 112–13)

and the old packs needed, according to *The Maystre of Game*, prickers and other servants to ride at their tails and ' hold them in '. They had their vices too. Some would flash ahead, overrun and overtop the scent, and required to be ' trashed ', that is to say burdened with a long strap, like a pointer's check-cord, to bring them back to the body of the pack. There were bawlers who would throw their tongues before the hare was found, and babblers or brabblers who would do likewise when she had been found but when they had no scent of her.

> He will spend his mouth, and promise, like Brabbler the hound ; but when he performs, astronomers foretell it.   (*Troilus* V. i. 101–3)

There were untrue hunters, who would leave the sweet scent of a hare, and speak to the rank scent of a fox.

> Sowter will cry out upon 't, for all this, though it be as rank as a fox.   (*Tw. N.* II. v. 137–8)

But the crime of all crimes was to hunt counter or, as it is now called, ' heel ' ; a fault which might set the whole pack wrong in working out the doubles of a hare.

> How cheerfully on the false trail they cry !
> O ! this is counter, you false Danish dogs !
>
> (*Haml.* IV. v. 109–10)

says the Queen in *Hamlet*, when she hears that the rabble acclaims Laertes king. ' Hunting change ' is nearly as grave a fault as ' hunting counter '. The expression never occurs in the whole of Shakespeare's works ; but no certain inference can be drawn from this omission as to his knowledge of deer hunting.

But these hounds of old time had their virtues too, and their masters could appreciate them.

> *Lord.* Huntsman, I charge thee, tender well my hounds :
> Trash[1] Merriman, the poor cur is emboss'd,
> And couple Clowder with the deep-mouth'd brach.
> Saw'st thou not, boy, how Silver made it good
> At the hedge-corner, in the coldest fault ?
> I would not lose the dog for twenty pound.
> *First Hunt.* Why, Bellman is as good as he, my lord ;
> He cried upon it at the merest loss,

---

[1] The passage is corrupt, and ' trash ' is conjectural only. There is one undoubted instance of ' trash ' in Shakespeare, viz. *Temp.* I. ii. 81.

And twice to-day pick'd out the dullest scent :
Trust me, I take him for the better dog.
    Lord. Thou art a fool ; if Echo were as fleet,
I would esteem him worth a dozen such.
But sup them well, and look unto them all :
To-morrow I intend to hunt again.
                    (*Tam. Sh.* ind. i. 16–29)

This lord, as the 'hedge-corner' seems to indicate, had been hunting the hare. Here, then, we learn that when a hound was dead beat, which is the meaning of embossed, he was allowed to go to kennel uncoupled, but attached to a trash or check-cord, presumably to lead him by, for he can hardly have needed steadying. It is to be hoped that he was left at home next day, or he must have been, as was the case with Roderigo, 'not like a hound that hunts, but one that fills up the cry' (*Oth.* II. iii. 372–3). The 'deep-mouth'd brach' needs no further description, such a voice being unusual in her sex. If, as seems likely, she were a wise and steady old lady, we may assume that Clowder was a puppy. Echo was probably an old hound whose nose had survived his legs. Bellman seems to have combined good speed with a good nose, so that the huntsman may well have been justified in esteeming him the best of the pack. It is interesting to see how many of the names of the hounds mentioned by Shakespeare still survive, particularly Ringwood, Merriman, and Bellman, though Sowter, Clowder, Fury, Tyrant, Echo, Silver, and Mountain are more doubtful.[1] But in truth there is nothing new under the sun. Substitute the word fox for stag, and who would say that the following passage, written by Jacques du Fouilloux in the sixteenth century, had not been written in the twentieth ?

In these days I see that a stag is not hunted fairly nor according to his desert ; for men do not give hounds time to do their work, and so those are but two or three that carry the line of scent ; the more so that now there are so many men on horseback who know nothing of horn-blowing, hallooing, or riding to hounds. These ride among the hounds, crossing and scattering them so that they can neither run nor hunt, and therefore I say that it is the horses that do the hunting and not the hounds. Huntsmen nowadays take no

---

[1] Judge Madden doubts whether Mountain be not a misprint for Mounter ; but Mountain appears in the account of the trencher-fed pack in *Handley Cross* ; a fragment which is as excellent and as valuable for the history of the chase as anything outside Shakespeare.

pleasure in seeing hounds hunt. It is enough for them to see a stag taken and killed, so as to earn their masters' good pleasure and make their own profit, and when once a stag is roused, they desire nothing but his death, which was not the way of our forefathers.

Such a complaint is old as humanity itself :—

> Aetas parentum, peior avis, tulit
> Nos nequiores, mox daturos
> Progeniem vitiosiorem.

It is probably nearer to the truth that in all ages good sportsmen, like good men, are rarer than bad ; but good there have been in all times, and among the best of the sixteenth century we must certainly rank William Shakespeare.

BIBLIOGRAPHICAL NOTE.—As is stated in the body of this paper, our early works upon Venery are borrowed to all intent entirely from the works of Gaston Phœbus, Count of Foix, and of Jacques du Fouilloux ; and it is really unprofitable to take notice of any others. The names are given of the English writers who made, or are reputed to have made, translations or adaptations of them ; and there is no more to be said. Our ancestors borrowed from the French much of the terminology of the chase, but from their Norman conquerors and not from books. They may have borrowed some of the French methods also, but they changed them and wrought them up into new methods of their own, of which we know little and are unlikely ever to know much more. If any one desires to study an exhaustive bibliography of old works on the chase, he will find it in *Arrian on Coursing*, by a Graduate of Medicine, 1831 ; but if any reader supposes that by the study of these old books he will arrive at any knowledge of English Venery in the sixteenth century, or in any other century, he is greatly mistaken. We have practically no original literature of the chase until the eighteenth century, and it is idle to pretend that we have. The only original book on English woodcraft is C. PALK COLLYNS's *Notes on the Chase of the Wild Red Deer*, 1862, and even that is stuffed with extracts from Turbervile. BECKFORD's *Thoughts on Hare and Fox Hunting*, 1781, new edd. 1879, &c., is the parent of all subsequent works on the subject.

§ 2. FALCONRY

BY

The Hon. Gerald Lascelles

' Hawking,' wrote Richard Brathwait, a writer of the true Elizabethan temperament, in his *The English Gentleman*, 1630, ' is a pleasure for high mounting spirits ; such as will not stoope to inferiour lures, having their mindes so farre above, as they scorne to partake with them.'

' I have bought me a hawk and a hood and bells and all, says Master Stephen, the simple country squire, in Ben Jonson's *Every Man in his Humour* (i. i. 43 ff.) ; ' I lack nothing but a book to keep it by. . . . Why, you know an a man have not skill in the hawking and hunting language nowadays, I'll not give a rush for him.'

So great a hold had falconry taken upon the minds of country folk in Elizabethan times that its technical terms were habitual to ordinary conversation. To the reader or playgoer of Shakespeare's time the technical terms describing the training of hawks for the sport of falconry were household words.

But to follow with understanding the various technical phrases it is necessary to be somewhat familiar with the ordinary processes of training the hawks used in falconry, as laid down in the pages of contemporary manuals. In the main, these processes, with the terms applied to them, have been followed up to the present day, with perhaps a little improvement—taught partly by modern experience and partly by the knowledge gained by our intercourse with the East and our knowledge of Indian and Persian methods. For it must never be forgotten that falconry was essentially an Oriental sport, and the management of hawks an art that came into Europe from the East—at what date is unknown, but possibly before the Christian era.

The principal Elizabethan writer on falconry was the miscellaneous writer, George Turbervile, the first edition of whose *Booke of Faulconrie or Hauking for the onely delight and pleasure of all Noblemen and Gentlemen* appeared in 1575. A great part of this work was a reproduction of the mediaeval French works of Guilliaume Tardif and Jean de Franchières, just as most of Turbervile's *Noble Arte of Venerie* was a reproduction of Jacques du Fouilloux, woodcuts and all. Turbervile does not pretend to originality, but owns that his book is collected out of the best authors, as well Italians as Frenchmen, of whom he gives a list. The next work of importance is Simon Latham's *Falconry, or the Faulcons Lure and Cure in two Bookes*, the first book treating of ' all Hawkes in generall, especially the Haggard Faulcon gentle ', and the second book treating of diseases of hawks. An appendix dealt with all hawks unmentioned in the first book. Latham's work was first published in 1615, and is a genuine original work, though the author quotes largely from other works, all by foreigners. Another book of authority was *An Approved Treatise of Hawkes and Hawking*, by Edmund Bert, which came out in 1619. This is almost entirely original. It treats of the training of the short-winged hawks, viz. the goshawk and sparrowhawk. Bert was a gentleman who lived at Collier Row, near Romford, in Essex, and who seems to have been recognized as the great expert of his time, and also to have done no little dealing in his goshawks, for some of which he obtained large sums. Bert's book and Latham's are the standard English works of the seventeenth century, and embody the best hawking experience of Shakespeare's era.

In England, as in other countries, the stand-by of the falconer was that species which naturalists call the peregrine falcon, a bird of almost universal distribution, still a common breeder on our coasts, and, as the autumn migration sets in, widely distributed over Europe, where it is captured at various places. For centuries past the principal place where hawks have been captured as a matter of business is—as its name indicates—Valkenswaard, in Holland ; but no doubt in old days every falconer was on the look-out for the migratory flocks of birds with their attendant pirates, and captured the hawks as opportunity served. So also in modern times these hawks have been captured in Northamptonshire, in Wiltshire, and in Normandy, and they could probably be taken in small numbers in many other places.

To the modern falconer these peregrines are divided into

The Booke of Faulconrie or Hau-
KING, FOR THE ONELY DE-
light and pleasure of all Noblemen and Gentlemen:

Collected out of the best aucthors, asvvell Italians as Frenchmen,
and some English practises withall concernyng Faulconrie, the contentes
whereof are to be seene in the next page folowyng.
By *George Turberuile* Gentleman.
NOCET EMPTA DOLORE VOLVPTAS.

Imprinted at London for Christopher Barker, at the signe of
the Grashopper in Paules Churchyarde. *Anno.* 1575.

three kinds—the passage hawk, a hawk that is captured on migration after having preyed for itself ; the eyas, a hawk taken from the nest and reared by hand ; and the haggard, which is merely a passage hawk of mature age that has gone through at least one moult.   In Turbervile's time the subdivision was more minute.   The whole species went under the name of Falcon or Tercel gentle.

> Hist ! Romeo, hist ! O ! for a falconer's voice,
> To lure this tassel-gentle back again.
>
> (*Rom. & Jul.* II. ii. 158–9)

Turbervile's first subdivision was that of eyasses, i. e. hawks taken and reared entirely by hand from the eyrie.   In Shakespeare's time the modern practice of flying eyasses 'at hack' seems to have been unknown.   This 'hack' is a state of liberty which the young hawks enjoy for some fortnight or three weeks, being allowed to roam wherever they please so long as they return to the food set out for them and thus show that they have not learned to prey for themselves.   By this treatment modern eyasses are practically of the same class as Turbervile's second category of Ramage hawks,[1] which was formed of birds that have left the eyrie and flown at large, preying for themselves until the end of August.   Such hawks are more difficult to man and handle than the home-bred eyas, but ' whoso can use them with pacience and judgement shall find them passing good '.

Thirdly, there were Soar hawks, that is to say, hawks of the first year caught wild between the end of August and the end of November, the period of the autumn migration.   These hawks are the passage hawks of modern falconers, and have been considered in all times the best variety of hawk to train, having been wild long enough to be excellent at flying and capturing any wild quarry, yet not so old as to be very shy, stubborn, and difficult to train.   As Turbervile says, they ' are of good disposition and will do verye well and are in their prime and full pryde for beautie and goodnesse '.

Fourthly, there are 'Marzaroli', said to be an Italian designation for the same hawks caught between November and May ; they are said to be ' very tedious and paynefull ',

---

[1] ' Ramage is when a hawk is wild, coy or disdainful to man and contrary to be reclaimed.'   Simon Latham, *Hawking Terms.*

the reason being that they come at a time of year when it is difficult to do much work with them as their training progresses.

Fifthly, when caught between May and December of the year succeeding their birth they were called Entermewers, because their first moult was as yet incomplete, though commenced.

Lastly, when fully moulted at least once, they are called Haggards, and some early writers, and especially Latham, have an exceedingly high opinion of this class of the falcon gentle—rather more so than is entertained by modern practitioners.

It stands to reason that the longer a bird has been at large preying for herself, and possibly for a young brood also, the more care, skill, and trouble will be required to train her; she may even be untrainable, or more trouble to reclaim than she is worth. Many such have been known. Shakespeare often uses the term ' haggard ' to signify wildness and inconstancy :

> If I do prove her haggard,
> Though that her jesses were my dear heart-strings,
> I'd whistle her off and let her down the wind,
> To prey at fortune. *(Oth.* III. iii. 260–3)

And again :

> I know her spirits are as coy and wild
> As haggards of the rock. *(Much Ado* III. i. 35–6)

On the other hand, if a fine-tempered, naturally docile haggard be found, there is no great difficulty to a skilled hand in training her, except that it takes a long time to overcome that nervousness and dread of man which is ingrained in her. When the haggard is once trained the falconer finds himself with no amateur like the eyas, which needs first to be tamed and then taught how to fly, but with a professional expert that cannot be defeated by the shifts and artifices, or left behind by the speed, of any feathered fowl. Hence Latham, a great authority, but in this instance peculiar, extols the haggard, and places her before every other variety of hawk. Turbervile, on the other hand, gives the first place to the soar hawk, or passage falcon, and the second to the haggard.

Turbervile's verdict agrees exactly with the experience and practice of succeeding generations of falconers, although

Latham no doubt had some reason for forming so decided an opinion in the shape of some particular hawk or hawks of his own. Many a good haggard has been trained during the last few decades, but for all that there is more certainty of success with the soar hawk.

The first thing in the process of training was to affix to the legs of the hawk the jesses or short straps of leather which remain always on her, and by which she is held. Witness the quotation cited above, ' Though that her jesses were my dear heart-strings ' (*Oth.* III. iii. 261). In Shakespeare's time varvels or little rings of silver were attached to the ends of the jesses, and on these the name of the owner was often engraved. If a wild-caught hawk was taken she was at once seeled thus. A needle and fine thread was passed through the lower eyelid, which consists merely of thin skin insensible to pain, passed over the crown of her head, and through the lower eyelid of the other eye. By drawing the thread fairly tight, both eyes are nearly closed by the lower eyelids being drawn nearly over them. By loosely tying the thread and then twisting up the ends the eyes are kept nearly closed, and by loosening the twisted thread day by day a little more daylight is given, until the thread is entirely removed as training progresses. Shakespeare repeatedly employs this technical verb of seeling :

> The wise gods seel our eyes ;
> In our own filth drop our clear judgements ; make us
> Adore our errors.   (*Ant. & Cleop.* III. xi. 112–14)

Or again of Desdemona, who

> could give out such a seeming
> To seel her father's eyes up close as oak. (*Oth.* III. iii. 209–10)

Again, of sleep Henry IV says :

> Wilt thou upon the high and giddy mast
> Seel up the ship-boy's eyes, and rock his brains
> In cradle of the rude imperious surge. (*2 Hen. IV*, III. i. 18–20)

In addition to seeling, a hood was placed on the hawk's head to ensure her perfect quiescence when not taken on hand, the seeling being intended as a temporary control midway between the blindfolding of the hood, which is in constant use, and the glare of open day, which to a newly-caught hawk would be alarming. The hood was an object as familiar as the hawk itself. Juliet, appealing to night, says :

> Hood my unmann'd blood, bating in my cheeks,
> With thy black mantle ; till strange love, grown bold,
> Think true love acted simple modesty.
>
> (*Rom. & Jul.* III. ii. 14–16)

With hood, jesses, and varvels provided, the work of manning the hawk is begun. She must be taken on the fist, and gently stroked with a feather or hand until she begins to submit to such treatment. At first it may be she will flutter wildly or bate from the fist. Gently and quietly she must be replaced and handled till custom begets familiarity, and she begins to feed on the piece of meat held to her feet. Sometimes all does not go well, and she must be brought to her bearings by fatigue—never by starvation, for that is her ruin. She must be watched or kept awake at night till by sheer weariness she settles down into tameness and docility. No one has ever better described the process than Petruchio in *The Taming of the Shrew* (IV. i. 196–201) :

> Another way I have to man my haggard,
> To make her come and know her keeper's call ;
> That is, to watch her, as we watch these kites
> That bate and beat and will not be obedient.
> She eat no meat to-day, nor none shall eat ;
> Last night she slept not, nor to-night she shall not.

And Desdemona says :

> My lord shall never rest ;
> I'll watch him tame, and talk him out of patience.
>
> (*Oth.* III. iii. 22–3)

The man who undertakes the task of taming a haggard must make up his mind to sacrifice a good deal of his night's rest in the early stages of the process. Should all go well, however, in a few weeks our hawk will display no fear of men or dogs, even when bareheaded in the open air. A pair of bells of shrill tones will have been attached to her legs in anticipation of the day when she shall first be flown at quarry, and perchance bring it to ground amid thick covert, where she might long be searched for unsuccessfully without the aid of the bells. 'As the ox hath his bow, sir,' says Touchstone, ' the horse his curb, and the falcon her bells, so man hath his desires ' (*A. Y. L.* III. iii. 85–7).

Early falconers seem to have fancied that the sound of

the bells terrified the quarry crouching on the ground when the hawk was waiting overhead.   Thus

> Harmless Lucretia, marking what he tells
> With trembling fear, as fowl hear falcon's bells. (*Lucr.* 510–11)

And again :

> Neither the king, nor he that loves him best,
> The proudest he that holds up Lancaster,
> Dares stir a wing if Warwick shake his bells.
>   (*3 Hen. VI*, i. i. 45–7)

When this stage has been reached, there is no more in the way of training to be done but to accustom the hawk to fly to the lure (either a dead bird, or a weight covered over with wings of game birds or fowls to resemble a bird), and not to leave it on the falconer's approach.   At first she is for safety's sake confined by a creance or long light line, but ere long she is flown loose altogether and will come to the lure as far as she can see it.

> As falcon to the lure, away she flies ;
> The grass stoops not, she treads on it so light.
>   (*Ven. & Ad.* 1027–8)

But great care will be taken by the falconer that his hawk is in the pink of condition and keenness, lest any untoward mishap should occur, and the falcon feel inclined to revert to her ancient independence rather than keep her attention fixed on the lure and on that alone.   That excellent falconer Petruchio bore this well in mind when he said :

> My falcon now is sharp and passing empty,
> And till she stoop she must not be full-gorg'd,
> For then she never looks upon her lure. (*Tam. Sh.* iv. i. 193–5)

If these early stages are successfully passed through, our hawk, be she eyas or haggard, falcon gentle or goshawk, is ready to be entered to the quarry which she is destined to pursue.   For, to attain excellence, each hawk must be kept at her own particular quarry, and to that alone—or rather, perhaps, to her particular mode of flight.   All hawks fly with the keenest zest the particular quarry to which they are most accustomed.

In the case of the falcon gentle there are two modes of hawking to which she can be trained—one might almost say two different professions which she can adopt—and it depends much upon her temperament, and on her style and powers of flight, which line she is most likely to succeed in.

Here the judgement and experience of the falconer must be his guides, and upon his discrimination at this juncture the future of the hawk may depend. One is the flight at the high mountee, that is, at the heron, the bittern, or their modern substitutes, the rook, the crow, or the sea-gull. In this form of sport, the hawk is flown out of the hood, or directly off the fist as the quarry rises, or passes over, at a distance of perhaps a quarter of a mile. The other method of flight is that at game of all kinds, as wild ducks; this is the hawking at the river in which our ancestors took immense delight. No more spirited account of a flight at brook has been penned than that by Michael Drayton, Shakespeare's fellow-poet of Warwick-shire, in his *Poly-Olbion* (song xx). In this system the game is either marked down, or, in the more orthodox fashion, found by a setting-dog. The hawk is then flown, and is trained to wait on steadily over the head of her master at a great height, whence she can descend in an irresistible stoop as her master flushes (or puts up) the quarry directly beneath her.

The first method of flight and class of quarry pursued thereby requires hawks of the greatest swiftness and power of wing to enable them to mount rapidly and overtake their quarry, perchance in the very clouds. The second system requires hawks of higher training, greater docility, and perhaps longer experience than those which are flown only out of the hood. Turbervile, in his introductory poem, well describes the various flights :

What sense so sad, what minde soe mar'd, but sets his sorowes by
When once the Falcon free begins to raid amid the skie,
To turn and winde a birde by sleight, and eke at last to slay
With strong encounter, doves and ducks, and every other prey ;
The pretty Partridge, Rayles and Quayles, that haunt the open field,
And from his mountey to enforce the Hearon haught to yield,
By binding with hir close in cloudes, in maner out of sight,
For noble Peeres and chiefest states a passing pleasant flight.
So small a birde, so large a fowle, at such a lofty gate,
To reache and rappe and force to fall it is a game of state ;
No fellow to the flight at Brooke, that game so full of glee ;
It is a sport the stooping of a royst'ring hawk to see ;
And if she misse, to marke hir how she then gets up amaine,
For best advantage to enew the springing fowle againe.

Each to his taste. Perhaps the balance of opinion throughout all time has been in favour of the high mountee, when in spiral rings the hawks follow their quarry into and above the very clouds. Ring after ring do they make, and still the gallant quarry is above them ; yet, at last, the dot in the sky, which represents the hawk that has climbed highest, seems to poise itself and fall like a bullet towards the larger speck representing the quarry. A second stoop is made by her mate, to whom she has given the opportunity by driving the quarry downwards, and the whole flight and the motions of the birds become more visible, till at last two of the dashing figures melt into one, the third is instantly merged in the *mêlée*, and the three birds descend, bound together, slowly out of the ether to the earth.

The flight at the partridge, or at the river or brook, was differently conducted. The followers of the sport would for the most part be on foot, instead of being mounted, as was necessary for the flight at the heron. Dogs also were essential ; the setting-dog to find the game in the first place, and more particularly spaniels to rouse it after the hawk had driven it into the water or into some covert.

The essence of a good hawk for game of any kind or for the brook is in the steadiness with which she will wait over her master's head until he springs the game for her, and in the pitch or height at which she will do it. The higher she will go, the more ground she will cover below her, and the swifter and more irresistible is her stoop or descent. Again Shakespeare offers abundant illustration in such lines as these :

How high a pitch his resolution soars!
(Rich. II, I. i. 109)

A falcon, towering in her pride of place,
Was by a mousing owl hawk'd at and kill'd.
(Macb. II. iv. 12–13)

Between two hawks, which flies the higher pitch, . . .
I have perhaps some shallow spirit of judgement.
(1 Hen. VI, II. iv. 11–16)

But perhaps the whole idea of the sport of game hawking, or flying at the brook, is best given in that admirable passage describing a return from hawking, which opens the second act of *2 Henry VI* (II. i. 5–15) :

King. But what a point, my lord, your falcon made,
And what a pitch she flew above the rest !

HAWKING AT THE RIVER by JOANNES STRADANUS

To see how God in all his creatures works !
Yea, man and birds are fain of climbing high.
   Suffolk. No marvel, an it like your majesty,
My Lord Protector's hawks do tower so well ;
They know their master loves to be aloft,
And bears his thoughts above his falcon's pitch.
   Gloucester. My lord, 'tis but a base ignoble mind
That mounts no higher than a bird can soar.
   Cardinal. I thought as much ; he'd be above the clouds.

Apart from the undercurrent of political irony that flows through the conversation, it is a capital reproduction of such a conversation as might be held by any party of enthusiasts coming home from a successful day's hawking ; one, too, that had not been without a spice of imprudence and danger, and therefore, since no harm had resulted, had afforded the keener relish.

All hawking is sadly dependent on the weather, and wind is the worst enemy of the sport. Although sometimes no harm may result, it is only at the risk of losing valuable hawks and having little sport that hawks can be flown in windy weather. The Queen opened the conversation just cited with the observations :

Believe me, lords, for flying at the brook,
I saw not better sport these seven years' day :
Yet, by your leave, the wind was very high,
And, ten to one, old Joan had not gone out.[1]

                                        (*2 Hen. VI*, II. i. 1–4)

Old Joan, or possibly John, we may conclude was an experienced falconer—perhaps an employee whose advice on this occasion was disregarded, perhaps a rival falconer—but at any rate one who knew his business and the risks that would be run by the rash (but successful) party that braved the elements.

Wild-fowl of all kinds are a favourite quarry of the falcon. Probably these hawks when in a wild state live mainly by catching them. Nor, in a suitable place, are wild ducks

---

[1] Some commentators on this passage have held that ' Old Joan ' was some favourite old falcon that it was thought inadvisable to risk on a stormy day. This, however, we think is a mistake. A trained falcon does not ' go out ', but is taken out or not, by her owner or trainer. Moreover, if in the mews there was an old, experienced, and reliable hawk of considerable value, it would be the very one that could most safely be risked on a doubtful day, and least likely to be lost. ' Old Joan ' was certainly a falconer, whether male or female, and one well known for caution and experience.

a difficult quarry, if there be plenty of assistance at hand to serve the hawk by speedily flushing the quarry after the hawk has driven it into the water or rushes. To do this thoroughly requires judgement, and the impetuosity bred of excitement must be curbed, or the hawk will be hindered, not assisted. So in *2 Henry VI* (II. i. 43–5) the Cardinal says :

> Believe me, cousin Gloucester,
> Had not your man put up the fowl so suddenly,
> We had had more sport—

a remark that, differently expressed perhaps, follows on many a flight at fowl or game. A flight of this kind is a merry sport, however. Turbervile's description is no bad one :

In my concept no pleasure like to hawks, I tell you trew ;
It sets the senses all to work ; there none may idle bee ;
The tongue it lures, the legges they leap, the eie beholds the glee,
The eares are busied eke to hear, the calling spaniel's quest.
Do tell me then what sense it is that respite has to rest.
And more than that, the heart it leapes and laughs for joy to think
How such a slender hawk should cause so huge a fowl to shrinke.[1]

A good description of hawking in Shakespeare's England is offered by one Thomas Nash, who called himself Philopolites, and is to be distinguished from the well-known satirical writer of Elizabeth's reign.   He wrote thus of the sport of falconry in his *Quaternio, or a Four-fold Way to a Happie Life* (1633) :

And to hear an accipitrary relate again how he went forth in a cleere, calme and sunshine evening about an hour before the sun did usually maske himself, unto the river, where finding of a mallard he whistled off his falcon, and how shee flew from him as if shee would never have turned head againe ; yet presently upon a shoute came in ; how then by degrees, by little and little, by flying about and about, shee mounted so high, untill shee had lessened herselfe to the view of the beholder, to the shape of a pigeon or partridge, and had made the height of the moone the place of her flight, how presently upon the landing of the fowle shee came down like a stone

---

[1] ' Hawking at the river ' has always been a favourite form of hawking among Anglo-Indian falconers. In some parts of India in the cold weather ducks are very numerous ; portions of the country are suitable for hawking, and the different varieties most interesting. In the winter of 1888–9, two British officers, with no large establishment of hawks, killed a total of 322 head, of which many were herons and peewits flown ' at the high mountee ', but more than half were wild-fowl divided into no less than twelve different varieties.

and enewed it.[1] And suddenly got up againe, and suddenly upon a second landing came downe againe, and missing of it, in the down-come recovered it beyond expectation, to the admiration of the beholder. And to heare him tell a third time how he went forth early in a winter's morning to fly the cocke, where having by a little white feather in his tayle discovered him on a brake, he cast off a tassel gentle, and how he never ceased in his circular motion untill he had recovered his place ; how suddenly upon the flushing of the cocke he came downe, and missing of it in the down-come, what working there was on both sides, how the cocke mounted, as if he would have pierced the skies ; how the hawke flew the con-trary way untill he had made the wind his friend ; how then by degrees he got up, yet never offered to come in till he had got his advantage of the higher ground, how then he made in ; what speed the cocke made to save himselfe and what hasty pursuit the hawke made, and how after two long miles flight he killed it, yet in killing of it, killed himselfe.

But all hawking was not after this fashion. Besides the falcon gentle and its congeners, the short-winged hawks, viz. the goshawk and sparrow-hawk, were used for taking birds in a much more lucrative if perhaps less sporting fashion than the flights with the more noble long-winged hawk. It was, however, no doubt excellent fun, even if it had a flavour of pot-hunting about it. In *The Merry Wives of Windsor* (III. iii. 243–6) Master Page says :

I do invite you to-morrow morning to my house to breakfast ; after, we'll a-birding together : I have a fine hawk for the bush.

A goshawk, no doubt, was his hawk, or perchance a sparrow-hawk.

A sportsman might have the best of diversion with a sparrow-hawk, of which the male—the smallest and most insignificant, yet a very smart little hawk—was called the musket. If taken from the nest as an eyas, it would be also one of the tamest and most docile of hawks. How apt, then, is the term ' eyas-musket' when applied to a smart yet obedient little page in *The Merry Wives of Windsor* (III. iii. 22) :

Mrs. Page. Here comes little Robin.
Mrs. Ford. How now, my eyas-musket ! what news with you ?

' A hawk for the bush' aptly describes the mode of using the short-winged hawks of either kind. They are

---

[1] To ' enew ' was to drive the quarry into covert or water, where it was kept down, till again roused by the falconer with his spaniels. The term occurs once in Shakespeare (*Meas. for M.* III. i. 89), but in the Folios is disguised under the erroneous form ' emmew '.

essentially hawks of the woodland or enclosed country rather than the open heaths or downs, where the noble falcon delights to take her prey. Their flight is very swift for a short distance, but is not prolonged, and they can dash through thick covert with the ease and swiftness of a woodcock. Their flight being so short, they can be used very many times during the day, and are in fact most formidable engines for taking game. Flown at such quarry as partridges, which outfly her, a goshawk will follow the covey till it dashes into some hedge or brake for refuge, when she will take stand on an adjoining tree and await her opportunity. This soon comes by the aid of the falconer and his spaniels,[1] who drive out (or catch) one of the covey, when it is hard but that she will take it at the retrouve. More than that, she can be quickly rewarded and ready to fly again, when another of the covey may be flushed for her, since, when once driven in, they will lie like stones on their refuge. The process may be repeated till most of that covey is accounted for by one or two goshawks, a form of hawking that may aptly be termed ' birding '. Pheasants can be flown even in covert in the same way, but it was often the custom to use the spaniels quietly to drive the pheasant to perch, and then use the goshawk to take him from where he sits. Rabbits in numbers can be taken unerringly. Even hares can be held by a powerful female bird. Hence it will be seen that a good hawk for the bush was a most useful addition to the modest establishment of a country gentleman of the standing of Master Page, who did not own land enough to cumber himself with an appanage of falcons and falconers.

The short-winged hawks are trained differently from falcons. They are at first very timid and difficult to handle. They are generally carried bareheaded, and always so when out hawking, so that they may dash from the fist like the bullet from a gun.[2]

Simon Latham's *New and Second Booke of Falconry* (1618), appended to his *Falconry* (first published in 1615), is mainly devoted to the training of the goshawk, and contains much

---

[1] As will be gathered, well-trained spaniels were a most essential factor in the sport of hawking with the goshawk. Turbervile is loud in praise of them, and, like Latham, gives many directions for their breaking and training.

[2] In India the sparrow-hawk is carried *in*, not *on*, the hand, and is ' bowled ' at the quarry like a cricket ball—a most deadly method of taking quail, &c.

good advice ; yet Edmund Bert is the standard writer on
the training of these hawks (*An Approved Treatise of
Hawkes and Hawking*, 1619). A trainer of goshawks was
looked on as quite a different person from a falconer, and
was termed an Austringer, Astringer, Ostringer, or Ostreger,
derived ultimately from the Latin 'astur', a goshawk, which
appears in French as 'autour'.[1] Thus in *All's Well that
Ends Well* (v. i) we have (in the First Folio text) the stage
direction 'Enter a gentle Astringer'.[2] Related to this
word is the old word 'estridge', which Shakespeare makes
use of in two passages, apparently in the sense of goshawk.
Thus Enobarbus says :

> To be furious
> Is to be frighted out of fear, and in that mood
> The dove will peck the estridge ;
> > (*Ant. & Cleop.* III. xi. 194–6)

the goshawk is the fiercest and most powerful hawk in whose
talons an unfortunate dove could find itself. Again, Sir
Richard Vernon describes the Prince of Wales's adherents as

> All furnish'd, all in arms,
> All plum'd like estridges that wing the wind,
> Bated like eagles having lately bath'd.
> > (*1 Hen. IV*, IV. i. 97–9)[3]

There is no explicit mention of the smaller falcons used
in hawking, the merlin and the hobby, in the writings of
Shakespeare. Though the merlin was a great favourite
with ladies of the period, there is no reference to it. But
there is a striking allusion to the method of fowling with
the hobby in *Henry VIII* (III. ii. 280–3), where Surrey says :

> If we live thus tamely,
> To be thus jaded by a piece of scarlet,
> Farewell nobility ; let his Grace go forward,
> And dare us with his cap like larks.

[1] In French sporting parlance the two forms of hawking and the art of
training hawks for them are still always kept distinct as 'La Fauconnerie'
and 'L'Autourserie'.

[2] This passage has proved a stumbling-block to many editors. Many
modern editions have, even in despair, cut it down to 'Enter a gentleman',
But Shakespeare's meaning was as clear to all of his own time as it is to this
day among all who have had anything to do with hawking and its history,
or as 'enter a huntsman' or a 'gamekeeper' would be to the modern public.
The point was that the 'astringer' whom Helena had seen in the French
Court was a gentleman, and therefore a fit person to be entrusted with the
message she desired to send to the King.

[3] 'Estridge' is otherwise a common variant in Elizabethan English for
'ostrich'.

The method of taking larks with the hobby was known as
'daring'. The hawk was trained to wait on, above the
falconer, just as the falcon gentle was used for flying at the
brook or at game. The presence of their swift enemy
overhead so terrified or 'dared' the larks that they crouched
upon the ground and remained almost immovable. Two
men then took a trammel net, or oblong net of considerable
size, the lower edge of which was weighted with plummets.
The net was borne a little above the ground, and as the
weighted cord touched and flushed the cowering larks they
rose directly into it, and a whole flock could be taken at
a haul.

BIBLIOGRAPHY.—Apart from the works of TURBERVILE, LATHAM, and
BERT, which are already mentioned in the text, the chief Elizabethan books
on hawking include GERVASE MARKHAM'S *Countrey Contentments*, 1611 ; and
The Gentlemans Academie ; or the Booke of S. Albans, 1595, which mainly
reprints Dame Juliana Berners's treatise on hawking, hunting, &c., first pub-
lished in 1486. Modern books which deserve study are JAMES EDMUND
HARTING'S *Ornithology of Shakespeare*, 1871 ; and his *Bibliotheca Accipitraria ;
A Catalogue of books . . . relating to Falconry, with notes, glossary*, &c., 1891 ;
SALVIN & BRODRICK'S *Falconry in the British Isles*, 1855 ; the present writer's
'Falconry' in the Badminton Library volume on *Coursing and Falconry*,
1892; and Mr. JUSTICE MADDEN'S *Diary of Master William Silence : a study
of Shakespeare and of Elizabethan Sport*, new ed. 1907.

§ 3. COURSING, FOWLING, ANGLING

BY

A. FORBES SIEVEKING

COURSING

THIS was one of the most popular sports of the period. The Laws of the Leash, which embodied the accepted rules of coursing, were drawn up in Elizabeth's reign by Thomas, Duke of Norfolk, and coursing became one of the prominent features of the Cotswold games. We get a glimpse of the interest taken by country gentlemen in the Cotswold coursing matches in the opening scene of *The Merry Wives of Windsor* :

Slender. How does your fallow greyhound, sir ? I heard say he was outrun on Cotsall.
Page. It could not be judged, sir.
Slender. You'll not confess, you'll not confess.
Shallow. That he will not : 'tis your fault, 'tis your fault. 'Tis a good dog.
Page. A cur, sir.
Shallow. Sir, he's a good dog, and a fair dog.

' We use three maner of courses with Greyhounds here in England,' says Turbervile, ' that is at the Deare, at the Hare, and at Foxe or other vermine.' The only form of coursing that we find in Shakespeare is what is generally understood by the term, that is, the pursuit of the hare with greyhounds, by sight, as distinct from the hunting of the hare, which is treated in the section of this chapter dealing with hunting.

Caius states that the greyhound ' for his incredible swiftness, is called *Leporarius* ; because the principal service of them dependeth and consisteth in starting and hunting the hare '. Shakespeare puts it thus :

Say thou wilt course ; thy greyhounds are as swift
As breathed stags, ay, fleeter than the roe.

(*Tam. Sh.*, Ind. II. 49–50)

The coursing greyhound furnishes him with some of his

most striking imagery. King Harry exclaims to his yeomen troops before Harfleur :

> I see you stand like greyhounds in the slips,
> Straining upon the start. The game's afoot.
> *(Hen. V, III. i. 31–2)*

A very similar metaphor is put into the mouth of Queen Margaret after the battle of Towton :

> Edward and Richard, like a brace of greyhounds
> Having the fearful flying hare in sight, . . .
> Are at our backs. *(3 Hen. VI, II. v. 129–33)*

The leash usually coupled together three dogs, so that the word formed a common periphrasis for the number three.[1] Turbervile admits that

if the Greyhoundes be but yong or slowe, you may course with a lease at one Hare, but that is seldome seene, and a brase of Dogges is ynow for suche a poore beast.

The slips, as the name suggests, were so constructed that the hounds could be readily let go as soon as the game was started. The impetuous temper of Hotspur is well characterized in his father's words :

> Before the game's afoot thou still lett'st slip ;
> *(I Hen. IV, I. iii. 279)*

and Coriolanus says of Titus Lartius :

> Holding Corioli in the name of Rome,
> Even like a fawning greyhound in the leash,
> To let him slip at will. *(Cor. I. vi. 37–9)*

The letter-loose of the greyhounds, now called the slipper, was formerly known as the fewterer.

The chief technicalities of the sport are abundantly represented in Shakespeare. Rosencrantz thus reports the approach of the Players :

We coted them on the way ; and hither they are coming, to offer you service, *(Haml. II. ii. 338–40)*

meaning that he had turned them from their intended route after outstripping them. Turbervile explains the term thus :

A Cote is when a Greyhounde goeth endways by his fellow and giveth the Hare a turne . . . but if he coast and so come by his fellowe, that is no Cote.

---

[1] Thus we have a 'leash of drawers' whose names are 'Tom, Dick, and Francis' (*I Hen. IV*, II. iv. 7–9).

To coast was to turn aside in such a manner as to cut off the corner and so intercept the hare :

> And all in haste she coasteth to the cry.
>
> (Ven. & Ad. 870)

Golding gives a vivid account of a coursing match, with a full use of the terms of art :

> I gat me to the knap
> Of this same hill, and there beheld of this straunge course the hap,
> In which the beast seemes one while caught, and ere a man would think,
> Doth quickly give the Grewnd the slip, and from his bighting shrink :
> And like a wilie Foxe, he runnes not forth directly out,
> Nor makes a windlasse over all the champion fieldes about,
> But doubling and indenting still avoydes his enmies lips,
> And turning short, as swift about as spinning wheele he whips,
> To disapoint the snatch. The Grewnd pursuing at an inch
> Doth cote him, never losing ground : but likely still to pinch
> Is at the sodaine shifted of, continually he snatches
> In vaine : for nothing in his mouth save only Aire he latches.

In more than one passage Shakespeare also alludes to the sudden snatch of the greyhound as he comes up with the quarry. Benedick praises Margaret's jest :

> Thy wit is as quick as the greyhound's mouth ; it catches.
>
> (Much Ado v. ii. 11–12)

Henry V alludes to the ' pilfering borderers ' as ' coursing snatchers ' (*Hen. V*, i. ii. 143) ; and Aaron, catching at the hunting figure in Demetrius's speech, seems to be piecing it out with a coursing metaphor, when he eggs on Tamora's sons in their designs on Lavinia with the suggestion :

> Why, then, it seems, some certain snatch or so
> Would serve your turns.   (*Tit. Andr.* ii. i. 95–6)

The hare-finder, mentioned in *Much Ado about Nothing* (i. i. 186), must, according to Markham, ' give the Hare three sohows before he put her from her Lear ' to make the greyhounds gaze.

<h2 align="center">FOWLING</h2>

Some of the most usual bird-catching devices in use in Shakespeare's day are grouped together in the lines :

> Poor bird ! thou'dst never fear the net nor lime,
> The pit-fall nor the gin.   (*Macb.* iv. ii. 34–5)

Other methods and implements mentioned or alluded to in Shakespeare are bat-fowling, the bow and bolt, the stone-bow or birding-bow, and the shot-gun, the decoy, and the stalking-horse.

The springe was the common engine for snaring the woodcock and snipe. The woodcock's lack of intelligence was proverbial, and the bird's name was one of the many synonyms for ' fool '.

> O ! this woodcock, what an ass it is,
>
> *(Tam. Sh.* I. ii. 164)

says Grumio of Lucentio, disguised as a tutor. When Malvolio catches sight of Maria's concocted letter lying on the ground, Fabian exclaims :

> Now is the woodcock near the gin.   *(Tw. N.* II. v. 93)

Laertes, when wounded with his own poisoned weapon, laments that he is 'as a woodcock to' his 'own springe' *(Haml.* v. ii. 320–1).

The springe probably consisted, like its modern substitute, of a pliant rod planted upright in the ground, and having the top, to which a noose is attached, bent down and secured by a catch or trigger which is released by the action of the bird or animal. The rod flies up and the noose is drawn tight on the victim. It is uncertain whether the gin is the same contrivance as the springe, or, as some think, a steel trap very like a modern rat-trap.

The pitfall survives in the cruel brick trap. It was so arranged that a board or trap-door fell over an enclosed space, imprisoning or crushing the bird.

Of the weapons used in fowling or birding, the bird-bolt, a blunt-headed arrow, is in *Much Ado about Nothing* (I. i. 42) humorously contrasted with the ' flight '—an arrow for long-distance shooting—and in *Twelfth Night* (I. v. 99) with ' cannon-bullets '. Biron speaks of Cupid's dart as his ' bird-bolt ' :

> Proceed, sweet Cupid : thou hast thumped him with thy bird-bolt under the left pap.   *(Love's L. L.* IV. iii. 23–5)

The stone-bow, a cross-bow from which small stones or pellets were shot, is mentioned in *Twelfth Night* :

> O ! for a stone-bow, to hit him in the eye !   (II. v. 52)

The bird-bolt was much used for shooting small birds in the hedges.

Or if thou wilt goe shoote at little Birds
With bow and boult (the Thrustle-cocke and Sparrow)
Such as our Countrey hedges can afford's ;
I have a fine bowe, and an yvorie arrow

writes Barnfield in *The Affectionate Shephearde* (1594).

Fire-arms were coming into vogue for fowling, but their efficiency was low. Such was the birding-piece of the day, which Mistress Ford speaks of as being discharged in the chimney on the return of the sportsmen (*M. Wives* IV. ii. 57–60). Barnfield, when he tells how

To catch the long-billd Woodcocke and the Snype, . . .
The Partridge, Phæsant, or the greedie Grype,

does not refer to them, but advocates setting ' springes in a frostie night '.

The caliver, apparently the lightest of portable fire-arms except the pistol, was used as a fowling-piece. William Fulbecke in 1602 speaks of one ' that shooteth in a Caleever at birdes ', and Falstaff says his recruits are ' such as fear the report of a caliver worse than a struck fowl or a hurt wild-duck ' (*1 Hen. IV*, IV. iii. 20–2).

The practice of bat-fowling or ' bat-folding ' mentioned in *The Tempest* (II. i. 193) was carried on at night, when the birds, stupefied by glaring torches, were roused out of their roosting-places and beaten or ' batted ' down as they flew about the lights. Another somewhat similar method was ' low-belling ', mentioned in an Act of 1581, and so called from the ' low-bell ' carried by one of the fowlers. The birds, ' what with the bell, and what with the light, . . . will be so amazed, that when you come near them they will turn up their white bellies ', [1] and are then captured in nets.

Commonest of all was the practice of taking small birds with bird-lime. The glutinous substance is smeared on twigs which are then placed in bushes or other likely alighting places. Mariana in *All's Well that Ends Well* (III. v. 24–5) says that maidens ' are limed with the twigs that threaten them ', and King Henry VI says in reference to his suspicions of Gloucester's designs :

The bird that hath been limed in a bush,
With trembling wings misdoubteth every bush.

(*3 Hen. VI*, v. vi. 13–14)

---

[1] T. S., *Jewell for Gentrie* (1614).

The stale is a decoy-bird, either a living bird, a stuffed bird, or the figure of a bird used to entice others into a net ; the inanimate decoy was sometimes placed near springes or limed twigs. The ' faucon free ', says Surrey, ' for no stale doth care'. The device is alluded to in connexion with the limed bush in the following passage :

> Madam, myself have lim'd a bush for her,
> And plac'd a quire of such enticing birds
> That she will light to listen to their lays,
> And never mount to trouble you again.
>
> (*2 Hen. VI*, i. iii. 91–4)

The word became common for any kind of decoy, as in the passage where Prospero says to Ariel :

> The trumpery in my house, go bring it hither
> For stale to catch these thieves. (*Temp.* iv. i. 186–7)

The stalking-horse is best described in the words of Markham ; like the stale, it is either a live animal or an artificial imitation of it ; the latter is represented in the picture by Stradanus which accompanies this article.

The Stalking-Horse is any old Jade trayned up for that use, which will gently walke up and downe in the water ; and then you shall shelter your selfe and your Peice behind his fore shoulder. Now forasmuch as these Stalking horses are not ever in readinesse, in this case he may take any pieces of oulde Canvasse, and having made it in the shape or proportion of a Horse, let it be painted as neere the colour of a Horse as you can devise.

The stalking-horse is named only once, when the Duke says of Touchstone :

> He uses his folly like a stalking-horse, and under the presentation of that he shoots his wit. (*A. Y. L.* v. iv. 112–14)

One other definite reference to this mode of approaching wild-fowl occurs in *Much Ado about Nothing* :

> Stalk on, stalk on ; the fowl sits. (ii. iii. 101–2)

ANGLING

There is nothing in Shakespeare's works to warrant the assumption that he was an expert angler, or that he was much interested in the sport.

References to angling are for the most part commonplace, and the illustrations drawn from it chiefly turn upon the recognized metaphorical uses of ' angle ' and ' bait '.

Veſte boues operit, dum furuos fallit odores Venator, piſcias dum garrula ab ilice prædæ

THE STALKING HORSE by JOANNES STRADANUS

Ursula in *Much Ado about Nothing* (III. i. 26–8) thus describes the fisherman's happiest moments :

> The pleasant'st angling is to see the fish
> Cut with her golden oars the silver stream,
> And greedily devour the treacherous bait ;

and in *Venus and Adonis* (526) we have the observation,

> No fisher but the ungrown fry forbears.

In *Titus Andronicus* (IV. vi. 89–90) we read of

> Words more sweet, and yet more dangerous,
> Than baits to fish.

The picture of Benedick lurking in the arbour, eavesdropping, while Don Pedro, Leonato, and Claudio converse for his benefit, and the situation of Beatrice in the next scene, are both summed up in the language of angling (*Much Ado* II. iii. 121–2, III. i. 26–33). Again, the refusal by Adonis of Cytherea's favours is expressed in the words,

> The tender nibbler would not touch the bait.
> (*Pass. Pilgr.* iv. 11)

To ' angle ' for a person's thoughts, as Cressida confesses doing (*Troilus* III. ii. 162), to ' angle ' for another's life, as Hamlet says his step-father has done for his (*Haml.* v. ii. 64–6), are figures of speech that betoken no special knowledge or experience of the angler's art. Similarly Bertram says of Diana,

> She knew her distance, and did angle for me ;
> (*All's W.* v. iii. 214)

and Polixenes fears that Perdita is ' the angle that plucks our son ' to the shepherd's cottage (*Wint. T.* IV. i. 51). A possible exception to the general statement is the speech of Leontes, in which, speaking of the freedom he allows Hermione with Polixenes, he uses the words,

> I am angling now,
> Though you perceive me not how I give line,
> (*Wint. T.* I. ii. 180–1)

in which the necessity of giving way to the rush of a large fish when first struck seems to be alluded to.

The species of fish named, and the few angling terms used, lead to the conclusion that it was bottom-fishing and not fly-fishing with which Shakespeare was familiar. For him, the trout was a fish to be groped for or taken by tickling (*Meas. for M.* I. ii. 96, *Twel. N.* II. v. 25–6). Amongst his coarse fish is the pike, which, as is implied in the following words of Falstaff, makes prey upon the dace :

If the young dace be a bait for the old pike, I see no reason in the law of nature but I may snap at him.

(*2 Hen. IV*, III. ii, ad fin.)

The wary character of the carp is touched upon in *Hamlet* (II. i. 63) :

Your bait of falsehood takes this carp of truth,

and the fact that it was most commonly bred and stocked in fishponds is no doubt alluded to in *All's Well that Ends Well* (V. ii. 20–4) :

Here is a purr of Fortune's, sir, or of Fortune's cat . . . that has fallen into the unclean fishpond of her displeasure. . . . Pray you, sir, use the poor carp as you may.

The gudgeon—one of the young angler's favourites on account of its bold biting—is selected as a type of what is easily deluded—

But fish not, with this melancholy bait,
For this fool-gudgeon, this opinion ;

(*Merch. of V.* I. i. 101–2)

and the minnow appears only as a type of smallness (*Love's L. L.* I. i. 249, *Cor.* III. i. 88).

Among the references to bait and baiting, one kind only is named, the worm. Hamlet, in the grave-digging scene, says :

A man may fish with the worm that hath eat of a king, and eat of the fish that hath fed of that worm. (IV. iii. 29–31)

Shakespeare's ignorance or neglect of angling and his complete disregard of fly-fishing are remarkable, seeing that, as early as the middle of the fifteenth century, careful instruction was given for the making of ' dubbes ', that is, artificial flies, by the author of the little treatise called *Fysshynge with an angle*; and the advanced state of the art as described by Peacham only six years after Shakespeare's death, and later by Walton, is evidence that there was progress and development during the sixteenth century.

BIBLIOGRAPHY.—*Coursing.* An account of the coursing which formed part of the Cotswold Games as presided over by ' Captain ' Dover is contained in *Annalia Dubrensia*, 1636. The history of the sport is treated in *Arrian on Coursing* by a Graduate of Medicine [Rev. W. Dansey, M.B.], 1831, a work invaluable for its preface, notes and bibliography. The volume *Coursing and Falconry*, in the Badminton Library, 1892, is a useful manual.

Fowling. The most instructive works are J. E. HARTING's *The Ornithology of Shakespeare critically examined*, 1871, and D. H. MADDEN's *The Diary of Master William Silence*, 1897.

Angling. The chief books of the period are : L[EONARD] M[ASCALL]'s *A Booke of Fishing with Hooke and Line*, 1590, &c. ; J[OHN] D[ENNYS]'s *The Secrets of Angling*, 1613 (in metre), reprinted by Arber in *An English Garner*, 1870, vol. i, pp. 141–98 ; *The Pleasures of Princes, or Good Mens Recreations : containing a Discourse of the Generall Art of Fishing with an Angle or otherwise*, 1614, by Gervase Markham, who also converted Dennys's verse into prose in the 2nd ed. of his *Countrey Contentments*, 1623.

Modern works to be consulted are Sir Harris Nicolas's and Major's editions of Walton's *Compleat Angler*, and, for angling in Shakespeare, CANON H. N. ELLACOMBE's *Shakespeare as an Angler*, 1883.

§ 4. ARCHERY

BY

COLONEL H. WALROND

IN Shakespeare's time archery was in a critical condition. For many years, ever since the passing of the statute of Winton, in the reign of Edward I, the bow had been considered the principal weapon of the English, and the one on which they depended in order to defeat their enemies. Successive enactments were passed enforcing its practice. These did not prove effective, and one of the first statutes passed in the reign of Henry VIII (3 Henry VIII, c. 3) was to enjoin stricter attention to them. The results, however, do not seem to have been satisfactory, and in 1541 another Act (33 Henry VIII, c. 9) was passed to further the maintaining of artillery (in which archery was then included) and to prevent the practice of unlawful games. This was in force at the time of Shakespeare's birth, and for many years after. By this Act it is provided :

That every Man being the King's Subject, not lame, decrepit nor maimed, nor having any other lawful or reasonable Cause or Impediment, being within the Age of sixty years (except Spiritual Men, Justices of one Bench and of the other, Justices of the Assize and Barons of the Exchequer) shall from the Feast of Pentecost next coming, use and exercise shooting in Long-Bows, and also have a Bow and Arrows ready continually in his House, to use himself, and do use himself in shooting ; and also the Fathers, Governors, and Rulers of such as be of tender age, do teach and bring them up in the Knowledge of the same shooting : and that every Man having a Man-child or Men-children in his House, shall provide, ordain, and have in his House for every Man-child being of the Age of seven Years and above, till he shall come to the Age of seventeen Years, a Bow and two Shafts to induce and learn them, and bring them up in Shooting, and shall deliver all the same Bow and Arrows to the same young Men to use and occupy ; and if the same young Men be Servants, that then their Masters shall abate the Money that they shall pay for the same Bows and Arrows out of their Wages ; and after all such young Men shall come to the Age of seventeen Years, every of them shall provide and have a Bow and four Arrows continually for himself, at his proper Costs and Charges, or else of the Gift or Provision of his Friends, and use and occupy the same in shooting as is before rehearsed ; and if the Master suffer any of his Servants taking Wages, being in Household, and under the Age of seventeen Years ; or the Father suffer any of his Sons being in his Houshold, and under the Age of seventeen Years to lack a Bow and two Arrows, contrary to the Form of this Estatute, by the Space of one Month together ; then the Master or Father in whom such Negligences shall be, shall for every such Default forfeit vi. s. viii. d., and that every Servant passing the Age of seventeen Years, and under the Age of sixty Years, and taking Wages, which can or is able to shoot, and shall lack a Bow and four Arrows by the Space of one Month together, for every such Default shall forfeit and lose vi. s. viii. d.

The next section provides, that no one under 24 shall shoot at any standing Prick, except it be at a Rover, more than once when he shall change his mark, under a penalty of iv. d. ; that no one above 24 shall shoot at any mark of eleven score or under with any Prickshaft or Flight, under a penalty of vi. s. viii. d. ; that no one under 17 shall use a yew bow under a penalty of vi. s. viii. d. unless his father or mother shall be possessed of £10 a year in land, or he himself of 40 marks ; and that the inhabitants of every city, town, and place put and keep up butts, and shoot at them or elsewhere, on holy days and other times convenient.

The statute then goes on to say, after forbidding aliens, without the king's licence, the use of bows under penalties of fine and forfeiture :

That no Manner of Person or Persons, of what Degree, Quality, or Condition soever he or they be, from the Feast of the Nativity of St. John the Baptist now next coming, by himself, Factor, Deputy, Servant or other Person, shall for his or their Gain, Lucre or Living, keep, have, hold, occupy, exercise or maintain, any common House, Alley, or Place of bowling, coyting, cloysh, cayls, half bowl, tennis, dicing, table, or carding, or any other Manner of Game prohibited by any Estatute heretofore made, or any unlawful new Game now invented or made, or any other new unlawful Game hereafter to be invented, found, had or made, upon Pain to forfeit and pay for every Day keeping, having or maintaining, or suffering any such Game to be had, kept, executed, played or maintained within any such House, Garden, Alley or other Place, contrary to the Form and Effect of this Estatute, Forty Shillings.

The above statute seems stringent enough for any purpose, but it was not apparently sufficient to restore the popularity of the bow. It is clear from the statements of contemporary writers, that the former statutes were neglected, and that what archery there was, was concerned more with shooting at short distances and for wagers, than developing the muscular power necessary to use and master the old English longbow. The neglect of archery, which had been deplored by Sir T. Elyot in *The Governour* (1531), still continued,

O what cause of reproche shall the decaye of archers be to us nowe livynge? Yet what irrecuperable damage either to us or them, in whose time nede of semblable defence shall happen? Whiche decaye, though we all redy perceive, feare, and lament, and for restaurying thereof cesse nat to make ordinaunces, good lawes, and statutes, yet who effectuelly puttethe his hande to continual execution of the same lawes and provisions? or beholdyng them dayly broken, wynketh nat at the offendours?

The fact no doubt was that the inferiority of the bow against fire-arms was beginning to be recognized, though this was not generally acknowledged till long after Shakespeare's death. His allusions to fire-arms are few, and do not convey that he had much idea of their value, as when he makes Ford say:

Why, this boy will carry a letter twenty mile as easy as a cannon will shoot point-blank twelve score. (*M. Wives* III. ii. 33-5)

Nor is this to be wondered at, for, though hand fire-arms had been introduced into England more than a century before, they were very imperfect, the powder was bad, and their loading and discharging was a lengthy affair, and in the end the flight of the projectile was so erratic that a hundred years after Shakespeare's death a hot discussion was still going on as to the relative merits of the bow and fire-arms.

It might from this be inferred that at the period with which we are dealing bows and arrows had ceased to be of any consequence for warlike purposes. This was far from being so; they still formed an important, if a secondary means, for the defence of the country. Fresh enactments were passed in 1571 enforcing the previous Acts for the importation of bowstaves, and regulating their price. By these Acts, merchants were bound to import from countries from which bowstaves were procured, with each ton of merchandise, four, and with each tun of malmsey or Tyre wine, ten bowstaves. In the following year a return was called for of the number of bowstaves imported, from which it appears that 1,950 were brought from Embden, 1,975 from Suningborge, 2,060 from Danske, 2,000 from Hambrough, and an unspecified number from Dorte, besides the 'Cologne staves' brought down the Rhine, which were held to be the best. Keeping up the butts and shooting on holy and other days was also enforced at this time. From a list of the levies to repel the Armada in 1588 it appears that the proportion of trained men armed with bows was roughly from one-half to a fifth; the rest carried fire-arms and bills. In London fire-arms predominated, while in the country the proportion of bows was greater. Clearly the bow was still an important weapon, and in 1599 the stores at the Tower included about 8,185 bows, 6,000 bow-staves, 196 gross of bow-strings, 14,000 sheaves of livery arrows (each of 24 shafts), &c., but at the beginning of the seventeenth century archery, for purposes of war, rapidly declined.

From G. Markham, *The Art of Archerie*, 1634. (The bracer and shooting-glove are shown.)

Bows are either made entirely of wood, whether of one piece or more, or are composite, i. e. fashioned out of horn, wood, and sinew; the latter kind is used by Orientals, and is much the more powerful. Of this fact Shakespeare seems to have been aware, for Puck says:

> I go ; I go ; look how I go ;
> Swifter than arrow from Tartar's bow.
>   (*Mid. N. D.* III. ii. 100–1)

The English longbow is the weapon mentioned in the Statutes, and throughout this chapter. It was made of one piece of wood, preferably yew, varying in length,

according to the height of the shooter, from 5 ft. 6 in. to
6 ft. 8 in. Its weight (the number of pounds necessary
to draw the arrow to the head) was from 55 to 90 lb., to
suit the user. Staves were difficult to procure straight
and without knots ; hence the stringency of the Statutes
as to their importation, as, owing to our climate, English
yew was very inferior to foreign.[1]

Essential parts of an archer's equipment are the bracer
or arm-guard, which is fastened to the left arm to protect
it from the impact of the string when the arrow is loosed,
and the shooting-glove, which was to protect the three
first fingers of the right hand when drawing and loosing
the string. Of the arm-guard, a fine example remains to
us. It was left at Bolton Hall in Yorkshire by one of the
attendants of Henry VI, after the battle of Hexham.
It is made of ' cuir bouilli ' ; the inner part, which received
the blow of the string, is plain, while the outer is carved
with the king's device and I.H.S. HELPE in gothic letter.
As a rule, a plain piece of leather served the purpose,
but many bracers were of silver or ivory, with various
designs on them. Of the old shooting-glove no example
is known. In later times a small pocket was provided in
the back.

There were three chief methods of shooting, Prick or
Clout, Butt, and Roving. Prick or Clout shooting was
carried on at from 160 to 240 yards, the mark being
18 inches in diameter, made of canvas stuffed with straw,
and having a small white circle painted on it, in the centre
of which was a wooden peg ; to ' hit the white ' meant to
hit the white mark (the ' white ' or ' blank ') ; to ' cleave
the pin ', to strike the peg. The object of this practice
was to ' keep a length ', or shoot many arrows the same
distance. Butt shooting was more for accuracy ; the butts,
made of earth and banked with turf, were built from 100
to 140 yards apart. A paper disk, sometimes marked
with concentric circles, was placed on these, and to hit this
disk was again called hitting the white (*Tam. Sh.* v. ii. 187).
Roving was shooting over open ground at unknown distances, except in the Finsbury and St. George's fields,

---

[1] There is some question as to the meaning of ' hold, or cut bowstrings '
(*Mid. N. D.* i. ii. 115), but no doubt it implies ' come rain, hail, or shine ',
as it was not unknown for an archer to cut a rival's bowstring.

for which regular guides existed, showing the distance of each of the standing marks from the others.

Arrows were made of many and various woods, and they had different heads : for clout, prick, and roving, light ones were used, for butt shooting they were heavier, and still more so for war, when the heads were barbed. It was probably to a falling arrow of the former description that the Duke alludes when he says :

> Believe not that the dribbling dart of love
> Can pierce a complete bosom   (*Meas. for M*. i. iii. 2–3)

—the arrow falling feebly, and thus unable to pierce a corselet.

Arrows were commonly called Shafts, a Flight consisting of two or three arrows, matched, and found to fly exactly alike (cf. *Merch. of V*. i. i. 142). For cross-bows they were stouter and shorter, and called Bolts. Hence, proverbially, ' making a shaft or a bolt ' meant doing one thing or the other, as, if the wood was too short for the one, it could still make the other (*M. Wives* iii. iv. 24).

Roger Ascham was the first English writer on archery ; his book *Toxophilus* was first published in 1545, and was reprinted several times from 1571 onwards. He presented it to Henry VIII, who was much pleased with it, awarded the author a pension, and in 1548 appointed him reader to Princess, afterwards Queen, Elizabeth. This book is written in the form of a dialogue between Philologus and Toxophilus, is a most comprehensive treatise, and is the foundation of every book on the subject that has since been written. Living in the time he did, when every young man should have been an archer, probably Shakespeare was one, and the thorough knowledge of the sport displayed by him in his writings appears to prove it. But, more than this, many passages point to his having been actually conversant with *Toxophilus*. Thus, with respect to the wind and ascertaining its direction, Ascham says ;

You must take hede also yf ever you shote where one of the markes or both stondes a lytle short of a hye wall, for there you may be easlye begyled. Yf you take grasse and caste it up to se howe the wynde standes, manye tymes you shal suppose to shoote downe the wynde when you shote cleane agaynst wynde.

To this there is a close parallel in *The Merchant of Venice*, where Salanio says :

> I should be still
> Plucking the grass to know where sits the wind, (i. i. 17–8)

while in the same play Bassanio says :

> In my school-days, when I had lost one shaft,
> I shot his fellow of the self-same flight
> The self-same way with more advised watch,
> To find the other forth, and by adventuring both,
> I oft found both. (I. i. 141–5)

Again we read in *Toxophilus* :

a perfyte archer muste firste learne to knowe the sure flyghte of his shaftes, that he may be boulde alwayes, to trust them—

the fact being that it is always necessary to match arrows, few flying exactly alike, and as Ascham says :

You must have diverse shaftes of one flight fethered with diverse winges, for diverse windes.

With these we may compare Canterbury's speech in *Henry V* :

> I this infer,
> That many things, having full reference
> To one consent, may work contrariously ;
> As many arrows, loosed several ways,
> Fly to one mark ; as many ways meet in one town ;
> As many fresh streams meet in one salt sea ;
> As many lines close in the dial's centre ;
> So may a thousand actions, once afoot,
> End in one purpose, and be all well borne
> Without defeat. (I. ii. 204–13)

Ascham says :

The diversitie of mens standyng and drawyng causeth diverse men loke at theyr marke diverse wayes : yet they al lede a mans hand to shoote streight yf nothyng els stoppe. So that cumlynesse is the only judge of best lokyng at the marke.

The last paragraph might well have been in Shakespeare's mind when he makes King Lear say :

That fellow handles his bow like a crow-keeper. (*Lear* IV. vi. 88–9)

Other instances of similarity of words and phrases could be given. The following shows perfect mastery of detail :

Shallow. Death is certain. Is old Double of your town living yet ?
Silence. Dead, sir.
Shallow. Jesu ! Jesu ! dead ! a' drew a good bow ; and dead ! a' shot a fine shoot : John a Gaunt loved him well, and betted much money on his head. Dead ! a' would have clapped i' the clout at twelve score ; and carried you a fore-hand shaft a fourteen and fourteen and a half, that it would have done a man's heart good to see. (*2 Hen. IV*, III. ii. 45–55)

Here the allusion is to prick shooting. To hit the clout with a 'fore-hand shaft' at twelve score was a fine performance, as this was a much heavier arrow than that used in 'under' hand shooting, the difference of under hand and 'over hand' shooting being, that in the former the bow-hand was placed so high that aim had to be taken *under* the bow-hand, while in the latter the aim was taken *over* the hand, the arrow forming as it were the fore-sight. This kind of shooting was the usual one at butts, owing to the reduced elevation required, but at pricks none but a powerful and skilful archer could use it. The passage also shows the prevalence of betting at archery. In this kind of shooting, which was also called 'flight',[1] it was common to have a marker, whose business it was to show the shooter where his arrow had fallen, 'aim' being called when the arrow was in good line. To this custom reference is made by King Philip when he says,

> Peace, lady! pause, or be more temperate :
> It ill beseems this presence to cry aim
> To these ill-tuned repetitions ;   (*John* II. i. 195–7)

and in Ford's speech :

> Well ; I will take him, then torture my wife, pluck the borrowed veil of modesty from the so seeming Mistress Page, divulge Page himself for a secure and wilful Actaeon ; and to these violent proceedings all my neighbours shall cry aim ; (*M. Wives* III. ii. 42–7)

and again, when Malcolm exclaims :

> This murderous shaft that 's shot
> Hath not yet lighted, and our safest way
> Is to avoid the aim : therefore, to horse. (*Macb.* II. iii. 148–50)

It would be hard to find a better description of a shooting match than the following :

> *Costard.* By my troth, most pleasant : how both did fit it !
> *Maria.* A mark marvellous well shot, for they both did hit it.
> *Boyet.* A mark ! O ! mark but that mark ; a mark, says my lady !
> Let the mark have a prick in 't, to mete at, if it may be.
> *Mar.* Wide o' the bow hand ! i' faith your hand is out.
> *Cost.* Indeed a' must shoot nearer, or he'll ne'er hit the clout.
> *Boy.* An' if my hand be out, then belike your hand is in.
> *Cost.* Then will she get the upshoot by cleaving the pin.
>   (*Love's L. L.* IV. i. 133–40)

The upshoot was the best shot, up to any point in the contest.

---

[1] He set up his bills here in Messina and challenged Cupid at the flight ; and my uncle's fool, reading the challenge, subscribed for Cupid, and challenged him at the bird-bolt. (*Much Ado* I. i. 39–42)

References to flight and butt shooting are common : to the first by Petruchio :

'Twas I won the wager, though you hit the white ;
(Tam. Sh. v. ii. 187)

and to the second by Mercutio :

Alas ! poor Romeo, he is already dead ; stabbed with a white wench's black eye ; shot through the ear with a love-song ; the very pin of his heart cleft with the blind bow-boy's butt-shaft ;
(Rom. & Jul. ii. iv. 13–17)

and by York :

I am your butt, and I abide your shot.   (3 Hen. VI, i. iv. 29)

That efforts were made to carry out the enactments made for the encouragement of archery is proved by many of the churchwardens' and parish accounts of the period. Under date 1583, for instance, at Eltham, the following entries appear :

Paid for felling three trees for the Butts, and cutting them out	o	o	12
For carting the same timber	o	o	12
To Hampshire, for 2 day work to make the posts and rails and setting them up	o	2	4
Paid to 4 men that digged turf and labred at the Butts, and for 100 and a half of nails	o	4	9
Paid in charges for the suppers of all them that wrought at the Butts, which were three or more than we hoped, becas we could end in one day	o	2	2
For the two barres for the Butts with the staplest iron work thereto	o	2	2
Paid to Henry Byrde for ditching before the Butts in Easterfylde	o	o	12

Sometimes the butts were not considered enough to shoot at, and in one entry we find :

Item, making a Turk for shott, boards, nails and making xviii d.

During the reigns of Henry VIII and his successors, numerous archery pageants took place, and Shakespeare must have had opportunities of witnessing such performances. Though primarily shows, their main object was to foster the practice of archery. Henry VIII, himself a skilful and enthusiastic archer (for we are told that he shot as well as any of his guard), took part in them. These efforts to bring archery before the public were nothing new, though they appear to have reached their height in these reigns.

May-Day had been kept up as an English festival for many years, the popular hero, Robin Hood, and his merry men being gradually incorporated in the show. Of these pageants the chronicler Hall gives us several accounts.

Henry VIII also it was who granted the charter for the encouragement of archery to the Honourable Artillery Company, by which the Finsbury and other archers were enabled to use the fields round Clerkenwell for practising the sport. And when keeping his court at Windsor, he

caused sundry matches to be made concerning shooting in the long bow ; and to which came many principal archers, who being in game and the upshoot given, as all men thought, there was one Barlo yet remaining to shoot, being one of the King's guard ; to whom the King very graciously said, ' Win them all and thou shalt be Duke over all Archers.' This Barlo drew his bow, and shooting won the best. Whereat the King greatly rejoiced, commending him for his good Archery ; and for that this Barlo did dwell in Shoreditch, the King named him Duke of Shoreditch.

On another occasion, the King being at Mile End, was pleased with the shooting of a body of archers styling themselves Prince Arthur's knights. These two bodies under their respective chiefs held various pageants, with which Shakespeare was evidently familiar. Of one of them, which took place on September 17, 1583, a description is preserved. Notice was given by the Duke of Shoreditch (Barlo's successor) in good time, calling on the Marquesses of Clerkenwell, Hogsden and Shackelwell, the Earl of Pancridge, and other Barons and noblemen of his associates to meet him at Merchant Tailors' Hall, when

there repaired unto him all those that were appointed for the conducting of his Person to the place of meeting, as Barons and a multitude of good archers under his own Ensign, who with the sound of Trumpets, Drums and other necessary instruments, passed along Broadstreet, Moorgate to Finsbury Fields, and the place of meeting, Smithfield, from which they marched via Cheapside, Leadenhall, and Houndsditch.

Finally the procession arrived at the Hogsden Fields, where the butts and tents were set up. While on the ground the Duke of Shoreditch was informed of the arrival of a deputation from his rival potentate, Prince Arthur, who craved admission, and offered, to be shot for in all friendship, five gold bows and the same number of silver arrows.

446 1

Allusion is made by Shallow to a similar pageant :

I remember at Mile-end Green, when I lay at Clement's Inn,—I was then Sir Dagonet in Arthur's show.[1] (*2 Hen. IV*, III. ii. 301–3)

That ladies used the bow at this period we find numerous proofs in contemporary writers. Sir F. Leake, writing to the Earl of Shrewsbury in 1605, thanks him for the gift of a very great and fat stag :

the well-comer being stricken by yo. right honourable Ladies handes . . . howbeit I knoe her Ladyshipp takes pitie of my bucke sense the last tyme yt pleased her to take the travell to shote att them. I am afreyde that my honourable Ladies my Ladies Alathea and my Ladies Cavendishe wyl commande their aroe heades to be verie sharpe : yett I charitable trust such good Ladies wylbe pitifull.

Queen Elizabeth herself is mentioned in a manuscript belonging to the Berkeley family as having shot deer in the Park, and indeed it was a common practice with ladies. In *Love's Labour's Lost* we find the Princess so engaged.

Princess. Then, forester, my friend, where is the bush
That we must stand and play the murderer in ?
Forester. Hereby, upon the edge of yonder coppice ;
A stand where you may make the fairest shoot.
Prin. I thank my beauty, I am fair that shoot,
And thereupon thou speak'st the fairest shoot.
For. Pardon me, madam, for I meant not so. . . .
Prin. But come, the bow : now mercy goes to kill,
And shooting well is then accounted ill.
Thus will I save my credit in the shoot :
Not wounding, pity would not let me do't ;
If wounding, then it was to show my skill,
That more for praise than purpose meant to kill. (IV. i. 7–29)

This passage and the following refer to the usual method adopted by shooters of taking a sheltered stand while the game was driven towards them by beaters.

1st Keeper. Under this thick-grown brake we'll shroud our-
selves ;
For through this laund anon the deer will come ;
And in this covert will we make our stand,
Culling the principal of all the deer. (*3 Hen. VI*, III. i. 1–4)

To ' take a stand ' is essential for good shooting, as Falstaff tells us :

I am glad, though you have ta'en a special stand to strike at me, that your arrow hath glanced. (*M. Wives* V. v. 259–61)

---

[1] In a will of 1552 occurs a bequest of 20s. to be spent in Mile End for the Knights of the Round Table : see *Archaeologia*, vol. xxxix, p. 34, note.

Shakespeare's references to the use of the bow as a warlike weapon are fairly numerous, and show a good knowledge of the subject, though the glory of the longbow as *the* weapon of the English had by this time departed.

Longbow-men. From a broadsheet (Wood 401 in the Bodleian Library).

The following is a fine description of the order of battle, while Richard's exhortation to the archers is terse but to the point :

> I will lead forth my soldiers to the plain,
> And thus my battle shall be ordered :
> My foreward shall be drawn out all in length
> Consisting equally of horse and foot ;
> Our archers shall be placed in the midst.
>
> (Rich. III, v. iii. 292–6)

> Fight, gentlemen of England ! fight, bold yeomen !
> Draw, archers, draw your arrows to the head !
> Spur your proud horses hard, and ride in blood ;
> Amaze the welkin with your broken staves.
>
> (ibid. 339–42)

To sum up, there was no lack of bow-shooting during Shakespeare's time. Every one was an archer, or would have been, if the statutes for its encouragement had been carried out. Butts and marks were provided at the public expense, pageants and shows enough to satisfy the most exacting were common. Nor was the excitement of betting on one's shot unknown, while there were plenty of prizes to be won. It was also an institution at our public schools. At Eton what are now called the 'Playing' fields were then the 'Shooting' fields, and at Harrow archery was enjoined under the statutes of the school, drawn up by the founder John Lyon in 1590, a silver arrow being annually shot for, a custom which was duly observed till 1766. In sport also the longbow was in common use, though it was being gradually superseded by the crossbow.

BIBLIOGRAPHY.—The first manual of Archery, *L'Art d'Archerie*, was printed by Victor le Noir and published at Paris about 1525. In 1545 Roger Ascham brought out his *Toxophilus*, since reprinted many times, which, though improved upon by modern writers, is as a practical guide the foundation of them all. Several contemporary writers discuss the relative merits of the bow and fire-arms : among them Sir JOHN SMYTHE, in *Certain Discourses concerning the Formes and Effects of divers sorts of Weapons*, 1590, *Certain Instructions*, 1591, and in an unpublished work in MS. Harl. 135, Sir R. WILLIAMS in *A briefe Discourse of Warre*, 1590, and HUMFREY BARWICK in *A briefe Discourse*, 1590 (?), to which Sir JOHN SMYTHE'S MS. is a reply. Later W. NEADE in *The Double-armed Man*, 1625, and R. MASON in *Pro Aris et Focis*, 1798, return to the same subject. The various issues of *Ayme for Finsburie Archers*, 1604, &c., and WILLIAM WOOD'S *The Bowman's Glory*, 1682, tell us of the distances shot, and the pageants of that body ; *London's Artillery*, 1616, relates to the Fraternity of St. George, and R. ROBINSON'S *The Auncient Order, Societie, and Unitie Laudable of Prince Arthure, and his Knightly Armory of the Round Table, with a Threefold Assertion frendly in favour and furtherance of English Archery at this day*, 1583, translated from *La Devise des Armes des Chevaliers de la Table Ronde*, though professedly dealing with archery, is largely concerned with heraldry.

The best modern practical books are BUTT'S *Theory and Practice of Archery*, 1887, *Archery* in the Badminton Library, 1894, which contains a comprehensive bibliography, and, as an elementary guide, *Archery for Beginners*, 1900. Many useful articles, both practical and of general interest, appear in *The Archers' Register*, 1864–1915. In W. L. RUSHTON'S *Shakespeare an Archer*, 1897, an attempt is made, with some success, to prove that Shakespeare and Roger Ascham knew each other, or at any rate that the former was acquainted with the latter's *Toxophilus*.

§ 5. FENCING AND DUELLING

BY

A. FORBES SIEVEKING

FENCING

FENCING is properly taking up postures of fence, and the word 'fence' is merely 'defence' clipped.[1] The substantives are used indifferently by Shakespeare and his contemporaries :

> He . . . gave you such a masterly report
> For art and exercise in your defence,
> And for your rapier most especially.
> > (*Haml.* IV. vii. 95–8)

> I'll prove it on his body, if he dare,
> Despite his nice fence and his active practice.
> > (*Much Ado* v. i. 74–5)

The art of fencing had made sufficient progress in Henry VIII's reign for Roger Ascham in his *Toxophilus* (1545) to compare its growing popularity with the waning of archery :

For of fence, all mooste in everye towne there is not onely Masters to teache it, wyth his Provostes, Ushers, Scholers, and other names of arte and Schole, but there hath not fayld also whyche hathe diligently and favouredly written it, and is set out in Printe that every man maye rede it.

The professors of the art were incorporated [2] under Letters Patent of July 1540, by Henry VIII, to teach the Noble Science of Defence, in which scholars took degrees and proceeded to be Provosts of Defence. This title was 'wonne by public triall of their proficiencie and their skill at certain weapons, which they call Prizes', at the last of which 'they do proceed to be maisters of the science of defence or maisters of fence'. When Saturninus con-

---

[1] Instead of 'fencer' Shakespeare once uses 'scrimer' (or, as the First Folio spells it, 'scrymures '), apparently because the speaker is talking of the Norman experts in the art (*Haml.* IV. vii. 100) ; he may even have been copying *escrimeur* from Sainct-Didier. Like its unclipped form 'escrimer', it appears to be hapax legomenon.

[2] The incorporation was consolidated by Queen Elizabeth. The late Captain Alfred Hutton printed the rules and constitutions of the school, and the orders of the various prizes in *The Sword and the Centuries* (1901), pp. 259–85.

gratulates Bassianus on having played his prize (*Tit. Andr.*
I. i. 399), he employs the technical term for qualifying for
the patent as a member of the fencing fraternity.

The chief places where fencers exercised in London were
Ely Place in Holborn, the Belle Savage on Ludgate Hill,
the Curtain in Holywell, the Grey Friars within Newgate,
the Bull in Bishopsgate Street, Bridewell, the Artillery
Gardens, Leadenhall, and, above all, Smithfield, the original
site of the earlier jousts and tournaments.

West Smithfield, according to Fuller, was formerly called
Ruffian Hall, where such men usually met, casually or
otherwise, to try masteries with sword and buckler : more
were frightened than hurt, hurt than killed therewith, it
being accounted womanly to strike beneath the knee.

Here were practised many weapons—the ancient long-
sword and back-sword, rapier and dagger, the case of
rapiers (as a pair were called), single rapier, the sword and
buckler or target. Amongst those who gained the rank of
Master on one or other of these exercising grounds were
Shakespeare's contemporaries Robert Greene and Tarlton,
the comedian. John Blinkinsop, whom Ben Jonson speaks
of as ' Blinkinsops the bold ' (*New Inn* II. iii), in 1579
played his master's prize at the Artillery Gardens against
six other masters, at four kinds of weapons, viz. the two-
hand sword, the back-sword, the sword and buckler, and
the quarterstaff.

One of Sir Thomas Overbury's 'Characters' (1615) is
'An Ordinary Fencer', in the days when fencers were
statutably classed with players as rogues and vagabonds.
In this ' Character ' there occurs the same phrase that is
used by the ' popinjay with the pouncet-box ', who pestered
Hotspur on the field of battle—

> telling me the sovereign'st thing on earth
> Was parmaceti for an inward bruise.
>
> (*1 Hen. IV*, I. iii. 57–8)

Overbury's words are : ' For an inward bruse, lambe-
stones and sweetbreads are his only *Sperma Ceti*.' He
concludes :

One signe of a good nature is, that hee is still open breasted
to his friends ; for his foile, and his doublet, weare not above
two buttons [cf. *infra*, pp. 396–7] : and resolute he is, for he so
much scornes to take blowes, that he never weares Cuffes. . . .

Lastly, these Fencers are such things, that care not if all the world were ignorant of more Letters than onely to reade their Patent.

A treatment of the practice of the ' noble science ' falls naturally into two divisions, the one dealing with the weapons, the other with the methods of fighting and the various attacks and parries or guards.

Of the fashion in weapons and the supersession of the one kind by the other, the sword and buckler by the rapier (and dagger), Stow[1] gives the following account :

And whereas untill the twelfe or thirteenth yeere of Queene Elizabeth, the auncient English fight of Sword and Buckler was onely had in use, the Bucklers then being but a foote broad, with a pike of foure or five inches long, then they began to make them full halfe ell broad, with sharpe pikes ten or twelve Inches long, where-with they meant either to breake the swords of their enemies, if it hit upon the pike, or els suddenly to run within them and stabbe and thrust their Buckler with the pike into the face, arme or body of their adversary ; but this continued not long, every Haberdasher then sold Bucklers. For, shortly after, began long Tucks, and long Rapiers, and he was held the greatest Gallant, that had the deepest Ruffe and longest Rapier : the offence to the Eye of the one, and the hurt unto the life of the Subject, that came by the other, caused her Majesty to make Proclamation against them both and to place Selected grave Citizens at every gate, to cut the Ruffes and breake the Rapiers points of all passengers that exceeded a yeard in length of their Rapiers, and a nayle of a yeard in depth of their Ruffes.'[2]

The introduction of the rapier into England took place early in the reign of Elizabeth, if not in the reign of Henry VIII. It will surprise none that Shakespeare is guilty of the anachronism of arming his characters with it in *Richard II*, *Henry IV*, and *Henry V*, or that he is guilty, too, of the still more glaring inconsistency of giving to Chiron in *Titus Andronicus* (II. i. 39) the ' dancing-rapier ', the light ornamental blade of the Elizabethan courtier.

An early synonym of ' rapier ' is ' tuck ', which appears in Scotch documents from 1508 as ' towke ', ' touke ', and seems to be derived from an Old French *étoc*, variant form of *estoc*. Cotgrave, in his dictionary of 1611, has ' *Espée*

---

[1] *Annales*, continued by Edmund Howes, 1631, p. 869.
[2] The order as to cutting down ruff and rapier was ruthlessly carried out, even against so important a personage as the French ambassador, who in 1580 was stopped at Smithfield by the officer ' that sitteth to cut sourdes '. (Edmund Lodge, *Illustrations of British History* (1791), vol. ii, 228.)

Espagnole, a Rapier or Tucke'; and it is very probable that the rapier found its way into England first from Spain. This would be confirmed by Darcie's statement that it was introduced by Rowland Yorke, who had fought on the Spanish side in the Low Countries.[1]

Sir Toby says to Viola, ' Dismount thy tuck ' (*Tw. N.* III. iv. 247)—a euphemism for ' Strip your sword stark naked ', and Falstaff in his anger chooses as one of his ' base comparisons ' for the prince ' You vile standing-tuck ', an abusive alternative for ' You tailor's yard, you sheath, you bow-case ' (*1 Hen. IV*, II. iv. 277–8). It is difficult to determine in the present state of the evidence whether ' stuck ' in the following passage from *Twelfth Night* and in *Hamlet* IV. vii. 161, ' If he . . . escape your venom'd stuck ', is an alternative spelling of ' stock ', the stoccado (see p. 401), or rather a derivative of the French *estoc* mentioned above, or the Spanish *estoque*. Sir Toby says :

Why, man, he's a very devil; I have not seen such a firago. I had a pass with him, rapier, scabbard, and all, and he gives me the stuck in with such a mortal motion that it is inevitable.

(*Tw. N.* III. iv. 307)

—as in a modern bout we should say ' he gives me his blade '.

There are many allusions in both general and technical literature to the momentous change from sword and buckler to rapier and dagger. Such is Jonson's exhortation in the Introduction to *Bartholomew Fair*, not to look back to the sword-and-buckler age of Smithfield. Justice Shallow's memory took him back to the time when ' with my long sword I would have made you four tall fellows skip like rats ' (*M. Wives* II. i. 235–6). The gallant of the new fashion who made great show with the latest style of fencing while he kept his pages on short commons is catalogued as ' Master Starve-lackey the rapier-and-dagger man ' in Pompey's list of some who were ' all great doers in our trade, and are now for the Lord's sake ' (*Meas. for M.* IV. iii. 15–21).

How the sword and buckler were yielding ground among gentlemen and being left to the serving men is plainly told by Grassi's ' Introducer ' in the Advertisement to the

---

[1] Camden's *Annales*, translated by A. Darcie, 1625.

THE
CHOOLE OF THE NOBLE
and Worthy Science of Defence.

ng the first of any English-mans inuention, which professed the sayd
Science; So plainly described, that any man may quickly
come to the true knowledge of their weapons, with
small paines and little practise.

n reade it aduisedly, and vse the benefit thereof when occasion shal serue, so shalt
thou be a good Common-wealth man, liue happy to thy selfe,
and comfortable to thy friend.

so many other good and profitable Precepts and Counsels for the managing of Quarrels,
and ordering thy selfe in many other matters.

Written by IOSEPH SVVETNAM.

LONDON,
Printed by NICHOLAS OKES. 1617.

Reader. The degradation of the old weapons gives point
to Falstaff's sarcasm ' that same sword-and-buckler Prince
of Wales ' (*1 Hen. IV*, I. iii. 230). In *Romeo and Juliet* we
have a perfect epitome of the cause and materials for
fighting, of the quarrels that arose, and of the weapons
used in their liquidation in Shakespeare's days : the
serving men of the house of Capulet with their swords and
bucklers, the citizens with clubs or wasters, bills and partisans, old Capulet with his long sword (used with two
hands), Gregory and his ' swashing blow ' (I. i. 69),[1] Tybalt
with his sword swaying about his head and cutting the
winds, while others were exchanging thrusts and blows ;
and the rapier of the gallant Mercutio, like Rostand's
Cyrano, desiring to

> Tomber la pointe au cœur en même temps qu'aux lèvres.

But there were upholders of the old weapons even among
the experts, for George Silver argues that the sword and
buckler had the advantage against sword and dagger, for
although the dagger ' served well at length to put by
a thrust ', the buckler ' by reason of his circumference
and weight being well caried defendeth safely in all times
and places . . . from all manner of blowes and thrusts
whatsoever.' And again :

If we will have true defence, we must seeke it where it is, in short
swords, short staves, the half pike, partisans, gleves, or such like
weapons of perfect length, not in long swords, long rapiers, nor
frog pricking poinards. . . . English maisters of defence are profitable
members in the Commonwealth, if they teach with ancient English
weapons of true defence, weight and convenient lengths within the
compasse of the statures and strength of man.

Grassi, too, devotes a chapter to ' the manner how to
handle the Two-hand Sword in single combat ' ; yet he
is constrained to say that ' the Rapier is generally allowed
as a weapon because most perilous, therefore most feared,
and thereupon private quarrels and common frayes soonest
shunned '.

We are prone to associate Sir Philip Sidney, the mirror
of Elizabethan knighthood and chivalry, with the rapier
rather than the sword and buckler, but in a letter to his
brother, ' Sweet Robin ', October 18, 1580, we find him

[1] The same word recurs in Rosalind's ' a swashing and a martial outside '
(*A. Y. L.* I. iii. 123) and the ' three swashers ', Bardolph, Pistol, and Nym
(*Henry V*, III. ii. 31).

thus commending the older English weapon with its cutting edge :

When you play at weapons, I would have you get thick caps and brasers, and play out your play lustily, for indeed ticks and dalliances are nothing in earnest, for the time of the one and of the other greatly differs ; and use as well the blow as the thrust ; it is good in itself, and besides encreaseth your breath and strength, and will make you a strong man at the tourney and barriers. First, in any case practice the single sword, and then with the dagger ; let no day pass without an hour or two such exercise ; the rest study or confer diligently, and so shall you come home to my comfort and credit.

The foil, a light sword blunted or ' bated ' with a button, was a recognized fencing weapon as early as the reign of Elizabeth. In *Much Ado* (v. ii. 13) Margaret says that Benedick's wit is for bluntness like ' the fencer's foils, which hit, but hurt not '. The essence of the King's plot against Hamlet is that, in the fencing bout to be arranged between him and Laertes, the latter shall contrive to find a buttonless foil, ' a sword unbated ' (*Haml.* iv. vii. 138). In one place in *Hamlet* the word is rather used with vagueness, as one might say ' blade ' : ' the adventurous knight shall use his foil and target' (*Haml.* ii. ii. 343).

Two methods of fence strove for the mastery in England, the Spanish and the Italian. George Silver's *Paradoxes of Defence*, 1599, was the protest of an Englishman, having the perfect knowledge of all manner of weapons, against the lessons of the Italian teachers, and an admonishment to his countrymen to beware

how they forsake their owne naturall fight, that they may be casting off these Italianated weake, fantasticall and most divellish and imperfect fights and by exercising of their owne ancient weapons be restored, or atchieve unto their naturall and most manly and victorious fight againe.

In Silver's time there were three Italian Teachers of *Offence* in England : the title ' Master of *Defence* ' he appropriates to the English teachers. Rocko was the first; the second was Jeronimo, Rocko's boy, or usher (as we should now say ' Prévôt ' or Provost), who taught as his substitute in Blackfriars ; and the third was Vincentio Saviolo. Rocko came to England thirteen years before Silver wrote, and taught the nobles and gentlemen of the court, whom he caused ' to weare leaden soales in their shoes to make them more nimble'. His college, for he

thought it a disgrace to keep a fence school, was founded
in Warwick Lane, and this college was hung round with his
pupils' arms, under which were their rapiers, daggers, mail
gloves, and gauntlets. Benches and stools round the room
were filled with spectators of his teaching. Silver relates
how one Austen Bagger, 'a verie tall gentleman of his
handes', challenged Rocko, who with his two-hand sword
'let flie' at Bagger's sword and buckler, but the latter
closed with him, struck up his heels, cut him over the
breech, and trod upon him. Bagger's words, 'Thou that

*A guard for the short sword and dagger to encounter against the long Rapier
and Dagger, or else the long sword and Dagger.*

From J. Swetnam, *The Schoole of Defence*, 1617.

takest upon thee to hit anie Englishman with a thrust upon
anie button', recall Mercutio's description of Tybalt:

More than prince of cats, I can tell you. O, he is the courageous
captain of compliments. He fights as you sing prick-song, keeps
time, distance, and proportion; rests me his minim rest, one, two,
and the third in your bosom; the very butcher of a silk button,
a duellist, a duellist; a gentleman of the very first house, of the
first and second cause. *(Rom. & Jul.* II. iv. 20–7)

Massinger, in *The Unnatural Combat*, puts into the mouth
of the Pope:

He can teach
Our modern duellists how to cleave a button,
And in a new way never get found out
By old Carranza.

Sir John Harington (*Nugae Antiquae*) speaks of a fencer declaring ' on which button he will give the venew '.

We have a picture of Saviolo in his school by Florio, in his *Second Frutes*, 1591. Giordano and Edward go to a fence school, that of Master V. S., ' at the Signe of the red Lyon, in the little streate where the well is ' ; he plays at rapier and dagger, or rapier and cloak, 'he can give a thrust (*stoccata*) and ward it (*pararla*), knows all the advantages, how a man must charge (*investir*) and enter upon (*incalzar*) his enemy '. The master, it is said, ' will hit any man bee it with a thrust (*punta*), a stoccada, with an imbroccada or a chargeing blow, with a right or reverse blowe, be it with the edge, with the back, or with the flat.' Besides this, he shoots well, ' in a peece, in great ordinance, is an excellent souldier, dances both galliards and pavins, vaults most nimblie, and capers verie loftilie.'

For some time it looked as if the Spanish system of swordsmanship expounded in the works of Carranza and Don Luys Pacheco de Narvaez would ultimately prevail in England. This may be called the Geometrical or Euclidian School of Fencing, based as it was upon the theorems of geometry. The adversaries come on guard at the extremities of the diameter of an imaginary circle, the length of the diameter being determined by the two arms extended horizontally sword in hand. In a combat the two adversaries moved round in a circle and endeavoured not to come uncovered within touch of one another's weapons. Fletcher, in *The Queen of Corinth*, asks (adapting Spanish fencing terms to forms of speech) :

> Has he given the lye
> In circle, or oblique, or semi-circle,
> Or direct parallel ? You must challenge him ; (iv. 1)

and Ben Jonson (*New Inn* II. ii) has :

> He does it all by lines and angles, Colonel,
> By parallels and sections : has his diagrams.

Jeronimo de Carranza was the favourite Spanish master under Philip II (1527–98), and his book, *De la Filosofia de las Armas*, was first published in 1569. Later comes Luys Pacheco de Narvaez (commonly called by English contemporary writers ' Don Lewis ') who published his *Libro de las Grandezas de la Espada* at Madrid in 1600, and also edited Carranza.

The Spanish attack consisted in three kinds of passes or paces (*pasada*),—for, in the geometrical system, the step, or movement of the foot, mathematically measured, was the main principle of the attack,—viz. the *pasada* of about twenty-four inches ; the *pasada simple*, of about thirty inches ; and the *pasada doble*, formed of the first two, and performed by the two feet alternately.

When Captain Bobadill is giving Malton a fencing lesson after the manner warranted by the great Carranza, and tells him ' a well experienced hand will pass upon you at pleasure ', Malton asks, ' How mean you, Sir, pass upon me ? ' To which Bobadill replies : ' Why thus, Sir, make a thrust at me—come in upon the answer, control your point, and make a full career [i. e. lunge] at the body ; the best practised gallants of the time name it the passado, a most desperate thrust, believe it.' [1] Mercutio speaks of ' the immortal passado ', and Shakespeare has the word again in *Love's Labour's Lost* : ' the passado he respects not ' (I. ii. 188). But, although he makes Armado declare that Cupid's butt-shaft, being too hard for Hercules' club, is therefore too much odds for a Spaniard's rapier, it may be said in general that the fencing allusions in Shakespeare are usually to the Italian, while Jonson's are to the Spanish method. Ben Jonson alludes to both Carranza and Don Lewis in *The New Inn*, styling the latter ' the sole Master now of the World '.

Don Lewis's teaching was more favourable to the use of the point than Carranza's ; their system was reduced to its absurdity in the seventeenth century by Girard Thibault d'Anvers, whose superb volume remains as a monument, on the one hand, of his fencing fatuity, and, on the other, of the arts of Crispin van de Passe and the Elzevirs (1628).

It was not merely the decline of Spanish fashion and influence at Elizabeth's accession that led to the rejection of Spanish and the adoption of Italian methods of fight. The travelled and practical-minded Englishman was not slow to discover that if the Spaniard led the way in fighting ' by the book ' of geometry, rather than of arithmetic, the Italian master who had found his way into England,

---

[1] *Every Man in His Humour* I. iv. The whole of Bobadill's inimitable fencing lesson should be studied, and Mathew's eulogy of a ' hanger ' compared with Osric's (*Haml.* v. ii. 157 ff.).

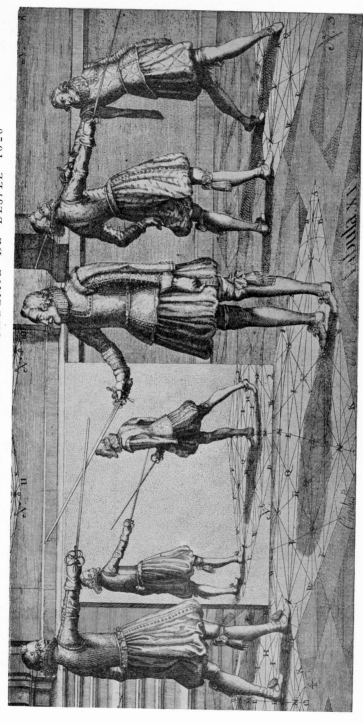

THE SCHOOL OF GEOMETRICAL FENCING

under the patronage of the Earl of Essex, was immeasurably superior in the practical art of killing his man.

Italian methods were first interpreted to English ears by the Modenese fencing-master Giacomo di Grassi, whose *True Arte of Defence*, englished by J. G(eronimo), was published in London in 1594, a year before Saviolo's 'Practise'. Grassi is generally held to have inspired Sainct-Didier and Saviolo. He was the first to take into consideration 'lines' of attack in fencing, which he differentiates into high, low, inside, and outside; on the other hand, he distinguishes only three 'wards' (guards or parries)—the high, low, and broad or wide ward. But the main advance in Grassi's work is his advocacy of the use of the point in attack, in preference to the edge. In this he is to be contrasted to some extent with Saviolo, who, asserting that the rapier alone was 'the true foundation and the true beginning from whence you may learn all things belonging to this art, tells us that it was made 'with two edges and one point', and that the whole art of the single rapier consisted in 'down-right or cross-blows, thrusts, foynes, or overthwart prickes'. Saviolo makes his scholars use the edge as well as the point of their blade, but he cautions them against the use of *mandrittaes* or *rinversoes* as dangerous, 'for to use the point is more readie and spendes not the lyke time'.

The following passage will give the modern fencer as good an idea of the teaching of Saviolo as any other, but, though nominally written in English, it requires frequent reference to Florio's *Worlde of Wordes* or *First Fruites* :

> Also if you should deliver a stoccata to your enemie, and that he should break it with his Rapier, immediately you might remove with your lefte foot, your left hand waiting on the weapon of your enemie, and give him an imbroccata or foine under or above his Rapier, and may be master of his weapon. But if your enemie strike a mandritta at the legges, if you strike it by with your weapon, he may give you a venew either by stoccata or imbroccata.

Silver condemns the evil custom in the fencing schools of forbidding the thrust (and favouring only the cut) with the Single Sword, Sword and Dagger, and Sword and Buckler, whereas at the Single Rapier, and Rapier and Dagger, they forbid the blow (i. e. the use of the edge). Silver contends that whichever method is best, is best with all weapons. 'There is no maner of teaching', he says, 'comparable to

the old ancient teaching, that is, first their quarters, then
their wardes, blowes, thrusts and breaking of thrusts, then
their closes and gripes, striking with the hilts.' Falstaf
says to the Prince, ' Thou knowest my old ward ' (*1 Hen. IV*
II. iv. 219), and would no doubt have been on Silver's side
in carving other men's doublets.

' Ward ', now more familiar in its French form ' guard '
means the attitude taken up to protect oneself from a blow.[1]
The old ward, or guard, had in it something of the offensive,
and was not, like the modern parry, merely defensive—
' the idea of self-defence being entirely merged in that of
offence to the enemy '—and there were often as many set
guards as there were known ways of delivering hits. The
Bolognese Viggiani, for instance, has seven guards offensive
and defensive, whereas Marozzo had taught six, Agrippa four.

The word Venew (venue or veney) Shakespeare uses both
literally and metaphorically for a ' hit ' or ' touch ', and
once for a ' bout ' (*M. Wives* I. i. 298). Bobadill expresses
disgust at the term :

Venue ! Fie, most gross denomination as ever I heard : O, the
stoccata while you live, sir, note that. (*Every Man in his Humour* I. i)

With him as with Mercutio :

Alla stoccata carries it away, (*Rom. & Jul.* III. i. 79)

as he bids Tybalt pluck his sword ' out of his pilcher [i. e.
scabbard] by the ears '. Armado, a fantastical Spaniard,
has ' A sweet touch, a quick venew of wit ! snip, snap,
quick and home ! ' (*Love's L. L.* v. i. 62–3), which recalls the
fact that a *riposte* in fencing has been likened to an epigram
or repartee in action.

In the First Quarto of *Hamlet*, when the fencing match
is being arranged, the wager is to be ' that young Laertes
in twelve venies, at Rapier and Dagger do not get three
odds of you '. In the later form of the play the King stakes
six Barbary horses against ' six French rapiers and poniards,
with their assigns, as girdle, hangers and so ', that ' in
a dozen passes ' between Hamlet and Laertes, ' he shall
not exceed you three hits ' (*Haml.* v. ii. 156–74).

---

[1] Shakespeare has six instances of the fencing ' ward ', as against two of
' guard '. The following may be noticed here : ' Come from thy ward ' (i. e.
Come off thy guard) (*Temp.* I. ii. 468). ' Drive her then from the ward of
her purity ' (*M. Wives* II. ii. 262–3). ' The best ward of mine honour ' (*Love's
L. L.* III. i. 139). ' He 's beat from his best ward ' (*Wint. Tale* I. ii. 33).

'Foin', an old word (as old as Chaucer) for thrust, occurs as noun and verb in Shakespeare. In Marston's *Scourge of Villanie* the lash of his satire falls upon a certain 'Bombast foil-button', who, 'for want of talk-stuff, falls to foinery.' 'Sir boy, I'll whip you from your foining fence', cries old Antonio in his rage to Claudio (*M. Ado* v. i. 84). And the host in *The Merry Wives* includes the term in his fencing ecstasy:

To see thee fight, to see thee foin, to see thee traverse; to see thee here, to see thee there; to see thee pass thy punto, thy stock, thy reverse, thy distance, thy montant.   (II. iii. 24-7)

This last word, 'montant', which occurs also in its fuller form of *montanto* in the mouth of Captain Bobadill, means an upright blow or thrust, and is the name jokingly selected by Beatrice for Benedick, whom she dubs *Signior Mountanto*, to indicate his fencing reputation (*M. Ado* I. i. 30).

The foin, the venue, the stoccata (or stock), and the punto, —all nearly synonymous,—together with the punto reverso (*Rom. & Jul.* II. iv. 28) or back-handed thrust, and the montanto, exhaust the list of Shakespeare's hits. Other terms, common enough with his contemporaries, such as the mandritta (the thrust from right to left) or the imbroccata (the charging blow), are absent from his works.

DUELLING

The gentleman will for his honour's sake have one bout with you; he cannot by the duello avoid it.   (*Tw. N.* III. iv. 340-2)

On the relation between fencing and duelling Montaigne wrote:

The honour of combates consisteth in the jealousie of the heart, not of the science. And therefore have I seene some of my friends, renowned for great Masters in this exercise, in their quarrels to make choice of weapons that might well take the meane of this advantage or oddes from them ... that their victorie might not rather be imputed to their fencing then ascribed to their valour. And in my infancy our nobility scorned the reputation of a fencer, though never so cunning, as injurious; and if any learnt it they would sequester themselves from company, deeming the same as a mystery of craft and subtility, derogating from true and perfect vertue.[1]

Brantôme tells us that he undertook his treatise on

---

[1] Florio's *Essayes of Montaigne*, 1603, Bk. II, chap. xxvii (*Cowardize the Mother of Crueltie*).

duels in order to arrive at a decision upon the disputed point which he had often heard debated, ' si l'on doit pratiquer grandes courtoisies, et en user parmy les duels, combats, camps clos, estaquades (i. e. estocades) et appels ' —in other words, if duels were to be conducted with courtesy, fairness, and honour as between gentlemen, or with brutality and every base ruse and advantage as between cut-throats and assassins. And indeed, to judge from Brantôme's own ' contes duelatiques ', which have been described as ' story after story of cold-blooded assassination, thinly disguised by a few artificial formalities ',[1] it was high time that a little more sense of the obligations of nobility, whether of birth or of mind, should enter into the relations of men who fought to the death upon frivolous or serious grounds. Chivalry towards women had long preceded the cultivation of the point of honour amongst men, and Selden shows how the modern extra-judicial duel was dependent upon chivalrous ideas for its origin :

For truth, honour, freedom and courtesy being incidents to perfect chivalry, upon the lye given, fame impeached, body wronged or courtesy taxed . . . a custom hath been among the French, English, Burguignons, Italians, Almans, and the Northern people to seek revenge of their wrongs on the body of their accuser, and that by private combat *seul à seul* without judicial lists appointed them.[2]

Hence the attention paid by writers upon social ethics to the precedence and punctilios of the duel and its antecedents ; the cause of quarrel, the challenge and its acceptance, and the choice of weapons. Giving the lie in some form or other was the final and irrevocable provocation, the dishonour of which bloodshed alone could wipe out. This is over and over again insisted upon in contemporary text-books upon ' honour and civility '. So we find Bryskett in *A Discourse of Civill Life* (1606) saying :

It is reputed so great a shame to be accounted a lyer, that any other injury is cancelled by giving the lie ; and he that receiveth it standeth so charged in his honour and reputation, that he cannot disburden himself of that imputation, but by striking of him that hath so given it, or by chalenging him the combat.

In *The Booke of Honor and Armes* (1590), which is now usually attributed to Sir William Segar, and which most probably Saviolo had before him when he wrote his

---

[1] G. H. Powell, in *Quarterly Review*, Oct. 1901, p. 435.
[2] *The Duello or Single Combat*, 1610.

' Practise ', a whole chapter is devoted to ' the nature and diversitie of lies ', where they are divided into Conditional and Certain lies, either of which may be general or special. To these a third kind is added, called ' Vain lies '. An example of a General and Certain lie is this : ' Thou hast spoken in prejudice of mine honor, honestie and credite, and therefore doest lie.' This has no force. ' Thou hast said that at the Battaile of Montcontour I abandoned mine Ensigne and cowardly ran away ' is an instance of a lie special, which Saviolo copies very closely. The ' Conditional lie ' is the occasion of much disputation because it is not in force till the condition is verified : ' Therefore it behoveth Gentlemen and other persons of honor or credite to shunn all conditional lies.' Instances of ' Vain lies ' are : ' If thou wilt not say I am an honest man, thou liest in thy throat.' Or ' Draw thy weapon, and I will presentlie prove thee a Liar and a Varlet '. The nature of the lie being to rebuke injury, if it did not have that effect it became an injury itself, and might be returned by another lie. This looks like the early state of the ' Tu quoque '.

The receiver of the lie had the right to become the challenger.[1] The letter of challenge, which takes the place of the ancient cartel, ought to use all plainness of words and phrases, leaving aside eloquence and ambiguities of speech . . . ; ' all speeches or writings of or to an enemie should be in good honourable terms.' This hardly coincides with Sir Toby's views or his advice to Sir Andrew Aguecheek (who in his challenge to Viola is so anxious to keep within the law or to the windy side of it) to swear horribly as he draws :

for it comes to pass oft that a terrible oath, with a swaggering accent sharply twanged off, gives manhood more approbation than ever proof itself would have earned him. (*Tw. N.* III. iv. 199–203) .

Sir Toby is rather more cautious and less aggressive in his suggestions as to the form of the challenge itself :

Go, write it in a martial hand ; be curst and brief ; it is no matter how witty, so it be eloquent, and full of invention : . . . if thou thou'st him some thrice, it shall not be amiss ; and as many lies as will lie in thy sheet of paper. (*Tw. N.* III. ii. 47–52)

---

[1] The word *challenge*, modern etymology teaches us, is originally the same word as *calumniate*.

This, we may say with Rosalind, is rather

a boisterous and a cruel style,
A style for challengers. (A. Y. L. iv. iii. 32–3)

In Possevino's *Dialogo dell' Honore* (Venice, 1559), from which it is not impossible that Saviolo, Favin, Segar, and other Elizabethan writers drew their inspiration—(although the writer is himself accused of plagiarism)—we find, in addition to a definition of the 'duello', the following passage on lies : ' Of lies, some are affirmative, some negative, some general, some particular—and of the latter some are absolute, some conditional.' Touchstone's enumeration of the preliminary stages or degrees, the seven causes of the quarrel,—a quarrel ' in print, by the book '—comprised the ' retort courteous ', the ' quip modest ', the ' reply churlish ', the ' reproof valiant ', the ' countercheck quarrelsome ', the ' lie with circumstance ', and the ' lie direct '. The Clown concludes his exposition with

All these you may avoid but the lie direct ; and you may avoid that too, with an 'if'. . . .Your 'if' is the only peace-maker ; much virtue in 'if'. (A. Y. L. v. iv. 101–109)

It would seem that the circumstantial lie is meant to represent the conditional lie of the books.

The duel in Elizabeth's reign had almost passed from its original form, derived through the Normans, of judicial combat[1] held to decide a charge of treason against the sovereign or a legal right or wrong, into the personal stage, when it decided the point of wounded honour between one individual and another. It was no longer loyalty or the law that the duello vindicated, but personal honour, pride, or vanity.

Of the early judicial form of the duel Shakespeare gives us one example. The knightly or chivalrous preliminaries are shown in the opening scene of *Richard II*, where Bolingbroke challenges Mowbray in presence of the King with all the pomp and ceremony of mediaeval forms :

What my tongue speaks, my right drawn sword may prove ;

and the cause has to be arbitrated by blood between

---

[1] Spelman tells us how, in 1571, one of the last judicial duels, which was adjudged to be decided before the Justices of the Common Pleas as umpires, in Tothill Fields, proved abortive owing to the non-appearance of the petitioner, who was consequently non-suited. Actually it was only by statute of George III that the judicial combat was finally put an end to as a form of legal procedure.

loyalty and treason. The gage is thrown down by Bolingbroke, who declares to Mowbray :

> If guilty dread have left thee so much strength
> As to take up mine honour's pawn, then stoop :
> By that, and all the rites of knighthood else,
> Will I make good against thee, arm to arm,
> What I have spoke, or thou canst worse devise.
> *Mow.* I take it up ; and by that sword I swear,
> Which gently laid my knighthood on my shoulder,
> I'll answer thee in any fair degree,
> Or chivalrous design of knightly trial.
>
> (Rich. II, I. i. 73–81)

And then the charge of treason is brought in detail, and
after the King has failed to get the two knights to throw
down each other's gage, and make peace, they are cited by
the King to the lists at Coventry on St. Lambert's Day
to see

> Justice design the victor's chivalry.   (ibid. 203)

In *The Second Part of King Henry VI* we have an example
from a lower rank of life, in the serio-comic duel between
Horner the Armourer and his prentice Peter, in which the
King, as equal dispenser of justice to all his subjects high
and low, asks his uncle Gloucester how he should act, and
is advised—

> And let these have a day appointed them
> For single combat in convenient place ;
> For he hath witness of his servant's malice.
> This is the law, and this Duke Humphrey's doom.
>
> (I. iii. 211–14)

Ultimately Horner fights in a drunken state, is struck
down by Peter, and admits his guilt (*ibid.* II. iii. 59–98).

The examples of the contemporary duel (in *As You Like It*
and *Twelfth Night*) have already been referred to, and in
these it appears that Shakespeare deliberately set out to
ridicule current practice. Whether it was owing to the
direct encouragement of the Queen, or to the introduction
of the easily manipulated and universally worn rapier as
the favourite weapon of a gentleman, it is a fact that
duelling in these days almost bore the aspect of a social
contagious disease.

James I, however, regarded duelling as ' a vaine that
bleeds both incessantly and inwardly ', and resolutely dis-
countenanced the practice ; his *Proclamation against private*

Challenges and Combats appeared in 1613 (in conformity with which Lord Sanquhar was executed for the ' murder ' of his fencing master), and in 1615, when Bacon was attorney-general, the Star Chamber ' with one consent did utterly reject and condemne the opinion that the private duel in any person whatsoever had any ground of honor '.

James Howell considered the Frenchman a far fairer duellist than the Spaniard, who has his ' doublet quilted, his coat of mail, his cassock, and strives to make himself impenetrable '.[1] George Silver, over forty years earlier, speaks of the strange vices and devices of Italian, French, and Spanish fencers ;[2] but on the other hand he extols the Spaniards' bravery in fight ' with their bodies straight upright, narrow spaced with their feet continually moving, as if they were in a dance holding forth their armes and rapiers verie straight against the face or bodies of their enemies '. Herein we see the influence of Carranza's system.

What has been said sufficiently shows the intimate connexion existing in Shakespeare's day between the art of fencing and duelling—an alliance which in England at least has long been broken, although on the Continent the sword is sometimes the final arbiter of ' honour and honourable quarrels '. The two great contemporaries of the sixteenth century, Montaigne and Shakespeare, both laid their finger on the vital difference between fencing and duelling in words which have a curious ring of resemblance. Shakespeare's are put into the mouth of Justice Shallow :

> In these times you stand on distance, your passes, stoccadoes and I know not what : *'tis the heart, Master Page ; 'tis here, 'tis here.*
>
> (*M. Wives* II. i. 232–4)

Montaigne, through his mouthpiece Florio, thus distinguishes between true and false honour :

> It is a pranke of skill and knowledge to be cunning in the art of fencing, and which may happen unto a base and worthlesse man. *The reputation and worth of a man consisteth in his heart and will ; therein consists true honour.*[3]

[1] *Instructions for Forreine Travell*, 1642.
[2] *Paradoxes of Defence*, 1599.   [3] *Essayes*, Bk. I, chap. xxx.

BIBLIOGRAPHY.—The chief contemporary English works dealing with Fencing or Duelling or both are *The Booke of Honor and Armes, wherein is discoursed the Causes of Quarrell and the Nature of Injuries with their Repulses,* 1590, ascribed to Sir W. Segar; MATTHEW SUTCLIFFE'S *Practice, Proceedings and Lawes of Armes, described out of the doings of most valiant and expert Captaines*, 1593; *Vincentio Saviolo, His Practise, in two bookes: the first intreating of the use of the Rapier and Dagger, the second of Honour and Honourable Quarrels*, 1595, a book which with the following is indispensable for the study of fencing and duelling in Shakespeare and Jonson; GEORGE SILVER's *Paradoxes of Defence, wherein is proved the true ground of fight to be in the short ancient weapons, and that the short sword hath the advantage of the long sword or long rapier, and the weaknesse and imperfection of the rapier fight displayed*, 1599; also his *Brief Instructions upon my Paradoxes of Defence*, first printed from the manuscript by Captain (now Colonel) Cyril Matthey in 1898; Sir ROBT. COTTON's *Of the Antiquity, Use and Ceremony of Lawful Combats in England*, 1601 (Stow MS. 569, f. 35); Sir W. SEGAR's *Honor military and civill*, 1602; SELDEN's *The Duello or Single Combat from antiquitie derived into this Kingdome of England, with severall kindes and ceremonious formes thereof*, 1610; FAVYN's *Theater of Honour and Knighthood*, 1623; JOSEPH SWETNAM's *The Schoole of the Noble and Worthy Science of Defence*, 1617. The legal aspect of duelling can be studied in *A Brief of two proclamations and his Majesty's edict against Duels*, 1613, and in Sir F. BACON's *Charge concerning Duels, with the Decree of the Star Chamber thereupon*, 1614. Much information concerning this edict and on James I's and Bacon's attitude in regard to duels may be found in the prologue and notes to *Worke for Cutlers* (1904), edited by the present writer.

The Italian code of honour or punctilio of the duel are treated in G. B. POSSEVINO (the Elder)'s *Dialogo dell' honore, nel quale si tratta à pieno del Duello*, 1553. (In JOHN KEPERS's *Courtiers Academie* (1598), translated from Count Annibale Romei's *Discorsi* (1587), it is stated that the Bishop of Caserta claimed to have written Possevino's Booke of Honour. Romei's chapter ' of Combate ' is a discussion of the principles governing the arguments of Susius, Pigna, Paris de Puteo, and Possevino.) FRANÇOIS DE LA NOUE's *Discours politiques et militaires*, 1587, should also be consulted. For Fencing, HENRI DE SAINCT-DIDIER's *Traicté contenant les secrets du premier livre sur l'espée seule*, 1573, is an adaptation of CAMILLO AGRIPPA's *Trattato di Scientia d'Arme*, 1553, and GIACOMO DI GRASSI's *Ragione di adoprar sicuramente l'arme*, 1570. *Giacomo di Grassi, his true Arte of Defence . . . Englished by J. G.*, appeared in 1594.

The Spanish geometrical system of fence is expounded in JERONIMO DE CARRANZA's *De la Filosofia de las armas*, 1569, and LUYS PACHECO DE NARVAEZ's *Libro de las grandezas de la Espada*, 1599. Carranza's mechanical method was reduced to sheer absurdity in the magnificently futile GIRARD THIBAULT's *Académie de l'Espée*, 1628.

Works treating specifically of the history of the duel are P. BOYSSAT's *Recherches sur les Duels*, 1610; JEAN SAVARON's *Traicté contre les Duels*, 1610; VITAL D'AUDIGUIER's *Le vray et ancien usage des duels*, 1617; and BRANTÔME's famous *Discours sur les Duels* (vol. vi in the 1822 edition of his works, vol. viii, 1858). Of later writers may be mentioned COCKBURN's *History and Examination of Duels*, 1677 and 1888, and J. G. MILLINGEN's *History of Duelling*, 1841, and his article in the *Edinburgh Review*, no. lxxv.

The following are the modern historical works that must be consulted for a complete view of the subject: articles in the *Encyclopaedia Britannica* (1910) by F. STORR on *Duel*, and Sir FREDERICK POLLOCK on *Sword*; articles *Escrime* and *Duel* in *La Grande Encyclopédie* and in Larousse's *Dictionnaire Universel du XIXe Siècle*; EGERTON CASTLE's *Schools and Masters of Fence*, new ed., 1893, indispensable for a proper understanding of the various European systems and changes; Captain ALFRED HUTTON's *Old Sword Play*, 1892, and *The Sword and the Centuries*, 1901; *Fencing* in the Badminton Library, 1890, and a series of articles and studies which appeared in the *Saturday Review* between 1882 and 1895; G. LETAINTURIER-FRADIN's *Le Duel à travers les Ages*, 1892. See also C. A. THIMM's monumental *Bibliography of Fencing and Duelling*, 1896.

§ 6. HORSEMANSHIP, WITH FARRIERY

BY

A. FORBES SIEVEKING

BREEDS OF HORSES

THE breeds of horses known in England in Shakespeare's day were, according to Blundeville, the Turkey horse, Barbarian or Barb, Sardinian, Neapolitan, the Spanish Jennet, the Hungarian, the High Almaine or German horse, the Friesland, the Flanders, the Sweacian or Sweathland (Swedish) horse ' of a mean stature and strength ', and the Irish hobby.

Of all these, the Barbary horse or Barb was undoubtedly Shakespeare's favourite. With such affection and intimacy does he dwell upon its merits that it is probable that the poet at one time possessed a roan barb. The groom says to King Richard II :

> When Bolingbroke rode on roan Barbary,
> That horse that thou so often hast bestrid,
> That horse that I so carefully have dress'd ;

and the King replies :

> Rode he on Barbary ?   Tell me, gentle friend,
> How went he under him ?
> *Groom.* So proudly as if he disdain'd the ground.
> *K. Rich.* So proud that Bolingbroke was on his back.
> (*Rich. II*, v. v. 78–84)

The Barb was a little horse, but swift, and was esteemed in the manage for its ability to make a long career. ' Six Barbary horses ' was the wager made in *Hamlet* (v. ii. 154–7) against ' six French rapiers and poniards ' ; and Othello is referred to as a Barbary horse [1] (*Oth.* I. i. 112). The Neapolitan horse is described by Blundeville as ' a trim horse being both comely and strongly made ', gentle and courageous, with a long slender head, the nether part bending like a hawk's beak.

Their sure footmanship, their well-reining, their lofty pase, their clean trotting, their strong gallopping, and their swift running well

---

[1] Thus suggesting a not uncommon cross between an Eastern horse—usually a Barb—and an English mare (see Madden, p. 259).

THE NEAPOLITAN HORSE

THE SPANISH HORSE

considered, . . . they excel numbers of other races even so farre as the faire Greihoundes the fowle Mastiffe curres.

Markham calls the old Neapolitans the schoolmasters of all Christendom in the art of horsemanship, and through Grisone and Pignatelli they were certainly our teachers in the manage art. This reputation did not prevent Portia from rejecting the Neapolitan Prince with the disdainful words :

Ay, that's a colt indeed, for he doth nothing but talk of his horse ;   (*Merch. of V.* I. ii. 43–4)

nor did it weigh in the scale that he was able to shoe him himself. Markham places the coursers of Naples next to the English horse, although ' his legs to an over-curious eye might appear a little too slender '. The Spanish jennet for his fine making, lightness, and swiftness was very much esteemed.

A breeding jennet, lusty, young, and proud

is Shakespeare's description of the mare in *Venus and Adonis* (l. 260). His pace was neither trot nor amble, but ' a comely kind of going like the Turk '. The pace of the Hungarian was a hard trot. He had a great hooked head, a mane hanging down beneath his knees, and a long bushy tail. The Almaine or German horse was very strongly made and ' more meete for the shock—" grating shock of wrathful iron arms " (*Rich. II*, I. iii. 136)—than to pass a cariere or make a swift manage '. The Flanders horse was ' of a greater stature and more puissant ' than the German, and used as a draught horse. The Friesland horse, of mean stature but ' wel compackt ' and with good legs, could make a good career, and do the curvet as well as the Spanish jennet. The Sweathland or Swedish horse, but lately introduced into England, was not well conditioned, and most commonly ' pied ', with white legs and body of another colour.

Besides these Shakespeare mentions by implication the Moorish or Morocco horse, the most famous contemporary instance of which was Bankes's performing and calculating horse Marocco or Morocco. He is alluded to in innumerable places. Hall writes ' of strange Moroco's dumb arithmetic' (*Satires* IV. ii). He was also the subject of a pamphlet, *Maroccus Extaticus, or Bankes Bay Horse in a Trance* (1595). This horse would restore a glove to the due owner, after the master had whispered the man's name in his ear :

would tell the just number of pence in any piece of silver coin newly showed him by his master.'[1]

Moth says to Armado :

How easy it is to put ' years ' to the word ' three ', and study three years in two words, the dancing horse will tell you.

(*Love's L. L.* I. ii. 56–9)

The same horse is perhaps alluded to as ' bay Curtal and his furniture' (*All's W.* II. iii. 65). A curtal horse was one with its tail docked.

Another kind is the Galloway nag, which is mentioned by William Harrison in his *Description*.[2] ' Know we not Galloway nags ? ' asks Ancient Pistol (*2 Hen. IV*, II. iv. 204), and Gervase Markham gives us the answer :

There is a certain race of little horses in Scotland called Galway Nagges, which I have seen hunt the Buck and Stagge exceedingly well, and indure the chase with good Courage.

Drayton contrasts the Galloway with other nags :

Nor yet the level South can show a smoother race
Whereas the ballow nag outstrips the winds in chace ;
As famous in the West for matches yearly tried,
As Garterley, possess'd of all the Northern pride :
And on his match as much the Western horseman lays,
As the rank-riding Scots upon their Galloways ;

(*Poly-Olbion*, III. 23–8, 1612)

which reminds us that horse-racing began in Scotland before it did in England, and that James I, on his accession, probably made it popular more quickly in the south, especially in Newmarket, than it would have otherwise been.

Shakespeare never once speaks by name of the Great Horse, as the old English war-horse, used for tournaments and service, was called, and of which we read so much in Blunde-ville and Markham. By the latter he is referred to as—

The true English horse, him I mean that is bred under a good clime, on firme ground, in a pure temperature, is of tall stature and large proportions.

The great horse was probably the model for Antony's horse :

a creature that I teach to fight,
To wind, to stop, to run directly on,
His corporal motion govern'd by my spirit.

(*Jul. Cæs.* IV. i. 31–3)

[1] Kenelm Digby, *Treatise on Bodies*, p. 393.
[2] See Chapter XV, § 3. I.

THE FLANDERS HORSE

THE BARBARY HORSE

Continuous efforts were made by kings and parliaments from Henry II to Elizabeth to promote the breeding of great horses. These horses may first have been imported from Normandy, where the Northmen had long before brought the large black German horses. Thus early did the Normans earn a reputation for breed of horses and horsemanship, which was still maintained in Shakespeare's day :

> *King.* Here was a gentleman of Normandy :
> I've seen myself, and serv'd against, the French,
> And they can well on horseback ; but this gallant
> Had witchcraft in 't, he grew unto his seat,
> And to such wondrous doing brought his horse,
> As he had been incorps'd and demi-natur'd
> With the brave beast ; so far he topp'd my thought,
> That I, in forgery of shapes and tricks,
> Come short of what he did.
> *Laer.*   A Norman was't ?
> *King.* A Norman.
> *Laer.* Upon my life, Lamord.
>
> (*Haml.* IV. vii. 82–92)

' A horse ', says Blundeville,

is coloured according as he is complexioned . . . and he is complexioned according as he doth participate more or less of any of the four elements. If the earth predominates he is melancholy, heavy and faint-hearted and his colour is black, russet, a bright or dark dun. If he has more of the water, he is phlegmatic, slow, dull, apt to lose flesh, and his colour usually milk white. If of the air, he is sanguine, pleasant, nimble and of a bay colour. If of the fire, he is choleric, therefore light, hot and fiery, a stirer, seldom of great strength, and a bright sorrel colour.

In *King Henry the Fifth* the Dauphin's horse, it will be recalled, is compact of the two elements, air and fire :

Dau. I will not change my horse with any that treads but on four pasterns. *Ça, ha !*[1] He bounds from the earth as if his entrails were hairs : *le cheval volant*, the Pegasus, *qui a les narines de feu !* When I bestride him, I soar, I am a hawk : he trots the air ; the earth sings when he touches it ; the basest horn of his hoof is more musical than the pipe of Hermes.

Orl. He 's of the colour of the nutmeg.

Dau. And of the heat of the ginger. It is a beast for Perseus : he is pure air and fire ; and the dull elements of earth and water never appear in him but only in patient stillness while his rider mounts him : he is indeed a horse ; and all other jades you may call beasts (III. vii. 11–26).

[1] This is the French form of one of the ' aids ' of the voice (see p. 423).

If he participate in all the four elements equally, he is perfect, and commonly one of the following colours : a brown bay, a dapple-gray, a black full of silver hairs, a black like a Moor or a fair roan—' which kind are most commendable, most temperate, strongest, and of gentlest nature '. Next comes the bright bay, dark bay, the bright sorrel, the flea-bitten white, the white liard like silver, with black ear-tips, mane, tail, and all four feet.

But the bay was accounted the best, especially when marked by a white star in the forehead, which leads us to the question of ' cloud-in-the-face '. A horse with a cloud in his face was one with no white star in the forehead. Such a horse, it was held, was ' furious, dogged, full of mischiefe and misfortune'. All this helps to explain the allusion in *Antony and Cleopatra* :

> *Eno.* Will Caesar weep ?
> *Agr.* He has a cloud in 's face.
> *Eno.* He were the worse for that were he a horse ;
> So is he, being a man.   (III. ii. 50–3)

It was one of the regular tricks of Smithfield horse-dealers to make a false star in the forehead, and the older books give directions how this may be done.

THE MANAGE

The Italian art of training the horse in the manage, as practised and described by Grisone, Fiaschi, Caracciolo, and Claudio Corte, was acclimatized in England by Henry VIII, who introduced to court as his Riding Master Robert Alexander, ' sometime Grison's scholler ',[1] a pupil of the Neapolitan master Pignatelli, and father of three sons, who became established amongst us as teachers. Our 'Italianate' nobility, moreover, learnt to know and love the art upon their foreign travel. Sidney was an early convert, and became the patron of two Italian riding-masters in England, Romano and Prospero. In his forty-ninth sonnet[2] he shows how love itself may be translated into

---

[1] Who brought the proudest coursers to his becke
And with his hand, spur, voice and wand did tame
The stately steedes that never brookt the checke.
(Nicholas Morgan's *Perfection of Horsemanship*, 1609)

[2] I on my horse, and Love on me doth trie
Our horsmanship, while two strange works I prove,
A horsman to my horse, a horse to Love.

From A DE PLUVINEL'S *MANEIGE ROYAL* 1623 by CRISPIN VAN DE PASSE

THE VOLTE IN THE CADENCE OF THE CURVET AT THE PILLAR

' terms of manage ',[1] and he delighted

> To turn and wind a fiery Pegasus
> And witch the world with noble horsemanship,
> (1 Hen. IV, IV. i. 109–10)

having when at the emperor's court been the pupil of John Pietro Pugliano, an esquire of the stable.[2]

In 1565, the year after Shakespeare's birth, Thomas Blundeville had made the teaching of Federico Grisone's *Gli Ordini di Cavalcare* (1550) accessible to English readers in *The Fowre Chiefyst Offices belongyng to Horsemanshippe*, a book with which there is good reason to think that Shakespeare was familiar. Compare, for instance, the passage descriptive of Adonis's horse with the ' points ' in Blundeville :

> Round-hoof'd, short-jointed, fetlocks shag and long,
> Broad breast, full eye, small head, and nostril wide,
> High crest, short ears, straight legs and passing strong,
> Thin mane, thick tail, broad buttock, tender hide :
>   Look, what a horse should have he did not lack,
>   Save a proud rider on so proud a back.
> (Ven. & Ad. 295–300)

Blundeville's description is :

> Round hooves, short pasterns with long fewter lockes, broade breast, great eies, short and slender head, wide nostrils, the creast rising, short ears, strong legs, crispe mane, long and bushy tail, great round buttocks.

The Italians distinguished four kinds of manage : in the first the horse was taught to double his turns ; ' another is when they make him to gallop the field going in and out, as they do in skirmish ; the third is when they make him to leape aloft and to fetch diverse saultes; the fourth is when they pase, trot or gallop him a good while to and fro, in one selfe path . . . turning him at each end thereof, either with single turn, whole turn, or double turne ' (Blundeville, book II, ch. xx).

The English at first called only the last a manage, subdivided into three kinds : manage with half rest, manage with whole rest, and manage without rest—to each of which Blundeville devotes a chapter. This division,

---

[1] Cf. ' Speak terms of manage to thy bounding steed ' (*1 Hen. IV*, II. iii. 54).
[2] See *An Apologie for Poetrie*, ad init.

Markham says, breeds confusion; and he accordingly
reduces them to two, *manage open*, and *manage close* :
open, when you turn *terra terra* ; or close, when you turn
upon the *incavalare* and *chambetta*, which are the closest
of all turns, and may be done in a flying manner, even upon
one foot : ' the turn *Terra, Terra*, in the outmost circle of
the Strait Ring, and the *Incavalare* and *Chambetta* in the
changes, wherein he is forc't to lap one leg over another,
or else to lift up the inmost leg from the ground, while
he brings the outmost over it.'

The first lesson was to teach the colt ' to tread loftily,
to keep one path and to trot cleane, and then to be light
at stop, when checked in the career '.

He hath rid his prologue like a rough colt ; he knows not the stop,
says Lysander (*Mid. N. D.* v. i. 119–20) ; the term occurs
again in *A Lover's Complaint* :

What rounds, what bounds, what course, what stop he makes !
(l. 109)

and in a double sense in :

Come, the full stop.   (*Merch. of V.* III. i. 17)

In another lesson the horse is taught to advance before
and to yerk behind, upon which Mr. Justice Madden has the
following observation : ' And inasmuch as this yerking is an
artificial development of a motion to which the horse is by
nature occasionally too prone, Gervase Markham counsels
to make your horse yerk out behind, yet " so as it may
be perceived it is your will and not the horse's malice " ;
as it was on the field of Agincourt, when the wounded
steeds of the French

Fret fetlock-deep in gore, and with wild rage
Yerk out their armed heels at their dead masters,
Killing them twice.   (*Hen. V*, IV. vii. 83–5)

When your horse knows how to turn readily on both
hands with single turn and double turn, and is perfect in
the manage already described, you then teach him ' to passe
a swift cariere ', which, according to Gervase Markham,
is ' to run your horse forthright at his full speed, and then
making him stop quickly suddenly firme, and close on his
buttock '. Again and again Shakespeare uses the image of
the career :

stopping the career
Of laughter with a sigh.   (*Wint. Tale* I. ii. 286–7)

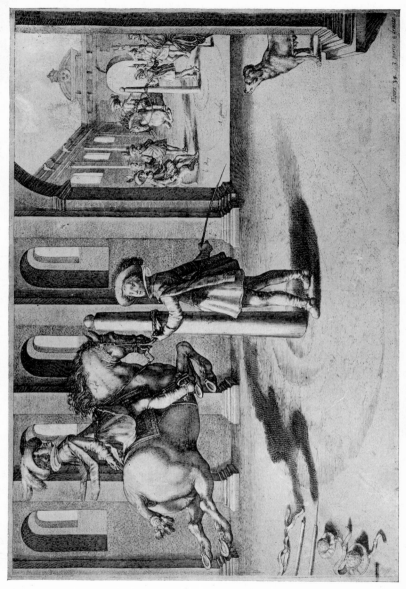

From A DE PLUVINEL'S *MANEIGE ROYAL* 1623 by CRISPIN VAN DE PASSE

THE CAPRIOLE OR GOAT-LEAP AT THE PILLAR

Sir, I shall meet your wit in the career, an you charge it against me.   *(Much Ado* v. i. 138–9)

Shall quips and sentences and these paper bullets of the brain awe a man from the career of his humour ?   *(ibid.* II. iii. 260–2)

               Full merrily
Hath this brave manage, this career, been run.
           (Love's L. L. v. ii. 482–3)

What rein can hold licentious wickedness
When down the hill he holds his fierce career ?
            (Hen. V, III. iii. 22–3)

' And finally,' sums up Blundeville,

f your horse be nimble, and apt thereto by nature, you may make him a Stirer, by teaching him to bound aloft, to yerke withall, to gallop the gallop galliard, to fetch the Capriole [goat leap], to do the Corvette [curvet] [1]—and such kinds of saults ; and in all his doings from the beginning to the ending you must see that hee reane [rein [2]] well and beare his head steadily, which is the foundation of all the rest.

A high crest was one of the distinguishing beauties of the horse, a mark of mettle *(Ven. & Ad.* 297), and lowering the crest was a sign of inferiority and submission. It is applied figuratively by Shakespeare when he speaks of ' hollow men ', who,

               like horses hot at hand,
Make gallant show and promise of their mettle ;
But when they should endure the bloody spur,
They fall their crests, and, like deceitful jades,
Sink in the trial.   *(Jul. Caes.* IV. ii. 23–7)

So also a horse

        his mettle from his rider takes,   *(Lover's Comp.* 107)

and when

           allow'd his way,
Self-mettle tires him.   *(Hen. VIII,* I. i. 133–4)

' Falling of the crest ', from the farrier's point of view, s when the upper part of the neck leans to one side or the other or falls down flat, and comes from old age or poverty ; t was counteracted by plaiting weights into the mane.

---

[1]   His manly marrow . . .
    Which should sustain the bound and high curvet
      Of Mars's fiery steed.   *(All's W.* II. iii. 298–300)
[2] i.e. submit to the rein.
    He will bear you easily and reins well.   *(Tw. N.* III. iv. 362)
To bear the head ' is used with a similar implication :
    Ajax is grown self-will'd, and bears his head
    In such a rein, in full as proud a place
    As broad Achilles.   *(Troilus* I. iii. 188–90)

Shakespeare marks the contrast :

> His ears up-prick'd ; his braided hanging mane
> Upon his compass'd crest now stand on end.
>
> *(Ven. & Ad.* 271–2)

> For that will . . . make him fall
> His crest that prouder than blue Iris bends.
>
> *(Troilus* I. iii. 378–80)

The horse's chief lesson was in the art of pacing, which Shakespeare alludes to in the following passage :

> For those that tame wild horses
> Pace 'em not in their hands to make 'em gentle,
> But stop their mouths with stubborn bits, and spur 'em,
> Till they obey the manage.   *(Hen. VIII,* v. iii. 21–4)

One of the ' x properties of a woman ', which, according to Fitzherbert *(Booke of Husbandry,* 1534), a horse should possess, was to be ' well paced '. This may have been in Shakespeare's mind when he wrote of a woman,

> My lord, she 's not paced yet ; you must take some pains to work her to your manage. *(Pericles* IV. vi. 68–70)

> The third o' the world is yours, which with a snaffle
> You may pace easy, but not such a wife.
>
> *(Ant. & Cleop.* II. ii. 67–8)

The paces given by Markham are the Trot, Rack, Amble, and Gallop.

The favourite pace in Elizabethan days was the amble. It differs from the trot, in which the horse takes up his feet crosswise, in that he moves the fore and hind legs simultaneously first on one side and then on the other, and sets them down together. The horse

> in that motion must lift and wind up his forefoot somewhat hye from the ground, but his hinder foot he must no more but take from the ground and as it were sweep it close by the earth . . . this ambling motion in his smoothe stealing away, and as it were with a soft and tender touching of the ground, carries his burthen away gently without shaking.

Armed with this definition, we are in a position to appreciate the force of Benedick's retort to Claudio :

> Sir, your wit ambles well ; it goes easily ;
>
> *(Much Ado* v. i. 162)

and of Rosalind's explanation that ' Time ambles withal . . . with a priest that lacks Latin, and a rich man that hath not the gout ', whereas ' he trots hard with a young maid between the contract of her marriage and the day it is solemnized ' (*A. Y. L.* III. ii. 330–41).

Markham further discriminates the ' thorough ' from the ' broken ' amble, and describes the various methods of teaching the pace—' by the help of a new plowde field ', from the gallop or by over-riding, by the use of weights, out of the hand, with the help of the hand only, or most commonly, by means of ' trammels ' used to connect or strap together the legs on each side either above the hocks and knees or just above the fetlocks.[1]

The Irish hobby, being ' tender-mouthed, nimble, light, pleasant, and apt to be taught ', was the favourite ambler. Markham considers that geldings were ' more naturally addicted to ambling then any stoned horse whatsoever '. Hence the pertinence of Master Ford's

I will rather trust . . . a thief to walk my ambling gelding, than my wife with herself (*M. Wives* II. ii. 320–4).

Markham defines the ' rack ' or ' racking ' pace as intermediate between the trot and amble.

The ' false gallop ', the early name for a canter, is twice used figuratively by Shakespeare:

Beat. What pace is this that thy tongue keeps ?
Marg. Not a false gallop ;   (*Much Ado* III. iv. 92–4)

and

This is the very false gallop of verses. (*A. Y. L.* III. ii. 120)

Just as a rider now breaks into a canter from a trot, so formerly he was said to break into or rise from his trot or amble to his false gallop.[2]

It is again a metaphor derived from horsemanship when a man is described as

breath'd, as it were,
To an untirable and continuate goodness ;
(*Timon* I. i. 10–11)

and ' continuate ' suggests a horse's staying power, or its lasting long, as when Benedick says :

would my horse had the speed of your tongue, and so good a continuer (*Much Ado* I. i. 148–9).

---

[1] Many in an Elizabethan audience listening to Macbeth's words,
        If the assassination
    Could trammel up the consequence, and catch
        With his surcease success,   (*Macb.* I. vii. 2–4)
would at once have called up to their mind's eye the horse ' trammelled ' for the amble, rather than the fishing or bird net, from which Shakespeare's image is taken.   [2] Richard Sadleir, *De procreandis . . . et tractandis equis*, 1587.

'Breathed' means in good wind, and in good training:

> And on thy well-breath'd horse keep with thy hounds,
>
> (*Ven. & Ad.* 678)

and figuratively it is said of untrained and unexercised minds:

> Hard-handed men, that work in Athens here,
> Which never labour'd in their minds till now,
> And now have toil'd their unbreath'd memories
> With this same play, against your nuptial.
>
> (*Mid. N. D.* v. i. 72–5)

Closely connected with 'breathing' a horse, or rather a horse's breathing or wind, is the 'sob' used by Dromio of Syracuse, who describes the bailiff's man:

> The man, sir, that, when gentlemen are tired, gives them a sob,[1] and rests them. (*Com. of E.* IV. iii. 22–4)

This term is fully substantiated by Markham in his *Cavelarice*:

> If your horse cannot move easie with a winde, but if he want staies or Sobbes.

And Browne, in his *Fiftie Yeares Practice* (1624), is still more explicit and graphic:

> Give me that horse, that will ride of an easie gallop from the hand, and so to the middle of his speede, and so to the very height of his speede; alwayes carying light of your hande, and ever yeeld willinglye to your hand whensoever you see occasion to take him up to give him a sobe.

SADDLES, BITS, STIRRUPS, AND SPURS: AIDS AND CHERISHINGS

> Your beards deserve not so honourable a grave as to stuff a botcher's cushion, or to be entombed in an ass's pack-saddle.
>
> (*Cor.* II. i. 98–100)

says Menenius to the tribunes, choosing the poorest form of saddle for the embellishment of his comparison.

Of the favourite saddle in Shakespeare's day we give an illustration from Markham, who speaks of it under the name of Prospero's saddle. After the manner of many English treatises on technical subjects in the sixteenth century, the illustration is taken direct from a foreign

---

[1] 'Bob' and 'fob', with various other conjectures, are usually to be met with in modern texts in place of the original reading.

source, the *Cavalerice* of Salomon de la Broue, who says
that the saddle was invented by Seigneur Maxime, Écuyer
to Amiral and Duc de Joyeuse. Other saddles in use for
the different purposes indicated by their names, were the
' Morocco' saddle, differing in the size of the pillows and

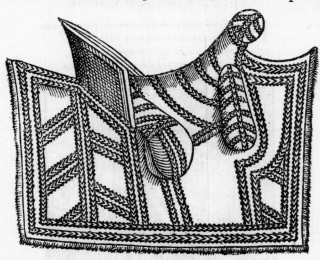

the height of the hind-crupper; the French pad, which was
best fitted for travellers, the seat being stuffed with down
and quilted; the large and plain Scotch saddle; and the
hunting or racing saddle, the ' lightest and nimblest'.

> The iron bit he crushes 'tween his teeth,
> Controlling what he was controlled with.
>
> (*Ven. & Ad.* 269–70)

Bits, of which Blundeville enumerates and figures (after
Grisone) many specimens, were either ' close' or ' open '—
the latter being also called ' port-bits', some whole and
some broken, to give the tongue greater freedom.

The English bit-makers called all kinds of square bits
' upset mouths', some of which were locked together with
one plight within another. Gervase Markham disapproved
of all upset mouths, ports, trenches, and ' byts of crueltie',
which Shakespeare must have had in his mind when he
wrote of the ' stubborn bits ' in the passage already quoted
(*Hen. VIII*, v. iii. 23). Bits were cannon bits, scatches
(Ital. *scaccia*), or (according to their shape) melon, pear,
olive, campanel or bell bits, bastonets, cat's feet, and goose-

necks, and all their elaborate parts had technical names
—such as the cheeks, eyes, jeives, rols, rings, the port,
buttons, &c. The close bits were for horses with good
mouths ; a cannon with compassed cheeks was recom-

Ephippiarius. Der Sattler.

Hvc ades à veterum qui natus origine Regum,
    Sortis es eximio munere factus eques.
Hic accepta viris, et ephippia grata puellis,
    Stratag̃ magr animũ apta parantur equis.

Impositis long.as melius quibus itur in or.as,
    Miles et in bellum trux equitare potest.
Prima Peletronias antiquus ephippia rumor,
    Arte noua gyros et reperisse refert.
Hi docuêre solo quibus insultaret aperto
Gressibus, atg̃ modũ se glomeraret equus.

The Saddler, by Jost Amman.

mended for a gentle mouth—and, for a tender mouth, a
melon or olive bit with a water chain. Our illustration
represents the first form of cannon bit figured in Blundeville. In Shakespeare we find references to the 'gimmal'
(i.e. twin) bit (*Hen. V*, IV. II. 49), and to the 'half-checked'
(or 'cheeked') bit (*Tam. Sh.* III. ii. 58).

A half-*cheeked* bit has been explained as a bit in which the bridle is attached half-way up the cheek, thus giving insufficient control; but a better explanation can be inferred from Markham's *Cavelarice*, where he speaks of three cheeks of bits, (1) a ' straite cheeke ' for a colt, (2) the ' broken cheeke ', to be used with the flying trench, and (3) the perfect or ' travelling cheeke '. ' The straighter the cheek is, the more it putteth up the head, neck and muzzel.' Here is reproduced his picture of these three cheeks. Nothing would be easier than for the ' broken cheek ' to get literally broken in half at its weakest point, and thus make a half-cheeked bit.

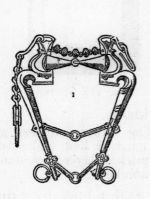 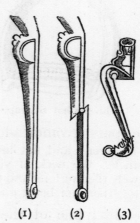

(1)   (2)   (3)

> their poor jades
> Lob down their heads, dropping the hides and hips,
> The gum down-roping from their pale-dead eyes,
> And in their pale dull mouths the gimmal bit
> Lies foul with chew'd grass, still and motionless.
> (*Hen. V*, IV. ii. 46–50)

The gimmal bit is one in which two parts or links were united as in the gimmal ring, but its identity with any of the known bits has not been clearly established. The curb is mentioned seven times by Shakespeare. Touchstone says that a horse has his curb just as the ox has his yoke and the falcon her bells (*A. Y. L.* III. iii. 86); the Duke in *Measure for Measure* compares laws to

> The needful bits and curbs to headstrong steeds. (I. iii. 20)

On the other hand, the snaffle is mentioned only once, in the passage from *Antony and Cleopatra* quoted on p. 416. The play of *Edward III* (I. ii. 29) characterizes it as 'light-borne'.

Of stirrups Markham recognizes two main types, 'the perfite stirrop' and 'the evill stirrop'; the former by its form gives the foot perfect freedom of entrance and exit, and requires no extreme pressure or treading upon, but only the lightest touch; the latter, shaped like a scutcheon turned upside down, is of one width and gives no sure foothold. The two forms are reproduced here:

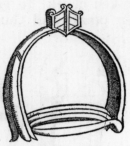
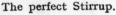

The perfect Stirrup.   The evil Stirrup.

The spurs recommended by Markham

must be strong and flat inward, bending with a compasse under your ancle; the neck of your spurre must be long and straight, the rowels thereof long and sharp, the prickes thereof not standing thick together, nor being above five in number.

The discipline of the horse is maintained by punishment or 'corrections', helps or 'aids', and encouragements or 'cherishings'. 'A cowardly horse must be corrected courteously.' It is as true of a man or woman as of a horse or mare:

> Our praises are our wages: you may ride 's
> With one soft kiss a thousand furlongs ere
> With spur we heat an acre.   (*Wint. Tale* I. ii. 94–6)

Two stanzas of *A Lover's Complaint* may be said to supply a general introduction to this part of the subject—the relation of a horse to his rider:

> Well could he ride, and often men would say
> ' That horse his mettle from his rider takes:
> Proud of subjection, noble by the sway,
> What rounds, what bounds, what course, what stop he makes !'
> And controversy hence a question takes,
> Whether the horse by him became his deed,
> Or he his manage by the well-doing steed.

But quickly on this side the verdict went :
His real habitude gave life and grace
To appertainings and to ornament,
Accomplish'd in himself, not in his case :
All aids, themselves made fairer by their place,
Came for additions ; yet their purpos'd trim
Piec'd not his grace, but were all grac'd by him.   (ll. 106–19)

The ' aids ' or ' helps ', according to Grisone and other Italians, were seven—the voice, or tongue, the rod, wand, or switch, the bridle, the calves of your legs, the stirrups, the spurs, and the ground. Thus : ' Switch and spurs, switch and spurs ', exclaims Romeo in his breathless snipsnap with Mercutio (*Rom. & Jul.* ii. iv. 75). The voice was either a correction or help—roughly delivered *Ha Traytor, Ha Villain*, for obstinacy—' but if you crie, *Hoe, Hoe*, or *Hey, Hey*, or *Via, Via*, then 'tis a help in . . . any ayre or sault whatsoever. But if you will cherrish, then you must in the myldest manner that may be, cry, *Holla, Holla*, or *So boy, so boy*, and such like.' Sadleir, encouraging his horse to a quicker trot, writes, ' Praesertim cum voces has ædimus *hey* aut *huff*.' When these words are forcibly brought out the body, thighs, knees move in such a way that the horse feels a certain exciting motion. The Dauphin uses ' Ça, ha '—a French form of encouraging voice ' aid ' (*Hen. V*, iii. vii. 13). Michael Baret gives as corrections of the voice, ' Will you, Roague.' ' Backe ! I say, stand,' &c. The two forms of ' cherishing ' were with the voice and the hand : ' Cherish him with some little tickling,' says Astley, ' or some scratching with the end of your rod, or with your fingers upon the withers, or thereabouts in the necke.' Adonis uses his ' flattering Holla ' or his ' Stand, I say ! ' and Richard II once made his roan Barbary ' proud with clapping him ' (*Rich. II*, v. v. 86).

FARRIERY

Grumio declares that his master, Petruchio, would marry for money

an old trot with ne'er a tooth in her head, though she have as many diseases as two-and-fifty horses.   (*Tam. Sh.* i. ii. 80–2)

The proneness of the horse to disease was proverbial. The Fool in *King Lear* says that

He's mad that trusts in the tameness of a wolf, a horse's health,
a boy's love, or a whore's oath.   (III. vi. 20–2)

A Yorkshire Tragedy (1608), once attributed to Shakespeare, has

O stumbling jade, the spavin o'ertake thee ! The fifty diseases
stop thee !

and Hazlitt says that there is an old book entitled *The
Fifty Diseases of a Horse* by Gervase Markham ; but Markham's *Maister Peece* has 173 chapters ' of cures Physical '
in his First Book, and 199 chapters of ' Cures Chirurgical '
in his Second Book.

When Shakespeare makes Biondello catalogue the ail-
ments of the horse on which Petruchio came mounted to
fetch his bride, his language is highly technical, but it
bears the mark of knowledge and experience, and is not
lifted straight out of a text-book :

his horse hipped with an old mothy saddle and stirrups of no kindred ;
besides possessed with the glanders and like to mose in the chine ;
troubled with the lampass, infected with the fashions, full of wind-
galls, sped with spavins, rayed with the yellows, past cure of the
fives, stark spoiled with the staggers, begnawn with the bots,
swayed in the back, and shoulder-shotten ; near-legged before.
                              (*Tam. Sh.* III. ii. 50–8)

A horse was said to be hipped when his hip-bone was
dislocated so that he halted much and trailed his legs.

Some thought that glanders was an inflammation of
the ' kernels ' on each side of the throat underneath the
roots of the tongue ; Markham disagreed and called such
inflammation the strangle, and the glanders he defined as
' a Running Imposthume, ingendred either by cold, or by
Famine '.

' When the matter from the nose is dark, thin and
reddish, it is called the mourning of the chine,' a disease
held to be incurable ; some farriers termed it ' the moist
malady ', which may account for Shakespeare's ' mose
in the chine '.

' The Lampasse proceedeth of the abundance of bloud,
resorting to the first forrowe of the mouth . . . next unto
the upper foreteeth ', causing a swelling ' so as he cannot
chaw his meat ' ; the remedy is to sear away the swelled
flesh with a hot iron.

' The Farcy (of our ignorant Smiths called the Fashions)

is of all outward Sorrances [i.e. diseases] the vilest, the most poysonous, infectious, and the most dangerous ', says Markham, and quotes Blundeville as follows :

This is a kind of creeping ulcer growing in knots, following alongst some veine, and it proceedeth of corrupt blood or else of some outwarde hurt, as spur-galling.

Spur-galling was the injury caused by excessive use of the spur, so that the flesh was chafed. Richard II complains that he was not ' made a horse ',

> And yet I bear a burden like an ass,
> Spur-gall'd and tir'd by jauncing Bolingbroke.
>
> (*Rich. II*, v. v. 93–4)

' The windgall . . . is a bladder full of corrupt jellie, wherof som be great and some be smal, or do grow in each side of ye joint.'

' Sped with spavins ' means crippled with swelling of the joints. There is a wet and a dry spavin. Shakespeare has another instance of the disease in *Henry VIII*, where Lord Sands, speaking of the English returned from France, says

> They have all new legs, and lame ones : one would take it,
> That never saw 'em pace before, the spavin
> Or springhalt reign'd among 'em.   (I. iii. 11–13)

The springhalt—or, as the more usual form was, the stringhalt—called also the ' maryhinchcho ', was a sudden twitching up of the horse's hind legs, 'as if he did tread upon needles.'

The fives or vives, says Blundeville, consists of ' certaine kirnelles growing under the horses eare . . . fulle of little white graines, like white salt kirnels. The Italians call them *Vivole.*'

' Rayed with the yellows ' means fouled with the jaundice ; the staggers resulted from dizziness attributed to ' corrupt blood ' ; the bots are parasitic worms or maggots.

A horse was said to be ' swayed in the back ' when, by reason of a wrench or strain in the lower part of the back below the short ribs, he swayed ' backwards and sidelong '.

' Shoulder-shotten ' appears to denote a dislocation of the shoulder. Many attempts have been made to explain ' near-legg'd before ', but none are satisfactory.

A few other terms relating to injuries received by horses

require explanation. The wringing of the withers, to which Shakespeare refers twice (*1 Hen. IV*, II. i. 8; *Haml.* III. ii. 256), was the galling or pinching by a badly fitting saddle of the part where the shoulder-bones join the neck.

Foundering, or lameness caused by inflammation of the feet, was another common ailment; the term was used generally for any lame condition (cf. *Temp.* IV. i. 29). Falstaff boasts that he has ' foundered nine score and odd posts ' in his haste (*2 Hen. IV*, IV. iii. 39). Over-riding is referred to in *Henry V* in the speech of the Constable of France, when he thus contrasts the spirits of the English and the French :

> Can sodden water,
> A drench for surrein'd jades, their barley-broth,
> Decoct their cold blood to such valiant heat ?
> And shall our quick blood, spirited with wine,
> Seem frosty ? (III. v. 18–22)

Many horse-drenches (*Cor.* II. i. 132) are given in the old books, but they do not include barley-broth.

BIBLIOGRAPHY.—The foundation of all succeeding sixteenth and seventeenth-century treatises in Italian, French, or English is FEDERICO GRISONE'S *Ordini di Cavalcare, et modi di conoscere le nature de' cavalli, emendare i vitii loro, et ammaestrargli per l'uso della guerra et commodità degli huomini*, 1550. It was faithfully rendered into English, with identical illustrations, by THOMAS BLUNDEVILLE in *The Fower chiefyst offices belongyng to Horsemanshippe . . . The office of the Breeder, of the Rider, of the Keper and of the Ferrer*, 1565–6. Next in order of date of the Italian authorities come the following. CESARE FIASCHI'S *Trattato dell' imbrigliare, maneggiare, e ferrare cavalli*, 1556, gives more space to bits and bitting than to horsemanship proper; a French translation, *Traicté de la manière de bien emboucher, manier et ferrer les chevaux*, was made by FR. DE PROVANE, 1567. GIOVANNI BATTISTA FERRARO'S *Delle razze, disciplina del cavalcare et altre cose pertinenti ad essercitio così fatto*, 1560. PASQUAL CARACCIOLO's *La Gloria del Cavallo*, 1556–7, has the unappealable authority of Sir Philip Sidney and commends itself to literary riders by its incomparable index. CLAUDIO CORTE's *Il Cavallerizzo*, 1573, was dedicated to Charles IX, and its author was in the service of Robert Dudley, Earl of Leicester, Master of the Horse to Queen Elizabeth. THOMAS BEDINGFIELD translated it in a very ' brieflie reduced ' form as *The Art of Riding*, 1584. Its influence upon Sidney and his contemporaries is demonstrated in an article in *The Quarterly Review*, Jan. 1895, by the present writer and F. H. Cripps-Day, where will be found an epitome of the literature of the manage art. The rarest of all Elizabethan manage books is JOHN ASTLEY's *The Art of Riding*, 1584. A book valuable for its treatment of the paces is RICHARD SADLEIR's *De procreandis, eligendis, alendis, frænandis et tractandis equis experientia*, 1587. CHRISTOPHER CLIFFORD's *Schoole of Horsmanship*, 1585, NICHOLAS MORGAN'S *The Perfection of Horse-Manship*, 1609, and MICHAEL BARET's *An Hipponomie or the Vineyard of Horsemanship*, 1609, and the superbly illustrated *Maneige Royal*, 1623, of ANTOINE PLUVINEL, are also important.

A new departure may be made with SALOMON DE LA BROUE's *Le Cavalerice François*, 1593–4, from which the veteran compiler GERVASE MARKHAM borrowed much. When he was 25 Markham wrote *A Discource of Horsmanshippe*, 1593 ; much of it was re-issued in 1596 as *How to Chuse, Ride, Traine, and Dyet both Hunting Horses and Running Horses*, and *How to . . . Trayne . . . Horses to Amble*, 1605. His next book on equine subjects was *Cavalarice, or the English Horseman*, 1607, the title being borrowed from La Broue. Works on farriery followed : *The Methode oi Epitome*, 1616, *The Faithfull Farrier*, 1635, and others. *Le Marescale or the Horse Marshall, containing those secrets which I practice, but never imparted to any man* is still in manuscript and in the possession of the Executors of the late Sir Clements Markham.

Eighteenth and nineteenth-century works that must be consulted are RICHARD BERENGER's *The History and Art of Horsemanship*, 2 vols., 1771 ; Rt. Hon. D. H. MADDEN's *The Diary of Master William Silence*, 1897 ; Sir WALTER GILBEY's *The Great Horse . . . from the time of the Roman invasion till its development into the Shire horse*, 2nd ed., 1899 ; WM. RIDGEWAY's *The Origin and Influence of the Thoroughbred Horse*, 1905, a scientific work on comparative and historical hippology. For the bibliography of the subject F. H. HUTH's *Bibliographical Record of Hippology*, 1887, is invaluable.

§ 7. BEARBAITING, BULLBAITING, AND COCKFIGHTING

BY

SIR SIDNEY LEE

THE baiting of bulls and bears by dogs was recognized by Shakespeare's contemporaries as a legitimate sport. The practice was of classical antiquity. As early as 1174 William Fitzstephen, in his *Descriptio Londoniae*, mentioned the baiting of bulls and bears among the established pastimes of Londoners in winter. The sport was long encouraged by English sovereigns and their Courts, and enjoyed the almost universal patronage of the middle and lower orders of society. Throughout the sixteenth century the recreation was, in fact, a leading national amusement. James Howell seems in error in describing it as 'peculiar to the English'. In Spain it was much practised and developed into the bullfight, which still persists in the peninsula and in South America. Yet bearbaiting and bullbaiting were pursued in England with an earnestness which was hardly known elsewhere.

In 1506 Erasmus noticed in his *Adagia* that many herds of bears were maintained in England for purposes of baiting. In Henry VIII's reign the mastership of the royal game of bears, bulls, and mastiff dogs became a Court office, and it was so maintained through and after Shakespeare's lifetime. In 1526 fresh stability was given to the pastime by the erection under royal patronage, in the Manor of Paris Garden on the Bankside in Southwark, of a circus or amphitheatre which was thenceforth devoted to exhibitions of contests between mastiff dogs and bulls or bears. Accommodation was provided there for a thousand spectators. The entrance fee was soon fixed at a penny, with an extra penny for the best places in the galleries. About 1570 a second circus was added in an adjoining field, to be applied to bullbaiting, while the older ring was used almost entirely for bearbaiting.

Contests between bulls or bears and dogs were likewise held in royal and private parks, to which the public were admitted free, as well as in open spaces in town and country. But Paris Garden remained the popular head-quarters of the twofold sport until 1642, when the Bear Garden was closed by order of the Long Parliament.

In Shakespeare's time promoters of public amusement seem to have placed the attractions of bullbaiting and bear-baiting on much the same level as dramatic performances. Philip Henslowe, the leading theatrical manager of South-wark, and his son-in-law Edward Alleyn, the great actor, divided their energies for a substantial part of their careers almost equally between the production of stage plays and the organization of baiting matches on the Bankside. In December 1594 they secured a substantial interest in Paris Garden, and though they failed in 1598 in a joint application for the mastership there of the royal game of bears, bulls, and mastiff dogs, they purchased the office of the holder in 1604, and wholly controlled the sport for nearly seven years. Early in 1611 Alleyn sold his interest in the Bear Garden to Henslowe, who in the spring of 1613 took a new partner, a waterman, named Jacob Meade. Henslowe and Meade then demolished the main buildings in Paris Garden, and erected on their site a new edifice called ' The Hope ', which they contrived to adapt for stage plays as well as for baiting matches.

With the ordinary procedure of the sport Shakespeare shows much familiarity. At the opening of a match, the bear, which was kept in training by the keeper or bear-ward, was attached by a long chain to a stake in the middle of a ring. Macbeth is reminiscent of this feature of the arena, when he utters the despairing cry :

> They have tied me to a stake; I cannot fly,
> But bear-like, I must fight the course.
>
> (*Macb*. v. vii. 1–2)

To like purpose Gloucester exclaims in *King Lear* (III. vii. 54) :

> I am tied to the stake, and I must stand the course.

Active operations began with the letting loose upon the chained bear of four, five, or six mastiff dogs. The bear often ' pinched ' or clawed one or two of the dogs to death at the first onset, and the rest retreated to bark at their foe at a safe distance. Richard III compares his father, the Duke of York, in battle, to

> . . . a bear, encompass'd round with dogs,
> Who having pinch'd a few and made them cry,
> The rest stand all aloof, and bark at him.
>
> (*3 Hen. VI*, II. i. 15–17)

But the pause in the strife was not prolonged; fresh dogs replaced those which were mutilated or slain until the bear was either mastered or proved himself invincible. In case of the bear's death or disablement, the game was continued with another bear, and at times as many as thirteen appeared in the ring in succession. The bears' wounds seem rarely to have proved fatal, and the bear-wards carefully tended them in the bearhouse for further encounters. Achilles has the baited bear in mind when he laments (*Troilus* III. ii. 228–9) :

> I see my reputation is at stake ;
> My fame is shrewdly gor'd.

The exhibition was at times diversified by the introduction of a blind bear, which was also secured to a stake by a long chain, and was attacked by men armed with whips. Occasionally the blind bear broke from its chain and ran amok among the crowd, with disastrous results. Bulls, which played a comparatively small part in the proceedings, were treated in the same fashion as the bears. Their horns were their chief weapons of offence, and had more deadly effect than the bears' claws. Paris Garden in its flourishing days was equipped with only three bulls to twenty bears, while the mastiffs numbered seventy. Sometimes the bear-baiting or bullbaiting exhibition closed with the pursuit by the dogs of a horse running free with an ape on his back. ' Pleasant sport with the horse and ape ' was no infrequent item on the programme.

Both Queen Elizabeth and King James I and their courtiers did all they could to encourage the sport. The Queen while a youthful princess witnessed a display of bearbaiting in the park at Hatfield along with her sister, Princess Mary, and both their highnesses expressed them-selves ' well content ' with what they witnessed. During the reigns of Queen Elizabeth and her successor the baiting of bears or bulls invariably formed part of great official entertainments. Very early in her reign, on April 25, 1559, Queen Elizabeth provided in the grounds at Whitehall a

Sic ferus exardet in auro taurus aperto.   Cum sua terribili prelii irritamina cornu

BULLFIGHTING by JOANNES STRADANUS

baiting of bears and bulls by English dogs in honour of the French ambassador, and next day the distinguished visitor went to Paris Garden to see a similar entertainment. All foreign tourists sought a like ' pleasant ' experience. When the Earl of Leicester entertained his sovereign at Kenilworth in 1575 a fiercely contested bearbaiting took place in the park for the Queen's delectation. Again, in Greenwich Park, on May 8, 1586, an elaborate exhibition was arranged in honour of an ambassador from Denmark. The royal hostess attended in person, and an immense crowd of ordinary people was admitted to the spectacle. The ' shrill shouts ' of the onlookers betrayed their joy and delight. The entertainment ended with the diversion of ' the horse with the ape on his back '. In 1599 Queen Elizabeth visited Paris Garden.

Men of fashion, tradesmen, mechanics, apprentices, were all united in an enthusiastic patronage of the sport. Sir Toby Belch and his foolish dupe, Sir Andrew Aguecheek, wasted much time at it (*Tw. N.* i. iii. 101). Bearbaitings were haunted by the knave Autolycus. The motley audience delighted in the ' biting, clawing, roaring, tugging, grasping, tossing, and tumbling of the bears and the bulls ', as well as in ' the nimbleness and wait of the dog to take his advantage '. The crowd rejoiced to see the bear ' work and wind himself ' from his assailants, and they eagerly watched him ' when he was loose ' shaking ' his ears twice or thrice with (of) the blood and the slaver hanging about his physiognomy '. The ' bellowing, bawling, yawling, yelling ' of the excited spectators caused residents in the neighbourhood of Paris Garden the utmost annoyance, and made a bear garden a proverbial synonym for a place of disorder. When the porter in *Henry VIII* reproved the noisy rabble in Palace Yard on the approach of the coronation procession of Queen Anne Boleyn, he taunts the crowd with mistaking ' the court for Paris Garden ' (v. iv. 2). In *Troilus and Cressida* (v. vii. 10–21) Thersites imitates the confused cries of the mob at a bullbaiting when he punctuates the fight between Menelaus and Paris with such ejaculations as these : ' Now, bull ! now, dog ! 'Loo, Paris, 'loo ! . . . 'loo, Paris, 'loo ! The bull has the game : 'ware horns, ho ! '

The distinctive names which were allotted to the bears played a large part in popular parlance. At the end of the sixteenth century fighting bears called respectively George Stone, Harry Hunks, Tom of Lincoln, and, above all, Sackerson, were for the sporting public of London vulgar idols. Abraham Slender, Anne Page's foolish suitor, who loved the sport well, boasts that he had seen Sackerson loose twenty times, and had taken him by the chain amid the frightened shrieks of women onlookers (*M. Wives* I. i. 309–11). Ned of Canterbury, Don Jon, and Blind Robin were among Sackerson's honoured successors.

From the reign of Edward VI Puritan preachers denounced the brutality of the pastime and urged its suppression. 'What Christian heart', asked Philip Stubbes in his *Anatomie of Abuses* (1583) 'can take pleasure to see one poor beast rend tear and kill another and all for his foolish pleasure?' 'And to be plain,' the Puritan censor added, 'I think the devil is the master of the game, bearward and all. A goodly pastime, forsooth.' The chief matches invariably took place on Sundays, a fact which accentuated the Puritan hostility. Edward Hake, in *Newes out of Powles Churchyarde* (1579), inveighs against the practice, especially on the sabbath:

> What else but gaine and money gote
> Maintains each Saboth day
> The bayting of the Beare and Bull?
> What brings this brutish play?

On Sunday, January 13, 1583, an accident at Paris Garden gave new point to the Puritan outcry. The scaffolding of the crowded amphitheatre suddenly collapsed 'when the dogs and bear were in the chiefest battle', and five men and two women were killed. The Corporation of London, which cherished Puritan sympathies, frequently expressed strong disapproval of the pastime. But Paris Garden was out of their jurisdiction. Complaint was often made by the city authorities that the matches drew together immense crowds, which helped to spread the plague and other diseases. When in the summer of 1583 the Privy Council ordered the Corporation to enforce in the city the laws for the practice of archery, the Lord Mayor, in reply, laid the blame for the neglect of archery on the growing vogue of bearbaiting. But the Court and upper classes took another view of the situation. The sport was defended as 'a sweet and comfortable recreation fitted for the solace and comfort of a peaceable people'. The fact that the exhibitions drew large crowds of the working class on holidays was held to be a safeguard against worse disorders. The Privy Council declined to restrain the pastime, which enjoyed royal sanction.

In 1591 the growth of theatres on the Bankside was creating a formidable competition with the attractions of Paris Garden. The Privy Council accordingly forbade the opening of theatres on Thursdays, so as to promote public support on that day of ' the game of bearbaiting and like pastimes which are maintained by her Majesty's pleasure and were suffering neglect '. The bear gardens remained open on other days than Thursday. Till the end of the sixteenth century and for the first thirty years at least of the seventeenth century, Sunday was still devoted to this recreation in Southwark.

King James was loyal to the tradition of his predecessor in his encouragement of bearbaiting, and made some effort to improve upon the sport. The Scottish king was deeply interested in the menagerie of lions and other wild animals which was long maintained at royal expense in the Tower of London. On his first visit to the Tower, on March 13, 1603–4, the King experimented with a baiting of lions, with which he thought to vary the accepted practice of bear-baiting and bullbaiting. By royal order Edward Alleyn brought from Paris Garden to the lion's den at the Tower three of ' his fellest dogs ', which were incited to attack a lion in the King's presence. The King professed himself anxious to test the remark of a foreign writer that English mastiffs were as courageous as lions. The trial which King James devised was pursued rather half-heartedly, and was drawn in the lion's favour. Two of the dogs died of their wounds. Next year the King ordered the construction of a special den at the Tower for the purpose of baiting the lions with ' dogs, bears, bulls, boars, &c.' The initial encounter there, between a lion and three mastiffs, which took place in the presence of the King and a large company, again gave the lion the victory. Four years later, on June 23, 1609, the whole of the royal family, with a large company, revisited the Tower to witness a match between a lion and ' a great fierce bear ', which belonged to the royal menagerie, and had lately fallen into disgrace by killing a child. On this occasion the combatants refused to engage in earnest, and by the King's directions the bear

' was baited to death upon a stage ' a few days later. Despite Puritan protests, public sentiment clearly encouraged the employment of bears, bulls, and dogs, if not of lions, for purposes of sport in ways which have long since been discredited as brutal barbarity.

In Shakespeare's England, cockfighting, or, as it was familiarly called, ' cocking ', was practised as generally as bearbaiting, and enjoyed as much popular favour. Throughout Shakespeare's lifetime ' cocking ' was a widespread Sunday recreation, both in London and in the country. In much the same fashion as bearbaiting, the pastime was condemned for its brutality by Puritan preachers, and was defended for its manliness by profane writers.

Like bearbaiting, cockfighting boasted a classical descent, and established itself in England in the early Middle Ages. James Howell's claim for the sport that it was ' peculiar to the English ', has even less to support it than his like claim on behalf of bearbaiting. Fitzstephen, in 1174, described how London schoolboys brought every Shrove Tuesday ' cocks of the game to their master and all the forenoon they delighted themselves in cockfighting '. The boys were often content with an inferior form of the pastime, and confined themselves to ' cockthrowing ', i. e. flinging missiles at the cocks. Shrove Tuesday was specially associated with ' cocks of the game ' down to the eighteenth century but the cockfighting season rapidly extended to all months of the year save June and July. The sport was finally organized in Henry VIII's reign, when the first cockpit was constructed by the King for its regular exercise. Before 1536 Henry VIII built a cockpit in St. James's ' Fields ' or Park (near what is now Birdcage Walk), open ground which the King had added to the precincts of the Palace at Whitehall. The royal cockpit survived till 1816. The building was elaborately contrived, and was from the time of Queen Elizabeth frequently devoted to dramatic performances as well as to cockfighting matches. Throughout the sixteenth century noble sportsmen purchased at high rates cocks of the game or gamecocks which were systematically trained and trimmed for fighting, and heavy wagers were laid by their owners on promising birds. Although there is no proof that Queen Elizabeth personally interested herself in the sport, it grew in all directions in her time. Cockpit became numerous in London. The three which attained chief notoriety were situated respectively in Jewin Street, Shoe Lane, and St. Giles in the Fields. The last was early in James's reign converted into the Phoenix or Drury Lane Theatre, and stage plays alternated there with cockfighting matches. There were occasional exhibitions at Paris Garden. Stow wrote in 1598: 'Cocks of the game are yet cherished by divers men for their pleasures, much money being laid on their heads when they fight in pits, whereof some be costly made for that purpose.' 'Cocking in hoops [i. e. rings] is now all the play', wrote Sir John Davies in his Epigrams in 1596. Shakespeare bears witness to the Londoner's familiarity with the cockpit, when he describes as 'this cockpit' the theatre at which his play of *Henry V* was first produced in 1599 (*Hen. V*, 1st Chorus, line 11). The dramatist makes an intimate reference to the sport when Cloten deplores in his clownish arrogance that his rank precludes him from fighting ordinary persons: 'Every Jack-slave hath his bellyful of fighting, and I must go up and down like a cock that nobody can match' (*Cymb.* II. i. 23–5).[1] The boisterous cries of the spectators, when cockfights were in progress, are often noticed by the Elizabethan dramatists. Ben Jonson makes Volpone (*Volpone* II. ii. 327) complain of the everlasting voice of Lady Politick Would-be:

> The bells, in time of pestilence, ne'er made
> Like noise, or were in that perpetual motion!
> The Cockpit comes not near it.

A further impetus was given to the practice of the sport in Shakespeare's England by James I's enthusiastic patronage. He appointed a 'cockmaster', a royal officer who was responsible for the breeding, feeding, and training of gamecocks for fighting in the royal cockpit. Throughout his reign cockfighting was a favourite pastime of the King. In the spring of 1617, when he paid a visit in state to the city of Lincoln, he directed a 'cocking' to take place at an inn-yard in his presence, and 'appointed four cocks to be put in the pit together, which made his Majesty very merry '.

---

[1] Plutarch seems to have suggested Antony's reflection that Octavius Caesar's cocks
> do win the battle still of mine
> When it is all to nought.

(Ant. & Cleop. II. iii. 36–7)

Fighting cocks were in the seventeenth century chiefly bred in Norfolk, and in 1607 George Wilson, vicar of Wretham in that county, championed the pastime in a work entitled *The Commendation of Cocke and Cock-fighting wherein is shewed that cocke-fighting was before the coming of Christ.* The author describes many matches which he has witnessed, and especially commends a gamecock named Tarlton, after the comedian, because before combat it was wont to drum loudly with its wings. Like bearbaiting, cockfighting was often classed as an amusement that could compete with dramatic performances. The royal favour which was bestowed on the game led other writers to extol its merits. In 1614 Gervase Markham, a writer on very various subjects, included among his *Pleasures of Princes or Good Mens Recreations* an account of the 'choyce ordering, breeding, and dyetting of the fighting cocke'.

Like other sports which collected crowded audiences in towns, cockfighting had to be suspended in times of plague. It was not prohibited altogether by law until 1654, but public taste then rendered the legal restriction inoperative. The sport flourished through the eighteenth century, and when the statute of 1849 forbade its open practice, it was still on occasion indulged in surreptitiously.

BIBLIOGRAPHY.—JOSEPH STRUTT's *Sports and Pastimes of the People of England*, 1801, gives a general account of bullbaiting, bearbaiting, and cockfighting. See also STOW's *Survey of London*, 2 vols., ed. C. L. Kingsford, 1908. The best contemporary descriptions of bearbaiting exhibitions will be found in ROBERT LANEHAM's *Description of the entertainment at Kenilworth*, 1575 (ed. F. J. Furnivall, New Shakspere Society, 1890, pp. 16–17), in NICHOLS's *Progresses of Queen Elizabeth*, vol. ii, 459–60, and in PAUL HENTZNER's *Travels in England* (in 1598) (in W. B. RYE's *England as seen by Foreigners*, 1865). There are many other references to bearbaiting in the royal presence in NICHOLS's *Progresses, of Elizabeth*, 3 vols., 1823, and *of James I*, 4 vols., 1828. For the history of Paris Garden, see WILLIAM RENDLE's *The Bankside, Southwark and the Globe Playhouse* (Appendix I to Part II of the New Shakspere Society's reprint of Harrison's *Description of England*, 1878); J. P. COLLIER's *Annals of the Stage*, 3 vols., 1831; and T. FAIRMAN ORDISH's *Early London Theatres*, 1894. Contemporary memoranda respecting the control or regulation of the Bear Garden will be found in HENSLOWE's *Diary* (ed. W. W. Greg), 1904; *The Alleyn Papers at Dulwich College*, calendared by G. F. Warner, 1881; the *Remembrancia of the City of London* (1579–1664), 1878; and the *Acts of the Privy Council* (temp. Eliz.), ed. J. R. Dasent, 1892–1905.

The best contemporary accounts of cockfighting will be found in the books of George Wilson and Gervase Markham mentioned in the text.

§ 8. DANCING

BY

A. Forbes Sieveking

Dancing was practised by all classes in Shakespeare's England, and the steady growth in its popularity excited he gravest misgivings among Puritan preachers and amphleteers. Dancing schools were opened in London, nd skill in what the Puritans derided as this 'noble cience of heathen devilry', 'the horrible vice of pestiferous ancing', was reckoned an essential mark of good breeding. hose who denounced the practice admitted that, were it used in a mean in time and place convenient', it might rove 'a wholesome recreation of the mind and also an exer- ise for the body'. But it was argued that in high and w society alike indulgence in the amusement was exces- ive, that lascivious dances had been borrowed from foreign untries and were threatening the nation's morality, and at the Sabbath was habitually desecrated by the infatua- on. At Court, dancing found an enthusiastic patroness Queen Elizabeth, and she readily countenanced its ractice on Sunday afternoons. When she visited her vourite, the Earl of Leicester, at Kenilworth in 1575, rds and ladies danced before her on the Sabbath day ith a 'lively agility and commendable grace', which as 'as strange to the eye as pleasant to the mind'. hroughout Shakespeare's life, both under Queen Eliza- eth and her successor, dancing was regularly pursued Sundays. John Stow, in his *Survey*, regrets the ecay of the practice of the maidens of the City dancing holy days after evening prayer 'for garlandes hanged wart the streetes', and fears that worse is done indoors. Queen Elizabeth prided herself on her grace as a dancer, d danced with vigour till near her death. When a false port was spreading that she was suffering from lameness, e proved its falsity by her lively paces at a courtier's edding feast. The favour which the Queen bestowed on r Christopher Hatton was attributed at the time to her admiration for his triumph in a galliard. On September 19, 1602, the Earl of Worcester writes of much dancing of country dances in the privy chamber at Nonesuch, before the Queen's Majesty, who is exceedingly pleased therewith.

When James I entertained the Constable of Castile after signing the peace with Spain at Whitehall, a great banquet took place on Sunday, August 19, 1604, and was followed by a ball. Queen Anne distinguished herself in dancing several brawls, in one of which her partner was the Earl of Southampton. Henry, Prince of Wales, showed agility at both the galliard and the coranto.

The dances of Shakespeare's time fall under two heads, People's or Folk dances, and Society or Court dances, the latter for the most part derived from the Latin countries where they had themselves arisen from a popular origin. Of the folk dances the most elaborate is the Morris Dance or Morisco. Its name undoubtedly indicates a 'Moorish' origin, and it may have been introduced into northern countries from Spain. In the English morris dance there figured at one time or another a Negro or Moor, a hobby-horse, dragons, Robin Hood, Friar Tuck, Little John, and Maid Marian. This combination produced a rough *balle d'action* not unlike the combination of various elements in a modern pantomime. The performers danced to an accompaniment of bells of different sizes and tones known as the fore bell, the second bell, the treble, mean, tenor, bass, and double bells. The hobby-horse, an important feature, was formed by a man inside a frame fitted with the head and tail of a horse, and with trappings reaching to the ground and hiding the feet of the actor, who pranced and curvetted about.[1] A character in a tragedy called *The Vow Breaker* by William Sampson (1636), proclaims his skill as a hobby-horseman thus :

Have I borrow'd the fore horse bells, his plumes and braveries nay, he's had his mane new shorne and frizl'd. . . . Am I not going to buy ribbons and toyes of Sweet Ursula for the Marian—and shall I not play the hobby-horse ? . . . Provide thou for the Dragon and leave me for a hobby-horse.

Will Kemp, a member of Shakespeare's company of actors, who describes himself as ' Head Master of Morris

[1] ' The hobby-horse is forgot' (*Love's L. L.* III. i. 32, *Haml.* III. ii. 146) perhaps a quotation from some ballad satirizing the Puritan's opposition to morris-dancing.

Kemps nine daies vvonder

Performed in a daunce from
London to Norwich.

Containing the pleaſure, paines and kinde entertainment
of *William Kemp* betweene *London* and that Citty
in his late Morrice.

Wherein is ſomewhat ſet downe worth note; to reprooue
the ſlaunders ſpred of him: many things merry,
nothing hurtfull.

Written by himſelfe to ſatiſfi: his friends.

LONDON

Printed by *E. A.* for *Nicholas Ling,* and are to be
folde at his ſhop at the weſt doore of Saint
Paules Church. 1600.

dancers, High Headborough of Heighs, and only tricker
of your trill-lilles and best bell-shangles, between Sion and
Mount Surrey', speaks of meeting a country lass, on his
dance to Norwich from London (1599), who borrowed of him
a 'leash of his bells' and was 'Marian in his Morrice dance',
and of yet another at Chelmsford he says, 'I was soon won to
fit her with bells; besides she would have the old fashion,
with napkin on her arms, and to our jumps we fell!'

Morris-dancers contributed to the Maypole festivities,
such as took place in Cornhill and are described by Stow, and
more fully by Philip Stubbes. The Maypole, beribboned
and beflowered, was drawn to its position by twenty or
forty yoke of oxen, their horns decorated with nosegays,
and followed by a crowd of men, women, and children.
And then they 'fall to daunce about it, like as the heathen
people did at the dedication of the Idols'. Shakespeare
in *Henry V* (II. iv. 25) has an allusion to the ordinary
event of a 'Whitsun morris-dance', and again to 'a morris
for May-day' (*All's Well* II. ii. 26). The Duke of York,
in his description of Jack Cade's achievements, says that
after he had been shot full of arrows,

> In the end being rescu'd, I have seen
> Him caper upright like a wild Morisco,
> Shaking the bloody darts as he his bells.
>
> (*2 Hen. VI*, III. i. 364–6)

James I, in his *Declaration to His Subjects concerning
lawful Sports to bee used* (1633), especially sanctions May-
games, Whitsun ales, and morris dances, and the setting up
of maypoles as 'lawful recreations after the end of divine
service'.

The simplest form of country dance is that in which
the dancers form a circle; this was called a Round or
Roundel. The first edition of *The English Dancing-Master*
(1651) has thirteen rounds, for six, eight, or 'as many
as will'. Titania asks for 'a roundel and a fairy song'
(*Mid. N. D.* II. ii. 1), and the witches in *Macbeth* perform
their 'antick round' (IV. i. 130).

The Hay or Hey, a round dance in which the dancers
performed winding evolutions in and out, seems to have
been of French origin. 'Les Hayes' is one of the 180
dances in Rabelais' famous list, and Clément Marot had
spoken of a 'haye d'Allemaigne'. It was sometimes danced

like a reel. Sir John Davies speaks of these dances as
'winding heyes' and 'wild whirling heyes'. In the
presentation of the Nine Worthies in *Love's Labour's Lost*,
Dull consents to 'make one in a dance, or so', or, says he,

> I will play the tabor to the Worthies, and let them dance the hay.
> (v. i. 164–6)

It is not clear how far the hay differed from the hay-de-
guy or hay-de-guise, which was an equally popular dance
in the sixteenth and seventeenth centuries. Kemp says
of one of his lasses :

> Yet she thumped it on her way
> With a sportly hey de gay.

The Trenchmore is an old English country dance—
first mentioned by that name in the middle of the sixteenth
century. Selden in his *Table Talk* records its prevalence at
Charles I's court, where it had superseded the graver dances :

> The Court of England is much alter'd. At a solemn Dancing,
> first you had the grave Measures, then the Corrantoes and the
> Galliards, and this is kept up with Ceremony ; at length to Trench-
> more and the Cushion-Dance, and then all the Company Dance,
> Lord and Groom, Lady and Kitchin-Maid, no distinction. So in
> our Court in Queen Elizabeth's time, Gravity and State were kept
> up. In King James's time things were pretty well. But in King
> Charles's time, there has been nothing but Trench-more, and the
> Cushion Dance, omnium gatherum, tolly, polly, hoite come toite.

The Trenchmore, according to *The Dancing-Master*, is to
be danced 'longways for as many as will'. Shakespeare
has no mention of it.

Jig [1] seems to have been applied to various lively dances.
Though jigs are now almost confined to Ireland, the Scotch
are older ; Shakespeare alludes to a Scotch jig (*Much Ado*
II. i. 79), which was a round dance for a large number of
people. Jigs were variously named, as the Cobbler's
Jigg, Nobody's Jigg, Solomon's Jigg, and took their titles
also from kings and queens. Morley (1597) couples together
'hornepypes and jygges'. Shakespeare's only reference
to the hornpipe is in *The Winter's Tale* (IV. ii. 48), where
the clown singles out one of the sheep-shearers as a Puritan,
who 'sings psalms to hornpipes' after the manner of the
adherents of Geneva, who sang their new 'godly ballads'
to old dance tunes.

---

[1] The jig performed at the end of a play must be carefully distinguished :
see Chapter XXV.

The Dump was a slow mournful dance. The nature of the steps of this dance is not certainly known. Dr. Naylor suggests two features, a tapping of the foot, and a slow sliding step, alternating with a quicker movement. Shakespeare employs the word to denote the correspondingly mournful music that would accompany it. Proteus recommends the Duke of Milan to try a serenade :

> Visit by night your lady's chamber-window
> With some sweet consort : to their instruments
> Tune a deploring dump.   (*Two Gent.* III. ii. 83–5)

Peter, Capulet's servant, first played by Will Kemp, speaks ironically of a ' merry dump ' (*Rom. & Jul.* IV. v. 108), and in *The Rape of Lucrece* (l. 1127) we find

> Distress likes dumps when time is kept with tears.

This brief account of country dances may be fittingly concluded with two quotations. The first is a dialogue from Heywood's *A Woman Kilde with Kindnesse* (1607), and gives us a summary of the more popular ones :

Jack Slime. Come, what shall it be ? ' Rogero ' ?

Jenkin. Rogero ! No ; we will dance ' The Beginning of the World '.

Cicely. I love no dance so well as ' John, come kiss me now '.

Nich. I that have ere now deserv'd a cushion, call for the Cushion dance.

R. Brick. For my part, I like nothing so well as ' Tom Tyler '.

Jen. No, we'll have ' The Hunting of the Fox '.

Jack Shine. ' The Hay ' ! ' the Hay ' ! There 's nothing like ' the Hay '. . . .

Jen. Let me speak for all, and we'll have ' Sellinger's Round '.   (I. ii)

The second is a description by the author of *The Dancing-Master* of the movement in Sellinger's Round, which is typical of those country dances, of which Sir Roger de Coverley is the most familiar to our generation :

> The dancers take hands, go round twice and back again ; then all set, turn, and repeat ; then lead all forward, and back, and repeat ; two singles and back, set and turn single and repeat ; arms all and repeat.[1]

Upon few subjects does Shakespeare more persistently

---

[1] Shakespeare has a remarkable isolated reference to a dance of local Italian origin. Bottom invites Duke Theseus to ' hear a Bergomask dance between two of our company ' (*Mid. N. D.* v. i. 361–2). The Bergomask was an old Italian dance borrowed from the peasants of Bergamo in Lombardy, which was once a dependency of Venice and supplied the buffoons of Italy with their jargon.

From the PICTURE in the FITZWILLIAM MUSEUM CAMBRIDGE

THE PALACE OF SHEEN

MORRIS DANCERS ARE SHOWN IN THE FOREGROUND

expend his punning propensity than upon the dancing names and terms current in his day, like measure, brawl, cinquepace, and caper ; but it is with society dances that this form of wit is chiefly occupied. We learn much from him of ' treading a measure ', which was to perform all that was most solemn and ceremonious in the way of rhythmical movement. Sir John Davies dwells upon the gravity of ' the measure ' and the solemnity of its pace :

> But after these, as men more civil grew,
> He [Love] did more grave and solemn measures frame
>
> .   .   .   .
>
> Yet all the feete, whereon these measures go
> Are only spondees, solemn, grave, and slow.

In *Love's Labour 's Lost* the King sends to the Princess the message :

> Say to her, we have measur'd many miles,
> To tread a measure with her on the grass.

and the word-play is prolonged over many lines (v. ii. 183–223). Beatrice frivolously prescribes, as a cure for the Prince's impatience, that he be told ' there is measure in everything, and so dance out the answer' (*Much Ado* II. i. 75–6). Benvolio harps upon the same string :

> But, let them measure us by what they will,
> We'll measure them a measure, and be gone.
>
> (*Rom. & Jul.* I. iv. 9–10)

Beatrice, in confidential talk with Hero, compares wooing, wedding, and repenting to a Scotch jig, a measure, and a cinquepace :

The first suit is hot and hasty, like a Scotch jig, and full as fantastical ; the wedding, mannerly-modest, as a measure, full of state and ancientry ;

but the conclusion is not very happy, for the cinquepace, being the most joyous part of the galliard, is hardly comparable to repentance, which,

with his bad legs, falls into the cinquepace faster and faster, till he sink into his grave. (*Much Ado* II. i. 79–84)

Cinquepace—also written cinqua-pace, cinque-pas, sinquapace, sincopas, and sink-a-pace—was the name by which the original galliard was known. Praetorius says that a galliard has five steps, and is therefore called a cinque-pas, but it may be that in later times the galliard was so much altered by the addition of new steps, that the original form of the dance came to be distinguished by the name cinque-pas.

The Pavane, pavin, or paven (as it was variously written), is one of the oldest of the ' danses nobles' or 'danses basses', as they were called to indicate both their high descent, gravity, and low practice on the ground, and to distinguish them from the 'danses baladines'. It was a stately, dignified, processional dance, suitable to the gala-mantles of princes and the robes of magistrates. 'Every pavane has its galliard', says the Spanish proverb, as if to say every solemnity must have its moment of levity. The measured steps were two simple and a double one forward, and the same number backward, to the music of hautboys and trumpets. The name has been derived by some from Padova (Padua), in support of which in a MS. collection of airs and dances by Dowland and Holborne a piece is called 'Padovana de la Milanessa'.[1] A more favoured suggestion is that the dance is Spanish in origin, invented by Fernando Cortez in the sixteenth century, and that the name comes from ' pavo ', a peacock, the dancers facing one another and forming a kind of wheel, the arm rounded beneath the cape or mantle, and the hand resting on the sword-hilt, and so causing the point to raise the cloak like a peacock's tail. Puttenham speaks of the Italian pavane as being danced by measures in princes' courts, and Ascham wonders, and leaves us wondering, whether the music of the pavane is 'like the musike of the Lydians or the Dorians'. Catherine de Médicis excelled in its performance accompanied by the tambourin, and Brantôme expresses his admiration at a pavane danced by or before Henri II and his sister, when the ' turns were so well danced, the steps so deftly executed, the pauses so exactly observed, that one knew not which most to marvel at, the fine part in movement or the majesty in repose, the former a picture of hilarity, and the latter of gravity and dignity'. But gradually the gravity of the pavane yielded to the briskness of the galliard, which was added to it as the last movement, and figures borrowed from other dances overlaid its primitive solemnity.

[1] In Alford's 'Instructions for the Lute' (1568) the name is spelt both *Paduane* and *Pavane*.

The only time Shakespeare mentions the pavane is in the following quotation from *Twelfth Night* :

Clown. O! he's drunk, Sir Toby, an hour agone: his eyes were
    set at eight i' the morning.
Sir Toby. Then he's a rogue, and a passy-measures pavin.

(v. i. 206–9)

Much ingenuity has been exercised in the elucidation of this passage, but it cannot be said that a satisfactory solution has been arrived at.[1] 'Passy-measures' is the English form of ' Passamezzo ', the name of an early Italian dance, probably a variety of the pavane, performed less solemnly and more quickly, as Arbeau says, and called in English a passy- or passe-measures paven.

The Brawl, another of the ' danses basses ', is in French ' bransle ' ('bransler ', to vibrate). As early as 1531 Sir Thomas Elyot in *The Governour* speaks of ' base daunses, bargerettes [i. e. pastoral dances], pavions, turgions, and roundes' as having 'a concinnitie of mouving the foote and body, expressing some pleasaunt or profitable affectes or motions of the mind'. The macaronic poet, Antony de Arena, whose work Camden says he ' kept as a jewel ', has left the following description of a brawl :

Modus dansandi Branlos.

Ipse modis branlos debes dansare duobus,
    Simplos et duplos usus habere solet.
Sed branlos duplos, passus tibi quinque laborent ;
    Tres fac avantum, sed reculando duos.
Quatuor in mensura ictus marchabis eundo,
    Atque retornando quatuor ipse dabis.

The name became the generic term for all dances led by one or two dancers, whose movements were followed and repeated by the others. A succinct description of it is to be found in Marston's *Malcontent* (1604) IV. ii :

Why, 'tis but singles on the left, two on the right, in a figure of eight.

---

[1] Dr. Naylor points out that the strains of the passamezzo are constructed like the ordinary pavane, and consist of eight bars each ; and that Sir Toby, in his semi-sober state, and with his musical proclivities, compares mentally the clown's remarks about the surgeon's eyes being ' set at eight ' with the fact that the pavane is also set at eight, as stated in Morley's *Practicall Musicke*, ' Fewer than eight [semi-breves] I have not seen in any pavan.'

Halliwell quotes an old description of steps of the dance, ' two single and a double forward, and two single syde, reprynce back', and thinks that it is only necessary to have seen a drunken man to understand the allusion.

It may be regarded as the most ancient type of figure dance, and in one form or other was danced in Italy, France, and England till the seventeenth century, when it passed through the transition stage of ' branle à mener ' into the ' menuet ' or minuet.   The French branle on festive occasions began with a double-branle, followed by a simple-branle ; next came the gay-branle, and finally the branle of Burgundy or Champagne.   The first pair led throughout, and the dance often finished by all joining hands and dancing in a round.· This is depicted in an oil-painting in the Louvre, by Clouet, representing a court-ball in the reign of Henry III at the Duc de Joyeuse's wedding (1581).

In Shakespeare's time the name of the dance had become mixed up with the older word ' brawl ' meaning quarrel, and thus furnished ready raw material for the manufacture of a Shakespearian pun, which has ever since been protected. ' Master, will you win your love with a French brawl ? ' asks Moth of Armado in *Love's Labour's Lost*. ' How meanest thou ', retorts his master, ' brawling in French ? '   But the imp explains that what he means is ' to jig off a tune at the tongue's end, canary to it with your feet ' (III. i. 8–14).

The conclusion of the brawl was in French sometimes called ' tourdion ' (which we find in Sir Thomas Elyot as ' turgion ').   This was a gliding form of the galliard—unless the latter be considered as a lofty or leaping form of tourdion —consisting of five steps (De Arena's ' passus tibi quinque laborent ').

Riche, in his *Farewell to Militarie Profession* (1581), finds the complex Galliard beyond his range :

Our galliardes are so curious, thei are not for my daunsyng, for thei are so full of trickes and tournes, that he which hath no more but the plaine sinquepace is no better accoumpted of than a verie bungler.

The ' nimble galliard ' (*Hen. V*, I. ii. 252) was first known in Italy as the Romanesca, from its source in the Campagna, and was danced to the same music as the tourdion and having one movement called the ' greue ' or ' ruade '— the first a sort of kick in front, and the second a kick behind. Ben Jonson, in *Cynthia's Revels*, sketches a traveller as ' grievously torturing strangers with inquisition after his

grace in the galliard ', and Sir Thomas Overbury's ' Fine
Gentleman ' carries pumps in his pocket, and lest he should
take fiddlers unprovided, whistles his own galliard.

Capriole, a term also used in the manage, and probably
the source of ' caper ', means properly a goat's leap.   As

CAPRIOLE.

Capriol.

I'apprendray voluntiers ceste capriole puis qu'elle porte mõ
nom: Mais qu'appellez vous cadance.

From ' Thoinot Arbeau ', *Orchésographie*, 1588.

a dancing movement it consisted in beating the feet together
in the air ; it was introduced into some galliards.

Sir Toby Belch. What is thy excellence in a galliard, knight ?
Sir Andrew Aguecheek. Faith, I can cut a caper.

and Sir Toby punningly replies :

And I can cut the mutton to 't.   (*Tw. N.* i. iii. 129–32)

We are reminded of Sir Willoughby Patterne by Sir Toby's
compliment :

I did think, by the excellent constitution of thy leg, it was formed
under the star of a galliard. . . . Let me see thee caper. (142–4, 151–2)

Sir John Davies devotes two stanzas to eulogy of the
galliard :

But for more diverse and more pleasing show,
A swifte and wandering dance she did invent,
With passages uncertain to and fro,
Yet with a certain answer and consent
To the quick music of the instrument.

Five was the number of the Music's feet,
Which still the dance did with five paces meet.

A gallant dance, that lively doth bewray
A spirit and a virtue masculine,
Impatient that her house on earth should stay,
Since she herself is fiery and divine,
Oft does she make her body upward fine;
With lofty turns and capriols in the air,
Which with the lusty tunes accordeth fair.

The galliard ultimately merged into the volte, and only
one step, called the 'pas de gaillard', has been preserved,
which Littré defines technically thus—'un assemblé, un pas
marché, et un pas tombé'.

The Volte was the form of the galliard which originated in
Provence [1] or in Italy. It was danced throughout Europe
in the sixteenth century, and consisted in a turn of the body
with two steps, a high spring, and a pause with feet close
together. It was the rage at the court of Charles IX, and
Marguerite de Valois excelled in it. At the ball given on
August 14, 1572, in honour of the double marriage of the
King of Navarre with Marguerite de Valois, and of the
Prince de Condé with Maria of Cleve, the volte was danced
so thoroughly by the latter that she was obliged to retire
and change her dress. A picture in the museum at Rennes
shows a nobleman and lady dancing the volte at the critical
point of the dance. Davies thus describes the dance:

Yet is there one the most delightful kind,
A lofty jumping or a leaping round,
Where arm in arm two dancers are entwin'd,
And whirl themselves with strict embracements bound.
And still their feet an anapest do sound;
An anapest is all their music's song,
Whose first two feet are short and third is long.

Shakespeare uses the form lavolt or lavolta. Troilus declares
that he has no accomplishments; 'I cannot sing,' he says,

Nor heel the high lavolt. (*Troilus*, IV. iv. 86)

In *Henry V* lavoltas and corantos are coupled together:

They bid us to the English dancing-schools,
And teach lavoltas high and swift corantos;
Saying our grace is only in our heels,
And that we are most lofty runaways, (III. v. 32-5)

---

[1] Antony de Arena had sung with justifiable patriotic pride:
De Dansando tamen Provencia nostra triumphat,
Palmam dansandi semper habere solet.

as they are by Morley in the following technical description :

Like unto this [viz. the *bransle double*], but more light, be the voltes and courantes, which being both of a measure, are, notwithstanding, daunced after sundrie fashions, the volte rising and leaping, the courante travising and running, in which measure also our countrey dance is made.

The Courante or Coranto was a dance performed in 2/4 time, whereas the volte was in 3/4, and the step was a hopping one. 'Thoinot Arbeau' tells us that in his youth the courante was preceded by a sort of pantomime or ballet danced by three young men and three girls standing in a row. The courante was either simple or figured. In *Twelfth Night*, Sir Toby, in a speech made up of dancing terms, places the galliard and the coranto in immediate context, but not necessarily in contrast :

Why dost thou not go to church in a galliard, and come home in a coranto ? (I. iii. 138-9)

In Davies's *Orchestra* we meet the coranto under the guise of 'current traverses' :

What shall I name those current traverses,
That on a triple dactyl foot do run
Close by the ground with sliding passages,
Wherein that dance's greatest praise hath won
Which with best order can all orders shun ;
For everywhere he wantonly must range
And turn and wind with unexpected change.

Pepys in his diary relates how his wife's dancing-master 'would needs have me try the steps of a Coranto', about the music of which he says elsewhere he had an argument whether 'the law of a dancing Corant is to have every bar to end in a pricked crochet and quaver'.

The Allemande was a German dance, early transplanted to Switzerland and France ; it was danced by several couples simultaneously, the gentleman leading the lady by the hand, which he never quitted during the dance, and the other pairs following forwards and backwards, keeping time with their steps and a 'greue' (lifting the foot without a spring). 'The Alman', says Morley, 'is a more heavie daunce than this [the galliard], fitlie representing the nature of the people whose name it carieth'.

The Canary was a lively Spanish dance, the idea of which is said to have been derived from the aborigines of the Canary Islands. Arbeau believes that 'the name was

derived from a ballet composed for a masquerade, where the
dancers were dressed like the kings and queens of Mauritania,
or else as savages, with plumage of divers colours'.

Ford puns on ' wine ', ' pipe ', and ' canary ', meaning
whine, pipe (for dancing to), and the canary that he meant
Falstaff to dance :

Host. I will to my honest knight Falstaff, and drink canary with
  him.
Ford (aside). I think I shall drink in pipe-wine first with him ; I'll
  make him dance. (*M. Wives* III. ii. 91–5)

and Lafeu speaks of a medicine, to wit a woman's charms,
that will

make you dance canary
With spritely fire and motion.   (*All's W.* II. i. 77–8)

BIBLIOGRAPHY.—Dancing was generally considered a part of a liberal
education, and is therefore treated in educational books such as Sir THOMAS
ELYOT's *Governour*, 1531 (the edition by H. H. S. Croft, 1880, has valuable
notes on the history of dancing), and PEACHAM's *Compleat Gentleman*, 1622, &c.
Its use is condemned in more or less severe language by JOHN NORTHBROOKE
in *A treatise wherein Dicing, Dauncing, Vaine Plaies or Enterludes . . . are
reprooved*, 1579, by PHILIP STUBBES in *The Anatomie of Abuses*, 1583, and
others.
    The first English work entirely devoted to dancing is Sir JOHN DAVIES's
Orchestra, 1594, written in verse ; reprinted by Arber in *An English Garner*,
vol. v., pp. 19–58, 1882. The main authority for the figures and music of the
old country dances is *The English Dancing-Master*, put forth by John Playford,
long after Shakespeare's death, in 1651 ; a second edition appeared in 1652.
    The most valuable contemporary treatise for the history and execution of
society dances in Shakespeare's time is JEHAN TABOUROT's (' Thoinot Arbeau ')
*Orchesographie et traite en forme de dialogue par lequel les personnes peuvent
facilement apprendre et practiquer l'honneste exercice des danses*, 1588. Important
Italian works are FABRITIO CAROSO DA SERMONETA's *Il Ballarino*, 1581 (which
gives full direction for the Passa-Mezzo), and CESARE NEGRI's *Nuove Inventioni
di Balli*, 1604. (James I's copy of the latter is in the British Museum.) A much
earlier work (in macaronic verse) dealing with the ' danses nobles ' was composed by the Provençal ANTONIUS DE ARENA (de la Sable) under the title
Ad suos Compagnones . . . bassas Dansas et Branlos practicantes, 1529
RABELAIS in bk. v, ch. xxxiii bis of *Pantagruel* gives a list of 180 dances
Le Duchat's ed., 1741, has valuable notes. A translation from French, *The
maner of dauncynge of Bace daunces after the use of fraunce*, was issued by
Robert Copland in 1521.
    There are many foreign (chiefly French) histories of dancing. The best
history of dancing that has yet appeared in English is Mrs. LILLY GROVE's (Lady
Frazer) *Dancing*, 1895, in the Badminton Library. GASTON VUILLIER's *A History
of Dancing from the Earliest Ages to our own times* contains a sketch of Dancing
in England by J. GREGO, 1898. The articles on the names of dances in
Grove's *Dictionary of Music* should be consulted. Dancing figures largely
in BURNEY's *General History of Music*, 4 vols., 1776–89, and Sir JOHN
HAWKINS's history, 5 vols., 1776 ; it is the subject of bk. iii, ch. xv, of
STRUTT's *Sports and Pastimes*, ed. J. C. Cox, 1903 (pp. 174–94). E. W
NAYLOR's *Shakespeare and Music*, 1896, is indispensable for a right under
standing of Shakespeare's allusions to dancing.

§ 9. GAMES

BY

A. Forbes Sieveking

THE etymological meaning of Game is probably ' communion of men '. The educational writers of the Renaissance laid emphasis on another kind of communion which was held to be the highest object of play, namely, communion of body and mind. Thus Montaigne in his essay *Of the Institution of Children* :

All sports and exercises shall be a part of his study. . . . I would have the exterior demeanor or decencie, and the disposition of his person to be fashioned together with his mind : for, it is not a mind, it is not a body that we erect, but it is a man, and we must not make two parts of him.

Richard Mulcaster, in his *Positions*, has a very similar reflection on exercise and the training of the body :

The soule and bodie being coparteners in good and ill, in sweete and sowre, in mirth and mourning, and having generally a common sympathie, and a mutuall feeling in all passions : how can they be, or rather why should they be severed in traine ?

Shakespeare knew the value of a ' game play'd home ' (*Wint. Tale* I. ii. 248), where each man's aim is to ' carry out ' his ' side ' (*Lear* v. i. 61).

Games were divided broadly by Vives into lawful and unlawful games ; to the first class belong all games of ball, leaping, running, and gymnastic exercises ; to the second belong dice and cards, all games of chance, and, strange to say, swimming. Roger Ascham's list of noble exercises includes

to ride cumlie : to run faire at the tilte or ring : to plaie at all weapones : to shote faire in bow, or surelie in gon : to vaut lustely : to runne : to leape : to wrestle : to swimme : To daunce cumlie : to sing, and playe of instrumentes cunnyngly : to Hawke : to hunte : to playe at tennes, and all pastimes generally, which be joyned with labor, used in open place, and on the day light, conteining either some fitte exercise for warre, or some pleasant pastime for peace.

Among Shakespeare's contemporaries who were proficient

in sport and physical accomplishments, Sir Philip Sidney's eminence is well known, and received this tribute from his brother poet Spenser (*Astrophel* ii. 73–8) :

> In wrestling nimble, and in renning swift,
> In shooting steddie, and in swimming strong :
> Well made to strike, to throw, to leape, to lift,
> And all the sports that shepheards are emong.
> In every one he vanquisht every one,
> He vanquisht all, and vanquisht was of none.

Sport was fostered by such periodical meetings as that which took place in the Cotswolds at Whitsuntide. The Cotswold Games probably date back at least to the last quarter of the sixteenth century. After James I's accession, Robert Dover, an attorney, called 'Captain' by courtesy, who first lived at Barton-on-the-Heath, Warwickshire, and was thus a neighbour of Shakespeare, but afterwards settled at Stanway, in the heart of the Cotswolds, obtained permission from the King to direct the sports, and superintended them for forty years, in royal cast-off clothes, which he is said to have worn with more dignity than the monarch. The games were originally only athletic exercises, such as wrestling, leaping, cudgel-playing, sword-and-buckler, pitching the bar, throwing the sledge (hammer), and tossing the pike ; but coursing and dancing were added later. Justice Shallow includes among the 'swinge-bucklers' in the Inns 'Will Squele a Cotswold man' (*2 Hen. IV*, III. ii. 23–4) ; and when Slender asks Page, 'How does your fallow greyhound, sir ? I heard say he was outrun on Cotsall' (*M. Wives* I. i. 92–3), he alludes to the Cotswold coursing matches.

No better epitome of the popular indoor and outdoor games and pastimes current in Shakespeare's time can be given than is contained in the following verses from *The Letting of Humours Blood in the Head-Vaine*, by Samuel Rowlands (1600) :

> Man, I dare challenge thee to throw the sledge,
> To jumpe or leape over a ditch or hedge ;
> To wrastle, play at stooleball, or to runne,
> To pitch the barre, or to shoote off a gunne ;
> To play at loggets, nineholes, or ten pinnes,
> To trie it out at foot-ball, by the shinnes ;
> At Ticktacke, Irish, Noddie, Maw, and Ruffe :
> At hot-cockles, leape-frogge, or blindman-buffe

To drink halfe pots, or deale at the whole canne :
To play at base, or pen-and-Ynk-horne sir Ihan (John) :
To daunce the Morris, play at barly-breake,
At all exploytes a man can thinke or speake ;
At shove-groate, venter poynt, or crosse and pile,
At ' beshrow him that 's last at yonder style ' ;
At leapynge ore a Midsommer bon-fier,
Or at the drawing Dun out of the myer ;
At ' shoote-cocke, Gregory ', stoole-ball, and what not,
Picke-poynt, toppe and scourge, to make him hott.[1]

In one of Ben Jonson's masques, *Love Restored*, we find
a very pretty contrast drawn between court and country
sports. ' Are these your court-sports ? ' cries Robin Good-
fellow,

Would I had kept mee to my gamboles o' the countrey still,
selling of fish, short service, shooing the wild mare, or roasting
of robin red-brest. . . . I am . . . Robbin good-fellow, hee that
sweepes the harth, and the house cleane, riddles for the countrey-
maids, and does all their other drudgerie, while they are at hot-
cockles.

And Plutus, masquerading as Cupid, paints this alluring
picture of frugal pastimes :

Why should not the thriftie and right worshipfull game of Post
and payre content 'hem ; Or the wittie invention of Noddy, for
counters ? or God make them rich, at the Tables ? but Masking
and Revelling ! Were not these Ladies, and their gentlewomen
more housewifely employ'd . . . i' their chambers, at home, and
their old night gownes, at Draw-gloves, Riddles, Dreames, and
other prettie Purposes ?

The outdoor sports and indoor games of country life
at the close of the sixteenth century are given at length
in *Cyvile and Uncyvile Life* (1597), and the reader is
referred to Chapter I, pp. 34–5, for the catalogue of
them. With this we may compare the list which Burton
gives in his *Anatomy of Melancholy*, published twenty-five
years later. Besides hawking, hunting, fowling, fishing,
ringing, bowling, shooting, there are

Keelpins, tronks, coits, pitching bars, hurling, wrestling, leaping,
running, fencing, mustring, swimming, wasters, foiles, foot-ball,
balown, quintan, &c. ;

and among amusements for the winter we have :

Cards, Tables, and Dice, Shovelboord, Chess-play, the Philosophers
game, small trunks, shuttle-cock, balliards, musick, masks, singing,

---

[1] The last two lines were added later.

dancing, [Y]ulegames, frolicks, jests, riddles, catches, purposes, questions and commands, merry tales.

Praise of sport rightly used is not hard to seek among writers of this period, but none perhaps sums up the matter better than Thomas Fuller, who, though he was born only eight years before Shakespeare's death, may be fitly quoted here :

Running, leaping and dancing, . . . are all excellent exercises. And yet those are the best recreations which, besides refreshing, enable, [or] at least dispose men to some other good ends. Bowling teaches men's hands and eyes mathematics and the rules of proportion : swimming hath saved many a man's life . . . : tilting and fencing is war without anger ; and manly sports are the grammar of military performance.

We British people like to think of ourselves as the originators, as we assuredly are the organizers and perfecters, of our sports and games. But it must be said at the outset of this brief treatise that it is an undoubted fact that in Tudor days we derived our recreations and pastimes, as we did our intellectual culture and social refinements, from Spanish, Italian, and French sources. Horsemanship, as has been seen, came through Italy, from the East ; falconry and fencing from Italy, France, and Spain ; tennis from Italy and France. There was an organized ' wall-game ' at football in Florence long before it reached Eton ; Giovanni de' Bardi's *Discorso* (1580) shows strategic and tactical football played in Florence at a time when in England it was chiefly pursued by the rabble in the streets. Billiards and cards came direct from Spain.

It will be convenient here to begin with games that demand, above all, strength of body.

GAMES OF STRENGTH

Running is commended by Sir Thomas Elyot as ' bothe a good exercise and a laudable solace '. Foot-racing is among the most ancient of sports, and has been practised in England from the earliest times. Shakespeare, with characteristic brevity, gives us a picture of runners exhausted at the end of their course :

Forspent with toil, as runners with a race,
I lay me down a little while to breathe.

(*3 Hen. VI*, II. iii. 1–2)

There is much truth in the proverb, 'Où l'on trouve la lutte, cherchez le Celte', for it is doubtful if Wrestling would have survived as a sport but for the Celtic inhabitants of Brittany and Cornwall and the Celto-Scandinavians of Cumberland and Westmoreland. Cornwall, whose arms at the battle of Agincourt, as we learn from Drayton, were two wrestlers, was recognized at a very early date as producing fine wrestlers.

In the fifteenth and early sixteenth centuries, wrestling was a common interlude in, or even an integral part of, a joust royal. And so it is with the wrestling match in Lodge's *Rosalynde* (1590), where Torismond, King of France, appoints 'a day of wrestling and of tournaments'. A Norman champion was to stand against all comers. 'He straight coped with a lusty franklin, gave him the fall, and killed him with the weight of his corpulent personage.' The younger brother leaped into the place and first brought the Norman to the knees, but fear of disgrace doubled the Norman's strength, so that he threw his opponent down and broke his neck. The people murmured at this 'massacre', but Rosador 'vailed bonnet to the King, and lightly leaped within the lists'. The Norman 'roughly clapped to him with so fierce an encounter, that they both fell to the ground'. At last Rosador roused himself and threw the Norman, falling upon his chest 'with so willing a weight, that the Norman yielded Nature her due and Rosador the victory'. A garland was the prize.[1]

This incident, itself based on a passage in *The Tale of Gamelyn*, is the source of the wrestling episode in *As You Like It* (I. ii), in which Shakespeare introduces comments upon the propriety of ladies being present at such a dangerous kind of sport. Le Beau tells how the eldest of three proper young men

wrestled with Charles, the Duke's wrestler ; which Charles in a moment threw him and broke three of his ribs, that there is little hope of life in him : so he served the second and so the third.

Touchstone asks 'But what is the sport, monsieur, that the ladies have lost ?' and makes the wise comment : 'It is the first time that ever I heard breaking of ribs was sport for ladies.' However, the ladies do stay and see the 'sport', and, though Celia and Rosalind try to dissuade Orlando, he tries

In England in earlier days, as we learn from Chaucer, the prize was a ram.

a fall with the rib-breaker, with the result that the latter is
served in his own way, and Rosalind admits to Orlando
that he has 'wrestled well and overthrown more than his
enemies'.

The result of the match illustrates the dictum of Sir
Thomas Elyot, who recommends the use of wrestling in
war, in case 'a capitayne shall be constrained to cope with
his adversarye hande to hande', since 'the weaker person
by the sleyght of wrestlynge hath overthrowen the stronger'.

The 'fall' consisted in either the adversary's back or
one shoulder and the contrary heel touching the ground.
The 'foil' was a fall that was almost but not quite a flat
fall. Carew, in his *Survey of Cornwall*, says :

> If he be endangered and make a narrow escape, it is called a
> foyle. . . . Many sleights and tricks appertaine hereunto, in which
> a skilfull weake man will soone get the overhand of one that is
> strong and ignorant. Such are the Trip, fore-Trip, Inturne, the
> Faulx, forward and backward, the Mare and divers other like.

'To give the foil' and 'to put to the foil', which occur
in the plays (*Temp.* III. i. 46, *1 Hen. VI*, v. iii. 23), are used
metaphorically for any kind of check. We cannot always
be sure of the source of the metaphors which Shakespeare
puts into the mouths of the vulgar, but it is probable that
the Porter in *Macbeth* is at grips with wrestling when he
says that 'being too strong for him [i. e. drink], though
he took up my legs sometime, yet I made a shift to cast
him' (II. iii. 45–7).

Wrestling matches were held in Clerkenwell from early
times, and wrestlers came together from many parts.
The Londoners were sometimes beaten and riots were not
uncommon. Hentzner, in his *Itinerary*, records the presence
of the Lord Mayor in state on horseback at a meeting in
Clerkenwell.

A practical knowledge of the art of Swimming on the part
of Shakespeare might be wellnigh proved from the description of Ferdinand's escape from the wreck in *The Tempest* :

> I saw him beat the surges under him,
> And ride upon their backs : he trod the water
> Whose enmity he flung aside, and breasted
> The surge most swoln that met him : his bold head
> 'Bove the contentious waves he kept, and oar'd
> Himself with his good arms in lusty stroke
> To the shore   (II. i. 121–7)

To swimme with his hands together.

From C. Middleton's translation of Everard Digby's *De Arte Natandi*, 1595.

In the next scene Trinculo asserts that he

swam ashore, man, like a duck : I can swim like a duck, I'll be
sworn.   (II. ii. 137–8)

Another indication of familiarity with the practice of the
art appears in the expression 'swims against the stream'
(*2 Hen. IV*, v. ii. 34) ; and Wolsey, in his soliloquy, compares
himself to

> little wanton boys that swim on bladders, . . .
> But far beyond my depth.   (*Hen. VIII*, III. ii. 360–2)

Swimming on bladders and hurdles is depicted in the
Historia de Gentibus Septentrionalibus of Olaus Magnus
(1555), and a soldier upright in the water is shown inflating
a leather buoy through a tube.   The allusion in *Macbeth*
(I. ii. 8–9) to

> two spent swimmers, that do cling together
> And choke their art,

and the lines

> Like an unpractis'd swimmer plunging still,
> With too much labour drowns for want of skill
>
> (*Lucr.* 1098–9)

reveal either the close observer or the experienced
swimmer.   Shakespeare may have seen Everard Digby's
De Arte Natandi (1587), with its curious woodcuts, or its
English translation of 1595, in which various feats of
fancy swimming are described, as 'to turne in the water
like a Roach ', ' to turne the Bell turne in the water ',
' to tumble in the water ', ' to make a circle in the water
with the feete ', ' to swim like a dog ', ' to pare his toes in
the water ' ; and the learner is shown how 'to tread the
water '.

In the sixteenth century Sliding as a term included
Skating, for it was not till near the close of the seventeenth
century that the word ' skate ' was borrowed from Holland.
The point is illustrated by the following passage from
Stow's *Survey* (in a translation of Fitzstephen's account
of the sports and pastimes followed in the city in his
days) :

When the great Fenne or Moore, which watereth the wals of the
Citie on the North side is frozen, many yong men play upon the
yce, some striding as wide as they may, doe slide swiftly : others
make themselves seates of yce as great as Milstones : one sits
downe, many hand in hand doe draw him, and one slipping on a

sudden, all fall togither : some tie bones to their feete, and under their heeles, and shoving themselves, by a little picked Staffe, doe slide as swiftly as a bird flieth in the ayre, or an arrow out of a Crossebow.

Shakespeare has one reference to the sport :

> The fool slides o'er the ice that you should break.
>
> (*Troilus* III. iii. 216)

BALL GAMES

Of all the Ball games, Tennis is perhaps the most interesting and the most important.

All the available evidence points to the game having been borrowed directly from France. Its very name is not improbably taken from French ' tenez ', take, that is, receive the ball. There is a passage in *King Henry the Eighth* which bears witness to a current belief that tennis came from France. Sir Thomas Lovell says :

> They must . . . leave those remnants
> Of fool and feather that they got in France, . . .
> . . .   renouncing clean
> The faith they have in tennis and tall stockings.
>
> (I. iii. 23–30)

The name of the game in French is ' jeu de paume ', palm-play,[1] which suggests that it originated in a hand-ball game resembling Fives. There is some difference of opinion whether the game of fives or an early form of lawn tennis is described in the following passage from Nichols's *Progresses of Queen Elizabeth* :

Ten of my Lord of Hertford's servants, all Somersetshire men, in a square greene court, before her Majestie's windowe, did hang up lines, squaring out the forme of a tennis-court, and making a cross line in the middle. In this square they (being stript out of their dublets) played five to five, with the hand-ball, at bord and cord (as they terme it), to the so great liking of her Highnes.

Mulcaster commends

the little hand-ball, whether it be of some softer stuffe, and used by the hand alone, or of some harder, and used with the rackette, whether by tennice play with another, or against a wall alone.

---

[1] The palme play, where, dispoyled for the game,
    With dazed eies oft we by gleames of love,
Have mist the ball, and got sight of our dame,
    To baite her eyes, whiche kept the leads above.
                (Earl of Surrey's *Poems* in *Tottel's Misce* .,
                        Arber, 1895, p. 13)

From being a game penalized by law under the early
Tudors, like many other games that were considered to
distract the people from military exercises, tennis became,
in the course of the sixteenth century, one of the most
fashionable.   Prince Henry, son of James I, ' the English
Marcellus ', was a keen tennis-player, and was thought to
have brought on his untimely death by over-indulgence in
the game.[1]

In one of the dialogues of Juan Luis Vives (1539), a
speaker who has come from Paris describes the Braccha[2] as
the most famous private ground for games.   The teacher
of tennis there, it seems, furnished the players with felt
shoes for play on a smooth tiled pavement, and with caps
held on by a band under the chin; the balls are described
as being smaller than the wind-balls (or balloons), and
harder—being made of white leather and 'stuffed' not
with wool torn from rags, but chiefly dog's hair,[3] the
ball being struck, not with the fist or palm of the
hand, but with a net (i. e. a racquet) 'woven from
strings such as are found on the six-stringed lyre '.
A rope is stretched across the court, over which the
ball must be sent, within two limits or boundaries. The
game is marked ' 15, 30, 45 or (advantage), equality of
numbers, and victory ', which is twofold, according as a
game or set is won.   The ball is either taken full, or at the
first bound.

There is a remarkable parallel in language between a
passage in Puttenham's *Arte of English Poesie* (1589) and
a speech in *All's Well that Ends Well* (II. iii. 314–15).
Puttenham illustrates the figure of Antanaclasis, or the
Rebounde, as follows :

Ye have another figure which by his nature we may call the
Rebound, alluding to the tennis ball which being smitten with the
racket reboundes backe againe, and where the last figure before
[syneciosis] played with two wordes somewhat like, this playeth
with one word written all alike but carrying divers sences as thus :
The maide that soone married is, soone marred is.

---

[1] When James I writes of ' the Caitche or Tennis ' (*Basilikon Doron*,
1599), he is using the Old Dutch word ' kaetse ', from French ' chasse ',
whence also the English ' chase '.
[2] The *Bracque* tennis-court, so called from its sign, a setter, was in the
Faubourg Saint-Marcel.   Rabelais mentions it (*Gargantua* I. xxiii).
[3] Cf. 'The barber's man hath been seen with him; and the old ornament
of his cheek hath already stuffed tennis-balls.' (*Much Ado* III. ii. 45–7)

Parolles, commenting on Bertram's violent decision to leave his newly-wed wife and go to the wars, exclaims :

> Why, these balls bound ; there 's noise in it. 'Tis hard :
> A young man married is a man that 's marr'd.

Tennis also suggests homelier reflections, as in Prince Henry's speech to Poins :

> What a disgrace is it to me . . . to bear the inventory of thy shirts ; as, one for superfluity, and the other for use ! But that the tennis-court-keeper knows better than I, for it is a low ebb of linen with thee when thou keepest not racket there.
> (2 Hen. IV, ii. ii. 15–24)

The insolence of the Dauphin in sending ' a tunne of tennis balles' to Henry V occasioned the following dramatic retort of the King, which is an epitome of the chief terms of play current in Shakespeare's time :

> When we have match'd our rackets to these balls,
> We will in France, by God's grace, play a set
> Shall strike his father's crown into the hazard.
> Tell him he hath made a match with such a wrangler
> That all the courts of France will be disturb'd
> With chaces.[1] (Hen. V, i. ii. 261–6)

The court is an enclosed oblong building, having on one side and at the two ends an inner wall between which and the outer wall is a sloping roof, the ' penthouse '.[2] Pericles, when tossed by the rackety waves, speaks of himself as

> A man whom both the waters and the wind,
> In that vast tennis-court [the sea], have made the ball
> For them to play upon. (Pericles ii. i. 64–6)

In the inner wall are openings, called hazards, such as the *trou*, or hole near the floor, and later, galleries. The chase is the second impact on the floor (or in a gallery)

---

[1] The incident which calls forth this speech is related at length in Hall's *Chronicle*, taken from the contemporary account of Thomas Otterbourne in 1414 (Harl. MS. 3643). It is also found in Caxton's Continuation of Higlen's *Polychronicon* (1482), in Holinshed, in *The famous Victories of Henry the Fifth* (1598), on which Shakespeare's play is founded, and in Drayton's *Battaile of Agincourt*, which has strong affinity to Shakespeare's verses :
> . . . Ile send him Balls and Rackets if I live,
> That they such Racket shall in Paris see,
> When over lyne with Bandies I shall drive,
> As that before the Set be fully done
> France may perhaps into the Hazard runne.

[2] Otterbourne's word is *tecta*. It was called ' the house ' in Shakespeare's time. Cotgrave defines a sense of ' Jeu ' as ' the upper end of a Tennis court (next to the house) or so much of it as is comprised within the streake of chaulke, &c., drawne overthwart the court '.

of a ball which the opponent has failed or declined to return ; its value is determined by the nearness of the point of impact to the end wall. A chase does not count to either player until the players have changed sides. A player wins a chase, on sides being changed, if he can cause his ball to rebound nearer the wall than the ball did in the chase for which he is playing. Florio gives an excellent view of the game in Shakespeare's time, in his *Second Frutes* (1591), where the value of chases is discussed.

To ' bandy ' meant to strike the ball to and fro.

> Well bandied both ; a set of wit well play'd,

says the Princess in *Love's Labour's Lost* (v. ii. 29), in commendation of the contest between Rosaline and Katharine. Juliet complains of the Nurse's slowness, and continues :

> Had she affections, and warm youthful blood,
> She'd be as swift in motion as a ball ;
> My words would bandy her to my sweet love,
> And his to me. (*Rom. & Jul.* II. v. 12–15)

Antonio Scaino in his treatise on ball-games gives Football a special chapter as being a game unlike all others. The ball he describes weighs ten ounces and is six inches in diameter, and is softer and more elastic than the ball used for *pallone* or balloon.[1] He specifies the arena at Padua and the season of Lent as fit place and time for its performance, by 20, 30, or 40 players. He speaks of ' segne ' or goals into which the ball is to be driven by any and every part of the player's body, as well while it is flying in the air, as after the first, second, or any number of rebounds. The ball is not allowed to be thrown when caught, and if this is done the game becomes a ' scaramuccia ', in which word for ' skirmish ' we detect the modern ' scrimmage '. For details of the battle, recourse must be had to the book itself ; here we can only indicate the distribution of the players into forwards (' antiguardia '), the stalwart half-backs (' gagliardi ') and runners, and behind these the backs or rear-guard (' retroguardia '). This definitely organized game, which is even more fully

---

[1] Markham describes ' Baloone ' as ' a strong and mooving sport in the open fields, with a great Ball of double Leather filled with Winde, and so driven too and fro with the strength of a mans Arme arm'd in a Bracer of Wood, eyther of which actions must be learnt by the Eye and practise not by the Eare or Reading '.

VEDVTA DELLA PIAZZA DI S.ᵗᵃ CROCE DELLA CITTA DI FIRENZE NEL ATTO DI PRINCIPIARE IL GIOCO DEL CALCIO S.ᵗᵃ 16 60 00

FLORENTINE RENAISSANCE FOOTBALL

described by Giovanni de' Bardi in the work from which we give an illustration, is in direct contrast with the disorderly games of football as practised in this country at that time.

If an inference may be drawn from Dromio of Ephesus' comparison of himself to a football in *The Comedy of Errors*, it seems probable that the ball had by Shakespeare's day already passed the early naked-bladder stage :

> Am I so round with you as you with me,
> That like a football you do spurn me thus ?
> You spurn me hence, and he will spurn me hither :
> If I last in this service, you must case me in leather.
>
> (II. i. 82–5)

Football is treated hardly by most of the schoolmasters of later days, although we find Mulcaster raising his voice in 1581 in its favour against Sir Thomas Elyot's strictures of fifty years before, to the effect that football, so far from being ' nothinge but beastly furie and exstreme violence ', could not have

> groune to the greatnes that it is now at . . . if it had not had great helpes, both to health and strength,

and in his view ' the abuse of it is a sufficient argument that it hath a right use '.   He moreover advocates

> a trayning maister, a smaller number of players sorted into sides and standings, not meeting with their bodies so boisterously to trie their strength.

We are not surprised that Stubbes should regard it as one of his many ' devilish pastimes ', but it is clear from Shakespeare's allusion to football in *King Lear* (I. iv. 95–6) that the game was far from being regarded as a gentle or even a legitimate sport.   To the cautious King James, football was ' a laming exercise not to be used by a Prince ', although he expresses royal approval of

> running, leaping, wrastling, fencing, dauncing, playing at the caitche or tennise, archery and palle maille, and such other faire and pleasant field games.

BOWLS, QUOITS, ETC.

We find many references to the game of Bowls in Shakespeare's works, and a good case might be made out for his having been a practical bowler.   The conditions of the game are frequently taken to represent the vicissitudes of fortune, as in :

> *Queen.* What sport shall we devise here in this garden,
> To drive away the heavy thought of care ?
> *First Lady.* Madam, we'll play at bowls.
> *Queen.* 'Twill make me think the world is full of rubs,
> And that my fortune runs against the bias.
> (Rich. II, III. iv. 1–5)

> Nay, sometimes,
> Like to a bowl upon a subtle ground,
> I have tumbled past the throw.   (*Cor.* v. ii. 19–21)

The effect of the Bias of the bowl is forcibly illustrated in the Bastard's soliloquy in *King John* (II. i. 574–80) :

> Commodity, the bias of the world ;
> The world, who of itself is peized well,
> Made to run even upon even ground,
> Till this advantage, this vile-drawing bias,
> This sway of motion, this Commodity,
> Makes it take head from all indifferency,
> From all direction, purpose, course, intent ;

and in Petruchio's comment on his wife's temper :

> Well, forward, forward ! thus the bowl should run,
> And not unluckily against the bias.   (*Tam. Sh.* IV. v. 24–5)

In two places Shakespeare puts the word to strained and fanciful uses :

> Blow, villain, till thy sphered bias cheek
> Outswell the colic of puff'd Aquilon.   (*Troilus* IV. v. 6–8)

> But in this extant moment, faith and troth,
> Strain'd purely from all hollow bias-drawing,
> Bids thee, with most divine integrity,
> From heart of very heart, great Hector, welcome.
> (ibid. 167–70)

The Rub is any obstacle or impediment which diverts the bowl from its course. It is a feature that lends itself to punning and metaphorical application.

> *Costard.* She's too hard for you at pricks, sir : challenge her to bowl.
> *Boyet.* I fear too much rubbing.   (*Love's L. L.* IV. ii. 142–3)

Henry V, when the conspiracy of Scroop and his confederates has been detected, exhorts his lords to proceed to the French campaign, and adds :

> We doubt not now
> But every rub is smoothed on our way.
> (Hen. V, II. ii. 187–8)

The best-known instance of all is in Hamlet's great soliloquy:

> Ay, there's the rub.   (*Haml.* III. i. 65)

The Jack—the smaller bowl placed as a mark for the
players to aim at—was also called the Master or Mistress.
Shakespeare plays upon the latter word when he makes
Pandarus encourage Troilus in his addresses to Cressida:
with the words:

> So, so; rub on, and kiss the mistress. (*Troilus* III. ii. 50)

'Kiss' is a technical term when one bowl touches another
one or the jack.

From more than one passage we gather that the
game was considered suitable for women (*Rich. II*, III.
v. 1–5; *Love's L. L.* IV. ii. 142–3). It was played both
in the open and in closed alleys. Bowling-alleys were often
the scene of gambling and dissipation, and, in spite of
many Acts of Parliament, the evil continued to flourish.
Gosson, in his *Schoole of Abuse* (1579), says:

> Common Bowling Allyes are privy Mothes, that eate uppe the
> redite of many idle Citizens, whose gaynes at home are not able
> to weighe downe theyr losses abroad, whose Shoppes are so farre
> from maintaining their play, that their Wives and Children cry
> out for bread, and go to bedde supperlesse ofte in the yeere;

and Stow in his *Survey* complains that owing to the en-
closing of the common grounds

> our Archers, for want of roome to shoote abroade, creepe into bowling
> allies, and ordinarie dicing houses, nearer home, where they have
> roome enough to hazard their money at unlawfull games.

Shakespeare refers to such gambling in *Cymbeline* (II.
i. 1–8):

> Was there ever man had such luck! when I kissed the jack,
> upon an upcast to be hit away! I had a hundred pound on 't;
> and then a whoreson jackanapes must take me up for swearing,
> as if I had borrowed mine oaths of him and might not spend them
> at my pleasure.
> *First Lord.* What got he by that? You have broke his pate
> with your bowl.

There is no mention in Shakespeare of Ninepins or
kittles. Similar games were Kayles, Cloish, and Loggats.
Kayles[1] seems to have been played with six, eight, or
any number of pins, placed in a single row. In cloish—or
closh—a bowl was used as the missile, instead of the stick

---

[1] From the French 'quilles'.

employed in kayles. In loggats, bones were substituted
for wooden pins by boys and rustics, and another bone
was thrown at them. This use of bones explains Hamlet's
question,

Did these bones cost no more the breeding but to play at loggats
with 'em ? (*Haml.* v. i. 97–9)

Clarendon says the game resembled bowls, played not on
a green, but on an ash-strewn floor. In his account, the
jack is a disk of lignum vitae, and the loggat a truncated
cone of apple-wood.

Kayle pins passed through the form of kettle- or kittle-
pins into ' skittles'. Skittle-pins were sometimes made
from bones, as appears from *The Merry Milkmaid of Islington* (1680) :

I'll cleave you from the skull to the twist, and make nine-skittles
of thy bones.

Proficiency in the game of Quoits was one of the accomplishments which—so Falstaff said—endeared Poins to
Prince Henry (*2 Hen. IV*, II. iv. 266). Earlier in the same
scene, Falstaff, combining metaphors from quoits and
shovel-board, emphasizes Doll Tearsheet's wish to get rid
of Pistol by throwing him downstairs :

Quoit him down, Bardolph, like a shove-groat shilling.

(ll. 205–6)

Shakespeare only once alludes to Billiards, in one of
his most conspicuous anachronisms. Cleopatra, in her
moods, says to Charmian after she has called for music :

Let it alone : let 's to billiards. (*Ant. & Cleop.* II. v. 3)

Cotgrave defines ' Billiard ' in 1611 as ' the sticke where-
with we touch the ball at billyards ' ; this was later called
a mast or mace. The game was perhaps originally played
out-of-doors on a green, and may owe its green cloth to
such an origin.

Other games which were originally played in the open air
and subsequently became indoor pastimes are Troll-madam,
Nine-holes, and Merels. Troll-madam, troll-in-madam, troll-
my-dames, or *Gallice* trou-madame, was a game played
chiefly by ladies, and consisted in ' trolling ' or rolling
metal or wooden ball along a board or bench having eleven
holes at one end. Shakespeare refers to it in *The Winter's
Tale* (IV. ii. 90–3) :

Clown. What manner of fellow was he that robbed you ?

Autolycus. A fellow, sir, that I have known to go about with troll-my-dames.

Another method of playing this game was by trolling the balls through arches in an upright board. It had other names, as Trunks, Holes, and Pigeon Holes.

Nine-holes was a very similar game, in which the players endeavoured to roll small balls into nine holes in the ground, each of which had its own scoring value. It was also played on a square fixed on the ground, in which nine holes, all numbered, were arranged in three rows. Drayton, in the following lines of the *Poly-Olbion*, gives us an appealing picture of its attraction for rustics :

> The unhappy wags, which let their Cattell stray,
> At Nine-holes on the heath whilst they together play

Merels was a game for two players or parties, each of whom had the same number of pebbles, disks, pegs, or pins. It was also known as Nine Men's Morris, Fivepenny Morris, and Three Men's Morris, according to the number of ' men ' used. The usual form of the diagram on which it is played is a square with one or more squares inside it. The pegs or stones placed at set points are moved by one side so as to take up the men of the other. Cotgrave speaks of ' the boyish game called Merilles, or fiue-pennie Morris ' as being ' played here most commonly with stones, but in France with pawnes, or men made of purpose, and earmed Merelles '.[1] Various local varieties have been described by antiquarian writers. In the open-air form of the game the squares are made in the turf with knives. Titania says that, owing to the floods,

> The nine men's morris is fill'd up with mud.
> (*Mid. N. D.* ii. i. 98)

The popular amusement of Shovel-board or Shuffle-board consisted in driving a coin or disk by a blow with the hand along a highly polished board into compartments marked out at one end of it. It was also known by many synonyms—Shove-board, Shove-groat, Slide-groat, Slide-thrift, and Slip-groat. The coin most commonly used was a shilling, and especially, it seems, a shilling of Edward VI. It was called a ' shove-groat shilling ' (*2 Hen. IV*, ii. v. 205), or ' shovel-board shilling ', and, for the nonce, in

---

[1] *Marelle* in modern French means hopscotch.

The Merry Wives of Windsor (i. i. 160), an 'Edward shovel
board'. The ease with which the coin slid along the smooth
board is well illustrated by Ben Jonson in *Every Man i*
his Humour :

[They] made it run as smooth off the tongue as a shove-groa
shilling,

and by Middleton and Dekker in *The Roaring Girle* :

Away slid my man, like a shovel-board shilling.

DICING AND CARDS

Sir Hugh Plat, author of *The Jewell House of Art an*
Nature (1594), having heard of ' a pair of cards, wherof
most of the principall Grammer rules have been printed
conceived the idea of turning to educational account th
chief instrument of gambling. His suggestion was t
convert the devil's bones into a hornbook, by making fou
large dice of bone or wood and

upon everie square, one of the smal letters of the crosse row to b
graven ... and the child using to play much with them, ... wil soo
gain his Alphabet, as it were by the way of sport or pastime.

Dice-play was probably the commonest form of gambling
Falstaff declares that he 'diced not above seven times a week
(*1 Hen. IV*, iii. iii. 18), and Edgar confesses that in time past

Wine loved I deeply, dice dearly.   (*Lear* iii. iv. 90–1)

The terms of its language are the most apt to describe i
metaphor the gamble for success or the final attempt t
retrieve shattered fortunes. So, to take one exampl
King Richard exclaims :

Slave ! I have set my life upon a cast,
And I will stand the hazard of the die.

(*Rich. III*, v. iv. 9–10)

Nor could Shakespeare easily miss the opportunity
punning which the word ' die ' offered. And so, whe
Pyramus ends his song with ' Now die, die, die, die, die
Demetrius quibbles ' No die, but an ace, for him ; for h
is but one', and Lysander goes on, 'Less than an ace, ma
for he is dead ; he is nothing ' (*Mid. N. D.* v. i. 313–7
And again :.

Take thou the destin'd tenth,
And by the hazard of the spotted die
Let die the spotted.   (*Timon* v. iv. 33–5)

Many and various were the stakes placed upon a throw
of the dice. In Stow's *Survey*, we read there was a
'clochier' with four bells near St. Paul's School, and 'the
common speech then was' that Sir Miles Partridge threw
dice with Henry VIII, and set a hundred pounds upon
he cast, against the great Jesus bells in the tower of
St. Paul's, London, and won them; but 'the ropes afterwards catched about his neck' wrote Fuller in *The De-
generous Gentleman*, for in the fifth year of Edward VI, he
was 'executed at Tower Hill for matters concerning the Duke
of Somerset'.

The chorus in *King Henry the Fifth*, describing the scene
before the battle of Agincourt, says that

The confident and over-lusty French
Do the low-rated English play at dice, (IV. chor. 18–19)

and when it is seen that the French have lost the fight,
the over-confident Dauphin, referring to the victorious
English, exclaims:

Be these the wretches that we play'd at dice for?
(ibid. IV. v. 8)

The falseness of dice and of 'dicers' oaths' had become
a proverb (*Wint. Tale* I. ii. 133–4, *Haml.* III. iv. 45), for
cheating with false or loaded dice had been reduced to a
fine art. There were many kinds of false dice; fourteen
are enumerated in Dekker's *The Belman of London* (1608),
and the more usual are given by Samuel Rowlands in *The
Letting of Humours Blood* (1600), in the following verses:

But come to Dice; why that's his onely trade,
Michell Mum-chaunce, his owne Invention made.
He hath a stocke, whereon his lyving stayes,
And they are Fullams, and Bard quarter-trayes:
His Langrets, with his Hie-men and his low,
Are ready what his pleasure is to throw:
His stopt Dice, with Quick-silver never misse.[1]
He calles for, Come on five; and there it is:
Or else heele have it with five and a reach,
Although it cost his necke the Halter stretch.

The nature of langrets is explained in *A Manifest Detection of Dice Play* (c. 1550), attributed to Gilbert Walker:

A well favored die that semeth good and square: yet is the
bored longer on the cater [4] and tray [3], then any other way,
and therefore holdeth the name of a langret.

[1] Cf. Ascham's *Toxophilus* (1545): dise stopped with quicksilver and
heares [i. e. hairs].

Of the bard (i.e. barred) dice or bars there were many species. Greene says :

The Chetor with a langret, cut contrarie to the vantage, will cros-bite a bard cater tray.

Unfortunately Greene, 'for some speciall reasons', was more reticent about 'Cheting Law' than other forms of cozenage, and so he leaves the terms Bard-dice, Flats, Fargers, Langrets, Gourds, Demies, and many others, untranslated into the vernacular.

Cogging the dice was the use of some sleight of hand to control the falling of the bones. Again in *Dice Play* we read :

When fine squariers only be stirring, ther rests a great help in cogging,—that is when the undermost dy standeth dead by the weighty fall of his fellow ; so that if vi. be my chaunce, and x. yours, graunt that upon the die I cogge and keepe alway an ace, deuce or tray, I may perhaps sone cast vi. but never x.

Besides, there were sliding, foisting, and coyting.

Hazard is a dicing game, one term of which, 'main chance', has become a commonplace of ordinary language. The caster, before throwing the dice, called a main, which was a number from five to nine inclusive. The player then threw with two dice, and if he threw a nick, that is, a throw which is either the same as the main, or else a number which has a fixed correspondence to it, he won ; but if he 'threw out', i.e. threw two aces, or a deuce and an ace,[1] he lost. If the caster neither nicked nor threw out, the number thrown was his chance, and he then continued to play until either the chance came up, in which case he won, or the main, when he lost the game. Rambures, on the eve of the battle of Agincourt, asks :

Who will go to hazard with me for twenty prisoners ?

and the Constable of France, playing on the word, replies :

You must first go yourself to hazard, ere you have them.

(*Hen. V*, III. vii. 98–101)

And Hotspur asks :

> Were it good
> To set the exact wealth of all our states
> All at one cast ? to set so rich a main
> On the nice hazard of one doubtful hour ?

(*1 Hen. IV*, IV. i. 45–8)

---

[1] The names for these throws are 'ames-ace' (*All's W.* II. iii. 85) and 'deuce-ace' (*Love's L. L.* I. ii. 50).

Mumchance was a similar game to hazard, in which strict silence was observed. Novum (*Love's L. L.* v. ii. 545), or Novum quinque, was a game in which the two principal throws were nine and five. Passage was played by two persons, with three dice, and the players had to throw doublets over ten to win.

Tray-trip was a dice game, probably won by throwing a trey, i. e. a three. Sir Toby asks :

Shall I play my freedom at tray-trip, and become thy bond-slave ?   (*Tw. N.* II. v. 209–10)

' Trey ' is illustrated by the following passage :

Biron. White-handed mistress, one sweet word with thee.
Princess. Honey, and milk, and sugar ; there are three.
Bir. Nay then, two treys, an if you grow so nice,
Metheglin, wort, and malmsey : well run, dice !
There 's half a dozen sweets.
Prin.   Seventh sweet, adieu :
Since you can cog, I'll play no more with you.
                                              (*Love's L. L.* v. ii. 231–6)

From about 1500 till Restoration times, a pack of cards was commonly known as a ' pair of cards ', as in Italian it was called ' un paio di carte da giuocare '. In Tudor days it was also a bunch or a deck. There was also a specialized use of ' deck ' for the portion of the pack which, in some games, is left over after dealing, and of this use there is one instance in Shakespeare :

Alas ! that Warwick had no more forecast,
But, whiles he thought to steal the single ten,
The king was slily finger'd from the deck. (*3 Hen. VI*, v. i. 42–4)

The same use is illustrated in the following passage from *Selimus* (1594) :

Will fortune favour me yet once againe ?
And will she thrust the cards into my hands ?
Well, if I chance but once to get the decke,
To deale about and shuffle as I would ;

and Armin in *The Two Maids of More-clacke* (1609) has :

Ile deale the cards and cut ye from the decke.

Shakespeare in many places applied the language of card-playing to matters of life and conduct. Lewis, contemplating a bid for the English crown, says :

Have I not here the best cards for the game
To win this easy match play'd for a crown ?
And shall I now give o'er the yielded set ? (*John* v. ii. 105–6)

Aaron, reflecting on his handiwork in egging on Tamora's sons, says :

> That codding spirit had they from their mother,
> As sure a card as ever won the set. (*Tit. Andr.* v. i. 99–100)

It will be observed that 'set' was formerly used with something like the meaning of rubber.

The origin of the Elizabethan proverbial 'cooling card' is obscure : it is only clear that it implied some event that was damping to the spirit.

> There all is marr'd ; there lies a cooling card.
> (*1 Hen. VI*, v. iii. 84)

Roger Ascham, comparing the attractions of cards and shooting, describes how—

> A man, no shoter, (not longe agoo) wolde defende playing at cardes and dise, if it were honestly used, to be as honest a pastime as youre shotinge : For he layed for him, that a man might pleye for a litle at cardes and dyse, and also a man might shote away all that ever he had. He sayd a payre of cardes cost not past ii. d. and that they neded not so moche reparation as bowe and shaftes, they wolde never hurte a man his hande, nor never weare his gere A man shulde never slee a man with shoting wyde at the cardes.

The next two or three pages of *Toxophilus* are the fairest possible summing up of the case, *pro* and *con*, of archery *versus* cards and dice. Camden, however, adds 'the one satyric touch' to this picture by telling us, in his digression on Ascham's death, that he lived and died a poor man, through love of dicing and cockfighting.

John Northbrooke, in *A Treatise against Diceing* (1579), justifies his denunciation of 'the plaie of cards' as an 'invention of the devill' by the plea that

> the kings and coate cards that we use nowe were in olde time the images of idols and False Gods . . . chaunged into Charlemaine, Launcelot, Hector, and suchlike names.

Card-games were in great vogue at Court, and Primero was among the first favourites with royalty and other persons of distinction. The date of its introduction is uncertain, but it was a game familiar to Sir Thomas Elyot, and Shakespeare with some historical probability makes Bishop Gardiner tell us that he left Henry VIII playing primero with the Duke of Suffolk (*Hen. VIII*, v. i. 7–8). Queen Elizabeth was fond of taking a hand at primero, but not recklessly.

A GAME OF PRIMERO

In the *Sydney Papers* [1] we read of a quarrel in which Lord Southampton, the patron of Shakespeare, 'strooke' Ambrose Willoughby, who with Sir Walter Rawley and Mr. Parker was at primero in the Presence Chamber, for persisting in playing when the Queen had gone to bed. Falstaff deplores the decline in his fortunes ever since he forswore himself at primero (*M. Wives* IV. v. 104–5). It was a great gambling game, and large stakes were often played for. 'If her Majestie', wrote Sir John Harington in *A Treatise on Playe* (printed in *Nugæ Antiquæ*),

would play at Primero in that proportion of her estate as I have seen some of her mean subjects in theyr poor callinges, she showld play a dukedom at a rest, and a barrony stake, and then I know none able to hold play with her.

Harington commends Sir Christopher Hatton for his wisdom in that when he placed £1,000 of his own at the disposal of his gambling guests, he rated it 'at xii*d*. the pownd', so that the amounts played for might seem great.

Primero [2] was a Spanish game closely resembling the later ombre. There were the greater and lesser primero—the former played with figured cards. At the latter the highest card was seven. The seven, six, and five had treble values, the ace counted sixteen, and the deuce, trey, and four had their nominal values. Each player had four cards dealt to him, and then he had to show them. He whose cards were of different suits won the prime; if they were all of one colour, he won the flush, which was the best hand, although it might be numerically inferior to the others. Research has not yet revealed the full details of the play.

An important term is 'rest', which was the name given to the stakes kept in reserve; when these were lost the game terminated. One's rest, therefore, became anything that one stood to win or lose, and 'to set up one's rest' was to venture one's final stake, to stake one's all, and was a phrase which naturally lent itself to extensive word-play.

One of Sir John Harington's Epigrams describes the story of Marcus's life at Primero:

Till of his age, quite was consum'd the prime,
Then he more warily his rest regards ;

[1] vol. ii, p. 83.
[2] The Spanish name is ' primera ', the Italian ' primiera ', and the French prime ' (Rabelais).

and has finally to 'set up his rest' at the Counter or
Debtor's prison ; and Shakespeare, among others, has the
following allusive references to the term :

When I cannot live any longer, I will do as I may : that is my
rest.   (*Hen. V*, II. i. 16–17)

The man, sir, that, when gentlemen are tired, gives them a sob
and rests them [1] ; . . . he that sets up his rest to do more exploits
with his mace than a morris-pike.   (*Com. of E.* IV. iii. 22–7)

O ! here
Will I set up my everlasting rest,
And shake the yoke of inauspicious stars
From this world-wearied flesh.
                                        (*Rom. & Jul.* V. iii. 109–12)

Cheating at primero is enlarged upon in *A Manifest
Detection of Dice Play* :

Primero, now as it hath most use in court, so is there most disceyt
in it ; some play uppon the prickes, some pinch the cards privily
with their nayls,—some turne up the corners,—some mark them
w[h] fine spots of inke. . . . At trump, saint, and such other like,
cutting at y[e] neck is a great vantage, so is cutting by a bum card
(finely) under and over, stealing the stocke of the decarded cardes,
if there brode lawes be forced aforehand.

Maw was another card-game of this period. It was
played with a piquet pack of thirty-six cards, by from two
to six persons, who were divided into partners. It was
also called Five Cards. Another game of the piquet class
was Saunt or Sant, otherwise spelt saint, sent, and cent.

Gleek was a game played by three persons ; forty-four
cards were used, each player receiving twelve, whilst the
remaining eight formed a common stock. It was known
as halfpenny-, penny-, twopenny-, &c., gleek, according to
the amount staked.

When you please, Sir, I am,
For three peny Gleeke, your man,

says one of the characters in Jonson's *The Devil is an Ass*
(v. ii). Shakespeare seems to use the word only in the
sense of gibe or jest, although some think there are allusions
to the game.[2]

Trump not only meant trump-card, but was also one

---

[1] Cf. p. 418 *supra*.
[2] Cf. *Mid. N. D.* III. i. 154 ; *Hen. V*, V. i. 78 ; *1 Hen. VI*, III. ii. 123 ;
Rom. & Jul. IV. v. 115.

of the names of a game,[1] otherwise called Ruff, which was
the precursor of whist. It seems certain that ' trump '
is an alteration of ' triumph ', which is used in the same
way. An Italian game called ' trionfi ' occurs as early as
1526, and Florio in his *Worlde of Wordes* (1598) translates
trionfo as ' a trump at cards, or the play called trump or
ruff '. This may be the same game as *la triomphe* of the
early editions of the *Académie des Jeux*, which is called by
Cotton ' French Ruff ', and resembles écarté. Trump and
Ruff are in some way contrasted in the following passage
of Nashe's *Martin Marprelate* (1589) :

Leaving the auncient game of England (Trumpe) where everie
coate and sute are sorted in their degree, [they] are running to their
Ruffe where the greatest sorte of the sute carrieth away the game.

Noddy, Post and Pair, Loadum, and a host of other
card games flourished during the Shakespearian period.

TABLE GAMES

Queen Elizabeth played at Draughts and Chess with
Roger Ascham, but James I thought chess was

overfond, because it is over-wise and Philosophique a folly : . . .
it filleth and troubleth mens heades with as many fashious toyes of
the play, as before it was filled with thoughts on his affaires.

(Basilikon Doron, 1599)

Rowbothum dedicated his translation of Gruget's treatise
to Robert Dudley, Earl of Leicester, because he could
' play excellently at this game of ye Cheast ' ; and Arthur
Saul dedicated *The famous game of Chesse-play* (1614) to
Lucy, Countess of Bedford.

The writings of Shakespeare's literary contemporaries
abound in punning references to the terms of the game.
' Chess ', says Greene in *A Groats Worth of Wit* (1592),

is a game . . . that the first danger is but a checke, the worst,
the giving of a mate ;

and Gascoigne in his *Flowres* (1572) laments that 'deadly
hate'

> Did play checke mate
> With me poore pawne.

[1] Latimer shows the twofold use in his *Sermon on the Card*, 1529. There
seems to be an allusion to ' triumph ', a trump-card, in *Antony and Cleopatra* :
> She, Eros, has
> Pack'd cards with Caesar, and false-play'd my glory
> Unto an enemy's triumph.   (IV. xii. 18–20)

An allusion in *Pappe with an Hatchet* (1589) is more elaborate :

If a Martin can play at chestes, as well as his nephewe the ape, he shall knowe what it is for a scaddle [i. e. mischievous] pawne, to crosse a Bishop in his owne walke. Such dydoppers must be taken up, els theile not stick to check the king.

A notable instance of a game played out on the stage is to be found in John Fletcher's *The Spanish Curate* (1622). Bacon also, in his essay *Of Boldness* (1625), draws a simile from the game :

With Bold men . . . they stand at a stay ; like a Stale at Chesse, where it is no Mate, but yet the Game cannot stirre.

Shakespeare has, however, but one unquestionable example of the game, the memorable stage-direction in *The Tempest* (v. i) :

Here Prospero discovers Ferdinand and Miranda playing at Chesse.

For the rest, there is the dubious reference in *King Lear* (I. i. 157–8), when Kent says :

My life I never held but as a pawn
To wage against thine enemies ;

and in *The Taming of the Shrew* (I. i. 57–8) there is a possible pun on 'stalemate' in Katharina's petulant demand to her father, who had just announced his determination not to bestow his younger daughter till the elder is disposed of :

I pray you, sir, is it your will
To make a stale of me amongst these mates ?

Down to the middle of the seventeenth century Backgammon was known as Tables. It is played by two persons on a board consisting of two 'tables' hinged together and hence called 'a pair of tables', each table being marked with six points, coloured alternately black and white.

There is one mention of it in Shakespeare. Biron, speaking of Boyet, says :

This is the ape of form, monsieur the nice,
That, when he plays at tables, chides the dice
In honourable terms.   (*Love's L. L.* v. ii. 236–8)

Backgammon figures among the occupations of an idle fellow who spends his life in play, depicted by Harington in *A Treatise on Playe* :

In the morninge, perhapps, at chesse, and after his belly is full then at cardes, . . . then for some exercyse of his armes at dyce, and . . . for a little motion of his body, to tennis ; and . .

The famous game
of Cheſſe-play,

Truely diſcouered, and all doubts reſolued;

So that by reading this ſmall Booke thou
ſhalt profit more then by the playing
a thouſand *Mates*.

An Exerciſe full of delight, fit for Princes, or any
perſon of what qualitie ſoeuer.

Newly publiſhed by A. S. Gent.

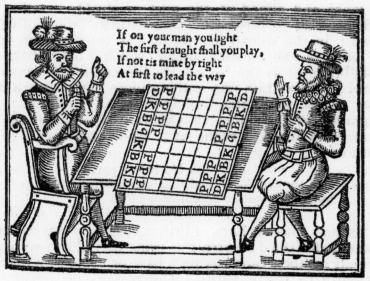

If on your man you light
The firſt draught ſhall you play,
If not tis mine by right
At firſt to lead the way

Printed at London for *Roger Iackson*, and are to be
ſould at his ſhop neere Fleetſtreet-Conduit. 1614.

then, to coole himselfe a little, play at tables; and being disquieted in his paciens for overseeing synk and quater, or missing two or three fowle blotts, then to an enterlude, and so . . lyke to a mill horse, treddinge alwayes in the same stepps.

Similar games were Irish and Lurch.

Tick-tack was an old variety of backgammon, and was played on a board having holes along the edge, in which pegs were placed for scoring. The mention of 'tick-tack' in *Measure for Measure* (I. ii. 202) bears an allusion to another Elizabethan application.

RUSTIC AND CHILDREN'S GAMES

Running at the Quintain was one of the knightly exercises of the Middle Ages. The quintain consisted originally, it appears, of a post, and later of a shield attached to a post and moving in a circle on a pivot. The rider couched his lance and aimed at the post or shield; in the first form he tried to break his lance without interrupting his career; in the second his object was to escape by speed the blow of the rotating shield, which would strike the unskilful tilter in the back. By the end of the sixteenth century the quintain was nothing more than a rough rural sport which was often indulged in at weddings. For Cotgrave (1611) it was 'a Quintane (or Whintane) for countrey youthes to runne at'; and Shakespeare's only mention of it is:

My better parts
Are all thrown down, and that which here stands up
Is but a quintain, a mere lifeless block.
(*A. Y. L.* I. ii. 266–8)

Prisoners' Base or Bars, or Prison-base, as it was variously named, is described by Strutt as being played by two parties of equal number, each having a base or home at a distance of twenty to thirty yards. The players on either side, joining hands, extend themselves in length opposite one another, one of them always touching the base. Any one loosing hands and 'giving chase' is followed by one of the other side, and he by a second opponent, and so on, each person trying to catch the enemy he started after, and if successful, scoring one for his side. In Essex the game was played with two prisons, marked by stakes

driven into the ground, and every person touched is sent
to one of the prisons. In *Cymbeline* it is the 'country
base':

> Lads more like to run
> The country base than to commit such slaughter.
>
> (v. iii. 19–20)

Adonis's 'trampling courser' is made 'to bid the wind
a base' (*Ven. & Ad.* 303), that is, he challenges the wind
to pursue him—a figure which we find again in 'I bid the
base for Proteus' (*Two Gent.* I. ii. 94), where there is a
pun upon 'bass' in the musical metaphor just before.

A proclamation under Edward III (1331–2) prohibited
the game from being played near the Palace of Westminster during the session of Parliament.

Prisoners' base is often coupled with barley-break, as
by Drayton in *The Muses Elizium* (1636):

> Nimphes that . . . disposed were to play
> At Barly-breake and Prison-base.

The old game of Barley-break, or Last-in-hell, is thus
described:

It was played by six persons, three of each sex, coupled by lot.
A piece of ground is divided into three compartments, the middle
one being called 'hell'. The couple condemned to hell try to
catch the others advancing from the extremities; if they succeed
the hell-pair change places with the couple taken. In the catching,
the middle pair were not to separate before they succeeded, while
the others might loose hands at any time if pressed. When all had
been taken the last couple was said to be 'in hell', and the game
ended.

A poetical description of the game is given by Sir Philip
Sidney in his *Arcadia*:

> Then couples three be streight allotted there,
> They of both ends the middle two do flie,
> The two that in mid place, Hell called, were,
> Must strive with waiting foot, and watching eye
> To catch of them, and them to hell to beare,
> That they, as well as they, Hell may supplye.

So Thomas Randall in an eclogue in *Annalia Dubrensia*
(1636), speaking of the decay of the Cotswold Games and
their revival under 'Captain' Dover, attributes their
decay to 'some melancholly swains' who

> . . . teach that Dauncing is a Jezabell,
> And Barley-breake, the ready way to Hell.

Blind-man's-buff was in Shakespeare's time Hoodman Blind and Hobman Blind. The first of these is used by Shakespeare in *All's Well that Ends Well* :

> Hoodman comes ! *Porto tartarossa* ;　　(IV. iii. 137–8)

and in Hamlet's passionate appeal to his mother when he bids her ' look on this picture, and on that ' :

> What devil was't
> That thus hath cozen'd you at hoodman-blind ?
> 　　　　　　　　　(*Haml.* III. iv. 76–7)

The game has had many names. Cotgrave (1611) gives :

> *Clignemusset*, the childish play called Hodman blind, Harrie-racket, or, are you all hid.

The modern name of the game is found in Rowlands's *The Letting of Humours Blood* (1600) ; a variant is Blind-man-Buffet. According to John Taylor, the Water-poet, the name of the inventor of ' the unmatchable mystery of Blind-man-Buffe ' was Gregorie Dawson.

Hide-and-seek is perhaps the same as Hamlet's ' Hide fox and all after ' (*Haml.* IV. ii. 32). ' All hid, all hid ',—Biron's comment on seeing Longaville conceal himself, as the King and he himself have previously done, was the hide-and-seek cry.

Dun is in the Mire is as old as Chaucer. Gifford,[1] who had played at the game, gives a description of it to the following effect. A log of wood to represent Dun, the cart-horse, is brought into the room, and the cry raised that he is stuck in the mire. Two of the company advance to draw him out, with or without ropes. They fail, and ask help. All join in, trying to lift the log, which they let fall on one another's toes.

Shakespeare's one reference to the game is put into the mouth of Mercutio, the prince of punsters, who, when Romeo declares :

> The game was ne'er so fair, and I am done,

sees his chance and retorts :

> If thou art Dun, we'll draw thee from the mire.
> 　　　　　　　　　(*Rom. & Jul.* I. iv. 39–41)

---

[1] *Works of Ben Jonson*, 1816, vii. 283.

Richard Mulcaster devotes a whole chapter of his *Positions* (1581) to the Top and Scourge:

He that will deny the top to be an exercise indifferently capable of all distinctions in stirring, the verie boyes will beate and scourge him to, if they light on him about lent, when Tops be in time.

The whipping of tops still comes in about March; in Selden it takes a place with the eating of fritters, the roasting of herrings, and Jack-a-lents, which were connected with the beginning of the Lenten season.

Shakespeare's 'whirligig of time' (*Tw. N.* v. i. 389) is after all only a whipping-top. The 'schoolboy's top' (*Wint. Tale* ii. i. 102) is associated in Falstaff's recollection with other joys of his school-days:

Since I plucked geese, played truant, and whipped top, I knew not what it was to be beaten till lately. (*M. Wives* v. i. 26–8)

Whipping a gig, as a pastime eminently proper to infancy, is recommended by Holofernes the schoolmaster to Moth, the irrepressible page:

Thou disputest like an infant: go, whip thy gig;
(*Love's L. L.* v. i. 70–1)

and earlier in the same play 'Hercules whipping a gig' (iv. iii. 167) is one of the typical instances of incongruity imagined by Biron.

'What an arm he has!' says a Servant in admiration of Coriolanus:

He turned me about with his finger and thumb, as one would set up a top. (*Cor.* iv. v. 160–1)

Top-scourging was not only a juvenile pastime. A large top was kept in every parish to keep out-o'-work labourers out of mischief, and the proverbial expression 'to sleep like a town top' arose from the custom. Sir Toby Belch alludes to this when he says:

He's a coward and a coystril, that will not drink to my niece till his brains turn o' the toe like a parish-top.

(*Tw. N.* i. iii. 43–5)

Little more than a mere mention must suffice of some of the many minor games practised by rustics or children. There were Blow-point, which Strutt thinks consisted in 'blowing an arrow through a tube at certain numbers by way of lottery'; Dust-point, which was played by boys, says Cotgrave, 'laying their points in a heape of dust, and throwing at them with a stone';

Hot-cockles, in which one player, lying face downward or kneeling blindfold, is struck by others, and must guess the name of the striker; Push-pin (*Love's L. L.* IV. iii. 169), in which each player tries to push his pin across another player's, the ancient Drawgloves, which was simply a race in drawing off gloves; Cherry-pit (*Tw. N.* III. iv. 131–2), Cherry-stone, or Cherry-stone Pit, consisting in tossing cherries into a hole; and Leap-frog (*Hen. V*, v. ii. 141–4). The formula used in Handy-dandy, a game in which children close hands and guess the contents, which is as old as *Piers Plowman*, is introduced in the midst of Lear's colloquy with Gloucester :

What ! art mad ? A man may see how this world goes with no eyes. Look with thine ears : see how yond justice rails upon yon simple thief. Hark, in thine ear : change places ; and, handy-dandy, which is the justice, which is the thief ?

(Lear IV. vi. 154–9)

The Wild Mare was the see-saw. Falstaff says that the Prince loves Poins because, for one thing, ' he rides the wild mare with the boys' (*2 Hen. IV*, II. iv. 268). Sidney thinks of it when he describes the efforts of a shipwrecked person to save himself by making his way along a floating mast ; he writes :

bestriding the mast, I gat by little and little towards him, after such manner as boies are wont . . . when they ride the wild mare.

(Arcadia, bk. ii, ch. xxiv)

BIBLIOGRAPHY.—On games in general there is much information to be gathered from the three Tudor pedagogic works, Sir THOMAS ELYOT'S *The Governour*, 1531, ROGER ASCHAM'S *The Scholemaster*, 1570, and RICHARD MULCASTER'S *Positions*, 1581 ; with these must be classed the *Linguae Latinae Exercitatio*, 1539, of the Spanish scholar JUAN LUIZ VIVES, which was put into English under the title of *Tudor School-boy Life* by Prof. Foster Watson in 1908, and ERASMUS'S *Colloquia* (*Lusus Pueriles*). On gymnastics the *De Arte Gymnastica*, 1569, illustrated ed. 1573, of HIERONYMUS MERCURIALIS is interesting but not reliable ; it was analysed and in part translated into English by J. W. F. Blundell in 1864. *Annalia Dubrensia*, 1636, gives an account of the yearly celebration of the Cotswold games ; it has poetical contributions by Jonson, Drayton, Randolph, and others. JAMES I's *Basilikon Doron*, 1599, 1616, and PEACHAM'S *The Compleat Gentleman*, 1622, &c., give much information on various pastimes. RANDLE HOLME'S *The Academy of Armory*, 1688, furnishes many illustrations of the implements, as well as details of the playing, of games.

STOW'S *A Survey of London*, 1598, &c., records the history of games pursued in London from the earliest times. Of modern historical accounts STRUTT'S *The Sports and Pastimes of the People of England*, 1801, ed. J. Charles Cox, 1903, and D. P. BLAINE'S *An Encyclopaedia of Rural Sports*, and STONEHENGE'S various *British Rural Sports* ending with *The Encyclopaedia of Sports*, 1910, &c., are indispensable. Lady GOMME's *The Traditional Games of England, Scotland, and Ireland*, 2 vols., 1894, 1898, is a treasury of research.

On the origins, THOMAS HYDE's *De Ludis Orientalibus* in his *Shahiludium*, 1694, is a learned discourse on games derived from Oriental sources, and JOANNES MEURSIUS's *De Ludis Graecorum*, 1622, is equally valuable for games of Greek and Roman origin. There is an illuminating article by Sir E. B. TYLOR on 'The History of Games' in *The Fortnightly Review*, 1879. A representative example of the pre-eminence of France in the history and literature of games must be added here, viz.: His Excellency J. J. JUSSERAND's *Les Sports et Jeux d'Exercice dans l'ancienne France*, 1901.

For particular games the following works are all of importance: for wrestling, FABIAN VON AUERSWALD's *Ringerkunst*, 1539, with plates by Cranach (fully described by the present writer in *The Field*, 25 April, 1914), NICOLAES PETTER's *Klare Onderrichtinge der voortreffelijcke Worstel-Konst*, 1674, with illustrations by Romeyn de Hooge, and Sir THOMAS PARKYN's *The Inn-Play; or, Cornish-Hugg-Wrestler*, 1713; for swimming, there is the contemporary *De Arte Natandi* of EVERARD DIGBY, 1587, translated into English by Christopher Middleton, 1595, and the comprehensive handbook *Swimming*, 2nd ed., 1904, by RALPH THOMAS; for leaping, vaulting, and tumbling, ARCANGELO TUCCARO's *Trois Dialogues de l'Exercice de sauter et voltiger en l'Air*, 1599 (see *The Field*, 25 May, 1915), and WILLIAM STOKES's *The Vaulting Master*, 1652. For ball games ANTONIO SCAINO DA SALO's *Trattato del Giuoco della Palla*, 1555, a very rare work, is especially valuable for tennis; it is analysed in what is perhaps the most complete work ever written on a ball game, JULIAN MARSHALL's *The Annals of Tennis*, 1878; it should be noted that the *Maison Académique*, 1659 (the first of a long series, under varying titles, of *Académie des Jeux*), reprints the 'ordonnance' of tennis made in 1592 and published by C. Hulpeau in 1632. For football GIOVANNI DE' BARDI's *Discorso sopra 'l Giuoco del Calcio Fiorentino*, 1580 (described by the present writer in a series of articles on 'The Origins of Football' in *The Field*, 1912), is the main contemporary authority. For the history of bowling, JAMES A. MANSON's *The Complete Bowler*, 1912, is the best modern work.

Indoor games, billiards, chess, cards, and dice, are fully described in CHARLES COTTON's *The Compleat Gamester*, 1674. H. J. R. MURRAY's *A History of Chess*, 1913, covers the whole vast field of this subject and almost makes recourse to the earlier works unnecessary; among which, however, must be mentioned JAMES ROWBOTHUM's *The Pleasaunt and Wittie Playe of the Cheasts* (from the French of Gruget after the Italian of Damiano da Odemira), 1562, and ARTHUR SAUL's *The famous game of Chesse-play*, 1614.

On playing cards the authorities are: NIGI SERMOLLINI's (Messer Pietro-paulo da San Chiroco) *Capitolo del Giuoco della Primiera*, 1534, LE DUCHAT's notes to Rabelais, 1741, BULLET's *Recherches historiques sur les Cartes à Jouer*, 1757, S. W. SINGER's *Researches into the History of Playing Cards*, 1816, W. A. CHATTO's *Facts and Speculations on the Origin and History of Playing Cards*, 1848, and Lady CHARLOTTE SCHREIBER's *Playing Cards of various Ages and Countries*, 3 vols., 1892, 1893, 1895. On dicing, besides the books mentioned in this article, the following should be consulted: LORENZO SPIRITI's *Le Passetemps de la Fortune des Dez*, 1559, LAMBERT DANEAU's *A right excellent Invective against the wicked Exercise of Dice-Play* (in *True and Christian Friendshippe*), 1586. R. GREENE's *A Notable Discovery of Coosnage*, 1591, is a repertory of Elizabethan cheating and swindling of all varieties.

XXVIII

ROGUES AND VAGABONDS

BY

CHARLES WHIBLEY

IN the sixteenth century rogues and vagabonds infested every corner of England. They packed the towns ; they haunted the countryside to the common danger of peaceful citizens. 'Worke is left at home undone,' wrote Rowlands in his *Martin Mark-all* (1610), 'and loyterers laze in the streete, lurke in the Ale-houses, and range in the high-waies.' It is difficult to say by what means these vagabonds inflicted the heavier injury on the commonwealth—by their idleness or their depredations. Of many kinds, they were driven by many causes to their shiftless, wandering life. The largest class of all was the 'masterless' men, who refused to come beneath the yoke of labour, and who hoped by threats or begging to extort the bread which they would not earn with their hands. 'Work they will not,' wrote Edward Hext, a justice of the peace for Somersetshire in 1596 ; 'neither can they, without extreme pains, by reason their sinews are so benumbed and stiff through idleness, as their limbs being put to any hard labour will grief them beyond measure : so as they will rather hazard their lives than work.' In brief, they preferred death before toil, and thought it better to confess a felony which was a hanging matter, than to perform the tasks allotted them in the house of correction.

Another dangerous mob of 'vagrom men' (*Much Ado* III. iii. 26) consisted of the disbanded soldiers, who esteemed it a disgrace, after the free life of camps, to resume their humble crafts. They, like their masterless fellows, refused to abandon the freedom of idleness, and since they were strong in arm and resolution they

deprived of peace and comfort all those who dwelt in up-
land towns and little villages. And after them came the
bands of adventurers, whose trades made vagabondage
inevitable, men whole and mighty in body, who used no
' merchandise, craft, or mystery whereby they might get
their living'. These were of various character and many
pursuits—fencers, who for centuries were accounted the
promoters of idleness, ballad-mongers, and minstrels, who
carried sedition up and down the country in their songs,
bearwards, whose bears devoured many a child playing at
the roadside, common players, who belonged to no baron
of this realm, ' bawkers,' who haunted bowling-alleys to
cozen the poor fools who resorted thither for sport, scholars
of Oxford and Cambridge, who went abroad begging, without
the authority of the Vice-Chancellor, shipmen, pretending
losses at sea, together with a vast mob of jugglers, tinkers,
and petty chapmen. A motley crew, indeed, which, while
it levied an infamous toll upon rich and poor, indued the
roads of England with the colours of romance, and lent the
excitement of uncertainty to the lives of the people.

Thus year by year the rogues and vagabonds increased in
number, until in 1596 it could be said with truth that ' the
able men that were abroad, seeking the spoil and confusion
of the land, could, if they were reduced to good subjection,
give the greatest enemy her Majesty hath a strong battle,
and (as they were then) were so much strength to the enemy '.
In the meantime the gipsies were gathering in force, and
leading their free lawless life under the stars. It was in the
beginning of the sixteenth century that they made their
first appearance, and the mystery of their coming and going
was still unsolved. Though they were called Egyptians, or
in derision, Moon-men, there were few who believed in their
eastern origin. ' Ptolomy, I warrant,' says Dekker, ' never
called them his subjects, no, nor Pharao before him.' And
the same writer, declaring that their complexion is filthier
than the tawny face of a red-ochre man, is sure, in defiance
of the truth, that it is not their own. ' Yet are they not
borne so,' says he, ' neither has the Sunne burnt them so,
but they are painted so.'

Concerning their organization and pursuits there is little
difference of opinion. Their head-quarters were in the
Derbyshire Peak, whence they travelled southward over

the country—' Egiptian grass-hoppers that eate up the
fruites of the earth '—frequenting fairs and pillaging farm-
yards.   It was an order among them, that ' none eate meat,
as Pigges, Capons, Geese or such like, unlesse he purchase
it by privie pilfery, or cleanly conveyance '.   They travelled
in companies of a hundred or more, men and women, and
detached flying squadrons of four or five to do the work of
cozenage by which they eked out the living they made by
the roadside.   They lightly deceived the common people,
' wholly addicted and given to novelties, toyes, and new
fangles,' whom they delighted with the strangeness of their
headgear, and of whose credulity they took an easy advantage.   Wherever they went they practised legerdemain, or
fast and loose, they professed a knowledge of physiognomy,
palmistry, and other abused sciences, and by foretelling in
the hand destinies, deaths, and fortunes, they robbed poor
country girls of money and linen.   In brief, they were
' charmers ', as Othello called the Egyptian who gave the
fatal handkerchief to his mother :

> She was a charmer, and could almost read
> The thoughts of people ; she told her, while she kept it,
> 'Twould make her amiable and subdue my father
> Entirely to her love.   (*Oth.* III. iv. 58–61)

Shakespeare, as always, took the humaner view.   That the
gipsies were more harshly spoken of in general than they
deserved is not wholly strange.   They were the enemies at
once of the law-maker and the law-breaker.   The sturdy
rogue, thinking that they took the bread out of his dishonest
mouth, hated them as bitterly as did the constable, whose
duty it was to arrest them.   And so strong was the general
feeling against them that they would have one and all gone
to the gallows, had not the lawyers declared them not
chargeable with felony, because, Scotland being their last
home, they had not come into England from beyond the sea.

Many causes contributed to the vast increase of rogues
and vagabonds.   The old spirit of almsgiving, lavish and
improvident, was no more.   The territorial aristocracy had
not yet recovered from the heavy blow dealt by the Wars of
the Roses.   The dissolution of the monasteries had destroyed
the aristocracy of the Church.   Stow unfeignedly regrets
the ancient habit of generosity which persuaded the great
men of our realm to give relief to the poor.   ' I myselfe,' he

writes, ' in that declining time of charity, have oft seene at the Lord Cromwel's gate in London, more than two hundered persons served twise every day with bread meate and drinke sufficient, for hee observed that auncient and charitable custome as all prelates, noble men, or men of honour and worship his predecessors had done before him.' For good or evil this ancient custom was dead. The poor, brought up to rely upon the munificence of others, found the doors of their benefactors closed suddenly against them, and were forced into the devious paths of begging and extortion.

The abbots, moreover, had been kindly landlords. They had always been ready to come to the aid of their tenants and had done their best to lessen the risks which still beset the craft and mystery of farming. They did not hesitate to remit their rents, when bad seasons had made payment a hardship, and the confiscation of their land drove many an honest tiller of the soil to begging. But great as was the injury inflicted upon agricultural England by Henry VIII's policy, there was another and deeper reason for the prevailing distress. Though it was hardly recognized at the time, a silent and far-reaching revolution was in progress. The merchants of England were acquiring a wealth and influence which had never been theirs, and they marked the first step which they took in prosperity by the purchase of land. With all speed they bought farms ' out of the hands of worshipful gentlemen, honeste yeomen, and poor laborynge husbands '. An immense increase of manufactures, had it not been checked at will by extortionate taxation, might have provided fresh work for idle hands, but the moment of transition, as always, was attended with great difficulty, and the new owners of the soil felt no inherited responsibility for the welfare of those who had served their predecessors. The old relations which had bound the husbandman to his land were passing away ; the merchant, proud of the wealth which he had acquired himself, did not understand the obliga- tion of generosity ; the labourers whom he found attached to the soil were as nothing to him, nor did he scruple to turn them straightway adrift. ' Some also', wrote Harrison, ' doo grudge at the great increase of people in these daies, thinking a necessarie brood of cattell farre better than a superfluous augmentation of mankind.' Such men he likened unto the pope and the devil, and rightly did he see in them a danger for the future. 'If it should come to passe', he added, 'that any forren invasion should be made, which the Lord God forbid for his mercies sake!—then should these men find that a wall of men is farre better than stackes of corne and bags of monie, and complaine of the want when it is too late to seeke remedie.'

And they were likely to find more money than corn. For everywhere the plough was being suppressed ; pasture was replacing arable ; and many a labourer was driven upon the pad, to learn in starvation the hard shifts of beggary and crime. A single boy can mind a flock of sheep ; the fair tillage of the soil was work for many men. The danger in which the ruin of agriculture placed the country was early understood. A petition presented to Edward VI's Council in 1550 boldly attributed the decay of England to the great multitude of sheep which were fed on her pastures. Its authors saw no profit either in sheep or shepherds. They demonstrated that the increase of sheep meant dearer wool, dearer mutton, dearer beef, and fewer eggs for a penny. Moreover, it caused 'great decay to artyllary : for that do we reken that shepherdes be but yll artchers'. And even then, thought they, we were but on the threshold of the havoc wrought by these silly sheep. They declared that since the reign of Henry VIII every town and village in England, to the number of 50,000, had suppressed one plough. And of these 50,000 ploughs—such is their tragic conclusion—

everye ploughe were able to maintain 6 persons : that is to saye, the man, the wyfe, and fower other in his house, lesse and more. 50 thousande plowes, six persons to every plough, draweth to the nomber of three hundred thousand persons were wont to have meate, drynke, and rayment, uprysing and down lying paying skot and lot to God and to the Kynge. And now they have nothynge, but goeth about in England from dore to dore, and axe theyr almose for Goddes sake. And because they will not begge, some of them doeth steale, and then they be hanged, and thus the Realme doeth decay, and by none other wayes els, as we do thynke.

Such were the main causes of roguery and vagabondage. Ingenious persons, who did not always separate causes from symptoms, were not at a loss to discover others. This one declared it was the fault of the tippling houses ; that one ascribed all the evils of the commonwealth to the sorry justice that was meted out to the wrongdoer ; and many others

N.º 64

189

100

A FORGED PASSPORT WITH WHICH A VAGABOND TRAVELLED THE
LENGTH OF ENGLAND IN 1596

were sure that the only begetter of England's poverty and distress was the ever-increasing size of London. There was, indeed, a steady, unceasing influx of artificers, unskilled labourers, and insolvent loafers into the metropolis. The suburbs were infested with loose dissolute people, harboured in 'noysom and disorderly howses'. This overcrowding involved a double loss. The smaller towns in the kingdom with difficulty found enough labourers to do their proper work, while London swarmed with idle rogues, who hung about the taverns, ordinaries, dice-houses, and bowling-alleys to do what mischief they might. And thus it was that the statesmen of Elizabeth's reign attempted the hopeless task of checking the growth of London. They devised the most ingenious schemes, they passed what they deemed the wisest bills, and all in vain. They ordered that no new house should be built within three miles of London or Westminster, that no single house should be converted into two, that all shops and sheds, erected within seven years, should be razed to the ground, and that all unfinished buildings, or new foundations, should be pulled down. Schemes and Acts of Parliament were alike ineffective. Nothing could check the growth of London, and with her growth the rogues and vagabonds marvellously increased.

If it was impossible to abolish the prevailing poverty, the statesmen of the sixteenth century did their best to mitigate it. They spared no pains to come at an exact knowledge of the wandering rogues, who covered England like a plague of locusts. In 1571 a determined effort was made in every parish, in every wapentake, in every county, to make a census of all 'rogues, vagabonds, and mighty valliant beggars', and to examine, whip, stock, and punish them according to law. And the punishment was in no sense indiscriminate. The poor were distinguished and classified with care and prudence. They were divided, as Harrison tells us, into three sorts. First came those who were poor by impotency—the fatherless child, the aged, the blind and the lame, the incurably diseased. Then there were those impoverished by casualty—the wounded soldier, the decayed housekeeper, the sick person grievously visited. And finally the thriftless poor had to be reckoned withal, the rioters, who had consumed their livelihood, the vagabonds that would abide nowhere, the canting crew of rogues and strumpets, who lived on the highroad or in the woods, and levied a shameless toll upon society.

For all these was decreed relief or restraint according to their needs. The threefold object of Elizabeth's poor-laws was to feed the hungry, to punish the evildoer, and to exact payment from the unwilling rich. They were thus an inglorious mixture of enforced charity and the branding-iron. The first Act of Elizabeth's reign, for instance, provided that all who would not work should be adjudged vagabonds, that the poor and aged, forbidden to beg, should be relieved in the parishes of their birth; that collectors of alms should be appointed on the Sunday after Midsummer Day, and fined £10 if they refused to serve; that the Bishop or his Ordinary should exhort the wealthy to subscribe, each according to his means, for the relief of the poor. Those who declined to pay were treated none too harshly. For their amiable guidance, the statute enacted that if any person, properly exhorted, should, ' of his froward, wilful mind, obstinately refuse to give weekly to the relief of the poor, according to his ability; the Bishop, or his Ordinary, shall bind him, by recognisance, to appear at the Quarter Sessions : and at the said Sessions, the Justices shall charitably and gently persuade and move him '. If gentle persuasion was of no effect, the recalcitrant alms-giver was taxed a weekly sum and shut up in prison until it was paid. One other necessary provision was added : if a parish was cursed with more poor than it could support, certain persons were licensed to beg within the limits of the county, and were bidden for their better control to wear badges on their breast and back. Here was a great loophole for corruption. The forgery of licences became a profitable trade, carried on by a set of scoundrels, called ' Jarkemen ' in the canting tongue, whose skill, as Harman testifies, might have been more worthily and profitably employed.

Such was the Act which formed the basis of legislation for many years. Its scope was increased and modified from time to time. Now, to prevent the increase of ' masterless ' men, wages were regulated by law, and no person was permitted to depart out of service, ' onles he have a Testemoniall under the Seale of City or Towne corporate '. Now the definition of vagabond was so widely extended as to include every man and woman who did not follow an acknowledged trade, craft, or mystery. Again, the punishment of vagrancy varied in severity from year to year, which proved that legislation was still in the region of experiment. In 1572 rogues and vagabonds were condemned to be grevouslye whipped, and burnte through the gristle of the right Eare with a hot Yron of the compasse of an Ynche about. At a second offence they were adjudged felons without benefit of clergy. Even these penalties were too light for James I, who in the first year of his reign ordained that rogues should be branded in the left shoulder with a great roman R of the breadth of an English shilling; and when this failed to cleanse the highroad, he bade them summarily be banished to Virginia.

Charity and the branding-iron were, as might have been expected, wholly ineffectual. The severest punishments meted out to the scoundrel, the heaviest tolls levied upon the wealthy, neither cured nor discouraged the crime of vagabondage. A larger measure of relief was deemed necessary, and so it was that in 1598, in the thirty-ninth year of Elizabeth's reign, overseers were appointed in every parish, who should impose a rate, to provide sufficient flax, thread, wool, and iron, on which the poor might work, to apprentice destitute children, and to keep the aged, lame, and blind from starvation. As an offset to this humane provision the penalties against roguery were made yet harsher. 'Every vagabond found begging' —thus ran the law—' is to be stripped naked from the middle upwards, and openly whipped, until his or her body be bloody, and then passed to his or her birthplace or last place of residence, and in case they know neither, they are to be sent to the House of Correction for a year, unless some one gives them employment sooner.' This Act, important of itself, gains increased importance from the fact that, with certain changes and additions, it was presently converted into the celebrated Act of 1601, which for more than three centuries has shaped our policy. Passed as an experiment, and, according to the general practice of England, in the panic caused by several bad harvests, it was made perpetual in the reign of Charles I, and remains, despite the many changes of thought and creed, upon our Statute-book.

Meanwhile, the line which separated vagabondage from crime grew thinner with the years. The wanderers, whose very idleness was an offence against the law, turned readily to more evil practices. Many a simple trade, innocent of

itself, assumed an air of roguery, when it was pursued on
the highroad. 'The tinker in his budget, the pedlar in his
hamper, the glass-man in his basket, and the lewd proctors
which carry the broad seal and green seal in their bags, cover
an infinite number of felonies.' And whatever trifles these
scoundrels picked up they disposed of easily enough. There
were receivers in every ale-house, in every bush, who not
merely sold the 'purchases' of their colleagues, but, like the
old Jew whom Edward Wakefield found in Newgate, and
Dickens's own Fagin, instructed the youth in light-fingered
arts. 'These rabble are', in fact, 'the very nurseries of
rogues,' and the canting tongue was their fruitful method of
instruction. 'If you can cant,' wrote Rowlands, 'you will
never worke,' and true it was that they who had been long
enough on the road to learn the dialect of the canting-men
never settled themselves to labour again. Thus the vast army
of outlaws ever increased, and England won an unenviable
supremacy in the kingdom of crime.

Yet all men were not permitted to come within the guilty
circle. In the sixteenth and seventeenth centuries thievery
was a science as well as an art. It was hedged about with
a hundred technicalities; it was organized strictly into a
close corporation; it imposed on all those who embraced
it its own laws, its own customs, its own language. Before
a rascal could be admitted of the tribe, he underwent a sort
of apprenticeship, he performed the proper rites of initiation.
The Upright Man, of whom more presently, could make
whom he would free of the guild. Did he meet a rogue
sturdy or impotent, who still dwelt without the pale, he
carried him straightway to the bousing-ken. 'Then', says
Harman, 'doth this upright man call for a gage of bowse
whiche is a quarte pot of drinke, and powres the same upon
his peld pate, adding these words :—" I. G. P. do stalle thee
W. T. to the Roge, and that from hence forth it shall be
lawefull for the to Cant "—that is, to aske or begge—" for thy
living in al places ".' After this the initiate might be promoted to the highest order of roguery; with talent and
courage he might even become an Upright Man himself,
and administer the laws of his tribe to all the 'rowsey
ragged rabblement of rakehelles' which followed him.

That we possess so precise a knowledge of the fraternity
of vagabonds, of its kinds and craft, is due to Thomas

NICHOLAS BLUNT ALIAS NICHOLAS GENNINGS AS
UPRIGHT MAN AND COUNTERFEIT CRANK

Harman, whose *Caveat or Warening for commen cursetors vulgarely called Vagabones* (1566) bears upon every line the stamp of truth and authenticity. Harman, in brief, is the Hakluyt of roguery. He did for the underworld of Shakespeare's England that which the author of the *Voyages* achieved for the world of adventure. Like the honest man that he was, he acknowledges the good work done by Awdeley, his predecessor. 'There was a fewe yeares since a small breefe', says he, 'setforth of some zelous man to his countrey, of whom I knowe not, that made a lytle shewe of there names and usage, and gave a glymsinge lyghte, not sufficient to perswade of their pevishe peltinge and pickinge practyses, but well worthy of prayse.' This is a fair estimate of Awdeley's *Fraternitye*. It is a 'glimsing light' and 'well worthy of praise'. Harman cherished a larger ambition. His book is a book of acute observation and varied experience. He sets down nothing that he has not seen with his eyes and heard with his ears. There is an intimacy in his descriptions which convinces the reader that he writes out of fullness of knowledge. He has met his rogues face to face, has spoken with them, and marked well their peculiarities. When in his list of names he sets down John Stradling with the shaking head, and Harry Walles with the little mouth, when he records that Robert Brownswerd weareth his hair long, and that John Browne is a great stammerer, he intensifies the impression of truth. Who and what he himself was remains uncertain. The few hints which he gives us are insufficient for a portrait. He lived at Crayford in Kent, a near neighbour of the right honourable and singular good lady, Elizabeth, Countess of Shrewsbury, to whom his dedication is addressed. He had been in the Commission of the Peace, and bore arms, which he tells us were engraved upon his pewter plate. In brief, says he,

beinge placed as a poore gentleman, [I] have kepte a house these twenty yeares, where unto poverty dayely hath and doth repayre, not without some reliefe, as my poore callinge and habylytie maye and doth extende.

And having occasion through sickness to tarry at home, he talked and conferred daily with many wily wanderers of both sorts, men and women, boys and girls. He had no difficulty in surprising their secrets and measuring their ambitions, which he reveals, with no other motive (he is

sure) than that 'their undecent, dolefull dealing and execrable
exercyses may apere to all as it were in a glasse'. But no
sooner does he take pen in hand than the artist which is in
him gets the better of the Justice of the Peace, and he describes his fleeting fellowship, his Cursetors, with the zest and
enthusiasm which are bred of sympathy. It is true that he
preserves scrupulously and unto the end the farce of moral
sentiments, but these sentiments carry no more weight than
do the dull, inapposite moralizings of the Newgate Calendar.

Like most of his contemporaries, he disclaims any attempt
at fine writing. He is content to be neither ' homely ' nor
'darke'. He refuses to use such words, like 'robardesmen'
and 'drawlatches', as were familiar in Edward III's time.
For the rest he confesses a love of plain order and common
words. 'Eloquence have I none,' he says ; 'I never was
acquaynted with the muses ; I never tasted of Helycon.'
Here he strays from the truth. Throughout his book he
betrays a love of artifice and ingenuity. He has a pretty
taste for alliteration, and his sense of style is so acute that
we owe to him our first vocabulary of the pelting speech.
And what a gallery of portraits he has bequeathed to us,
drawn each one of them with a cunning hand and a sureness of
technical knowledge unsurpassed ! The Ruffler is first of 'this
odious order ', 'the worthiest of this unruly rablement '. He
has either fought in the wars or has been a serving-man, and
having shaken off all toil, lives by extorting defiantly where
he thinks he may be bold, or by asking elsewhere a tearful
charity for his maimed and bruised limbs. If twined hemp
do not prevent him, he becomes in due course an Upright Man,
a hero of great authority, whose behest all rogues obey, who
travels the country, attended by his Mort or Doxy, who will
turn his hand to pilfering clothes or breaking houses, and
whose pride it is that, scorning the offer of meat and drink,
he will accept nothing in charity save money. Then follow
the Hookers or Anglers, habited in frieze jerkins and gally
slops, who mark by day what they carry off at night on
their iron-hooked staves ; the Priggers of Prancers, who
lurk in the highways, and ride away on their booty three
score miles or more ; the Palliards or Clapperdogens, ragged
in patched clothes, who for gain and to be pitied bliste
their legs with spearwort or arsenic ; the Abraham Men,
who feign to have been mad and ask at the farm-house

for bacon, cheese, or wool, or anything that they may turn to money; the Fresh-water Mariners, whose ships have sunk in Salisbury Plain; the Counterfeit Cranks, who pretend sickness and never go abroad without a piece of white soap which should make them foam at the mouth and so deceive the common people; the Dummerers, who hold their tongues down doubled and show a forged writing that they were dumb, together with a vast mob of Tinkers and Swadders, of Morts, Doxies, and Dells, who practise their trades of theft and beggary in every shire of England. And in their wake come an army of roaring boys and bullies, Corinthians or Ephesians of the true Church, as Shakespeare called them, who bouse in taverns, ruffle it at ordinaries, take their pleasure at their ' manner of Picked Hatch ', and who are always ready to empty a pocket or cog the dice.

Varying in skill and livery, they had a common purpose— to live without work, and a common end—the gallows. Harrison cites Cardan, an insecure authority, as saying that Henry VIII hanged up threescore and twelve thousand of them in his time, and admits that there is commonly not one year ' wherein three hundred or foure hundred of them are not devoured and eaten up by the gallowes in one place and other '. But wherever they went, whatever they did, they remained a class apart, separated from the rest of the world by strange names and a secret speech. No better means of defence against the world of honesty, no better method of helping the hopeless beggar along the high-road, could have been devised than the Canting tongue or Pedlars' French, ' compact thirtie yeares since ', says Harrison, ' of English, and a great number of od words of their owne devising, without all order or reason : and yet such is it as none but them-selves are able to understand '. If we might believe Harri-son, ' the first deviser thereof was hanged by the necke; a just reward no doubt for his deserts '. But we may not believe Harrison. The pelting speech was not devised by one man, and cant words came into our English language long before the sixteenth century. They were derived from many and far distant sources. Each influx of foreign beggars added something to the Pedlars' French. Ireland and Wales contributed a large share to the slang of the Canting Crew. French words crossed the Channel, or travelled southward from Scotland. The vagrant Monks, sent tramping up and down England at the dissolution of the monasteries, invented many a useful Latinism, and the old soldiers brought back from their campaigns strange, foreign words, half remembered and sometimes misunderstood. Above all, it should not be forgotten that the dialect of the rogues and vagabonds was not the same as the gipsy tongue, which did but increase its variety, and that it kept alive many specimens of provincial English which otherwise had perished.

Thus the rogues and vagabonds, a close body, were walled about with a language and a nomenclature of their own. In the same spirit of technical exclusiveness each manifestation of their skill was controlled by rule and described in terms of which the people, their victims, knew nothing. The cony-catchers, cross-biters, and shifters, who haunted London, chased their prey and played their confidence-tricks in obedience to an inexorable convention, which proves that the skilled industries of the underworld were highly organized and that their practitioners were closely banded together. ' If you marvel at these misteries and queynt words,' says Greene, ' consider, as the carpenter hath many terms familiar enough to his prentices, that others understand not at al, so have the cony catchers, not without great cause; for a falsehood once detected can never compass the desired effect.' So they called their knaveries by the names of arts or laws,[1] of which names the most have long since lost their meaning. For instance, the craft of cheating at cards was called Barnard's law, and those who took part in it went by strange titles. The first of the cozeners was called the Taker-up or Setter. ' O! 'tis our setter: I know his voice,' says Poins of Falstaff in *1 Henry IV* (II. ii. 56). His business it was to decoy the victim. Then came the Verser to his help, a man of more worship than the Taker-up, and wearing the countenance of a landed man. And when they were set the Barnard stumbles in, habited like an aged farmer, and a pretended stranger to them all. Those who in our own days have seen the three-card trick played will recognize the procedure, and know that for the cozen there is no way of escape. The rest, in fact, was easy, and if the cozen lost ungraciously at cards, there stood

---

[1] In the eighteenth century the word ' law ' was changed to ' lay '. The figging law of the cony-catchers became the figging lay of Jonathan Wild.

a Rutter at the door with drawn sword ready to force a quarrel on an ostler or on his own shadow, so that, in the turmoil of the fray, the Barnard may steal away with the spoil.

To cut off ones head, and to laie it in a platter,
which the iugglers call the decollation of Iohn Baptift.

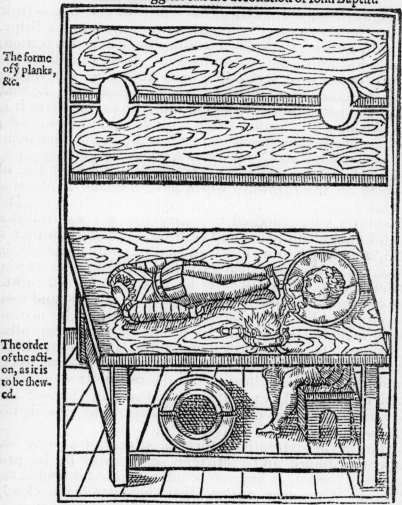

The forme of ẙ planks, &c.

The order of the action, as it is to be shewed.

A juggler's trick. From Scot's *Discoverie of Witchcraft*, 1584.

That is a typical example of cheating law, and Vincent's law matches it in curiosity. It was a species of cozenage practised by those who frequented bowling-alleys, and it

446.1

K k

explains why those resorts, innocent enough of themselves, were condemned as lewd and unlawful places. The Bawkers, as they were called, who took the chief part came into the alley, like honest citizens eager for the sport. No sooner does the game begin, than the Gripes, who are their accomplices, shout the odds aloud, and quietly take up whatever bets are offered. Thus they entice the Vincent, who is their victim, to his undoing. ' I take six to one,' says the Gripe. 'I lay it,' answers the Vincent, and one thing only was certain, that he lost whom the Vincent backed. In the same lingo the simple practice of shop-lifting was known as the Lifting Law, and they who followed it are thus described: he that steals the parcel is known as the Lift; he that receives it is the Marker; the Santar stands without and carries it off; and the goods thus stolen, or purchased, to use the euphemism of Bardolph and Nym, was known as the garbage.

The High Law was the most famous of all—the law of robbing on the highway, which gave England a perverse celebrity until the end of the eighteenth century. The adventurer who practised this dangerous art was called a High Lawyer, and to succeed he needed nothing less than a bold, stern look, a stout heart, and a good sword. He was, in truth, the plain antithesis of the palliards and dummerers who mumped at the roadside; yet he, too, though freedom was the essence of his craft, subscribed to the articles, and used the jargon of his law. The names and duties of his accomplices were duly set forth. He who set a watch was called a Scripper, the watch was known as the Oak, and the victim was the Martin, who, when he yielded, was said to stoop. From these confused images and the restraints which they imposed the High Lawyer presently emancipated himself, and he remained for two centuries the independent sovereign of the road.[1]

Thus in the sixteenth century the science of roguery was patiently studied and thoroughly understood by its professors. The art, as happens so often, lagged far behind the science. When men analyse their handicraft too closely they are wont to forget their skill. Yet signs of improvement were not lacking, and the fact that the pickpocket was throwing the cutpurse into contempt proves that at least

[1] The activities of the Elizabethan highwayman are described in Chapter VII.

one branch of roguery was pursued with lightness of hand and courage of heart. The historians, in brief, separate, by a sharp contrast, the Nip and the Foist. The object of both was the same—a heavily laden purse; but while the Nip was content to use a knife and cut the purse, the Foist drew the pocket into his hand. The artistic superiority of the Foist was evident, and he was not slow to claim it. He called himself always a Gentleman Foist, and so bitterly did he disdain the clumsiness of his brother Nip, that he would not carry a knife in his pocket, wherewith to cut his meat, lest he might be suspected of putting it to any improper use. Here breathes the spirit of true artistry, and it is not surprising that the rhapsodist describes the perfections of the Foist with a thinly veiled enthusiasm.

'An exquisite Foist', says Greene, 'must have three properties that a good surgion should have, and that is an Eagles eie, a Ladies hand, and a Lyons heart : an Eagles eie to spy a purchase, to have a quick insight where the boung [1] lies, and then a Lyons heart not to feare what the end will bee, and then a Ladies hand to be little and nimble, the better to dive into the pocket.' In short, the true Foist had nothing to help him save what Hamlet called his ' pickers and stealers ' (*Haml.* III. ii. 355–6), and he deserved all the credit that his sleight of hand won for him. The Nip, on the other hand, could not work without a clumsy apparatus. Ben Jonson calls him a ' knight of the knife ', or ' child of the horn-thumb ', referring of course to the guard or stall which was his protection against the sharp edge of the knife. Yet even the Nip was forced to do his work with celerity. ' I warrant him a quick hand,' says Overdo of Ezekiel Edgworth in the play, and quick as he was Ezekiel did not escape the eye of the critic. However, it was a time of change, and some there were who employed both methods. If the Foist would never stoop to nip, the Nip sometimes aspired to the higher game. Autolycus, a finished artist only in speech, used the knife as well as his hand. ' In this time of lethargy', said he, ' I picked and cut most of their festival purses ' (*Wint. Tale* IV. iii. 628–30). And, despite the jealousy which divided them, the Foists and the Nips met on common ground. As has been said, they sought the

---

[1] The boung is the purse, still known as the bung in the flash speech of to-day.

same end by different roads, and so they instituted a kind
of brotherhood amongst themselves, and kept their own
meeting-place.   Once their Hall was near Bishop's Gate,
if we may believe Greene, but, when that became too
familiar, they removed to Kent Street, to the house of one
Laurence Pickering, the brother-in-law of Ball, the hangman,
who accounted for the most of them in the end.

Both the Foist and the Nip worked with an accomplice,
whom they called a Stall, and whose business it was to jostle
and perplex the victim while his purse was being removed.
Oftentimes, too, the ballad-monger was their ally, who
gathered a crowd about him and held its attention.   In
Bartholomew Fair, Nightingale, the ballad-man, calls Edgworth, the civil cutpurse, his secretary, and, as Mooncalf
says, ' they are never asunder '.   By a fine irony Edgworth
tickles Cokes in the ear with a straw, to make him draw his
hand from his pocket, at the very moment when the ballad-
man is singing his ' Caveat for Cutpurses ' to the famous tune
of ' Pagginton's Pound '.   ' Repent then,' says Nightingale,

> Repent then, repent you, for better, for worse,
> And kiss not the gallows for cutting a purse.
> Youth, youth, thou hadst better been starv'd by thy nurse,
> Than live to be hanged for cutting a purse.

And Cokes cries aloud, ' O Lord ! my purse is gone, my purse,
my purse, my purse ! '

Wherever men were gathered together on business or
pleasure, there the Foists and the Nips plied their trade.
Paul's was their favourite haunt at the hour of noon, and
during Term time they found great profit at Westminster
Hall.   The Tiltyard knew them, and Tyburn on execution
days.   They frequented fairs, and assemblies of all sorts.   So
rapidly did their fame increase, that to lose a purse seemed
as intimately a part of London as its fog.   In 1598 Paul
Hentzner visited Bartholomew Fair, and thus recorded his
experience :

> While we were at this show, one of our company, Tobias Salander
> Doctor of Physic, had his pocket picked of his purse, with nine
> crowns, which, without doubt, was so cleverly taken from him by
> an Englishman, who always kept very close to him, that the Doctor
> did not perceive it.

Poor Salander, the first foreigner to suffer from a craft
which ever since has won for England a world-wide renown

*   *   *   *   *   *

The age of Shakespeare produced many admirable artists in crime; yet none of them was more bravely characteristic of the age than was Mary Frith, the famous Moll Cutpurse, a true Elizabethan in courage and flamboyancy of spirit. Everything about her was great— her knowledge, her voice, her heart. She was born four years after the destruction of the Armada, and she died a brief year before the return of Charles II to his rightful throne. Her activities thus covered a long period, and as she was the heroine of a comedy of Middleton, so, says rumour, with her own voice she bade the rebel Fairfax stand and deliver. A woman neither in kind nor manner, she well earned her title of ' Roaring Girl ', and she was ready to drink her tobacco or draw her sword with any roysterer in London. ' She has the spirit of four great parishes,' says the dramatist, 'and a voice that will draw all the city.' She cherished also a natural love of skill, and did her best, by discouraging the Nip, to admit the Foist to the fullness of his glory. ' The best signs and marks of a happy industrious hand', she wrote, ' is a long middle finger equally suited with what they call the fool's or first finger.' Later artists called these twain ' the forks '. But it was not long before Moll retired from the eager practice of her craft. She quickly discovered that hers were the gifts of command and government, and thus she made herself the head of a vast gang, which for many years was a terror to Brentford and Shooter's Hill. Not merely did she plan the robberies which her henchmen carried out, but she disposed of their purchases, either to their just owners, if the reward were sufficient, or to certain cunning merchants whom she knew. Thus for many years she ruled the underworld of England with an iron hand, and in the heyday of her youth shared the sovereignty of the realm not unfittingly with the austere, implacable Elizabeth herself.

Such are some of the rogues who trampled honesty under foot in Shakespeare's time. That he knew them and their exploits is certain; it is certain also that he saw them, as he saw all men, in an atmosphere of romance. Ben Jonson, stern realist that he was, paints them in their true colours. You know that Jordan Knockem and Zekiel Edgworth plied their trade in the streets and fairs of London. Falstaff is the High Lawyer purged of reality. The fat knight bade no man stand

and deliver save on the highroad of poetry. His humour
throws a radiance over his worst villanies. A word elevates his
greed, his cowardice, his falsehood, to sublimity. No sooner
does he come upon the stage than 'nimble fiery and
delectable shapes' (*2 Hen. IV*, IV. iii. 108) emanate from his
brain. 'We that take purses', says he, 'go by the moon
and the seven stars, and not by Phoebus, he, "that
wandering knight so fair"' (*1 Hen. IV*, I. ii. 15–17). Himself and his friends are 'Diana's foresters, gentlemen of the
shade, minions of the moon' (*ibid.* I. ii. 29–30). Even when
he would mend his ways it is but in thought and for a
moment. 'I must give over this life,' he says, 'and I will
give it over; by the Lord, an I do not, I am a villain: I'll
be damned for never a king's son in Christendom' (*ibid.* I.
ii. 106–9). Before the end of the sentence his humour has
changed, and there follows a dialogue which sets this
wayward 'tun of a man' vividly before us:

> *Prince.* Where shall we take a purse to-morrow, Jack?
> *Fal.* Zounds! where thou wilt, lad, I'll make one; an I do not,
> call me a villain and baffle me.
> *Prince.* I see a good amendment of life in thee; from praying to
> purse-taking.
> *Fal.* Why, Hal, 'tis my vocation, Hal; 'tis no sin for a man to
> labour in his vocation. (*ibid.* I. ii. 110–17)

Thus robbery and repentance are alike the fruit of his fancy.
Why should he rob, if he may not repent? Why should he
repent, if he may not rob again? It is but as the mood
takes him, and for all his fat body, for all the weight of flesh
that 'lies three fingers on the ribs' (*ibid.* IV. iii. 78–81), he is
capricious as a child, mobile as the changing wind.

And so the plot is laid. In Poins's exhortation is summarized the whole art and science of the road:

> My lads, my lads, to-morrow morning, by four o'clock, early at
> Gadshill! There are pilgrims going to Canterbury with rich offer-
> ings, and traders riding to London with fat purses: I have vizards
> for you all; you have horses for yourselves. Gadshill lies to-night
> in Rochester; I have bespoke supper to-morrow night in East-
> cheap: we may do it as secure as sleep. If you will go I will stuff
> your purses full of crowns; if you will not, tarry at home and be
> hanged. (*ibid.* I. ii. 137–47)

Such is the prelude to the famous episode of the man in
buckram.

And Gadshill is a match in vaunting cowardice for the

THE BELMAN
OF LONDON.

Bringing to light the moſt notorious
villanies that are now practiſed
in the KINGDOME.

Profitable for Gentlemen, Lawyers, Merchants, Citizens, Farmers,
Maſters of Houſholds, and all ſortes of ſeruants, to marke,
and delightfull for all men to Reade.

Lege, Perlege, Relege.

Printed at London for NATHANIEL BVTTER. 1 6 o 8.

fat knight.   He is a true Trojan, a veritable roaring boy.
' I am joined with no foot-land-rakers,' he brags, ' no long-
staff sixpenny strikers, none of these mad mustachio-purple-
hued malt worms ' (*ibid.* II. i. 81–3).   For all his brave
words he loves fighting as little as the others, and, like Peto,
cares not who sees his back.   Yet it is Bardolph that is
the mean-souled, irredeemable villain of the gang.   A born
rogue, he has lived in the hedge-row.   Falstaff has seen
other days, and loves adventure as he loves sack.   When
he is out at heels, he must cony-catch.   As he says,

I myself sometimes, leaving the fear of God on the left hand
and hiding mine honour in my necessity, am fain to shuffle, to
hedge and to lurch.   (*M. Wives* II. ii. 23–6)

Bardolph has no honour to hide.   He shuffles willingly and
by the light of nature.   Purse-picking is for him a plain pro-
motion.   He confesses that he has been a clapperdudgeon
and feigned wounds.   Seven years before he had tickled his
nose with spear-grass to make it bleed, and beslubbered his
garments with it.   Even when the warlike Harry 'assumed
the port of Mars', it was the hope of petty theft that drove
him and Nym to France.   'They will steal any thing and
call it purchase,' complains the Boy.

Bardolph stole a lute-case, bore it twelve leagues, and sold it
for three halfpence.   Nym and Bardolph are sworn brothers in
filching, and in Calais they stole a fire-shovel ;—I knew by that
piece of service the men would carry coals,—they would have me
as familiar with men's pockets as their gloves or their handkerchers.
(*Hen. V*, III. ii. 45–53)

And their very meanness makes Bardolph and the rest the
best foil for Falstaff, whose gay-hearted magnanimity not
even cowardice can impair, who, old as he is, confronts the
travellers on Gadshill with a 'What ! ye knaves, young
men must live ' (*1 Hen. IV*, II. ii. 99–100); and in the
midst of riot cries,

A plague of sighing and grief ! it blows a man up like a bladder.
(*ibid.* II. iv. 370–1)

Falstaff is of an heroic mould.   He transcends the scale
of human life.   Autolycus brings us back to the earth again.
Save in speech, he goes not beyond the general experience of
his time.   This ' snapper-up of unconsidered trifles ' is, as
it were, an epitome of vagabondage ; he resumes the
rogueries of Harman's *Caveat* in his proper person ; he is

a cozener, that will turn his hand to anything. His traffic is sheets. 'When the kite builds,' says he, 'look to lesser linen' (*Wint. Tale* IV. ii. 23–4). And being born of Shakespeare's fancy, he cannot but set his cozenage to music :

> The white sheet bleaching on the hedge,
> With heigh ! the sweet birds, O, how they sing !
> Doth set my pugging tooth on edge ;
> For a quart of ale is a dish for a king. (*ibid*. IV. ii. 5–8)

When the Clown surprises him, he is grovelling on the ground, playing a trick that the counterfeit crank did not disdain. 'O ! help me, help me ! ' he cries, ' pluck but off these rags, and then death, death ! ' (*ibid*. IV. ii. 56–7). To courage and virtue he makes no pretence. ' I must confess to you, sir, I am no fighter,' says he : ' I am false of heart that way ' (*ibid*. IV. ii. 116–17). Much as he loves the crime, he dreads its consequences. ' Gallows and knock are too powerful on the highroad,' he admits : ' beating and hanging are terrors to me ' (*ibid*. IV. ii. 28–30). At the same time he finds Honesty a fool, and ' Trust, his sworn brother, a very simple gentleman ' (*ibid*. IV. iii. 608–10). If he is honest himself, it is ' by chance ', and he takes a noble pride in his own superiority, when he envisages the Clown and the Shepherd :

> How bless'd are we that are not simple men !
> Yet nature might have made me as these are. (*ibid*. IV. iii. 774–5)

Nor does he underrate the difficulties of his craft :

> To have an open ear, a quick eye, and a nimble hand, is necessary for a cut-purse ; a good nose is requisite also, to smell out work for the other senses. (*ibid*. IV. iii. 688–91)

In just such words as these does Greene appreciate the qualities of the Foist, and it is evident that Autolycus had the whole duty of the cony-catcher at his fingers' ends. Above all, this filcher, this ballad-singer, this counterfeit crank, is endowed with a fine sense of irony. When the Clown picks him up after his feigned beating, he empties the Clown's pocket, and then gallantly refuses the offer of money.

> No, good sweet sir : no, I beseech you, sir, . . . offer me no money, I pray you ! that kills my heart. (*ibid*. IV. ii. 85–9)

In *King Lear* we may watch the same process at work, yet more intimately. Mad Tom is at once closer to and more remote from his model even than Autolycus.

The hapless figure, strange to us, was familiar in its essence to all those who frequented Shakespeare's theatre.[1] Awdeley, in *The Fraternitye of Vacabondes*, gave Shakespeare the rough sketch : 'An Abraham man'—thus he writes—' is he that walketh bare armed, and bare legged, and fayneth hym selfe mad, and caryeth a packe of wool, or a stycke with baken on it, or such lyke toy, and nameth himselfe poore Tom.' Harman adds that the Abraham men beg at farmers' houses, and that if they espy small company therein ' they wyll with fierce countenaunce demaund some what'. Now see what Shakespeare makes of the Abraham man in the person of Edgar :

> The country gives me proof and precedent
> Of Bedlam beggars, who with roaring voices,
> Strike in their numb'd and mortified bare arms
> Pins, wooden pricks, nails, sprigs of rosemary ;
> And with this horrible object, from low farms,
> Poor pelting villages, sheep-cotes, and mills,
> Sometime with lunatic bans, sometime with prayers,
> Enforce their charity. Poor Turlygood ! poor Tom !
>
> (*Lear* II. iii. 13–20)

There is a close resemblance of fact between the verse and the prose, but in fancy how far are they remote ! By every touch Shakespeare emphasizes poor Tom's madness, and suppresses the beggar that is in him. It is the Bedlamite, not the rogue, that stands before us.

> Fathom and half, fathom and half ! Poor Tom !
>
> (*ibid.* III. iv. 37)

—thus he sings on the borderland of sense and nonsense. Even when he begs, his voice rather claims pity than utters threats. 'Who gives anything to poor Tom ?' he asks. '. . . Tom's a-cold. . . . Do poor Tom some charity, whom the foul fiend vexes' (*ibid.* III. iv. 49–61). He shows his misery and hunger through a veil of fancy.

> Poor Tom ; that eats the swimming frog ; the toad, the tad-
> pole, the wall-newt, and the water. (*ibid.* III. iv. 132–4)

The revenge which society takes upon him seems actual enough. He is ' whipped from tithing to tithing, and stock-punished, and imprisoned' (*ibid.* III. iv. 138–9). Yet even this toll of vengeance is levied by the imagination.

---

[1] That there was no doubt about the personage whom Edgar represented is evident in Act IV, Scene i, line 26, where the Old Man at his first appearance on the stage recognizes the Bedlamite : ' 'Tis poor mad Tom,' he says.

You cannot believe that it is Shakespeare's Poor Tom who is whipped and stocked. He still remains etherealized, a poetical symbol of Bedlam. Lear, with the intuition of madness, sees through his rags, his ' Persian attire ', to the disembodied spirit within, and says :

Thou owest the worm no silk, the beast no hide, the sheep no wool, the cat no perfume . . . ; thou art the thing itself ; unaccommodated man is no more but such a poor, bare, forked animal as thou art. (*ibid*. III. iv. 106–11)

After crime the punishment. And though of old it was a commonplace that every rogue was at last ' trussed up in a Tyburn tip ', Shakespeare fills us with surprise that so many vagabonds were called to account. The skill of the rogue was ill-matched by the pompous simplicity of the law. ' The thief doth fear each bush an officer,' says Shakespeare (*3 Hen. VI*, v. vi. 12), and if the officer were no better than Dogberry or Elbow, he was less formidable even than a bush. The constable, the headborough, and the watch are mere figures of fun in the plays. ' If we know him to be a thief,' asks the watch, ' shall we not lay hands on him ? ' ' Truly, by your office, you may,' answers Dogberry; ' but I think they that touch pitch will be defiled. The most peaceable way for you, if you do take a thief, is, to let him show himself what he is and steal out of your company' (*Much Ado* III. iii. 58–64). Shakespeare's constables, in brief, are no better able to keep the peace than a policeman in a modern pantomime. Their skill is an inspired misuse of words, the utmost of their endeavour is to raise the parish. Again, the poet indulged his fancy, proving his romantic sympathy for the thief by his ridicule of the thief-taker. For in Dogberry's despite the rascals who levied toll on rich and poor went not unpunished.

When once the malefactor was caught he suffered summary punishment. The prisons of the seventeenth century were places of brief resort. There the thief sojourned on his way to the gallows, and the debtor until he had satisfied the demands of his creditors. Nor were they managed with any regard to the comfort of their occupants. Those who had no money in their pockets found in them little enough to eat. There remains a prisoners' petition, which reveals their pitiful condition. It runs thus :

In all lamentable manner most humbly beseecheth your good

Worship, wee, the miserable multitude of very poore distressed prisoners, in the hole of Wood-street Counter, in nomber fiftie poore men or thereabouts, lying upon the bare boordes, still languishing in great neede, colde, and miserie, who, by reason of this daungerous and troublesome time, be almost famished and hunger-starved to death ; others very sore sicke, and diseased for want of reliefe and sustenance, by reason of the great number, which dayly increaseth, dooth in all humblenes most humbly beseech your good worship, even for Gods sake, to pitie our poore lamentable and distressed cases ; and nowe helpe to relieve and comfort us with your Christian and Godly charitie against this holie and blessed time of Easter.[1]

This is a sincere cry from the heart, which went not unregarded. To alleviate the distress a humane clause was inserted in the famous act of the forty-third year of Elizabeth's reign, directing a sum of money to be raised by a weekly rate for the relief of the poor prisoners in the King's Bench and Marshalsea. On the other hand, a prison was not too harsh a dwelling-place for those who had money to spend. There was at least the freedom of squalor. Barnardine in *Measure for Measure* ' hath ever-more had the liberty of the prison '. If leave were given him to escape he would not take it. ' Drunk many times a day, if not many days entirely drunk,' he was unmoved even when he saw the warrant of execution (IV. ii. 154–60). And when at last the hangman calls for him in seeming earnest he is deaf to the summons.

I have been drinking hard all night, and I will have more time to prepare me, or they shall beat out my brains with billets. I will not consent to die this day, that's certain. (*ibid.* IV. iii. 57–61)

In the jails of the sixteenth century, if there was greater cruelty, there was, to be sure, less formality than to-day. Crime and the law were more closely connected. A prisoner if he would turn hangman, had a fair chance of saving his life. ' Thou shalt have the hanging of the thieves,' says the Prince to Falstaff, ' and so become a rare hangman ' (*1 Hen. IV*, I. ii. 75–6). And in *Measure for Measure* Pompey is offered his freedom on the familiar condition. But Abhorson, the executioner, likes not his new col-league. ' A bawd, sir ? ' says he to the Provost, ' Fie upon

---

[1] *A Collection of Seventy-nine Black-Letter Ballads and Broadsides, printed in the Reign of Queen Elizabeth, between the Years 1559 and 1597.* London 1867, pp. 16–17.

him! he will discredit our mystery' (IV. ii. 29–30). The
jailers, whether pardoned criminals or not, erred not
on the side of clemency. They were made, says William
Fennor, of the same stuff as the fabric, stone and iron,
and as the jails themselves were 'noisome and unsavoury',
it was well that they were for the most part mere
halting-places between the offence and the scaffold. The
ancient laws of England were like the laws of Draco in their
simplicity. Rogues and vagabonds were, at their first offence,
branded, or stocked. They might be whipped at the cart's
tail, or be asked to preach in a pillory for lack of pulpit.
But a second offence brought them within the reach of felony,
and felony meant the gallows. So even a poor masterless
man, if he disdained work, was compelled at last to groan
out of a cart up the heavy hill. Truly, felony was a large
and comprehensive term. Breach of prison, hunting by
night with painted faces, carrying of horses into Scotland,
stealing of hawks' eggs, conjuring and witchcraft, diminution
of coin, stealing of cattle, robbing by the highway, or on the
sea, or of dwelling-houses, letting out of ponds, cutting of
purses, deer-stealing by night, counterfeiting of coins, im-
penitent roguery and idleness—all these were felonies and
punishable according to law with a hempen rope. In England,
then, the gibbet was, with one exception, universal. At
Halifax alone the felon climbed no triple tree. If he was
convicted of stealing thirteen-pence-halfpenny or upwards he
was beheaded upon the next market-day. The instrument of
his suffering was, as Harrison describes it, not unlike the
guillotine, and it is satisfactory to reflect, when the pin was
pulled out

the head blocke wherein the ax is fastened dooth fall downe with
such a violence, that if the necke of the transgressor were so big
as that of a bull, it should be cut in sunder at a stroke, and roll
from the bodie by an huge distance.

The felon's death, if brutal, was instantaneous, and it
was probably only the honourable tradition of the gallows
that made the malefactors of England beware of Halifax.
But the malefactors of England, though they feared not
death, refused obstinately to be tortured. By an ancient
statute jailers were held guilty of felony, if they inflicted
pain upon any prisoner for the revealing of his accomplices.
'The nature of Englishmen', says Sir Thomas Smith, 'is to

neglect death, to abide no torment.' And with a just pride the author of *The Commonwealth of England* declares that 'in no place shall you see malefactors goe more constantly, more assuredly, and with less lamentation to their death than in England'. In brief, it was not a time of sentimentality. He who had done wrong thought it no shame to pay the penalty. And the scoundrels of Elizabeth's reign, though they were a burden on the country, though in artistry they yielded to their successors, yet knew how to make a noble and becoming end. If it were their fate to dance without the music or to tend the sheep by moonlight, they did not whine of wasted opportunities, they did not complain of the harshness of the law.

BIBLIOGRAPHY.—The chief contemporary authorities for the practices of organized roguery are JOHN AWDELEY's *The Fraternitye of Vacabondes*, 1561, and THOMAS HARMAN's *A Caveat or Warening, for commen cursetors vulgarely called Vagabones*, 1566. Both these works have been reprinted by the Early English Text Society (1869) and by the New Shakspere Society (1880). Numerous pamphlets by Elizabethan writers of repute described the criminal fraternity of London. Chief among these are ROBERT GREENE's *A Notable Discovery of Coosnage*, 1591, *The Defence of Conny-catching*, 1592, and *A Disputation betweene a Hee Conny-catcher and a Shee Conny-catcher*, 1592; THOMAS DEKKER's *The Seven Deadlie Sinnes of London*, 1606, *The Belman of London*, 1608, *Lanthorne and Candle-Light; or, the Bell-Mans Second Night Walke*, 1609; and Samuel Rowlands's works, especially his *Martin Mark-all, Beadle of Bridewell*, 1610. For the prisons of the time or somewhat later the reader may consult W. FENNOR's *The Compters Common-Wealth*, 1617, and GEFFRAY MYNSHULL's *Essayes and Characters of a Prison and Prisoners*, 1618. The Roxburghe Collection of Ballads (Ballad Society, 1871–99) and *The Shirburn Ballads*, ed. Andrew Clark (1907), should also be consulted. Elizabethan statutes for the punishment of 'rogues, vagabonds and sturdy beggars', as well as those for the relief of the poor, are printed in G. W. PROTHERO's *Select Statutes ... illustrative of the Reigns of Elizabeth and James I*, ed. 2, 1898. A picture of the life of Elizabethan rogues is given by FRANK AYDELOTTE in *Elizabethan Rogues and Vagabonds*, 1913. Sir F. M. EDEN's *The State of the Poor*, 3 vols., 1797, contains many valuable documents. C. J. RIBTON-TURNER's *A History of Vagrants*, 1887, is a general history of the class.

XXIX

BALLADS AND BROADSIDES

BY

C. H. FIRTH

SHAKESPEARE was as familiar with the English ballads of his time as Burns was with the songs of Scotland. Besides continually citing stanzas from them, he mentions their tunes or employs their language. Falstaff and Sir Toby Belch, Hamlet and Mercutio all freely echo contemporary ballad-literature. To a student of Shakespeare's plays, however, the chief value of the ballads of his time does not consist either in the light they throw on particular passages or in the explanation they supply of particular phrases. The ballads do something more than this : they supply evidence on the character of Shakespeare's audience. These remnants of the popular literature of the time show how the people lived, and what they thought, the stories with which they were familiar, and the allusions which they could understand.

Most of the ballads written in Shakespeare's days have perished, but enough survive, in one shape or another, to enable us to form general conclusions on the nature and the development of the species. Furthermore, the printers of ballads, in order to obtain copyright, were obliged to enter the titles of their productions in the register of the Stationers' Company, and the entries indicate the subjects of ballads now lost, and at times the manner in which the subjects were treated. Besides this, the date of the registration enables us to determine when a particular ballad was produced, and whether it preceded or followed others of somewhat similar title and subject.[1] Of the Elizabethan ballads which survive, some exist in the original

---

[1] Unluckily the records of the Stationers' Company are defective. Between 1570 and 1576 there is a hiatus in the register, and during a large part of the reign of James I the custom of registering ballad-titles fell into disuse.

broadside form, others in seventeenth century reprints, or in 'garlands' and similar collections, while some few are preserved in manuscript.

Little is known of those who produced this mass of popular literature. Ballads are for the most part anonymous. During the early part of Elizabeth's reign the author of a ballad frequently put his name at the end: in this way we know the names of Leonard Gybson, William Fulwood, T. Ryder, Bernard Garter, Stephen Peele, and others. 'Finis, quod John Barker', or 'Finis qd W. Elderton' are examples of signatures. It soon became usual to put initials only. William Elderton's productions are signed 'W. E.', Thomas Deloney's, 'T. D.' Later it became the general practice to omit any signature, except in the case of a few men whose names had a distinct commercial value, such as Martin Parker.

Elderton and Deloney are the representative ballad-writers of the Elizabethan age, not only because they wrote more or wrote better than the rest, but because something is known about them. Elderton, according to Stow, was at one time an attorney, at another time he is said to have been master of a company of comedians. He wrote from 1559 to 1584, and died before 1592. Over twenty of his ballads have survived: the earliest are stiff and full of classical allusions; the later are vigorous and humorous, have an excellent swing and a rich vocabulary. He was frequently scurrilous, and sometimes indecent. There is extant a 'Supplication' addressed to Elderton by another ballad-writer, William Fulwood. A hosier named Leach, a simple man with no more wit than to call a spade a spade, had termed some of Elderton's verses 'filthy rhymes', and Elderton had replied with acrimony. Fulwood intervened to justify Leach, and to exercise his wit on Elderton's 'rich nose'. To this 'ale-crammed nose' Gabriel Harvey and other critics refer, and it became the tradition that Elderton 'armed himself with ale when he ballated, as old father Ennius did with wine'.[1]

Deloney's name is better known, yet personally he is not so definite a figure as Elderton. Nashe terms him 'the ballading silkweaver of Norwich'; Kemp refers to him in 1600 as 'the great ballad-maker', and as recently dead.

[1] Cf. Harvey, *Four Letters*, ed. Grosart, i. 201.

The earliest ballad of Deloney's we possess was printed in 1586, but the most remarkable of his ballads are the three on the Spanish Armada, printed in 1588. In 1596 the Lord Mayor suppressed one of Deloney's ballads, because it made the Queen ' speak with her people in dialogue in very fond and indecent sort '. The printer was imprisoned, and the author in danger of prison ; this perhaps it was that led Deloney to the safer trade of writing prose romances, such as *Jack of Newbury, Thomas of Reading,* and *The Gentle Craft.* Two little collections of ballads owed their existence to him, *The Garland of Good Will* and *Strange Histories.* Of the first the earliest extant edition is dated 1604, of the second 1602. Not all the ballads which these collections contain can be assumed to be Deloney's, though most of them undoubtedly are his, and it is certain that many of Deloney's ballads were not included. These ballads are for the most part simple and straightforward narratives, the best of them inspired by a patriotic fervour which lifts them above the commonplace. Deloney had also a certain power of telling a story, and Drayton found his style ' full of state and pleasing '.

Ballads multiplied exceedingly as the reign of Elizabeth drew towards its close. To write them or to sing them became a profitable trade. The minstrel of the middle of the century led a hard life. One of the profession, Richard Sheale, for instance, in the curious autobiographical poem lamenting a robbery of which he had been the victim, describes his manner of living, and his poverty. Nevertheless, a generation or two later it had become a profitable trade both for ballad-maker and ballad-singer. Chettle, writing in 1592 his *Kinde-Hart's Dreame,* complains that ' a company of idle youths, loathing honest labour, and despising lawful trades, betake themselves to a vagrant and vicious life, in every corner of cities and market towns of the realm, singing and selling ballads. . . There is many a tradesman, of a worshipful trade yet no stationer, who after a little bringing up apprentices to singing brokery, takes into his shop some fresh men, and trusts his servants of two months standing with a dozen gross of ballads. In which if they prove thrifty he makes them petty chapmen '. He goes on to mention two young men, ' the one with a squeaking treble, the other with an

446.1   L l

ale-blown bass', who bragged that they earned 'twenty shillings a day' by the exercise of these natural gifts.

Even the authors of popular ballads made money out of them. In *The Returne from Parnassus* (ed. Macray, p. 51), Luxurio, wishing to live well, scorns to be a scholar or schoolmaster, and aspires to write ballads. In one scene he is introduced with the boy he hires to sing his productions.

'Come boy,' he says, 'if thou chante it finely at the fayre wee'll make a good markitt of it. . . . I am sure I have done my parte, for I am sure my pen hath sweated through a quire of paper this laste weeke ; and they are noe small verses like "Captains couragious, whome death coulde not daunte" [i.e. the first line of 'Mary Ambree'], but verses full of a poeticall spirit ; such that if Elderton were alive to heare, his blacke potts shoulde put on mourninge apparell, and his nose for verie envie departe out of the worlde.'

'I warrante youe', replies the boy, 'I'le purchase suche an auditorie of clowns that shall gape, nodd, and laughe ! One shall crye "a goodlie matter", another "bravely wanton", and a thirde "commende the sweet master". I'le make every hoydon bestowe a fairinge on his dore, his wall, his windowe.' So he strikes up :

> Nowe listen all good people
> Unto a strange event,
> That did befall to two yonge men
> As they to market went.

The roguish pedlar, Autolycus, is Shakespeare's contribution to the gallery of Elizabethan ballad-mongers. Printed ballads are the most popular of his wares, and his singing of them at the sheep-shearing feast in *The Winter's Tale* is applauded ecstatically by his peasant audience. 'He sings several tunes faster than you'll tell money,' says one hearer ; 'he utters them as he had eaten ballads and all men's ears grew to his tunes ; . . . he hath songs for man or woman, of all sizes ; no milliner can so fit his customers with gloves.' 'I love a ballad but even too well,' interposes the admiring clown, 'if it be doleful matter merrily set down, or a very pleasant thing indeed and sung lamentably.' The shepherdess Mopsa urges the clown to buy some ballads of the accomplished packman. 'I love a ballad', she adds, 'in print, a-life, for then we are sure they are true' (*Wint. Tale* IV. iii. 181–263). There is another description of a 'ballad-man' and his audience in Ben Jonson's *Bartholomew Fair*. In one scene (II. i), Nightingale, 'a sweet singer of new ballads allurant', gives a list of his stock. In another (III. i) he sings to a circle of enthusiastic hearers 'A Caveat for Cutpurses'.[1] One of his auditors, Bartholomew Cokes, an esquire of Harrow, joins in the chorus :

> Youth, youth, thou hadst better been starv'd by thy nurse,
> Than live to be hanged for cutting a purse.

Squire Cokes is a lover of ballads, but demands a good picture at the head of one as well as a taking tune. ' Do you remember ', he says to his sister, ' the ballads over the nursery chimney at home o' my own pasting up—there be brave pictures.' While he listens, eager to buy the whole bundle of ballads, his purse is stolen. Grave scholars like Selden and Prideaux sometimes formed part of such an audience, for both were great collectors. In 1600 Sir William Cornwallis, the essayist, draws the moral which such scenes suggested to him.

I have not been ashamed to adventure mine eares with a ballad singer, and they have come home loaden to my liking, doubly satisfied, with profit and with recreation. The profit, to see earthlings satisfied with such coarse stuff, to heare vice rebuked, and to see the power of vertue that pierceth the head of such a base historian and vile auditorie. The recreation, to see how thoroughly the standers by are affected, what strange gestures come from them, what strayned stuff from their poet, what shift they make to stand to heare, what extremities he is driven to for rime, how they adventure theyr purses, he his wits, how well both their paines are recompenced, they with a filthie noise, he with a base reward. (Cornwallis's *Essays*, No. 15)

At times more than one minstrel took part, and a ballad developed into a duet, or a semi-dramatic performance, in which several performers united. To these the name of 'jig' was usually given, which has been defined as 'a dramatic ballad or a ballad drama written to dance music, and capable of presentation by dance action on the stage.' In one example, 'Mr. Attowell's Jigge', the characters are 'Francis, a gentleman ; Richard, a farmer ; and their wives '. In 'Rowlands Godson' there are three characters, Bess, Bess's husband, and John, Bess's lover. In 'Clod's Carrol' there are two characters only : it is described as

---

[1] Cf. the version in *Roxburghe Ballads* iii. 491.

' a proper new jigg to be sung between a man and a woman
that would need be married '. Some jigs extend to the
length of twenty-six or twenty-eight verses.

It is not easy to define a ballad. So far as substance is
concerned the distinction between the ballad and various
forms of lyric is not very sharply drawn. Many of the pieces
included in Tottel's *Miscellany* (1557) were republished as
ballads during the early years of Elizabeth's reign, and on
the other hand a collection such as Clement Robinson's
Handefull of pleasant delites (1584) contains many things
originally printed as broadside ballads. Sir Edward Dyer's
poem, ' My mind to me a kingdom is ', was printed as
a ballad in William Byrd's *Psalms, Sonets, and Songs*
(1587), and Richard Barnfield's ' As it fell upon a day '
became, with additions, *A Lover's Newest Coranto.*

The productions of poets and courtiers were drowned
in a flood of ballads written expressly for the populace.
A large portion of these consisted of amatory ditties. ' A
Newe ballade of a Lover extolling his Ladye ' (1568),
' A very proper Dittie to the tune of Lightie Love ', and
' Adewe, Sweete Harte ' (1569), are good examples of the
nature of these compositions during the earlier part of
Elizabeth's reign. Mixed with them were stories of the
quarrels of husbands and wives, such as ' The Pinnyng of
the Basket ', and ' A mery balade how a wife entreated
her husband to have her own wyll ', or fabliaux such as
' A mery new Song how a Bruer meant to make a Cooper
cuckold, and how deere the Bruer paid for the bargaine '.
Many of these ditties were immoral and indecent. A collection of songs issued about 1558 was called *The Court of Venus*.
' No filthy mind a songe can crave, but therein he may find
the same ', said the author of an answer to it called *The
Court of Virtue*. A divine, named Thomas Brice, printed a
ballad ' Against filthy writing and such like delighting ', in
which he asked if the English people were heathens, and
whether Christ or Cupid was lord. In his *Anatomie of Abuses*,
Philip Stubbes vigorously denounces the immorality of the
popular ballads; and Nashe, who was not prudish, condemned
some of them. 'I could hardly be perswaded', he wrote in
1592, 'that anie professor of so excellent a science [as
printing] would be so impudent to print such ribauldrie as
Watkin's Ale, The Carman's Whistle, and sundrie such

other.'   Ballads of this kind naturally lent themselves to personal scurrilities. Falstaff threatens to avenge the tricks which Prince Hal and his companions play upon him by having ' ballads made on you all, and sung to filthy tunes ' (*1 Hen. IV*, II. ii. 51).   Cleopatra and her handmaiden are terrified by the thought that ' scald rimers ' may ' ballad us out o' tune ' (*Ant. & Cleop.* v. ii. 215).

Some attempt to check these unseemly productions was made by the Stationers' Company.   On December 3, 1595, it ordered that the press and the types of Abel Jeffes should be seized, he having printed ' divers lewd ballads and things very offensive '.   In 1597, William Blackwell was

From ' A most excellent Ditty of the Lovers promises ' and ' The Ladies prudent answer to her Love ' (*Roxburghe Ballads* I. 205).

fined 2*s*. 6*d*. for selling a ballad called ' Lusty Larrance ' ; in 1600 three printers were fined 5*s*. apiece for selling ' a disordered ballad of " The Wife of Bathe " '.   But since their authors did not usually attempt to register them, most ballads of this kind escaped the Company's control.   Moralists who wished to combat this evil were driven to put their exhortations into the form of ballads in order to reach the minds of the people.   They published ballads against particular sins, against slander, against whoredom, against unthriftiness, and so on.   Or else they produced general exhortations to repentance and warnings of the wrath to come

> Good people all, repent with speede
> All carefull Christians, marke my song
> Awake, awake, O England.

These ballads and many others like them, as one of their editors observes, ' discharged the functions of the modern pulpit.'

Another way of counteracting the immorality or frivolity of particular ballads was to moralize them. This was done upon a great scale in Scotland, where in *Ane Compendious Buik of Godly and Spirituall Sangis*, printed in 1567, a number of popular ballad tunes were wedded to new words of a religious instead of an amatory nature.[1] In England the process was not carried out on so comprehensive a scale, but there are examples of its application in particular cases. For instance, the ballad entitled ' Row well, ye Mariners ', published in 1565–6, was moralized at once as ' Row well, Christ's Mariners ' and ' Row well, God's Mariners ', and the words of several political ballads set to this tune are extant. ' Fain would I have a prettie thing to give unto my Ladie ' became next ' Fain would I have a godly thing to give unto my Ladie ', and finally ' Fain would I have a virtuous wife adorned with all modestie '. A love song with the burden, ' Dainty, come thow to me ', became a devotional one with the burden, ' Jesu, come thow to mee '. Shakespeare quotes in *King Lear* (III. vi. 28), ' Come o'er the bourn, Bessy, to me ', an old love song which, when Elizabeth ascended the throne, was converted into a political dialogue between the Queen's Majesty and England, and also moralized as a dialogue between Christ and mankind.

Quite apart, however, from moralization, a popular ballad was immediately answered, imitated, and continued, till air and words became familiar to everybody. Two of those referred to by Shakespeare supply good examples. In *As You Like It* (III. iii. 105) Touchstone quotes ' O sweet Oliver, leave me not behind thee '. This was the title of a ballad entered by Richard Jones on August 6, 1584, and on August 20 Henry Carr entered an answer to it. Two years later, on August 1, 1586, a third publisher registered ' O swete Olyver, altered to the Scriptures '. Still more popular were the ballad and the tune of ' Greensleeves ', mentioned by Falstaff and Mrs. Ford in *The Merry Wives of Windsor* (II. i. 64, v. v. 22). This ballad was registered on September 3, 1580, as ' a new

---

[1] Known also as *The Gude and Godlie Ballatis*, and re-edited in 1897 by A. F. Mitchell.

northern dittye of the Lady Grenesleves ' : on the same day
another publisher registered 'Ladie Greene sleeves answere
to Donkyn hir frende '. ' Greene Sleves moralised to the
Scripture' followed on September 15, and ' Greene Sleves
and Countenaunce in Countenaunce is Greene Sleves ' on
September 18. On December 14 yet another version was
entered, and on February 13, 1581, came ' Reprehension
against Green Sleves ', by Elderton. The series ended on
August 24, 1581, with a ballad entitled :

> Green sleeves is worn away,
> Yellow sleeves come to decay,
> Black sleeves I hold in despite,
> But white sleeves is my delight.

At times old ballads were wholly rewritten and set to
new tunes—a practice to which Armado bears witness
when he proposes to have ' newly writ o'er ' the ancient
ditty of ' The King [Cophetua] and the Beggar ', which in its
original shape no longer serves ' for the writing nor the
tune ' (*Love's L. L.* I. ii. 115–21).

The ballads which Shakespeare quotes are always those
which were most popular and best known. Amatory and
religious ballads were longer lived than the rest, because
they dealt with subjects of perennial interest. But a very
great number of ballads were merely concerned with matters
of temporary interest.[1] They filled the place of the modern
newspaper, or were substitutes for prose pamphlets of
news. A prose narrative of an event was often followed
and sometimes accompanied by a verse narrative of the
same in the shape of a ballad. For instance, on April 13,
1598, Thomas Purfoot entered a prose pamphlet called ' The
true and lamentable discourse of the burning of the town
of Tiverton ', and on the 28th of the same month, ' The
ballad of the burning of the town of Tiverton '. Sometimes the two were entered on the same day. ' Master

---

[1] John Earle, in his *Microcosmographie* (1628) well described a little later
in his ' character ' of a ' pot-poet ' (No. xxviii) the wide range of the ballad-
maker's topics: ' The death of a great man or the burning of a house
furnish him with an argument, and the nine muses are out strait in mourning
gowns, and Melpomene cries fire ! fire ! . . . He is a man now much employed
in commendations of our navy, and a bitter inveigher against the Spaniard.
His frequentest works go out in single sheets, and are chanted from market
to market to a vile tune and a worse throat ; whilst the poor country wench
melts like her butter to hear them. And these are the stories of some men of
Tyburn, or a strange monster out of Germany ; or, sitting in a bawdyhouse,
he writes God's judgments.'

Styrrop' entered on August 22, 1596, 'the Victorie against Rynebeck', and then 'any ballad that shall be made thereof'.

Public calamities, such as the destruction of a town, were good subjects, for at the moment every one was interested in them. The burning of the town of Beccles in Suffolk in 1586 was the subject of two ballads, both of which are still extant. One of them was the earliest known work of Thomas Deloney. In 1570 Richard Tarlton wrote a ballad on 'the fierce floods which lately flowed in Bedfordshire, in Lincolnshire and many other places'. This too has survived, but most of the many ballads printed on events of this kind have perished. Of the four ballads on the earthquake of April 6, 1580, nothing but the titles survive. One began :

> Quake, quake, 'tis tyme to quake,
> When towers and townes and all doo shake.

Another began :

> Come from the playe, come from the playe,
> The house will fall, so people say.

It is clear that the earthquake was long remembered, and that Shakespeare's allusion to it in *Romeo and Juliet* (I. iii. 23) — ' 'Tis since the earthquake now eleven years ' — was readily understood by playgoers. At the end of Shakespeare's professional career, a characteristic ballad which commemorated in detail the burning of the Globe Playhouse in 1613 was widely circulated in manuscript versions under the title of 'Sonnet on the Pitiful Burning of the Globe Playhouse in London '.

Few events or exploits were deemed by the mob to be fully authentic without the ballad-maker's certificate. Falstaff desires, by way of attestation of his capture of that most furious knight, Sir John Colevile, that the achievement should be enshrined in 'a particular ballad with mine own picture on the top on't, Colevile kissing my foot ' (*2 Hen. IV*, IV. iii. 52–4). The sudden surprises of the catastrophe in *The Winter's Tale* evoke from an onlooker the regret : ' Such a deal of wonder is broken out within this hour that ballad-makers cannot be able to express it ' (v. ii. 25–7).

Events which happened on the Continent were also made known to the people through ballads, such as those relating the incidents of the struggle between the Huguenots and the Catholics in France, or of the struggle between the Spaniards and Dutch in the Low Countries. Most of them have perished, but half a dozen are still extant. These are : ' A Warning to London by the fall of Antwerp ' (1577) ; ballads on the battle of Ivry (1590), on the capture of Calais by the Spaniards in 1596, and on the siege of Rheinberg by Prince Maurice in 1601 ; ' News from Flanders,' which is an account of the victory of Prince Maurice at Nieuport in 1600, and ' The wofull Complaynt of France ', which laments the assassination of Henri IV by Ravaillac in 1610.

Naturally ballads on the wars in which England was directly concerned, and on the conspiracies which threatened to produce a civil war at home are more numerous. The Register of the Stationers' Company shows that the rising in the North in 1569 was the subject of about twenty ballads, of which eight are still in existence, besides the long narrative ballad printed by Bishop Percy. Four-and-twenty ballads dealing with the struggle against the Spanish Armada and the victory over it were registered in 1588, and four of them still exist. Of this struggle Deloney was the laureate ; three of the ballads are from his pen, and it is probable that he was also the author of the ballad on the capture of Cadiz by Essex in 1596.

Each of the conspiracies against Queen Elizabeth led to a series of executions, which in turn produced a crop of ballads. ' England's Lamentation for the late Treasons conspired against the Queen's Majestie by Francis Throgmorton ' (1584), ' A proper new Balad breefely declaring the Death and Execution of 14 most wicked Traitors ' (1586), and ' A Warning to all false Traitors ' (1588), are good examples of their species. All inculcate the same moral :

> You traitors all that doo devise,
> To hurt our Queene in treacherous wise,
> And in your hartes doo still surmize
>   Which way to hurt our England,
> Consider what the ende will be
> Of traitors all in their degree,
> Hanging is still their destenye
>   That trouble the peace of England.

The most notable of these troublers of the peace of England was the Duke of Norfolk, executed in 1572, upon whom there is a curious ballad by Elderton called 'The Dekaye of the Duke'. Queen Mary Stuart's execution was celebrated in 'An Excellent Ditty made as a general rejoicing for the cutting off the Scottish Queen', but no copy of this ditty has survived. On the other hand there are two versions extant of a ballad on the murder of Lord Darnley; the first, preserved in Percy's folio MS., was probably written in Scotland; the second, printed in London about 1579, was apparently altered in order to meet some scruples raised by the licenser.

The censorship exercised by the Government on all expressions of opinion about things which could be construed to be matters of State was a permanent check to the publication of ballads which touched public men or political events. No ballad on Essex's death could be registered until after the death of Elizabeth, ballads on the coronation of James I were kept back till they had been duly authorized, and those published in 1603 concerning the trial of Grey, Cobham, and Ralegh were called in and suppressed. Further, as Deloney's case showed, ballad-writers, like playwrights, might be called to account for any innocent reflections or allusions which happened to be misinterpreted or resented by persons in authority.

This minute and suspicious control was hardly necessary. Nothing could exceed the loyalty of the Elizabethan balladwriters. 'A Prayer and also a thanksgiving unto God for his great mercy in giving and preserving our Noble Queen Elizabeth to live and reyne over us' (1577); 'A godly ditty or prayer to be song unto God for the preservation of his Church our Queene and Realme'; 'A pleasant newe ballad of the most blessed and prosperous Raigne of her Majestye' (1600), and many other productions of the same kind, attest this devotion to the Queen. A ballad, like a play, often ended with a prayer for the Queen, quite irrespective of its subject.

> Lord save our gracious soverayne,
> Elizabeth by name,
> That long unto our comfort,
> She may both rule and raigne,

ends the exhortation to repentance entitled 'The Belman's Good Morrow', and 'A most strange and trew ballad of a monstrous Child borne in Southampton' concludes in

a similar fashion. The Queen's escape from a gun acci-
dentally fired by a waterman while she was passing on the
Thames in July, 1578, her reception by the citizens of
London in 1584, her visit to the camp at Tilbury in 1588,
are all celebrated in ballads with a fervour and sincerity
which cannot be mistaken for the expression of a conventional feeling.

The natural correlative of love for this ' peerless pearl of
princes ' was hatred of her enemies both at home and
abroad.   Popular sentiment was anti-Papal and anti-
Catholic.   The excommunication of Elizabeth by Pius V
in 1570, and the publication in England of his bull for
her deposition gave rise to four ballads, in which the
Pope was denounced and derided.   They supply a perfect
commentary on Act III, Scene i, of Shakespeare's *King
John*, and show how the scene between Pandulph and the
king must have pleased the taste of an Elizabethan audience about the year 1590.   Another little group of ballads
written by Anthony Munday dealt with the execution of
Edmund Campion, and produced by way of replication
verses in favour of the sufferer written by Catholic pens.
Anti-Catholic feeling was strengthened by the war with
Spain, and still more by the Gunpowder Plot.   But out of
nine ballads entered in the Stationers' Register on the subject of the Plot, and those who suffered for it, only one
has survived, and that in a very imperfect condition.   It
is ' The Shamefull Downefall of the Pope's Kingdome con-
tayning the life and death of Steeven Garnet, the Pope's
chiefe Priest in England '.   Garnett is alluded to in *Macbeth*
(II. iii. 10–13) in the Porter's speech as

an equivocator, that could swear in both the scales against either
scale ; who committed treason enough for God's sake, yet could not
equivocate to heaven.

Two other ballads against the Pope, printed about the
beginning of King James's reign, are preserved in the
Pepysian collection.

It would not be safe to infer from the printed ballads that
England was politically unanimous, and that there was
neither religious nor social discontent.   Only the supporters
of the Government could express their opinions freely.
Catholics who lamented the sufferers for their creed, or the
destruction of the magnificent fabrics raised by the devotion

of the faithful in earlier ages, had to lament in verses circulated in manuscript, while their opponents could answer them in print. Deloney's ' Pleasant Song between Plain Truth and Blind Ignorance ', written in 1588, represents in a moderate form what the average Elizabethan Protestant thought about the controversy between the supporters of the old Church and the defenders of the Reformation.[1]

Social discontent, too, had to express itself in a general or an indirect form. ' A balade declaring how neybourhed love and trew dealyng is gone ' afforded opportunity for denunciation of rackrenting landlords and rich oppressors of the poor (1561). One in praise of the Golden Age served to compare things as they were with things as they ought to be. ' The poore people's complaynt, bewayling the death of their famous benefactor, the worthy Earl of Bedford ' (1585), and ' The crie of the poore for the death of the right Honourable Earle of Huntingdon ' (1596), show what model noblemen were expected to be. The second Earl of Southampton, the father of Shakespeare's friend, is the subject of a ballad-epitaph praising him for his justice and liberality to the poor.

It was possible to praise good landlords individually and by name, but bad landlords could only be attacked by creating imaginary types. ' A Lanthorne for Landlords ' warned them neither to eject widows who could not pay their rent nor to store up corn against a dear year. The ' miserable wretch ', whose story was related, turned the widow's house into a barn,

> And filled it full in harvest time
> With good red wheat and corne,
> To keep it safely from the poore
> Untill there came a yeare
> That farmers might oppress them all,
> And make all victualls deare.

Fire from heaven consumed his barn and heavy judgements fell upon his family. One is reminded of the ' farmer that hanged himself on the expectation of plenty', mentioned in *Macbeth* (II. iii. 5). In default of an English example to

[1] *The Garland of Good Will*, Percy Society's reprint of 1851, p. 89. A more elaborate example of a controversial dialogue of the same sort is ' An Answere to a Romish Rime ', reprinted in Farr's *Select Poetry, chiefly devotional, of the Reign of Queen Elizabeth*, 1845, ii. 267. Another instance is ' An answer to a Papisticall Byll, cast in the streetes of Northampton ', reproduced in the Britwell Court collection edited by H. L. Collmann.

serve as a warning, the ballad-maker found or invented
a foreign one. 'The wrathfull Judgement of God upon
Bishop Hatto' was a ballad licensed on August 15, 1586,
though the oldest version of it which has survived was
printed about a century later. Again, in 1607, at the time
of the revolt against enclosures in the midland counties,
a ballad was produced entitled, ' God's judgementes showed
against a covetous incloser of common pasture in Germany
who was strangely trod to death of one of his own cattel.'
Yet another method of attacking the enemies of society
was the scriptural parallel. An attack on corruption in
high places might be made by telling the story of Gehazi :

> Was not the bryber Gehazie,
> Rewarded justly of the Lord,
> Whch for example verelie
> The Holie Scripture doth recorde ?

His sin and his punishment are related, and the ballad
closes with the hope that the Queen and her council will
take care ' in this lande brybers to expell '.

Though there are a number of ballads inspired by the
desire to preach a social or economic doctrine, most of
the narrative ballads originated simply in the desire
to tell a story. For the people ballads supplied the place
of novels, and their authors derived their themes from
every possible source. The Bible was continually drawn
upon. The stories it contained were familiar enough to
be intelligible to every one, and sufficiently interesting to
attract when they were put into metre. Sometimes a
number would be strung together in one ballad, as in
' A pleasant Posie or sweet Nosegay of fragrant smellyng
Flowers gathered in the Garden of heavenly pleasure, the
holy and blessed Bible '. Sometimes a single incident was
selected for treatment. Gradually the moral became less
obtrusive, and the intrinsic charm of the story the obvious
motive for retelling it. A series of simple narrative ballads,
dealing with the adventures of the chief characters mentioned in the Old Testament or the Apocrypha, came into
existence. One of the earliest and most popular of this
kind of ballads was ' The Constancy of Susanna ', of which
the first line is quoted by Sir Hugh Evans in the first quarto
of *The Merry Wives of Windsor* (ed. Greg, line 717), and again
by Sir Toby Belch in *Twelfth Night* (II. iii. 87).

> There dwelt a man in Babylon
> of reputation great by fame,
> He took to wife a fair woman,
> Susanna she was called by name.

Another ' pious chanson ' was ' Jeptha, Judge of Israel ', which Hamlet quotes to Polonius (II. ii. 431–6). There are many more written in the same style and on the same model. When a singer began,

> In Nineve old Toby dwelt ;

or

> When Samson was a tall young man ;

or

> When King Nebuchadnezzar was puffed up with pride,

an Elizabethan audience settled down to hear an old story with a sound moral in nineteen or twenty stanzas.

The Greek and Roman classics were used for the same purpose as the Bible. At first biblical and classical characters or incidents were often combined. Elderton, in ' The Panges and Fits of Love ', leads off with the case of King Solomon :

> Was not good kyng Salamon
> Ravished in sondry wyse,
> With every livelie paragon
> That glistered before his eyes ?
> If this be trewe, as trewe it was,
> Lady ! lady !
> Why should not I serve you, alas,
> My deare lady ?

Then come the classical examples. One verse runs :

> Knowe ye not how Troylus
> Languished and lost his joye,
> With fittes and fevers mervailous
> For Cressida that dwelt in Troye ?

Another inquires :

> What say you then to Piramus
> That promised his love to mete,
> And founde by fortune mervailous
> A bloudie clothe before his feete,
> For Tysbie's sake himself he slewe,
> Ladie, ladie !
> To prove that he was a lover true,
> My deare ladie.

When Mercutio takes leave of Juliet's nurse, singing derisively, ' Lady, lady, lady ' (*Rom. & Jul.* II. iv. 152), the wag doubtless has the refrain of this ballad in mind.[1]

Each of the legends mentioned in 'The Panges and Fits of Love' was also treated in separate ballads. One of the oldest Elizabethan ballads is that beginning 'When Troilus lived in Troy town', and one on Pyramus and Thisbe is found in Clement Robinson's *Handefull of pleasant delites*. Every Elizabethan lover knew about Troilus long before Shakespeare made a play about him, and there was nothing absurd in supposing that Elizabethan artisans

From 'The Lamentable History of Titus Andronicus' (*Roxburghe Ballads* I. 392): see p. 531 infra.

were familiar with the story of Pyramus. Amongst the ballads which survive are one on Apelles and Pygmalion, another on Diana and Actaeon, and others on Aeneas, 'the wandering Prince of Troy', and 'Constant Penelope', the 'looking-glass for ladies'. But these survivors are but a tithe of the ballads on classical legends which were published during the early part of Elizabeth's reign. In the one year 1569–70, no less than seven were entered in the Stationers' Register: 'The tyranny of Judge Appius'; 'The Miserable State of King Midas'; 'The unfortunate

---

[1] 'Lady, lady,' is however, the refrain also of the ballad of 'The Constancy of Susanna', to which reference has been made already (see p. 525).

End of Iphis'; 'The Death of Acrisius'; 'Ptolemy King of Egypt'; 'Synorix and Camma,' and one which began 'No man could get Atalanta by running.'

When the classics had been thoroughly ransacked, or classical stories had ceased to attract, English history supplied fresh materials. Fair Rosamund and Jane Shore were made heroines of romance : the downfall of the proud Spensers, the lamentable Fall of Queen Eleanor, Edward III's courtship of the Countess of Salisbury, and Edward IV's wooing of the Fair Maid of London, and many similar incidents were narrated. Deloney, who wrote a large number of these historical ballads, including all that are best known, took Holinshed, Stow, or Grafton, and turned a story into verse, sometimes adopting the very words of one of the chroniclers, sometimes altering and adding details. He did not scruple to take his subjects from very recent history, such as the May Day riots against foreign merchants in 1517, or the wanderings of the Duchess of Suffolk during the Marian persecution. Eight or nine of these historical ballads are contained in *The Garland of Good Will*. His *Strange Histories* contains a consecutive series of ten more, extending from the Norman Conquest to the rebellion of Wat Tyler. *The Crowne Garland of Golden Roses : Gathered out of Englands Royall Garden*, which Richard Johnson published in 1612, contained a number of additional ballads on the events of the fifteenth and sixteenth centuries, and carried the metrical history of England down to the reign of Queen Elizabeth. No doubt some of these ballad narratives were from Johnson's pen, though he is best known as the author of the prose romance entitled *The Seven Champions of Christendom*, which had appeared in 1596.

English history was not an inexhaustible source ; from the first it had been supplemented by legend and romance. The Robin Hood cycle was enlarged by the addition of fresh lays, as, for instance, Robin's adventure with the Pinder of Wakefield. Adam Bell rivalled Robin in popularity, and both Mercutio and Benedick cite him as a model marksman (*Rom. & Jul.* II. i. 13, *Much Ado* I. i. 269). The old romance of Roswall and Lilian became in 1580 the ballad of the Lord of Lorne and the false Steward. 'Guy of Warwick' was condensed into a ballad in 1592. A ballad on Patient Grissell was entered about 1566, though that we have is probably of later date, and perhaps by Deloney. The ballad of 'The Judgement of God shewed upon one John Faustus, Doctor in Divinity', dates from 1589, or possibly 1580. Shakespeare's favourite, 'King Cophetua,' which he cites five times in four different plays (*Love's L. L.* I. ii. 115, IV. i. 66; *Rom. & Jul.* II. i. 14; *Rich. II*, v. iii. 80; *2 Hen. IV*, v. iii. 103), appeared first as 'A Song of a King and a Beggar', and was doubtless written by Richard Johnson, whose *Crowne Garland* contains the oldest extant version of it. The reference to it in *Love's Labour's Lost* seems to show that it was written somewhere about 1590. Malory's *Morte d'Arthur* supplied a source for some ballads. Deloney drew from it the episode of Sir Lancelot's combat with Tarquin, and Falstaff quotes the first line of his ballad in *2 Henry IV* (II. iv. 36), 'When Arthur first in court began'. Johnson's *Seven Champions of Christendom* was another fount of inspiration. 'Why do you boast of Arthur and his knightes,' began a ballad called 'Saint George's Commendation', published in 1612. A ballad on St. Denis was printed about the same time, and there are others on Saint George. It was also in 1612 that another famous legend was naturalized. On August 21 in that year there was registered 'Wonderfull Strange Newes out of Germanye of a Jewe that hath lived wanderinge ever since the passion of our Saviour Christ'.

At a pinch the ballad-writer was capable of inventing a plot instead of borrowing one. 'Maudlin, the merchants daughter of Bristow', who was called 'the touchstone of true love', is a simple love-story of the rhymer's own devising (published in 1595). The story of the fair Widow of Watling Street and her three daughters (published in 1597), the 'most sweet Song of an English merchant born at Chichester', and the 'lamentable ballad of the Lady's Fall', are good specimens of these home-made romances. Another very popular story was 'Young Bateman', one of the many ballads 'against the hard hearts of maids' who preferred rich old men to comely proper young ones, and were duly punished for the bad choice. This was originally entitled 'A godly warning for all maidens by the example of God's judgement shewed on one Jerman's wife of Clifton in the county of Nottingham', and purported to relate an event which had really happened; it was entered in the Stationers' Registers, June 8, 1603. Authors discovered that the life of the time supplied better subjects than chronicles or romances, and that a recent domestic tragedy was of all topics the most attractive and the most moving. The most famous of all ballads, namely, 'The Babes in the Wood', appeared in October, 1595, and was registered as 'The Norfolk Gentleman his Will and Testament, and how he committed the keeping of his children to his owne brother, who delte most wickedly with them, and howe God plagued him for it'. The murder of a husband by his

From 'The Norfolke Gentleman' (*Roxburghe Ballads* I. 284).

wife, or a wife by her husband, if there was some story of love or jealousy behind it, was at once seized upon as a fitting theme. The murder of Mr. Page of Plymouth in 1591 furnished Deloney with the stuff of two ballads, one the Lamentation of Eulalia Page, the other that of George Strangwidge, for whose sake she consented to her husband's death. Often the same event attracted both the balladmaker and the dramatist. In 1604 Walter Calverley murdered two of his young children and stabbed his wife. 'A ballad of a lamentable Murther donne in Yorkeshire by a gent uppon two of his own Children' was registered on July 3, 1605, and on May 2, 1608, there followed the well-known drama, *A Yorkshire Tragedy*, which the publisher impudently assigned to Shakespeare's pen. At times a long interval elapsed between the event and its re-narration in ballad or play. Thomas Arden was murdered in 1551, the tragedy of *Arden of Feversham* appeared in 1592, the ballads apparently not till 1633. If there were some cases in which a popular ballad either supplied the basis of a play or suggested its composition, there were even more in which a play was popularized in the shape of a ballad. The ballad on Dr. Faustus preceded Marlowe's play by eight or nine years, since it was registered in 1580, but Kyd's *Spanish Tragedie* gave birth to the ballad of the same title ; and the comedy of *Mucedorus* was printed in 1598, while the ballad is evidently much later. The play and the ballad of *Titus Andronicus* were both entered on the same day, February 6, 1594, by the same printer, John Danter. ' A newe ballad of Romeo and Juliet ' was entered on August 6, 1596, a year before Shakespeare's play was printed, but probably some time after it had been put on the stage. In the case of *The Merchant of Venice*, the ballad of ' Gernutus ' is no doubt older than the play, but the name given to the inexorable Jew shows that the ballad is connected with the play called *The Three Ladies of London*, rather than with Shakespeare's. So, too, the ballad of ' King Leare and his Three Daughters ' is clearly later than Shakespeare's play, and was most likely suggested by it.

While players and ballad-writers often employed the same sources, the authors of the ballads made greater use of contemporary events. There are more topical ballads than there are topical plays. In the first place the communication of news was one of the chief objects of the ballad-writers ; in the second place an episode was enough for him, while the dramatist needed an incident containing the elements of a plot. The dying speech of an ordinary criminal was sufficient matter for a ballad. The confession of George Sanders, the ' lamentation of Henry Adlington ', fencer, who was hanged for murder, and the lament of William Wrench, a soldier executed for desertion, are examples. One of the earliest of these laments is the 'sorrowfull sonet made at Cambridge Castle ' by George Mannington, beginning ' I waile in wo, I plunge in pain ', which was entered in the Stationers' Register in 1576, and is preserved by its inclusion in the *Handefull of pleasant delites*.[1] In *Eastward Hoe* (v. i.), Quicksilver, the debauched apprentice, shows his penitence for his sins against his master by singing a confession modelled on Mannington's, and earns his master's forgiveness thereby. No criminal who had any title to fame left the world without 'the meed of some melodious tear'. Luke Hutton, the highwayman, executed at York in 1595, was not only the reputed author of a poem and a prose tract, but the subject of a play and a ballad. His 'Lamentation' is an autobiography in verse,

From 'The Spanish Tragedy' (*Roxburghe Ballads* I. 364).

reciting the robberies committed by himself, and the twelve ruffians he called his 'twelve Apostles'.

> There was no squire nor barron bold,
> Ah woe is me, woe is me, for my great folly!
> That rode that way with silver and gold,
> Be warned, young wantons, hemp passeth green holly!
> But I and my twelve Apostles gaie
> Would lighten their load ere they went away.

Nine score indictments and seventeen were read against him, and each was found felony, but he felt secure of pardon in a higher court, and ended:

> When on the ladder you shall me view
> Think I am nearer heaven than you.

There was a good deal of sympathy for criminals whose crimes had something spirited and romantic about them

---

[1] Ed. Arber, pp. 57–9.

John Musgrave, executed at Kendal for robbing the king's receiver, was celebrated in a ballad with the refrain, ' Farewell the flower of serving men '. We are told in another ballad that 'a thousand hearts were sorry', and 'a thousand lasses wept full sore ' for the death of ' a worthy gentleman named George Stoole ', executed at Newcastle for stealing sheep and horses on the Border. It is exceptional to find a ballad on a highwayman so hostile and unsympathetic as that on Philip Collins, alias ' The Devil of the West '.

Massinger introduces into his *Bondman* (v. iii) a criminal who begs that he may not be executed twice over :

> At the gallows first, and after in a ballad
> Sung to some villainous tune. There are ten groat-rhymers
> About the town, grown fat on these occasions.
> Let but a chapel fall, or street be fired,
> A foolish lover hang himself for pure love,
> Or any such like accident, and before
> They are cold in their graves some damn'd ditty 's made
> Which makes their ghosts walk.

Princes and nobles suffered from rhymers in the same way. There are ' A most Royal Song of the Life and Death of our late renowned Princess Queene Elizabeth ' and ' A Short and sweet Sonnet ' made by one of her Maids of Honour to be sung to the tune of ' Phillida flouts me '. King James himself is said to have written a ballad on the death of his son Prince Henry, entitled, ' The good Shepherd's sorrow for the Death of his beloved Son '. There are also extant funeral ballads on the Earls of Arundel, Southampton, Bedford, and Huntingdon, on Bishop Jewell, on Sir Francis Walsingham, on the Lady Mayoress, and on a foreign merchant named Benedict Spinola. The custom of actually hanging memorial verses on the tombs of the dead encouraged their production. In *Much Ado about Nothing*, Leonato bids Claudio mourn for Hero in this way :

> If your love
> Can labour aught in sad invention,
> Hang her an epitaph upon her tomb. (v. i. 295–7)

There is a good example of these compositions amongst the *Shirburn Ballads,* one of which is headed, ' The Lover being sorrowfull for the death of his Lady E. C., writeth this Epitaph followinge '.

Another class of ballads consists of relations of prodigies

and strange events. The pack of Autolycus, besides containing ' the prettiest love songs for maids ', included one narrative of a fish that appeared upon the coast, and sang a ballad against the hard hearts of maids, and another telling how a usurer's wife was brought to bed of twenty money-bags at a birth (*Wint. Tale* iv. iii. 264–84). The printers of ballads and broadsides recorded monstrous births as attentively as grave historians of the time noted meteors and comets and sights in the air.

Sometimes the event is related and the monster described entirely in verse, as in ' The true description of a monsterous Chylde ' born in the Isle of Wight in October, 1564, or ' The true description of two monsterous Children lawfully begotten betwene George Stevens and Margerie his wyfe ', born at Swanbourne in Bucks on April 4, 1566. Pictures of the monsters are often given as illustrations to the ballads. Sometimes a prose description is preceded or followed by a verse exhortation to take heed of these warnings of the wrath of God and repent betimes. The monstrous pig with ' a head much like to a dolphin's head ', born not far from Charing Cross in 1562, was a sign not difficult to interpret :

> What might these monsters to us teache
> Which now are sent so rife,
> But that we have Goddes word well preacht
> And will not mend our life ?

So with the child born at Maidstone, October 24, 1568 :

> This monstrous shape to thee, England,
> Playn shewes thy monstrous vice,
> If thou ech part wylt understand
> And take thereby advice.

The huge mouth typified the greediness of the English people, the fingerless hands its laziness, other deformities signified kindred vices. Occasionally a monster was treated not as a warning against vices in general, but as a manifestation of the consequences of some particular sin. ' Prides fall : or a warning to all English women by the example of a strange monster borne of late in Germany by a proud marchant's wife,' is a story told to show ' England's fayre daintye dames ' the result of too much devotion to new fashions in dress and other ' worldly toyes '.

Incidents of this nature were as commonly told entirely

in prose as in verse. There is no rule : the choice of the form seems to have depended on the taste or capacity of the publisher. A monstrous pig born at Hampstead in 1562, a child with a ruff born at Mitcham in 1566, and a 'marvellous strange fish' captured between Calais and Dover in 1569 (which certain men of Captain Hawkins's called a shark), were all recorded in prose only. As a rule, however, the prose broadsides of the reigns of Elizabeth and James deal with less trivial matters. Many are official or semi-official. A large number of proclamations issued by the government have survived. Lord Crawford's elaborate catalogue enumerates 440 published during the reign of Elizabeth and 467 during that of James I, indicating in each case where the original broadside is to be found.

Akin to proclamations are the advertisements and orders issued by minor authorities, ecclesiastical or civil. Instances of this are an admonition published by the Bishop of London in 1563 about the measures to be taken in order to escape the contagion of the plague, and a notice by the Archbishop of Canterbury explaining the degrees of affinity. Instructions as to the manner of executing the laws against vagrants, an explanation of the advantage of observing fish-days, tables of the fees chargeable by watermen between London and Gravesend, or by the officials of the customs in the port of London, were printed in the same form. For calendars and ready reckoners of every kind it was also the most convenient shape, since they could be pasted up on walls for reference. ' A Caveat for the Borrower ; or a perfect Table of Usurie ', and ' A Necessary Instruction to cast account by, serving for all such as are unskilful in the Art of Arithmeticke ', no doubt helped to furnish London shops.

Excepting the proclamations, very few of the broadsides relate to political affairs : it is rather as illustrations of social or economic history that they are valuable. There are, however, several which relate to the foundation of new colonies. One is an offer made by Sir Thomas Smyth and his son in 1572 to adventurers willing to join in establishing a colony in Ulster. There are also four advertisements, published by the Virginia Company, stating the advantages promised to emigrants, the progress of the enterprise, and a ' declaration for the certaine time of drawing the great standing Lottery ', which was intended to attract subscribers to the Company.[1]

Portraits of eminent personages were also issued as broadsides. Those of George Clifford, Earl of Cumberland, Robert Cecil, Earl of Salisbury, Prince Henry, and Queen Anne are still extant. In 1563 a portrait of Queen Elizabeth was entered in the Stationers' Register. ' Loe here the pearle whom God and Man doth love ' began the verses beneath it. But Elizabeth disliked these rude representations of her features. The draft of an undated proclamation has been preserved in which ' payntors, pryntors and gravors ' are forbidden to produce such pictures, until ' some cunning person mete therefor shall make a naturall representation of her Majestys person, favour, or grace ', as a pattern for others to copy.[2]

Royal pedigrees were less liable to exception than royal portraits, and obviously better suited for publication in the form of broadsides than in any other shape. On the occasion of the marriage of the Princess Elizabeth with the Elector Palatine three pedigrees of the kind were published. One showed that both the Princess and the Elector were descended from Edward III, the other traced the descent of the Princess from Henry VIII, giving rude woodcuts of the sovereigns mentioned. The title of James I was set forth in a similar fashion. There is ' an excellent new ballad shewing the petigree of our royal king James ', tracing it back to John of Gaunt. There is also as a companion to it, a broadside representing the various branches of the royal house of Stuart, and exhibiting the descent of King James from Banquo. It is headed ' Regiae Stuartorum Familiae ... Genealogia ', was evidently published about the time of James's accession, and probably suggested the passage in Shakespeare's play in which the witches show Macbeth the vision of the eight kings of Banquo's issue ; it is preserved in the Sutherland Collection in the Bodleian Library.

[1] The Virginian broadsides are printed in full in Alexander Brown's *Genesis of the United States*, 1890, pp. 354, 445, 608, 797. He also gives a facsimile of that relating to the Lottery, p. 761.

[2] The portrait of Elizabeth by Hillyard, which is No. 101 of the Broadsides of the Society of Antiquaries, was apparently published after the Queen's death.

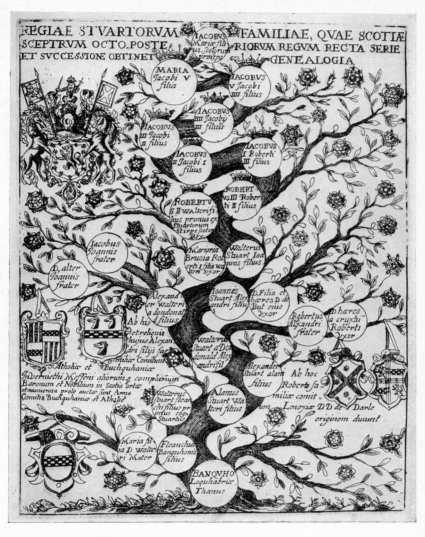

THE PEDIGREE OF JAMES I

BIBLIOGRAPHY.—BISHOP PERCY, who published his *Reliques of Ancient Poetry* in 1765, devoted a portion of that collection to ballads which in some way or other seemed to throw light on the works of Shakespeare. 'This second book', he wrote (vol. i. p. 118), 'is set apart for the reception of such ballads as are quoted by Shakespeare, or contribute in any degree to illustrate his writings.' The Bishop made no attempt to include all the numerous ballads quoted by Shakespeare.

The best account of the great collections of sixteenth- and seventeenth-century ballads, many of which are entered in the Stationers' Company Register, is contained in Mr. CHAPPELL's introduction to the *Roxburghe Ballads*. The Roxburghe and other collections in the British Museum, Wood's collection in the Bodleian Library, and the Pepysian collection in the library of Magdalene College, Cambridge, all contain some Elizabethan and many Jacobean ballads. But of the ballads printed during Queen Elizabeth's reign, most of those which are still extant are in the collections of Mr. Huth, Mr. Christie Miller, or the Society of Antiquaries. Those in Mr. Huth's possession were reprinted in 1870 by Joseph Lilly under the title *A Collection of seventy-nine Black-Letter Ballads and Broadsides printed in the reign of Queen Elizabeth*. Those in Mr. Christie Miller's possession were printed for the Roxburghe Club in 1912, under the editorship of Mr. H. L. Collmann, and with the title, *Ballads and Broadsides chiefly of the Elizabethan Period . . . now in the Library at Britwell Court*. Of those in the possession of the Society of Antiquaries, fifteen—ten belonging to Elizabeth's reign, four to that of Mary, and one to that of Edward VI—were reprinted by SAMUEL PARK in his edition of the *Harleian Miscellany* (vol. x), and some others by JOHN PAYNE COLLIER in *Old Ballads from Early Printed Copies*, published by the Percy Society in 1840. Of the twenty-five ballads which Collier's collection contains, twenty were printed during the reign of Queen Elizabeth, many of which are from Mr. Christie Miller's library.

In a paper entitled 'The Ballad History of the Reigns of the Later Tudors', the present writer endeavoured to collect the ballads referring to political events from 1547 to 1603 (*Royal Hist. Soc. Trans.* 1908–9).

Elizabethan and early Jacobean ballads derived from manuscript sources are to be found in *The Shirburn Ballads*, edited by the Rev. ANDREW CLARK, in 1907, from a manuscript in the possession of the Earl of Macclesfield, and in the second volume of *Ballads from MSS.*, edited by Mr. W. R. MORFILL for the Ballad Society in 1873. Some ballads of this period are included in *Bishop Percy's Folio MS.*, edited by Dr. FURNIVALL and Mr. HALES, 1867–8, and the volume of *Songs and Ballads chiefly of the Reign of Philip and Mary*, edited by THOMAS WRIGHT, from the Ashmolean MSS., 1860, contains a few which belong to the early years of Queen Elizabeth. In 1869 there was printed for private circulation a book entitled *Twenty-five Old Ballads and Songs*, from manuscripts in the possession of J. Payne Collier. In the notes to his *Extracts from the Registers of the Stationers Company*, published by the old Shakespeare Society in 1848–9, the same editor printed a certain number of ballads from a manuscript volume said to have been written in the reign of James I (see *Extracts*, vol. ii, pp. vii, ix). As these are of very little interest and their genuineness is very doubtful, none of them are referred to in this chapter.

Since the ballads were meant to be sung, CHAPPELL's *Popular Music of the Olden Time*, 1855–9, new edition 1893, is an indispensable companion to the reprints of the contemporary broadsides, and a necessary help in ascertaining their dates and fixing their relationship. Many tunes are hopelessly lost; those of which some record exists in printed or MS. music-books are brought together in his pages, with notes on the various ballads sung to each air.

The ballad-maker, Thomas Deloney, is the subject of an elaborate monograph by RICHARD SIEVERS (Berlin, 1904). A collection of the works of Thomas Deloney, edited by F. O. Mann, was published by the Clarendon Press in 1912. The Percy Society reprinted Deloney's *Strange Histories* (1607), and his *Garland of Good Will* (1603), in 1841 and 1851 respectively, as well as RICHARD JOHNSON's *Crowne Garland* (1612) in 1842. Another useful contemporary collection of ballad-poetry, CLEMENT ROBINSON's *Handefull of Pleasant Delites* (1584), was reprinted by Arber in 1878. Professor HERFORD's *Literary Relations of England and Germany*, 1886, and Miss P. SHEAVYN's *The Literary Profession in the Elizabethan Age*, Manchester, 1909, throw occasional light on the topic of this chapter.

Of contemporary proclamations and broadsides, the chief collections are those in the British Museum, the library of the Society of Antiquaries, the Bodleian, and the library of Queen's College, Oxford. The proclamations of Queen Elizabeth were collected into a folio volume by Humphrey Dyson in 1618. Those of James I from 1603 to 1612 were similarly collected by ROBERT BARKER, and a large number of them are reprinted at length in RYMER's *Foedera*.

For valuable lists of extant broadsides as well as proclamations see *Bibliotheca Lindesiana—Catalogue of English Broadsides*, 1505–1897 (privately printed 1898), *Tudor and Stuart Proclamations*, calendared by ROBERT STEELE under the direction of the Earl of Crawford, Oxford, 1910, and LEMON's *Catalogue of Printed Broadsides in the possession of the Society of Antiquaries*, 1866.

XXX

SHAKESPEARE'S ENGLISH

BY

HENRY BRADLEY

THE expression 'Shakespeare's English', in its most usual acceptation, denotes the vocabulary, grammatical forms, and idioms, occurring in the writings of Shakespeare himself. In the present chapter, however, it will be applied, in a somewhat wider sense, to the language of Shakespeare's England ; to the English which he spoke, heard, and read, as well as to that which he wrote. The characteristics which distinguish Shakespeare's English from the English of earlier times will be noted only occasionally, and where special reason exists for doing so ; our chief concern will be with the points of difference between the language of the sixteenth century and that of the present day.

PRONUNCIATION

When we try to call up in imagination the conversation of the men and women of the Elizabethan time, we find it quite natural, and indeed inevitable, to think of them as using many words and forms of speech which are no longer current ; but it hardly occurs to us that even when their sentences were word for word such as we might use ourselves, there must have been a remarkable difference in their manner of uttering them. Nor, when we read a play of Shakespeare with our modern pronunciation, have we ordinarily any consciousness that we are not reproducing the very sounds that were heard by the audiences at the Globe Theatre. Yet it has long been well known to scholars, and is now beginning to be known more widely, that the changes which the English language has undergone in pronunciation during the last three centuries are quite as

striking as those other changes which our reading of the
older literature enables us to recognize. Although the
knowledge of the phonetics of Elizabethan English cannot
be of much service in the elucidation of the writings of the
period, and can only now and then add even to our appreciation of the melody of the verse, it may contribute not
a little to the vividness and truth of our imaginative
reproduction of the past. It is therefore quite worth
while to try to ascertain as far as possible how the English
language sounded three centuries ago. The investigation,
however, is not free from serious difficulties. Paradoxical
as the statement may sound, it is much less easy to determine approximately how the English language was pronounced by Shakespeare and his contemporaries, than how
it was pronounced in the days of Chaucer or in the days of
King Alfred. Absolute precision, of course, is not to be
hoped for in the results of investigation of the pronunciation of any long-past age. But while there is no substantial
difference in the conclusions of modern scholars as to the
phonetic system of English in the ninth or in the fourteenth
century, the pronunciation of the Elizabethan age is, in
several details, still a matter of dispute. This is the more
remarkable, because for the sounds of the later period we
possess a considerable body of evidence of a kind which is
altogether wanting for those of earlier times. In the sixteenth and seventeenth centuries there were many writers
who endeavoured, with no little ability, to give a minute
account of the English pronunciation of their own day,
partly by description of the organic formation or the
acoustic effect of the sounds, and partly by comparison
with the sounds of foreign languages. The testimony of
these writers, however, is not always easy to interpret,
owing to the inadequacy of their means of expression ;
and even where its import is unequivocal, there is sometimes reason to doubt whether the witnesses were capable
of appreciating correctly the sounds which they describe.
One result of investigation that appears to be well established is that the pronunciation of the educated classes was
considerably less uniform three hundred years ago than it
is now. Several of our authorities expressly recognize the
existence—in cultivated circles—of modes of pronouncing
the vowels different from those which they themselves

recommend ; and the wide divergence in the evidence respecting the nature of certain sounds cannot always be attributed to defective observation. Even at the present day the pronunciation of English among highly educated persons is far from being absolutely uniform, though the progressive increase in facility of communication between different parts of the country, and other causes, must in the course of three hundred years have had no little effect in reducing differences. It is probably safe to assume that even in the inmost circle of the Court there were many whose speech was strongly marked by the dialectal peculiarities of the part of England from which they came, and that the pronunciation of the mercantile classes in London was much less of one type than it would have been found to be a century or two later. Besides the differences that originated in local dialects, there were others produced by fashionable affectation or caprice. We read, for instance, of modes of utterance that were favoured by ' fine ladies ' (*quaedam mulierculae delicatiores*), and some of those who had travelled abroad took pleasure in speaking their native tongue with the accent of a Frenchman or an Italian. There were also pedants who took the written form of words as a guide to pronunciation, and insisted on sounding the letters which in unaffected speech had become silent ; and in a few words, such as *fault*, they actually succeeded in inducing the educated classes in general to follow their example.

There are, however, some facts about the Elizabethan pronunciation of English that may be regarded as securely established. The consonants, in general, were sounded just as they are now ; but some words which contain written consonants that are now silent were then pronounced as they are spelt. No one in Shakespeare's time would have made a pun on *knight* and *night*,[1] for *k* was pronounced before *n* as in the German *knabe* ; and it is probable that the *g* was sounded in words like *gnat* and *gnaw*. The dropping of the *l* in *should* and *would* seems to have been only a vulgarism, or at best a licence to be tolerated only in careless speech. What is curious is that in *could* also the *l* seems to have been sounded, though etymologically it has no

---

[1] Some have found such a pun in *1 Hen. IV*, I. ii. 27-8, ' vs that are Squires of the Nights bodie ' ; but the notion is obviously baseless.

right to be there. The *gh* in words such as *light, night* had
in some dialects ceased to be pronounced at least as early
as the first half of the fifteenth century ; Shakespeare has
many rhymes like *night* and *white*, but during and after his
lifetime there were many who continued to pronounce the
gh like the German *ch* in *licht*, or with some fainter modification of this sound. In 1621 Alexander Gill condemns
the pronunciation ' laff ' for *laugh* as provincial, and adheres
to the older rendering of the *gh* (like the *ch* in *loch*) ; but
Shakespeare treats *laugh* as a rhyme to *staff*. Presumably
he also pronounced *laughter* with an *f*, but his rhyming
daughter and *after* does not afford sufficient reason for in-
ferring that he said ' dafter ', although that pronunciation
did exist in his time, and is still preserved in dialects. The
more likely explanation is that it was thought allowable,
for the sake of rhyme, to adopt the colloquial (now vulgar
or dialectal) pronunciation of *after* as ' a'ter '. It will be
remembered that in the nursery jingle ' Jack and Gill ',
after rhymes with *water*. The endings *-tion, -sion* were in
deliberate speech disyllabic, *nation*, for instance, being
' na-si-on ', *question* ' ques-ti-on ', *mansion* ' man-si-on ',
vision ' vi-zi-on '; for metrical purposes these endings could
be treated as monosyllabic, but there is no trace as yet
of the modern pronunciation with *sh* or *zh*. The *r* was
perhaps not by all persons sounded exactly in the same
way ; but it seems to have been a real consonant in all
positions, so that there was no such confusion between
alms and *arms*, or between *Lear* and *Leah*, as there is in
the London English of the present day.

In the pronunciation of the vowels the past three centuries have brought greater changes than in that of the
consonants. The short vowels, however, have not altered
much. Such words as *bad, bed, bid, bodkin, bush*, as Shakespeare pronounced them, would probably not sound strange
to our ears, though words like *bush* and *brush*, *pull* and *dull*,
probably made faultless rhymes in the educated English of
the sixteenth century, as they do still in the rustic dialects
of the midlands. The ' long *a* ' in *hate* was the sound of
the *a* in *hat* lengthened ; in certain parts of Yorkshire this
pronunciation may still be heard. We now make no difference between *queen* and *quean*, and as confusion between
these words would be particularly inconvenient, the latter

of them has become obsolete in the spoken language. Archaizing writers may venture to use it in print, but only because English spelling is not phonetic. In Shakespeare's time the words were different in sound. The Anglo-Irish dialect still keeps up the old distinction between the vowel in the words spelt with *ea* and that in the words spelt with *ee*; the word *seem* having its usual pronunciation, while *seam* sounds something like 'same'. Probably these words were in the sixteenth century pronounced exactly in what is now the Irish way. How the long *i*—the vowel in *time*, and in the pronoun of the first person—was pronounced is a question on which opinions differ greatly, but we are expressly told that there were several ways of rendering it. Even now, many varieties of this sound may be heard from educated people. It is always, however, some sort of diphthong, and so it was already in the Elizabethan age, though perhaps none of the different pronunciations then in use coincided exactly with ours. In Chaucer's time this vowel was still sounded as it is in French or Italian; that is to say, like the *i* in *machine* as rendered by northern speakers. In Shakespeare's time the evidence goes to show that some persons pronounced *time*, *ride* very much as a lower-class Cockney of to-day pronounces *team*, *read*, i.e. with the sound of the *i* in *pin* followed by the consonant *y*, while others came much nearer to our present fashion of utterance. It would appear that our modern way of pronouncing the long *i* was then peculiar to Scotchmen; at any rate this, or something very like it, seems to be indicated by such spellings as *whayet*, *whayle* (for quiet, while) in the speeches of Bohan in Greene's *James the Fourth*, and *ay* for the pronoun I in those of Captain Jamy in *King Henry V*. The synonym of 'yes', now spelt *aye* or *ay*, was written *I*, and did not differ in sound from the pronoun. The long vowel expressed in writing by *o* or *oa* still retains its sixteenth-century sound in the word *broad*, but in all other words it has altered greatly. Shakespeare's pronunciation of *coal* and *bold* would sound to our ears like *call* and *bald*, while his pronunciation of the latter words was what we should express by the spelling *cahl* and *bahld*. The sound of the letter *u* in words like *tune* was what it still remains in midland dialects; it might be expressed by such a spelling as 'tiwn'. The pre-

fixing of *r* made no difference : *rule* and *fruit* were sounded
'riwl' and 'friwt'. At the beginning of a word, this
vowel did not, as at present, take a *y* sound before it.
Union, which we now pronounce 'yoonion', was in the
sixteenth century 'iwnion'. Some of the orthoepists of
that period identify the English long *u* with the French *u*,
but it is doubtful whether they appreciated the sound
correctly. There is no doubt that in Middle English the
long *u* was really pronounced as it is in French, and possibly
in some dialects or in some classes of society this earlier
sound was still retained down to the Elizabethan period ;
but it was probably not in general use. There were several
different ways of pronouncing words containing the combination *ai* or *ay*, and we find that some of our authorities
stigmatize as either vulgar or affected the pronunciations
which others regard as correct. Perhaps the most common
mode coincided with the modern Cockneyism which comic
writers represent by such spellings as *rilewye* and *dye* for
'railway' and 'day'. It seems certain that most persons
made a marked difference in sound between the *ai* and the
ordinary long *a* ; a pun on *sail* and *sale*, for instance,
would hardly have been recognized. There were some who
made no distinction between the sound of *ai* and that of *ea*.
The often-quoted Shakespearian pun on the words *reason*
and *raisin* ('if reasons were as plentie as black-berries',
1 Hen. IV, ii. iv. 264) is, however, not really to the point.
The Old French word for 'grapes' had the two dialectal
forms *resin* and *raisin*, both of which came into English.
Hence the word was often spelt and pronounced 'reason' ;
and as late as 1828, though in writing the form with *ai*
had long been the only one in use, Webster's Dictionary
says that *raisin* was pronounced like *reason*. The combination *ei* had with some speakers the same sound as *ea*
(whence the frequent spelling 'receaue', 'conceat') ; others
made it a diphthong more or less like our modern *ei* in
weigh. The diphthong *oi*, *oy*, as in *point, boy*, was sounded
ooi, that is to say like the *ui* in *ruin* spoken quickly as
a monosyllable. The pronunciation of *ou* or *ow* varied
according to its etymological origin. When it descended
from the Old English *āw* or *āg*, as in *know, soul, own*, it had
the sound of the modern *o* in *not*, or that of *au* in *pause*,
followed by the consonant *w*. When it came from the Old

English *ū* or the French *ou,* as in *now, doubt,* it was sounded like the *oo* in *good* with a *w* after it.

Probably most attentive readers of Shakespeare will have observed that the metre requires certain words of two or more syllables to have a different accentuation from that which now prevails. Our modern pronunciation of *ádvertise* and *advértisement* obscures the relation between the two words ; if the spelling did not help us we should hardly know that they are connected. It was otherwise in the sixteenth century, when both words were accented on the second syllable. In *3 Hen. VI,* v. iii. 18 we read, ' We are aduértis'd by our louing friends.' In several words, as *córrosive* (which was colloquially shortened to *corsy*), there is evidence that the now obsolete mode of accentuation indicated by the metre was really normal in the sixteenth century. But there are many words of Latin or French origin in which the stress was variable, so that the poets could place the accent on one syllable or another as the necessities of rhythm demanded. Shakespeare, for instance, has *cómmendable* and *comméndable, cónfessor* and *conféssor* ; the adjective *complete* has the stress on the first syllable when it precedes a noun, and on the second syllable in other circumstances. As our knowledge of the Elizabethan accentuation of such words is mainly derived from the practice of the poets, it is often uncertain which of the alternative pronunciations was the normal one.

It may be remarked that the modern practice of obscuring the vowels of the unstressed syllables (which is one of the points in which our pronunciation most strikingly contrasts with that of Chaucer's time) was already fully established in the sixteenth century. The play on *dollar* and *dolour* in *The Tempest* (II. i. 18–19) would have been impossible two hundred years earlier.

It is unnecessary here to go more fully into the question of the Elizabethan pronunciation of English. The general result of the researches that have been made on the subject may be expressed by saying that if a courtier or a scholar of Shakespeare's time could come among us speaking as he spoke when alive, his utterance would sound to us like a mixture of vulgarisms and peculiarities of various provincial dialects.

ORTHOGRAPHY

Most people are aware that the orthography of the Elizabethan age differed a good deal from our own, but, owing to the general custom of using modernized editions, comparatively few readers of Shakespeare are at all familiar with it. There are probably many persons who unconsciously assume that our modern spelling already existed in the sixteenth century as a sort of ideal standard of correctness, although in practice it might not be rigorously followed. The fact is, of course, that at that time the modern notion of correctness in spelling was only beginning to be developed. So far as classical derivatives are concerned, indeed, the etymology served to some extent as a standard, though even scholars seem sometimes to have been careless of it. But in general any spelling that fairly represented the sound of a word, according to current analogies, was considered as correct as any other. ' Grone ' was as good a form as ' groan ', and ' boan ' as good as ' bone '. No doubt every writer had his own habitual mode of spelling certain words, and sometimes one out of the possible alternative forms came to be more frequently used than the rest ; but no hard and fast rules were generally recognized. It is mainly in this absence of uniformity that the spelling of the sixteenth century differs from that of later times ; there were very few words that were *never* written as they are now. The later printers, to whom, much more than to the writers, the regulation of English orthography is due, made few absolute innovations ; they merely selected for exclusive use some one of the alternative ways of spelling a word. If an Englishman of the year 1600 could have had before him a play of Shakespeare printed as it appears in a modern edition, the general effect of the spelling might strike him as rather odd, but he would have no difficulty in reading it ; though a modern reader who for the first time takes up a book printed in the orthography of the sixteenth century usually finds its peculiarities seriously embarrassing. The uniformity of present-day spelling has had the result of establishing, in the minds of practised readers, a direct association between the graphic form of words and their meaning, so that when we read a printed page we usually apprehend the sense before we have had time to translate the visible symbols into sounds ; we mentally hear or pronounce only a small portion of what we read. Any deviation from the customary spelling of words is therefore apt to check the rapidity of our understanding of the author's meaning.

Perhaps the features that contribute most to the uncouth appearance which a page of Elizabethan print wears to unaccustomed eyes is the use of *i* for *j*, and the absence of the modern distinction between *u* and *v*. Of course the student very quickly learns to reconcile himself to forms like *iuyce, aduyce, vniust*, but their constant recurrence is at first disturbing. The early type-founts, both black-letter and roman, had the character J, j, following the usage of MSS., but it was merely a different form of *i*, and was used both as a vowel and as a consonant. Most of the printers of the late sixteenth and the early seventeenth century dispensed with the *j* altogether in English words ; in the Shakespeare Folio of 1623 it occurs only (and that very seldom) as an italic capital. The characters V, v, and U, u, were regarded as different forms of one and the same letter. Some few printers of the latter part of the sixteenth century used the form *v* for the consonant and *u* for the vowel, as we do ; but it was not until about 1630 that this practice was generally adopted. The rule that was followed consistently in print (though not equally so in contemporary handwriting) was to use *v* at the beginning of a word and *u* in other positions ; the regular forms, for instance, were *vnder, vain, viuid, reuiue*.

When, at the end of the fourteenth century, the final *e* ceased to be pronounced, it still continued to be written ; and as the sound no longer showed whether the word had a final *e* or not, the letter was often added or omitted arbitrarily. Owing to the fact that in nearly all the words which in the correct traditional spelling ended in *e* after a single consonant, the preceding vowel was long, it became customary to use the addition of a silent *e* as one of the ways of marking vowel-length.[1] When the vowel was *a* or *i*, this was the only method available :[2] *hate* and *write*, for

---

[1] Consistency would have required that the shortness of the vowel in *give, live, love* should be shown by dropping the *e*. But so long as non-initial *v* continued to be written *u* this was obviously impossible, and afterwards the conservative instinct prevented the change from being made.

[2] Another notation for long *i* occurs in a few words, as *spight, spright*, for spite, sprite ; this survives in the modern spelling of *sprightly* and *delight*.

instance, had necessarily to be spelt as we still spell them. But in other words there were alternative means of indicating quantity: e.g. *oa* could be written for long *o*, and *ee*, *ea* for the two varieties of long *e*. Where it made no difference to the sound, the silent *e* could be added or omitted, as the writer pleased. A free choice was allowed between *bone*, *boan*, and *boane*; between *meet* and *meete*, *break* and *breake* (the older *mete*, *breke* became rare in the sixteenth century, being phonetically ambiguous); between *wit*, *witte*, and *witt*; between *box* and *boxe*, *task* and *taske*. No doubt this variety of spelling saved the compositors some trouble in spacing out their lines; the choice among the different forms seems often to have been determined by typographical convenience.

From the twelfth century onwards the letters *y* and *i* (as vowels) had been (as they still are) exactly equivalent in phonetic value, and mediaeval scribes treated them as optional varieties of the same letter. Even in the writing of Latin, such spellings as *vnyus* were not uncommon; the substitution of *y* for *i* was a great help to legibility in handwriting that made hardly any difference between *im*, *mi*, *nn*, *uu*, *un*, *nu*. In the sixteenth century and later, we constantly find a word written with *i* and with *y* on the same page. In Shakespeare's time custom had begun to set limits to this diversity. Roman type is more distinct than black-letter, so that one of the motives for the frequent use of *y* ceased to operate. The pronoun I was no longer written *y*, and in the initial position and various other collocations *i* was almost universal. There remained, however, a wide field for freedom of choice; *heyre* and *heire*, *ioyne* and *ioin*, *dailie*, *dailye*, and *daylie* occur in many books quite promiscuously. The sixteenth-century writers made no attempt to discriminate homophones by difference of spelling, as in the later *die* and *dye*, *deer* and *dear*; and the ideographic use of the apostrophe to distinguish the possessive case from the nominative plural was unknown. Italics were freely used (as roman type had previously been used in black-letter texts) to distinguish proper names, quotations, headings of chapters, stage-directions, and the like; but hardly ever for the purpose of indicating emphasis, which is now their most prominent function. Initial capitals were regularly used for proper names, and irregularly for

The amendment of ortography.   10

two whick for the phrenzy. which,ph,is onely vfed in wordes borrowed of the Græke.

Ph.is neuer in Latine,but in wordes borowed from the Græke,and then is founded,as : f : of which feund,is onely,Φ,in the Græke.   *ph. foun= ded in La= tine.*

Th.hath two foundes in Jnglifh , not much noted of many men : yet fo founded of moft,or all fouthfaxons : fauing, that the common people vnlear= ned,in the eaft part of Suffex and Kent,doe fpeake words written with :th: as though in the fame place, d, were written, as for,this,that,thofe, thumbe, thorne : they fay,dis,dat,dofe, dumbe, dorne. For which J vfe : this, that, thor,thumb,thorn.The firft thrée wordes,(this,that,thor)differing fome= what in found,from the two latter,(thumb,thorn,) and therefore J make a comma,vnder the latter,or other turned difference . wherefore J giue to,th, a name of this fillable, thée, the accufatiue cafe of, thou : as in thefe wordes : Bothe thy father and thy mother lothe thée, for this thy breathing on them : which J write,thus : both thy father, and thy mother loth the, for this thy breathing on them.   *Th.oftwo foundes. D.abufed for, th. th,diffe= reth from th.*

J giue to,th,a name of the found of this fillable,théé: (the found of,f,being left out) in the fame name , the reft (thee) being fully founded : as in thofe words : A thoufand are loth to haue the tenth thiftle or thorne, that thou haft in thy thumbe : yet thou thinkeft , to blowe them through thicke and thinne, with a breath in thine anger. which J write,thus : A thorand ar loth tw hau the tenth thiftl or thorn,that thu haft in thy thumb : yet thy thin= keft,tw blow them throgh thik,and thin,in thyn anger,with a brech.   *Letters of olde, p, δ, and now new, th, th*

It appéereth by fir *Thomas Smithes*, and Maifter *Chefters*, bookes of ortogra= phy, that there hath bene vfed of olde time, two letters feruing to thefe two foundes,and figured,thus : p,δ, naming the laft,the,thorne,d,which hauing the ftrike thorough the head thereof, might well haue bene named as my, th, and by negligence of the writer,the ftrike not made , or a ftraunger teaching the fame,(and could not founde it rightly)vfed the founde,that we and ftran= gers giue at this day to,d,whereby the founde of,dis,dat,dofe, dumbe, dorne, aforefaide, in fome places grew in vfe. The like abufe of the writer, may we well geffe in the figure,p,who is nere the likeneffe of this figure,p,that quick writing with a turned fwte,by vfe in time,made one figure (that is,p,) ferue the turne of bothe the foundes : as may appéere by abbreuiations,figured by,p, and certaine bowels,fillables,and notes,fet ouer it, which yeildno part of the founde of the olde name of,p, (which is,wy) nor other founde of,y,whether it were bowell or confonant,but yeildeda perfect founde of my,th, and of the olde figure, p,as may appéere by thefe wordos : p y thinke p of y, y y man is p whome y féekeft , agréeing by no reafon to be written with, p, might very well be written or printed with, p, thus : p p δinke p of p, p p man is p whome p féekeft : for here is that oldeft letter,p, for which,th, is vfed in the olde,and J vfe th,) founded rightly, end, y, might be abufed in this place by   *Euery na= tion hath fom fpeci= all foundes in voice, not vfed of other nations.*

Odeff, y p δinke us is p of p. p of p. Did, p y ti us thinke y of p. new, thei that think thus of this.

F.j.   ftran=

substantives and (rarely) adjectives; most commonly they
denote some degree of emphasis, but the use is often
arbitrary. A stroke over a vowel was still often used to
indicate the omission of a following *n* or *m*. The use of
y (representing the Old English þ) for *th* survived only in
the forms *y*ᵉ for *the*, and *y*ᵗ for *that*; in MS. these were
extremely common, but the printers employed them more
sparingly.

GRAMMAR

With regard to its grammatical forms, the English of the
sixteenth century differs but little from the English of
the twentieth. Already in Caxton's day the process of dis-
carding the ancient inflexional endings had been carried
very nearly to the utmost conceivable extent; and the one
or two further changes in this direction that might have
taken place without loss of intelligibility still remain un-
accomplished, at least so far as educated speech is concerned. Some dialects, it is true, have dropped the distinctive ending of the third person singular of the present
tense—saying ' he do ' for ' he doth ' or ' he does '; but it
is not likely that this simplification will ever invade the
literary language. Speaking broadly, we may say that the
accidence of the English language was in Shakespeare's
time what it still is, and what it probably will be for
centuries to come. Such remarks as have to be made on
this part of the subject relate to matters of somewhat
minute detail.

The literary English of the sixteenth century—and, naturally, above all, the English of the stage—is, with regard to
its grammar, based on the colloquial English of the educated
classes in London. As represented two hundred years earlier
in the writings of Chaucer and Gower, this was already
a compromise between the midland and the southern
dialects, the former greatly predominating. In the time
of Shakespeare the blending of elements from different
parts of the country in the society of the capital had had
the result of introducing into the grammatical mixture some
forms of northern origin. The Londoner of Chaucer's time,
for instance, always said ' he liveth ', ' he walketh ', but
two hundred years later the common colloquial form was
that with the ending *s*, which did not form a syllable except

when the preceding consonant required this, as in *teaches, rises*. The old-fashioned *-eth*, however, in Shakespeare's time and long afterwards, continued to be regarded as more appropriate for dignified literary use. In the prose of Shakespeare's plays, indeed, which is mostly colloquial in tone, this ending is extremely rare ; but it occurs more than once in the more formal prose of the argument prefixed to *Lucrece*. Even in his verse, although *-eth* is, for metrical and euphonic reasons, not unfrequent, he commonly uses the monosyllabic form, which by its brevity is especially suitable to the condensed and fervid diction of the Sonnets.

It has often been remarked that while in the laboured and artificial prose of Shakespeare's contemporaries the ending *-eth* greatly predominates, the poetry of the same period admits the shorter form much more freely. The difference of usage is strikingly observable in the works of Lyly and Sidney, who wrote much both in prose and verse : it is only in their poetry that they allow themselves to make frequent use of the form which had become general in everyday speech. The ordinary prose style of Daniel and Jonson shows little trace of the fashionable affectations, and is marked by the regular occurrence of the *-s* inflexion ; but in their dedicatory epistles, which are more stilted in expression, the archaistic ending is common. Ben Jonson's remark in his English Grammar, that the third person ends in *-eth*, 'sometimes shortened to *-s*', is scarcely in accord with his own practice. Except *hath, doth*, and *saith* (which seem not to have been wholly obsolete in conversational use), the forms with *-eth* were no longer contracted to monosyllables, even in those verbs in which contraction had once been the general rule. The Old English euphonic change of the *th* of this inflexion into *t* after certain consonants, which was still regular in Chaucer's time (as in *arist, bit, stant*, for ariseth, biddeth, standeth), is exemplified in Elizabethan English only by the verb *list* : 'Goe to bed when she list, rise when she list, all is as she will' (*M. Wives* II. ii. 124-5). Even this was becoming obsolete, for Shakespeare elsewhere has *listeth* and *lists*.

In the formation of past tenses and past participles, the English of Shakespeare's time shows many differences from that of the fourteenth century, in addition to those that were necessitated by regular phonetic change. It is true that the transference of a verb from the 'strong' to the 'weak' conjugation had been less frequent than perhaps might have been expected ; and even where it did occur, the phenomenon was in many instances merely temporary, the later language having rejected the innovation. Thus, while Shakespeare has (though only exceptionally) the form *shaked*, modern educated English recognizes only the older *shook* and *shaken*. Similarly, the forms *beated* (*Sonnet* lxii), *becomed* (*Ant. & Cleop.* III. vii. 26), *blowed* (*Hen. V*, III. ii. 101), *weaved* (*Pericles* IV. Prologue 21) survive only as vulgarisms, the literary language retaining the original strong inflexion. On the other hand, *helped*, which in Shakespeare occurs rarely beside the olden *holp*, *holpen*, is now the ordinary form. The few examples of change in the opposite direction—from 'weak' to 'strong' —have found general acceptance : we still say *wore, worn, strove, striven,* instead of the original *weared, strived.*

Another class of innovations in conjugation, much more frequently occurring than that which has just been referred to, arose from the confusion between the forms of the past tense and the past participle. Owing to the fact that in weak verbs these forms had become identical (' I loved ', ' I have loved '), there was in the sixteenth century a strong tendency to treat the equivalent forms in strong verbs as interchangeable. To some extent this has affected the later language : we now say *held* instead of *holden*, *stood* instead of *standen*, *struck* instead of *stricken* ; and, contrariwise, we use the (shortened) participial form for the past tense in *bit, found, broke, bore,* and many other instances. But in the Elizabethan age, and indeed long afterwards, literary usage permitted many substitutions of the preterital for the participial form which now occur only in uneducated speech. Shakespeare has, for instance, ' These errors are *arose* ' (*Com. of E.* V. i. 391), ' Thou hast perpendicularly *fell* ' (*Lear* IV. vi. 55), ' Had she then *gaue* ouer ' (*Ven. & Ad.* 571), ' He hath *wrote* ' (*Lear* I. ii. 96), ' He might haue *tooke* his answer long ago ' (*Tw. N.* I. v. 284), ' Be *shooke* to ayrie ayre ' (*Troilus* III. iii. 226). It is noteworthy that we do not meet with these forms in the Bible of 1611, which is also archaistic in its use of the older preterites *bare, brake, spake,* &c., for which Shakespeare commonly has *bore, broke, spoke,* &c. The modern language has restricted these shorter forms to the past tense, employing *borne*, *broken*, *spoken* for the participle, although in most of the other classes of strong participles the dropping of the *-en* is now the rule rather than the exception.

Owing to the enthusiastic study of the works of Chaucer, Gower, and Lydgate in the sixteenth century, the language of many of the Elizabethan poets is marked by the free use of verbal inflexions that had long been obsolete in speech and in prose writing. This fashion, however, apparently did not commend itself to Shakespeare's taste. Almost the only instances of deliberate grammatical archaism to be found in the writings attributed to him occur in the lines spoken by 'Gower as prologue' in *Pericles*, which are almost certainly by another hand. The attempt at antique colouring is not very successful; the prologues are written in the newest of English, oddly diversified by the introduction of one or two obsolete inflexions, such as the infinitives *speken* and *killen*, and the present plurals *perishen*, *escapen*. The old participial prefix *y-* occurs here in *y-slaked* and in the past tense *yravished*; elsewhere in Shakespeare it is found (except for the common *ycleped*) only in *2 Henry VI* (I. i. 33), ' Her words *yclad* with wisedomes Maiesty '. Some writers have mentioned *waxen* in *Midsummer-Night's Dream* (II. i. 56) (' And then the whole quire hold their hips, and loffe, And waxen in their mirth ') as an example of grammatical archaism. But the frequent use of *waxen* by Arthur Golding (whose language is not otherwise archaistic) seems to indicate that it was apprehended rather as a poetical synonym of *waxe* than as an inflected form of that verb. In matters of grammar, as well as in matters of vocabulary, Shakespeare looks forward, not backward.

The conjugation of the verb *to be* in the English of Shakespeare differs in several points both from the usage of earlier times and from that of the later literary language. As in the modern West Midland dialects, *be* often occurs for *is* and for *are*, though in the singular Shakespeare seems to use it only after *I think*. In the second person of the present indicative the Old English *bist* had long been obsolete; Shakespeare has only *art* (Old English *eart*), but in the subjunctive he uses the new form ' if thou *beest* ', which is found later in a well-known passage of Milton. Instead of the Middle English (*thou*) *were*, the sixteenth century had the two new formations *wert* and *wast*. The latter is rare in Shakespeare, and possibly was not really used by him at all, as nearly all the examples occurring in modern texts are derived from the Folio, which several times substitutes *wast* for the *wert* of the older texts. The past participle sometimes appears with the spelling *bin*, which represents a pronunciation that is still common.

Some of the forms of the Old English verb *witan*, to know, were still frequently used by writers of the sixteenth and seventeenth centuries, though it is doubtful whether they were in colloquial use ; they have rather the appearance of being rhetorical archaisms. The original conjugation of the verb was entirely lost, the several forms being apparently not recognized as belonging to the same word. If the Old English inflexions had survived unaltered except by change of pronunciation, the present tense would have been *I wot, thou wost, he wot, we wit* or *weet* ; the past tense *wist* ; and the infinitive *wit* or *weet*. In the first person singular the form *wot* continued in use, but in the third person it survived only in *God wot*. Shakespeare has (*he*) *wots, you wot, thou wot'st*, and (*Lucr.* 1345) the present participle *wotting*, but these seem to be merely artificial literary forms. Although the past tense *wist* is retained in the Bible of 1611, it is found in Shakespeare only once : ' And if I wist he did ' (*1 Hen. VI*, IV. i. 180), where, however, *wist* is a conjectural reading for *wish*. The infinitive *to weete* occurs once (*Ant. & Cleop.* I. i. 39) ; the form *wit* (apart from the phrase ' to wit ' = namely) appears only in *Pericles* IV. iv. 31, ' Nowe please you wit The epitaph is for Marina writ '. The old adverb *iwis*, certainly, was at the end of the sixteenth century written *I wis*, and was probably supposed to be the present tense corresponding to the past tense *I wist*.

English, as compared with most other European languages, is very defective in its means of expressing the future tense. The auxiliaries *shall* and *will*, which are our only available signs of this tense, have the disadvantage that they both convey other notions than that of mere futurity : *shall* originally implied obligation, and *will* intention or willingness. If there were no traditional custom to guide us in the selection of the auxiliary, it would be necessary, every time we had to put a verb in the future tense, to bethink ourselves which of the two irrelevant notions would in the particular circumstances be the less inconvenient. In the hurry of speech we should often choose wrongly, and even when we made the best choice possible, our hearer might sometimes remain uncertain whether we meant to express simple futurity or something else. The modern convention—the result, so to speak, of ages of experiment—is that *I shall*, *you* and *he will* are, as a general rule, to be used and interpreted as signs of the future tense, while *I will*, *you* and *he shall* normally express a resolve or purpose on the part of the speaker. This rule (which is subject to many qualifications) renders the meaning of *shall* unambiguous, but it is often doubtful whether *will* is a mere sign of the future or retains its original sense. As every reader of Shakespeare or the English Bible must have perceived, the use of *shall* and *will* three centuries ago was not the same as it is now. Such a sentence as ' And if I die, no soule shall pittie me ' (*Rich. III*, v. iii. 202) sounds to us like an Irishman's English, or at least would do so if we believed the passage to be prose. When it is understood that in Shakespeare's time *shall* was the natural expression for the idea of something certain or inevitable in the future, it becomes obvious that the substitution of *will* in this line would greatly weaken the effect. In Shakespeare *will* seldom serves as a simple sign of the future, except where volition might, at least metaphorically, be attributed without incongruity. There are some exceptions which at first sight appear surprising, though they are not difficult to account for. Thus, in ' Perchance I will be there as soone as you ' (*Com. of E.* iv. i. 39), the use of *will* strikes us as singularly inappropriate. But the alternative *shall* was in the sixteenth century so associated with the idea of certainty that it would have seemed out of place in a sentence in which contingency was prominently expressed. It seems probable, also, that the colloquial contraction *Ile* (for *I will*) was more extensively used than it would have been if a contracted form for *I shall* had been current.

In Old English the verb represented by *shall* meant ' to owe ', and (when followed by an infinitive) ' to be bound or obliged '. When it came to be used as a mere sign of the future, it necessarily became obsolete in its full original sense. In the Elizabethan period it was, however, still often used (like the corresponding German *soll*) where we should now say 'is to', as in 'What is he that shall buy his flocke and pasture ?' (*A.Y.L.* II. iv. 89).

The uses of *should* and *would*, both in Elizabethan and in later English, are much more varied than those of the corresponding present tenses, because the same forms serve for the indicative and subjunctive, and the past subjunctive in English expresses many varieties of meaning. The functions of *should* and *would* form one of the most intricate parts of English grammar. We can only give here a few illustrations of the changes in usage with regard to these auxiliaries that have taken place in the past three centuries. The obsolete use of *shall*, already noted, in the sense of the modern 'is to', is found also in the past tense. Thus in the Bible we read, 'Art thou he that should come, or look we for another ?' In the passage, 'You should refuse to performe your Fathers will if you should refuse to accept him' (*Merch. of V.* I. ii. 98–100), two differences between the old and the modern idiom are exemplified. We should now say (unless using a deliberate archaism) 'you would be refusing' and 'if you refused', or (more idiomatically) 'if you were to refuse'. In the first clause, *you should* could now only mean 'you ought to', and even if we substituted *you would*, the conditional sentence would suggest that the refusal 'to perform' was a distinct action from the refusal 'to accept'. In the second clause, 'if you should refuse' would now be inadmissible, because *should* when preceded by *if* is taken to refer to the future and not to the present. We say, for instance, 'If it should rain, take a cab'. The meaning may be equally well expressed by 'if it rains', only that *should* indicates either an unlikely or an unwelcome contingency. This use had not been developed in Shakespeare's time ; when *should* referred to the future it was equivalent to the modern *were to*. Our *should* corresponds to the older *shall* in such a sentence as ' If you shall chance (Camillo) to visit Bohemia' (*Wint. Tale* I. i. I).

In two adjectives Shakespeare's English still retains traces, which have since been lost, of the primitive inflexional system. While *more* is used as the comparative of *much*, and therefore occurs mainly with nouns in the singular, the comparative of *many* is normally *moe* or *mo*, which accordingly is used with plural nouns. We read, for in-

stance, ' My love is more than his ', beside ' Mo suns than
one '. Similarly, while a singular noun is qualified by
enough (' There is not *enough* leek to swear by '), the form
used with a plural noun is *enow* (' We have French quarrels
enow '). The same distinctions are observed in the English
Bible of 1611 ; [1] but as the modern printers have substituted
' more ' and ' enough ' for *moe* and *enow*, these forms are
not among the archaisms that are familiar to Bible readers.
In Johnson's Dictionary (1755) *enow* is still recognized as
' the plural of enough ', and a few writers of the eighteenth
century continued to use it, though it now survives only
in dialects. The form *moe* was obsolescent early in the
seventeenth century, and in several passages where it occurs
in the first editions of Shakespeare's plays, the Folio of 1623
replaces it by *more*. Although *moe* and *enow* have the
appearance of being similar in function, being both used to
qualify plural nouns, their formal history is not at all
parallel. *Moe* (which is not, as is sometimes supposed,
a shortened form of *more*) was originally an adverb, but
could be used (like the Latin *satis* in *satis virium*) as a quasi-
substantive followed by a noun in the genitive plural.
When the Old English case-inflexions became obsolete,
moe assumed the appearance of being an adjective in concord with the following noun. So long as *more* continued
to be often used in its original sense of ' greater ', the
retention of *moe* as the comparative of *many* was useful
in preventing ambiguity : thus *more reasons* meant ' greater
reasons ', but *moe reasons* meant ' reasons in greater number '. *Enow*, on the other hand, is historically a real
plural form ; it descends from the Old English plural
genōge, while *enough* descends from the Old English singular
form *genōh*.

In the sixteenth century the old comparative *farre* (from
Old English *fierra*) was not quite obsolete, though it had
come to coincide in sound with the positive *far*, from Old
English *feorr*. Shakespeare, however, has only one example :
' Farre then Deucalion off ' (*Wint. Tale* IV. iii. 444).
Near and *next* could still be used as the comparative and
superlative of *nigh*, as in ' Be ne're the neere ' (*Rich. II*,
v. i. 88), ' The next way ' (*Wint. Tale* III. iii. 131), though

---

[1] It is true that *enow* occurs only once, and that in the Apocrypha (*Ecclus.*
xxxv. 1); but *moe* is somewhat frequent.

ordinarily *near* was employed as a positive form, with the regular comparison *nearer, nearest.*

In the declension of the pronouns, the early editions of Shakespeare exhibit one or two archaic forms which later editors have suppressed. The very awkward ambiguity that existed in Chaucerian English, owing to the twofold use of *her* as a feminine genitive singular and as a genitive plural, persisted for a long time in southern and even in midland use. In 1485 Caxton still uses *her* for their. The Oxford Dictionary gives no later example. But when we find in Shakespeare as many as three instances of *her*,[1] for which modern editors have, in accordance with the sense, substituted *their*, one can hardly help doubting whether these can really be due to misprints or to loose syntax, or whether the plural *her* may not have survived in the poet's native dialect. It is not unlikely that just as the colloquial *'em* (for *hem*) is still commonly supposed to be a shortening of *them*, so *'er* may have been regarded as a careless pronunciation of *their*. The original form of the neuter pronoun, *hit*, is found only once in Shakespeare (*Macb.* I. v. 48); but it was not uncommon in the sixteenth century, and the instances would probably be more numerous were it not that the pronoun rarely bears the sentence-stress, as it does in this passage. In Scotland *it* is still pronounced 'hit' when emphatic, and this pronunciation may have been common in England down to Shakespeare's time.

The Old English genitive of *hit* was *his*, and this form often occurs in Shakespeare. But it was already felt to be inconvenient, on account of its coincidence with the masculine pronoun, and the awkwardness was often avoided by the use of such substitutes as *of it* ('and the tears of it are wet ') and *thereof*. The modern *its* first appears, so far as is known, in Florio's Italian dictionary of 1598, and Florio uses it also in his translation of Montaigne. The Bible of 1611 contains no example of the form, and it is very doubtful whether Shakespeare ever wrote it, though it occurs ten times in plays printed after his death. The use of *it* as a possessive, which is still common among the uneducated, is found in several passages. Most of them, indeed, are playful or familiar in tone, as when a child is addressed or

[1] The references are: *1 Hen. VI*, I. i. 83 ; *Oth.* III. iii. 66 ; *Troilus* I. iii. 118.

spoken of ; but some are not to be accounted for in this
way, and the examples in the Bible ('that which groweth
of it owne accord', Lev. xxv. 5) and in writers of the period
show that the use was not yet confined to trivial occasions.

WORDS AND THEIR MEANINGS

While the grammatical differences between Shakespeare's
English and our own often escape notice, many of the
lexical differences force themselves on the attention even
of a careless reader. Obsolete words, and words used in
senses strikingly different from those which they now bear,
occur so frequently in the writings of Shakespeare and his
contemporaries, that no one can fail to perceive that there
has been a good deal of change in the English vocabulary
and use of words since the early years of the seventeenth
century. The change, however, has been much more extensive than is revealed by these obvious phenomena.
A reader who has not studied the language historically
will usually attribute to a word its modern sense if the
context will admit of it ; and very often a passage misinterpreted in this way presents no awkwardness that
occasions suspicion, especially if recourse is had to the convenient assumption of poetical licence or of carelessness on
the author's part. Although gross misunderstandings may
occur but rarely, the reader of Elizabethan literature is
constantly liable to fail to apprehend the precise shade of
meaning in which a word is used or the precise tone of feeling which it implies. Commentators and glossarists can do
but little for us here ; the attempt to point out every subtle
distinction between the modern and the earlier use of words
would be insufferably tedious and pedantic.

It is impossible in this chapter to treat at length of the
differences in vocabulary and in use of words between the
English of the sixteenth century and that of later times,
because these differences mainly concern unconnected
matters of detail which do not admit of being reduced to
any general statement. There are, however, one or two
points that seem to call for mention, either on the ground
of their exceptional significance, or because they are often
overlooked.

Among the changes in the meaning of words that have

taken place since Shakespeare's time, there are few that more frequently cause embarrassment to unlearned readers than those affecting certain adverbs which originally expressed an easily definable ' notional ' sense, but have come to be used as mere particles, the exact force of which hardly admits of being stated in words. In the sixteenth century these adverbs had already acquired a weakened sense, but since that time this sense has undergone a further development. For example, the original meaning of the adverb *still* is that which survives in expressions like ' to stand still ', i. e. without motion. By a very easy transition, the word came to mean ' without change ' ; a step further, and we arrive at the sense which it ordinarily has in Shakespeare, ' without intermission or ending', 'always'. From this meaning, by the same process of development as may be observed in the French *toujours*, was evolved the sense in which we now use the word, and which we might paraphrase by ' now as heretofore '. It is quite common to miss the force of a passage of Shakespeare by taking *still* in its modern sense. Polonius's ' Still harping on my daughter' (*Haml.* II. ii. 190–1) is an instance, though here the misunderstanding is of little importance. In some other passages the attribution of the modern sense to the word involves greater damage to the effect. It is true that in some instances Shakespeare seems to use the word exactly, or almost exactly, as we now use it ; but in these cases there always remains some colouring of the older use, which must be borne in mind if we are not to miss something of the writer's intention.

Another word that has had much the same kind of history is *even*. Its primitive sense is, of course, ' evenly, on a level '. Hence comes the now obsolete use for ' equally', as in *The Merry Wives* (IV. vi. 27), ' Her Mother, (euen strong against that match And firme for Doctor Caius) hath appointed ' &c. The most frequent sense of the word in Shakespeare would now naturally be expressed by some such word as ' just ', ' exactly', ' quite'. Not very remote from this is the use so familiar to us from the Bible, in which *even* preceded a repetition or an explanation, with a sense akin to that of ' namely' or ' that is to say', as in *Gen.* xxi. 10, ' The son of this bondwoman shall not be heir with my son, even with Isaac '. Now all these uses, once so common, are quite foreign to natural modern speech, though some of them may occur as literary archaisms. The only function of *even* in ordinary English is to emphasize the statement of an extreme case, as in 'even his best friends condemn him', 'even if this be admitted', 'he did not even answer my letter'. This sense of the word seems to have been unknown before the Elizabethan period, and did not become common till much later. Shakespeare, who is in language one of the most modern writers of his time, has a few clear instances of it, besides some that are doubtful. In the archaistic language of the Bible of 1611 it does not occur at all, though there are passages in which modern readers are apt to fancy that they find it. The translators probably regarded it as a questionable innovation, as they avoid it in some places where it would have been particularly convenient, e. g. *Gal.* ii. 13, 'insomuch that Barnabas also was carried away with their dissimulation.' (The Revised Version of 1881 reads 'even Barnabas', which is much more lucid.) The notion which we now express by *even* is of such constant recurrence in our everyday speech that it is very difficult for us to avoid reading it into passages in which the word has quite another sense.

Somewhat similar is the history of the sense-development of *rather*. The word etymologically means 'more quickly', and in the sixteenth century it was still often used for 'earlier', 'sooner'. An example of this is probably to be found in *Macbeth* (1. vii. 62), 'when Duncan is asleepe, (Whereto the rather shall his dayes hard Iourney Soundly inuite him)'. But the most common use of the word was in the sense 'more readily', 'preferably', and (through such expressions as 'I would rather say') it came to be used to introduce a statement or appellation considered more true or more proper than that with which it is contrasted. Those senses still survive in use, but in colloquial language by far the most frequent use of the word is as a synonym of the earlier *somewhat*, as in 'The day was rather cold'. This appears first about the middle of the seventeenth century, and was apparently evolved from the phrase 'I rather think'.

One of the striking features of the literary English vocabulary of the sixteenth century, as contrasted with that of earlier periods, is the great and progressive increase in the number of words taken directly from Latin. In the preceding centuries, the great majority of the words of Latin origin used by English writers had come in from French; many of them make their first appearance in the vast body of translations from that language published by Caxton. It is true that the fifteenth century produced a large crop of immediate translations from Latin, principally works of religious edification ; and the authors of these versions, though writing mainly for the unlearned, sometimes allowed themselves to give an English form to words in their originals for which they found no satisfactory vernacular equivalent. There were, too, a few pedants who ran riot in the introduction of words of learned sound without any regard to fitness or to intelligibility. All this, however, was merely exceptional. It was not until the reign of Henry VIII, when the new humanistic culture became a powerful influence in England, that there was any great influx of words of immediate Latin derivation which took a permanent place in the language. Sir Thomas More, whose most famous book was written in Latin, is, so far as is known, the first user of many of the classical derivatives which are still current. The same practice was continued by scholars like Elyot; and even Ascham and Wilson, who protested against pedantic extravagance in this direction, did not wholly abstain from enriching their native language by anglicizing Latin words. The great army of skilled translators, among whom may be mentioned Udall, Robinson, and Arthur Golding, all contributed their share of learned neologisms, and gave wider currency to those which had been introduced by other writers. In the last decade of the sixteenth century it may be said with little exaggeration that any well-known Latin compound or derivative verb or noun might have been used in an English form without occasioning surprise in the minds of educated readers.

Of the innumerable Latin verbs that came into English during the sixteenth century, very many were adopted first in the passive participle. Thus in an Act of Parliament of 1536 we read of places ' where yowth and good wyttes be *educate* and norysshed ', though the verb does not otherwise occur until half a century later, the oldest known example being in Shakespeare. Again, Elyot in 1531 writes ' The king of Mede had *depopulate* the country ', the first instance of the verb in *The Oxford English Dictionary* being dated 1545.

This use of adapted forms of Latin participles in their strict participial function would now sound strange, such words (except for occasional poetic archaisms) being employed only as adjectives. It goes back to the fourteenth century ; Chaucer and Trevisa have several instances. The reason why these participles, down to the end of the sixteenth century or later, were not felt to be un-English in form was that many verbs ending (phonetically) in *t* could still form their past participle (and their past tense also) without the addition of -*ed*. This mode of conjugation is now confined to a very few verbs, as *cast, put, set,* but as late as the Elizabethan time it was optionally admitted in many other instances. Thus Shakespeare writes *acquit, heat, contract,* where we should say *acquitted, heated, contracted,* and in the Bible we read ' He hath *whet* his sword '. Hence a participle that ended in -*ate* did not sound irregular to an English ear ; all that was required to make it normal was the assumption that it belonged to a verb of the same form. For example, when in 1527 Bishop Gardiner, in a letter to the King, requests that a certain person's expedition 'may be the more *accelerate* ', he is virtually using a verb *to accelerate,* even though he might have hesitated to employ any other form of it than the participle. Just about the same time, Sir Thomas More writes : ' Their maner of liuing must nedes accelerate this dredfull day.' It is of course quite possible that Gardiner and More were not really the first writers to use the word in English ; but in any case the example shows how the adoption of Latin participles involved the formation of corresponding verbs. When a number of verbs had arisen by this process, they furnished a pattern to be followed in anglicizing Latin verbs generally. Hence it is that while in the other modern languages the verbs adopted from Latin appear in forms based on the present stem, in English they are very often derived from the passive participle.

When such a verb as *depopulate* had once been formed, a participle with the ending -*ed* soon arose alongside the original shorter form, and in the course of the sixteenth century these extended forms became normal except in rhetorical or poetic use. There are several instances of the short participle in Shakespeare—' This report Hath so *exasperate* their King' (*Macb.* III. vi. 38) ; ' This Chaos, when Degree is *suffocate,* Followes the choaking' (*Troilus* I. iii. 125) ;

Of an old man carying deth.

When an old man carying a fagot of wood on hiz shoulderz out-of a wood or grou[n] waz wery with the long way, caled deth. Lo deth cam thicher, and asketh the cauz whær-for he caled her. Then the old man sayeth, that thu wyldst lay-on this fagot of wood vpon my shoulderz.

The moral.

The fabl mæneth, that euery man iz very-dezyrous of lyf : thouh he be subiect tu a thozand dangerz yet he al-way eschewyth or flyeth from] deth.

From BULLOKAR'S *AESOP'S FABLES* 1585

/ an aduertizment touching d'order
ov de foluing tabl.

/ bikauz de voëls and konsonants ar deveided intu suc parts az befor, dis tabl duts kip dem in de leik order : tu-uit first a, e, i, o, u, and den de four perz huic ar mad uid a stoping bret: tu uit b, p : d, t : g, k : and z, c. / den d'uder tri trulei bredd pers, tu uit d, ts : v, f : and z, s. / den de. 5. semi-uokals l, m, n, r, and d, and de tu breds ð, and b: aulso, for dat in d'order befor iuzd, dez niu leters ar not komprehended. / huer-for dis tabl is plased and set in suc order as foluëts.

R. 4. / a

From HART'S *ORTHOGRAPHIE* 1569

'Lest that your goods too soone be *confiscate*' (*Com. of E.* I. ii. 2) ; 'I am alone *felicitate*' (*Lear* I. i. 77). But these, and all the other similar examples, occur in verse, and it is note-worthy that in *1 Henry IV* (v. i. 72), where modern editors rightly follow the Quarto in reading 'These things indeed you have *articulate*', the Folio of 1623 substitutes *articulated*. Whether these forms are to be regarded as contracted participles of the English verbs or as adoptions of Latin participles is a question that cannot always be answered, and indeed it is very unimportant, as the two formations were probably not consciously distinguished by the writers who use them.

The words of Latin derivation that were first introduced, or first came into common use, in the sixteenth century were commonly employed with a distinct recollection of their etymology, and might bear any of the senses which they had in the classical language. Many of these words have, in the course of three hundred years, undergone some restriction or change of meaning which causes the earlier use to seem to us obscure or eccentric. Although we may be aware that the literal sense of *aggravate* is 'to make heavier', this is not commonly present to our minds when we use the word. The meaning it has for us is determined not by etymology but by traditional association. We speak of aggravating a burden or an evil, but we could no longer say, as Shake-speare does, 'Then soule liue thou vpon thy seruants losse, And let that pine to aggrauat thy store (*Sonnet* cxlvi).' *Continent*, both as adjective and substantive, is now confined to certain specialized meanings, which hardly suggest to us the literal senses, 'containing, holding in check', 'that which contains' ; so that passages like 'My desire All continent Impediments would ore-beare' (*Macb.* IV. iii. 64), or 'They [the rivers] haue ouer-borne their Continents' (*Mid. N. D.* II. i. 92), have a curiously foreign sound. Another Latin present participle that could be used in Elizabethan English with all the latitude permitted by its etymology is *apparent*. We now use the word almost exclusively in implied oppo-sition to *real*, but in the sixteenth century it was chiefly real things that could be said to be 'apparent'—i.e. obvious or evident. When the Duke says (*Two Gent.* III. i. 116), 'One cannot climbe it Without apparant hazard of his life', he is very far from treating the danger as imaginary. The verb *to intend* has now only the sense of 'purpose', and readers unacquainted with the Latin phrase *iter intendere* might easily mistake the meaning in *Antony and Cleopatra* (V. ii. 200), 'Caesar through Syria Intends his iourney', and still more easily in *Sonnet* xxvii, 'My thoughts . . . Intend a zelous pilgrimage to thee'. The cognate noun, *intention*, has the obsolete sense of 'intentness of gaze' in *The Merry Wives* (I. iii. 71), 'with such a greedy intention'. The etymological sense of *rapture*, the act of carrying off as spoil, as in *Pericles* (II. i. 167), 'And, spight of all the rapture of the sea, This iewell holdes his buylding on my arme', is strange to us; and hardly less strange is the figurative use in 'Your pratling Nurse Into a rapture lets her Baby crie' (*Cor.* II. ii. 226). *Diffidence*, which in the sixteenth century meant distrust or suspicion, is now limited to distrust of oneself.

If our space permitted us to examine in this manner every word of Latin derivation occurring in the writings of Shakespeare and his contemporaries, we should hardly find one that was not sometimes used with shades of meaning which are unknown in more recent literary English. The readers and hearers were expected to understand words of this kind mainly by the help of their knowledge of Latin. Although Shakespeare was no pedant, the modern reader who is not familiar with Latin is at a considerable disadvantage in the minute interpretation of his text. At the same time, the classical scholar who is only in the second place a student of English is apt to have his own misleading prepossessions, against which it is desirable to guard. We sometimes meet with expressions of regretful admiration for the superior 'correctness' of the Elizabethan use of Latin derivatives as contrasted with the manner in which the same words are now employed. This feeling is to a great extent the offspring of a fallacy. We cannot indeed deny that the English language has gained enormously in power of expression by the liberty allowed to the Elizabethan writers of drawing at will on the resources of the learned language. But it is really a mark of immaturity and imperfection in a language that a large portion of its literary vocabulary has to be interpreted by a mental recourse to a foreign tongue. It was well that in the sixteenth century English should 'borrow' (as we aptly say) largely from Latin; but it was not until the loans became converted into gifts—that is to say, until the genius of the language became free to treat the adopted words as its own, to extend or limit their meanings in accordance with its own needs, emancipated from the dead hand of etymology—that they constituted a real accession of wealth.

The demand for variety and force of expression, created by the new literary ambitions of the Elizabethan age, led to the enrichment of the vocabulary by other means than the adoption of foreign words. The prefixes *dis-* and *re-*, which had previously been rare except in words taken from French or Latin, rapidly came to be applied without restriction to verbs and verbal nouns, whatever their etymology. On the pattern of the words of French origin beginning with *en-*, were formed a multitude of new words like *enthrall, enskied, enseat, ensheltered*. The native suffixes, *-ful, -less, -ness, -hood*, were used with greatly increased frequency; and the language regained much of its long-lost facility in the formation of compounds. It is, moreover, mainly to this period that we owe the development of the attributive or quasi-adjectival use of the substantive (as in 'household words'); and this attributive use was extended to other parts of speech, and even to phrases, as in Shakespeare's 'far-off mountains', 'the world-without-end hour'. The more timid spirit of later times rejected many of the verbal audacities of the sixteenth century, and in truth they were not always felicitous. But no other half-century has done so much for the permanent enrichment of the language as that which is covered by Shakespeare's lifetime.

COLLOQUIAL ENGLISH

At no period—not even in our own time, which has an unexampled abundance of prose fiction dealing with all aspects of contemporary life—has the colloquial vocabulary and idiom of the English language been completely preserved in the literature. The homely expressions of everyday intercourse, the phrases of temporary currency alluding to recent events, the slang words and uses of words characteristic of particular classes of society—all these have been only very imperfectly recorded in the writings of any age. Of the familiar speech of the Elizabethan period we know— thanks especially to the comic scenes of the dramatists—

considerably more than we do of that of any earlier time. Yet how little we really know of it will be evident if we consider how often we find that a single passage, interpretable only by doubtful conjecture, contains the only trace of some colloquial word or phrase that must have been perfectly intelligible to the original readers. Of one of the non-literary varieties of the English of the sixteenth century, the cryptic jargon of thieves and vagrants, we know a good deal from the vocabularies of Awdeley (1561) and Harman (1567), and from Copland's *Hye Way to the Spittel House* (1517); in the seventeenth century, but still in Shakespeare's lifetime, some further particulars, apparently authentic, are furnished by Rowlands's *Martin Mark-all*. Although some of Shakespeare's literary contemporaries, as Greene and Dekker, were interested in this jargon, and Fletcher (though, it would seem, without any first-hand knowledge) turns it to dramatic account in *Beggars Bush*, there is hardly a trace of it in Shakespeare's own writings. The scenes of *The Winter's Tale*, in which Autolycus appears, might have given opportunity for introducing it, if the poet had cared to do so, but they contain nothing of the kind except the word *prig*, in the sense of thief. Perhaps there may be an inaccurate reminiscence of the slang vocabulary in Autolycus's words, ' My Reuennew is the silly Cheate ' (IV. iii. 28), but this is uncertain. One or two words, like *filch* and *rogue*, which were originally thieves' cant, had become literary English before Shakespeare began to write, so that his use of them calls for no remark. Certain terms of gaming slang had similarly obtained general currency in a figurative sense. The verb *to foist*, which meant to conceal a die in the hand (Dutch *vuisten*, from *vuist*, fist), is still common, though its literal meaning is forgotten ; Shakespeare has it only once, in a sonnet. *To cog*, which denoted some other mode of cheating at dice, is now obsolete, but Shakespeare uses it several times.

Although the ' Pedlar's French ' of Awdeley and Harman is, as we have seen, no part of ' Shakespeare's English ' in the narrower sense, it is not without historical interest. Many of its words, as *towre*, to see, *mort*, a woman, are of quite obscure etymology. A certain number of latinisms, as *pannam*, bread, *cassons*, cheese, *commission*, a shirt (from *camisia*), show that the scholar-vagrant was not unknown in England, though he was not so familiar a figure here as in France or Germany. As in earlier times, the Low Countries contributed largely to the disreputable part of the population of England, and the cant of the sixteenth century has a few words imported from Dutch, as *kinchin*, a child, *cranke*, a malingerer, *dell*, a young woman, *bung*, a purse. The vagrant language, as exhibited by the writers above mentioned, seems to owe nothing whatever to the gipsy tongue. The fact is all the more curious, as Andrew Borde in 1547 quotes a genuine specimen of Romany, which he calls ' Egyptian '. For obvious reasons, we do not find here the Hebrew words that are so conspicuous in the contemporary *Rotwelsch* of Germany. With regard to those parts of it that are founded on the ordinary vernaculars, the vagrant slang of all European countries is surprisingly similar in its manner of construction, and among the fantastic English coinages that have almost exact parallels in French or German, we may quote *darkmans*, the night, *lightmans*, the day, *glasyers*, the eyes, *stampes*, the feet, *smelling cheat*, the nose, *pratling cheat*, the tongue, *grunting cheat*, a swine, *cackling cheat*, a hen (*cheat* being used as equivalent to ' thing '). Nearly all the words of ' Pedlar's French ' can be traced back no further than to the sixteenth century. The natural inference that they are not much older would, however, be unsafe, as one of them, *bouse*, to drink (a loan-word from Dutch), happens to be preserved in a solitary instance of about the year 1300. The vagrant jargon may, for all we know, have existed from a very early time ; but England produced no Villon.

Quite distinct from the secret jargon of the disreputable classes, though in some respects comparable with it, is the slang of general society or of particular sections of society, which has its origin in a feeling of impatience with the restraints of conventional propriety. Although the slang word often begins as a humorous metaphor, the motive for its continued use is not so much the appreciation of the jest which it embodies as a desire to outrage the accepted standards of expression, and to escape the irksomeness of always having to call things by their proper names. A slang term, in fact, is related to its more respectable synonym very much as a person's nickname is to his name. The sixteenth century was certainly a much more ceremonious age, both with regard to speech and manners, than the present ; but the tyranny of fixed rules of any sort always provokes a disposition to revolt, and (as has already been remarked) the slang vocabulary of Shakespeare's time was probably much more extensive than the literature shows. We can hardly suppose, for instance, that the fancy of the Elizabethan age was less fertile in the invention of jocular terms relating to drunkenness than that of succeeding times, but in the writings of Shakespeare's contemporaries we find only very few. *Foxed*, *columberd*, and *disguised* occur early in the seventeenth century, but Shakespeare himself uses none of them (though he has the substantive *disguise*, explained by Johnson as 'disorder from drink'). *Fap*, in *The Merry Wives* (I. i. 184), was probably soldiers' slang for 'drunk', but there is no other trace of its existence. Jocular synonyms for 'money' abound in the slang vocabulary of most countries and periods, but *chink* (of obvious origin) seems to be the only one recorded from the sixteenth century ; the frequent use of the Dutch *gelt* in this sense is probably not to be regarded as slang. Two or three jocular synonyms for 'head' are of common occurrence : *costard*, literally 'apple', *mazard*, a mazer or bowl, and *sconce*, which may be a use either of the word meaning 'a small fort or earthwork', or of that meaning a lantern. *Noddle*, *noll*, and *pate*, though now confined to ludicrous use, were originally employed quite seriously. Of the military slang of the Elizabethan period there is, considering the abundance of warlike scenes in the plays, and the opportunities offered by characters like those of Parolles and Bobadill, singularly little record. *Fox*, for a sword, is probably slang ; *toasting-iron* in the same sense (*John* IV. iii. 99) may be merely an individual jest.

Under the head of slang may, without serious inaccuracy, be reckoned the enormously extensive vocabulary of profane oaths and euphemistic or burlesque substitutes for them. Many hundreds of expressions of this kind are to be found in the Elizabethan writers. Those in which the name of God appears in the possessive, as in *God's blood*, *God's body*, *God's wounds*, themselves number at least two hundred. Most of these are varied by the substitution of some unmeaning syllable, like *Cock's*, *Gogs*, *Ods*, for the Divine name. There are other forms in which the possessive is reduced to 's or *z*, as in *'sdeath*, *'slife*, *zounds*, and still others in which it is dropped altogether. These are by no means the only types of asseverative swearing, and the imprecatory oath, serious and jocular, has hardly fewer varieties. In a complete dictionary of the current English of Shakespeare's time the words of this peculiar kind would occupy a quite appreciable proportion of the space. They are now nearly all obsolete. The Act of Parliament of 1606 (3 Jac. I, c. 21), which forbade the jesting and profane use of the names of God, Christ, or the Holy Ghost or the Trinity in any stage play or show, doubtless had some effect in discouraging the habit of blasphemous slang; but neither this statute, nor even the religious sentiment which prompted it, had more than a subordinate place in the combination of causes that brought about the disappearance of the vocabulary of sixteenth-century profanity.

The colloquial English of the sixteenth century is marked by a profusion of reduplicating formations, most of which are not found in earlier writings, though it is likely enough that some of them had long existed. Shakespeare has *helter-skelter*, *hugger-mugger*, *hurly-burly*, *skimble-skamble*, ' the *tag-rag* people ' ; in the writings of his contemporaries we find many other similar forms, such as *fiddle-faddle*, *flim-flam*, *higgledy-piggledy*, *riff-raff* (which occurs in the fifteenth century), *thwick-thwack*. Very few of these have quite gone out of use, though some are no longer common.

Many familiar terms, on the one hand of endearment, and on the other hand of contempt or abuse, which belonged to the everyday speech of the Elizabethan age, now survive, if at all, only as literary archaisms. *Bully* (apparently a sixteenth-century adoption from Dutch) has long ceased to be a jovial term of address in the sense of ' friend ' or 'comrade'. Most of the epithets of affection in Shakespeare's time—*sweeting*, *chuck*, *pigsnye*, *pinkeney*, *fondling*, are now obsolete ; and it seems very strange to us to find *fool* used as an expression of tender compassion, as in many passages of Shakespeare and other writers of his day. The language of the sixteenth century had a rich store of vituperative words that have not survived, as *coystrill*, *meacock*, *scroyle*, *hilding*, *cullion*, *mome*. On the other hand, *scoundrel*, a word of quite obscure etymology, which first appears in two books by different authors published in 1589, is still current English, and (owing perhaps to its sonority) has come to express a stronger degree of moral reprobation than originally belonged to it.

DIALECT

The fashion of representing rustic speech in literature appears, so far as the extant evidence goes, to be no older than the middle of the sixteenth century, though there are grounds for believing that in the non-literary drama of earlier times the uncouth dialect of the country bumpkin may often have been made to contribute to the amusement of the audience. In the play *Respublica*, written in 1553, and in Pikeryng's *Horestes* (1567), the peasant speakers are characterized by the peculiarities which are now confined to the south-west (Somerset, Wilts, Dorset, and parts of the adjacent counties), but which originally prevailed over the whole of England south of the Thames. The chief features of the rustic dialect of these plays are the substitution of *v* and *z* for *f* and *s* ('vather', 'zummer'), the form *ich* for the pronoun I, and the contractions *cham*, *chave* or *cha*, *chad*, *chill*, *chud* for I am, I have, I had, I will, I would. This dialect, except for the contracted forms, is identical with that of the Kentish *Ayenbite* of 1340, and it appears in the 'Kentish Wooing Song' published as late as 1611. It is very doubtful whether we can regard this song as a correct representation of the speech of Kent at the time when it was written; but, however this may be, it is probable that what we now regard as the south-western dialect extended much farther east in the sixteenth century than it does at present. The playwrights of the Elizabethan period, and indeed of much later times, commonly employ it when they bring rustic speakers on the stage, and Golding, in his translation of Ovid's *Metamorphoses* (1567), puts it into the mouth of the herdsman Anetor in the eleventh book. It seems, in fact, to have become a fixed convention that the speech of country people should be represented in no other way. In *Gammer Gurtons Needle*, probably written in 1560, though not published until 1575, Hodge and the village gossips speak this dialect, though the play was acted at Cambridge, and the author seems to have been a northern man. The dialect, however, is far from accurate, and contains several forms that can never have been really in use. On the other hand, it is curious that in *Ralph Roister Doister* (1553), the writer of which, Udall, was a southerner by birth and residence, the only distinct bit of provincial dialect (the refrain 'I mun be married a Monday') is decidedly northern. Spenser, though the discourse of his shepherds is full of northernisms, does not really attempt to write in dialect, and throughout the Elizabethan age the countryman of literature, if he does not speak ordinary English, always talks in the traditional southern fashion. The first extensive attempt in dramatic writing to represent any midland or northern variety of provincial English occurs in Jonson's *Sad Shepherd*, where the shepherds of Sherwood Forest speak a jargon which, so far as it is anything at all, is Scotch.

Although Shakespeare renders with much humour the broken English of Welsh and French speakers, and in Captain Jamy makes an attempt to represent the Scottish dialect, he does not appear to have felt any interest in rustic English. The language of his peasants usually does not differ, except in homeliness of expression, from that of the educated speakers. The shepherd in *The Winter's Tale* uses the northern *barne* for 'child', but in other respects his English is of the ordinary type. In *King Lear*, however, the disguised Edgar talks southern dialect in his altercation with the Steward (IV. vi. 240–6) : 'Chill not let go Zir, Without vurther 'casion'; 'and 'chud ha' bin zwaggerd out of my life, 'twould not ha' bin zo long as 'tis, by a vortnight'. If the reading of the Folio be original, the dialect is not very accurate (dramatic propriety, perhaps, hardly requires that it should be so) : in the sentence 'Ice try whether your Costard, or my Ballow be the harder' (247–8), the form *ice* for 'I shall', and the word *ballow*, seem to be peculiarly northern or midland. The Quartos, however, read *ile* and *bat* or *battero*, so that possibly the inaccuracy may not be due to the poet. It is noteworthy that once (in Lady Capulet's speech to the nurse, *Rom. & Jul.* I. iii. 9) Shakespeare has *thou'se* for 'thou shalt', not as a provincialism, but merely as a colloquial form. It would be rash to assert that we have here a trace of the poet's native midland dialect, but it seems not impossible.

The question whether the language of Shakespeare's writings has any features characteristic of the part of the country in which he was born is not easy to answer with confidence. There are, no doubt, many Shakespearian words and phrases that are not now current in standard English, but are preserved in the dialect of Warwickshire and the adjoining counties. Too much importance, however, must not be assigned to coincidences of this kind. Every local dialect retains some words or expressions that were once part of the general language ; and even if we could prove that some word used by Shakespeare had survived exclusively in his native district—which of course we never can—there would still be room for doubt whether this was anything more than an accident. At the same time, it must be admitted that some of the points of agreement between Shakespeare's diction and the folk-speech of Warwickshire are decidedly remarkable. Among the many coincidences pointed out in Mr. Onions's *Shakespeare Glossary*, there are three that seem especially significant, because the expressions referred to are apparently found in no other writer than Shakespeare. The disrespectful title ' Mounsieur Basimecu ' (*baisez mon cul*), applied by Jack Cade to ' the Dolphine of France ' (*2 Hen. VI*, iv. vii), is clearly identical with *bozzimacu*, used at Birmingham as a jeering cry addressed to an Italian organ-grinder.[1] Iago's ' speake within doore ' (*Oth.* iv. ii. 144), meaning ' speak softly ', finds its parallel in the equivalent phrase ' speak within the house ', still current at Birmingham. The Warwickshire ' on a line ', meaning ' in a rage ', supplies justification for the reading of the Folio in *The Merry Wives* (iv. ii. 22), ' Your husband is in his olde lines againe ', and in *Troilus and Cressida* (ii. iii. 140), ' Yea watch His pettish lines ', in both which places the modern editors have altered *lines* into *lunes*.

A few more examples may be quoted of Shakespearian words which seem never to have been common in literary use, and which, according to *The English Dialect Dictionary*, are current dialectally chiefly in Warwickshire and the adjacent counties. *Bemoil*, to cover with mud (*Tam. Sh.* iv. i. 77), for which *The Oxford English Dictionary* gives only one other example (dated 1636), is preserved in southeast Worcestershire (only a few miles from Stratford), and in the neighbouring Staffordshire ; elsewhere, it would appear, only in Lincolnshire. It should, however, be noted that the verb *moil*, without the prefix, occurs frequently with this sense in the sixteenth and seventeenth centuries,

---

[1] From a note by Professor Henry Jackson in *The Modern Language Review*, January, 1911, p. 96, it appears that *bozzimacu* was vulgarly used at Sheffield nearly sixty years ago in the original sense of the French phrase.

and survives in many modern dialects. *Dowle*, a filament of a feather ('one dowle that's in my plumbe', *Temp.* III. iii. 65), of which only one instance earlier than Shakespeare has been found, is but scantily evidenced in literature. Its present dialectal range comprises Warwickshire and four conterminous counties, together with Shropshire, Herefordshire, and Wiltshire. A curious confusion between this word and *down* occurs in *2 Henry IV*, as printed in the Folio : a *dowlney* feather' ; 'that light and weightlesse *dowlne*' (IV. v. 31–2). *Nayword*, a byword, a watchword, occurs first in Shakespeare (in three places) and the instances in later writers seem to be echoes of his use. If we disregard Forby's questionable statement that it was vernacular in East Anglia in his time, its currency appears to be confined to Warwickshire, Worcestershire, Shropshire, and Cheshire. *Blood-bolter'd*, the epithet applied by Macbeth to the apparition of Banquo (IV. i. 123), is probably a compound formed for the occasion, but *boltered* in the sense of 'clotted' is current in Warwickshire, and apparently little known except in that county and the immediate neighbourhood. The play on the similarity of the words *sheep* and *ship*, which occurs in *Love's Labour's Lost* (II. i. 217–18), in *The Two Gentlemen of Verona* (I. i. 72–3), and in *The Comedy of Errors* (IV. i. 94–5), would hardly have suggested itself to one who was not familiar with the west midland pronunciation according to which the two words are sounded alike. A rustic of the Malverns will still speak of 'the 'ill ship' for the mountain sheep.

It is, of course, possible that there may be other genuine traces of west midland dialect in Shakespeare's works than those that have just been cited. On the other hand, it is equally possible that some of our supposed examples may be fallacious. There is certainly no antecedent reason for expecting the amount of provincialism in the plays to be other than very small. A playwright would naturally be careful to avoid any peculiarities of diction which his London audiences might find obscure or ludicrous, and anything of this kind which he introduced inadvertently would probably be brought to his notice by the actors. On the whole, therefore, it seems more likely that our list of probable vestiges of Stratford dialect requires shortening than that it admits of being greatly extended.

BIBLIOGRAPHY.—Of Elizabethan works on English grammar and orthography, the most important are RICHARD MULCASTER'S *The First Part of the Elementarie, which entreateth chefelie of the right writing of our English Tung,* London, 1582 ; EDMUND COOK'S *The English Schoolmaster. Teaching all his Scholars, of what age soever, the most easie, short and perfect order of distinct Reading, and true Writing, our English-tongue, that hath ever yet been known or published by any,* London, 1597 (often reprinted) ; BEN JONSON'S *The English Grammar made for the benefit of all strangers,* first published posthumously in 1640. Much phonetic information is embodied in several schemes of spelling reform which were published in Shakespeare's lifetime. Of these the most interesting are Sir THOMAS SMITH'S *De recta et emendata linguae Anglicae scriptione,* which was appended to his *De recta et emendata linguae Graecae pronunciatione,* Paris, 1568 ; JOHN HART'S *An orthographie, conteyning the due order and reason, howe to write or painte thimage of mannes voice, moste like to the life or nature.* Composed by J. H., 'Chester Herault', London, 1569; WILLIAM BULLOKAR'S *Booke at Large, for the Amendment of Orthographie for English speech,* London, 1580. Equally important with these, though not published in Shakespeare's lifetime, is ALEXANDER GILL'S *Logonomia Anglica,* London, ed. 1, 1619, ed. 2, 1621 (a valuable edition by O. Jiriczek, Strassburg, 1903).

The chief modern works on Shakespeare's English are Dr. E. A. ABBOTT'S *Shakespearian Grammar,* London, ed. 2, 1870 (since often reprinted), and Prof. WILHELM FRANZ'S *Shakespeare-Grammatik,* ed. 2, Heidelberg, 1909, which contains a valuable bibliography. On the pronunciation the best books are A. J. ELLIS's *Early English Pronunciation,* 1867–1889, and WILHELM VIËTOR'S *Shakespeare Phonology,* Marburg, 1906; many of the views of these writers are contested, with great ability, in R. E. ZACHRISSON'S *Pronunciation of English Vowels, 1400–1700,* Göteborg, 1913; see also H. C. WYLD'S *Short History of English,* London, 1914, ch. vii. For the vocabulary constant reference should be made to *The Oxford English Dictionary,* as well as to ALEXANDER SCHMIDT'S *Shakespeare-Lexicon,* 2 vols., ed. Sarrazin, Berlin, 1902, and C. T. ONIONS's *Shakespeare Glossary,* Oxford, 1911 ; a useful glossary of obsolete words and senses is R. J. CUNLIFFE'S *New Shakesperean Dictionary,* London, 1910.

INDEX OF PASSAGES CITED FROM SHAKESPEARE'S WORKS

INDEX OF PROPER NAMES

INDEX OF SUBJECTS AND TECHNICAL TERMS